Richard Miller Devens

Cyclopedia of commercial and business anecdotes

Vol. I

Richard Miller Devens

Cyclopedia of commercial and business anecdotes
Vol. I

ISBN/EAN: 9783337215569

Printed in Europe, USA, Canada, Australia, Japan

Cover: Foto ©Suzi / pixelio.de

More available books at **www.hansebooks.com**

CYCLOPÆDIA

OF

COMMERCIAL AND BUSINESS

ANECDOTES;

COMPRISING

INTERESTING REMINISCENCES AND FACTS,

REMARKABLE TRAITS AND HUMORS,

AND

Notable Sayings, Dealings, Experiences, and Witticisms

OF

**MERCHANTS, TRADERS, BANKERS, MERCANTILE CELEBRITIES, MILLIONNAIRES,
BARGAIN MAKERS, ETC., ETC.**

IN ALL AGES AND COUNTRIES.

DESIGNED TO EXHIBIT, BY

NEARLY THREE THOUSAND ILLUSTRATIVE ANECDOTES AND INCIDENTS,

THE

PIQUANCIES AND PLEASANTRIES OF TRADE, COMMERCE, AND GENERAL
BUSINESS PURSUITS.

ASTOR,	GIRARD,	McDONOGH,	BARING,
ROTHSCHILD,	BIDDLE,	TOURO,	LORILLARD,
OUVRARD,	LABOUCHERE,	LONGWORTH,	PERKINS,
BATES,	APPLETON,	BAYARD,	LEROY,
BARKER,	LAFITTE,	STEWART,	RUSSELL,
LENOX,	COOPER,	SHAW,	STEIGLITZ,
HOWQUA,	GRESHAM,	LOWELL,	BUSSEY,
GOLDSCHMID,	PEABODY,	MORRIS,	VANDERBILT,
HOPE,	NOLTE,	RIGGS,	JEEJEEBHOY,
HOTTINGUER,	BROOKS,	GIDEON,	GRINNELL,
GRACIE,	RIDGWAY,	SLATER,	LEE,
COUTTS,	GRAY,	FRANCIS,	FUGGER,
BELMONT,	CHILD,	DEXTER,	TATTERSALL,
MORRISON,	HUDSON,	WHITNEY,	HOPPER,
DE MEDICI,	LAWRENCE,	STURGIS,	COPE,

ETC., ETC., ETC.

Long life to Commerce! What lives not through it? What is all fresh life, all movement, in reality, but trade, exchange, gift for gift!—BARNES.

Come, ANECDOTE! with all thy graces come,
Relieve the grave—to mirth thy rights afford,
And crown the sparkling glass and hospitable board.—COOKE.

I am persuaded that every time a man smiles—but much more so when he laughs—it adds something to this fragment of life.—STERNE.

A dinner of *fragments* is often said to be the best dinner.—"GUESSES AT TRUTH."

By FRAZAR KIRKLAND.

EMBELLISHED WITH PORTRAITS AND ILLUSTRATIVE CUTS.

VOL. I.

NEW YORK:
D. APPLETON AND COMPANY, 443 & 445 BROADWAY.
LONDON: 16 LITTLE BRITAIN.
1864.

PREFACE.

THE design and scope of this work will be found as clearly indicated and as amply set forth on the Title page, as is requisite to the most complete understanding of the plan which it involves and the character of the matter embodied in its pages. As there stated, it is a collection, original and selected, of the choicest, most striking and *recherché* ANECDOTES relating to BUSINESS MEN and COMMERCIAL PURSUITS, from the earliest trading transactions of which any record can be found down to the present time. It is in no sense intended as a work of biography, history, statistics, or collated facts, only so far as either of these has been found associated, anecdotically, with some episode of Business Character or Dealing, illustrative of the latter in their various aspects of the gay, the ludicrous, the witty, the ingenious, the droll, the original, the unique — laughter-provoking, side-shaking, wonder-exciting, &c.; with such these pages abound.

The Anecdotes here given necessarily pertain both to persons and things—alike to the *Celebrities* of traffic in all ages and nations, and to the multitudinous *Objects* which give to traffic its name and import. Every country, as well as people, has here its personal representative—exhibiting, in all their kaleidoscopic lights and shades, the idiosyncrasies, customs, and animus peculiar to it, in bargain and sale; every clime its happy illustrations, in the productions native to it, or which enter into its commercial exchange : the whole forming, as it were, a sort of mental Pantechnicon, or Bazaar, where are to be seen delineated, in endless variety, and as pictures hung upon a wall, the curiosities incident to the genius and craft of THE MART!

Perhaps no volume ever issued from the American press has furnished, in a compendious form, so fruitful a display of the unique and marvellous in human nature, on its *commercial* side, as this. Indeed, it has the merit, whatever that may be, of being the first work of the kind which has ever appeared, in this or any other country, devoted to *the Humorous phase of Trade and Traders*. Collections of anecdotes having reference to art, science, literature, morals, the drama, etc.,— some of them possessing high merit, and attaining a wide circulation—

have at different times been sent forth for public favor; but not one, it is believed, of all these, has ever touched, or but very slightly, the field of pleasantries and piquancies here spread out to view. Our volume, therefore, being thus *sui generis*, offers no opportunity of winning praise by comparison, or of suffering from disparagement by contrast with any other work of its kind. But, however the fact might be in this respect, it would not stand in the way of an honest claim in behalf of the work, of being as perfect in its character as the sources of material available to that end would permit. No time has been spared, no means and facilities left unimproved, no expense or labor withheld, to render these pages tempting to every lover of pithy, pointed, sparkling, and mirthful reading.

It is not too much to say, that the anecdotes, witticisms, and memorabilia, which are here presented, of such monarch merchants as Astor, Rothschild, Girard, Baring, Lafitte, Jacob Barker, De Medicis, Lorillard, Howqua, Bates, Peabody, Lawrence, Hope, Touro, &c., &c., would form, of themselves alone, one of the most delectable of volumes. But these are only a few out of many *scores* of mercantile notabilities who have flourished during the past, or are yet on the stage of action, and of whom it is the object of this book to present the most lively and pleasing incidents illustrative of their professional character, moods, and dealings. And here it will not be impertinent briefly to observe, that, as every undertaking must have its limits, so in the case of the present work, it has been found a point of necessity to exercise a restraining hand, that the several divisions might not become too bulky or diffuse. Arising from this consideration, there are some characters, more or less noteworthy, whose names are not here to be met with, but to which we would gladly have given place. It is believed, however, that this omission rarely involves a name of extensive renown, but applies rather to those whose fame, living or posthumous, is restricted to particular localities or circles; and, as almost every business community, large or small, is known thus to have its "representative men," —those of strongly marked individuality in their calling,—it is apparent that no task could be more impossible than to attempt to give, without discrimination, the current reminiscences of such a multitude.

In the prosecution of our purpose, every important catalogue, both American and foreign, has been carefully consulted, with a view to examining whatever might promise aid to our efforts; and not a single library of note, in our largest cities, has been left unexplored for material, in the way of biography, travels, adventure—fresh, racy, and relevant—in the preparation of this work. Besides these invaluable means, the best private sources within the circle of men of letters have been resorted to, and the suggestions and assistance thus personally extended have added greatly to the pleasantness of our task, as well as to the value of its results.

But the perplexities attending a nice discernment in the selection of matter for this volume have by no means been slight. The first requisite, of course, in the qualities of an anecdote, is that of truth. Where this is wanting, the narration, however agreeable or well told, falls off at once ninety per cent. in its interest and import. It becomes a mere fable, and should be thus entitled. The number of so-called "anecdotes" coming within this latter class, and which might have had their nominal appropriateness in these pages, is very large; they have been rejected in every case where they could not stand a fair test of authenticity. Many others, of the genuine cast, have been abridged or condensed; and others still have been revised or rewritten, so as more nearly to conform to fact and reason, or that they might appear in a more perspicuous dress to the reader. There is yet another class—and one which forms an exception to the observation just made with reference to credibility—namely, the bristling fantasiæ of commercial satire, burlesque, &c., which have been allowed a welcome place in almost every department. These explain themselves, and may be said to constitute one of the richest and most attractive features of the work.

It is believed that the general arrangement and classification of this volume are scarcely susceptible of improvement. They are such as to relieve the matter of all stiffness, formality, and tediousness, while they at the same time open up, at the reader's will or fancy, and in pleasing diversification, all the various spheres and phases of commerce, business life, and its individual appertainments. It is not claimed, however, that there are no instances to be found, where portions of one department might not as appropriately—and perhaps more so—have had a place under some other specialty. The difficulties of perfect precision in this respect, in such a work, are obvious, and were frequently felt in the allotment of its contents. For any incongruities that may thus be manifest, a lenient criticism is asked.

Our acknowledgments are due, and are here most gratefully tendered, to those librarians in our principal cities who have so freely and courteously opened the treasures of their alcoves to our use; and also to the many editors, authors, and merchants, who have not only encouraged us by their warm approval of our work, but have favored us with their advice and friendly offices, and with the happy effusions of their pens, with which to enliven our volume.

The magnificent collections of standard periodical literature, now to be found complete in almost all our great libraries, and embracing full sets of the Edinburgh, Westminster, Gentleman's, Fraser's, Blackwood's, Eclectic, Harleian, Jerrold's, Dublin, Punch, Notes and Queries, Chambers', Household Words, The Leisure Hour, &c.,—these, in addition to our American publications of similar character, furnish a vast and bountiful storehouse, inviting and rewarding the research of the scholar. All these have been made readily accessible to us; and, though the labor of painstakingly examining their contents has certainly been formidable, it has yet been richly remunerative for the purposes of this volume.

The choice sippings of Punch will be relished by all who love to drink at that fountain of mirth, satire, and facetiæ; and Mrs. Partington, that brusque old wit—or witch—will be found to grace, by her weird presence, the same exhilarating category. The pages of the now venerable, but always sprightly and inimitable Knickerbocker, have been drawn upon for some of those "saws" whose teeth always have a point; and the "Drawer" of Harper's, that charming repository of keen blades and fancies, has been approached like a bundle of golden jack-straws, from which we might extract, here and there, a dainty waif, without taking all. From the files of Hunt's and Homans' magazines, we have culled not a few of the admirable morceaux of commercial biography and the humors of mercantile genius, which give to those serials so peculiar a value; and the same observation is pertinent to the more youthful Continental, especially the series of brilliant personal sketches from the facile pen of Mr. Frothingham. Of the writings of Mr. Richard B. Kimball and "Walter Barrett," from which we have taken an occasional anecdote or vivacious passage, it may truly be remarked that those authors have succeeded in imparting the delight of romance to the counting-house themes which they have made their specialty; and the great popular favor which their works have received, evinces the widespread taste for the pleasantries of commercial literature, under the inspiration of a genial hand.

Having wrought, to the best of our ability, in the field from which this CYCLOPEDIA OF ANECDOTES has been garnered, it is sent forth with the consciousness that, whatever defects or deficiencies may be discoverable, it has at least been the aim of the editor, from the inception of the volume to its completion, to spare neither time, labor, nor cost, in rendering it as rich and perfect of its kind as seemed humanly possible.

IT is generally admitted by those qualified to speak authoritatively in such matters, that the term ANECDOTE may be used to designate collections, either of the recorded acts of noted individuals, of remarks made by them, or of extracts from their private writings as well as their published works; or generally, of particulars respecting them and their calling—detached incidents, narratives, and experiences; personal tastes, traits, and habits; eccentricities, witticisms, &c., &c. It is thus, in its most enlarged and comprehensive sense, that the word is employed in this volume, and applied distinctively to those engaged in BUSINESS PURSUITS.

That the ancients were given to the wit and raillery conveyed through anecdotes, may reasonably be supposed from the fact that no less a person than Julius Cæsar compiled a book in which he related the *bon-mots* of Cicero ; and Quintilian informs us, that a freedman of that celebrated wit and orator composed three books of a work entitled De Jocis Ciceronis; and Gellius has filled his Noctes Atticæ with anecdotes which he heard from those distinguished characters whose society he frequented in Rome. Procopius gave the title of Anecdotes to a book he published against Justinian and his wife Theodora; and other similar collections of incidents in the lives of eminent men have been published. Muratori gives the title, Anecdota Greca, to several writings of the Greek Fathers found in the libraries, and first given to the world by him. Martene and Durand have given a Thesaurus Novus Anecdotorum. Becker, Bachmann, Heinbach, and others, have made collections, and called them Anecdota. The Orientalists, more than others, were particularly fond of these agreeable collections; and the fanciful titles with which they labelled their variegated miscellanies, sufficiently attest their delight.

The first eminent person of modern times, whose jests and opinions have in this way been transmitted to posterity, is Poggio Bracciolini, who was secretary to five successive popes. He and his friends were accustomed to assemble in a hall to discuss the news and scandal of the day, and at these meetings they communicated to each other entertaining anecdotes. The pointed jests and humorous stories which occurred in these unrestrained conversations were collected by Poggio, and formed the chief materials of his Facetiæ, printed in 1470.

One of the most curious of such collections is considered to be the Walpoliana, founded upon the life and sayings of Horace Walpole, who was distinguished for his resources of anecdote, wit, and telling remark, as well as for his epistolary qualifications. The most celebrated of the French collections of anecdotes is the Menagiana—the best known, the fullest, and most valuable. Other works of this kind that may here be named are the Conversations of Luther, Boswell's Life of Johnson, Selden's, Johnson's, and Cowper's Table Talk, the Percy and Arvine collections, &c., &c.

It would be a tedious as well as profitless task, however, to go over the dusty past, with a view to describing the character, or discussing the merits, of the various works of this kind which have appeared at different times and in different countries. It will suffice our immediate purpose to say, that, among them all, no volume of anecdotes, wit, and amusement, relating to the votaries of Trade and Commerce, as such, is numbered, notwithstanding the universality of those occupations, and the vast numerical preponderance of those engaged in them.

The present volume, then, may be said to be the first in the pleasing domain of Commercial Incident, Novelty, and Humor. And if it be true, as has by some one been remarked, that there is no species of composition so delightful as that which presents us with personal anecdotes of men notable in their peculiar calling—illustrating the genius of their adaptation to and success in such calling, as well as their domestic traits, and peculiarities of temper—then a claim for no small credit may with justice be put forth in behalf of the present work, the abundant pages of which are stored with the rarest, the best, and most striking of such memorabilia. They will be found to be a "salad" alike for the "solitary" and the "sociable"—entertaining, from their variety, and curious, as presenting a lively image of those whom they thus portray, in their most interesting relations and doings. If men reason more correctly on paper, they usually display their feelings and convictions with more truth in that unpremeditated conversation, and in those natural outgushings of wit, which they give play to in the familiar haunts of business, and under the free-and-easy influence of home surroundings. Few are so cautious or artificial that they do not sometimes drop the mask in the society of their friends, and express just what they think or feel, when they entertain no apprehensions of being watched and noted. In many instances, however, anecdotes are to be regarded rather as affording an idea of the *casual* turn of thinking and acting, of those whose conversations they detail, or whose deeds they record, than as authorities for settled opinions. Thus, a spirit of contradiction, a wish to display ingenuity, to astonish, or merely to support conversation, may often lead men to maintain ideas in colloquial intercourse, which they perhaps never seriously held, or at least would be ready to disclaim on mature deliberation.

It being the nature of anecdotes to involve or exemplify more or less of Wit, it is well for those who use or listen to them to bear in mind that such an element is rarely calculated to have any influence on reasoning, other than to disturb it. To determine, however, the precise character, or to give a definite *meaning*, to the term wit, is indeed difficult. According to one, both fancy and judgment are comprehended under that name; but this idea is far from being the one generally adopted, and the word has perhaps passed through more significations than any other in the English language. At one time, it used to denote a superior degree of understanding, and more particularly a quick and brilliant reason; but it came subsequently to be regarded as consisting in lively and ingenious combinations of thought; and was afterward very neatly described to be such an assemblage of ideas as will give delight and surprise; and from this it has ultimately come to be regarded as ludicrous surprise.

But, in addition to the pleasure to be derived from anecdotes on account of the wit which may characterize them, and which carries with the recital both relish and stimulus, there is also the very active element of Curiosity, in the constitution of the human mind, and which craves and welcomes every opportunity of gratification. This feeling of curiosity oftentimes rises to eagerness and enthusiasm. There is an anxiety to know all that is possible to be learned of those who have occupied a prominent position in their sphere of life. It is not, merely, that every circumstance derives value from the person to whom it relates; but an apparently insignificant anecdote often throws an entirely new light on the character of a man's actions. Great deeds, though they shed a broad and lasting lustre round the reputation of those who have achieved them, yet occupy but a small part of the life of any individual; and mankind are never unwilling to penetrate through this bright halo surrounding one or more illustrious deeds, to see how the interior or remaining intervals are filled up; in a word, to look into the every-day details, to detect incidental foibles, and to ascertain what qualities such persons have, or had, in common with the great mass of men, as well as distinct from them.

D'Israeli very philosophically remarks, that "every class of readers requires a book adapted to itself." It was in this conviction that the book now offered to that numerous and influential portion of every community—the Business class—had its origin; fortified by the well-known fact, that anecdote forms an element of positive force and profitable effect in the transactions of the counting-room and shop—as much so, perhaps, as in any other profession. And why should it not be so? An anecdote in point, occurring to a man of business, when he is plying the arts of trade, whether as buyer or seller, will naturally give spur to his thoughts, and perhaps be the means of balancing things in his favor, when all other expedients and every other recourse would have proved unavailing. This is a principle as rational as truth itself, and the value of which will be found most amply unfolded in the contents of this volume.

That all pleasantries ought to be short, has long since passed into an axiom. Due regard has been paid to this sentiment, in the preparation of these pages. Nor has it been any part of the purpose of this volume, to make it a mere lumber room of the relics and dotage of far-back ages—a few things good and fresh mixed up with many stale and inferior wares. A special characteristic, too, of mercantile or business men, is that of action—of ready doing, rather than loquacious talking; a quality of which Rothschild, of the Old World, and Girard, of the New, may be cited as memorable examples. Anecdotes are brief, or should be—all over in a short time; and, if they hit the mark, the object is gained. This collection treats of the business classes on a similar plan: their acts, sayings, achievements, fortunes, customs; shop talk and "conversations commercial;" curious annals and interesting data in all the departments of trade; all the turnings and windings of mercantile life; apt maxims, ingenious or philosophical thoughts; testimonies and examples of virtues, of vices, and of abuses, in all their ramifications; types, pictures, and images; signs, shows, and wonders; all things, in short, that have either wit, or humor, or sparkling ideas in them, or a more original or novel spirit than ordinary, here enter as ingredients, and are interwoven in pleasing variety—a distillation of whatever is pointed or pungent—the milledulcia extracted from the choicest and innumerable sources.

The opening department of this volume—that which presents Business Celebrities in their more distinctively biographical aspect—forms one of the most interesting of the series. It is the vestibule, or porch, as it were, to the rest; and the endeavor has been to arrange it with that care and completeness which should distinguish matter of such a character. To render biography generally attractive, it is indispensable that its basis should be that of truth. Without this, it necessarily wants the great superiority of the narrative of real events over that of mere fictitious creations; viz., that of recording what has actually occurred in real life. How important an element this is in awakening the sympathies, may be seen in children, who, when particularly fascinated by any story they are told, almost invariably end by asking, " But is it all true ? " The fact, also, that biography deals with personal characters, admits of its expansion into many topics, both interesting and amusing. As the delineation of character is its object, and the events of individual life its principal subject, it not only admits of, but requires a thousand incidents and descriptions, which are essential to a right understanding of the characters portrayed. Such details enable the reader to clothe the characters in which he is interested in the actual habiliments in which they were arrayed; they bring before one's eyes the business occupations and resorts, the dwellings, the firesides, the traits of domestic association, and other data, which go to make up the warp and woof of life.

Nor is it less instructive than pleasant, to be, as it were, introduced thus familiarly to the companionship of men who have been or are distinguished in the sphere occupied by them. If they be men of sterling and intrepid qualities, it is a privilege to be made acquainted with the motives of their actions, to follow them from their starting point, to mark the difficulties and opposition they encountered in their struggle for advancement—the energy and skill by which they were overcome, and the courage that animated them to persevere in their efforts. By their failures, also, warning is obtained of the various quicksands and dangers that beset the path of commercial life.

Thus considered, the lives of noted business men supply abundant and striking material for the pen of the writer. It is true, that only here and there does such a life present itself among that class—so full of versatile and remarkable experience—as to afford substance for an elaborate and formal biography. Such as the latter have sometimes been written, exhibiting a most frugal proportion of kernel to shell—mere rivulets of fact in meadows of verbiage, and bringing positive discredit both upon the author and his subject. But, notwithstanding this, there are very many characters which afford, respectively, some trait, habit, or individuality, capable, when presented in a lively manner, of furnishing entertainment and profit in the highest degree; as the numberless specimens here spread out before the reader will attest.

It may safely be asserted, that no character of fiction, made ever so dazzling by the imagery of the novelist, presents to the mind such marvels as may be found in the solid realities of experience pertaining to an Astor, a Rothschild, a Lawrence, a McDonough, a De Medicis, a Girard, and their compeers, the chronicles of whose great and unfaltering career loom up so conspicuously in these pages. Nor is the mind less startled at the history of the magnificent success of a Morris, a Law, a Lafitte, a Goldschmid, a Fordyce, a Hudson, and others, and their subsequent downfall and ruin. Not only are such narratives adapted to intellectually impress—to captivate, to excite, to confound, to arouse to wonderment, to amuse—but they may be made subservient to positive profit; in business parlance, they may "be made to pay!". An aquaintance with the ways and means which have characterized the career of successful business men —their apt sayings, or more apt silence; their penetration of human character, and art of imperceptibly influencing its sensibilities and moods to their own ends; their genial sallies and happy repartees; their shrewd plans, skilful combinations, ingenious finesse, and general *modus operandi* of "turning a trade;" such an acquaintance cannot but be a capital desideratum to all who move in a kindred path.

The plan which has been adopted of dividing the contents of this work into different sections, each devoted to a particular specialty, is one which will enable the reader to strike easily at every salient point in the anecdotical field of commerce and commercial character thus spread before him. Of the bearings of the first department, we have already spoken; the others admit, severally, of similar explanatory detail with respect to their prescribed object and the illustrations afforded by their contents. But, not to attempt to specifically portray or analyze the features of each department by itself, into which this volume is divided—the fascinating data which open up in the memorials of world-renowned merchants, bankers, and millionnaires—the arts and humors of money dealing—the captivating examples of success based on the practice of the more rigid qualities—the low craft and bold criminalities both of ancient and modern traffic—the whims and ingenuities of business phraseology—the unique thoughts and things pertaining to commercial transit—the curious phenomena of trade and merchandise in their legal bearings—the exhibition of the private or domestic side of mercantile characters—the novelties and erratic expedients characteristic of bargain makers in different countries—the vagaries and hazards of insurance—the incidents of clerk life, shop experience, &c., together with the variegated jottings of trade and its votaries, as related to "the rest of mankind;"—without attempting to depict the results, or point out the peculiar entertainment presented by each one of these, separately, it may be remarked, in conclusion, that perhaps the portion of this volume which exhibits the phenomena of commercial dealings in their most extraordinary developments, is comprised in the recital of the manias, bubbles, panics, and delusions, which have from time to time swept the business world like a tornado, carrying before it the verdant like chaff, and ultimately the most sagacious and wary.

Now that those delusions are past, it is difficult to conceive how mercantile men could be led to entertain such visionary expectations, and to pay immense premiums in distant and hazardous undertakings, of which they knew little or nothing. A blind ardor seemed to take possession of men's minds; every rumor of a new project was taken at once as the presage of sudden and inexhaustible wealth. People supposed they were forthwith to lay their hands on treasure that waited simply their bidding. The rise, in many cases, exceeded cent. per cent. Many who were most eager in pursuit of shares, intended only to hold them for a few hours, days, or weeks, and then profit from the advance which they anticipated would take place, by selling them to others more credulous or bold than themselves. The confidence of one set of speculators confirmed that of others. Meanwhile, the indiscriminating rapacity of the public was fed by every conceivable art. Madness ruled the hour. The poor and the rich rushed wildly to invest their all; and even mendicants rolled proudly, for a while, in fictitious wealth! But, as in all such cases since the world was, the shadows of doubt began, in time, ominously to cast themselves athwart this bright picture, and soon deepened into the dark and lurid clouds of stern reality. People turned ashy pale. Consternation took the place of confidence, and Panic spread out her spectral wings. Thus, one by one these airy bubbles exploded, leaving the wail of desolation, of gaunt despair, and of ghastly suicide, in their fatal train. The pen of the romancer, in its most unrestrained flights, would fail to equal, in startling wonders, the chronicles of commercial tragedy which have their appropriate department in this volume.

CONTENTS.

PART I.

*ANECDOTES AND REMARKABLE REMINISCENCES OF THE EARLY CA-
REER OF BUSINESS CELEBRITIES IN ALL AGES AND COUNTRIES.*

ASTOR, ROTHSCHILD, OUVRARD, BATES, BARKER, TOURO, McDONOGH, HOWQUA, GOLD-
SCHMID, HOPE, HOTTINGUER, COUTTS, MORRISON, DE MEDICIS, GIRARD, BIDDLE,
LABOUCHERE, LAFITTE, APPLETON, COOPER, GRESHAM, PEABODY, NOLTE, GRAY,
VANDERBILT, BEATTY, LAWRENCE, LOWELL, WHITNEY, GIDEON, BARING, MORRIS,
LORILLARD, STEIGLITZ, PERKINS, JEEJEEBHOY, BROOKS, LONGWORTH, ETC., ETC., ETC.

B

xvi CONTENTS.

PART II.

ANECDOTES AND INCIDENTS OF BUSINESS PURSUITS IN THEIR MONEY RELATIONS.

BANKS, BANKERS, BROKERS, SPECIE, NOTES, LOANS, EXCHANGE, DRAFTS, CHECKS, PUBLIC SECURITIES, AND CURRENCY IN ALL ITS FORMS AND PHASES; WITH JOTTINGS OF THE MOST CELEBRATED MILLIONNAIRES AND MONEY DEALERS—THEIR BUSINESS MODES AND CHARACTERISTICS, MAXIMS, COLLOQUIES, WIT, ECCENTRICITIES AND FINESSE.

PART III.

ANECDOTES AND ILLUSTRATIONS OF THE SUCCESSFUL BUSINESS QUALITIES.

INTEGRITY, ENTERPRISE, ENERGY, PERSEVERANCE, COURAGE, SHREWDNESS, PUNCTILIOUS-
NESS, PRUDENCE, AMBITION, GRATITUDE, BENEVOLENCE, GENEROSITY, ECONOMY; WITH
PENCILLINGS OF STRIKING BUSINESS ADVENTURES, VICISSITUDES, EXPLOITS AND
ACHIEVEMENTS, BOTH SERIOUS AND COMICAL.

PART IV.

ANECDOTES OF TRADE AND BUSINESS IMMORALITIES.

THE RAREST INSTANCES OF INGENIOUS BUSINESS FRAUD, FORGERY, COUNTERFEITING, AND
  SMUGGLING; USURY, ARTIFICE, TRICKS, AND MALPRACTICE; WITH EXAMPLES, EX-
  TRAORDINARY AND AMUSING, OF AVARICE, COVETOUSNESS, PARSIMONY, EXTORTION,
  PRIDE, RUDENESS, VIOLENCE AND EXTRAVAGANCE OF BUSINESS MEN.

CONTENTS. **xxi**

PART V.

ANECDOTES OF FAMOUS COMMERCIAL RESORTS AND LOCALITIES.

THE EXCHANGE, CUSTOM HOUSE, BOARDS OF TRADE, MARKETS, ETC.—THEIR ANNALS, USAGES, PECULIARITIES; WITH PERSONAL MISCELLANIES, APHORISMS, ODDITIES, WHIMS AND CAPRICES OF THEIR HABITUÉS.

·PART VI.

ANECDOTES OF COMMERCIAL ART AND PHRASEOLOGY.

ADVERTISEMENTS, SIGNBOARDS, TRADEMARKS, TOKENS, ENVELOPES, LABELS, INSCRIPTIONS, MOTTOES AND TERMS—QUAINT, CURIOUS, GROTESQUE, INGENIOUS AND LAUGHABLE.

PART VII.

*ANECDOTES AND THINGS MEMORABLE CONCERNING BUSINESS TRANSIT
AND COMMUNICATION.*

SHIPPING, STEAMBOATS, RAILWAYS, EXPRESSES, COACHES, OMNIBUSES, ETC.—THEIR
OWNERS, OFFICERS, PATRONS, AND ATTACHÉS.

LIST OF ILLUSTRATIONS.

PORTRAITS ON STEEL.

WOOD ENGRAVINGS.

PART FIRST.

———•———

Anecdotes and Remarkable Reminiscences of the Early Career of Business Celebrities in all Ages and Countries.

PART FIRST.

Anecdotes and Remarkable Reminiscences of the Early Career of Business Celebrities in all Ages and Countries.

ASTOR, ROTHSCHILD, OUVRARD, DATES, BARKER, TOURO, MCDONOGH, HOWQUA, GOLDSCHMID, HOPE, HOTTINGUER, COUTTS, MORRISON, DE MEDICIS, GIRARD, BIDDLE, LABOUCHERE, LA-FITTE, APPLETON, COOPER, GRESHAM, PEABODY, NOLTE, GRAY, BRUCK, BEATTY, STEWART, LAWRENCE, LOWELL, WHITNEY, GIDEON, DEXTER, BARING, MORRIS, LORILLARD, STEIGLITZ, PERKINS, LONGWORTH, ETC., ETC., ETC.

———That *captivating art* which consists in the delineation of individual traits and achievements.—EDIN. REVIEW.

The man who has not anything to boast of but his illustrious ancestors, is like a potato—the only good belonging to him is under the ground.—SIR T. OVERBURY.

Let not those blush who *have*, but those who *have not*, a lawful calling.—TATTLER.

Still let the mind be bent, still plotting where,
And when, and how, the business may be done.—HERBERT.

Robert Morris, the Financier, of Philadelphia.

THIS eminent financier was born in Liverpool, Eng., in 1734. Of his family, very little is known, except that his father was a respectable English merchant, and for a long time held the agency of a very considerable tobacco house in that place. The nature and extent of his concerns required his frequent visits to this country; and it was in one of these trips that his son Robert, at the age of thirteen, became the companion of his voyage, and received an introduction to the scene of his future greatness. His father, by a melancholy accident, lost his life about two years after he had established himself in this country as a merchant. Soon after this sad event, Robert was received into the counting house of Charles Willing, at that time the most distinguished merchant in Philadelphia, to whom he appears to have been indentured; and, after remaining in this subordinate station the usual term of years, he was established in business by his patron, in conjunction with his son, Thomas Willing.

Embarked in an extensive and profitable West India business, Mr. MORRIS made several voyages as supercargo in the ships belonging to the company, in one of which he was unfortunately captured by the French, and, during a close imprisonment for some time, suffered cruelty of treatment not justified by the laws of war, nor the usages of civilized nations. In this state of distress, without a shilling, by exercising his ingenuity, and repairing the watch of a Frenchman, he raised the means of his own liberation, and enabled himself to return to Philadelphia and resume his mercantile life.

Under his active superintendence, the house of Willing and Morris rapidly rose to the summit of commercial reputation. Their foreign freightage employed an incredible number of ships;

1

while the able management of their finances at home, procured them the confidence and credit of the world. At the age of thirty-six, he married the daughter of Colonel White ; she was the sister of the venerable Bishop White. At the close of 1775, he was sent to Congress, and, after rendering important services during the war, he was, in 1781, unanimously elected, by Congress, superintendent of national finance.

He still continued his commercial business, having formed a connection with the Messrs. Hazlehurst. In 1786 he was elected a member of the Convention which framed the Federal Constitution, and in 1788 was appointed United States senator. His public duties, however, caused that inattention to his private affairs, which finally resulted in those great embarrassments of mind and circumstances which weighed upon his declining years. In his old age, Mr. Morris embarked in vast land speculations, which proved fatal to his fortune. The man to whose financial operations our country has been said to owe as much as to the negotiations of Franklin, or even the arm of Washington, passed the latter years of his life in prison, confined for debt. He died on the 8th of May, 1806, in the seventy-third year of his age.

Mr. Morris was of large frame, with a fine, open, bland countenance, and simple manners ; for nearly half a century, until the period of his imprisonment, his house was a scene of the most liberal hospitality.

P. C. Labouchere, the Youthful Prince Merchant.

In his youth, LABOUCHERE commenced his commercial training in Nantes, but subsequently engaged to become a clerk, for a period of three years, to take charge of the commercial correspondence of Hope & Co., the world-renowned bankers of Amsterdam. Shortly before the close of this term young Labouchere gave his principal a hint that a moderate increase of salary was desirable. An answer was promised for the next morning. When he went at the appointed time to receive the anticipated reply, old Mr. Hope laid before him for his signature, a contract already drawn up, in which he named him as his partner, with a suitable share in the profits, and intrusted him with the signature of that vast and princely house. Labouchere was at that time only twenty-two years of age, yet ere long assumed the eminent position of head of the firm—one of the first in the world, and studied the manners of a French courtier previous to the Revolution ; these manners he soon made so thoroughly his own, that they seemed to be a part of his own nature. He made a point of distinguishing himself in everything he undertook by a certain perfection, and carried this feeling so far, that, on account of the untractable lack of elasticity in his body, and a want of ear for music, which nature had denied him, he for eighteen years deemed it necessary to take dancing lessons, because he saw that others surpassed him in that graceful accomplishment. He married a daughter of the Barings : his whole career, both public and private, was one of almost unexampled brilliancy.

Howqua, the senior Hong Merchant.

This immensely wealthy and powerful Chinese merchant, whose mercantile fame was so extensive in both hemispheres as long as he lived, was descended from a respectable Fo-kien family, long resident in the principal black-tea district, and his grandfather was one of the Amoy Hong, who, with the progenitors of the Canton Hong merchants, Poon-ke-qua, Chunc-qua, and Minqua, were ordered by the emperor to remove to Canton, when all intercourse was forbidden with the English and Dutch at the port of Amoy.

HOWQUA had attained his seventy-fifth year when he died, at Canton. For a long time he had been in a feeble state of health, with extremely attenuated frame, but with an unimpaired intellectual vigor up to his last illness. His fortune was variously estimated, but his investments in the British and foreign funds were very great, and it was the belief of those who were most personally intimate with him, that his wealth did not fall short of twenty-five million dollars. With a very small exception, all his riches were the result of his own industry and enterprise. The war with the English involved him in a loss of two million dollars, and his proportion of the Canton ransom was eight hundred thousand dollars.

One of the peculiar characteristics of Howqua was an inveterate aversion to new customs and modern fashions,—clinging with the most conservative tenacity to the old, corrupt system, by which his vast wealth was mainly accumulated. He was the organ of communication between the government and the foreign merchants, possessed great power and influence among his countrymen, was a large landed proprietor, and had founded and endowed a temple to Buddha, in the suburbs of Canton.

It seems almost incredible, but it is not the less true, that, to the last, he directed his vast and complicated trade, which almost encircled the globe, alone. His knowledge, and even familiarity with mercantile details connected with the trade of foreign ports, was truly astonishing. Sound judgment, true prudence, wary circumspection, and a wise economy, were distinguishing traits of his mercantile character. By Englishmen, Howqua was not liked. His predilections were American—and justly so, seeing that he was indebted, in an early stage of his career, to an American citizen, for information he sought in vain from the English.

James Wood, the Gloucester Millionnaire.

JAMES WOOD, the celebrated shopkeeping millionnaire and sole proprietor of the Old Gloucester (Eng.) Bank, —the oldest private bank, with the exception of Childs', in England—amassed a property of five million of dollars. From the earliest period in his business career to the day of his death, he kept a shop such as comes within the description of a chandler's shop, in which he sold almost everything, from a mousetrap to a carriage; not that his premises were large enough to contain all the various stores in which he dwelt, nor indeed was it requisite that they should—for his wealth was sufficiently known to all the large manufacturers and traders, so that they were at all times ready to supply him with goods to any amount. At one end of this motley shop, the business of the 'Old Gloucester Bank,' as it was familiarly called, was transacted; and the whole establishment was managed by himself and two clerks or assistants. He was very penurious, and never married, entertained no company, visited no one, spent his whole time in his bank or shop, and his Sundays in a long walk in the country. His will involved much litigation, and, as a consequence, proved a prolific source of employment to the gentlemen of the greenbag.

Coutts, the English Banker.

The father of Mr. COUTTS, the founder of the celebrated English banking house which bears his name, was a merchant of some eminence in the city of Edinburgh. He had four sons; the two youngest, James and Thomas, were brought up in their father's office. James, at the age of twenty-five, went to London, and settled in St. Mary Axe, as a Scotch merchant, and subsequently started as a banker on the same spot, and it is believed in the same house where the business of the bank is now carried on. Some few years after,

Thomas joined his brother as a partner in the establishment, under the firm of 'James and Thomas Coutts, Bankers.' On the death of James, Thomas was left sole proprietor of the bank. Mr. Coutts, the founder of this eminent house, was plain in his person, sedate in his deportment, punctual to an extreme nicety in the discharge of all the duties of his immense and successful business, frugal and sparing in his personal expenditure, singularly calm and clear in his judgment, careful of his health—and still more of his reputation. To these traits the great prosperity and wealth to which Mr. Coutts attained are due.

It is related, as an illustration of Mr. Coutts' character, that one day, while sitting at dinner with a company of bankers whom he had invited to his hospitable board, he was informed by one of his guests, that a certain nobleman had applied to his house for a loan of thirty thousand pounds, and had been refused. Mr. Coutts took no particular notice of this at the time, but the moment his guests had retired, which was about ten o'clock, he started off to the house of his lordship, and inquiring for the steward told him his business, adding, " Tell his lordship, that if he calls on me in the morning, he may have what he requires." On the following morning, the nobleman went to the bank. Mr. Coutts received him with great politeness, and taking thirty one-thousand pound notes from a drawer, presented them to his lordship, who was most agreeably surprised, and asked, " What security am I to give you ? " " I shall be satisfied with your lordship's note of hand," was the reply. This was instantly given. The nobleman then said, " I find I shall only require, for the present, ten thousand pounds of the money; I therefore return you twenty thousand pounds, with which you will be pleased to open an account in my name."

This handsome act of Mr. Coutts was not lost upon his lordship, who, in addition to paying in, within a few months, two hundred thousand pounds to his account, being the amount of the sale of an estate, recommended several of the nobility to patronize Mr. Coutts ; and further, his lordship related the interesting circumstance to King George the Third, who also patronized him by keeping a large amount of money in Mr. Coutts' bank. The king, however, afterward closed his account with Mr. Coutts, it having come to his knowledge that the latter advanced the sum of one hundred thousand pounds toward Sir Francis Burdett's election to parliament. In place of Mr. Coutts, the king opened an account with a banker at Windsor, but this banker, to the great mortification of the king, subsequently failed, considerably in his majesty's debt.

Tattersall, the Auctioneer, London.

The present noted auctioneer in London, known as TATTERSALL, is a son of the founder of the great establishment, who died while enjoying the sumptuous surroundings in which his princely fortune enabled him to indulge.

Nobody who sees Mr. Tattersall presiding in his rostrum during the sale of horses, can resist the conviction that Nature intended him for an auctioneer of those noble animals. In the rostrum, he is obviously in his proper business sphere. He enters on his vocation with heart and soul, each succeeding day. He has no idea of happiness beyond the auction yard. The very sight of the hammer, or rather of himself wielding the hammer, is to him an enjoyment of the first magnitude. His own voice, when expatiating in praise of any horse that " *is* to be sold," has inexpressible charms to his ear. There is not a sound in the world that he will acknowledge to be half so musical to him,—except it be the sound of some voice whose proprietor is making a

" handsome bidding " for the animal in the market.

Mr. Tattersall, though a man of few words compared with the voluble school of auctioneers in general, is a very adroit and successful knight of the hammer. He is dexterous in discovering who among all that surround him are the parties really intending to buy, and to them in succession he addresses himself. His very look, unaccompanied by a single word, has, in innumerable cases, appealed so forcibly to some bystander, as to draw out " another guinea for the horse," even when the person had fully resolved in his own mind not to advance, on any earthly consideration, a single sixpence more. He holds in contempt all bombastical diction, as in poor taste, a waste of time, and a positive insult to the persons assembled. Besides, he is convinced that by his own plain and homely, but expressive style, he " fetches " a far better price for his " fine animals," than he would by the most high-sounding clap-trap sentences that could be strung together. He usually contents himself with mentioning the pedigree of the horse, praising him as one of the finest ever known; affecting to be quite shocked at the idea of selling him at the price offered; assuring the company that it would be positively giving him away, which of course neither he nor the proprietor can afford to do; and regretting that he cannot bid himself. When an extra quality of horse is " up," Mr. Tattersall's art of winning upon the good graces of the company is inimitable; an example of which is furnished among the AUCTION anecdotes in this volume.

By all his acquaintance, Mr. Tattersall has the reputation of being an excellent-hearted man, and is a great favorite, personally, with all who visit his premises, or have occasion to do business with him. He is a dark-complexioned man, with a rather full face, and wears a reserved expression. He is slightly under medium size, of somewhat stout build, and very lame. The number of horses he sometimes sells in one day is one hundred to one hundred and eighty.

Jacques Lafitte, the French Banker.

Important results often follow from the most trifling incidents. A remarkable instance of this kind is that afforded in the history of LAFITTE, one of the most memorable among the names of French bankers, and which was the foundation of the colossal fortune he afterward accumulated, and of the scarcely less than imperial position which he at one time held in the councils of the realm.

When he came to Paris, in 1798, the extent of his ambition was to find a situation in a banking house; and to attain this object, he called on M. Perregeaux, the rich Swiss banker, to whom he had a letter of introduction. This gentleman had just taken possession of the hotel of Mademoiselle Gurmard, which had been put up in a lottery by that lady, and won by the fortunate banker. It was to this most charming habitation, which has since been demolished, that M. Lafitte paid his first visit in Paris, and, as it were, took his first step in the brilliant Parisian world. The young provincial— poor and modest, timid and anxious— entered by that gateway which had witnessed so many convivialities in the last century.

He was introduced into the boudoir of the danseuse, which had become the cabinet of the banker, and there modestly stated the object of his visit. " It is impossible for me to admit you into my establishment, at least for the present," replied the banker; " all my offices have their full complement. If I require any one at a future time, I will see what can be done; but, in the mean time, I advise you to seek elsewhere, for I do not expect a vacancy for a long while."

With a disappointed heart, the young

aspirant for employment left the office; and while, with a dejected air, he traversed the stately courtyard, he stooped to pick up a pin which lay in his path, and which he carefully stuck in the lappel of his coat. Little did he think that this trivial action was to decide his future fate and open up so famous a destiny to him; but so it was. From the windows of his cabinet, M. Perregeaux had observed the movement of the young man. The Swiss banker was one of those keen observers and quick interpreters of human actions, who estimate the value of circumstances apparently trifling in themselves, and which would pass unnoticed by the majority of mankind. He was delighted with the conduct of the young stranger. In this simple action, he saw the revelations of a character. It was a guarantee of a love of order and economy, a certain pledge of the qualities in especial which should be possessed by a good financier. A young man who would thus painstakingly pick up a pin, could not fail to make a good clerk, merit the confidence of his employer, and reach a high degree of prosperity. In the evening of the same day, M. Lafitte received the following note from M. Perregeaux:—

" A place is made for you in my office, which you may take possession of to-morrow morning."

The anticipations of the banker were not disappointed. The young Lafitte possessed every desirable quality, and even more than was at first expected. From a simple clerk, he soon rose to be cashier, then partner, then head of the first banking house in Paris; and afterwards, in rapid succession, a Deputy, and President of the Council of Ministers—the highest point to which a citizen could aspire. Rarely have riches been placed in better hands—rarely has banker or prince made a more noble use of them. In 1836, M. Lafitte founded the joint-stock bank which goes by his name, and of which he was the head

and principal partner. His fortunes changed materially, for the worse, after the Revolution. He died in May, 1844, and was buried with great magnificence in the cemetery of Père la Chaise. He left one daughter, who married the prince of Moskowa, the son of Marshal Ney.

William Forbes, Scotch Banker.

The private banking house once universally known in Scotland under the lead of SIR WILLIAM FORBES, had a somewhat peculiar genealogy, reaching far back into the last century, and even faintly gleaming through the obscurities of the one before it, when mercantile efforts and speculations were taking their birth amidst the embers of scarcely extinct civil wars and all kinds of private barbarisms. The genealogy is traced to the firm of John Coutts & Co., of Edinburgh, in 1742, and the concern appears to be the main stock from which branched off the eminent London banking firms of Coutts & Co. and Herries & Co. It was the first banking house in Edinburgh.

Born in 1734, and fatherless when four years of age, Sir William had but little other means of help than the usual Scotch thrift. He rose, however, to be the head of the house which he had entered as an apprentice, without a capital, at fifteen; recovered the lost fortunes of his family, aided materially in establishing those of his country on a solid basis, and even became the sole preserver of much of her literary history which must otherwise have perished.

Originally confined to commercial dealing and general business traffic, the sole transactions of the house finally came to be those of banking. It subsequently yielded, once or twice, to the temptation of mercantile or merchandize speculation, but suffered from it, and ever afterward refused to engage, directly or indirectly, in anything but banking. Mr. Forbes died, in 1806, at the age of sixty-seven, and to his virtues Scott has paid a merited tribute in the dedication of one of the cantos of Marmion.

M. Steiglitz, Richest of Russian Merchants.

What the name of Rothschild is in other countries, and that of Astor in America, the name of STEIGLITZ is in Russia, and has been for half a century. It would doubtless still continue to hold this pre-eminence, but for the voluntary retirement of the proprietor, two or three years since, with a fortune computed, by Russian authorities, at scores of millions of dollars,—acquired by his connection with all the great financial concerns of the empire, and the numerous and extensive manufactories, sugar refineries, etc., which he carried on.

M. Steiglitz, senior, arrived in Russia about the commencement of the present century; he came from Hamburgh, and was a Jew by birth, but subsequently abandoned that faith and identified himself with Christianity. Immediately after his arrival in Russia he entered into business, and founded the great commercial and banking house which he bequeathed to his son, with the title of Baron, and a prodigious fortune. M. Steiglitz, junior, subsequently managed the house, and with such ability and success as to be able to retire with an estate valued at little short of *fifty millions of dollars.* This vast fortune consists in capital deposited in the imperial banks, in shares in the best Russian companies, and in landed estates, both in the south of Russia, in Livonia, and in Germany. He has the rank of Councillor of State, and is decorated with the grand cordon of the Order of St. Stanislaus. He married a Mdlle. Muller, belonging to a highly respectable, though not wealthy family, and has no children.

Solomon, the Merchant Sovereign.

KING SOLOMON was at once monarch and merchant; and it may easily be inferred, that no private merchant could safely compete with a prince so regal, who had assumed the mercantile character. By his intimate commercial union with the Tyrians, he was put into the most favorable of all positions for disposing of his goods. That energetic nation, possessing so small a strip of territory, had much need of various raw produce for their own wants. Another large demand was made by them for the raw materials of manufactures, and for articles which they could with advantage sell again; and as they were able, in turn, to sell so many acceptable luxuries to the court of Solomon, a most active exchange soon commenced. The carrying trade, which was shared between Solomon and the Tyrians, was probably the most lucrative part of the southern and eastern commerce. From Egypt, Solomon imported not only linen yarn, but even horses and chariots, which were sold again to the princes of Syria and of the Hittites; the light, strong, and elegant structure of the chariots rendering them very salable. Wine being abundant in Palestine, and wholly wanting in Egypt, was, no doubt, a principal means of repayment. That Solomon's trading correspondence also extended to Babylon, may be fairly inferred. He is said to have realized from a single voyage four hundred and fifty talents of gold, that is, *upwards of one hundred and twenty millions of dollars!* The business transactions of Solomon, it thus appears, were enormously large and lucrative; yet it does not appear that any fault was found with him on that account—particularly by his own subjects.

M. Bruck, Austria's Great Merchant Banker.

Some considerable number of years back, when the Greeks were in arms to assert their independence, a young man with a staff in his hand and a travelling knapsack on his back, presented himself at the office of a Greek merchant at Trieste, to whom he had a letter of introduction. Filled with youthful enthusiasm for the once glorious name of Greece, he was on his way to the Morea with the intention of joining the Greek insurgents.

The merchant, pleased with the youth's appearance, and perhaps influenced by the letter of introduction, thought it a pity that so much intelligence should be employed in warlike rather than in peaceful pursuits, and endeavored to dissuade him from his purpose. To give his argument its desired effect, he offered the adventurer a clerkship in his office. The offer was immediately accepted. The young man's name was BRUCK. He doubtless devoted himself with much zeal to the interests of his patron, for in a few years he became the head-clerk and manager of his business. A courtship shortly afterwards took place between him and the merchant's daughter, which ended in marriage with her and a partnership in business with her father.

This man became one of the ruling spirits in European commerce and finance, the extent of his business operations comporting with the high repute of the house with which he was identified. M. Bruck devoted himself to the formation of the Austrian Navigation Company; and he it was who established that well known commercial institution, the Austrian Lloyd's—for which he was indebted for a name to the mercantile phraseology of England,—and which he founded on principles similar to those by which the English Lloyd's is conducted. It is also due to his energy that railroads have been introduced and extended in Austria. And in addition to all this, his great financial and business talents caused him to be appointed Minister of Finance of the Empire,—like La-

bouchere in England, and Lafitte in France.

Jones Lloyd, London Banker.

The firm of JONES LLOYD & Co., consisting of two partners—father and son—has long held rank in London with those of the Coutts, Glyns, Denisons, Smiths, Barclays, Paynes, Willisses, and others, for immense extent of business and honorable dealing. The father has been mentioned as the only great banker in London who has made a fortune by banking, without having been bred to it. Banking sought him. He preserves, it is said, to this day, in his bedroom, a little table which used to stand many years ago in his shop at Manchester, and upon which, as people used to bring their money to him, his first accounts were kept. His wealth has been estimated at ten to twelve million dollars in ready money, the whole amount being kept floating in convertible securities for immediate use. Mr. Lewis Lloyd, according to his own account, began business in 1792, at Manchester, where having spent a year, he removed to London, where he concluded to remain, with a partnership in the Manchester firm. According to report, he was originally a Unitarian clergyman, but soon became tired of that vocation—finding it, as he is said to have sometimes confessed after dinner, "much more profitable and agreeable to spend his time in turning over bank notes, than in turning up the whites of his eyes." Mr. Lloyd seems to have been somewhat partial to this style of remark. Thus, when Frys and Chapman, the Quaker bankers, failed, a member of the society took his account to Mr. Lloyd: "We think you are right, friend," said the senior partner; "it is wiser to put thy money with a rich sinner than a poor saint."

James Lenox, Merchant, of New York.

The name of LENOX appears among some of the early Scotch emigrants, such as the Irvings, Masons, Douglasses, Grahams, &c. Robert Lenox became a distinguished New York merchant. His profits were wisely invested in land, and this became very valuable. His only son, JAMES, inherited the larger portion of this estate, whose increasing value made him a millionaire.

In his benefactions, Mr. Lenox is said to exercise close discrimination, and in this way has for years refused personal applications. This measure, indeed, was necessary, in order to escape a perpetual siege, which would soon have driven any man to distraction. He has been in the habit of considering written applications, and of selecting such as seemed worthy of his patronage. Mr. Lenox annually disburses, it is stated, an enormous sum in a most useful as well as most quiet manner. Indeed, his mansion has been described as one of the benevolent institutions of the day—its occupant being, to all intents and purposes, but an actuary, driven by perpetual duties and working with assiduity to fulfil an important trust. He is a thoroughly practical man, posted on all the details of business, and, inheriting the peculiar abilities and energy of his father, puts them to the best of use.

Mr. Lenox is a man of fine taste, and finds recreation in gathering rare books, of which he has a valuable collection, and he possesses, in addition, a splendid gallery of pictures, among these being two of Turner's landscapes.

Daniel Callaghan, the Irish Mercantile Celebrity.

One of the ablest and most accomplished merchants that Ireland ever produced was DANIEL CALLAGHAN, the elder,—shooting ahead of all the merchants in Ireland, by his native abilities, his shrewdness, enterprise, and tact. He set up, when but a stripling, in the butter trade, but was refused credit for the small amount of £400 at

Tonson & Warren's bank, as his first experience. He, however, finally obtained the aid he was in need of, and from that time pursued his business with great success. A great London merchant took the whole provision contract at that time, and the Cork merchants combined to engross the market. This was the moment chosen by Callaghan to reap the reward of the study he had bestowed, so inquiringly and systematically, upon the business of his choice. Alarmed at their position, one of the Londoners came over, and was still more dismayed when he reached Cork. Young Callaghan introduced himself, and, what was then thought a most presuming thing on his part, he gave a dinner to the Londoner, to which, however, he had some difficulty in getting guests. He soon showed the London firm the game it should play, and expounded all the resources in their power, to their enlightenment. A share of the contract was immediately given him, and, before the year expired, the same firm handed Callaghan £10,000, on his own word, after having hesitated, only nine months before, to take his bond with security for a few hundreds. There have been a few Irish merchants who have realized greater fortunes than Mr. C., who, at his culminating point, was rated at considerably above a million; but it was the splendid style in which he transacted his affairs, his off-hand dealing, his liberality and contempt for peddling, and his complete mercantile accomplishments, that placed him at the head of the Irish commercial world.

Henry Engelbert Haase, Banker, of Bremen.

Among those who have reached and passed through the "golden gate" of commercial success, is HENRY ENGELBERT HAASE, of Bremen, widely known at home and abroad, but whose career terminated so disastrously. By trade

10   COMMERCIAL AND BUSINESS ANECDOTES.

he amassed a large property, and was one of the most highly respected business men in Bremen—holding several public offices, was trustee of various funds, administrator of many estates, and guardian of a large number of orphan children. In fact, he abounded in both public and private charities, and he was always the one above all others to whom his friends intrusted their obligations when they were absent from the city. A certain coxcombry—for instance, he wore jewels and lace, which was not usual, and took every measure to conceal his age—was forgiven him, on account of the high esteem which he universally enjoyed. No one ever ventured in the slightest degree to ridicule Alderman Haase—in the opinion of every one, he stood higher than any other man in Bremen. He was remarkably hospitable; entertaining every week a distinguished company, and a degree of luxury was exhibited at his dinners, excusable only in a rich man without children. In his annual statement of the different trust funds he had in charge, he warmly solicited the inspection of the books, and often pretended that the value of the property had increased by advantageous purchase and sale of stocks, and frequently offered to show the overseers the certificates in various closets and oaken chests; but it was naturally deemed a gross imputation on such a wealthy trustee and sternly particular accountant, as well as a downright waste of time, to accept the offer. But at last, in one of the ways peculiar in such cases, an explosion took place, and his defalcations, squandered in luxury and "charity," were found to be immense. His house fell, and "great was the fall of it."

Preserved Fish, Merchant, of New York.

No name was better known in the mercantile community of New York than this, during the advanced life-

time of its owner. Mr. Fish was born in Rhode Island, July 3, 1766, of parents in obscure circumstances. He was at an early age apprenticed to the blacksmith business, but becoming dissatisfied with his employment and employers, he ran away, and shipped as a cabin boy in a whaling vessel. In this trade he made several voyages, gradually rising until he became master of a small whaling craft, and finally by his economy and industry accumulating a little capital.

In 1810, he quit his seafaring life and settled in New York, forming a business copartnership with his cousin, Mr. Joseph Grinnell, under the style of Fish & Grinnell, and which lasted until 1825, when Mr. Fish went to Europe and established a house in Liverpool, under the name of Fish, Cairns & Crary. He soon after returned to New York, forming a copartnership with Mr. Saul Alley and Joseph Lawrence, under the style of Fish, Alley & Lawrence, but which only continued for two or three years. As president of the Tradesmen's bank, to which position he was elected in 1829, his management was very successful, as the high dividends and large contingent fund of that institution, under his administration, show.

Mr. Fish was remarkable for great energy and decision of character, pursuing with ardor anything he undertook, and, like most men of this character, he was rather opinionative, and always firm in maintaining his own notions—possessing but little of the *suaviter in modo*, that *oily* process of operating which distinguishes the more polished man. Perhaps this trait which characterized Mr. Fish may be said to have been illustrated in the remark made by a certain eminent man, that "whenever I issue an order to a servant, I say *if you please*, and *if he don't please, I make him please.*" Still, in business qualifications, Mr. Fish had few superiors, and enjoyed the universal confidence of the mercantile community.

It may be said of him, that he was temperate in his habits, moderate in his desires, and neither parsimonious nor prodigal in his expenses; while his industry, economy and good judgment, enabled him to realize a fortune from which he derived an abundant income. He was three times married, but left no children. The story that he was picked up at sea, on a plank or in an open boat, and in that way acquired the name *Preserved*, was unfounded in truth; but its peculiarity probably added notoriety to a character already distinguished for consistency, a discriminating judgment and stern integrity.

The name of DAVID LEAVITT may also be here cited as that of one who exhibits in his habits of industry and his business judgment, as well as financial success, a parallel case with that of Mr. Fish. And to these distinguishing qualities as a business man, Mr. Leavitt unites the personal bearing of a bland and high-toned gentleman of the old school. Few names stand out brighter on the roll of illustrious American merchants, —attaining to wealth and distinction by every honorable means perseveringly applied,—than that of David Leavitt.

Amos Lawrence, Merchant, Boston.

According to the usual custom in New England, the first experience of AMOS LAWRENCE, in the sphere of business, was that of shop boy, and subsequently that of clerk. The firm by whom he was thus employed having, in course of time, become insolvent, Mr. L. conceived the idea of commencing business on his own account, and accordingly rented a shop on Cornhill, Boston. He was then, he says, in the matter of property, not worth a dollar. His father was comfortably off as a farmer, somewhat in debt, with perhaps four thousand dollars. His brother Luther was in the practice of law, getting forward, but not worth two thousand dollars; William had nothing; Abbott, a lad just fifteen years old, at school; and Samuel was a child of only seven years. Some four months before, Mr. Lawrence's father mortgaged his farm for the sum of one thousand dollars, and placed the proceeds in the hands of Amos, for his use in business. Although the latter was deeply affected by this act, which had been effected without consultation with any human being, he did not the less deeply regret it. He had no desire for aid that might cause others to suffer through their affording it. His own ideas on this point will be interesting: "My honored father brought to me one thousand dollars, and asked me to give him my note for it. I told him he did wrong to place himself in a situation to be made unhappy, if I lost the money. He told me he *guessed I would'nt lose it*, and I gave him my note. The first thing I did was to take four per cent. premium on my Boston bills—the difference then between passable and Boston money—and send a thousand dollars in bills of the Hillsborough Bank to Amherst, N. H., by my father, to my brother Luther, to carry to the bank and get specie, principally in silver change, for the bills, and he returned it to me in a few days. In the mean time, or shortly after, the bank had been sued, the bills discredited, and, in the end, proved nearly worthless. I determined not to use the money except in the safest way, and therefore loaned it to the Messrs. Parkman, in whom I had entire confidence. After I had been in business, and had made more than a thousand dollars, I felt that I could repay the money, come what would of it—being insured against fire, and trusting no one for goods. I used it in my business, but took care to pay off the mortgage as soon as it would be received."

Mr. Lawrence cleared fifteen hundred dollars the first year, and four thousand the second. Excessive credit he regarded as the rock upon which so many business men are broken. He therefore, at the commencement of his own business, adopted the plan of keeping an accurate account of merchandise bought and sold each day, with the profit, as far as practicable. This plan he pursued for a number of years; and he never found his merchandise fall short in taking an account of stock, which he did as often at least as once in each year. He was thus enabled to form an opinion of his actual state as a business man. He adopted also the rule always to have property, after the second year's business, to represent forty per cent. at least more than he owed—that is, never to be in debt more than two and one-half times his capital, a plan which saved him from ever getting embarrassed. The splendid fortune which Amos Lawrence amassed, during his business career, was thus founded in the most careful and upright regulations, and to these he rigidly adhered. He used his vast wealth for the best good of his fellow creatures; and his style of living, though elegant, as became one occupying so high a position, was marked by no extravagance. What his distinguished namesake, Cornelius W. Lawrence, has so long been in the commercial circles of the Empire State,—or its metropolis,—Amos Lawrence was in New England and its thriving capital. The history of both of these men is luminous with those traits and characteristics which lie at the foundation of prosperous commerce and individual renown.

Lorenzo de Medicis, "the Magnificent Merchant."

The MEDICI family is universally acknowledged to be the most splendid instance of commercial greatness which the world affords. The true source of the wealth and renown of the Medici was their superior talents, and the application of those talents to mercantile enterprise.

Cosmo de Medici and his grandson,

"the Magnificent Lorenzo," were practised and operative merchants, who by combining personal enterprise with the most exalted patriotism, and a love of trade with a devotion to science and literature, raised the city of Florence to an unexampled height of glory, and made themselves the first citizens of the world.

The high character of LORENZO, as a statesman and man of letters, was the means of obtaining from other countries privileges and advantages which rendered Florence the envy of the civilized world. The glory of the republic appeared at a distance to be concentred in himself. He seems to have arrived at proficiency in everything he undertook, and his individual success was made subservient to his country's good, his private gains being freely devoted to the defense of the state and the preservation of its honor.

Under the auspices of this family of merchants, literature, science, and the arts, flourished side by side with commerce. The Medicean Library, founded by Cosmo, and supported by his grandson, still exists in Florence, presenting the noblest of the many monuments of their glory, the most authentic depository of their magnificent fame.

Historians, poets, and philosophers, have combined to swell the notes of praise in honor of the merchant to whom posterity has awarded the title of "Magnificent." Thus, Voltaire says: "What a curious sight it is to see the same person with one hand sell the commodities of the Levant, and with the other support the burden of a state, maintaining factors and receiving ambassadors, making war and peace, opposing the pope, and giving his advice and mediation to the princes of his time, cultivating and encouraging learning, exhibiting shows to the people, and giving an asylum to the learned Greeks that fled from Constantinople! Such was Lorenzo de Medicis; and when to these particular distinctions, the glorious names of the father of his country and the mediator of Italy are appended, who seems more entitled to the notice and admiration of posterity than this illustrious citizen of. Florence?" This eulogy is as beautifully as it is wisely and truthfully penned.

The death of this great man, whose splendid career terminated at the early age of forty-four years, called forth from his townsman and contemporary, the wise but profligate Machiavelli, the following encomium : " No man ever died in Florence, or in the whole extent of Italy, with a higher reputation, or more lamented by his country. Not only his fellow citizens, but all the princes of Italy, were so sensibly affected by his death, that there was not one of them who did not send ambassadors to Florence, to testify their grief, and to condole with the republic on so great a loss." The busts and portraits of this illustrious merchant adorn almost every art-collection and gallery in the capitals of Europe.

Henry Hope, the Amsterdam Banker.

The great Amsterdam banking house of Hope & Co. was established in the seventeenth century by HENRY HOPE, a Scottish gentleman, a descendant of John de Hope, who came in 1537 from France to Scotland, in the train of Madeleine, queen of James V.

Mr. Hope was one of the most exalted of his class. It was he who opened the way for the autocratic power of Russia, under the empress Catharine II., to the confidence of the then wealthiest capitalists in Europe, the Dutch, and thereby laid the foundation of Russian credit. Always treated by the empress with great distinction, he was honored with the gift from her own hand, of her portrait, the full size of life. This picture occupied the place of honor in the superb gallery of paintings, fitted up by Mr. Hope in his palace " t'Huys ten Bosch," now a royal pleasure-place, which he had built in the domain of

Harlem. Upon his emigration to England, he took this splendid gallery, entirely composed of cabinet pieces, with him, having it at his residence in Cavendish Square.

To the tone of a refined gentleman and man of the world, he united a certain amiable affability, which won upon all who were numbered among his associates. The trouble of *his* heart, however, was the notorious relations of his niece, Madam Williams Hope, with a Dutch officer of dragoons, by the name of Dopff. The larger part of Hope's fortune, which he had bequeathed to Henry, the eldest son of this niece, and who died unmarried, passed, at the decease of the latter, to Adrian, the second son, who left no male heirs, but from whom it descended to Francis, the third son, born several years afterward, —this third inheritor being the rich and well known Mr. Hope, of Paris, the last member of that branch of the whole family.

One of the leading members of this vast establishment, in the early part of the present century, was Mr. Henry Hope, who was born in this country, being the son of a Scotch loyalist who had settled in Boston, Mass. This Henry Hope lived some time in the town of Quincy, Mass., and was a poor youth when he emigrated from that place to England, at the close of the last century. Mr. John Williams, an Englishman, who married his niece, and who assumed the name of John Williams Hope, and afterward that of John Hope, was the manager of the establishment. Among the silent partners of the house were Adrian Hope, Henry Philip Hope, and Thomas Hope, the author of " Anastasius." The oldest active member of the firm was Mr. Peter Cæsar Labouchere, the interesting circumstances relating to whom, in his elevation to this high position, are narrated on another page of this work.

The governments with whom this house entertain the most intimate financial relations, are those of Holland, Russia, and Spain. The Hope certificates, as the stocks are called, which the Russian government has given to the Dutch bankers, in acknowledgment of its debt, amount to about twenty-five millions of dollars. Although much less powerful in its monetary sway than the Rothschilds, the Hopes hold in some respects a position superior to the Jewish bankers. Sir Archibald Hope, and the Earl of Hopetoun (John Alexander Hope), are the present representatives of the English and elder branch of the Hope family. Some of the great financial transactions of this eminent house, as given in other parts of this volume, will be found to possess scarcely less interest than a romance.

Francis Child, the Founder of English Banking Houses.

The celebrity of the first London banking house belongs, by common consent, to Mr. FRANCIS CHILD. This gentleman, who was the father of his profession, and possessed a large property, began business shortly after the Restoration. He was, originally, apprenticed to William Wheeler, pawnbroker and banker, whose shop was on the site of the present world-renowned banking house. The foundation of his importance arose from the good old fashion of marrying his master's daughter, and through this he succeeded to his estate and business. The latter he subsequently confined entirely to the banking department. The principles on which he founded it, and the remarkable clauses in his will, by which he regulated its future conduct, show him to have been a man of the highest business character. It has maintained to the present day, amid all the chances and changes of banking, the same position and the same respectability which he bequeathed to it.   .

Stephen Whitney, Merchant, of New York.

STEPHEN WHITNEY was so long an habitué of Wall street, Front street, and Coenties slip, that even now (says a writer in the " Continental Magazine ") we almost momentarily expect to meet him. His office was held for years in the second story of a warehouse in Front street, a spot in whose vicinity he had passed nearly threescore years. Thither he had come, in his boyhood, a poor, friendless, New Jersey lad, had found friends and employment, had at last got to be a grocer, and had gradually accumulated a large capital by the closest economy. At this time, the war of 1812 broke out, and cotton became very low, in consequence of the difficulty of shipping it to England. Mr. Whitney had at that time a vast amount of outstanding accounts in the Southern States, and his debtors were glad to pay him in this depreciated article. We have been informed that Jackson's cotton defenses of New Orleans were of his property. As neutral ships were permitted to sail between the belligerent ports, Mr. Whitney exported large quantities of cotton to England, and held the balance of his stock until the close of the war, when it advanced enormously. This advance, together with the proceeds of his exports, at once made him a millionnaire, and the capital thus acquired never lost a chance of increase. Giving up the details of trade, Mr. Whitney bought large quantities of real estate, on which he erected warehouses and obtained a princely rental.

Francis Cabot Lowell, Merchant, of Boston.

This distinguished merchant was a native of Newburyport, Mass., where he was born in 1775, and died in Boston in 1817. In 1810, Mr. LOWELL visited England, on account of the state of his health; and on his return home, shortly after the commencement of the war of 1812, he became so strongly convinced of the practicability of introducing the cotton manufacture into the United States, that he proposed to his kinsman, Patrick T. Jackson, to make the experiment on an ample scale.

The result of his project was the establishment of manufactures at Waltham, and the foundation of the city of Lowell, which was named after himself. He visited Washington in 1816, and his personal influence with Mr. Lowndes, Mr. Calhoun, and other leading members of Congress, contributed largely to the introduction into the tariff act of that year of the protective clause which gave such an impetus to the cotton manufacture in the United States.

Johannes Fugger, and the Great Commercial Family of Fuggers.

The origin of the proverb "as rich as a Fugger" is in the name of a German family of immensely wealthy merchants. Its founder was JOHANNES FUGGER, a weaver of Graben, near Augsburg, who lived in the first half of the fourteenth century, and acquired a large property in lands by commerce in cloths. His son, of the same name, continued the occupation of weaver, to which he also added that of cloth merchant. Andreas, eldest son of the latter, lived about 1400, and was widely known as "*Fugger the Rich.*" The nephews of the last, Ulrich, Georg, and Jakob, born about the middle of the fifteenth century, covered the Baltic with their commerce, which extended also to Hungary, Italy, and even to India, and were able to influence the affairs of the empire by lending money to the princes, and were in course of time created nobles. After attaining to high political dignities, they continued their commerce, built in the Tyrol the splendid castle of Fuggerau, greatly embellished the city of Augsburg, and found a new source of wealth by working the mines of Iaathal, Falkenstein, and Schwartz. The only

heirs of these three brothers were two sons of Ulrich, Raimund and Anton. The latter raised the family to its highest degree of prosperity and power. The emperor Charles V. resorted to them both when pressed for money, yielded to them the privilege of coining, and made them counts and princes of the empire, and was lodged in the splendid mansion of Anton when he attended the diet of Augsburg. So wealthy were they, through the success attending their commercial enterprise, that "as rich as a Fugger" became a proverb. The most important branches of this family at present are the princely houses of Kirchberg and Babenhausen.

Benjamin Bussey, Merchant, of Boston.

BENJAMIN BUSSEY was for a long period known as one of the old school merchants of Boston—only a few of whom now remain as representatives of that highly honored and most worthy class.

He was in the early part of his life engaged in the occupation of a silversmith, and on going into business on his own account he had only a very small amount of paper money, which his father gave him, accompanied with the characteristic advice of that day, to be always diligent,—to spend less than he earned,—and never to deceive or disappoint any one. From his grandfather he also obtained the additional sum, at this time, of fifty dollars in silver money. Having purchased the necessary tools, he had only ten dollars left as his whole capital, and owed fifty dollars borrowed money. But he possessed an iron constitution, principles of strict integrity, and a spirit of perseverance which nothing could subdue or tire. In one year he made himself acquainted with all the details of a silversmith's art; he had by his good business management acquired some capital, and his success had been equal to his expectations. Articles of gold and silver wrought by his own hand—and well wrought, too,—may still be met with in and near Boston. In two years he purchased the real estate on which was his store. He subsequently engaged 'in trade, in Dedham, and afterward in Boston, soon reaching a high position as a merchant. His business rapidly increased, he became deeply concerned in commerce, dealt largely with England, France, and Holland, owned several large vessels, and was engaged in heavy and distant mercantile adventures—though all of them were legitimate business transactions, for he never speculated. He seldom gave or took credit. The immense fortune which he left ultimately goes, by his will, to Harvard University.

Peter Cooper, Merchant, of New York.

It is an interesting fact, that the first idea of PETER COOPER'S great University of Science, or "Institute," arose in his mind when he was young and thirsting for knowledge, which at that time he could not buy in New York, even with the money which he earned in his trade. One day, a friend told him of a visit he had lately made to Paris, where he had been able to learn whatever he wished, without money and without price, at the University endowed by the first Napoleon. Peter Cooper, with all the ardor of his aspiring mind, wished that there was such an opportunity in America, and this idea he said never left him afterward. When he began to be very successful, this idea began to take shape, till at last it has built that monumental palace of Science for " whosoever will "—the Cooper Institute, involving the munificent individual appropriation of six hundred thousand dollars, and which bids fair to rival, at some future day, the most magnificent universities of Europe. The successful glue-maker has always in a measure " stuck to his glue," and now not merely sits in the palace due

to his opulence and high position as a merchant, but is besides an intellectual noble of the first class.

George Peabody, American Merchant and Banker, of London.

GEORGE PEABODY was born in Danvers, Mass., Feb. 18, 1795, of parents in humble circumstances, though industrious and respectable. His father, however, died when George was in his teens, and, from the first, he was aware that in the battle of life before him he must depend on himself alone. Fortunately for himself and many others, he very early found that he *could* thus depend on his unaided efforts. Incidents strongly displaying ambition, energy, and perseverance, marked the whole course of his youth. The hard earnings of his boyhood were cheerfully devoted to the comfort of his mother, his brothers, and sisters; and he subsequently charged himself with their entire support, and cheerfully practised every self-denial that he might serve them. It is always safe to say, that the son and brother who has shown himself true to the claims of kindred, will be found wanting in none of the relations of life; and George Peabody is an eminent illustration of the truth of this saying.

.At the age of thirteen he became clerk for a grocer, and remained with him about three years. Afterward, he went with an uncle to Georgetown, and in course of time he attracted the attention of Mr. Riggs, the capitalist, with whom he finally went into business—Riggs furnishing the money and Peabody the brains. The house was removed to Baltimore, and prospered so well that branches were established in New York and Philadelphia. In 1837 he went to England to buy goods, and formed many acquaintances with its leading merchants and politicians. He now took up his permanent residence in England, and severed his connection with Peabody, Riggs & Co., in 1838.

He rendered important service in preventing the complete prostration of American securities, and particularly those of Maryland, in London, in 1837, but refused all compensation for what he did. While he has lived in England, his establishment has been a headquarters for Americans, whom he has always welcomed with a generous hospitality. The princely gift of seven hundred and fifty thousand dollars was made a short time ago to the destitute of London, but was not the first instance of his public spirited generosity. In 1852, he sent a toast to a semi-centennial festival at his native town, Danvers, which was to be opened at the table. It was: "Education, a debt to future generations;" and to pay his share of that debt, he inclosed twenty thousand dollars, to be expended in establishing an institute, library and lyceum for the town. The sum has since been increased to sixty thousand, with ten thousand dollars additional for a branch library at No. Danvers. Mr. Peabody subscribed ten thousand dollars toward the first Grinnell expedition to the Arctic sent in search of Franklin. In 1856, he gave three hundred thousand dollars, with a pledge to make it five hundred thousand, for the establishment of an institute in Baltimore, to be devoted to science, literature and art. A record of colossal munificence is that of George Peabody.

John McDonogh, Millionnaire, of New Orleans.

JOHN McDONOGH was born in Baltimore, Md., in 1779. The only incidents of his youth that are known are, that he was a clerk in a mercantile store in an inland town of Maryland; that he was noted then for eccentricities, and for an excess of imagination, which led to the apprehension that he was not entirely of sound mind. Still, his energy and intelligence secured him employment and the confidence of his employers.

About the year 1800 he was sent out to New Orleans by a house in Baltimore, with a letter of credit and considerable resources. He then engaged largely in business, but soon renounced his position as agent, and starting on his own account, became a leading and prosperous merchant. In a few years he accumulated a large fortune, say at least three hundred thousand dollars. He was one of the nabobs of the city, and his style of living, and his habits, conformed to his position and resources. His mansion was one of the most showy and luxurious in the city. He kept his carriages and horses, his cellar of costly wines, and entertained on a scale of great extravagance and sumptuousness. He was, in fact, the centre of fashion, frivolity, sociability, and even of the fashionable dissipations of the day. His person, which even in extreme old age was remarkable for dignity, erectness, and courtliness, was at this period conspicuous for all the graces of manhood. Owing to some peculiar experiences of a private nature—an account of which will be found in our ANECDOTES OF MERCHANTS IN THEIR DOMESTIC RELATIONS,—Mr. McDonogh eventually became secluded and morose, though prosecuting his acquisition of property with augmented vigor, his peculiar passion being that of accumulating countless acres of waste and suburban land. All his views regarded the distant future. The present value and productiveness of land were but little regarded by him. His only recreation and pleasure were in estimating the value of his swamp and waste land fifty, a hundred, and even a thousand years to come. This passion at last gained such an ascendency over him, that he seemed to court and luxuriate in waste and desolation. He would buy cultivated places, and let them go to ruin. He would build on his lots in the city miserable shanties and rookeries, which

2

would absolutely taint the neighborhood, and thus enable him to buy out
his neighbors at low rates.

He could not be induced, by any
offer or consideration, to alienate any
of the property he had once acquired.
Abstemious to a fault, and withholding
himself from all the enjoyments and
associations of the world, he devoted
his time to the care of his large estate,
to the suits in which such acquisitions
constantly involved him, working for
seventeen hours out of the twenty-four,
the greater part of which labor consisted in writing the necessary documents relating to his titles, and in
corresponding with his lawyers and
his overseers. For the fifty years of
his residence in New Orleans, he never
left the State, and rarely, if ever, passed
beyond the limits of the corporation.
He was not a usurer, a money lender,
nor a speculator. He acquired by
legitimate purchase, by entries on public
lands. He dealt altogether in land.
Stocks, merchandise, and other personal securities, were eschewed by him.
The wonder is, how, with a comparatively small revenue, his property not
being productive, and his favorite
policy being to render his lands wild
and unsuited for cultivation, he was
able to go on every year expanding the
area of his vast possessions.

Sampson Gideon, the Rival of Roths-child.

SAMPSON GIDEON, the great Jew
banker, as he was commonly called—
and the rival and enemy of Rothschild
—was the financial support of the illustrious Sir Robert Walpole, the oracle
and leader in all monetary matters, and
his name was as familiar in the last
century as those of Goldschmid and
Rothschild. A shrewd, sarcastic man,
possessing a rich vein of humor, the
anecdotes and reminiscences preserved
of him are, unhappily, few and far between. " Never grant a life annuity to
an old woman," he would say ; " they

wither, but they never die." And if
the proposed annuitant coughed with
a violent asthmatic cough on approaching the room door, Gideon would call
out, " Aye, aye, you may cough, but it
shan't save you six months' purchase !"

In one of his dealings with Mr. Snow,
the banker—immortalized by Dean
Swift—the latter lent Gideon £20,000.
Shortly afterward, the " forty-five "
broke out ; the success of the Pretender
seemed certain ; and Mr. Snow, alarmed
for his cherished property, addressed a
piteous epistle to the Jew. A run upon
his office, a stoppage, and a bankruptcy, were the least phenomena the banker's imagination pictured ; and the
whole concluded with an earnest request for his money. Gideon went to
the bank, procured twenty notes, sent
for a vial of hartshorn, rolled the vial
in the notes, and thus grotesquely
Mr. Snow received the money he had
lent.

The greatest hit Gideon ever made
was when the rebel army approached
London ; when. the king was trembling ; when the prime minister was
undetermined, and stocks were sold at
any price. Unhesitatingly he went to
Jonathan's, bought all in the market,
advanced every guinea he possessed,
pledged his name and reputation for
more, and held as much as the remainder
of the members held together. When
the Pretender retreated and stocks rose,
the Jew experienced the advantage of
his foresight, in immense gains.

Khan, the Great Persian Merchant.

When Georgia was invaded by Mo-
hammed, the founder of the present Persian dynasty, the only one of the Khoras-
sanian chiefs who was not obliged to
give hostages of fidelity was ISAAC
KHAN, chief of Turbet-e-Hyderee, a
man of low birth, who, by the pursuits
of commerce, had been able, like the
Medici family in Italy, to obtain a
territory of two hundred miles in

length, and to raise himself from being overseer of a caravansary, to the rank of an independent sovereign and the most eminent merchant and trader in the whole realm. His revenue was reckoned at one million dollars, two hundred thousand of which was realized from the merchandise in which he traded, and the rest from his land property, etc., which he had come in possession of by means of his vast and successful mercantile transactions. He had six thousand troops in his pay, but chiefly trusted to his policy for the maintenance of his power; nor did ever prince more securely reign in the hearts of his subjects, and of the merchants whom he had attracted to his new emporium. To these, as well as to pilgrims and beggars of every country and religion, his hall was always open; and it was 'his principal relaxation from the fatigues of public affairs and commercial traffic, to dine in company with the motley multitude,—conversing on equal terms with all, acquiring an accurate knowledge of everything which concerned the welfare of the people, and admired by his guests for his affability.

Jamsetjee Jeejeebhoy, the Great Parsee Merchant.

One of the most remarkable East India merchants, a native of the Parsee race and faith, and ranking with the highest and the most enlightened among Europeans of the same business calling, was JAMSETJEE JEEJEEBHOY. He was born at Bombay in 1783, and his father was so poor that he followed the profession of a " bottly-wallah," that is, a bottle-fellow, buying and selling old bottles. At the age of nineteen, Jamsetjee entered into partnership with his father-in-law, Framjee Nusserwanjee, and in the following years made several successful voyages to China.

Possessing those qualities most desirable in a merchant, integrity, judgment, and enterprise, he gradually extended his dealings to other countries, and drew in a rich harvest of gains. His ships, built by the excellent Parsee shipwrights of Bombay, traded with all parts of the East, and now and then sailed even round the Cape. Year after year he prospered, and when he had been twenty years in business, he had acquired a large and still increasing fortune. He did not, however, in winning his fortune, forget or mistake how to spend it.

In the course of a few years, Jeejeebhoy's benefactions amounted to some $300,000. The East India Government made a report of his enlightened munificence to the Home Government, and the latter conferred upon him the rare and distinguished honor of knighthood. It was the first instance, indeed, of any royal title being bestowed by the English government upon a native of India. The ceremony of presentation took place at the Governor's House. The circumstance was one not only highly gratifying to Sir Jamsetjee Jeejeebhoy himself, but to the native community in general, who are accustomed to attach an extravagant value to any such marks of honor. It was consequently determined by some of the most influential natives to offer him a testimonial at once of their respect for his character, and their gratification at the distinction he had obtained. A sum of fifteen thousand rupees was consequently raised, and invested—not in a silver service, a bust, or a statue, but—in a fund, the interest of which should be devoted to procuring translations of popular and important works from other languages into Guzeratte, the language chiefly in use among the Parsees.

Vincent Nolte, the Wandering Merchant.

VINCENT NOLTE has been termed "the wandering merchant." He was born at Leghorn, in Italy, and lived, successively, in Leghorn, Hamburg,

Trieste, Venice, Nantes, Paris, Amsterdam, London, Philadelphia, and New Orleans. He began his life as a clerk in the house of Otto Frank & Co., at Leghorn, in 1795; while drawing caricatures, the theatres, dress, and flirtation, formed his real occupation. His tailor's bill, at the end of a year, presented the not inconsiderable sum total of twelve coats of all colors, and twenty-two pairs of hose and pantaloons, which were just then coming into fashion,—rather fast life for a youth of sixteen. He saw Bonaparte at Leghorn, in 1796; saw Wellington and the allies at Paris, in 1815; fought under Jackson, at New Orleans, in 1814, and was with Lafayette, in Paris, during the revolution of 1830. How many times he crossed the Atlantic it would be difficult to say.

Mr. Nolte was termed "the giant of cotton speculation" at New Orleans; he was also a contractor for supplying the French army with muskets; the mercantile agent in Cuba and the United States of the house of Hope & Co., of Amsterdam; and agent of the Barings; an operator in stocks; a translator of manuscripts at Venice; a *Trésor de Numismatique et de Glyptique*; a writer on finance; and an editor. He stood in business and social relations with most of the great men of "high finance" of the last century—with the Barings, Labouchère, Hottinguer, Lafitte, Ouvrard, etc.

"Lord Timothy Dexter," the Eccentric Merchant, of Newburyport, Mass.

According to his own account, TIMOTHY DEXTER was born in Malden, Mass., Jan. 22, 1747. After having served as an apprentice to a leather dresser, he commenced business in Newburyport, where he also married a widow, who owned a house and a small piece of land, part of which, soon after the nuptials, was converted by him into a shop and tanyard for his own use.

By application to his business, his property increased, and the purchase of a large tract of land near Penobscot, together with an interest which he bought in the Ohio Company's purchase, eventually afforded him so much profit as to induce him to buy up public securities at forty cents for the pound, which securities soon after became worth twenty shillings on the pound. By these and other fortunate business transactions, he prospered so greatly, that property now was no longer the sole object of his pursuit; he exchanged this god of idolatry for that of *popularity*. He was charitable to the poor, gave liberal donations to religious societies, and handsomely rewarded those who wrote in his praise. His lordship —a self-conferred title—about this time acquired his peculiar taste for style and splendor, set up an elegant equipage, and, at great cost, adorned the front of his mansion with numerous figures of illustrious personages.

Some of his lordship's speculations in trade have become quite as celebrated for their oddity as those of Rothschild for their unscrupulous cunning. He once anxiously inquired of some merchants, whom he knew, how he should dispose of a few hundred dollars. Wishing to hoax him, they answered, "Why, buy a cargo of warming pans, and send them to the West Indies, to be sure." Not suspecting the trick, he at once bought all the warming pans he could find, and sent them to a climate where—there was every reason to suppose—ice would be far more acceptable. But "Providence sometimes shows his contempt of wealth, by giving it to fools." The warming pans met with a ready sale—the tops being used for strainers, and the lower parts for dippers, in the manufacture of molasses.

With the proceeds of his cargo of warming pans, Dexter built a fine vessel; and being informed by the carpenter that *scales* were wanting, he called on an acquaintance, and said, "My head workman sends me word that he wants 'wales' for the vessel. What does he mean?" "Why, whalebones, to be sure," answered the man, who, like everybody else, was tempted to improve the opportunity of imposing upon Dexter's stupidity. Whalebones were accordingly bought; but, finding that Boston could not furnish enough, he emptied New York and Philadelphia. The ship-carpenters, of course, had a hearty laugh at his expense; but, by a singular turn of fortune, this blunder was also the means of increasing his wealth. It soon after became fashionable for ladies to wear stays completely lined with whalebone; and as none was to be found in the country, on account of his having thus so completely swept the market, it brought a golden price. Thus his coffers were a second time filled by his odd transactions.

Joshua Bates, of the House of Baring & Co.

An honored member of the great firm of Baring Brothers & Co., London, is JOSHUA BATES. Mr. Bates is a native of Weymouth, Mass., where he was born in 1788, being the only son of Col. Joshua Bates, of that place. He received his early education under Rev. Jacob Norton, and at the age of fifteen entered the counting-room of William R. Gray, of Boston, an accomplished man of business.

Young Bates showed a remarkable aptitude for commercial knowledge and a commercial career, on which account he was intrusted with the extensive business concerns not only of his first employer, but of the latter's father also, the elder Mr. Gray, for a long time the leading merchant in New England and exceeded by but a few in the world, in respect to extent of shipping.

The war with England proving disastrous to mercantile pursuits, Mr. Bates was despatched to Europe, to look after Mr. Gray's extensive maritime interests in that quarter. This, of course, brought him into relations with some of the leading commercial and banking houses of Europe, especially of the Hopes and the Barings, who were greatly impressed with his remarkable talent and judgment in respect to whatever concerned the commerce of the world. In the year 1826, through the influence of Messrs. Baring Brothers & Co., he formed a house in London, in connection with Mr. John Baring, son of Sir Francis Baring, under the firm of Bates & Baring. On the death of the late Mr. Holland, these gentlemen were both made partners in the house of Baring Brothers & Co., and of which Mr. Bates has ever since been an active and efficient member, giving to it much of that commanding influence which it enjoys both in Europe and America. Mr. Bates has long been noted for his large-hearted charities on both sides of the Atlantic. His most munificent donations to the Boston Public Library are well known; but his benevolence has by no means been confined to that object alone.

Mr. Bates was married, in 1813, to Lucretia Augusta, of the Boston branch of the Sturgis family, by whom he has only one surviving child, Madame Van de Wyer, wife of the eminent statesman who has more than once been called to administer the government of Belgium, and more recently officiating as its diplomatic representative at the court of St. James.

James Morrison, "of twenty millions."

JAMES MORRISON, who well deserved the title given him of a "modern Crœsus," was until his death one of the extremely rich men of London. In mental character, and with boundless wealth entirely self-acquired, this great millionnaire was certainly remarkable as a man and a merchant. He was of common parents, originally of Scotch descent. Early transplanted to the English metropolis, at the end of the last century, the country boy first set foot in London unaided, in search of his fortunes. After the close of the great Continental wars, and the consequent rapid extension of population and wealth, Mr. Morrison was one of the first English traders who reversed his system of management, by an entire departure from the old plan of exacting the highest prices. His new principle was the substitution of the lowest remunerative scale of profit and a more rapid circulation of capital; the success of this experiment was soon seen in his enormously augmented trade. " Small profits and quick returns " was his motto, and he therefore became widely known as the " Cheap Merchant." From his earliest settlement in London, he was associated with the liberal party in politics,— even in the worst of times,—nor did his later gains of immense wealth ever vary his political principles. As a member of Parliament, he devoted himself to questions and measures relating to trade, foreign commerce, the currency, and railways. His accumulations amounted to the prodigious sum of twenty millions of dollars.

Mr. Morrison retired from active business several years since, but without withdrawing his capital from the mercantile house; and though managing his vast funds himself up to the time of his death (which recently occurred) with all the sagacity of earlier days, he became haunted with the idea that he should come to want. He finally commenced doing day labor on a farm held by one of his tenants, for which labor he was regularly paid twelve shillings a week, and this he continued up to the time of his last illness. For eighteen months before his death he was an habitual applicant for relief to the parish, assembling twice a week with the town paupers, and receiving with each one of them his two shillings and a quartern loaf. His friends indulged him in these fancies,

on the ground that it was the best choice of two evils. And yet he made a most judicious will, and his investments up to the last were characterized by great good sense.

The probate duty on Mr. Morrison's will exceeded five hundred thousand dollars. Among his possessions was his seat at Basildon Park, which cost over six hundred thousand dollars, and the furniture four hunded and fifty thousand. The mansion on this estate was left to his widow, with an annuity of fifty thousand dollars yearly. The estate itself was left to his son Charles, as well as the Islay estate in Scotland, which latter cost about two and a-half millions of dollars. This is let to numerous tenants, and from its extent and vastness may be termed a principality. His son Charles was likewise bequeathed the round sum of $5,000,000 under the will. Besides being possessed of Fonthill Abbey, Hone Park, Sussex, and his town palace in Harley street, Mr. Morrison had shares amounting to four hundred thousand dollars in the Victoria Docks, and large acquisitions in the United States.

———

Jacob Little, " of Wall Street."

The name of JACOB LITTLE has long been so largely and universally associated with the financial operations of which Wall street, New York, is the especial theatre, that that *locale* may with more appropriateness perhaps than any other be connected with his name and reminiscences.

Mr. Little was born in Newburyport, Mass., and, when twenty years of age, he went to New York to seek his fortune and give play to the business faculties and aptitude with which nature had endowed him. His means were small, but his intelligence was quick and made readily available to his circumstances and purposes. He became, in a short time, a clerk in the employment of Jacob Barker, and, under such tuition and example, it must indeed have been his own fault, if he did not find himself, at the close of his five years' service, prepared to follow *some* calling with shrewdness and success. His career shows that the opportunities thus enjoyed were not lost upon him. On leaving Mr. Barker, Mr. Little commenced the business of exchange and specie broker, on his own account, and in this sphere left nothing undone that could contribute to an energetic and successful pursuit of his business, and to securing the confidence of those who intrusted to him their orders and funds. His activity, decision, and good judgment, gave him a high place in monetary circles, wealth and favor rolled in upon him, and though he has more than once had to yield to the revulsions in the stock and money market, he has shown the rare quality of being as faithful to his creditors as to himself.

Mr. Little has been humorously written of as equally the hero and the dupe of the American stock exchange —the heir of Ouvrard—the confidant of bank presidents—the untiring projector of time bargains—and every now and then he becomes so jaded and out of breath, that he himself cannot be "called to time." He has for some forty years thrown an air of enchantment about speculation; has devised more pitfalls for the credulous, as well as for the cautious, than any man of his time—repeatedly losing or impairing his financial power, and as often regaining it. He was made to wrestle with fortune, and to fall with a laughing face. Hundreds of satellites revolve about him, set when he sets, and rise when he rises. If fate should compel him to a period of inaction, his condition would be most miserable.

The Rothschilds, Wealthiest Bankers in the World.

The house of ROTHSCHILD is the impersonation of that money power which governs the world. For nearly half a century their influence has been continually on the increase; and to them, more than to any monarch or minister of state, however potential, Europe is indebted for the preservation of peace between the great powers. To give even an outline of the immense and successful operations which have placed a German Jew, his sons, and grandsons, at the head of the moneyed interests of the world, it would be necessary to embrace the history of European finance since the year 1812.

Meyer Anselm Rothschild was the founder of this house, about the year 1740; he was a money-changer and exchange broker, a man of fair character, and in easy circumstances. After the battle of Jena, October, 1806, Napoleon decreed the forfeiture of their states by the sovereigns of Brunswick and of Hesse-Cassel, and a French army was put in march to enforce the decree. Too feeble to resist, the landgrave prepared for flight. But in the vaults of his palace he had twelve million florins—about $5,000,000—in silver. To save this great and bulky amount of money from the hands of the French was a matter of extreme difficulty, as it could not be carried away, and the landgrave had so little confidence in his subjects that he could not bring himself to confide his case to their keeping, especially as the French would inflict severe punishment on him or them who might undertake the trust. In his utmost need, the landgrave bethought himself of Meyer Anselm Rothschild, sent for him to Cassel, and entreated him to take charge of the money; and by way of compensation for the dangers to which Mr. Rothschild exposed himself, the landgrave offered him the free use of the entire sum, without interest. On these terms, Mr. Rothschild undertook the trust, and by the assistance of some friends, Jewish bankers at Cassel, the money was so carefully stowed away, that when the French, after a hurried march, arrived in the city, they found the old landgrave gone, and his treasure vanished.

At the time this large sum of money was placed in M. A. Rothschild's hands, he had five sons, of whom three, Anselm, Nathan, and Solomon, had arrived at man's estate. These he associated with himself. By their skilful management, the large sum of ready money at their disposal increased and multiplied with astonishing rapidity. The fall of Napoleon enabled the old landgrave to return to Cassel, and he gave the Rothschilds notice that he should withdraw the money he had confided to them; but before the notice expired, Napoleon's return from the isle of Elba so greatly alarmed the landgrave that he urged the Rothschilds to keep the money at the low rate of two per cent. per annum, which they did until his death, in 1823, when the Rothschilds refused to keep it any longer.

At the period of Meyer Anselm Rothschild's death, which occurred so unexpectedly, he saw his five sons placed respectively at the head of five immense establishments—at Frankfort, London, Paris, Vienna, and Naples, all united in a copartnership which is universally allowed to be the most wealthy and extensive the world has ever seen. And, whatever exceptions may be made to the manner in which the business of these houses has been conducted, in some operations which have marked their career, it must be admitted that rarely does a family furnish so many members who are competent, individually, to be intrusted with such vast financial concerns.

Although Mr. ROTHSCHILD was commonly termed a merchant, his most important transactions were in connection with stocks, loans, etc. It was here that his great decision, his skilful combinations, and his unequalled energy, made him remarkable. At a time when the funds were constantly varying, the temptation was too great for a capitalist like

Mr. Rothschild to withstand. His operations were soon noticed; and when the money market was left without an acknowledged head, by the deaths of Sir Francis Baring and Abraham Goldschmid—for the affairs of the latter were wound up, and the successors of the former did not then aim at the autocracy of the money market,—the name of Nathan Meyer Rothschild was in the mouths of all financial dealers as a prodigy of success. Cautiously, however, did the great banker proceed, until he had made a fortune as great as his future reputation. He revived all the arts of an older period. He employed bankers to depress or raise the market for his benefit, and is said to have purchased in one day to the extent of four million pounds. His transactions soon pervaded the entire globe. The old and the new world alike bore witness to his skill; and with the profits on a single loan he purchased an estate which cost seven hundred and fifty thousand dollars. Minor capitalists, like parasitical plants, clung to him, and were always ready to advance their money in speculations at his bidding. Nothing seemed too gigantic for his grasp—nothing too minute for his notice. His mind was as capable of contracting a loan for tens of millions, as of calculating the lowest possible amount on which a clerk could exist. Like too many great merchants and bankers, whose profits are counted by thousands and millions, he paid his assistants the smallest amount for which he could procure them.

Rothschild in London knew the result of the battle of Waterloo eight hours before the British Government, and the value of this knowledge was no less than *one million dollars, gained in one forenoon.* No bad loan was ever taken in hand by the Rothschilds; no good loan ever fell into other hands. Any financial operation on which they frowned, was sure to fail. And so conscious were they of their influence, that after the July revolution in 1830, Anselm Rothschild, of Frankfort, declared,—and the declaration was made to sound in imperial ears,—" The house of Austria desires war, but the house of Rothschild requires peace."

In addition to their five principal establishments, they have agencies of their own in several of the large cities, both of the old and the new world. As dealers in money and bills, they may be said to have no rivals, and as the magnitude of their operations enables them to regulate the course of exchange throughout the world, their profits are great, while their risks are comparatively small by the perfect manner in which their business is managed. Indeed, the only *heavy* loss they may be said to have experienced as yet—that is, heavy for *them*,—was through the February revolution of 1848, when it is said that, owing to the sudden depreciation of all funded and railroad property throughout Europe, their losses from March till December of that year reached the enormous figure of $40,-000,000. But great as their losses were, they did not affect the credit of the Rothschilds, and do not appear in any degree to have impaired their means. The members of the firm are numerous, as the third generation has been received into the copartnership, and, as the cousins mostly intermarry, their immense wealth will, for a length of time, remain in comparatively few hands. The affairs of this firm in the United States have for a long time been under the direction of August Belmont, of New York, by whom they have been managed with distinguished success.

G. J. Ouvrard, the "Napoleon of Finance."

M. GABRIEL JULIEN OUVRARD'S name has been associated with the most gigantic financial operations, in Europe, during the last half century,

and numberless interesting incidents have marked the chequered career of him who has been most appropriately designated the "Napoleon of Finance;" and when the vastness and novelty of his plans, the extraordinary quickness of his perception, the fertility of his resources, his masterly combinations, and the vigor and perseverance with which he wove out the brilliant but eminently practical conceptions of his genius, are considered, the epithet thus given him seems most happy.

That he has claims to universal celebrity as a financier, it is sufficient to say that he figured prominently in the great events of the French Republic—the Consulate—the Empire—the Restoration—and the Revolution of 1830; that, after having witnessed the horrors of the Reign of Terror, and aided in the downfall of Robespierre, he became the *Banker of the Republic*, with power to issue a paper currency of his own, admissible as a legal tender in payment of the taxes of the state—the associate of Barras, Cambacérès, and Talleyrand—a worshipper at the feet of " Notre Dame de Bon Sécours "—the votary of ." Notre Dame des Victoires " —the creditor of Bernadotte—the confidential agent of Charles IV. of Spain —the honored guest of Pozzo di Borgo, Metternich, and Louis XVIII.—the intimate friend of Châteaubriand—the Commissary-General of Napoleon at the Passage of the St. Bernard, the Camp of Boulogne, and on the decisive field of Waterloo—and the host of Wellington at Paris !

By a special contract with Charles IV. of Spain, M. Ouvrard became the business partner of his Majesty in the exclusive commerce of the Spanish possessions in the new world during the war with Great Britain. It was in reference to this contract, and while crumpling the document in his hand, that Napoleon observed to M. Ouvrard, in presence of the council of ministers, " You have lowered royalty to the level of commerce." Whereupon M. Ouvrard, to the surprise of all present, replied, in a firm but respectful tone, "Sire, commerce is the life-blood of states; sovereigns cannot do without commerce, but it can very well do without sovereigns."

M. Ouvrard lived to a very advanced age, using moderately the bounties and luxuries of affluence with which he was surrounded. The philosophical equanimity of his mind, and the iron frame in which it was cast, served him in all his varied experiences. His elegance of manner, dignified serenity of countenance, and the graceful charm of his advanced years, rendered his presence both illustrious and attractive. He was naturally indulgent, kind-hearted, condescending, and, like all thorough men of the world, inclined to treat with lenity the inexperience and errors of his fellows, and especially of his juniors. His memory was wonderfully retentive; and his conversation, founded on a vast experience of men and things, was rich in information and sparkling with wit, and without any affectation. Some of his transactions, however, cast a cloud upon the integrity of his business dealings—at least during one portion of his remarkable career.

Thomas Gresham, the Royal Merchant and Financier.

Sir THOMAS GRESHAM'S name stands out prominently in England's mercantile annals, as the founder of the Royal Exchange, and as a distinguished financier. His father had amassed great wealth and attained great eminence as a merchant and bill broker in the reign of Henry VIII., and he resolved to train his son to succeed him in the business so successfully pursued by himself. After a thorough collegiate education, young Gresham was apprenticed to his uncle, a knight, and a distinguished member of the "Merchants' Company." Under Edward VI., Gresham was employed on the same services as his

father had performed for that king's father, and in the course of Edward's short reign, he made no fewer than forty voyages to Antwerp, on the royal business. By his financial skill and foresight, he rendered great service to the revenues of the English crown, which he rescued from the extortions of Dutch and Jewish capitalists, and introduced with great effect the practice of raising money from native money lenders, in preference to foreigners, who exacted a ruinous rate of interest. Mary and Elizabeth continued him in his employment, and the latter knighted him in 1559. He had now accumulated an immense fortune and built himself a palatial dwelling—which, after his wife's death, was used as Gresham College, and the site of which is now occupied by the excise office. He lived there in great state, and, by command of Elizabeth, he often entertained the ambassadors and visitors of rank that thronged her court. To these circumstances Gresham owed his familiar title of the "*Royal Merchant and Financier.*"

Nicholas Biddle, the Financier, of Philadelphia.

The eminent financier, NICHOLAS BIDDLE, was born in Philadelphia, Jan. 8, 1786, and died there Feb. 27, 1844. On graduating at Princeton college, he studied for the legal profession, but being too young for admission to the bar, he accepted the post of secretary to Gen. Armstrong, Minister to France, and afterward filled the same position under Mr. Monroe, Minister to England. He afterward travelled much in Europe, and in 1807 returned to Philadelphia, and commenced his career as a lawyer. He edited the "Portfolio," compiled a Commercial Digest, and prepared the popular narrative of Lewis and Clark's Exploration. He was at different times a representative and senator in the Pennsylvania legislature, where he ably

supported various educational measures. He was a candidate for Congress
in 1817, but was defeated by the Federal party. In 1819, President Monroe
appointed him a government director
of the United States Bank, and in 1823
he became its president. This bank
continued until the expiration of its
charter, in 1836, when Congress renewed the charter, but President Jackson vetoed it. The Pennsylvania legislature then created a State Bank,
giving to it the name of the United
States Bank. Mr. Biddle, then at his
zenith as a financier, was urged to
accept the presidency of this institution, which he finally though reluctantly did, serving until 1836, when he
resigned on account of ill health. Two
years afterward, the bank, after many
struggles, ceased payment, and became
insolvent. Whether this was the result
of measures pursued during the administration of Mr. Biddle, or after it, or
of general causes affecting the condition of the whole country, were points
of vehement controversy still fresh in
the minds of business men. Mr. Biddle,
besides his career as a financier, was a
writer of considerable ability, an
agriculturist, and quite an adept in the
fine arts. He was president of the
trustees of Girard College, and determined the plan of the building in
accordance with his fine classic taste;
also the beautiful structure, the United
States custom-house.

The Barings, Merchants and Bankers, of London.

Various origins are attributed to the
members of the house and family of
BARING. It has been stated, and is generally believed to be the most authentic account concerning them, that they
were originally German weavers who
came over to London; and, being successful in business, were, through the
interest of William Bingham, of Philadelphia, appointed agents to the American government. During the loyal-

ty loan in 1797, the head of the house
made one hundred thousand pounds
for three consecutive days; and in 1806,
somebody sarcastically said, "Sir Francis Baring is extending his purchases
so largely in Hampshire, that he soon
expects to be able to inclose the country with his own park paling." Nearly sixty years ago, this gentleman, the
first algebraist of the day, retired from
business with a regal fortune, and died
shortly after his retirement. But the
great commercial house which he had
raised to so proud a position was continued by his sons, and may be considered the most important mercantile
establishment in the British empire;
and as an instance of the fortune and
capacity of its members, it may be
mentioned that the late Lord Ashburton, when bearing, as Sir Robert
Peel expressed it, "the honored name
of Alexander Baring," realized £170,-
000 in two years by his combinations
in French rentes.

Peter Baring seems to have been one
of the remotest ancestors of the Barings.
He lived in the years from 1660 to 1670
at Groningen, in the Dutch province of
Overyssel. One of his ancestors, under
the name of Francis Baring, was pastor
of the Lutheran church at Bremen, and
in that capacity was called to London,
where, among others, he had a son
named John. The latter, well acquainted with cloth-making, settled at
Larkbeer, in Devonshire, and there put
up an establishment for the manufacture of that article. He had five children—four sons, John, Thomas, Francis, Charles, and a daughter called
Elizabeth. Two of those sons, John
and Francis, established themselves,
under the firm of John and Francis
Baring, at London, originally with a
view of facilitating their father's trade,
in disposing of his goods, and so as to
be in a position to import the raw
material to be required, such as wool,
dye stuffs, &c., directly from abroad.
Thus was established the house which,

after the withdrawal of the elder brother, John, who retired to Exeter,—gradually under the firm-name of Francis Baring & Co., and eventually under that of Baring Brothers & Co., rose to world-wide eminence in commerce.

Isaac De Buirette, the Illustrious German Merchant.

The German mercantile house of DE BUIRETTE was, in the seventeenth century, as also in the beginning of the eighteenth, one of the most extensive and renowned on the continent of Europe. Its name, its influence, extended over the whole commercial world, and its credit was unlimited. In his time, Isaac De Buirette was considered the most accomplished merchant in all Germany. Under the firm of Blumart & De Buirette, he carried on the most important exchange business, and entered largely into great commercial undertakings and bold speculations. A second house was in the course of time established at Vienna, which acquired in a short period a great reputation, and was the most celebrated ware-emporium of that famed commercial metropolis. The king of Prussia made him his financial counsellor. His learning was ripe and varied. His correspondence was immense—extending to all places of trade in his part of the world, and also beyond, in all of which his high reputation was a proverb, and an unlimited confidence and credit in the mercantile world were his reward. The firm, in its later stages, and after the decease of Daniel De Buirette, consisted of his three sons, and existed for many years. It was a house whose fame will never be blotted out in the annals of German commerce.

James Beatty, Merchant, of Baltimore.

The name of JAMES BEATTY will long be known in the mercantile annals of Baltimore, as that of an unblemished merchant, who reaped the rewards of his good judgment and uprightness. An anecdote which he himself used to relate will be appropriate here as illustrating the secret of his success: At the time of the approach of the British forces toward Baltimore, the United States navy agent, Mr. Beatty, was placed in a somewhat unpleasant situation by repeated threats from the soldiers in the regular army, that unless they received, within a stated period, all the wages due them, they had determined to revolt. The amount of funds in his hands was far short of what was required, and the banks of the city were called upon to aid in making it up; but after this request had been complied with, there was still not enough to satisfy the demand. At this juncture, Mr. Beatty happening one day to meet Mr. James Wilson, the latter gentleman made inquiry as to how matters stood with him in relation to the raising of the funds. Mr. Beatty related the circumstances, upon which Mr. Wilson requested him to step to his counting-room, and he would give him a check for the sum yet wanting, which was over $50,000. Mr. Beatty went to the bank, and the check was duly cashed—the soldiers returning to duty —the battle of North Point was fought shortly afterward—the war was closed —and Government again became enabled to discharge all its minor debts in that section. Mr. Beatty made out a statement of the indebtedness of the Government to Mr. Wilson for his approval. "Mr. Beatty," said the patriotic merchant, "you have allowed me interest on the sum loaned; sir, I want *no interest*—the money was lying idle, and it was just as well that Government should have the use of it." It was doubtless Mr. Beatty's method to put himself in contact with men of this stamp, and his own probity and judgment secured their confidence as well as coöperation.

P. T. Barnum, the "Prince of Showmen."

Though only in his youth, and then but for a brief period and in a subordinate capacity, engaged in mercantile trade, the career of Mr. BARNUM, dating from his humble beginning, affords one of the most notable instances of business enterprise, perseverance, originality, tact and success. Indeed, the history of the American business world during the last quarter of a century would fail of one of its most piquant pages, without some reminiscences of the " Great Showman." He started in his business career without a cent, and was compelled to carry on the struggle alone. He commenced life as a clerk in a country store, and married at the age of nineteen. He published a newspaper several years in his native town, where he was fined and imprisoned for publishing his opinions too freely. Afterward he tried mercantile business on his own account, in both Connecticut and New York, with indifferent success. In 1835 he became engaged in a strolling exhibition; afterward in a circus, &c.; and in 1842, bought the American Museum in New York. This establishment began to thrive immensely under his management. In 1843 he picked up " Gen." Tom Thumb; exhibited him in his museum a year, then took him to Europe, where he remained three years, appearing before all the principal courts and monarchs of the old world, and returned with a fortune to his native country. In 1850, he engaged Jenny Lind, and with her made the most triumphant and successful musical tour ever known, clearing, it is said, some half a million dollars in nine months, after paying that lady over three hundred thousand dollars.

Stephen Girard, Merchant and Banker, of Philadelphia.

STEPHEN GIRARD was born in the environs of Bordeaux, May 24, 1750. Little or nothing is known respecting the condition of his parents. He is supposed to have left his native country at the age of ten or twelve years, in the capacity of cabin boy in a vessel bound for the West Indies. He soon after came to New York, as cabin boy and apprentice in the employment of Captain J. Randall. While with the latter, his deportment was distinguished by such fidelity, industry and temperance, that he won the attachment and confidence of his master, who generally bestowed on him the appellation of " my Stephen ; " and when he gave up business, he promoted Girard from the situation of mate to the command of a small vessel, in which he made several voyages to New Orleans, always applying himself with great soberness and diligence to the accomplishment of his ends.

Girard was self-taught, and the world was his school. His intuitive quickness of conception and his powers of combination were such as would cause a very little instruction to go a great way. It was a favorite theme with him, when he afterward grew rich, to relate that he commenced life with a sixpence, and to insist that the best capital a man can have is his personal industry.

The Water-Witch, or, at least, the captain of the Water-Witch, was always fortunate, and he soon became part owner. Such was his confidence in his " lucky star," as almost to amount to superstition. He first visited Philadelphia in 1769. He soon established himself in business, and was reputed a thriving man. In partnership with Isaac Hazelhurst, he purchased two brigs, in 1771, to trade to St. Domingo. Of one of them he took command himself. Both were captured and sent to Jamaica. For once his " lucky star " forsook him. All professions and all occupations, which afforded a just reward for labor, were alike honorable in his estimation. He was never too proud to work, even when he was the richest millionnaire in the land. During the revolutionary war, he bottled and sold cider and claret. In 1780, he was engaged in trade to St. Domingo and New Orleans. In 1790, on the dissolution of a partnership which had some time existed between himself and his brother, John Girard, he was found by their mutual umpire to be worth thirty thousand dollars.

At the time of the insurrection of the blacks in St. Domingo, he had a brig and schooner in port, in which many of the inhabitants deposited their most valuable goods, but were prevented by a violent death from returning to claim them. It is, however, not supposed that he received in this manner more than fifty thousand dollars. In the time of the fever, in 1793, when consternation had seized the whole population of the city, Girard, then an opulent merchant, offered his services as a nurse in the hospital; his offers were accepted, and, in the performance of the most loathsome duties, he walked unharmed in the midst of the pestilence. He used to say to his friends, "When you are sick, or anything ails you, do not go to the doctor, but come to me. I will cure you."

The terms of a bargain were to him a law, which he never violated; but in his breast there was no chancery jurisdiction for the decision of causes in equity. The misfortunes of a bankrupt, in his view, were follies, which excited no commiseration.

Having been successful in his commercial speculations, and by that means made immense additions to his property, in 1811, in expectation of a renewal of the charter of the old Bank of the United States, he purchased a large amount of the stock of that institution. The charter was not renewed, and the banking house coming into his hands by purchase, at a reduced price, the Bank of the United States became Stephen Girard's Bank. It was emi-

nently convenient to the public at the time it was established, and during the war was particularly useful to the government, supplying, in fact, the want of a national institution, at a time when it was especially needed. On the establishment of the last national bank, Mr. Girard, just at the close of the subscription, took the balance of the stock, namely, three million and one hundred thousand dollars.

Mr. Girard did much to ornament the city of Philadelphia, and his ambition during his long and untiring business career, seems to have been to die the richest man in the country and be remembered as the patron of learning and the benefactor of the poor. He died December 26, 1831, in the eighty-second year of his age, the Girard College and the city of Philadelphia being his principal devisees.

Alexander T. Stewart, Merchant, of New York.

In his early years, Mr. STEWART was engaged in teaching, but soon changed his employment for a small mercantile business. He commenced with but a limited capital, and opened a store on Broadway, in 1827. This little concern, in which he then was salesman, buyer, financier, and sole manager, has gradually increased in importance, until it has become the present splendid establishment, whose name and fame are heard everywhere.

The marble block which the firm now occupies was built nearly twenty years ago. It had been the site of an old-fashioned hotel called the "Washington," which was destroyed by fire. Mr. Stewart bought the plot at auction for seventy thousand dollars,—a small sum in comparison with its present value. To this was subsequently added adjacent lots in Broadway, Reade, and Chambers streets, and the present magnificent pile was reared. This establishment, large as it is, proved too small for the increasing business; hence another mercantile palace has been erected by Mr. Stewart, in Broadway and Tenth street. This is intended for the retail trade, and is, no doubt, the most splendid structure of the kind in the world. The down-town store is devoted to the wholesale trade. The firm of A. T. Stewart & Co. consists of Mr. Stewart and two partners, one of whom, Mr. Fox, resides in Manchester, and the other, Mr. Warton, in Paris. These gentlemen, together with agents in the principal cities of Europe, are constantly engaged in furnishing the house with supplies of goods. The amount of annual sales is estimated at from ten to twenty millions. In the retail department, the proceeds of which are included in this estimate, the daily sales vary, according to the weather and the season, from three thousand to twelve thousand dollars.

Mr. Stewart has attained his present position by patient toil and forty years of close application to business. His remarkably fine taste in the selection of dress articles, by means of which he was always able to have superior goods, probably led to his first success. He has everything reduced to a perfect system. Each branch of his trade is under a special manager, who is selected with a view to his qualifications for that department. The numerous failures which take place among the business men of New York give him his choice among them for his managers, so that he is always able to find the kind of men he needs and whom he can trust. He is an accurate judge of character, possessing a penetration which enables him to read men at a glance; so that it is rarely, if ever, that he is deceived. He sits close in his office, is seldom seen in the salesrooms, or among his clerks, yet seems to know everything that is going on throughout the establishment. Mr. Stewart is a native of Ireland.

Edwin D. Morgan, Merchant, of New York.

Mr. MORGAN is widely known both as a successful merchant and able statesman. His father, Jasper Morgan, an old and highly respected citizen of Connecticut, formerly lived in Berkshire county, Mass., and there it was that his son Edwin was born, in February, 1811. He received a fair education before he was seventeen, without going to college, and at about that age commenced his mercantile experience in a store in Hartford, Conn., at a salary of sixty dollars for the first, seventy-five for the second, and one hundred for the third year's service. A trip to the great city was not then made with the facility that it is now; but as he had served for two or three years in the store, and acquired the confidence of his employer, he was permitted to go to New York, and, to combine business with pleasure, was intrusted to make sundry purchases of tea, sugar, etc., and also corn, which was then becoming an article of import, instead of export. The visit was made, and Edwin returned in due time, by the old stage route. After being greeted and welcomed, his employer inquired as to the corn. The price was very satisfactory; but his employer doubted if the article would be of good quality at so low a rate. Edwin immediately drew a handful, first from one pocket and then from another, as samples, and the old gentleman expressed his approbation. It had been usual for the dealers to purchase two or three hundred bushels at a time, and he then inquired of Edwin as to the quantity, but was nonplussed by the answer that he had bought two cargoes, and that the vessels were probably in the river. "Why, Edwin," said the astonished old gentleman, "what are we to do with two cargoes of corn? Where can we put it? Where can we dispose of it?"

"Oh!" replied Edwin, "I have disposed of all that you don't want, at an advance; I have shown the samples to Messrs. A. & B., who wish three hundred bushels; C. & Co., three hundred, &c., &c. I could have disposed of three cargoes, if I had had them. I stopped into the stores as I came along, and made sales."

This was a new phase, and out of the old routine; but the gains and results were not to be questioned. The following morning, Edwin was at the store, as always, in season, and had taken the broom to sweep out the counting room, when his employer entered.

"I think," said he, "you had better put aside the broom; we will find some one else to do the sweeping. A man who can go to New York, and on his own responsibility purchase two cargoes and make sales of them without counselling with his principal, can be otherwise more advantageously employed. It is best that he should become a partner in the firm for which he is doing so much,"—and he did, though not yet of age.

When he had just attained to his majority, Mr. Morgan was elected to the city council of Hartford; and at twenty-two he married Miss Waterman, of that city, by whom he has but one surviving child—a son. He removed to the city of New York in 1836, establishing himself as a wholesale grocer, upon a small capital of four thousand dollars, but which his business qualities afterward greatly enlarged, and his fortune increased, until now the house of Edwin D. Morgan & Co. is one of the richest of the metropolis. In 1849, Mr. Morgan was elected a member of the then Board of Assistant Aldermen; in 1852, a member of the State Senate; in 1858, to the high position of Governor of the State; and he now fills the honored post of United States Senator. Such a career of combined mercantile success and political honors is rare indeed.

Nathan Appleton, Merchant, of Boston.

Mr. APPLETON was born in New Ipswich, N. H., in 1779, and was the seventh son of Isaac Appleton. At fifteen years of age he was examined and admitted into Dartmouth College. It was decided, however, that he should proceed no further in his collegiate studies. His brother Samuel, who had been in trade in New Ipswich, and was about to remove to Boston, proposed that he should accompany him. This was accepted, and, as he afterward said, "It was determined that I should become a merchant rather than a scholar." His brother commenced business in a small shop on Cornhill, Boston; it consisted mostly in purchasing goods at auction and selling them again to country dealers for cash and short credit, at a small profit. In 1799, his brother made a short visit to Europe, and left his business in the charge of Nathan. On the return of the former, he removed to a warehouse in State street, and proposed to the latter, who had become of age, to be a partner. This was accepted, and Nathan now had at hand opportunities for enlarging his observation and experience. He was sent out to England to purchase goods. Europe was in a state of war. The news of peace reached him, however, on landing, and changed the whole current and condition of trade. He postponed his purchases and travelled on the Continent; shortly afterward returning to America and resuming his mercantile career. In 1806 he married Maria Theresa Gold, eldest daughter of Thomas Gold, of Pittsfield, and for the health of his wife soon crossed the ocean again. In Edinburgh he met Mr. Francis C. Lowell, at the moment the latter was first conceiving the policy to which the cotton manufacture of New England owes its origin; with him he held an earnest and encouraging consultation in regard to it. As capital accumulated in his hands, he took an active part in connection with Mr. Lowell, Patrick T. Jackson, Paul Moody, and others, in establishing the cotton factory at Waltham, Mass. He says: "When the first loom was ready for trial, many little matters were to be adjusted or overcome before it would work perfectly. Mr. Lowell said to me that he did not wish me to see it until it was complete, of which he would give me notice. At length the time arrived, and he invited me to go out with him to see the loom operate. I well recollect the state of satisfaction and admiration with which we sat by the hour watching the beautiful movement of this new and wonderful machine, destined, as it evidently was, to change the character of all textile industry." Mr. Appleton was also one of the chief associates in the company which made the first purchases for a like purpose in Lowell. On different occasions he was elected a member of the Massachusetts legislature, and in 1830 was chosen a member of Congress. In 1842 he was again sent, to fill the vacancy occasioned by the resignation of Robert C. Winthrop. In this sphere, his mind naturally turned to the financial and commercial view of questions. He was a member of the American Academy of Science and Arts, and of the Massachusetts Historical Society. Mr. Appleton died in Boston, July 14, 1861, and left a very large fortune.

The name of WILLIAM APPLETON is justly entitled to a place in the records of this eminent commercial family. Few names, indeed, shine out with such conspicuous and unsullied lustre in the annals of American mercantile fame as this. For their enterprise, integrity, benevolence, and public spirit, they have never been surpassed by any of the "solid men of Boston," whose character reflects such honor upon American commerce, at home and abroad.

David Ricardo, English Financier.

DAVID RICARDO, celebrated alike as a merchant, banker, and financial writer, was born in London, of a Jewish family, in 1772. His father, a native of Holland, was for several years a prominent banker in London, and, designing his son for the same occupation, he sent him to Holland, where he might obtain the best commercial education. Soon after his return to England, he was taken into his father's office as a clerk, and, when of age, he was associated with him in business. He subsequently formed a matrimonial alliance with a lady of the Christian faith, which union was displeasing to his father, by reason of the latter's religious scruples,—the elder Mr. Ricardo having been born of Jewish parents, and continuing in that faith until his death. This breach between the father and the son,—which, however, was afterwards entirely healed,—necessarily caused the dissolution of their business copartnership.

But the character of the son, for industry, talent, and fair dealing, early secured to him the confidence of business men as well as that of the community, and he thus accumulated a magnificent fortune. He amassed his immense wealth by a scrupulous attention to what he called his own three golden rules, and the observance of which he used to press on his private business friends. These were: "*Never refuse an option when you can get it*,"—"*Cut short your losses*,"—"*Let your profits run on.*" By cutting short one's losses, Mr. Ricardo meant, that when a broker had made a purchase of stock, and prices were falling, he ought to re-sell immediately. And by letting one's profits run on, he meant, that when a broker possessed stock, and prices were rising, he ought not to sell until prices had reached their highest, and were beginning to fall.

Besides being an eminent banker,

3

Mr. Ricardo was a most profuse writer on finance and currency, and his works on these subjects gained for him a high repute. He was also of quite a speculative turn of mind—and in some respects strangely so—on religious themes. He is stated to have adopted the Unitarian system of belief, though usually attending the established or Episcopal church. On the other hand, he is said to have suggested, as an "improvement," a sort of intermediate faith between Judaism and Christianity; holding that Jesus Christ was a worthy man and an excellent teacher, whose precepts should therefore be regarded with great respect,—but that "he assumed too much in his claim to be the son of God, and therefore that the blame of his unhappy catastrophe was to be divided between his enemies and himself." The number of adherents to Mr. Ricardo's faith were very few, and his writings on this subject were far less brilliant in their results than those which constituted the staple of his counting-house ledgers.

Judah Touro, Merchant, of New Orleans.

A well written life of this remarkable man would make a volume of peculiar interest, especially to the mercantile class, of which he was long so honorable as well as successful a member. At first, he opened a small shop on St. Louis street, near the levee, where he began a brisk and profitable trade in soap, candles, codfish, and other exports of New England, making prompt returns to his friends in Boston. His fidelity, integrity, and good management, soon secured him a large New England trade, every vessel from that section bringing him large consignments, and many ships being placed at his disposal, as agent, to obtain cargoes and collect freight. His business was prosperous, his funds accumulated. He invested his surplus means very judiciously in ships and in real estate, which

rapidly advanced in value. His career, guided by certain principles to which he steadfastly adhered, was one of honest, methodical labor, and stern fidelity to the legitimate practices of trade, never embarking in any hazardous ventures or speculations, never turning aside from his chosen sphere of business, and adhering rigidly to the cash system.

Mr. Touro was as methodical and regular as a clock. His neighbors were in the habit of judging of the time of day by his movements. In his business he rarely employed more than one clerk, and even this one was generally a lad. It was his custom to open his store himself at sunrise and close it at sunset. He attended to all his affairs himself, and had them so well arranged that there was no possibility of any misunderstanding. He engaged in no lawsuits, though he lived in one of the most litigious communities in the world. He could not bear a disputatious, nor even a very earnest, discussion. On one occasion his friend, Dr. Clapp, became involved in a very warm discussion on a theological question with some clergymen of the city. Mr. Touro was greatly annoyed at the warfare of words and logic thus carried on, and begged Dr. Clapp to desist from a controversy which was so unpleasant to him.

Mr. Touro's hard experience of the discomforts attending voyages by sea, though it determined him to remain on land for the remainder of his life, could not eradicate from him that natural passion of a New Englander—as he was—to own ships. He had consequently invested largely of his means in this business, and owned some of the largest and best built ships that came into the port of New Orleans. It was rather an amusing peculiarity of his, that though he took great pleasure and pride in walking along the wharves and surveying the grand and symmetrical proportions of his noble ships, he could never be persuaded to go aboard and examine and admire their interior. Mr. Touro's career.was perhaps not so eventful as that of his townsmen John McDonogh and Jacob Barker, and yet, as an upright, enterprising, and successful merchant, there are few whose names can be placed in advance of his.

"Old Billy Gray," Merchant, of Boston.

Among the successful and honorable merchants of America, few have stood higher than WILLIAM GRAY—"Old Billy Gray," as he came to be universally called. He was born in Lynn, Mass., in 1751, and when quite a small boy was apprenticed to a merchant in Salem. He finished his commercial education with Richard Derby, of that port; and such was his character for enterprise and strict integrity during his apprenticeship, that when, soon after its close, he commenced business for himself, he had the entire confidence and good will of the whole community. Prosperity waited upon him in all his transactions, and in less than twenty-five years after he commenced business, he was taxed as the wealthiest man in Salem, notwithstanding some of the largest fortunes in the United States belonged to that town. His enterprise and industry were wonderful; and at one time he had more than sixty sail of square-rigged vessels on the ocean. For more than fifty years, he arose at dawn, and was ready for the business of the day before others had finished their last nap. Although he had millions of dollars afloat on the sea of business, he was careful of small expenditures—those leaks which endanger the ship—and his whole life was a lesson of prudent economy, without penuriousness.

During the embargo, Mr. Gray took sides with Jefferson, notwithstanding New England was all in a blaze against the president, and it was an injury to the amount of tens of thousands of dollars to the great merchant's business. In the midst of the commercial distress, he removed to Boston, and having pleased the people while a State senator, he was chosen lieutenant-governor of the commonwealth. He freely used his immense riches for the wants of Government, and it is said never took advantage of the exigencies of the times, to speculate in government securities. After the war of 1812-15, he engaged largely in business again, but he lost often and heavily. Yet he died a rich man, and universally respected, at his elegant mansion in Boston, Nov. 4, 1825, aged about seventy-four years. It has been stated that at one period in his early career, Mr. Gray was a poor shoemaker; but, notwithstanding his subsequent great wealth, and the magnificence of his dwelling, the old cobbler's bench which he formerly used long remained intact in a separate room, and was shown with pride to his visitors as the sign of what he once was.

"Rich Spencer," Merchant and Banker, of London.

JOHN SPENCER—afterward Sir John, and, in 1594, Lord Mayor of London—died possessed of property valued at several round millions, acquired by his tact and shrewdness in the pursuits of commerce. There is much that might be written respecting the humors and caprices of this noted representative of the commerce of that period,—one who rose to such eminence in the annals of wealth amassed by sharp dealing and still closer saving. In a curious pamphlet printed in 1651, and entitled "The Vanity of the Lives and Passions of Men," there is the following singular anecdote respecting this "Rich Spencer"—for so Sir John was usually called: In Queen Elizabeth's days, a private of Dunkirk laid a plot with twelve of his mates, to carry Spencer away, and which, if he had done, fifty thousand pounds, it is stated, would not have redeemed him. This private come over the seas in a shallop, with twelve musketeers, and in the night came into Baring Creek, and left the shallop in the custody of six of his men, and with the other six came as far as Islington, and there hid themselves in ditches, near the path in which Sir John came to his house (Canonbury House); but, as good fortune would have it, Sir John was forced, by some unusual demands of business, to stay in London that night. But for this, he would have been taken away and rigidly dealt with. The kidnappers, fearing they should be discovered, returned in the night time to their shallop, and went back to Dunkirk, minus their anticipated booty.

Jacques Cœur, French Merchant in the Middle Ages.

JACQUES CŒUR was the great French merchant and financier of the middle ages. He sprung from the people, and raised himself, by successful commercial enterprise, to a level with the princes of his age. He found French commerce behind that of every other nation; and left it prosperous and increasing. Direct and speedy communication with the East seems to have been his great idea. Modern Europe is still striving for it. He had, at one time, in his employment, three hundred factors; and the rest of the merchants of France, with the whole of those of Italy, are not supposed to have equalled this one man, in the extent of their commercial dealings. "As rich as Jacques Cœur," became a proverb. It was even believed, by some, that he had found the philosopher's stone; and popular tradition asserts that so great was the profusion of the precious metals possessed by him, that his horses were *shod with silver*—a common reputation, even at the present day, enjoyed by persons of singular wealth.

He showed himself worthy of his great mercantile eminence, by giving his wealth, thus acquired, freely for noble objects. He raised three armies for king Charles at his own cost; and he repaired and reëstablished, in his office of *Argentier*, the deranged finances of the kingdom. It was his money which enabled the French to profit by the genius and enthusiasm of Joan of Arc; and it was his honest sympathy, and steady, manly counsel, which seems to have sustained the tender and brave heart of the noblest of royal mistresses, in her efforts to save the king. On her death bed, she selected Jacques Cœur for her executor.

Jacques Cœur had, in the course of twenty years, more commercial power than all the rest of the merchants of the Mediterranean put together. Everywhere his vessels were respected as though he had been a sovereign prince; they covered the seas wherever commerce was to be cultivated, and, from farthest Asia, they brought back cloths of gold and silk, furs, arms, spices, and ingots of gold and silver, still swelling his mighty stores, and filling Europe with surprise at his adventurous daring and his unparalleled perseverance. Like his great prototype, Cosmo de Medicis, who, from a simple merchant, became a supreme ruler, Jacques Cœur, the Medicis of Bourges, became illustrious and wealthy, and sailed long in the favorable breezes of fortune, admired, envied, feared, and courted by all.

But his weakness seems to have lain in the direction of personal magnificence and splendor, and to this may be traced his fall. He did not allow sufficiently for the prejudices of his age, and at last armed them for his ruin. He is described to have far transcended, in his personal attendance and equipments, the chiefs of the most illustrious families of France; and when Charles made his triumphal entry into Rouen, the merchant Jacques Cœur was seen by the side of Dunois, with arms and tunic precisely tho same as his. His destruction was planned by a party of the nobles, and an indictment of all sorts of crimes preferred against him—among them, the charge of having poisoned Agnes Sorel. He narrowly escaped torture and death; and only this by confiscation of his treasures (which his judges divided among them), and perpetual banishment. This latter resolved itself ultimately into a sort of strict surveillance in a French convent, from which he at last escaped by the fidelity of one of his agents, who had married his niece. He was again characteristically engaging in active pursuits; and beginning life anew, on the coast of Asia Minor, when illness seized him in the island of Scio.

Peletiah Perit, Merchant, of New York.

The name of PELETIAH PERIT has been familiar in the business circles of New York for about half a century, and is one of the most honored. He was at one time a member of the firm of Perit & Lathrop, and in 1819 he became a partner in the house of Goodhue & Co. Mr. Perit (says the author of the " Old Merchants of New York ") was born in Norwich, Conn., and received a collegiate education at Yale College. In the first partnership of Mr. Perit with Mr. Lathrop, his brother-in-law, he was not successful, and during the war he was connected with an artillery company, and performed military service in the forts that protected the harbor. After he went with Mr. Goodhue, his commercial good fortunes returned, and their house coined money. In 1833 or 1834, the health of Mr. Perit declined, and he conceived the idea that it was necessary to take more active exercise, and in order to insure that daily, he purchased a piece of property on the North river, lying between Burnham's and the Orphan Asylum. It may have cost him perhaps ten thousand dollars. He sold it about

two years ago, and it is now supposed to be worth half a million dollars. This is a comment on persevering mercantile life. By a mere accident Mr. Perit buys a small lot of land, and makes more money than Goodhue & Co. ever made in fifty-three years' hard work! Probably no house has done a larger business with all parts of the world than Goodhue for the fifty-three years that it has existed in a continuous business. This house, so eminent, commanding means to an extent that an outsider has no conception of, has made merely moderate earnings in comparison with some lucky land hit, made by unknown and uncredited persons, that has realized millions. Since Mr. Perit sold his property in New York, he has removed to New Haven, Conn. He has done much for the benevolent enterprises of the day. He is unequalled as a merchant, and has been for many years honored with the presidency of the Chamber of Commerce.

Jacob Ridgway, Merchant, of Philadelphia.

This wealthy Philadelphia celebrity came from New Jersey at an early age, and commenced the life of a busy, bold, and enterprising merchant. He commenced on a small scale; but by his industry, integrity, economy, and attention to business, he rose rapidly. Dame Fortune smiled, and in course of time he took high rank among the shipping merchants of that period. He visited Europe, to superintend a branch of the house with which he was connected; and soon after, having the confidence of the merchants of his own country, Mr. RIDGWAY was appointed American consul at Antwerp, where he laid the foundation of his handsome fortune. He returned soon after, and retired from mercantile pursuits, settling himself in Philadelphia, and engaging extensively in plans for the improvement of it and the city of Camden, on the opposite side of the river Delaware. In proportion as his efforts and means were laid out in this direction, so did his fortune increase; and from being the owner, in early life, of a single farm, he acquired possessions and wealth, the extent of which has perhaps never but once been equalled in Pennsylvania, and in all human probability never will be by any one man again. He was a plain man—his dress and deportment were plain, and his manners free from *hauteur*. In his directorship of the Bank of Pennsylvania, in which he was a large stockholder, he exhibited much prejudice against granting discounts and accommodation to the rich and extensive operators, preferring the humbler mechanics, tradesmen, and merchants.

Abraham and Benjamin Goldschmid, old English Bankers.

For a long and important period, ABRAHAM and BENJAMIN GOLDSCHMID were the magnates of the English money market. Of singular capacity, and, for a time, of equally singular good fortune, the firm of which they were the members rose from comparative obscurity to be the head and front of the financial circle of the world's metropolis. They were the first members of the Stock Exchange who competed with the bankers for the favors of the chancellor, and diverted from their bloated purses those profits which were scarcely a legitimate portion of banking business. The combination of that powerful interest being thus broken up, the bargains for public loans became more open, and have continued so.

The munificence of the Goldschmids was constant and wide spread. Naturally open hearted, the poor of all creeds found kindly benefactors in these Jew capitalists. On one day, the grandeur of an entertainment given by them to royalty was recorded in the papers, and on the next a few words related a visit of mercy on their part to a condemned cell. At one time, their mansion, vying in architectural beauty with those of

regal occupants, was described; at another, some great and gracious act of charity was narrated. Entertainments to princes and ambassadors, reviving the glories of oriental splendor, were frequent; and galleries, with works of art worthy the magnificence of a Medici, graced their homes. They seemed, at least for a while, Fortune's chief and most special favorites. When, in 1793, the old aristocracy of England's traders fell, as in 1847, and the bank in one day discounted to the amount of more than twenty million dollars, the losses of this great firm amounted to only the trivial sum of fifty pounds sterling. Strange to relate, both of these brothers came to their death by violence at their own hands.

Judah M. Lopez, Speculator in Annuities.

The name of JUDAH MANASSEH LOPEZ is handed down to this day, in England, as that of a Lombard and Jew of "the baser sort," and a usurer—one in whose business dealings the art of deception seemed to have fairly culminated. Of the origin or the successive business steps in the career of this man we know little. His business consisted in the purchase and sale of annuities. He lent to merchants when their vessels failed to bring them returns in time to meet their engagements; and he advanced cash on the jewels of those whom a disturbed period involved in conspiracies which required the sinews of war. But annuities were his favorite investment; and to him, therefore, resorted all who were in difficulties and were able to deal with him. With the highest and the lowest he trafficked. He was feared by most, and respected by none.

One remarkable feature in this man's dealings was, that no one found it easy to recover the property once pledged, if it chanced to much exceed the amount advanced. In an extremity, Buckingham, the favorite of Charles, applied to and received assistance from the Jew on the deposit of some deeds of value. When the time approached for repayment, Lopez appeared before the Duke in an agony of grief, declaring that his strongroom had been broken into, his property pilfered, and the Duke's deeds carried away. But Buckingham had dealt too much with men of this class to believe the story on the mere word of Lopez. He therefore detained the usurer while he despatched messengers to the city, to search out the truth, placing the Hebrew at the same time under watch and ward, with an utter indifference to his comfort.

When the messengers returned, they avouched that all Lombard street was in an uproar at the violation of its stronghold. Still the Duke was dissatisfied, and resolutely refused to part with his prey until he had received full value for his deposit. In vain did the Hebrew demurely fall on his knees —in vain did he call on Father Abraham to attest his innocence; for, in the midst of one of his most solemn asseverations, Buckingham was informed that a scrivener urgently solicited an audience, and he saw at the same time that a cloud came over the face of Lopez.

The request of the scrivener being granted, to the Duke's astonishment he produced the missing document, explaining to his Grace that Lopez, believing the scrivener too much in his power to betray him, had placed it in his charge until the storm should blow over, but that, fearing the Duke's power and trusting to his protection, he had brought it to York House. On the instant, Buckingham confronted the two. The Jew's countenance betrayed his crime, and, fawning on the very hem of the Duke's garment, he begged for forgiveness, and crouched like a dog to procure it. It is intimated that from that time the Duke had his loans on more equitable terms and on smaller security, as he dismissed the Jew with a courtesy the latter did not deserve.

William B. Astor, Millionnaire, of New York.

Prince street, New York, is the locality of Mr. WILLIAM B. ASTOR's financial operations. The street itself is of but a third-rate character, and the houses are but of a common stamp. Near Broadway, however, one may notice a small brick office, neatly built, of one story, with gable to the street, but with doors and windows closed, and the whole appearance one of security. Near the door may be seen a little sign which reads thus: 'ENTRANCE NEXT DOOR. OFFICE HOURS FROM 9 TO 3." This "next door" to which we are referred is a plain three-story brick dwelling, with no name on the door, and might be taken for the residence of some well-to-do old-fashioned family. Hence one is quite startled to find that this is the headquarters of the chief capitalist of America. Entering the street door, one will find himself in a small vestibule, neatly floored with checkered oilcloth, and opening a door on his left, he will enter a well-lighted front room, destitute of any furniture but a counting-house desk and a few chairs. At this desk stands an accountant (or perhaps two) working at a set of books, and evidently enjoying an easy berth. He will answer all ordinary inquiries, will do the duty of refusing charitable demands, and will attend to anything in the ordinary run of business; but if one has anything special on hand, he will point to a door opening into a rear office. This apartment is of moderate size and of simple furniture. On the table are a few books, and on opening one of them, which appears well thumbed, it will be found to contain maps of plots of city property, carefully and elegantly executed, and embracing the boundaries of an enormous estate. Seated by the table may generally be seen a stout-built man with large and unattractive features, and upon the whole an ordinary face. He is plainly dressed, and has a somewhat careworn look, and appears to be fifty or sixty years of age. One naturally feels—that is, if he be a poor man—that it is quite a rare thing to address a capitalist, and especially when that capitalist is the representative, say of twenty-five millions of dollars. His daily income has been estimated at *six thousand dollars!*

The care of Mr. Astor's estate—the largest in America—is a vast burden. His tenements, of all grades, number several hundreds, ranging from the dwelling at three hundred dollars per annum, to the magnificent warehouse or hotel at thirty thousand dollars. To relieve himself from the more vexatious features of his business, he has committed his real estate collections to an agent, who does the work well, and who is, no doubt, largely paid. He, with his clerks, collects rents, and makes returns of a rent roll whose very recital would be wearisome. As a matter of course, such a man must employ a small army of painters, carpenters, and other mechanics, in order to keep up suitable repairs; and as Mr. Astor pays no insurance, the work of rebuilding after fires is in itself a large item. A large part of Mr. Astor's property consists of vacant lots, which are in continual demand, and which he generally prefers to hold rather than sell; hence he is much employed with architects and master builders, and always has several blocks in course of erection. This is a very heavy burden, and, were it not for the help derived from his family, would, doubtless, crush him. His son, John Jacob, is quite a business man, and bears his share of the load. In addition to this, Mr. Astor has the aid of a gentleman of business habits and character, once a member of one of the largest shipping houses in New York, who has become connected with the family by marriage. The la-

bors of all these parties cannot be more than adequate to the requirements of so enormous a property.

C. K. Garrison, Merchant, of San Francisco.

The financial and public position attained by Mr. GARRISON, of San Francisco, so well known as one of the mayors and leading merchants of that city, was due to his own perseverance, exhibited in a manner and to a degree rarely witnessed even in American mercantile character. Originating in New York, near West Point, his ancestors were among the regular "Knickerbockers" of that region—the Coverts, Kingslands, Schuylers, and others. The *paterfamilias* was at one time considered quite wealthy, but from heavy indorsements he became involved at an early period in the life of the subject now under notice. The latter, having to look to his own resources, left home at the age of thirteen, in the capacity of a cabin boy in a sloop. It was not, however, without great difficulty, that young Garrison obtained from his parents their consent that he might leave their home, and accept the situation he sought. "What," said his mother, with characteristic feminine perception, "would the Van Buskirks, the Kingslands, the Schuylers, the host of other respectable relatives, the thousand and one cousins, &c., &c., say, if it reached their ears that my son was a cabin boy?" From this small beginning he worked his way up, until he finally found himself in California, where, shortly after, on account of his great business tact, he was offered the Nicaragua Steamship Company agency, at a salary of $60,000 a year, for two years certain. In addition to this appointment, he received at the same time the agency of two insurance companies, at a salary of $25,000 per annum. At the age of forty-five, he found himself the possessor of a princely fortune; with a salary three or four times greater than that of the President of the United States; with a revenue besides, from other sources, of as much more; and occupying the position of Mayor of the city of San Francisco. This is success that rarely falls to the lot of those, even, who are what may be called the "successful" ones in commercial life.

William Hogg, the Pennsylvania Millionnaire.

More than seventy years ago, WILLIAM HOGG—who died at his residence in Brownsville, Pa., leaving an estate of more than a million dollars—crossed the Alleghany mountains with a small pack of goods, all he possessed, and which he bore upon his own back, and established himself at Brownsville, then called Red Stone. He soon after opened a small store, the first in that region of country, on the Monongahela river, transporting his goods from Philadelphia by means of packhorses, and increasing his stock, from time to time, until he became the wealthiest merchant in Western Pennsylvania—a rank which he prominently occupied in the latter period of his life. He was remarkable for his accurate habits of business, his persevering and indefatigable application, and his great sagacity in the management of his numerous and extensive establishments. Whether worth one dollar only, or a million, he held that frugality was the same virtue, and rigidly lived up to this principle.

Herodotus a Merchant.

The opinion—equally ingenious and probable—is advanced by Malte Brun, that the great father of history and geography, HERODOTUS, was a merchant. "At least," says he, "this supposition affords the most natural solution of his long voyages and numerous connections with nations by no means friendly to the Greeks." His silence respecting commerce is presumed to have arisen from the same motives which in-

duced the Carthaginians to throw every voyager into the sea who approached Sardinia, lest the sources of their commerce and riches should be discovered.

Jeejeebhoy Dadabhoy, Parsee Banker and Merchant.

JEEJEEBHOY DADABHOY, of Bombay, was a Parsee banker, merchant, agent, and broker, for more than forty years, and sustained important business relations to many European mercantile houses. So extensive were his transactions, that his name was well known in all the commercial towns of England, Scotland, France, Germany, Austria, Egypt, India, China, Mauritius, &c. A few years before his death, which occurred in 1849, at the age of sixty-four years, he retired from the firm of Messrs. Jeejeebhoy Dadabhoy, Sons & Co., but left his name by associating his sons, who have since carried on the business, the firm ranking among the first Parsee commercial houses in India.

Jeejeebhoy Dadabhoy was one of the most active among the native capitalists in the establishment of the various banks in Bombay; and he served his time as director respectively in the Oriental and Commercial Banks. To him and to Sir Jamsetjee Jeejeebhoy the people of Western India are indebted for the introduction of steam navigation for commercial and passenger traffic—the first, and by far the best paying of these steamers having been built by them. Jeejeebhoy Dadabhoy, the manager of this company, so judiciously conducted the business, that in the course of six years he divided profits amounting to nearly the outlay.

He shared, indeed, in every enterprise which promised to promote public advantage, however little his personal interests might be benefited. Among the commercial joint-stock companies, he was a large shareholder in the following: the Railway Companies, Cotton Screw Companies, Steam Navigation Company, Colaba Land and Cotton Companies, most of the Bombay Marine and Life Insurance Companies, the Bengal India General Steam Navigation Company, several Calcutta Insurance Companies, &c. His capital was likewise engaged in advances on coffee, sugar, &c., &c.

For nearly twenty years he was a member of the Parsee Punchayet, a position which frequently imposed important duties upon him for the general benefit of the Parsee community. He was also constantly called upon to arbitrate and settle matters in dispute between members of his caste, and his straightforward judgment invariably gained for him the esteem of those who had submitted their difficulties to his decision.

In matters of charity his purse was always open to the poor of his community. His name was likewise to be found on almost all the lists of public subscriptions and private charities, both European and native. At the time of his death, forty-two schools, in various parts of the Bombay Presidency, were wholly supported by his bounty.

He left a widow, four sons, three daughters, twenty-one grandchildren, and six great-grandchildren, to whom he bequeathed immense wealth. He likewise, by his will, left one hundred thousand dollars, to be invested in Government securities in the names of eight trustees, four of these being his sons, the interest of this amount to be annually divided in charities for the relief of the suffering of his caste.

Abbott Lawrence, Merchant, of Boston.

ABBOTT LAWRENCE, one of the most eminent of American merchants, was born in Groton, Mass., in 1792. His ancestors were people in humble circumstances, who had for one hundred and fifty years been settled in Groton as cultivators of the soil, and his father, Major Samuel Lawrence, served with credit in Prescott's regiment at Bunker Hill, and in many of the severest battles of the war of Independence. For a brief period in his boyhood, he attended the district school and the academy at Groton, and in his sixteenth year went to Boston, with less than three dollars in his pocket, and was bound an apprentice to his brother Amos, then recently established there in business. In 1814 he became one of the firm of A. & A. Lawrence, which for many years conducted a prosperous business in the sale of foreign cotton and woollen goods on commission. Subsequently to 1830, they were largely interested as selling agents for the manufacturing companies of Lowell; and, in the latter part of his life, Abbott Lawrence participated extensively in the China trade.

In addition to his business pursuits, Mr. Lawrence took a deep interest in all matters of public concern, and was at an early period of his career a zealous advocate of the protective system. In 1834, he was elected a representative in the twenty-fourth Congress, and was there a member of the important committee of ways and means. He also served for a brief period in 1839–'40. In 1842, he was appointed a commissioner, on the part of Massachusetts, on the subject of the northeastern boundary, in the discharge of which trust he rendered the most important service. In the Whig Nominating Convention of 1848, he was a prominent candidate for Vice-President of the United States, lacking but six votes of a nomination—the choice falling upon Mr. Fillmore. On the accession of General Taylor, whose election Mr. Lawrence had zealously advocated, a seat in the cabinet was offered to Mr. Lawrence, but declined by him. He was subsequently appointed the representative of the United States at the court of Great Britain, a position which he occupied with credit until October, 1852, when he was recalled at his own request. The remainder of his life was devoted to his private business.

The benefactions of Mr. Lawrence, for private and public purposes, were numerous and wisely bestowed, although, from the nature of the circumstances under which the greater part of his life was passed, the amount cannot, as in his brother Amos's case, be accurately estimated. In 1847, he gave to Harvard University fifty thousand dollars to found the Scientific School, bearing his name, connected with that institution; and he bequeathed a like sum in aid of the same object. He left a further sum of fifty thousand dollars, for the purpose of erecting model lodging houses, the income of the rents to be forever applied to certain public charities. He was greatly esteemed in private life for his benevolence of disposition and genial manners, and in his public relations commanded the respect of all parties. Mr. Lawrence died in Boston, August 18th, 1855.

Jacob Barker, Merchant, of New Orleans.

Mr. BARKER is descended from the same stock as Dr. Franklin, to whom he is proud to claim a certain family resemblance—and certainly in some of their personal characteristics there is a striking identity. He was brought up in the Quaker communion, to which, and to their unpretending costume, he long adhered.

At the age of sixteen he was adrift in the world, and came to New York, where he got employment with Isaac Hicks, a commission merchant, and, beginning the trade on his own account, in a small way, *before his majority* was in possession of four ships and a brig, and had his notes regularly discounted at the United States Bank. Sitting at his wedding dinner, August 27th, 1801 (he married Elizabeth, daughter of Thomas Hazard, of New York), with Mr. Henry Dewees, for whom he had heavily indorsed, news

was brought him of the ruin of them both; he passed the letter over to Mr. Dewees, drank wine with him, and took no further notice of the matter.

For some transactions concerning the North River Bank, Mr. Barker was once openly insulted by one David Rogers, to whom he sent a note demanding an explanation. No explanation came, but in place of it an indictment by the grand jury for sending a challenge. Mr. Barker defended himself with infinite subtlety on the trial, denying the fact of the challenge; but the jury would not be persuaded, nor the judges afterward, when he argued the question of law, and he was sentenced to be disfranchised of his political rights—from which sentence he was relieved by Governor Clinton. But at length, on the failure of the Life and Fire Insurance Company, he was indicted, with others, for conspiracy to defraud. The trial was long, the counsel wanted time to look over their notes, and it was suggested that Mr. Barker should begin his defence. He had no brief, and had taken no notes, but professed his readiness. "Yes," said Mr. Emmet, "if they were all to be hanged, Mr. Barker would say, hang me first!" His defence was a prodigy of ability. At the first trial the jury disagreed, on the second he was convicted, but a new trial granted. After the third the indictment was quashed.

Some years since he appeared in his own defence in a suit brought in New Orleans, and obtained a verdict after a long personal address to the jury, which is said to have made a most vivid impression both upon them and a numerous auditory. In reciting the chequered history of his life—his unrivalled commercial enterprise,—"that the canvas of his ships had whitened every sea, and that the star-spangled banner of his country had floated from the mast head of his ships in every clime,"—his aid in procuring a loan of five million dollars for the Government during the last war with England—he said he came to New Orleans poor, and in debt, that he had since made a great deal of money, and spent it in the support of his family and the payment of his debts outstanding in New York; that all those debts were now settled, as was proved, and that he owed nothing in the world at present but one account (on a note, he believed) of about a thousand dollars.

During the war, Nantucket was in want of supplies : Mr. Barker purchased the New York pilot boat Champlain, and caused her to be landed at Norfolk with flour, and despatched for that place. When near the island a heavy fog set in ; when it cleared away she was within a half gunshot of a British seventy-four, captured, and vessel and cargo lost.

Alexander Fordyce, the Shark of the Exchange.

The career of this notorious broker —one of the shrewdest ever known on the roll of British financiers—furnishes a dark phase in the dealings of the exchange. Bred a hosier at Aberdeen, he found the North too confined for such operations as he hoped at some future day to engage in ; and, repairing to London, as the only place worthy of his genius, obtained employment as clerk to a city banking house.

Here he displayed great facility for figures, with great attention to business, and rose to the post of junior partner in the firm of Roffey, Neale & Jaines. Scarcely was he thus established, ere he began to speculate, and generally with marked good fortune— and, thinking his good luck would be perpetual, ventured for sums which involved his own character and his partners' fortune. The game was with him ; the funds were constantly on the rise ; and, fortunate as daring, he was enabled to purchase a large estate, to support a grand appearance, to surpass nabobs in extravagance, and *parvenus*

in folly. He marked "the marble with his name," upon a church which he ostentatiously built. His ambition vied with his extravagance, and his extravagance rivalled his ambition. The Aberdeen hosier spent thousands of pounds in attempting to become a titled magnate, and openly avowed his hope of dying a peer. He married a woman of title ; made a fine settlement on her ladyship ; purchased estates in Scotland at a fancy value ; built a hospital ; and founded charities in the place of which he hoped to become the representative.

But a change came over his fortunes. Some political events first gave him a shake ; then another blow followed, and he had recourse to his partners' private funds to supply his deficiencies. On being smartly remonstrated with, a cool and insolent contempt for their opinion, coupled with the remark that he was quite disposed to leave them to manage a concern to which they were utterly incompetent, startled them ; and when, with a cunning which provided for everything, an enormous amount of bank notes, which Fordyce had *borrowed* for the purpose, was shown them, their faith in his genius returned with the possession of the magic paper—it being somewhat doubtful whether the plausibility of his manner or the agreeable rustle of the notes decided them.

Ill fortune, however, still continued to cast its gaunt shadow on Mr. Fordyce's track—the price of the funds would not yield to his fine combinations and plans. But with all his great and continued losses, he retained to the last hour a cool and calm self-possession. Utter bankruptcy finally followed, and the public feeling was so violent, as he detailed the tissue of his unsurpassed fraud and folly, that it was necessary to guard him from the populace. He broke half the commercial town. Two gentlemen, ruined by the broker's extravagance, shot themselves dead, and many of the wealthiest families were beggared. Nor is this surprising, when it is known that bills to the amount of *twenty millions of dollars* were in circulation, with the name of Fordyce attached to them—a name still synonymous with that of "the Shark of the Exchange."

Nicholas Longworth, Millionnaire, of Cincinnati.

NICHOLAS LONGWORTH, who recently died in Cincinnati, at the age of eighty years, was born in Newark, N. J., in the year 1783, and was brought up to the shoemaking business in his early life. His father, having been reduced to poverty, became a shoemaker, and had all his children educated to follow trades. It was intended that Nicholas should obtain his living as a regular shoemaker; but at an early age he improved the opportunity offered him of going to the South with a brother, and became a clerk in the latter's store in Savannah. After being in mercantile business at the South about two and a half years, he removed in 1804 to Cincinnati, then only a scattered and sparsely populated village of about seven hundred and fifty inhabitants, adjoining to Fort Washington, on the banks of the Ohio, where the Federal Government maintained a garrison, the expenditure of which at that and earlier periods formed no small share of the business of Cincinnati.

The beginning of Mr. Longworth's career in Cincinnati was a very curious one. He commenced the study of the law, under Judge Burnett, an eminent lawyer, and was admitted to the bar in advance of the ordinary period. Until 1819, he followed the law as his profession. Meantime he had married a widow of some means, and had devoted himself to speculations in lots, foreseeing that the value of real estate must enhance immensely. In this way he laid the foundation of his gigantic fortune. At that time, property was at a very low valuation, and many of Longworth's lots cost him no more than ten dollars each, which in a few years multiplied in value a hundredfold. His property increased so rapidly that in 1850 his taxes rated higher, perhaps, than those of any other man in the United States except William B. Astor, the taxes of the latter amounting to some twenty-three thousand, while those of Longworth were over seventeen thousand. The ground occupied by the celebrated Observatory of Cincinnati was a free gift from Mr. Longworth. He donated four acres of his land on Mount Adams for that purpose.

Mr. Longworth devoted much of his time to agriculture and horticulture—the grape and the strawberry especially. Every one has heard of his Catawba wine, both still and sparkling champagne. Indeed, Nicholas Longworth, Esq., the "fifteen millionnaire," is not half so well known as "old Nick Longworth," who did so much for the culture of the Catawba and Isabella grape in the Ohio valley. His gardens and hothouses abounded in the rarest exotics, and were freely accessible to visitors who wished to enjoy them, and, if his gardeners were not on hand to point out their beauties, it is very probable that Nicholas Longworth himself would perform the part of chaperon. Mr. Longworth was a ready writer, full of wit, humor, and sarcasm.

Mr. Longworth had four children—three daughters and one son. One of the daughters married Larz Anderson, of Cincinnati, brother of the hero of Fort Sumter, a prominent lawyer. The wealth of which Mr. Longworth died possessed is put down at fifteen millions; but it is probable that it may be quoted at a much higher figure. His city lots alone would probably amount to that sum. The value of his property in the suburbs of Cincinnati and the different counties of Western Ohio, from Hamilton county to Sandusky, would perhaps swell his estate to twenty millions.

John Overend, the Pioneer Bill Broker of London.

JOHN OVEREND's name stood, for a long time, at the head of the most ancient as well as extensive and renowned bill-brokering establishment in the world: Bill brokering in its present form was commenced about half a century ago. This house—Overend & Co. —so well known in Europe and America, was formed in the year 1807, under the firm of Richardson, Overend & Co. The partners were Thomas Richardson, a clerk in the banking house of Smith, Wright & Gray; John Overend, a clerk to a woollen dealer; and Samuel Gurney, then twenty-one years of age, the second son of Mr. John Gurney, a partner in the Norwich Bank. This bank was established in 1770, by Henry Gurney, who was succeeded by his son, Bartlett Gurney, and the latter, in 1803, took into partnership his cousin, John Gurney, and several other members of his family. Mr. John Gurney had previously been a woolstapler and spinner of worsted yarn. In this character he was acquainted with Mr. Joseph Smith, who was extensively connected with the trade of Norwich, and was engaged by the Norwich Bank to employ their surplus funds in discounting bills for his numerous connections. This business became so extensive that, upon the suggestion of John Overend, a firm was established expressly for the purpose of carrying it on, under the superintendence of the Norwich Bank. Mr. Samuel Gurney had, for three years previously, been a clerk to Mr. Fry, who had married Mr. Gurney's sister, the celebrated Elizabeth Fry. After the death or retirement of Mr. Richardson, the firm was Overend & Co. On the death of Mr. Overend, Samuel Gurney became the senior partner, until his death in 1856, when he was succeeded by David Barclay Chapman. The second house of this kind, in point of time, was that of Messrs. Sanderson & Co. The house of Alexander & Co.

has also long been eminent in the same kind of business founded by Overend.

"Old Mr. Denison," of St. Mary Axe.

"OLD MR. DENISON," as he was called by every one, for more than a generation, belonged to the primitive school of English bankers, who made his own fortune, and was remarkable for his economy and strict attention to business. He lived for years at his banking house in "St. Mary Axe," and was so provident as to go to market daily, basket in hand, for his family. But if he thus looked closely after small matters, it was because he held everything subservient to one great one—his bank and the accumulation of capital. Like many men who have a turn for economy, he was fond of boasting of the bargains he had bought. There has also been many a chronicle rehearsed of the trouble it used to give to the old gentleman to provide good things *cheap*, when his son, the present distinguished banker and political notability, entertained his west-end friends at dinner. For, with the honorable pride so frequently observed among Scotchmen, "old Mr. Denison" not only took care that his son's education should be excellent, but gave him a very fair encouragement to gain a footing in the best society—in which, too, he was as successful as he could have wished. He left a large property, which has been increased by his son, one of the richest London bankers— being commonly rated at three millions sterling—the greater part of which is always kept available for business purposes.

Lorillard, the New York Tobacconist.

The name of LORILLARD looms up very prominently in the annals of American mercantile biography, and few of the solid merchants of New York show a more honorable record of personal worth and financial success. It was one of Mr. Lorillard's favorite remarks, and well deserving of note, that his prosperity arose from his *not having made haste to be rich.* He entered upon business with a capital of a thousand dollars, increased by a loan from his brothers of double that amount; and from the skill, the foresight, and the diligence with which his business was conducted, and from some adventitious advantages, his own part of it was eventually multiplied more than a thousand-fold. "Lorillard, the New York Tobacconist," became, in course of time, a name widely known in both hemispheres, nor has it yet lost its prestige.

Simple in all his tastes and habits, well regulated in all his affections and desires, free from vanity, ostentation, and pride, he had no extravagant longings, either to urge him on in the eager pursuit of wealth, or to make him squander, in prodigality, the fruits of iniquity and fraud. Instead, therefore, of unduly extending his business, and, in haste to enrich himself, careless about the interests and claims of others; instead of running out into wild and visionary schemes, which are usually so tempting to the cupidity of business men, and staking the laborious acquisitions of a life upon the chances of a day, Mr. Lorillard was contented to follow the prudent methods of better times, to avoid unnecessary anxiety for the future, to keep innocency, and take heed to the thing that was right in regard to his neighbor.

Whenever, therefore, the profits of his business were not needed for the enlargement of his capital, he was in the habit of investing them in real estate, selected very often in obscure and retired places, which would be unattractive to the mere speculator, and with greater regard to the security of the property than the immediate prospect of gain. But, in most cases, this very moderation and prudence turned to a better account than the grasping calculations of avarice itself—his own

possessions increasing in value, securely and steadily, while those of others were often swept away by their extravagance and folly.

John Jacob Astor, Richest Merchant of America.

Mr. Astor was born near the ancient city of Heidelberg, Germany, in the year 1763, and his history embodies an invaluable moral for merchants generally, and for young men in particular. His parents moved in humble life. He came to this country when about nineteen years of age, at which time the State of New York was mostly a wilderness. He made frequent excursions up the Mohawk river, to traffic with the Indians for furs, and gradually enlarged his business as his means increased. After a while, the American Fur Company was formed, and he became a competitor with the great capitalists of Europe, who controlled the Northwestern and Canadian Fur Companies. Such was his enterprise, that he extended his business to the mouth of the Astoria river, and formed the first fur establishment then known as Astoria. For many years previous to the war of 1812, and subsequently, Mr. Astor was extensively engaged in the Canton trade, and during the war was fortunate in having several of his ships arrive here with valuable cargoes. The profits on these were enormous. Mr. Astor made large investments in Government stocks, which he purchased during the war with Great Britain, at sixty or seventy cents on the dollar, and which, after the peace, went up to twenty per cent. above par. On his death, most of his estate went to Mr. William B. Astor, his son, and consisting in a great measure of property not subject to regular appraisal, the estimates of its value have been very various. During the whole of his protracted business career, Mr. Astor was noted for persevering industry, rigid economy, and strict integrity. He had a genius bold, fertile, and expansive; a sagacity quick to grasp and convert a circumstance to the highest advantage; and a singular and never-wavering confidence of signal success in what he undertook.

As the result of only sixteen years of business life, Mr. Astor was worth one quarter of a million dollars, and is supposed, on a moderate estimation, to have left a fortune of twenty millions. It would be difficult to say whether the great part of his immense fortune was derived from his mercantile dealings or his investments in real estate. He early began and systematically followed up the policy of investing largely, not only in the inhabited parts of the city, where immediate income could be realized, but in unoccupied lots, or acres, rather, of fields out of town, which he saw, in anticipation, covered by the spreading city. He was under no necessity of mortgaging one property for the purchase of another—under no temptation to dangerously expand. Thus he was enabled to make investments which it has been said, no doubt with literal truth, centupled on his hands. At one time, it is stated, he was in the habit of investing two thirds of his net annual receipts in land, and in the course of all of his vast operations, with a large part of his fortune afloat on the ocean, he is said never to have mortgaged a lot. During the fifty years of his active business life, he hardly made a mistake or misstep through defect of his own judgment. Until his fifty-fifth year, he was at his office before seven o'clock. He was a great horseman, and in the constant habit of riding out for pleasure and exercise. In the strength of his general grasp of a great subject, he did not allow himself to be too much disturbed by the consideration of details. His mind worked so actively that he soon got through the business of a day, and he could leave his office earlier than many business men who did less.

Troubled and annoyed by petty trials, he was calm and self-possessed under great ones. "Keep quiet—keep cool," was the constant and familiar admonition from his lips. When the great trials came, his spirit rose with the emergency, and he was equal to the hour. Mr. Astor died in March, 1848, aged eighty-four years, and in his will bequeathed four hundred thousand dollars to found a free public library in the city of New York.

Samuel Appleton, Merchant, of Boston.

SAMUEL APPLETON, a rich merchant and distinguished philanthropist of Boston, was born in New Ipswich, N. H., in 1766. His father was a respectable farmer, and the son spent his youth amidst the severe toils attendant on the pursuits of agricultural life. Samuel shared his good fortune with his brother Nathan, who was his partner in mercantile business. Some amusing anecdotes are related of the early career of the subject of this notice, illustrative of his humble origin and his fidelity. One of these is, that, when fourteen years of age, his father hired him to assist a drover of cattle ten miles through the woods, for which service the father received twelve and a half cents. The boy satisfied the drover so well, that six and a quarter cents more were given him as a gratuity. This was perhaps the first money that he could call his own. When about twenty-one years of age, he left home and spent some time in clearing a lot of new land in Maine, on which was a log cabin; the nearest residence was distant two miles, and his only guide to it was the marked trees. He next became a country schoolmaster, but after a short time engaged in a small village store. His success was good; and in 1794 he removed to Boston, where, with his brother Nathan, under the firm of S. & N. Appleton, he embarked in commercial pursuits, and became one of the most thrifty merchants in that city. His wealth increased rapidly; and, from an early date in his accumulations, his charities gladdened the hearts of the widow and orphan. The Boston Female Orphan Society was one of the first to participate in his munificence. His native town, also, was occasionally remembered by him with filial affection. Indeed, he was always ready to give, according to his means, and when consistent with their claims, if the object presented was a good one. Being himself without children, most of his estate, amounting to a million of dollars, was distributed by his will as follows: he left to his widow specific bequests amounting to two hundred thousand dollars; also, many other bequests, to nephews, nieces and others, amounting to some three hundred and twenty thousand dollars more. Among these may be mentioned one of five thousand dollars "to his friend and pastor, Rev. Ephraim Peabody," and five thousand dollars to the servants living in the family at the time of his decease, to be distributed in the manner and according to the proportion to be fixed upon by his widow. He then bequeathed to his executors, manufacturing stocks valued at two hundred thousand dollars, to be by them appropriated for scientific, literary, religious, or charitable purposes,—and thus, through the long future, his wealth is to be beneficially employed. Mr. Appleton lived to the good old age of eighty-seven years.

Peter C. Brooks, Underwriter and Millionnaire, of Boston.

PETER C. BROOKS was born in North Yarmouth, Maine, January 6th, 1769, his father, Rev. Edward Brooks, being then a settled clergyman in that place. Soon after his birth, his father returned to Medford, Mass., his native town, to which the family was strongly attached, and there he died prematurely, in 1781, the son being only twelve years of age.

4

As soon as the subject of this sketch arrived at maturity, he repaired to Boston, gifted only with a common school education, and without pecuniary means, to seek his fortune. The rich men of that city were then in especial need of young men of talent and character, by whom they could be assisted in the care of their property and business. Mr. Brooks soon proved to them that he had business talents of the highest order, and these were united with great modesty, and an integrity that never received from youth to old age a single blemish.

At the time referred to, there were no insurance companies in Boston, and Mr. Brooks had the sagacity to see the need of a substitute, and hence established himself as an insurance broker, particularly for marine policies. Most of the capitalists had such confidence in his judgments, that they became underwriters in his office. With the rapidly increasing commerce of the country, the business of Mr. Brooks became large and lucrative, and, almost before he or any one else thought of it, he was a rich man. This was the foundation of an estate estimated, long before his death, to amount to three millions of dollars, more or less; but it was at least sufficient to furnish a moral to young men, which to them is worth more than any mere financial computation. It shows how a small business, shrewdly commenced and skilfully prosecuted, will ordinarily lead to competence, if not to affluence. The same good sense manifested by Mr. Brooks in his business affairs was also exhibited by him in regard to his daughters when contracting matrimonial alliances. He desired his daughters especially to select wise and good husbands, rather than heartless and brainless shadows of manhood, though possessed of wealth. In illustration of this, it may be mentioned that Rev. Nathaniel L. Frothingham, D.D., Hon. Edward Everett, and Hon. Charles Francis Adams, son of John Quincy Adams, were his sons-in-law. Although Mr. Brooks did not receive an university education, yet his attainments were better than many who had enjoyed those advantages. As a man of business he had not a superior; and in the social relations of life, he was an accomplished Christian gentleman.

Thomas H. Perkins, Merchant, of Boston.

Mr. PERKINS was one of the most sagacious, enterprising, and successful of Boston merchants, of which city he was a native. Colonel Perkins, as he was uniformly called, had two brothers, James and Samuel, both merchants. James, who died about the year 1825, and left a large fortune, was a liberal patron of the Boston Athenæum. Samuel acquired a fortune; but afterward incurred such heavy losses, that for many years he derived his chief support from a salary as President of the Suffolk Insurance Company. Colonel Perkins had three sisters, one of whom was the mother of John P. Cushing, the well-known millionnaire, who accumulated a large fortune in China; one was the wife of Benjamin Abbott, LL.D., for fifty years the celebrated principal of Phillips Academy, Exeter, N. H.; and the third sister was the mother of the philanthropic Captain Forbes, who commanded the Jamestown on her mission of benevolence to famished Ireland, in the year 1847.

Colonel Perkins commenced his commercial career in partnership with his elder brother, James, who was a resident of St. Domingo, when the insurrection occurred in that island, and was then compelled to flee for his life. They afterward embarked in the trade to the Northwest coast, Canton and Calcutta, in which they acquired great wealth. Soon after the death of his brother James, Colonel Perkins retired from active business. The Perkins family gave over sixty thousand dol-

lars to the Boston Athenæum. For more than sixty years was Colonel Perkins identified with the commercial history of Boston; and for a quarter of a century, or more, by common consent, occupied a prominent position as the leading merchant of New England.

Among the many incidents of his life, which mark and illustrate his private character, is the part he took in the erection of the Bunker Hill Monument, and the donation of his elegant estate for the use of the Boston Institution for the Blind. He was also, in 1827, the projector of the Quincy railway, the first enterprise of the kind in the United States. Subsequently, he was much interested in urging forward the completion of the Washington Monument; and was also the largest contributor to the Boston Mercantile Library Association. But his chief pleasure was derived from his free and constant private charities. His full heart kept his full hand always open.

Colonel Perkins visited Europe several times, and, while in Paris, on one of these tours, participated, with another Bostonian, in the pleasure of liberating from the conscription, George Washington, the eldest son of the Marquis de Lafayette. His last visit to Europe was made when in his seventy-seventh year; and it has been asserted that no American, occupying a private station, has been treated with such marked attention by the nobility and gentry of Great Britain, as was Colonel Perkins. He was not simply a talented merchant, but his taste led him to the study and to the advancement of literature, the sciences, and the arts. He died at Boston, in January, 1854, at the age of eighty-nine years, leaving a fortune of nearly two millions.

Jonathan Goodhue, Merchant, of New York.

THIS eminent and excellent merchant was a native of Massachusetts, having been born in Salem, June 21, 1783.

His father, Hon. Benjamin Goodhue, represented the State of Massachusetts in the United States Senate, two successive terms. Jonathan received his education at the village grammar school, and diligently improved the opportunities of educational advancement there afforded him, until, at the age of fifteen, he became a clerk of that excellent man and distinguished merchant, John Norris, of Salem. After serving in this capacity a few years, his employer sent him to Arabia, as supercargo, touching at the Cape of Good Hope and the Isle of France, and remaining some six months at Aden, Arabia, carrying on trade with the Mohammedans. Subsequently to this he went, in the same capacity, on a voyage to Calcutta.

In 1807, at the age of twenty-four, Mr. Goodhue removed to New York, and there commenced his successful career as an extensive, high-minded and opulent merchant, under the patronage of his former friend, Mr. Norris, together with such men as William Gray, of Boston, Joseph Peabody, of Salem, and others of kindred stamp in that section of the country; and one of his warmest friends in his newly chosen sphere of commercial operations was the late Archibald Gracie.

As soon as the peace of 1814 came with its blessings upon the country, Mr. Goodhue greatly extended his business, comprising voyages to almost all parts of Europe, the East Indies, Mexico, South America, etc. And such was the method which characterized Mr. Goodhue's business transactions, that, notwithstanding the long period covered by his career, and the consequent multiplicity and importance of the political and other events affecting commercial interests during that period, his credit remained unimpaired throughout the whole.

In his intellectual qualities, Mr. Goodhue was distinguished for simplicity, clearness and strength, and his love of acquiring information from books and intelligent acquaintances. He was an unflinching Federalist, and an advocate of the doctrine of free trade,—differing of course, in these respects, from the great body of his associates through life. But that he entertained these views of political and commercial policy conscientiously, no one ever for a moment doubted. The same quality of conscientious uprightness may be said to have shone conspicuously in all his personal, public, and business dealings. His tastes, too, were simple, and thus the affluence to which he attained was never accompanied by pride or extravagance; and though he shunned notoriety, he was always ready to fill those positions of philanthropic or financial trust in which he could be of benefit to his fellow-men,—a feeling which was illustrated by his long and honorable connection with some of the most important institutions in his adopted city. Mr. Goodhue died at the age of sixty-five years. Immediately after this event, a letter was found, written by Mr. Goodhue to his family, and in which, —with many other things equally characteristic of the goodly simplicity of his character,—he says: "In reference to the closing scene in this world, I wish to express my desire that there be no parade connected with the funeral performances. It would be my desire that none but the immediate relatives and friends should be called together when the usual religious services should be performed, and that no more than a single carriage should follow the hearse to the cemetery."

Erastus Corning, Merchant, of New York.

In 1807, when but thirteen years of age, Erastus Corning sought and found the opportunity to begin that industrious career, which he has so long and so admirably sustained. Troy at that time attracted the attention of many of the sagacious men of business of the Eastern States. It seemed by its position toward the Western and Northern trade, and the facilities for manufacture which clustered near it, to afford a sure recompense for the exercise of business energy; a result of which the success of the city has justified the prediction. Mr. Corning's relative, Mr. Benjamin Smith, appreciating the character and energy of his nephew, made him the companion of his removal from Norwich; and, as he fixed his abode in Troy, associated him with his business. Mr. Corning here, and then, entered upon that connection with the business of hardware which, with him, has been the progress from a moderate beginning to the head and control of the largest establishment in that section of the country. Seven years were passed in Troy. The same kind relative who had initiated him into the duties of a commercial life, accompanied him with his kindness to the last. Strengthened in fortune, and with a business habit which moulded readily to his character, and which was every day developing the resources of judgment and good sense which distinguished him, he removed to Albany—the city the annals of whose prosperity, and, better than that, of whose charities, cannot be dissociated from his life.

The house Mr. Corning entered, when he arrived at Albany, had at its head a remarkable man—a man of the first grade of merchants. John Spencer exhibited one of the best specimens of a merchant high in the order of commercial integrity. Nor is it strange that out of a house, conducted by such a man, so many fortunes have had origin. Many of those, now giving to various great measures of good the valuable influence of their wealth, as well as their example, traced from the house of John Spencer & Co. their career. On one occasion, Mr. Spencer was at the old Pearl-street House in New York, when that locality was the gath-

ering place of the merchants of Western New York. At the dinner table were collected such men as Christopher Morgan, and those who, like him, led the business of "the West"—a geographical designation applied, at that time, to New York State. The name of a merchant in Albany was mentioned, and Mr. Spencer asked in relation to his solvency and credit. He answered instantly: "As good as my own." Returning to Albany, he sent for that man, conversed with him of his affairs, entered fully into their actual condition, and finding them precarious and at peril, assumed the burden of his obligations, and placed him beyond cavil or danger. Such was John Spencer's estimate of the worth of a merchant's word, that even his opinion was to be—though at cost and loss—made sound and reliable.

The young man who, at the age of twenty, came to his establishment, was congenial to such honorable rule, and in two years after his entry to the house he became a partner, and the house of Erastus Corning—sometimes alone, but oftener with partners, giving to the business the same high and earnest direction—has continued in increasing prosperity, and with a range of business touching the very verge of the country. But it is to Mr. Corning, as a railway man, that the public eye has for many years been directed, and, so well known is his distinguished career in this sphere, that it would be wellnigh superfluous to attempt, in this place, any delineation of his great and sagacious abilities.

Archibald Gracie, Merchant, of New York.

THIS distinguished merchant and estimable man was born at Dumfries, in Scotland, in 1756. He received a mercantile education of high order, in a counting house at Liverpool. Among his fellow clerks were three other eminent merchants—the late Mr. Ewart, of the latter place; Mr. Reid, of Reid, Irving & Co., London; and Mr. Caton, of Baltimore, who married a daughter of Charles Carroll, of Carrollton.

Mr. GRACIE came to the United States soon after the peace which confirmed their independence, and married Miss Rogers, a sister of the late Moses Rogers Esq., of New York. He established himself first in Virginia; where, in the year 1796, he was ranked among our first merchants for credit and capital.

The geographical position of New York did not escape his foresight; for he early pronounced its destiny to be the commercial emporium of the Western World, and selected that port for the home of his mercantile operations, as well as permanently made it his residence. Here riches flowed in, and honor and usefulness were his rewards for a long term of years. Endowed with rare sagacity and sound sense, to which he added great experience, his commercial enterprises were laid with judgment, and executed with zeal. His signal flag was known in most of the ports of the Mediterranean and the Baltic seas, of the Peninsula, in Great Britain and China, and his name was synonymous with credit, probity, and honor. Even the Spanish Government, not usually over-confiding in foreigners, intrusted to him at one time their bills of exchange, drawn on Vera Cruz, to the extent of ten millions of dollars. These bills were brought in a French frigate to New York, in 1806, and Mr. Isaac Bell, who had charge of them, was upset in a boat, and a reward of two hundred dollars was offered to the finder of the trunk which contained them. It was picked up a fortnight after, at Deal Beach, near Long Branch. The bills were dried, and collected in specie by Mr. Gracie and two other distinguished merchants—Mr. Oliver, of Baltimore, and Mr. Craig, of Philadelphia.

But a season of reverses came. Embarrassed by the capture of ships and cargoes, and by the failure of foreign correspondents and domestic debtors—disaster upon disaster befalling the commercial community—his mass of wealth, accumulated by a long life of enterprise and industry, was entirely swept away in the common ruin—a sad verification of the proverb: "Riches take to themselves wings and fly away." But he never boasted of them, nor trusted in their continuance. Public confidence had often been manifested toward him by appointments to places of trust; and now his friends, whose esteem he never lost nor forfeited, sought to secure a continuance of his usefulness, and an asylum for his declining years, in the presidency of an insurance company, created for these purposes. But the effect of the blast which had prostrated him was not yet over; for here again adversity crossed his path, and the hazards of the ocean proved ruinous to the affairs of the office.

Benevolence and beneficence were the shining characteristics of Mr. Gracie. His dwelling was long the mansion of elegant, unostentatious hospitality, and his door never closed against the poor. It is no slight testimonial to his standing and worth, that he reciprocated honor in a long and confidential intimacy with Alexander Hamilton and Gouverneur Morris. Mr. Gracie died on the 12th of April, 1829, in the seventy-fourth year of his age.

Thomas P. Cope, Merchant, of Philadelphia

MR. COPE, formerly one of the most eminent of Philadelphia merchants, was a native of Lancaster county, Pennsylvania, and belonged to a highly respectable Quaker family. His ancestor, Oliver Cope, was one of the first purchasers from William Penn. On the maternal side, Mr. C. descended from the Pyms, who claim as an ancestor the celebrated parliamentarian, John Pym, whose name is connected with that of Strafford. In 1786, he was sent to Philadelphia, and entered a counting house. In 1790, he began business for himself, and built for his own use the store at the corner of Second street and Jones's Alley, then known by the euphonious designation of Pewter-Platter Alley. Here he transacted a large business, importing his own goods. In this location he continued until 1807, at which time he built his first ship, which he named for his native county, Lancaster. This same year he was elected to the State Legislature; and soon afterward he was solicited to accept a nomination for Congress, but preferred to superintend his extensive mercantile concerns. To Mr. Cope was Philadelphia indebted, in 1821, for the establishment of the first regular line of packet ships between that city and Liverpool, England.

About 1810, Mr. Cope removed his place of business to Walnut street wharf, where his sons now have their counting house, and where their packet ships lie when in port. This place had been remarkable as the scene of misfortune to nearly all its previous occupants, and so marked had the results been, so striking and so uninterrupted, that a dread had been excited in the minds of those the least tinctured with superstition. It was what was called an "unlucky place," and several of Mr. Cope's friends mentioned to him with some earnestness its bad character in this respect. "Then," said he, with his characteristic uprightness and fearlessness, "I will try to earn for it a better name." And although he was a wealthy man before he removed thither, yet that place is identified with his subsequent prosperity.

As a mercantile man, Mr. Cope was the contemporary and often the rival of Stephen Girard; he was also on terms of intimacy and friendship with that remarkable man. It was another proof of Mr. Girard's sagacity, that he selected Mr. Cope to be one of the executors of his will, and one of the trustees of the bank. It happened that after discharging with fidelity the duties which his friend and fellow merchant had thus devolved upon him, Mr. Cope became, for a time, President of the Board of Commissioners of the Girard Estate. To Mr. Cope, in an eminent degree, may be acceded the praise of bringing to a completion the Chesapeake and Delaware Canal; and the citizens of Philadelphia are not likely soon to forget the promptness and the efficiency of his efforts to secure the construction of the Pennsylvania Railroad. For a long time he was President of the Board of Trade, an active manager of the Pennsylvania Hospital, and was also President of the Mercantile Library Company from its foundation to his death.

His personal appearance was quite prepossessing; and not even the weight of eighty years deprived him of a buoyancy of spirits that made his company the delight of social gatherings. He died November 22, 1854.

Jacob Ridgway, Merchant, of Philadelphia.

JACOB RIDGWAY, son of John and Phebe Ridgway, of Little Egg Harbor, was born on the 18th of April, 1768, and was the youngest of five children. His parents were Friends, his father being an elder in the meeting. He was about seven years old when his father died. His father left a good farm, besides money at interest, for each of the three sons; and a small house and lot, with three thousand dollars, to each of the daughters. The family continued to live at the homestead, until the death of the mother, when the household was broken up; and Jacob, then about sixteen, went to Philadelphia, to live with his eldest sister, whose husband he had chosen as his guardian. His property was more than sufficient for his maintenance and education, and afforded a capital at last for commencing business.

He studied the wholesale dry goods business in the store of Samuel Shaw, and succeeded him in it as partner with his son, Thomas Shaw. Though only twenty-one, he was highly valued for his business capacity. After a few years he withdrew from this, and went into partnership with his brother-in-law, James Smith, in a grocery, on Water street. They continued this for some time, till, finding their funds increasing, they sold out to Joseph Pryor, and commenced the shipping business.

Smith & Ridgway continued as shipping merchants with great prosperity until the difficulties between France and England. Their ships were seized; and it became necessary for one of the firm to reside abroad to protect their property. Mr. Ridgway then removed with his family to London, where he conducted the business of the firm, and also that of other merchants. He spent much time in travelling, but finally settled at Antwerp, as consul for the United States. He there became a partner in the firm of Mertons & Ridgway, still continuing in the firm of

Smith & Ridgway, of Philadelphia. During this time he constantly sent on funds to be invested in real estate in Philadelphia. On his return, after several years' absence, he retired from business, finding sufficient employment in the care of his property.

It is related, as an instance of his decision and promptitude, that, while living as consul at Antwerp, he was informed of the seizure of a vessel consigned to his care, the cargo of which was very valuable. Instantly he despatched a courier to Paris to order relays of post-horses at the different stations, collected his papers, and travelled day and night, eating and sleeping in his carriage, until he reached Paris, where he procured an interview with Bonaparte, obtained authenticated papers for the ship's release, and returned to Antwerp with the same rapidity. Before his absence had been even suspected, and just as the captors were about breaking open the cargo and dividing the spoil, much to their surprise and disappointment, he appeared among them and countermanded their proceedings, producing his papers, and taking possession of the ship. Mr. Ridgway died in May, 1843, aged seventy-six years.

PART SECOND.

———•———

*ANECDOTES AND INCIDENTS OF BUSINESS PURSUITS IN
THEIR MONEY RELATIONS.*

PART SECOND.

Anecdotes and Incidents of Business Pursuits in their Money Relations.

BANKS, BANKERS, BROKERS, SPECIE, NOTES, LOANS, EXCHANGE, DRAFTS, CHECKS, PUBLIC SECURITIES, AND CURRENCY IN ALL ITS FORMS AND PHASES; WITH JOTTINGS OF THE MOST CELEBRATED MILLIONAIRES AND MONEY DEALERS — THEIR BUSINESS MODES AND CHARACTERISTICS, MAXIMS, COLLOQUIES, ECCENTRICITIES, WIT, AND FINESSE.

Money in thy purse will ever be in fashion.—RALEIGH.

Money, as money, satisfies no want, answers no purpose — can be neither eaten, drank, nor worn.—LAURINS.

It—money—is none of the wheels of trade; it is the oil which renders the motion of the wheels more smooth and easy.—HUME.

Then would he be a broker, and draw in
Both wares and money, by exchange to win.—SPENSER.

Whole droves of lenders crowd the banker's doors.—DRYDEN.

Drawing the Specie.

THERE was at one time, in the vicinity of Boston, a working man who had saved quite a sum from his earnings, and of this sum he deposited some fifteen hundred dollars in a bank, one of the officers of which was an old acquaintance. After a time, however, the depositor concluded to withdraw his money, stating that he wished gold, as he was to expend it in Maine, and there might be some trouble about bills if he took them. He was informed that the cashier's check would be as good as gold for the purpose, and in case of loss, be more secure, as payment could be stopped. But he desired to have the gold, which was at once counted out to him. The next the bank officers heard of him, he was under arrest, and the following facts were elicited : The story about taking the funds to Maine was simply an excuse for drawing specie. The gold had been secreted under the hay in the loft of a stable; and the man, visiting it in the night, had taken a lantern, the light of which had arrested the attention of another party who watched the movements, supposing the owner of the gold to be an incendiary, and took the man and his bag of double eagles forthwith to the police station house. After considerable parley and protestations of innocence on the part of the supposed culprit, the funds were retained as security for the owner's appearance in the morning. His statements concerning his treasure were verified the next day, and he was released. When remonstrated with for his imprudence in mistrusting a sound bank so capriciously, and leaving his money in a place so liable to destruction as a stable, he replied, that he thought that in case the barn was burned, his gold would *drop through*, and he could easily find it among the ruins!

The Great Bankers of the World in Rothschild's Parlor.

In the year 1824, the great bankers of the world met together to combine in the carrying out of a colossal operation for the French government, viz., to convert the state debt from five per cents. to three per cents.

It was proposed to pay off with a round sum those who were disinclined to exchange their claims which bore five per cent. interest for new three per cent. claims, and to take seventy-five francs for every hundred. The whole of the state debt amounted to 3,066,-783,560 francs; and as it was shown that only about one third of the state creditors would consent to the conversion, a payment in cash of 1,055,556,720 francs became necessary. In order to collect this important capital, the whole financial power of England, Holland and France was called into exercise. Invitations in all directions assembled the leaders of the Paris and London Exchanges—Messrs. Baring Brothers & Co. of London, Brothers Rothschild, and J. Lafitte & Co. of Paris,—to no very difficult task, namely, to arrange in three lists the capitalists of various lands with whom they were connected, especially those of London, Amsterdam, and Paris, at the head of each list being one of themselves.

These financial magnates sat daily in the parlor of the Brothers Rothschild, and sat the longer because of the inexhaustible eloquence of M. Lafitte, about the advantages to accrue from the conversion and all matters connected with it,—an eloquence which, as Mr. Baring afterwards remarked, drove them frequently into positive impatience.

The secret plan of the holders of the three per cent. debt was to raise it to eighty, and then to sell it, and so get rid of it. This price would give to buyers an interest of three and one-half per cent.; and if the portion of the debt to be paid off could not be raised, excepting by new three per cent. pur-

chasers at eighty, the consequence would be, that the five per cent. before the conversion would be worth the relative price of one hundred and six francs sixty-six and two-thirds, in order to get rid of the corresponding interest. This governed the operations of the London, Frankfort, Amsterdam, and Paris Exchanges. The capital destined for the conversion, and collected at the common cost of the representatives of the three lists, was estimated at one thousand millions. Speculators had conceived so favourable an idea of the three per cent. funds to be created—an idea based upon the belief that the undertakers would not bring it into circulation under eighty—that buyers were found in Amsterdam and Frankfort at eighty-one and eighty-two, and even eighty-three and a half. At the same time important sales were made of French five per cent. state paper, at the relative price of from one hundred and six francs sixty-seven, to one hundred and ten. Nothing more was to be had. The project, after much opposition, was sanctioned by the chambers of deputies and peers. For the business world, the consequence of this measure was immense losses for all the direct partakers in the conversion, and for all the first speculators. The five per cents. ran down to ninety-eight francs, and remained fixed at that price for a long time. As people had freely purchased in behalf of the conversion, it became necessary to turn the purchases made on time into money again.

Of the three chiefs of this celebrated coalition, Messrs. Baring and Lafitte suffered most, because of the immense expense caused by the collection of the thousand millions. But the Rothschilds were splendidly compensated by the sales of the three per cents. at eighty-one and eighty-two, and by the sale, at the same time, of a great quantity of five per cents. at one hundred and four—five—and six. As the three per cents. had just been called into existence they had nothing to furnish, and they could replace the five per cents. sold at ninety-eight francs. This plan of M. Rothschild was not imparted to the other two who were interested in the conversion, as is always required by the common understanding of a common participation in loss and gain—the two had been outflanked. The unconquerable aversion which the chief of the Hope house had long felt, to all business connections with the Rothschilds, was the cause of the Amsterdam firms having no part in the projected conversion, and consequently none in the losses. In the same way the house of Hottinguer & Co. refused any participation in the matter.

Nicholas Biddle and the Mississippi Loan.

To the prudence and clearness which characterized Mr. Biddle's course in the crisis of 1836-'7 has been attributed the fact that American credit was saved, and the mercantile interests of the United States preserved from ruin. The gratitude of the commercial houses thus carried through was limitless, and Biddle was always received with marked attention in New York, and throughout the States he was hailed as the greatest financier of the day—the Saviour of Commerce. Perhaps the height to which he was thus elevated made him dizzy, even generating the fancy that his popularity and moneyed influence could lift him to the presidential chair. To win the South, he made enormous advances to the cotton planters. His last measure for popularity was this: there was no American holder of the whole $5,000,000 to the State of Mississippi. Planters are naturally rather backward, and this begat public distrust. Then Biddle took the whole loan, reckoning on his influence and the indorsement of his bank to procure money from the capitalist. When he saw, however, that he had reckoned without his host, he determined to offer

a part of it to Hottinguer & Co., as equivalent for the bank exchanges. The French firm, however, already a little nervous, resolved to get rid of the whole burden, to let the bank paper be protested, and to send back the Mississippi paper. What followed is well known.

Goldschmid and Baring's Unfortunate Contract—Suicide of the Former.

SOME fifty years ago, the houses of Baring and Goldschmid were contractors for a ministerial loan of £14,000,000. But Sir Francis Baring dying, the support of the market was left to his companion. The task was difficult, for a formidable opposition had arisen, which required the united energies of both houses to repress, and to meet which one house was inadequate. It was the interest of this opposition to reduce the value of scrip, and it succeeded. Day by day it lowered, and day by day was Mr. Goldschmid's fortune lowered with it. He had about £8,000,000 in his possession ; and with the depression of his fortune his mind grew dispirited and clouded. Another circumstance occurred at this particular moment to increase his embarrassments. Half a million of exchequer bills had been placed in his hands to negotiate for the East India Company ; and the latter, fearing the result of the contest going on, claimed the amount. His friends did not rally around him, as might have been expected they would, at such a moment ; and Abraham Goldschmid, dreading a disgrace which his sensitive and honorable nature magnified a hundredfold, after entertaining a large dinner party, destroyed himself in the garden of his magnificent residence in Surrey.

Glances behind the Bank Counter.

A VERY readable account of some of the inside operations of a provincial bank is given in Chambers' Journal. We commence with "Old Levy," the official specie hunter: "Who can this little man be who comes forward, thumping down on the counter those immense bags of silver, and who has a man behind him bringing more?" This is "Old Levy," who collects silver for the bank, when hard pressed for that useful commodity. How he gets it all, or where, nobody cares to know; there it is. Hard work he must have, and not very great pay, for he receives only half a crown for every hundred pounds of silver he brings. But a very useful appendage to the bank is Mr. Levy, nevertheless.

There goes the messenger off to some branch with a remittance which probably has just been asked for by letter. There seems nothing very particular about him, and yet his non-arrival at the branch to-day would place the respectable manager there in a very uncomfortable dilemma. It is curious how little bother is made in sending him off. The manager quietly walks up to him and says laconically: "Ten thousand pounds in notes to go to Overdun Branch by next train; you have twenty minutes." The messenger sends out for a cab, stuffs the little bundle of notes into an inside breastpocket, and away he goes, as unceremoniously and unconcernedly as if he hadn't a penny about him.

Here comes the little telegraph lad, elbowing his way up to the teller, and pitching his missive imperiously across to him, as if he knew that his business was of primary consequence, and would be first attended to; and he is right. The dispatch is opened by the manager, and is from the London bankers, where all the bills are payable,— and he thus reads: "Your customer, Robert Banks's bill for three hundred pounds to Hayes & Co., is presented for payment; we have no advice from you to pay,—shall we do so?" "Very stupid of Banks," mutters the manager; but on referring to his account, he finds plenty of funds to meet it; so the care-

less friend is sent for, to give the necessary check and 'sanction for correcting his oversight. He comes in very hot, makes all kinds of apologies, and then another little missive is sent to the telegraph office, addressed to the bank's agents; it contains only the word "Pay," accompanied, however, by a private cipher, known only to the "confidentials" in both establishments, and without which no notice would be taken of it.

Vaults of the Bank of France.

THE silver coin of the Bank of France is heaped up in barrels and placed in spacious cellars, resembling the subterranean storehouse of a brewery, each tub holding fifty thousand francs, in five-franc pieces, and weighing about six hundred pounds. There are, at times, eight hundred barrels, piled up to the very crown of the arches, and rising much higher than a man's head. The visitor walks through a long alley of these barrels, for some time, until he comes to a large stone-floored apartment, wherein are to be seen large square leaden cases, resembling those used at vitriol and sulphuric acid works. Each of these holds twenty thousand bags of one thousand francs, and the whole are soldered up hermetically within the cases—several of these, it appears, not having been opened for nearly forty years, and will probably remain entombed one hundred years longer—the last of the stock to be disposed of or dipped into. In these leaden reservoirs the treasure of the Bank of France is kept perfectly dry, and free also from any variation of temperature. The stairs reaching to these regions of Plutus are narrow, and admit of only one person at a time, ascending or descending with a candle. This has been expressly contrived for protection and defence from insurgent mobs. In one of the treasure vaults are the precious deposits of the Rothschilds, and other wealthy capitalists, left for safety with the bank.

"Confidence" in Hard Times.

A LITTLE Frenchman loaned a merchant five thousand dollars, when times were good. He called at the counting house on the times becoming "hard," in a state of agitation not easily described.

"How do you do?" inquired the merchant.

"Sick—very sick," replied monsieur.

"What is the matter?"

"De times is de matter."

"*Detimes?*—what disease is that?"

"De malaide vat break all de marchants, ver much."

"Ah—the times, eh? Well, they are bad, very bad, sure enough; but how do they affect you?"

"Vy, monsieur, I lose de confidence."

"In whom?"

"In everybody."

"Not in me, I hope?"

"Pardonnez moi, monsieur; but I do not know who to trust à present, when all de marchants break several times, all to pieces."

"Then I presume you want your money?"

"Oui, monsieur, I starve for want of *l'argent.*"

"Can't you do without it?"

"No, monsieur, I must have him."

"You must?"

"Oui, monsieur," said little dimity breeches, turning pale with apprehension for the safety of his money.

"And you can't do without it?"

"No, monsieur, not von other leetle moment longare."

The merchant reached his bank book, drew a check on the good old "Continental" for the amount, and handed it to his visitor.

"Vat is dis, monsieur?"

"A check for five thousand dollars, with the interest."

"Is it bon?" said the Frenchman, with amazement.

"Certainly."

"Have you *de l'argent* in de bank?"

"Yes."

"And is it parfaitement convenient to pay de same?"

"Undoubtedly. What astonishes you?"

"Vy, dat you have got him in dees times."

"Oh, yes, and I have plenty more. I owe nothing that I cannot pay at a moment's notice."

The Frenchman was perplexed.

"Monsieur, you shall do me von leetle favor, eh?"

"With all my heart."

"Vell, monsieur, you shall keep *de l'argent* for me some leetle year longer."

"Why, I thought you wanted it!"

"*Tout au contraire.* I no vant *de l'argent.* I vant de grand confidence. Suppose you no got de money, den I vant him ver much—suppose you got him, den I no vant him at all. *Vous comprenez,* eh?"

After some further conference, the little Frenchman prevailed upon the merchant to retain the money, and left the counting-house with a light heart, and a countenance very different from the one he wore when he entered. His *confidence* was restored—he did not stand in need of the *money.* That's all.

Pursuit of Specie under Difficulties.

AN anecdote of a somewhat lively character is given of a Cincinnati broker, who favored the banks of Lafayette, Ind., during a financial excitement. The broker had with him about $2,500 in bills on the old State Bank, and some $4,500 on the Bank of the State. He stepped into the latter, and his eye brightened at the prospect of the yellow boys ranged in tempting piles before him, every dollar worth ten per cent. premium. He presented his notes, and the cashier recognizing him as one of the Cincinnati sharks, took up a bag of silver specially reserved for such chaps, and commenced redeeming one bill at a time. The broker expostulated. He wanted gold—offered to make a slight discount; but no, the cashier told him that the notes were worth one hundred cents to the dollar, and he proposed to redeem them in Uncle Sam's currency at that figure. He refused to take the silver, and depositing the red backs in an old carpet sack that looked as though it could a tale unfold of many a "run," the discomfited broker wended his way to the old State Bank. He presented his packages, marked "$2,500," and demanded the specie. The cashier of this bank promptly put *his* hook into the broker's nostrils, by setting out a couple of bags filled with dimes and half-dimes. Mr. Broker thus finding "a spider in his cake" here also, turned upon his heel in disgust—if not a better man, at least better "posted."

Specie in the Brokers' Windows.

IT has been said that next to owning gold, the highest pleasure in life is looking at it. Acting on this idea, especially in times when specie circulates scantily, knots of people stand, shoulder to shoulder, at the windows of the exchange brokers, and feast their greedy eyes with gold.

There it is, spread out in a flat, careless heap, with an ingenious affectation of profusion. Looking at it, tossed recklessly on the black velvet, as if thrown out of a shovel, one would hardly think that the owners attached much value to it. Its tempting abundance calls up visions of great vaults full of gold in the back office. The display in the window seems but a sample of tons more, which can be heard of by inquiring within. This is a high instance of art concealing art. The intention of the broker is to express the idea of boundless resources, and he does it. If he arranged the gold in his window, in the shape of a cornucopia, or piled it up in little uniform columns, set like the squares of a checker-board, the illusion of untold wealth would at once be dispelled. The gazers on the sidewalk would say, or think, "This is all the gold the man has. He is showing it off to the best advantage." So it seems that the arrangement of gold in a broker's window, like the tying of a cravat, must be done with a certain studied carelessness, or it will fall short of a perfect success.

Some brokers, who have investigated the subject with that attention which it deserves, as a legitimate department of the fine arts, obtain an admirable effect by scattering twenty-dollar gold pieces carelessly at the bottom of the heap, barely allowing the milled edge of the ground periphery to stick out from the mass of smaller coins above and around. The sidewalk man recognizes the sublime double eagle of the national currency at once. Perhaps he owned one like it years ago—or, more probably, he was slightly acquainted with some other man that once had one. At any rate, he has seen a twenty-dollar gold piece somewhere before, and its majestic outline is stamped upon his memory. From seeing these double eagles peeping out here and there, among the sprawling mass of coins, he derives, by a natural logical process, an impression of Ophirs and Golcondas within, which ten times the number of the same huge unattainable pieces would fail to create, if geometrically adjusted in cylindrical piles.

Loss of Bank Notes.

THE old Bank of the United States was chartered in 1791, and continued in active business operation during a period of twenty years. Its circulation never exceeded twenty millions. In 1823, by decree of court, the trustees of the bank were formally released from any obligation to redeem outstanding bills, as twelve years had elapsed from the expiration of the charter; and notice, by public advertisements, had been widely spread for seven years,—sufficient to meet almost every ordinary case, it would seem. The notes then unredeemed amounted to the large sum of $205,000. A fund of five thousand dollars was reserved for instances of peculiar hardship that might in future turn up; but the whole presented did not exceed eleven hundred dollars, of which the greater part was in the hands of an invalid revolutionary soldier, and liquidated in 1825. A note of ten dollars, however, was redeemed a short time since.

Lafitte in a Tight Place.

THE ancient and close connection between the banking houses of Lafitte of Paris and Coutts & Co. of London, who were intrusted with the wealth of the highest and richest nobles in England, had brought into their hands an immense capital, belonging to English travellers in France and Italy. Many of the travellers had settled in those countries, leaving their money in Lafitte's hands.

It was the common calculation, that fifty thousand Englishmen were living in France; and that if each were to spend but ten francs a day, fifteen millions of francs a month, and one hundred and eighty millions a year, of English gold, would be spent in France. It is evident, that if one-third of these people, or even fewer, were to leave their funds in Lafitte's hands, it would make up a capital far beyond the need of his banking business, and so his own capital might be untouched. But, in order to make it lucrative, Lafitte had loaned it on mortgages of every sort, had invested it in factories, had bought real estate, forests, etc., so that it was no longer of use in his business, but the foreign capital served for his operations. The July revolution

alarmed most of the English in France; they departed, and drew their money from the banker. This emigration became stronger every day, and emptied the portfolios and chests of the house. *For the first time, the credit of the mightiest French banking house was shaken,* and their embarrassment was notorious. Then the new king, Louis Philippe, came to the help of his friend Lafitte, who had greatly contributed to his elevation, and bought of him the part of the forest of St. Germain which he owned, for the sum of nine millions of francs. Even this help, however, was not needed, for the storm soon blew over.

Ouvrard the Banker, and Napoleon.

NAPOLEON once sent for Ouvrard the banker, ostensibly on diplomatic business. After a brief interview, Napoleon said:

"Can you give me any money?"

"How much does your imperial majesty require?" was Ouvrard's answer.

"To begin with," said the emperor, "fifty millions of francs."

"I could get that amount within twenty days, in return for five millions Rente," (of which the price was more than fifty-three francs,) "to be given me at fifty francs, and under the condition that the treasury shall pay Doumerc, whose creditor I am, the fifteen millions it owes him."

The agreement was at once concluded, and the terms drawn upon the spot, by a secretary of the emperor, the latter dictating every word, and signing the paper with his own hand. Napoleon, who had made himself fully acquainted with the condition of the public credit on the Paris Bourse, himself doubted the success of this proposition of Ouvrard's; but when the great banker continued, for seventeen days, to pay in two millions of francs daily to the treasury, Napoleon could scarcely master his astonishment. This

5

was, perhaps, the first time that he, who had never known any other way of filling the treasury than by contributions from the countries he overran, and the taxation of his own subjects, formed a correct idea of the power of credit.

Learning the Currency in a Small Way.

OF all the close dealers among us, the Dutchmen live on the least, and shave the closest. It is astonishing how soon they learn our currency. A good thing occurred, however, in this connection, with the keeper of a small lager bier saloon, in a certain neighborhood, who undertook to teach his assistant, a thick-headed sprout of " Faderland," the difference between " fivepence " and " sixpence."

" Yah ! " said John, with a dull twinkle of intelligence.

A wag of a loafer, who overheard the lecture, immediately conceived the idea of a " saw " and " lager bier " gratis, for that day at least. Procuring a three cent piece, he watched the departure of the " boss," and going up to John, he called for a mug of " bier," throwing down the coin, and looking as if he expected the change. John, who remembered his recent lesson, took up the piece, and muttering to himself, " Mit-out de vomans—'tish von sixpence," he handed over three coppers change.

How often the aforesaid was drank that day, we know not; it depended upon his thirst and the number of times he could exchange three coppers for three-cent pieces; but when the boss came home at night, the number of small coin astonished him.

" Vat ish dese, John; you take so many ? "

" Sixpence," replied John, with a peculiarly satisfied leer.

" Sixpence ! Dunder and Blitzen ! You take all dese for sixpence ? Who from ? "

" De man mit peard like Kossuth; he dhring all day mit himself."

" Der teufel ! You give him change every time ? "

" Y-a-h," said John, with a vacant stare.

" Der teufel catch de Yankees ! " was all the astonished Dutchman could say.

Punch's Money Vagaries.

THE early Italians, says " Punch," used cattle as currency, instead of coin ; and a person would sometimes send for change for a thousand-pound bullock, when he would receive twenty fifty-pound sheep ; or, perhaps, if he wanted very small change, there would be a few lambs among them. The inconvenience of keeping a flock of sheep at one's bankers, or paying in a short-horned heifer to one's private account, led to the introduction of *bullion*.

As to the unhealthy custom of " sweating sovereigns," it may be well to recollect that Charles the First was, perhaps, the earliest sovereign who was sweated to such an extent, that his immediate successor, Charles the Second, became one of the " lightest sovereigns " ever known in England.

Formerly every gold watch weighed so many " carats," from which it became usual to call a silver watch a " turnip."

" Troy weight " is derived from the extremely " heavy " responsibility which the Trojans were under to their creditors.

The Romans were in the habit of tossing up their coins in the presence of their legions, and if a piece of money went higher than the top of the ensign's flag, it was pronounced to be " above the standard."

Banking Habits of Girard.

THE habits characterizing Mr. Girard's attention to business were extremely regular in his counting room, and generally so in the bank, but not always. On discount days, he almost invariably

entered the bank between nine and eleven o'clock during the short days of winter, and six and nine during the summer months; he immediately proceeded to the despatch of business, and would then drive to his farm—for which purpose he would order his horse and chair to the bank at the exact hour that he calculated to finish his business. This routine he generally followed up, unvaryingly, throughout the whole year, never deterred by the inclemency of the weather or other circumstances.

During the first years of the existence of his bank, his visits, except on discount days, could not be calculated upon, but at a later day, as the course of trade induced him to abstract more of his capital from commerce, the pleasure he took in his banking and financial operations seemed to increase, and he then seldom failed to examine his balance sheet every day, and "bleed" some of the debtor banks of their specie. In this latter operation, however, it is claimed for him that he was never actuated by any spirit of envy or hostility, but exclusively by the broad and fair principle of equitable competition—to keep down the balances due him to a sum corresponding to the resources of character of the debtor bank, as well as to check that spirit of too liberal discounting, by which they often extended their business beyond the just proportion of their specie responsibility, and the ability of their capitals.

From the peculiar nature of a private institution like Girard's, the harvest of his business was during a scarcity of money in the market, or a scarcity of specie among the banks. His deposits bore no proportion to his capital, but his specie responsibility always far exceeded, even in a compound ratio, that of other institutions; so that, when the State banks began to curtail, Girard's bank began to extend discounts, and this he always did to the utmost limits of a sound discretion, but never to the extent of his ability. He never seemed

to evince any great anxiety as to the small or large amount of applications for discounts. If the offerings were limited, he was content to keep his surplus funds, and draw specie from the other banks, to stock his vaults for emergencies. If they were ample, he discounted freely, and paid away the specie he had before been employed in gathering. In this respect, he seemed to have as much elasticity of mind, as he was distinguished by eccentricity of conduct; and, like a true philosopher, was always prepared for the loss or the profit that happened to him.

When the State passed an act prohibiting individuals from discounting notes, as bankers, he altered his books as they stood, and his system, from that of discount to loaning operations—giving the customer full credit for the whole amount of the note, and the interest charged against him, as a check drawn.

Timely Hard-Money Loan.

ROBERT MORRIS's financial benefits rendered to our country were equal in importance, as affecting the great issue involved, to the military exploits of some of the ablest generals, in the conflict then waged. At one time, the public safety absolutely demanded a certain sum of hard money, and information of this demand was sent to Mr. Morris, in the hope that, through his financial credit, the money might be obtained. The communication reached him at his office, on his way from which to his dwelling-house, immediately afterward, he was met by a merchant of the Society of Friends, with whom he was in habits of business and acquaintance, and who accosted him with his accustomed phrase, "Well, Robert, what news?" "The news is," said Mr. Morris, "that I am in immediate want of a sum of hard money"—mentioning the amount—"and that you are the man who must procure it for me. Your security is to be my note of hand and my honor." After a short hesitation, the quaker gentleman replied, "Robert, thou shalt have it," and by the punctual performance of his promise, the great public exigency was met.

Logic of Specie Payments.

A PECULIAR circumstance once occurred in Mr. Rothschild's dealings with the Bank of England, in which the latter may be said to have been essentially outwitted by his superior finesse. Mr. Rothschild was in want of bullion, and went to the governor of the bank to procure on loan a portion of their superfluous store. His wishes were met; the terms were agreed on; the period was named for its return; and the affair finished for the time. The gold was used by the financier, his end was answered, and the day arrived on which he was to return the borrowed metal. Punctual to the time appointed, Mr. Rothschild entered, and those who know anything of his personal appearance may imagine the cunning twinkle of his small, quick eye, as, ushered into the presence of the governor, he handed the borrowed amount in bank notes. He was reminded of his agreement, and the necessity for bullion was urged. His reply was worthy a commercial Talleyrand: "Very well, gentlemen. Give me the notes! I dare say your cashier will honour them with gold from your vaults, and then I can return you bullion." To such a speech the only worthy reply was a scornful silence.

Roman Money Lenders.

THE Roman money lenders had no newspaper in which they could temptingly advertise "advances to gentlemen on personal security"—after the modern fashion; but they could stand in the Forum, and offer their shining coin to the passers-by—a more beguiling lure to ruin perhaps, in the case of the heedless, than an advertisement. What spendthrift could resist the sight and convenient form of the yellow metal, or hear the clink thereof unmoved? No stairs to mount—no grim clerk to face —no "sweating room" to be ushered into,—the money amiably and invitingly thrust under his very nose! They had a thriving business, those Roman money lenders; legal interest was one per cent. per month—and the rest *they* knew about. The penalties, too, of non-payment, were such, in those times, as make a very paradise of all modern Botany Bays.

Disinterested Brokers.

WHAT would the British Government do without its broker? There never is a difficulty in the money market but he disinterestedly comes forward, bearing his offers of relief, and spends his fifteen or twenty thousand pounds with no more concern than a school boy would drop his halfpenny at the nearest apple stand. This he does, not merely one day, or a couple of days, but will go on generously buying for weeks and weeks together.

He is the financial physician to the State, and no sooner does Government feel a little tightness in its chest, than with the benevolence of a Rothschild himself, he is ready to relieve it by immediately applying for an investment, —the happy application of which to the part affected, enables the patient to exclaim with as much saltatory glee as the dressing-gowned invalid in George Cruikshank's pictorial advertisement, "Ha! ha! Cured in an instant!"

He is the best friend that Madam Bank, the aged lady in Threadneedle street, ever had, and, supposing that elderly dame ever took it into her head to marry, it would be no matter of wonder that the government broker should prove to be the object of her affection.

His wealth must be something enormous, considering the amount he spends in the course of a twelvemonth; and his frugality must be almost as great as his wealth, for it is noticed that he never buys for any other purpose than that of paying into the savings banks. He must make money very fast, too, or else has an enormous " ready cash" business, that brings him in thousands every week throughout the whole year, inasmuch as it is a stereotyped fact that the government broker limits his operations generally to buying—for he is rarely caught selling. This is a proof of the sure principle upon which he always conducts his business, and the consequence is, that the interest which accrues is invariably not less sure than the principal.

Counting House Dinners.

A CHARACTERISTIC anecdote is told of Girard, which shows that he was not disposed to permit his appetite to interfere with his business. A merchant had made a large purchase of him ; and after waiting some time for Mr. Girard to send for his notes, and not residing far off, he carried his receipt book and waited upon Mr. Girard to pay him. As he entered his counting room, he found Girard at dinner, making his repast upon biscuit and cheese, from a small pine table, the drawer of which, as the merchant entered, Girard opened, and with a broad, off-hand sweep of his right arm, brushed in the fragments of his simple meal—thus consulting not only the economy of money, but the economy of time. It is not supposed but that the " fragments" were made to serve a prudent purpose at another time.

Securing Trustworthy Bank Officers and Safety of Capital.

CREDIT, respectability, reputation, rank, and religious exterior having been proved to be no pledge for the probity of bankers, the public have become very anxious to be informed of some *definite criterion*, by which they shall be assured of the trustworthiness of those in whose keeping they intrust the whole, or most, of their money.

Since, then, the grounds of confidence in bankers above enumerated are not to be depended upon, the gentleman in search of a banker is reduced, by a process of utter exhaustion, to resort, for guidance in his momentous inquiry, to physiognomical indications, but of these the only scientific basis is the system of phrenology.

This consideration has suggested the formation of a new joint-stock bank, to be entitled the " PHRENOLOGICAL BANKING COMPANY," the directors to consist of individuals whose heads are all highly developed in the moral and intellectual regions. No doubt can be entertained of the soundness of the principles on which a bank would be conducted by gentlemen of fine embossments laying their heads together.

Casts of the heads of the directors and other officers of the bank are to be exhibited for public inspection in the bank windows facing the street, and another set of them will be on view within, open, on application, to all parties desirous of taking shares, or depositing money with the company.

As most persons, however, are but imperfectly acquainted with practical phrenology,—in order to facilitate the examination of the development of the directors, casts of the heads of the most noted villains will be placed in juxtaposition with them, for the sake of contrast or comparison. The criminal heads will include those of bankers most recently convicted and therefore most familiar to the public, and, if procurable, those also of directors who have eluded justice.

The casts of the heads of the directors of this new bank are to be duplicated, and kept on sale at all the principal image shops, and at the bank itself. It is submitted that this provision for the publicity of the constitution of the establishment will be far more satisfactory than an ordinary advertisement of the heads of a banking association.

It cannot have escaped the notice of many persons, that bankers are very apt to be bald. This fact looks almost like a provision of nature for assisting observation so extremely important as that of the moral organization of a banker; and it is not unworthy of remark, that "conscientiousness," and all the other organs of the virtues, are seated at the crown of the head.

Pecuniary particulars are to be announced when a certain number of subscribers shall have come forward; all that is precisely stated at present concerning the resources of the company being, that it is composed of capitalists with capital heads, and that the services of Mr. Bumpass have been secured as provisional manager.

Novel Securities for Loans.

THE great banking house of Strahan, Paul & Bates, of London, came to a sudden and ignominious end, some years ago, on its becoming known that they had been guilty of disposing of securities intrusted to them as bankers, by their customers, for safe keeping, and for their use, but which they had appropriated to their own,—one of the highest criminal offences in England, and which was formerly punishable with death. The name of this firm was originally Snow & Walton. It was one of the oldest, wealthiest, and most honored banking houses in London, second only to Child & Co., who date from 1640. At the period of the Commonwealth, Snow & Co. carried on the business of pawnbrokers, under the sign of the "Golden Anchor." The firm, about the year 1679, suspended its payments, in common with most of the London bankers, owing to the circumstance of the seizure of their money by that most profligate and unprincipled ruler, Charles the Second. On an examination of the books of Strahan & Co., ren-

dered necessary by their failure, one was discovered of the date of 1672, which clearly shows that the mode of keeping accounts in those days was in decimals. It is also stated as a curious fact, in respect to the nature and quality of the articles pledged by the *élite* at the loan houses of that period (comprising some of a domestic as well as rather comical character), that one of the entries in the books in question runs thus: "March 10, 1672. To fifteen pounds lent to Lady ——, on the deposit of a golden *pot de chambre*." The blank, it is said, might be filled up with an existing Scotch title.

Pawning Money in Ireland.

THE fund of Irish anecdotes will probably never be so much drawn upon, but that there will be one left. Among a portion of the people of Galway, so little is the commercial value of money known, that they are constantly in the habit of pawning it. A traveller visiting that place, having been informed of the fact, was so incredulous as to its truth, that he went to a pawnbroker's shop to satisfy himself in regard to it. On asking the question, the shopman said it was quite a common thing to have money pawned, and he produced a drawer containing a £10 Bank of Ireland note, pawned six months ago, for ten shillings; a thirty shilling note of the National Bank, pawned for ten shillings; a thirty shilling Bank of Ireland note, pawned for one shilling; a £1 Provincial Bank note, pawned for six shillings; and a guinea, in gold, of the reign of George the Third, pawned for fifteen shillings, two months ago. Anything more blindly ignorant and absurd than this, it is scarcely possible to conceive. The £10 bank note would produce six shillings and sixpence interest in the year, if put into the savings bank, while the owner, who pledged it for ten shillings, will have to pay two shillings and sixpence a year for the ten shillings, and lose the interest on his £10 ; in other words, he will pay ninety per cent. through ignorance, for the use of ten shillings, which he might have for nothing, and realize besides, some five or six shillings for the use of his nine pounds ten shillings. The keeper of the establishment also stated that in many cases money was sold as a forfeited pledge ; that a man would pawn a guinea or fifteen shillings, keep it in pawn till the interest amounted to three or four shillings, and then absolutely and doggedly refuse to redeem it.

Business Aspect and Conduct of the Richest Banker in the World.

AT all times in the haunts of business, and especially on 'change, Nathan Rothschild was a marked object. There he stood, day after day, leaning against his pillar on the right hand, entering from Cornhill. He was a monarch on 'change ; and the pillar in question may be said to have been his throne—but in his case a solid one of granite. No consideration would induce him to do business anywhere else, so devotedly attached was he to that particular spot. There, with his back resting against the pillar, and with note book in hand, he was always to be seen, during the usual hour of business, entering into transactions of great extent with the merchants and capitalists of all countries.

Little would a stranger, who chanced to see the money potentate of the world standing on the spot in question, have fancied from his personal appearance, what an important influence he exerted on the destinies of Europe. No one could be more unprepossessing than he, —just such a man as the boys in the street would have thought a fine subject for a "lark," unless, indeed, they had been deterred by the lowering expression or sullen aspect of his countenance. He always looked sulky, never indulged in a smile, nor even relaxed the rigidity of his muscles. In private,

his intimate friends mention that he occasionally made an effort to smile, but never with any marked success, his smiles at best being hardly more than a species of spoiled grin.

His countenance wore a thoughtful aspect, but his whole appearance was that rather of a stupid, clownish-like farmer of the humbler class. His features were massy. He had a flat face, its conformation being peculiarly characteristic of the faces of the Jewish race of people. His features seemed to be huddled together, without anything like regularity in them. His nose had a good deal of the cock-up form. His mouth was rather large, and his lips thick and prominent. His forehead was of more than an average height, considering the altitude of his face. His hair had something like a darkish hue, and was generally short. His complexion was pale, except where it was slightly tinged with color by the weather. He was short and thick ; though being considerably under the general height, it is possible his pot-belly and corpulent aspect generally, may have made him appear shorter than he really was. He usually was to be seen in a great coat of a dark brown color ; and as he paid but little attention to his personal habiliments, his tailor had no difficult customer to please— that is, in respect to taste and style, though not on the question of price.

It was one feature in Nathan's conduct when on 'change, that he never, except when engaged in business, entered into any conversation whatsoever with any of the multitude surrounding him. There he stood, apparently as deeply lost in thought, and with as melancholy a countenance, as if he had been alone in the "vast wilderness" of shade referred to by Cowper, or been the "Last Man," described by Campbell. Whether his reserve was constitutional, or whether it arose from the pride of purse, or whether from the magnitude of the matters which must have been ever occupying his mind—or from the conjoint operation of these three,—can only be surmised.

Another Bank Project.

It has long been a reproach to roguery that it never permanently prospers; a fact which is owing to the improvidence which generally accompanies want of "principle."

Numerous examples however, in the commercial world, as well as elsewhere, prove that it is possible for a rogue, provided he be prudent, to get on as well as anybody else. And, as organization is as necessary as honor among thieves, an eminent pickpocket has suggested the propriety of establishing a STEALINGS BANK to be conducted on the principle of a Savings Bank, for the accumulation of the earnings of dishonest industry, as a provision for the depredator's declining years.

The direction of the Stealings Bank is, according to the plan announced, to be vested in a chairman, whose name, for obvious reasons, has not been made public, he being the greatest character in the fraternity concerned. This "gentleman" is to be assisted by an unlimited number of Vices of the lowest grade. The smallest deposits will be admissible, and plunder in kind will be regarded as an investment, and receive a fair moneyed equivalent—whereby, it is hoped, an end will be put to the extortions of less reputable establishments now so numerous. The bank will be open to yards of ribbon and bits of tape, and even to rags and bones. To sharp shop-boys, also, having access to tills, no less than the footpad and highwayman, this institution will be available, and will receive any amount of booty from the smallest theft to the highest burglary, swindling, or forgery transaction.

No distinction is contemplated between common thieves, sharpers, Funks and pickpockets, and those engaged in mercantile and financial pursuits, or speculators in Government and other official situations; and thus, to all dishonestly-disposed persons holding public or private berths of trust, the Stealings Bank holds out peculiar temptations and facilities. Magistrates' clerks likewise, and officers of certain law courts, whose fees come decidedly under the head of impositions, will find an appropriate receptacle for their gains in the proposed Stealings Bank.

Yankee Hoarding Specie.

Now and then some very remarkable cases of specie hoarding come to light. A Boston broker some time ago purchased a quantity of coin, of which the history was as follows: The coin was purchased of the heirs of an old man who died in Barnstable county, Mass. He was an old resident of that county, and lived to be ninety-four years old. He was the owner of the house and land which he occupied; but it was not supposed that he had much property beyond his real estate, although it was known that he was very close and miserly in his habits. After his death, his premises were searched, and specie of various kinds found to the amount of fifty thousand dollars. Many of the Spanish dollars were of ancient date; but they showed by their color and perfect stamp that they had not circulated much since the coinage. The Spanish gold pieces were wrapped in scraps of parchment, on which the value of each was marked; and the date indicated that they had been thus hoarded for a long period. In all probability, a large part of this gold and silver had been in his possession more than half a century.

George Peabody's Colossal Fortune.

When all American securities were cast down in the London market, from the unjust confusion of good with bad, arising from the repudiation of some of the States, George Peabody made the beginning of that colossal fortune, which he has proved he knows so well how to use. He made no secret, indeed, of the true state of affairs, and publicly as well as privately exerted himself for the maintenance of American credit. It was a sort of poetical justice, that rendered the instruments by which he proved to the world his confidence in his assertions, the means of his own exceeding great reward, in a solid pecuniary return.

California Gold Seventy Years Ago.

IN the "Voyage Round the World," by Captain George Shelvocke, begun in 1790, he says of California: The soil about Puerto Seguro, and very likely in most of the valleys, is a rich black mould, which, as you turn it fresh up to the sun, appears as if intermingled with gold dust, some of which we endeavored to purify and wash from the dirt; but though we were a little prejudiced against the thoughts that it would be possible that this metal should be so promiscuously and universally mingled with the common earth, yet we endeavored to cleanse and wash the earth from some of it; and the more we did, the more it appeared like gold. In order to be further satisfied, I brought away some of it, which we lost in our confusion in China.

How remarkably a mere accident thus prevented the available discovery, nearly a century back, of the magnificent harvest of gold since gathered and now gathering in California!

"Lives" of Bank Notes.

THE average period which each denomination of London notes remains in circulation has been calculated, and is shown by the following authentic account of the number of days a bank

note issued in London remains in circulation: £5 note, 72.7 days; £10, 77.0; £20, 57.4; £30, 18.9; £40, 13.7; £50, 38.8; £100, 28.4; £200, 12.7; £300, 10.6; £500, 11.8; £1,000, 11.1. The exceptions to these averages are few, and therefore remarkable. The time during which some notes remain unpresented is reckoned by the century. On the 27th of September, 1846, a £50 note was presented bearing date 20th January, 1743. Another, for £10, issued on the 19th of November, 1762, was not paid till the 20th of April, 1845.

There is a legend extant of the eccentric possessor of a £1,000 note, who kept it framed and glazed for a series of years, preferring to feast his eyes upon it, to putting the amount it represented out at interest. It was converted into gold however, without a day's loss of time, by his heirs on his demise —a fact which can very easily be credited.

Stolen and lost notes are generally long absentees. The former usually make their appearance soon after a great horse race, or other sporting event, altered or disguised so as to deceive bankers, to whom the bank furnishes a list of the numbers and dates of all stolen notes.

Bank notes have been known to light pipes, to wrap up snuff, and to be used as curl papers; and British tars, mad with rum and prize money, have not unfrequently, in the time of war, made sandwiches of them, and eat them between bread and butter. Carelessness gives the bank enormous profits, against which the loss of a mere £30,000 note is but a trifle. In the forty years between 1792 and 1832, there were outstanding notes of the Bank of England —presumed to have been lost or destroyed—amounting to £1,330,000 odd, every shilling of which was clear profit to the bank.

Bank Parlor in the Winter.

THE parlor of the Bank of England has always been a place of considerable "interest," and has been often described by those so fortunate as to visit it. But its aspect in winter has been portrayed by only one hand, the sparkling qualities of whose pen are only equalled by those of real "Punch." Of course, in the cold weather, the fireplace is the spot which first attracts and holds the attention, and there the observer perceives the conventional mode of keeping the pot boiling by means of money, most strikingly realized. A bank coffer filled with real coffee rests on the bars, which of course are made of real bullion, and the fire is kept alight by the agency of little bags of a material—one hundred in a bag—that may be seen piled up in the neighboring coal-scuttle, which is also of the same shiny material. On the rug before the fire-place is a little footstool with a delicious stuffing of bank notes—an article known to be extremely useful in keeping people on their legs and giving them a firm footing. The seats serve the purpose of chests as well as chairs, and are filled with the national currency—every seat in the bank parlor having a good stock of the precious metals for its foundation. The works of art in the bank parlor are rare, and the celebrated drawing of a bank note for one million pounds, inclosed in a frame of gold—similar in style to the bars of gold which form the window sashes—is the chief ornament to the walls of the apartment.

Avoiding Specie Suspension.

WHEN the combined influence of the non-intercourse act, the war, and the dissolution of the old Bank of the United States, caused the State banks to resort to a suspension of specie payments, in order to avoid total ruin and bankruptcy, Mr. Girard became greatly embarrassed as to the course he should pursue, to avoid the drain of his specie, and yet preserve his character for strict integrity of business dealing; but he was soon relieved of his inquietude by adopting the suggestion of Mr. Simpson, a most competent and respected adviser in such matters, viz., to pay out the notes of the State banks instead of his own, which he drew in, by paying the specie for them;—so that, at no period of the most disastrous financial crisis, was a bank note of Stephen Girard's ever suffered to become depreciated. This husbanding of his resources subsequently enabled him, in 1817, to contribute so materially to the restoration of specie payments.

The fact just mentioned is interesting, as showing that Girard was never seduced into an imprudent measure, by the prospect of immediate profit, but was satisfied to do what appeared to procure permanent advantage, though, for the time being, rather detrimental than profitable. Most men would have attempted to force their notes into circulation, and redeem them when presented for payment, with the common circulating medium of the country. But, acting according to the principle and method which he did, Stephen Girard's bank never refused to pay the specie for a note of Stephen Girard! It is also stated, that only in one instance was his name ever protested; but even then, it was not his name, but that of his agent in Europe, on whom he had drawn bills, that became dishonored—for, as soon as they were presented to him, after their return, he immediately paid them.

Curious Reasons for Borrowing Money.

MR. PETER C. BROOKS'S maxim was, that "the whole value of wealth consists in the personal independence it secures." An amusing and singular illustration of that distinguished merchant's maxim is thus given:—

A merchant named Porter once had

a clerical friend between whom and himself there existed great intimacy. Every Saturday night, as Porter was sitting balancing his cash, a note would come, requesting " the loan of a five dollar bill." The money was always restored punctually at eight o'clock on the Monday morning following. But what puzzled the lender was, the person always returned the identical note he borrowed. Since the discovery of this fact, he had made private marks on the note; still the same was handed back on Monday morning.

One Saturday evening, Porter sent a five dollar gold piece, instead of a note, and marked it. Still the very same coin was returned on Monday. Porter got nervous and bilious about it; he could hardly sleep at night for thinking about it; he would wake his wife in the middle of the night, and ask her what she thought of such a strange occurrence. He was fast boiling over with curiosity, when a note came from the reverend borrower, one Christmas eve, asking for the loan of *ten* dollars. A brilliant thought now struck him. He put on his great coat, resolving to call and demand an explanation of the mystery. When he was shown into his friend's study, he found him plunged in the profoundest melancholy.

"Mr. B.," said the lender, "if you will answer me one question, I will let you have that ten dollars! How does it happen that you always pay me the money you borrow on Saturday night in the very same coin or note on Monday?"

The parson raised his head, and after a violent internal struggle, as though he were about to unveil the hoarded mystery of his soul, said, in faltering tones, "Porter, you are a gentleman, a Christian, and a New Yorker—I know I can rely on your inviolable secrecy. Listen to the secret of my eloquence. You know that I am poor, and when, on Saturday, I have bought my Sunday dinner, I have seldom a red cent left

in my pocket. Now I maintain that no man can preach the gospel and blow up his congregation properly, without he has something in his pocket to inspire him with confidence. I have therefore borrowed five dollars of you every Saturday, that I might feel it occasionally, as I preached on Sunday. You know how independently I do preach—how I make the rich shake in their shoes. Well, it is all owing to my knowing that I have a five dollar bill in my pocket. Of course, never having to use it for any other purpose, it is not changed, but invariably returned to you the next morning. But, *to-morrow*, Mr. George Law is coming to hear me preach, and I thought I would try the effect of a *ten* dollar-bill sermon on him!"

Atchafalaya Currency by the Cord.

CAPT. SHALLCROSS, of the Mississippi steamer Peytona, is one of the crack captains on the river. Everybody knows him and he knows everybody—therefore everybody will be pleased with a little story about him. One day, the Peytona was steaming down past the cotton woods toward New Orleans, when she was hailed by another boat going up.

" Hallo ! Capt. Shall. ! "
" Hallo ! " was the answer.
" Got any Atchafalaya money ? "
" Yes, plenty."
" Well, pay it out; the bank's busted, or gwine to."
" Ay, ay," said Capt. Shallcross. " Clerk, have you got much of that money ? " " About a thousand dollars, I reckon, sir," said the clerk of the Peytona. " Well, stop at the first wood boat." And the Peytona puffed on, until a wood boat was seen moored to the shore, with piles of cord-wood around, and a small man, with his trousers rolled up, and his hands in his pockets, shivering on the bank beside his boat, in the chill December weather.

"Wood boat, ahoy!" sang out Capt. Shallcross.

"Hallo!" sounded the small man in the distance.

"Want to sell that wood?"

Small man in the distance—"Yas."

"Take Atchafalaya money?"

Small man in the distance—"Yas."

"Round to, pilot," said Capt. Shall.

The boats bound down stream always have to come around, with their bow pointed up stream, to resist the current of the Mississippi; sometimes they encounter a big eddy, and have to take a sweep of some miles before they reach the landing place. So it was in this instance.

"So you *will* take Atchafalaya money for wood, will you?" said the captain, as the boat approached the shore.

"Yas," said the small man.

"How will you take it?" asked Capt. Shall.—meaning at what rate.

"Take it even," quoth the small man.

"What do you mean by even?"

"*Cord for cord, Captain.*"

"Put her round again, pilot," said Capt. Shall.," "and wood up at the next wharf-boat; I reckon that some gabbler has *posted* this fellow on Atchafalaya."

Burning a Banker's Notes.

DURING one of the rebellions in Ireland, the rebels, who had conceived a high degree of indignation against a certain great banker, passed a resolution that they would at once burn his notes which they held; this they accordingly did—forgetting that, in burning his notes, they were destroying his debts, and that for every note which went into the flames, a corresponding value went into the banker's pocket and out of their own. This is what may be termed a genuine financial Hibernianism!

Money Changers in China.

THE Chinese do not recognize either gold or silver as current coin. Gold is considered merchandise, and its value varies like that of any other precious commodity in Europe. As to silver, it is never coined, but, to forward the purposes of commerce, it is generally divided into small ingots, which they can cut into morsels, as they choose, in order to make their payments exact. Thus all men of business carry with them a pair of small scales, of most exact balance, by means of which they settle all their accounts by weight. The changer may usually be seen examining a dollar, and grasping with one hand a species of shears, used as well for testing as dividing the coin of foreigners. A dollar is worth a number—more or less, according to the course of exchange—of the small copper coins which are seen threaded on the changer's desk. This coin is the only one legally current in China; it is round, with a hole in the middle, and is a little larger, but much thinner than an English farthing. These small coins are called lees; they are used separately for trade purposes, or strung in fifties, hundreds, or thousands. The lees are current only during the reign of the sovereign who issued them. The head of the reigning prince, however, is never engraved on the Chinese coin; the only distinguishing mark is that of the dynasty under which it was struck, with a couple of Chinese characters on the face, and as many Tartar characters on the reverse. The Chinese would think it a great mark of disrespect to the majesty of the emperor, as brother of the sun, to circulate his august effigy among the common people, and submit it to the plebeian fingers of hawkers, pedlers, and fishfags. Such a degradation is not to be thought of.

Bankers of the Old School.

THE London banker of the olden time, the successor to the Lombards, had but little resemblance to the modern gentleman who is known by the same title.

He was a man of serious manners, plain apparel, the steadiest conduct, and a rigid observer of formalities. On looking in his face, there could be read, in intelligible characters, the fact that the ruling maxim of life, the one to which he turned all his thoughts and by which he shaped all his actions, was, "that he who would be trusted with the money of other men should *look* as if he deserved the trust, and be an ostensible pattern to society of probity, exactness, frugality, and decorum."

He lived, if not the whole of the year, at least the greater part of it, at his banking house, was punctual to the hours of business, and always to be found at his desk. The fashionable society at the west end of the town, and the amusements of high life, he never dreamed of enjoying, and would have deemed it little short of insanity to imagine that such an act was within the compass of human daring, as that of a banker lounging for an evening in Fop's Alley, at the opera, or turning out for the Derby with four greys to his chariot, and a goodly bumper swung behind, well stuffed with pies, spring chickens, and iced champagne.

The material or architectural aspect of the business of banking in early times, is also, to modern ideas, as humble as it must have been picturesque. Instead of the handsome apartments, the highly polished and well-fitted counters, and well-dressed clerks of the modern banking-houses, there were the dark-featured Lombards, ranged behind their bags of money displayed on low benches in open shops, protected, perhaps, by occasional awnings, from the inclemency of the weather.

"The Lady's Broker."

MOST of the leading men who act as brokers in London go by nick-names; and the way in which these names sometimes originate, is quite curious. One of the fraternity has been dubbed "The Lady's Broker," in consequence of hav-

ing been employed, on one occasion, by Madame R., the lady of a deceased capitalist, in a speculation into which she entered on her own account, and without the knowledge of her husband. The speculation turned out so unfavorably, that neither the lady nor her broker could discharge their obligations; and hence, as in other cases where the broker cannot meet the engagements he has entered into for any other party, he must, to save himself from the blackboard, give up the name of his principal,—the broker was compelled to divulge the name of the lady speculator. From that day to this, he has gone under the name of the "The Lady's Broker." The husband, in this case, knowing he could not be compelled to pay for the illegal gambling of his wife, refused to advance a single farthing in liquidation of her debts.

Cashier Inviting a Run upon his Bank.

A BANK that was managed with great caution was once in what was supposed to be a peculiar position, when a friend of the cashier called upon him, and taking him aside, with a grave face, said, "I heard it asserted just now that you have not five thousand dollars left out of the one hundred thousand silver dollars that were lately paid into your bank, and I hastened to tell you, in order that you may show me your vaults, and give me the means to contradict the rumor."

"No," said the cashier, "the rumor is all true. What use do you suppose that I have for the silver?"

"Why, to meet the run upon your bank, which must certainly come when this state of your affairs is generally known," was the reply.

"*Let the run come,*" said the cashier; "and by way of beginning it, do you go into the street, collect all of our bills that you can find, and bring them to me, and I promise to give you the hard dollars for them."

After some time, his friend returned to say that he had not been able to find any of the bills of that particular bank, excepting a solitary one for five dollars, for which the silver was immediately offered him.

"Just so," said the cashier, "almost all the bills that I have issued have already been sent in, and I have paid out the silver for them. But in doing so, I have emptied most of these boxes of dollars. The money was given me to lend; and I have lent it for about four months. But I could not lend and keep it too. I have, therefore, very little gold or silver in the vaults. So long as I have the small amount that is necessary to redeem the few bills that remain out, and the two thousand dollars which I have earned for the stockholders, I am easy. You may go back to the street, if you will, and defy the world to break our bank. We shall lend nothing more until the promissory notes that we have taken as security begin to fall due. As they are paid in, with hard dollars, or the bills of other banks, we shall have the means to lend money again."

Obtaining Security to be a Broker.

AMONG the political opponents of George Hudson, the English railway monarch, when at York, was one who, when riches were discovered by him to be so easily realized on the stock exchange, sought the great metropolis to make his fortune, as others had, by becoming a broker. To London he went. But to be a member of the money market in that city, two sureties were required; and he could procure only one. The difficulty continued, and great was his disappointment. In his despair he thought of the railway king; and, as a last resource, on Mr. Hudson he waited, and told his mission.

"You've been no friend of mine," said Mr. Hudson, bluntly; "but I believe you're a good sort of fellow—call on me to-morrow."

The morrow came, and, full of anxiety, he waited on the autocrat. "Well," said Mr. Hudson, "it's all settled; I've arranged everything. Mr. —— will be your other security: go to him; I've told him to do it."

Mr. Hudson did not add, as he might, that he had in fact guaranteed the amount to the broker named by him, and was himself sole surety for the opponent he befriended.

London Bankers and Banking Houses.

THE oldest banking houses in London are Child's, at Temple Bar, Hoare's, in Fleet street, Strahan's—formerly Snow's, in the Strand, and Gosling's, in Fleet street. None date earlier than the restoration of Charles the Second. The original bankers were goldsmiths— "goldsmiths that keep running cashes"—and their shops were distinguished by signs. Thus, Child's was known by "The Marygold," still to be seen where the checks are cashed; Hoare's, by "the Golden Bottle," still remaining over the door; Strahan's, by "the Golden Anchor," to be seen inside; and Gosling's, by "the Three Squirrels," still prominent in the ironwork of their windows toward the street.

The founder of Child's celebrated house was John Backwell, an alderman of the city of London, ruined by the shutting up of the Exchequer in the reign of Charles the Second. Stone and Martin's, in Lombard street, is said to have been founded by Sir Thomas Gresham, and the grasshopper sign of the Gresham family was preserved in the banking house till late in the last century.

Of the west-end banking houses, Drummond's, at Charing-cross, is the oldest; and next to Drummond's, Coutts's, in the Strand. The founder of Drummond's obtained his great position by advancing money to the Pretender, and the king's consequent withdrawal led to a rush of the Scottish nobility and gentry with their accounts, and to the ultimate advancement of the bank to its present footing. Coutts's house was founded by George Middleton, and originally stood in St. Martin's lane, near St Martin's church; Coutts removed it to its present site.

The great Lord Clarendon, in the reign of Charles the Second, kept an account at Hoare's; Dryden lodged his £50 for the discovery of the bullies who waylaid and beat him, at Child's, Temple Bar; Pope banked at Drummond's; Lady Mary Wortley Montague, at Child's; Gay, at Hoare's; Dr. Johnson and Sir Walter Scott, at Coutts's; Bishop Percy, at Gosling's; the Duke of Wellington, at Coutts's; the Duke of Sutherland, at Drummond's; the Duke of Devonshire, at Snow's.

Paying Notes in Specie.

PHILIP HONE, speaking of the " blessed" days of specie currency, says: "The few notes which were given out by the merchants and shopkeepers—and the sequel will show how few they must have been—were collected of course through the bank. Michael Boyle, the runner, with his jocund laugh and pleasant countenance, called, several days before the time, with a notice that the note would be due on such a day, and payment expected three days thereafter. When the day arrived, the same person called again with a canvas bag, counted the money in dollars, half dollars, quarters, and sixpences (those abominable disturbers of the people's peace—bank notes being scarcely known in those days), carried it to the bank, and then sallied out to another debtor. And in this way all the notes were collected in the great commercial city of New York, in such a circumscribed circle did its operations then revolve. Well do I remember Michael Boyle, running around from Pearl street to Maiden lane, Broadway, and William street,—the business limits, happily for him, not extending north of the present Fulton street,—panting under the load of a bag of silver, a sort of locomotive sub-treasurer, or the embodiment of a specie circular."

Security for a Discount.

IT is very common among business men to give vent to a good deal of grumbling about the illiberal course which characterizes banks in hard times, toward their customers. An unfortunate customer of one of these institutions in Philadelphia, being somewhat irritated at the picayune policy pursued, resorted to the following desperate expedient, to see if there was any such thing as " raising the wind," in said concern. He drew a note for five dollars at thirty days, covered it down the back with first-class indorsements from his fellow sufferers, pinned it to a ten dollar bill of the same bank, as collateral, and then ventured to offer it for discount. That is what Jedediah Tompkins would call " hintin' round."

Jacob Barker's Forty Kegs of Specie.

MANY years ago Jacob Barker offered some good business paper for discount at one of the Wall street banks, and, when the board of directors met, they, after mature deliberation, threw the paper out, which displeased friend Jacob, and he consequently sought revenge, in a professional way, for what he took to be rather ungentlemanly treatment. A few days only elapsed, when Jacob presented forty thousand dollars of the bills of that same bank at its counter, and demanded the specie from the astonished officers; but nevertheless it was rolled out to him in kegs of one thousand dollars each,—the teller of the bank informing him that they were obliged to give him small coin, five and ten cent pieces.

Here was a dilemma, even for so bright witted and redoubtable a man as Jacob; but being equal to the emergency, Jacob ordered the porter to unhead the casks, which being done, Jacob took a handful of the coin from each, and requested the teller to place the remainder—which of course required, according to bank custom, to be counted—to his credit. It was said, at the time, that it required the whole available force of the institution to count the coin, and that many late hours were made. Whether Jacob ever offered any more notes for discount, or applied for any "accommodation" favors, at that bank—or whether he got them if he did,—we are only left to infer.

Final Argument at a Bank Counter.

On receipt of the news of the banks suspending specie payments, Mrs. Jones hastened to her savings bank, elbowed her way smartly to the desk, presented her book, and demanded her money.

"Madam," said the clerk persuasively, " are you sure you want to draw this money out in specie ? "

"Mrs. Jones," said a director, with an oracular frown, do you know that you are injuring your fellow depositors ? "

"And setting an example of great folly to less educated persons in this community ? " struck in another director.

" Let us advise you simply to reflect," interposed the clerk, blandly.

" To wait for a day or two at least," said the director

At last there was a pause.

Mrs. Jones had been collecting herself. She burst now. In a tone which was heard throughout the building, and above all the din, and at which her interlocutors turned asby pale, she said:

" *Will you pay me my money—yes or no ?* "

They paid her instantly.

First Jewish Bill of Exchange.

THE circumstance which gave rise to the introduction of bills of exchange in the mercantile world, was the banishment from France, in the reigns of Philip Augustus and Philip the Long, of the Jews, who, it is well known, took refuge in Lombardy. On their leaving the kingdom, they had committed to the care of some persons in whom they could place confidence, such of their property as they could not carry with them. Having fixed their abode in a new country, they furnished various foreign merchants and travellers, whom they had commissioned to bring away their fortunes, with secret letters, which were accepted in France by those who had the care of their effects. From this it is claimed that the merit of the invention of exchanges belongs to the Jews exclusively. They discovered the means of substituting impalpable riches for palpable ones, the former being transmissible to all parts, without leaving behind them any traces indicative of the way they have taken.

Leather Money.

On the authority of Seneca, a curious account is given of a period when leather, appropriately stamped to give it a certain legal character, was the only current money. At a comparatively recent date, in the annals of Europe, Fredich the Second, who died in 1250, at the siege of Milan, actually paid his troops with leather money. Nearly the same circumstance occurred in England, during the great wars of the barons. In the course of 1350, King John, for the ransom of his royal person, promised to pay Edward the Third, of England, three millions of gold crowns. In order to fulfil this obligation, he was reduced to the mortifying necessity of paying the expenses of the palace in leather money, in the centre of each piece there being a little, bright point of silver. In that reign is found the origin of the burlesque honor of boyhood, called "conferring a leather medal." The imposing ceremonies accompanying a presentation, gave full force, dignity, and value to a leather jewel, which noblemen were probably proud to receive at the hand of majesty.

The United Job and Lazarus Bank.

WITH a view to the special advantage of the small and uncertain capitalist, the United Job and Lazarus Bank has at last been established.

That distinguished British actuary, Mr. Fitzlocker, has calculated that the half-pence annually bestowed in charity upon persons of the mendicant class amounts, on an average, to no less a sum than £950,000, 14s. 2½d. This sum does not include the daily coppers expended upon the crossing-sweepers, that may fairly be put down at £50,000 more, sinking, for the sake of round numbers, the odd half-penny. Thus, a total is presented of £1,000,000, 14s. 2½d. Now, it is well known that the mendicant and crossing-sweeper class are, for the most part, a thrifty if not a penurious people. What is more common than to read of the apprehension or death of the beggar upon whose person or body are found rolls of bank notes and showers of sovereigns?

It is calculated that of the above £1,-000,000, not above one half is expended by the recipients for board, clothing, and lodging—leaving a fair margin of expense for an annual visit to a watering place. Thus, a clear half million is annually accumulating in old stockings, under worm-eaten floors, and in all sorts of impossible nooks and corners considered convenient only to Plutus.

Now, it is to afford safe and peculiarly profitable means of investment to the provident classes above named, that the United Job (it is requested that "Job" be taken in its purely patriarchal pronunciation)—the United Job and

6

Lazarus Bank is established. The persons most interested in the successful permanence of the institution, it cannot be doubted, will feel the fullest and deepest confidence in the character of the concern, upon a careful perusal of the circular containing the names of the officers; these include such individuals as Messrs. Crook-fingered Jack, Jemmy Twitcher, Wat Dreary, Ben Budge, Ben Booty, Reynard Foxleer, and others, with Mr. Filch as manager and cashier

Capital of European Bankers.

AN actual report of the general supervisor of the books of the several firms of the Rothschild, giving the aggregate amount of their capital or the sum at their instantaneous command, shows that capital to be a millard of francs, or two hundred million dollars. It is also stated that the similar capital of the two Péreires is at least one hundred millions of francs; of the Hottinguers, seventy-five millions; of Mirés and the Foulds still higher; and the Duke of Galiera, at the head of the Crédit Mobilier, is held to be prodigiously opulent. The Péreires have created for themselves a new fortune by the purchase of very extensive grounds within and without the walls of the capital, which they turn into streets and boulevards with a certainty of the earliest and most ample proceeds.

Dudley North's Opposition to Brokerage.

THE system of banking or brokerage by bills which was introduced in London in the sixteenth century, in place of the old method of paying in solid metals, encountered much opposition and clamor. Old fashioned merchants complained bitterly that a class of men who, thirty years before, had confined themselves to their functions, and had made a fair profit by embossing silver bowls and chargers, by setting jewels for fine ladies, and by selling pistoles and dollars to gentlemen setting out for the Continent, had become the treasurers and were fast becoming the masters of the whole city. These usurers, it was said, played at hazard with what had been earned by the industry and hoarded by the thrift of other men. If the dice turned up well, the knave who kept the cash became an alderman; if they turned up ill, the dupe who furnished the cash became a bankrupt. On the other side, the consequences of the modern practice were set forth in animated language. The new system, it was said, saved both labor and money. Two clerks, seated in one counting house, did what, under the old system, must have been done by twenty clerks in twenty different establishments.

Gradually, however, even those who had been loudest in murmuring against the innovation, gave way and conformed to the prevailing usage. The last person who held out, strange to say, was Sir Dudley North. When, in 1689, after residing many years abroad, he returned to London, nothing astonished or displeased him more than the practice of making payments by drawing bills on bankers. He found that he could not go on 'change without being stealthily followed round the piazza by goldsmiths—as the dealers in bullion were then called—who, with low bows, begged to have the honor of serving him. He lost his temper when some of these friends asked him where he kept his cash: "Where *should* I keep it," he sharply asked, "but in my own house?" and turned his heel upon the whole pack. With difficulty he was at last induced to put his money, just by way of trial, into the hands of one of the Lombard street men, as they were familiarly called. As ill luck would have it, the Lombard street man broke, and some of his customers suffered severely. Dudley North lost only fifty pounds; but this loss immovably confirmed him in his dislike of the whole art of "improved bank-

ing." It was in vain, however, that this old landmark stood up and exhorted his fellow citizens to return to the good old practice, and not to expose themselves to utter ruin in order to spare themselves a little trouble. He stood alone against the whole community.

Strongest Bank in the World.

THE Bank of Genoa, which has been in existence hundreds of years, has perhaps proved itself the strongest institution of the kind in the world. It is a remarkable fact in its history, that its administration has always been as permanent and unchangeable, as that of the republic has been agitated and fluctuating. No alteration ever took place in the mode of governing and regulating the affairs of the bank; and two sovereign and independent powers, at war with each other, have been within the walls of the city, without producing the slightest shock to the bank, or causing it to secrete any of its books or treasures.

Financial Physic.

IT is proposed to establish an altogether new method of inquiring into the state of the health of certain classes of the community. The following are some of the interrogatories to be addressed to the patient: How are your funds? Let me see your coupons. Put out your stock. Are your dividends all right? Have you any pain about your bonds? Any uneasiness referring to your foreign securities? What is the state of your corn market? Allow me to examine your shares. Let me feel your scrip. Have you any sinking in your mines? Any tightness at the back, or hollowness of the chest? How is your discount? Have you any appetite for speculation?

Brief Explanation of Banking.

OLD Mr. Lefevre, father of the former speaker of the House of Commons, and the principal founder of the house of Curries & Co., illustrated the simple theory of banking to a customer one day, in a manner rivalling the best treatises on that subject. The customer in question was one of those men who find it very convenient to have bad memories, and very tantalizing at times to have good ones. His account was almost always overdrawn, and whenever spoken to on the hitch thus occasioned, his answer was invariably the same—he really had forgotten how it stood. At last, Mr. Lefevre watched his opportunity, caught him one day at the counter, and said to him:

"Mr. Y—, you and I must understand one another something better than we now seem to. I am afraid you don't know what banking really is; give me leave to tell you. It's my business to take care of your money; but I find you are always taking care of mine. Now, that is not banking, Mr. Y.; it must be the other way. I'm the banker, not you. You understand me now, Mr. Y.; I'm sure you do!"

Jacob Little and the Missing Bank Bill.

OF this acute financier, an anecdote of the most extraordinary of his faculties—his quickness of perception—is related, as illustrating one of the secrets of his success. A man came to the counter with a draft for $650. He was handed at once a $500, a $100, and a $50 bill. The man left. In a few moments he returned, saying,

"Mr. Little, sir, I think you made a mistake. That was a draft for $650 I gave you, and you have given me only $150—and he held out the $100 and the $50 notes.

With almost fierce abruptness—the tone familiar to all who knew Mr. L.,

he asked the man, "Where have you been?"

"To the Bank of America, to deposit my money, and it was there I—"

Mr. Little did not wait to hear the end of the sentence. Dashing on his hat, he ran out, hastened to the bank, and returned, in almost less time, than it takes to tell the story, with the missing $500 in his hand.

"Here, sir," said he, to the overjoyed customer; "you dropped your bill at the bank, and if I had been a quarter of an hour later, you would never have seen it again—let me tell you."

New York Bankers and Western Court Houses.

THAT city bankers are called upon to loan for almost everything, far and near, is a fact which none know so well as themselves. Occasionally, however, an incident like the following, in their experience, comes to light. The agent of a county in one of the Western States, visited New York to negotiate bonds, and called on a leading banker, with the expectation of having the gold shovelled into his pocket, that he might go home by the next train.

"What do you want the money for?" asked the banker.

"To build a court house and jail," was the answer.

"And you have called on me for advice?"

"Yes, sir. Knowing you to be acquainted with the best houses, I thought you could refer me to them in a favorable manner."

"I will give you my advice and help you willingly."

"Thank you—thank you."

"It is this: Put your bonds in your pocket and go home. When you get there, take your bonds out of your pocket, and put them into the fire."

The banker's visitor opened his eyes and mouth.

"Yes, sir, put them in the fire. Then tax your people and build your court house and jail. We can't give you money for any such purposes, and you have no business to ask it. What do we care for a court house and jail out by the Mississippi River? This is the way with some of you Western men! Now go back and do as I tell you—burn your bonds and tax your people. Nobody here cares a picayune whether you have a court house or not. If it should do no better than some other court houses, justice won't be the gainer by it. I think it quite likely you would be better with a jail, and I'm sorry to have to say that I can't help you to build it."

Banks Failing.

"ARE you afraid of the banks failing?" asked a Boston cashier, as Mrs. Partington went to draw her pension. "Banks failing!" said the dame; "I never had any idea about it at all. If he gets votes enough, I don't see how he can fail, and if he don't, I can't see how he is to help it." "I mean," said he, "the banks that furnish paper for the currency." She stood a moment counting her bills. "Oh, you did, did you?" said she; "well, it's about the same thing. If they have money enough to redeem with—and heaven knows there's need enough for 'redemption' for a good many of them, and more 'grace' than they allow their customers—they may stand it; but doubtful things are uncertain." She passed off like an exhalation, and the cashier counted out $115.17 fifteen times while pondering what she said, in order to catch her meaning.

Spanish Reals versus Spanish Bonds.

ROTHSCHILD, though so deeply engrossed in money matters, occasionally has time to add to his quality of shrewdness that of being witty. On being called upon one time to give a good definition of the real and the ideal in sublunary matters, he, true to his profession, answered: "I cannot give you a more forcible example than this, namely—the 'real' is the current coin of Spain, and a Spanish bond, which is supposed to represent it, is the 'ideal.'"

Throwing out Jacob Barker's Notes.

THE bitter opposition of Jacob Barker to the renewal of the charter of the United States Bank is matter of history, and it came about in this wise: Although subject to occasional reverses, Mr. Barker prospered greatly in his business until he had the misfortune to incur the displeasure of Robert Lenox, a very rich Scotch merchant—strong-minded and intelligent, with a will and prejudices equally decided.

Mr. Barker had, as agent for the owner, chartered to James Scott, the ship Live Oak, of Portland, Me., for a voyage to St. Domingo and back. On her arrival off the port of destination she found it blockaded, and was ordered off, when, according to custom, she proceeded to the next port; finding that in the possession of the slaves, they having revolted, the captain prudently returned to New York with the outward cargo.

A question now arose, whether or not the ship was entitled to compensation. Mr. Barker applied immediately to his friend and professional adviser, Gen. Alexander Hamilton, for advice; that gentleman advised him to retain a sufficiency of the cargo to pay the amount of the charter, until he could advise and receive an answer from his employer, the owner of the ship. A portion less than the amount of charter was in money; it was retained.

The following day, Mr. Barker's notes offered for discount at the United States Branch Bank, where he kept his account, were all thrown out, which was followed up every discount day for two or three weeks, when Mr. B. began to feel its effects. Knowing Mr. Lenox to be the most influential director, he applied to that gentleman, without the least idea of the cause, or that he was the individual who had induced the rejection of the notes offered; named to him the liberality with which he had always been treated by the bank, the goodness of the notes offered and their rejection, adding that he . presumed there must be some hidden cause which he, Mr. L., could satisfactorily explain, if he knew what it was.

"Yes," said Mr. Lenox, "there is a cause, and if you expect any more discounts at the Branch Bank, you must deliver to Mr. Scott the money you withhold from him."

Mr. Barker, astonished at the avowal, inquired if the board of directors undertook to pass, *ex parte*, on differences which arose among merchants, neither of whom was of their number, and to enforce their decision against one of the parties, without having allowed him a hearing. Mr. Lenox replied that he believed every director at the board agreed with him in opinion.

Application was immediately made to Gen. Stevens, Thomas Buchanan, and other directors, who informed him that Mr. Lenox was mistaken; that they were opposed to all such assumption of power, and that if Mr. Lenox did not withdraw his objection, they would not allow the notes of his friends to be discounted. One or two opposing a note, it could not, by the rules of the board, be discounted. On the re-appointment of Mr. Lenox as a director by the mother bank at Philadelphia, Mr. Barker sought his redress by opposing a renewal of the bank's charter, which was soon to expire. This he did with untiring tact and energy, not ceasing his exertions until the fate of the bank was sealed by a rejection of the bill for the renewal of the charter by Congress. This was done by a majority of only one; and as Mr. Barker's half-brother, Gideon Gardner, was a member from Nantucket, and voted against the bank, it is not unreasonable to conclude that Mr. Barker's influence was not small, in overthrowing the first United States Bank.

Establishment of the Bank of England —Curious Facts.

AFTER much opposition, the Bank of England was established in 1694. Strange as it may seem, the act of Parliament by which the bank was established is entitled "An act for granting to their majesties several duties upon tonnage of ships and vessels, and upon beer, ale, and other liquors, for securing certain recompenses and advantages in the said act mentioned, to such persons as shall voluntarily advance the sum of fifteen hundred thousand pounds toward carrying on the war with France." After a variety of enactments relative to the duties upon tonnage of ships and vessels, and upon beer, ale, and other liquors, the act authorizes the raising of twelve hundred thousand pounds by voluntary subscription, the subscribers to be formed into a corporation, and be styled "The Governor and Company of the Bank of England." The sum of three hundred thousand pounds was also to be raised by subscription, and the contributors to receive instead annuities for one, two, or three lives. Toward the twelve hundred thousand pounds no one was to subscribe more than ten thousand pounds before the first day of July next ensuing, nor at any time more than twenty thousand pounds. The corporation were to lend their whole capital to government, for which they were to receive interest at the rate of eight per cent. per annum, and four thousand pounds per annum for management; being one hundred thousand pounds per annum on the whole. The corporation were not allowed to borrow or owe more than the amount of their capital, and if they did so, the individual members became liable to the creditors in proportion to the amount of their stock. The corporation were not to trade in any goods, wares, or merchandise whatever, but they were allowed to deal in bills of exchange, gold or silver bullion, and to sell any goods, wares, or merchandise upon which they had advanced money, and which had not been redeemed within three months after the time agreed upon. The whole of the subscription was filled in a few days. In Grocers' Hall, since razed for the erection of a more stately structure, the Bank of England commenced operations. Here, in one room, were gathered, with almost primitive simplicity, all who performed the duties of the establishment. "I looked into the great hall where the bank is kept," says the graceful essayist of the day, "and was not a little pleased to see the directors, secretaries, and clerks, with all the other members of that wealthy corporation, ranged in their several stations according to the parts they hold in that just and regular economy."

A writer in the *Gentleman's Magazine*, speaking of the external appearance of the bank, in 1757, describes it as comparatively a small structure, almost invisible to passers by, being surrounded by many others, viz., a church called St. Christopher le Stocks; three taverns, two on the south side (the Fountain) in Bartholomew lane, facing the church there, just where the great door of entrance is now placed, and about fifteen or twenty private dwelling houses. Visitors are sometimes shown in the bullion office the identical old chest, somewhat larger than a common seaman's, also the original shelves or cases, where the cash, notes, papers, and books of business were kept. Visitors are occasionally shown some notes for large amounts, which have passed between the bank and government. In the early history of the establishment any person in the possession of a bank note might demand only part of its amount, and the same plan might be resorted to with the same note until the whole of the sum due upon it was ab-

sorbed; some of these are still shown —on the last which came in there was only sixpence to receive. A bank of England note is never issued after it returns to the bank; it is then cancelled and destroyed, to make way for the next issue. Whenever a note is presented to the bank the corner is torn from it, the number is punched out, it is cancelled in the register book, and then sent down to the library, there to lie for ten years, until burned in the yard during the eleventh. About one thousand persons are employed in the establishment.

Bound not to Break.

THE banking operations of Jacob Barker, when he carried on business in Wall street, New York, met with much opposition from many of the bankers of that locality, and they managed once in a while to push Jacob pretty close to the wall. On one occasion, when the times were somewhat tight, and Mr. Barker was absent, attending to his duties as a member of the New York senate, a ship arrived from Liverpool with advice of the failure of his house at that place. This at once caused a very great run on Mr. Barker's bank—on receiving notice of which he returned to the city, was the first to land from the steamboat, and drove with great speed to Wall street, the carriage making its way through the crowd with difficulty.

He alighted at the bank door, to the surprise of all, and to the disappointment of his enemies, who were ranged on the opposite side of the street in momentary expectation of seeing the doors of the bank close. They had not heard of the boat's arrival, or of the river's being free from ice. He was too quick for them, and remarked to all how glad he was to see them, saying, "Come in, come in—come in and get your money;" caused the back room to be thrown open, and additional clerks to be placed there, with plenty of specie.. All that wished it were supplied. A great number put the notes in their pockets and went home, fully recovered from their alarm. Mr. Barker was "bound not to break," and, as his stores were full of goods—hemp, sail cloth, iron, sugar, tea, salt, etc.,—he sold a sufficiency of these at auction to replenish the vaults of his bank, and at once returned to the duties of his office. Jacob declared, with characteristic emphasis, that he was "bound not to break."

Weight of Miss Burdett Coutts's Fortune.

THE late Duchess of St. Albans left Miss Burdett Coutts the regal sum of £1,800,000, or some nine million dollars. The weight of this prodigious sum in gold, reckoning sixty sovereigns to the pound, is thirteen tons, seven cwt., three qr., twelve lbs., and would require one hundred and seven men to carry it, supposing that each of them carried the solid weight of two hundred and ninety-eight pounds. This large sum may also be partially guessed, by considering that, counting at the rate of sixty sovereigns a minute for eight hours a day, and six days, of course, in the week, it would take ten weeks, two days, and four hours, to accomplish the task. In sovereigns, by the most exact computation — each measuring in diameter seventeen-twentieths of an inch, and placed to touch each other—it would extend to the length of twenty-four miles and two hundred and fifty yards; and in crown pieces, to one hundred and thirteen and one half miles and two hundred and eighty yards.

Mr. Biddle's Wit.

"NICK BIDDLE" was a wit as well as a financier. During the session of the legislature of Pennsylvania, in the year 184-, a bill was up appropriating a large sum for continuing the State improvements. Mr. H., of Berks, an honest but unlearned German member, was very hostile to the bill, and in fact opposed to all State improvements, as they involved such an expenditure of money. He knew the wishes of his constituents, but his general knowledge was rather limited. While the bill was under consideration, Mr. Biddle of the city moved an ironical amendment, appropriating ten thousand dollars for the improvement of the *Alimentary Canal*. The member from Berks was instantly upon his feet, declaring his purpose to oppose any appropriation for the Alimentary or any other canal —energetically declaring the amendment to be unnecessary and against the wishes of the people. The amendment was instantly withdrawn, amidst the general mirth of the members at the expense of the honest member from Berks.

Bankers Snubbing Napoleon.

THE house of Hope & Co., of Amsterdam—always remarkable for great independence of character—effectually checkmated Napoleon in his presumptuous dictation to them as bankers. This powerful house, which may be said to have then stood at the head of the mercantile order throughout the world, and, in Holland, not only felt itself perfectly its own master, but considered itself equal in financial matters to any potentate on earth, and entitled to occupy a similar footing with them, could not recognize that it was in any manner bound by an imperial decree.

Yet Napoleon was weak enough to think differently. He had dictated a letter, addressed to Messrs. Hope & Co., in the handwriting of Mollieu, the successor of Barbe Marbais, who had been removed. This missive, worded in the language of a master to his servant, contained the following words:

"You have made enough money in the Louisiana business to leave me no room to doubt that you will, *without reservation*, comply with any order I may see fit to make."

He then sent this letter, without Ouvrard's consent, by an inspector of finance, to Amsterdam. However, the finance inspector was very coolly received, and had to come back without accomplishing anything. Soon afterward, Napoleon thought it advisable to send the Baron Louis—afterward Louis Philippe's first minister of finance —to Holland, to explore the ground, and discover what resources Ouvrard might have there. Baron Louis presented himself to the Messrs. Hope, and disclosed the object of his visit. Mr. Labouchère, the partner who received him, at once replied in the following admirable and high-minded mercantile decision :

"Whether we have money in our hands for Mr. Ouvrard, or not, baron, is not a matter for which we are obliged to render any account to you; and the inappropriateness of your present visit must have been apparent to yourself!"

This anecdote was related by Ouvrard himself, and was likewise repeated frequently by Mr. Labouchère, who could not suppress his commercial pride, whenever he got an opportunity, at this illustration of his independence of the man, at whose feet all Europe bent the knee.

Astor's "Secret Pain."

Mr. Astor was compelled, at one time, to repair to Paris, where he could avail himself, for a physical infirmity, of the skilful assistance of Baron Dupuytren. The latter thoroughly restored him, and advised him to ride out every day. He frequently took occasion himself to accompany his patient on these rides. One day, when riding, Astor appeared by no means disposed to converse; not a word could be got out of him—and at length Dupuytren declared that A. must be suffering from some *secret pain* or trouble, when he would not speak. He pressed him, and wor-

ried him, until finally Astor loosed his tongue :

"Look ye, Baron!" said Astor; "how frightful this is. I have here, in the hands of my banker, at Paris, about two million francs, and cannot manage, without great effort, to get more than two and one half per cent. *per annum* on it. Now, this morning, I have received a letter from my son in New York, informing me that there the best acceptances are at from one and a half to two per cent. *per month*. Is it not enough to enrage a man?" This revelation of course relieved the Baron's apprehension of any "secret pain or trouble" of a *physical* nature.

Jewish Perseverance and Shrewdness.

The clerk of an English banker having robbed his employer of Bank of England notes to the amount of twenty thousand pounds, made his escape to Holland. Unable to present them himself, he sold them to a Jew, doubtless at a price affording a good bargain to the purchaser. In the mean time every plan was exhausted to give publicity to the loss. The numbers of the notes were advertised in the papers, with a request that they might be refused; and for about six months no information was received of the lost property. At the end of that period, the Jew appeared with the whole of his spoil, and demanded payment, which was at once refused, on the plea that the bills had been stolen, and that payment had been stopped. The owner insisted upon gold, and the bank persisted in refusing.

But the Jew was an energetic man, and was aware of the credit of the corporation; he was known to be possessed of immense wealth. He went deliberately to the exchange, where, to the assembled merchants of London, in the presence of her citizens, he related publicly that the bank had refused to honor their own bills for twenty thousand pounds; that their credit was gone; their affairs in confusion; and that they had stopped payment. The exchange wore every appearance of alarm; the Hebrew showed the notes to corroborate his assertion. He declared that they had been remitted to him from Holland; and as his transactions were known to be extensive, there appeared every reason to credit his statement. He then avowed his intention of advertising this refusal of the bank; and the citizens thought there must indeed be some truth in his bold announcement.

Information reached the directors, who grew anxious, and a messenger was sent to inform the holder that he might receive cash in exchange for the notes. In any other country, the Jew would have been tried as a calumniator; but in England, the bank—the soul of the State—would have lost the cause. The law could not hinder the holder of the notes from interpreting the refusal that was made of payment according to his fancy; nothing could prevent him from saying that he believed the excuse was only a pretext to gain time; and though intelligent people could not credit the story, the majority would have been alarmed, and would not have taken their notes for cash. In short, the Jew was acquainted with the nation and its laws, and he gained his point.

Sir Robert Peel's Opinion of his Son as a Financier.

MR. PEEL's great currency measure, which he caused to be carried through Parliament by his influence and eloquence, was opposed by his distinguished father, and one of the most interesting features in the history of that celebrated measure is to be found in a petition from the merchants of the city of London, presented by the elder Peel, against its enactment. After stating that his petitioners were the best calculated to judge on so important a point,

and that a meeting, which he had attended for this purpose, was composed of the very men who had so nobly supported the government in 1797, he proceeded to say, in language as feeling as the subject was interesting, that 'he well remembered when that near and dear relation was only a child, he observed to some friends who were standing near him, that the man who discharged his duty to his country in the manner in which Mr. Pitt did, did most to be admired, and was most to be imitated; and he thought, at that moment, if his own life and that of his dear relation should be spared, he should one day present him to his country to follow in the same path. He was well satisfied that the head and heart of that relation were in their right places; and that though he had deviated a little from the path of propriety in this instance, he would soon be restored to it."

Peeresses Conducting Banking Operations.

Two of the richest bankers in London, a few years ago, were peeresses, namely, the Duchess of St. Albans and the Countess of Jersey—the latter, as the heiress of old Josiah Child, constituting the principal partner of the Child banking house. Both ladies were at one time said to be in the habit of paying periodical visits to their respective establishments, and are said to have been distinguished for the affability and good sense with which they sustained their positions, inspected the books, and entered into general business details. But this report was true, and that in part, only of the late Duchess of St. Albans. She was peculiarly fond of showing herself at the bank in the Strand, and putting questions to the partners and clerks, with whom she was no favorite—being, in truth, somewhat of a bore. Lady Jersey, as the representative of Sir Josiah Child's interest, only attends the bank once a year, when the accounts are balanced and the profits struck. On this occasion, the partners dine together at the bank, and the countess, as the principal partner, takes the head of the table. This lady's connection with the concern has the following history: The last Mr. Child left an only daughter, who was the heiress of his great wealth, and was married to the Earl of Westmoreland ; the eldest daughter of that marriage was the present Countess of Jersey, to whom the grandfather's interest in the bank descended.

Model English Banker.

THE model English banker of the present day, is educated at Eton, and makes love to lords. They borrow his money, and laugh at him as a " toady." He enters the banking house at twenty-one, and looks upon the clerks as servants—as breathing copying machines. He belongs to all sorts of clubs. He is a great authority upon wine, horses, and women. He keeps his yacht, and never stops in town after the opera. He walks through the city as if it belonged to him. He is great in jewelry, and very particular about his riding-whips. He wears in winter white cords and buckskin gloves, and subscribes to the nearest " hounds." His wristbands show an inch and a half. He marries a baronet's daughter, and talks nothing but the Blue Book ever afterward. He has a house in Belgravia and a seat in the North. His name, too, is generally amongst the " fashionables whom we observed last night at Her Majesty's Theatre." He has always a particular engagement at the West-end at two, at which hour his bay cab invariably calls for him. His *printed* charities are very extensive—one sum always for himself, another for the company. He is very nervous during panics, and when there is a run upon the bank, it is always owing to " the pressure of the times." He pays his creditors one half

crown in the pound, and lives on three thousand pounds a year, "settled on his wife"—perhaps, indeed, a model banker of this description never fell yet, whose fall was not agreeably softened by a snug little property " settled on his wife." The inference from this is, that the model banker is a most rigid cultivator of the matrimonial virtues, and if he forgets occasionally what he owes to himself and others, he remembers to a nicety what is due to his wife. It is only the system of double entry applied to banking.

Largest Dealer in Commercial Paper in the United States.

THE late Stephen Whitney, of New York, is supposed to have dealt more largely in commercial paper than any other man in that city, and perhaps in the Union. His habits of industry continued through life, and were a common theme of remark with those who observed him in his daily walk from his office to the great moneyed centre of America, where the price of paper and money rates regaled his cars. He was a good judge of paper, and needed no one to advise him. He touched nothing but what in commercial parlance is termed " gilt-edged," and of this he purchased almost daily for thirty years. These notes being made payable to the order of the drawers, needed no other indorsement, and hence might pass through a hundred hands without this fact becoming known. Mr. Whitney's bills receivable falling due in Wall street, must have been at the rate of thirty thousand per day, and his purchases of paper, of course, were about the same rate.

" Borrow Money ? Borrow Money ? "

ONE of the familiar cries of the London Stock Exchange is " Borrow Money ? Borrow Money ? " a singular one to general apprehension, but it must be understood of course, that the credit of the borrower must either be first rate or his security of the most satisfactory nature, and that it is not the principal who thus goes into the market, but his broker.

"Have you money to lend to-day?" is a question asked with a nonchalance which would astonish the simple man who goes to a "friend," with such a question quivering on his mouth. "Yes," may be the reply. "I want ten or twenty thousand pounds." "On what security?" for that is the vital question; and this point being settled, the transaction goes on smoothly and quickly enough.

Another mode of doing the business is to conceal the object of the borrower or lender, who asks, "What are. Exchequer?" The answer may be "forty to forty-two;" that is, the party addressed will buy one thousand pounds at forty shillings, and sell one thousand pounds at forty-two shillings. The jobbers cluster around the broker, who perhaps says, "I must have a price in five thousand pounds." If it suits them, they will say, "Five with me, five with me, five with me," making fifteen—or, they will say each, "Ten with me;" and it is the broker's business to get these parties pledged to buy of him at forty, or to sell to him at forty-two, they not knowing whether he is a buyer or seller. The broker then declares his purpose, saying, for example, "Gentlemen, I sell to you twenty thousand pounds at forty," and the sum is then apportioned among them.

Peep at the Treasure in Threadneedle Street.

"THE next room I entered"—says a visitor at the Bank of England—"was that in which notes are deposited which are ready for issue." "We have *thirty-two millions of pounds sterling in this room*," the officer remarked to me, "will you take a little of it?" I told him that it would be vastly agreeable,

and he handed me a million sterling (five million dollars), which I received with many thanks for his liberality; but he kind of insisted on my depositing it with him again—perhaps because it would be hardly safe, besides being burdensome, to carry so much money with me into the street, though that was a risk I would willingly have incurred. I very much fear I shall never see that money again. In the vault beneath the floor was a director and cashier counting the bags of gold which men were pitching down to them, each bag containing a thousand pounds sterling, just from the mint. This money seemed to realize the most dazzling fables of Eastern wealth.

Vast Wealth of Crœsus.

IN our jottings of millionnaires, it would seem as though these pages were incomplete without some data concerning him whose name has for centuries and generations—fresh down to the present day,—furnished the standard representative of vast wealth. Crœsus flourished about the middle of the sixth century B. C. The prodigious wealth which he had inherited had been increased by the tribute of conquered nations, by the confiscation of great estates, and by the golden sands of the Pactolus. Perhaps some idea of the extent of this wealth may be formed from the rich votive offerings which he is known to have deposited in the temples of the gods. Herodotus himself saw the ingots of solid gold, six palms long, three broad, and one deep, which to the number of one hundred and seventeen, were laid up in the treasury at Delphi. He also saw, in various parts of Greece, the following offerings, all in gold, which had been deposited in the temples by the same opulent man: a figure of a lion, probably of the natural size; a wine bowl of about the same weight as the lion; a lustral vase; a statue of a female, said to be Crœsus's baking woman, four and one-half feet high; a shield and a spear; a tripod; some figures of cows; and a number of pillars; and a second shield in a different place from the first, and of greater size.

Mode of Conducting Great Transactions by Rothschild.

WHEN engaging in large transactions, the method pursued by Rothschild was this: Supposing he possessed exclusively, which he often did a day or two before it could be generally known, intelligence of some event which had occurred in any part of the continent sufficiently important to cause a rise in the French funds, and through them on the English funds, he would empower the brokers he usually employed to sell out stock, say to the amount of five hundred thousand pounds. The news spread in a moment in financial quarters, that Rothschild was selling out, and a general alarm followed. Every one apprehended he had received intelligence, from some foreign part, of some important event which would produce a fall in prices. As might, under such circumstances be expected, all became sellers at once. This, of necessity, caused the funds—to use the customary phraseology,—" to tumble down at a fearful rate." Next day, when they had fallen perhaps, one or two per cent, he would make purchases, say to the amount of one and a half million pounds, taking care, however, to employ a number of brokers whom he was not in the habit of employing, and commissioning each to purchase to a certain extent, and giving all of them strict orders to preserve secrecy in the matter. Each of the persons so employed was, by this means, ignorant of the commission given to others. Had it been known the purchases were for him, there would have been as great and sudden a rise in the prices as there had been in the fall, so that he could not purchase to the in-

tended extent, on such advantageous terms. On the third day, perhaps, the intelligence, which had been expected by the jobbers to be unfavorable, arrives, and instead of being so, turns out to be highly favorable. Prices instantaneously rise again; and possibly they may get one and a half, or even two per cent. higher than they were when he sold out his five hundred thousand pounds. He now sells out at the advanced price the entire million and a half pounds he had purchased at the reduced prices. The gains by such extensive operations, when thus skilfully managed, are enormous.

Bank Teller's "Varieties."

FEW are aware of the perplexing difficulties of a bank teller. Besides the routine of business in connection with the clearing-house, which requires most judicious examination, the current business of the day goes on with increasing pressure from the outside. So long as he can dispose of the applications uninterruptedly, as they are represented, the lobby is comparatively quiet and free from obstruction; but even a momentary stoppage causes the crowd to gather, and soon ten or a dozen persons are waiting to be served in turn. Expressions of impatience are not uncommon. The teller is pronounced " slow "—" indifferent to the convenience of the customers "—" incompetent," and " tantalizing," by his deliberation of movement. Deliberation is the secret of his accomplishing so much. In truth, there is hardly a moment when he may not be said to be doing two or more things at once. The interruptions to which he is subjected are almost incessant. The cashier has just received advices of the issue of a number of duplicate checks by a corresponding bank, to replace the originals which have been lost in the mail. He brings the letter and list of duplicates to the teller, who is occupied several minutes in obtaining a clear understanding of the case. Some of the originals might be in the hands of persons then waiting to be served, and he must be able to detect them at sight.

"Will you pay me this check, sir ? I don't want to be kept here half a day!" growls a hot-tempered customer.

"Yes, sir," answers the teller, "if you will have the discrepancy corrected between the figures and the writing."

Another: "How did your exchanges come out the day before yesterday?" asks a messenger from another bank.

"A thousand dollars over."

"That's lucky! Our teller is short a thousand—that must be it."

"Well, if he can establish his claim, and no other bank contests, I'll pay it."

"I want five thousand dollars in gold for that check—not good," says another bank messenger.

The porter or specie clerk, who keeps the coin prepared for such demands, is absent, and the teller may be obliged to go to the vault for it.

In the next moment, a check which had been sent to another bank, through the exchanges, is returned for a written guarantee of indorsement. If satisfied of its correctness, the teller gives the guarantee. Otherwise he pays the money for it, and returns it to the dealer who had deposited it.

A stranger offers to the teller five hundred dollars in bills, to pay a check which he had drawn on the bank. Keeping no account, his money is refused, but he persists in an altercation about it, to the hindrance of those behind him.

A dealer wants thirty or forty thousand dollars in coin, to pay duties at the custom house. Another hands in a memorandum check that he has given out, but of which he wants to arrest payment. Another inquires whether a lost check, of which he had previously given notice, has been paid. A porter from the Merchants' Bank presents a dozen notes of different parties for certification, and he is immediately followed by one from another bank, with a bag of gold which he reports ten dollars short, and which may be the occasion of some dispute.

The other clerks have frequent necessity to communicate with the paying teller with respect to the state of accounts, and he with them.

A noisy colloquy ensues with a dealer whose check has been refused, because of his deposit having been credited to another party; and with another, whose account appears deficient, because a promised discount of paper has not been entered on the books.

"Here," says Mr. Bungle, returning a handful of rumpled bank bills and coin, "that money which you paid me is twenty dollars short." The teller examines it, and satisfies Mr. Bungle that the error was in his own counting.

Raising Money on Manuscript.

In ancient times, manuscripts were important articles in a commercial point of view; they were excessively scarce, and preserved with the utmost care. Usurers themselves considered them as precious objects for pawn. A student of Pavia, who was reduced by his debaucheries, raised a new fortune by leaving in pawn a manuscript of a body of law; and a grammarian, who was ruined by a fire, rebuilt his house with two small volumes of Cicero, through the pawnbroker.

Irish Banker Redeeming his Notes.

Says a sprightly writer who possesses a lively relish for the humorous in matters of business: I once accompanied a large party of English ladies and gentlemen to that enchanting spot, the Lakes of Killarney, where, having amused ourselves for a few days, we were on the point of returning to Dublin, when one of the party recollected that he had in his possession a handful of notes on a banker who was a kind of saddler in the town of Killarney. Accordingly, we all set out by way of sport to have them exchanged, our principal object being to see and converse with the proprietor of such a bank.

Having entered the "bank," which hardly sufficed to admit the whole company, we found the banking saddler hard at work. One of the gentlemen thus addressed him:

"Good morning to you, sir. I presume you are the gentleman of the house?"

"At your service, ladies and gentlemen," returned the saddler.

"It is here that I understand that the bank is kept."

"You are right, sir," was the reply; "this is the Killarney Bank, for want of a better."

"We are on the eve," said the spokesman, "of quitting your town, and, as we have some few of your notes which will be of no manner of use to us elsewhere, I'll thank you for the cash for them."

The banker replied "Cash, plase your honor, what is that? Is it anything in the leather line? I have a beautiful saddle here as ever was put across a horse, good and cheap. How much of my notes have you, sir, if you please?"

"There are no less than sixteen of your promises to pay, for the amazingly large sum of fifteen shillings and ninepence sterling money."

"I should be sorry, most noble," returned the banker, "to waste any more of your lordship's time or of those swate beautiful ladies and gentlemen, but I have an illegant bridle here as isn't to be matched in Yoorup, Aishy, Africay, or Merickay; its lowest price is fifteen shillings six and a-half pence—will say fifteen shillings sixpence to your lordship. If ye'll be plased to accept of it, then there will be twopence ha'penny or a three-pence note coming to your lordship, and that will clear the business at once."

This account of an Irish banker, although possibly somewhat overcharged, may be considered a pretty fair specimen of many who pretended to carry on the business of banking in that country, years ago.

Florentine Brokers and Money Loaners.

THE early prosperity of the Florentine brokers was great indeed. The useful invention of a system of exchange, first known, or at least perfected in Florence, raised her in commercial character; and strengthened by the sums of money which, at an advantageous interest, were loaned by the Florentine merchants to the largest houses, and not unfrequently to the governments of other countries, the body or board of Florentine brokers became at once among the most influential in the domestic affairs of the city, and among the most necessary to the rising commerce of Europe.

The mode of exacting security on loans is a notable circumstance, and shows, with unerring certainty, the exact value to commerce of the indefatigable exertions made by the money lenders of Florence. When Aldobrandino d'Este applied for the aid of the bankers of Florence, in addition to the mortgage of all his real estate, they required the person of his brother in pledge. The neglect of similar precautions had caused to Florence a loss that shook the whole fabric of commercial prosperity, when Edward of England, the conqueror of Cressy and Poictiers, and the ambitious aspirant to the realm and throne of France, permitted the great house of Peruzzi to fail in consequence of his inability to repay the moneys which they had furnished for his wars, and which amounted to a sum, calculated according to the present value of money, of not less than thirteen millions of dollars.

Conducting Business on the Paris Bourse.

THERE are some interesting peculiarities in the mode of doing business on the Paris Bourse, or stock exchange. The *agens de change* alone are authorized by law to purchase or sell public securities. All respectable business, whether for cash or the end of the month, is transacted by them—not, as in London, through the medium of the third party, called the jobber,—but directly with each other. They seldom communicate to their principals the names of the persons with whom they deal; but they report each bargain as it is made, and answer at the end of the month for the balance due to him. They are very cautious in doing business with the public, and they generally require a deposit, or *couverture*, as it is called, of from two to four per cent. of the sum bought or sold, before they will deal for the end of the month.

Their profits are enormous, as about sixty agents engross the whole respectable business of the Bourse, and as they encounter losses only when some great banker fails, or some brother *agent de change* stops payment.

The *agens de change* compose what is called the "*parquet*," but there is another body in the exchange called the *coulisse*, consisting of speculators of all classes and fortunes, who are beyond the law, and who do business with each other on parole. There are respectable men to be found in the *coulisse*, but many persons are admitted into it who have very little to recommend them. Their operations are all for time, and in the three per cents. only. Several members of the *coulisse* do business as brokers for speculators out of the market, but their chief occupation consists in catching for each other the turn of the market. It rarely happens that the *parquet* and the *coulisse* take the same view of public affairs; and the former, backed by the great capitalists, are usually the "bulls," while the latter usually are the "bears." In both, the small fry are sacrificed—sooner or later they are carried down the stream, as the rich bankers, at stated times, combine and execute them without mercy.

Terrible Revenge on a Bank by Rothschild.

AN amusing adventure is related as having happened to the Bank of England, which had committed the great disrespect of refusing to discount a bill of a large amount, drawn by Anselm Rothschild, of Frankfort, on Nathan Rothschild, of London. The bank had haughtily replied "that they discounted only their own bills, and not those of private persons." But they had to do with one stronger than the bank. "Private persons!" exclaimed Nathan Rothschild, when they reported to him the fact: "Private persons! I will make these gentlemen see what sort of private persons we are!"

Three weeks afterward, Nathan Rothschild—who had employed the interval in gathering all the five-pound notes he could procure in England and on the Continent—presented himself at the bank at the opening of the office. He drew from his pocket book a five-pound note, and they naturally counted out five sovereigns, at the same time looking quite astonished that the Baron Rothschild should have personally troubled himself for such a trifle. The baron examined one by one the coins, and put them into a little canvas bag, then drawing out another note,—a third—a tenth—a hundredth, he never put the pieces of gold into the bag without scrupulously examining them, and in some instances trying them in the balance, as, he said, "the law gave him the right to do." The first pocket-book being emptied, and the first bag full, he passed them to his clerk, and received a second, and thus continued, till the close of the bank. The baron had employed seven hours to change twenty-one thousand pounds. But as he had also nine employés of his house engaged in the same manner, it resulted that the house of Rothschild had drawn £210,000 in gold from the bank, and that he had so occupied the tellers that no other person could change a single note.

Everything which bears the stamp of eccentricity has always pleased the English. They were, therefore, the first day, very much amused at the little pique of Baron Rothschild. They however laughed less when they saw him return the next day at the opening of the bank, flanked by his nine clerks, and followed this time by many drays, destined to carry away the specie. They laughed no longer, when the king of bankers said with ironic simplicity: "These gentlemen refuse to pay my bills, I have sworn not to keep theirs. At their leisure—only I notify them that I have enough to employ them for two months!" "For two months!" "Eleven millions in gold drawn from the Bank of England which they have never possessed!" The bank took alarm. There was something to be done. The next morning, notice appeared in the journals that henceforth the bank would pay Rothschild's bills the same as their own.

Determining the Genuineness of a Check.

THE bank account of a highly respectable house was reported overdrawn for two thousand dollars; and one of the firm denied the genuineness of a particular check for that amount. A number of his checks were so arranged as to conceal all but the signatures, and he was requested to point out the forgery. He acknowledged his inability to discriminate between that and any other. On close inquiry it appeared that he had been in the habit of signing checks in blank to the order of his bookkeeper, to be used in his ab-

sence, and the one in question was of this description, excepting that it was payable to the bearer. He was asked if he could swear that the signature was not his own—to which he answered in the negative. Yet it was not made subject to order in his usual form, and he had no recollection of having signed it. Under these circumstances, the bank insisted that it was genuine, and the house submitted to the loss.

Modern Bank Directors' Parlor.

THE bank room, or parlor, of the Bank of England, is the grand centre around which the whole mechanism of that vast establishment revolves. There in solemn assembly sit, once a week, that august commercial body, reverently spoken of by all as the "board of directors;" there all the overdrawn accounts are gone over and commented upon; instructions are given for further advance or reduced balances; all the bills on hand, and the character of their acceptors, are regularly examined and criticized; grave deliberations are held as to the best means of investing any surplus funds; and last, but not least, to those immediately concerned, the question of salaries is there gone into, and duly disposed of. Very rarely, indeed, is a joke heard, or a pun perpetrated in this retreat, sacred to business alone; but should such an event ever occur, it would doubtless be some dry wit comprehensible only to financiers. The directors never die— that is to say, they never die out. So soon as a vacancy takes place, it is immediately filled, generally by the largest shareholder, if possessed of a reasonable amount of capacity for the position.

Detecting Bad Bills.

A BANK TELLER requires an instinctive faculty for the detection of spurious bills. To stand by and observe him counting, it might be supposed that he

Modern Bank Directors' Parlor.

could hardly get a glimpse of each, so rapidly do they pass through his hands. He looks as if he were trying how many times he could strike the ends of his fingers together in the twentieth part of a second; but you see a steady stream of bills issuing beneath them and gradually gathering into a pile.

There goes one aside, without perceptible pause in the handling! He checks the item on the list, and with his right hand thrusts the pile into a drawer, whilst with the left he tosses the single bill back to the depositor. "Counterfeit—five dollars off!"

He makes the entry, deducting it from the list, hands the book to the dealer, and takes the next in order, in which there is a package of mixed denominations of several hundred dollars. He gives it a smack on the counter to loosen the bills, and a peculiar toss, which makes them fall over like the leaves of a book, affording an instantaneous glance at their ends. His eye has caught in that instant an old acquaintance.

"Where did you get that altered bill?" he asks of the customer, meanwhile counting—"twenty, thirty, fifty,

fifty-five, sixty," and on he goes like lightning. The dealer looks astonished, not thinking that the question could possibly have reference to any bill in his money. The teller repeats, without ceasing his account for an appreciable instant—"one twenty, one thirty, two, five, one forty five—say, where did you get that altered bill?—sixty-five, one seventy, eighty, two thirty—*that*," he says, tossing it in his face—"two altered to ten; two eighty-five, two ninety-five, three, five, ten, three thirty-five—ten off, right;" and the deposit is entered, and the dealer's book is returned before he knows it, and the teller is in the midst of another count for the next customer in order.

This is very curious to an inexperienced observer. But there are certain well-known spurious and altered bank bills, which are distinguished by a quick teller, as well as the countenance of said teller's landlord who approaches to ask for his quarter's rent.

An Excited Specie Hunter.

DURING the heat of the specie excitement at Glasgow, a few years ago, a gentleman went into the Union Bank of that city, and presented a check of five hundred pounds. The teller asked him if he wished gold. "Gold!" replied he, "no; give me notes, and let the fools that are frightened get the gold."

Another gentleman rushed into the same bank in a great state of excitement, with a check for fourteen hundred pounds. On being asked if he wished gold, he replied, "Yes." "Well," said the teller, "there are one thousand pounds in that bag, and four hundred in this one." The gentleman was so flurried by the readiness with which the demand was granted, that he lifted up the bag with the four hundred pounds only, and walked off, leaving the one thousand pounds on the counter. The teller, on discovering the bag, laid it aside for the time. Late in the day the gentleman returned to the bank in great distress, stating that he had lost the bag with the one thousand pounds, and could not tell whether he left it behind him on leaving the bank, or dropped it while in the crowd. "Oh, you left it on the counter," said the teller quietly, "and if you will call to-morrow you will get your thousand pounds."

Renewing a Note.

As queer scenes occur in the daily proceedings of a bank, probably, as in almost any kind or place of business that can be named—the apparent monotonous routine of bank transactions being diversified by many an odd incident.

When the tellers get at their posts, and the hour for business has arrived, customers begin to drop in first one by one, and there are generally "cases" of some sort or other soon requiring special attention. Perhaps among them will come "Old Indian," as he is familiarly known at the institution, a man who has honorably acquitted himself in the military line, and one who

is liked by all at the bank, but who has got into difficulties, which, perhaps, he feels to be more galling than he ever did the fire of an enemy. Without preliminaries, he, soldier-like, comes to the point at once.

"I wish to pay the interest on that bill of mine you hold, and to renew it for three months longer."

"Very good, sir; I will find the bill." The teller now goes ostensibly for the document, but in reality to consult the manager's wishes on the subject: "Mr. Brookes has called to renew his note; shall I do so?" "Well, I suppose we must. You know we have a little security for it, and as he means to pay off gradually, we must try to oblige him."

Having thus "found the bill," the teller again goes to his desk, and draws out the new one, which the old gentleman signs, pays the interest on the first, and with a stiff "good morning," takes his leave. They all feel for him, but sometimes wonder, with all credit to his good intentions, whether he will ever do much more than *renew* his bills.

Franklin's Multitude of Capitalists.

"TIME is money," said Franklin; but it doesn't follow that the multitude of those who have so great a quantity of such "money" on their hands are all capitalists.

"Manifolding" Bank Notes.

THE use of bank notes, independently of their legitimate value, appears to be somewhat diverse. But perhaps the most extraordinary use to which they have been applied is to be found in the process termed "manifolding." A person carrying on a rather extensive business in the British provinces, being in want of cash, and having in his possession a fifty-pound note, came to the conclusion that he would cut it in two. With one part he went to a moneyed acquaintance told him he had just received it by post, and that the other would follow in a day or two, and it would be a great convenience if his friend could advance him cash to the amount on its security. The person to whom he applied consented to the request. Having been thus successful with one half, he determined to try the other; with it he proved equally fortunate, and thus his fifty-pound note produced him one hundred pounds. The game was too profitable to be given up at once; so he went to a banker, and demanded a one hundred pound note with the cash he had received. Again he had recourse to the process of cutting; again he victimized two acquaintances, and thus procured two hundred pounds for his original note. With the money thus acquired he departed, satisfied with having gained one hundred and fifty pounds thus easily.

Running a Bank.

THE Bank of England probably never passed through a more critical strait than the "run" made upon it by the Duc de Choiseul,—a French plan to destroy the institution, hoping thereby to obtain important State advantages for France over her rival. Some millions of livres added to the zeal of the French emissaries, who discovered a period when the bullion was somewhat low, and spread reports calculated to injure the standing of the corporation.

Collecting all the notes which they could possibly procure, they poured them into the bank, and carried away the gold with a parade which attracted the attention it sought. The old cry arose of a run upon the bank, and in a few hours the whole city was in motion. Volumes of paper were presented, and gold received in exchange. The consternation of the directors was in proportion to the suddenness of the attack. The alarm, far from being quieted, became every day more general. Post-chaises poured in from the provinces. The application for specie became more urgent. There was no mode of judging to what extent an attempt so unprecedented and so unexpected might be carried. The efforts of the national enemy seemed prospering, and for some days England appeared to be on the brink of the greatest evil which could happen.

Time was necessary to collect specie, and people were employed day and night to coin money. All the gold which by any stratagem could be gathered was brought into the bank. The method of paying by weight was discontinued. The sums claimed were delivered with greater deliberation; and the money placed guinea by guinea on the table. For nine days this fever continued; but the method adopted by the directors, with concurrent circumstances, gave time for the production of a large supply of gold. All the demands were met, and the claimants finding there was no cause for doubt, resumed their confidence in the bank.

Intruding into the Bullion Room.

THE directors of the Bank of England some time since received an anonymous letter, stating that the writer had the means of access to their bullion room. They treated the matter as a hoax and took no notice of the letter. Another and more urgent and specific letter failed to rouse them. At length, the writer offered to meet them in their bullion room at any hour they might please to name. They then communicated with their correspondent through the channel he had indicated, appointing some "dark and midnight hour" for the rendezvous. A deputation from the Board, with lantern in hand, repaired to the bullion room, locked themselves in, and awaited the arrival of the mysterious correspondent. Punctual to the hour a noise was heard below. Some boards in the floor without much trouble were displaced, and in a few minutes the Guy Fawkes of the bank stood in the presence of the astonished directors. His story was very simple and straightforward. An old drain ran under the bullion room, the existence of which had become known to him, and by means of which he might have carried away enormous sums. Inquiry was made. Nothing had been abstracted, and the directors forthwith rewarded the honesty and ingenuity of their anonymous correspondent—a working man, who had been employed in repairing sewers—by a present of eight hundred pounds.

Rothschild Trying to Raise a Small Loan.

THE name of Nathan Meyer Rothschild is found upon more money bills than passed through any twenty banking firms in London, during the period covered by his business career. But he was far from being celebrated for his proficiency in the art of writing. This defect, on one occasion in particular, caused him some little annoyance. He was travelling in Scotland, and, on his return, stopped at the town of Montrose; here, wishing to replenish his exhausted exchequer, he went to the bank, and requested cash for a draft of one hundred pounds on his agent in London. He was, however, much surprised at the refusal of the bank manager to honor his check, without, as that functionary said, having the genuineness of the signature—*which he was utterly unable to read*—previously accredited; and for this purpose it must be first forwarded to London. To this arrangement Mr. Rothschild was compelled to submit; and as, at that time, it took six days before an answer could be received from London, he was detained until the reply came, which, of course, proving favorable, he was enabled to pursue his journey.

Girard's Great Government Loan.

IT is a fact which may be put to the credit of Girard's patriotism, that in 1814, when the credit of the country was exhausted, the treasury bankrupt, and an invading army was marching over the land; when, in fact, subscriptions were solicited for funds to the amount of five millions of dollars, upon the inducement of a large bonus and an interest of seven per cent., and only twenty thousand dollars could be obtained upon that offer for the purpose of carrying on the war, Stephen Girard stepped forward and subscribed for the whole amount. When, too, those who had before rejected the terms were afterward anxious to subscribe, even at a considerable advance from the original subscription, these individuals were let in by him upon the same terms.

Coin Used by Judas.

THE "piece of silver," thirty of which were paid to Judas, in his trade of betraying Christ, was considered a peculiar piece by the Israelites, and was always spoken of in their holy books as the shekel of Israel, or holy shekel of the sanctuary. It was the amount which each Israelite, between the ages of twenty and fifty, was required to pay into the public treasury, as a ransom for their delivery, during their sojourn in the wilderness.

According to the British currency, a shekel was worth two shillings three pence three farthings,—equal to about fifty cents of our money. The coin was somewhat larger than an American half-dollar, and was smooth-edged. On one side it bore the emblem of Aaron's rod, as mentioned in Numbers, xvii. 8, surrounded with the inscription in Hebrew which is given in the eleventh chapter of Leviticus—with the words, "Shekel of Israel."

History of the Old Red Cent.

As the old "red cent" has now passed out of use, and, except rarely, out of sight, like the "old oaken bucket," its history is a matter of sufficient interest for preservation. The cent was first proposed by Robert Morris, the great financier of the Revolution, and was named by Jefferson two years after. It began to make its appearance from the mint in 1792. It bore the head of Washington on one side, and thirteen links on the other. The French Revolution soon created a rage for French ideas in America, which put on the cent, instead of the head of Washington, the head of the Goddess of Liberty—a French liberty, with neck thrust forward and flowing locks. The chain on the reverse was replaced by the olive wreath of peace. But the French liberty was short-lived, and so was her portrait on our cent. The next head or figure succeeding this—the staid, classic dame, with a fillet around her hair,—came into fashion about thirty or forty years ago, and her finely chiselled Grecian features have been but slightly altered by the lapse of time.

Origin of Paper Money.

The celebrated traveller, Marco Paulo, of Venice, was the first person who announced to Europe the existence of paper money in China, under the Moguls. It was subsequently introduced by the Moguls into Persia, where their notes were called djaou, or djaw, a word evidently derived from the Chinese word schaio—a word intended to signify the want of specie.

The fact of the Moguls having, in China and Persia, made use of paper money, has induced the belief that they were the inventors of it. But in the history of Tchinghiz-khan, and of the Mogul dynasty in China, published in the year 1739, the author speaks of the suppression of the paper money, which was in use under the dynasty of the Soung, who reigned in China previous to the Moguls; and he also mentions a new species of notes which were substituted for the ancient in the year 1264.

The original financial speculation of the Chinese ministry, to provide for the extraordinary expenditures of the state, which were exceeding the revenues, was in the year 119 before the Christian era. At this period were introduced the phi-pi, or value in skins. These were small pieces of the skin of deer, which were kept in a pen, within the precincts of the palace. They were a Chinese square foot in size, and were beautifully ornamented with painting and embroidery. The price of those skins was fixed at a sum equal in English money to about twelve guineas.

Ricardo's Three Golden Rules.

David Ricardo, the English Jew broker, accumulated an immense property. He had what he called his three golden rules in business, the observance of which he always pressed upon his private friends. These were : Never to refuse an option when you can get it; cut short your losses; let your profits run on. By cutting short one's losses, Mr. Ricardo meant that, when a broker had made a purchase of stock, and prices were falling, he ought to re-sell immediately. And by letting one's profits run on, he meant that, when a dealer possessed stock, and the prices were rising, he ought not to sell until prices had reached their highest, and were beginning again to fall.

M. Rothschild on the Secret of his Success.

On the occasion of a familiar interview, one day, between Sir Thomas Buxton and Rothschild, the latter said : "My success has always turned upon one maxim. I said, *I* can do what *another* man can, and so I am a match for all the rest of 'em. Another advantage I had—I was always an off-hand man; I made a bargain at once. When I was settled in London, the East India Company had eight hundred thousand pounds in gold to sell. I went to the sale, and bought the whole of it. I knew the Duke of Wellington *must* have it. I had bought a great many bills of his at a discount. The government sent for me, and *said* they must have it. When they had got it, they didn't know how to get it to Portugal, where they wanted it. I undertook all that, and sent it through France; and that was the best business I ever did in my life.

"It requires (continued Rothschild) a great deal of boldness and a great deal of caution to make a great fortune; and when you have got it, it requires ten times as much wit to keep it. If I should listen to one half the projects proposed to me, I should ruin myself very soon.

"One of my neighbors is a very ill-tempered man. He tries to vex me, and has built a great place for swine close to my walk. So, when I go out, I hear first, 'Grunt, grunt,' then 'Squeak, squeak.' But this does me no harm. I am always in good humor. Sometimes, to amuse myself, I give a beggar a guinea. He thinks it is a mistake, and for fear I should find it out, he runs away as hard as he can. I advise you to give a beggar a guinea sometimes—it is very amusing."

Application for a Discount, by Astor.

Mr. J. J. Astor's profits rolled in upon him at a rate which no one could have dreamed of, and he kept their amount a secret until he had so penetrated the frontier by his agencies that he controlled the whole fur-trade, when he occasionally acknowledged a degree of wealth which astonished those who heard. For instance, he had occasion at a certain time, to use a large amount of cash, and, what was very rare with him, applied to his bank for a heavy discount. The unusual circumstance and the sum demanded startled the cashier, who, in a plain business way, put the question: "Mr. Astor, how much do you consider yourself worth?" "*Not less than a million,*" was the reply. "A million!"—the cashier was overwhelmed. He supposed that he knew all his customers, and had rated Astor at hardly more than one-tenth of that sum.

Peculiar Management of the Bank of Amsterdam.

Previously to the year 1609, the great trade of Amsterdam brought thither large quantities of clipped and worn coin, from foreign countries. Thus, the whole currency became greatly debased; for, whenever any coin was issued fresh from the mint, as the metal' was worth more than its nominal and current value, it was immediately withdrawn from circulation, and exported, or melted down. In this state of things, merchants could not always find enough of good money to pay their bills of exchange.

To remedy the inconveniences in question, a bank was established in 1609, which received all money, at its real value in standard coin, and gave the owners credit for the amount, after deducting a small percentage for the recoining and other expenses. A law was passed, that all bills of exchange of the value of six hundred guilders, or above, should be payable only in bank currency—a regulation, which at once compelled all merchants to open an account with the bank. As the city of Amsterdam became bound for the solvency of the bank, and as the paper currency had many conveniences, the bank paper was always at a premium, and could be sold in the money market for more than its nominal value. Consequently there was no necessity to demand payment of the bills.

The bank professed to lend no part of the money that was deposited in its vaults, but to have the value in coin always in hand, for all its certificates of credit. It is believed that this was really the case; for, on one occasion, when political events caused a run upon the bank, some of the coins, then paid out, bore the marks of having been scorched by a fire, which had occurred soon after the institution was established.

Lost Bank-Note of Thirty Thousand Pounds.

A VERY wealthy English banker had occasion for thirty thousand pounds, which he was to pay as the price of an estate he had just bought; to facilitate the matter, he carried the sum with him to the bank, and obtained for it a bank note. On his return home, he was suddenly called out upon particular business; he threw the note somewhat carelessly on the chimney, but when he came back a few minutes afterward to lock it up, it was not to be found. No one had entered the room—he could not, therefore, suspect any person. At last, after much ineffectual search, he was persuaded that it had fallen from the chimney into the fire. The banker went to acquaint the gentlemen, who were associated with him as directors of the bank, with the misfortune that had happened to him; and, as he was known to be a perfectly honorable man, he was readily believed. It was only four-and-twenty hours from the time that he had deposited his money; they thought, therefore, that it would be hard to refuse his request for a second bill. He received it upon giving an obligation to restore the first bill, if it should ever be found, or to pay the money himself, if it should be presented by any stranger.

About thirty years afterward (the banker having been long dead, and his heirs in possession of his fortune), an unknown person presented the lost bill at the bank, and demanded payment. It was in vain that they narrated to this person the transaction by which that bill was annulled—he would not listen to it; he maintained that it had come to him from abroad, and insisted upon immediate payment. The note was payable to bearer; and the thirty thousand pounds were paid to him. The heirs of the deceased banker would not heed any demand upon them for restitution, and the bank was obliged to sustain the loss. It was discovered afterward that an architect, having purchased the banker's house, had it taken down, in order to build another upon the same spot, and found the note in a crevice of the chimney !

Merchants' Notes as Currency.

THE peculiarities of carrying on business in the United States and England respectively, are illustrated by the difference in passing good mercantile notes as a circulating medium. In England, a note of hand, when given for any business purpose, is not taken to some convenient banker's, to be discounted or sold, but is treated with that deference that is given to other kinds of notes signed by certain officials known as the president and cashier of a bank, for the simple reason that, if made by an honest, responsible man, it is worth just as much. The holder can, any day, in the neighborhood where its character may be known, without any previous negotiation, buy anything he pleases, and pay for it with this paper by simply indorsing it—because the second holder knows he can in turn do the same; and so it goes, getting farther and farther from home, until having passed through the hands of perhaps more than twenty different persons, and being literally covered with indorsements, it is finally lodged in the bank for collection. Such a note, of one thousand pounds, is frequently made to pay the indebtedness of twenty different men, not one of whom needs to know whether the bank is calling in or letting out its best money, or to care whether his banker is easy or "tight" in his financial condition.

Scenes after Discount Day.

DISCOUNT customers at New York banks are, in a good majority of cases, an eager set. The first crowd at the bank the morning after the board has sat, is composed of the most anxious dealers. It is important for them to know early, whether they must seek elsewhere the bread of commercial life for the day. They are followed by the less needy—the more deliberate, who know the value of "deportment" in a tight market. Here are some samples which will keep fresh for a long time : "Notes done, sir ?" is asked by the applicant, either verbally, or in pantomime. The affirmative causes a bright gleam of sunshine in the face of the questioner. But a negative to the next comer substitutes a scowl of disappointment : "What is the reason of that, sir ? Has the bank stopped discounting ?" "Market tightened up, sir. Deposits down. Offerings very heavy."

The customer departs with an audible growl of indignation at what he conceives to be "a denial of rights."

Another : "Good morning, Mr. Smith; what have you to say to me ?" "Nothing very encouraging, sir. The bank discounted one of your notes." "What —only one out of ten ?" "That's all. Very good proportion, I do assure you." "A single thousand ! And I want five to-day ! Where's the president ?" "In his room, sir. But I don't believe you'll gain anything by talking to him. Our receipts are very small just now, and the porter brings bad news from the clearing-house."

A third fills the little gate in the railing with a grim and threatening visage, but does not speak. The clerk knows him as a frequent applicant, and seldom a fortunate one ; the character of his account, as well as of his paper, being inferior, and presenting no claims worthy of consideration by the directors. He receives back his offering without remark, and departs in sullen silence.

Customer four : "Well, Smith, don't tell me my notes ain't done ! " "Wouldn't if I could help it, sir. Board did mighty little." "Hang the board ! Isn't there any explanation ? Don't they know the paper ? Is it too long ?" "No explanation given to me. Bank's short. Can't help it. Majority in the same boat." Customer leaves an oath behind him.

Neapolitan Cambiamoneta, or Money Changer.

ALONG the crowded streets of Naples the passer-by will occasionally see a great red umbrella mounted on a tall pole, and under which a very snug little business is carried on. A smart, respectable, middle-aged lady sits in state beneath this circumscribed, but brilliant, little awning, which lends a decidedly roseate hue, not only to herself but to her calling. The table at which she sits is, in fact, a "strong box" on wheels, and she herself is a banker in a small way—a street money-changer. On her little counter are disposed various money bags, with open mouths—a small one of gold, a larger one of silver, and a still larger of copper coins. Her transactions are as safe as they are simple. She does not lend out her money on usury; she does not gamble on the stock-exchange, or make "time bargains," or demand a high rate of interest for "accommodation," while she gives a low rate of interest on "deposits." She merely lays herself out to change one set of coins into their equivalents ; for this she receives a small banker's commission, and on this small commission she lives and thrives.

It is surprising how often her intervention is required in the daily busi-

NEAPOLITAN MONEY CHANGERS.

ness of life. Here is a laughing, rollicking, black-eyed servant girl come out, with a basket on her arm, to make her purchases in the market of Santa Lucia. Her money does not happen to be in an available shape, and the fishmonger cannot give change. But—"Ah! most fortunate! See, the Signora Marchetti! Ah, *'cellenza*, without your help I am lost. Oblige me, this holy morning, with some of your dear *carlini*. My *padrone* (master) is so impatient. Ah, *'cellenza*, how eagerly he craves his dinner." And so her "Excellency" is only too happy to oblige her friend, the brisk and vivacious little cook, while with the blandest of smiles she deducts from the change her own pretty little percentage.

Again, there is a tall, dark, suspicious-looking man, who finds that his long walk from Capua has made a hole in his shoe. Near by, too, there is a poor street cobbler, who is seated on his own tool-basket, with his little hammer, and his twine and wax disposed around him on the pavement. The dark Capuan kicks off his ailing shoe, plants his unshod foot on the ground by the shod one, and, in spite of the police, hums a proscribed ode to Masaniello, until the poor cobbler sets him comfortably on his feet again. Once more, the Signora Marchetti must be referred to, for the cobbler's pocket is as empty as himself, and not a "grana" lurks there to supply his employer with the requisite change, and to supply himself with the yet more requisite dinner of chestnuts; and thus, for an additional exchange of equivalents, the banker's commission glides into the Signora's waiting purse.

Largest Check ever Drawn.

IN the negotiations made a few years since by the English government for a loan of eighty million dollars, the successful contractors were the Messrs. Rothschild; and, having been sup-

ported by the subscriptions of friends, they were of course recognized as the acting firm in that important transaction. In paying the first deposit toward this amount to the government, the check they drew was for the sum of *six million dollars*. This bank check was probably the largest ever drawn at once by one private banking-house—or, if not, it was certainly for a very "considerable sum."

Lorillard Paying a Bequest in Bank Stock.

ON a certain occasion, Jacob Lorillard was appointed executor to an estate in which the widow had a life-interest, but where each of the children was to receive a thousand dollars on coming to age. When, in the first case, this period had arrived, one of the sons called on him for the amount of this bequest. "And what," he said, "do you wish to do with it?" "To purchase stock with it in a particular bank." "At what is it now selling?" "A hundred and ten." "Have you any objections to leave the money with me on interest till the 1st of May, and then I will let you have the stock at the same rate?" In the mean time it fell, as he anticipated, to eighty-four. When this change took place, the young man was greatly depressed. He called at the time appointed, to fulfil the engagement. "The stock is ready for you," Mr. Lorillard playfully remarked; "however, if you prefer it, I will release you from the contract, and the money may remain where it is." It may easily be conceived that the young man left him grateful and rejoicing.

Greatest Lending House in Europe.

THE great money-lending house at Naples was first established in 1539 or 1540. Two rich citizens, Aurelio Paparo and Leonardo or Nardo di Palma, redeemed all the pledges which were at that time in the hands of the Jews, and offered to deliver them, to the owners without interest, provided they would return the money which had been advanced on them. More of the opulent citizens soon followed their examples; many bequeathed large sums for this particular purpose; and Toledo, the viceroy, who drove the Jews from the kingdom, supported it by every method possible. This lending house, which has undergone so many variations, is the largest in Europe; and it contains such an immense amount and number of different articles, many of them exceedingly valuable, that it may be considered as a repository of the most important part of the movables of the whole nation.

Oldest Bill of Exchange in the World, 1325.

THE oldest copy of a formal bill of exchange known to be in existence, at present, is one dated at Milan, on the 9th of March, 1325, and runs in the original as follows:

" Pagate per questa prima litera [lettera] a di IX. Ottobre a Luca de Goro Lib. XLV. Sono per la valuta qui da Marco Reno, al tempo il pagate e ponete a mio conto e R. che Christo vi guarde Bonromeo de Bonromei de Milano IX. de' Marzo, 1325." Or, in English—

" Pay for this first bill of exchange, on the 9th of October, to Luca Goro 45 livres; they are for value received here from Marco Reno; at the time of maturity pay the same to my account, thanking you, may Christ protect you, Bonromeo de Bonromei of Milan, the 9th of March, 1325."

Unexpected Balance at Coutts's Bank.

LORD A. FITZCLARENCE happened to drop into Coutts's bank with his friend Mr. W., who wanted to draw some money, for which purpose he got a check from the cashier, and filled it up for two hundred pounds; on re-

ceiving which, he observed that he had something to say to one of the partners, and excused himself for stepping into an inner room a few minutes for the purpose. Lord A., left standing by the counter, remarked, laughingly:

" Well, it is a very pleasant thing to walk in and get helped to two hundred pounds in that way."

" If your lordship wishes to draw," replied the cashier, " I will hand *you* a check."

" Oh, yes! but as I do not keep an account here, that would be of very little use," said the lord; and the conversation went on, as his lordship thought, jocularly.

" I beg your lordship's pardon; but I should be very happy to cash it."

" But I tell you I have no money in the bank, and never had any at Messrs. Coutts's."

" Your lordship is mistaken; there is a larger sum than that standing on our books in your name;" and, consulting a large ledger, he pointed out the entry.

It turned out that Lord A.'s royal father had vested certain amounts for the younger branches of his family, and had somehow forgotten to mention the circumstance; and so it might have lain for a very long time, as it is a rule of the house never to announce moneys paid in.

Colloquies inside the Bank.

IN his various walks and contacts, the porter of a bank gains much knowledge of men and things, which, discretionally, or in answer to questions, he communicates to the bank officials, between whom and himself there is free and often confidential intercourse. Here is an amusing illustration, from no other pen than Gibbons's:

" What news at the clearing-house to-day, Mr. Donaldson?" asks the president. " I didn't hear anything particular, sir. It looks as if things might be a little excited and uncomfortable, that's all." "Ah! Well, that's a good deal. What makes you think so?" "A little sort of *snap*, sir. Some of the porters came in late, as though they'd been holding back for morning checks." "Did you hear anything in the street?" "I heard some talk about a failure among the brokers, but no name." "No steamer in?" "Well, yes, sir; but the boys ain't crying an extra yet. They've got a notice on the bulletins—' *Delhi not taken!* '"

The president catches a valuable hint from many a conversation, of which this is an example.

"Delhi not taken! Then, Mr. Cashier, I think you may answer Mr. Borrow, that we can't give him any privilege of over-draft, nor re-discount his paper. These country banks must learn to take care of themselves." An application for a credit of fifty thousand dollars, which had been lying in suspense, is thus decided by the state of things *in India.*

It is not unlikely that the porter will carry notices to parties within the next half hour, calling in one or two hundred thousand dollars of demand loans, so sensitive are bank officers to imaginary effects that may follow an announcement that some "Delhi" or other is "not yet taken."

Disadvantage of being a Bank Director.

THE Senate of the State once elected Mr. Matthew Carey, the eminent book publisher, a director of the Bank of Pennsylvania. He mentions, as a disadvantage to him from the position, the lenity shown by the other directors, whereby his debts rose extravagantly high. This evil he urges with great warmth and zeal, as the one which several times in his business life came near bringing him to bankruptcy. "I printed and published," he declares, "above twice as many books as were necessary for the extent of my business; and, in

consequence, incurred oppressive debts to banks—was laid under contribution for interest to them and to usurers, which not only swallowed up my profits, but kept me in a constant state of penury. I was in many cases shaved so close by the latter class, that they almost skinned me alive. To this cause my difficulties were nearly altogether owing, for I did a large and profitable business almost from the time I opened a bookstore."

He sets down another evil practice of his business career, which he cautions young traders to shun, as they would "temporal perdition." It is that of endorsation. "In this way, in fourteen years," he writes, "I lost between thirty and forty thousand dollars; and but for this I might have retired from business ten years earlier than I did; besides, in one of the cases of failure, I was brought to the verge of stoppage."

Royal Pawners and Brokers.

THE infection of gambling, in the different varieties of that practice, is so strong that Pope, who knew his countrymen well, declared that:

"*Statesman* and *patriot* ply alike the *stocks;*
Peeress and butler share alike the box;
And *judges* job, and *bishops* bite the town,
And *mighty dukes* pack cards for half a crown."

In the twelfth century Richard I. pawned the revenues of the crown for the payment of moneys borrowed to defray the expenses of the fanatical conquest of the Holy Land. Henry III. pawned the crown jewels and regal ornaments and robes of state. Edward I. borrowed money to pay the debts of his father, in order to get his soul "out of purgatory," as the record states. Richard II. was deposed for extorting one million one hundred thousand pounds sterling, under pretext of borrowing, which was never repaid. This was one of the chief causes of the York and Lancaster wars. In 1346 Edward III. ordered a sum of money to be lent to him. Henry IV. *obliged* the rich men of the kingdom to lend him money on the growing taxes. Henry VIII. escaped the punishment he so justly merited for defrauding his creditors; he compelled Parliament to pass two acts, offering him "all the money he had received in loans,"—thus discharging him of all obligations he had come under, and all suits that might arise thereupon. In money matters in Elizabeth's time, the people insisted upon the payment of the sums advanced to her predecessors, a demand she was wise enough to comply with.

Irishman at the Bank.

THE city banks have all kinds of customers. For instance, one in the shape of an Irish pig-jobber, a stranger, introduces himself, or rather his business, by laying his great whip on the counter, taking off an apology of a hat—so far as any known styles stand related to it,—and then, fumbling in the cavernous recesses of his dirty garments, lugs out a crumpled bundle of very nasty-looking notes.

"Could ye give me your bank notes for these, sur?" he asks, in his most insinuating manner.

"We never change notes to strangers."

"Why, they're good, ain't they?"

"Yes, doubtless; but we don't change notes of another bank."

"Well, sur, supposing I'd be after paying ye a little charges now, would ye do it for me?"

"Do you know any one in the town? If you can find any one known to us, who will write his name on the back of them, we might do it, perhaps."

"Yes, sure, sur, there's Mr. Murphy the pork butcher, sur."

"Well, he will do."

In due time he re-appears, with his friend Murphy, and with much satisfac-

tion pockets the new and clean notes. After paying his "charges," as he calls them, the warm heart of a son of Erin exhibits itself:

"Thank ye, sur; and, by jabbers, if ye'll come out wid me. I'll stand trate for brandy."

Juvenile Contempt of the Bank.

A SHOP boy, having a very rustic appearance in dress and manners, entered one of the banks in Dundee, Scotland, and, throwing a sixpence to the teller, asked, "A saxpence worth o' fardins." The teller very politely replied, "I can't do it. I have not so many," Shop boy, "Gie's back my saxpence, then." The boy, on opening the door to leave, looked over his shoulder, and staring at the teller, exclaimed, "Sic a bank!" Next day he had occasion to visit the same bank, and on being asked amid the laughter of the clerks "If he got his saxpence worth o' fardins?" replied contemptuously, "Ay did I. I got them in a little pie-shop."

Banks of Ease.

MANY years ago the first settlers in Western New York were obliged to take their grain a great distance in wagons to Albany, to find a market. The roads were bad, and the travelling dangerous. Three farmers of this region found a purchaser for their loads of wheat at Amsterdam, a village some twenty-five miles west of Albany, and were glad thus to dispose of it, and save themselves the trouble and travel. They took an order on the bank of Amsterdam for their pay, which was offered them in specie—silver; but they objected to taking it, as it was too heavy to carry, and they preferred the notes of the bank. And here the laugh comes in. The officers of the bank refused to give them the bills, because the farmers were going so far out into the wilderness, the bills would never come back to the bank again! The matter was finally compromised by the bank's paying each of them one dollar extra, on their consenting to receive silver instead of paper money. Surely, this bank might well be termed a Bank of Ease!

Russian Money Brokers.

THOUGH the ring upon one's finger is said to be unsafe in the Russian money-marts, it is clear that the silver rubles and ducats on the tables of the money-brokers are perfectly secure; for tables of this kind stand at the corners of all the streets, amidst the thickest of the throng, upon which columns and heaps of the different sorts of coin are invitingly exposed to the public gaze—a phenomenon that perhaps could not take place in any other great and crowded city. It would be easy for any one intent on plunder to upset the table, and tumble its valuable freight promiscuously into the mud; and no one, amidst the general confusion, could be expected to point out the rogue that was enriching himself with the scattered spoil.

And yet it is a fact, that though thousands of rubles are often placed under the care of lads only twelve years of age, not a broker would risk a farthing, if he did not think himself perfectly safe with his money amidst all these people and the attendant commotion. But the Russian rogue is a strangely discriminating fellow, who has not the least scruple to commit some actions that are palpably dishonest—for instance, to charge a buyer six times as much for a thing as it is worth, or to pick one's pocket of watch or purse,—while he thinks others most disgraceful, and is therefore, in certain points, as honorable and trustworthy as the most conscientious man that can be found. These money-brokers are under the protection of the public and of the thieves themselves. No doubt it has

often happened that such money-tables have been overthrown, and not a single copeck, much less a ducat, has been lost, because all the by-standers, in their sheep-skin dresses, assisted with the most courteous officiousness to pick up all the pieces of gold and silver out of the dirt.

Note Buyers.

THERE are men who spend their whole lives in Wall street, and who do nothing else but buy notes. They come in early and go out late. Their time is occupied in making fresh inquiries, and in haggling about the rate per cent. You can to-day see these persons, if you will take the trouble to station yourself on the spot, and I predict you will behold what will deeply interest you. Wait a few moments near this corner, and you will not be disappointed. There he comes, passing thoughtfully along the street. He has the appearance of a man laden with many cares. Look at him! He is respectably encased in a moderately warm suit of black. His head inclines forward; his eye has become stony; his nose pointed; his chin angular; his cheeks rigid; his lips wooden; his mind—alas! he has no longer any mind; but in place of mind he possesses an instinct so subtle and acute that it will detect a piece of "made" paper in the very curl of the signature. If you wish to see more of this sort, go and take a seat for an hour or two in one of the many small note-brokers' offices, which abound, and watch the arrival of others of these paper sharks. They come in hungry, eager, sharp, to hear and see what new offers. They have a large capital, perhaps hundreds of thousands of dollars, invested in notes, or represented by securities, which can be converted into cash in twenty-four hours, should it be required to buy more paper with. They are always moving about to pick up the note of some good mechanic, who they know for certain reasons is hard-up, and who is willing to bleed freely rather than to fail in a contract.

It is hardly necessary to say that, for the delineation of the above character, the credit belongs to Kimball's facile pen.

Jacob Lorillard's Note of Accommodation.

THE benevolent feelings manifested by Jacob Lorillard toward young beginners in business, who were needy and friendless, exhibit a very bright side to human nature. When a director of that institution, of which he was twice the president, he would frequently take a parcel of the small notes which were offered for discount by poor mechanics, who were obscure and unknown, and which, therefore, for the most part, would have been rejected, and make diligent inquiry, in person, as to their character and standing; and if he found that, with a proper regard to the interests of the bank, he could commend them to favor and confidence, he felt that he was abundantly rewarded for all his pains.

On one occasion, a person whose note had been refused where it was offered for discount, and who, it appears, had no peculiar claims on his kindness and influence, though possessing his confidence, called on him for the favor of a line of recommendation, which would be sure to procure the desired accommodation. He at once, as it seemed, complied with the desired request; instead of being a line of recommendation, however, it was afterward discovered to be a note of Mr. Lorillard, for the amount which was needed. The person immediately returned, and pointed out the mistake. "Never mind," said Mr. Lorillard, "if they will not discount your note, see whether they will not mine."

Losing a Bank Customer.

MR. CHICKERING, of piano-forte fame, one day presented a large number of notes for discount at one of the banks in Boston, where he had done his business. The president asked him who was to endorse the notes. Mr. Chickering replied, "I shall endorse them myself." "That will never do," said the president. Mr. Chickering simply responded, "Very well," took the notes, and carried them to another bank, which immediately gave him all the money he needed. On another occasion, a bank with which he had long had transactions, and to which he had as usual applied through his clerk for an accommodation, sent for Mr. Chickering, and said to him, "Security was wanted." Mr. Chickering replied, "I shall give you none; I have done my business at this bank for a long time; and if you do not know me, I shall apply where I am better known." The consequence was, the necessary discount was at once given by another bank, to which he transferred his business. This business was worth at least ten thousand dollars a year. Soon after this, a director of the bank which refused him, called on Mr. Chickering, to induce him to restore his business, under the assurance that for the future the bank would grant whatever accommodation might be wanted. Mr. Chickering, however, declined the proposed arrangement, not wishing to do business at an institution willing to suspect his responsibility.

Endorser's Qualifications.

A WORTHY but poor minister once requested the loan of fifty dollars from the cashier of a country bank; and in the note requesting the favor, he said that if the cashier would oblige him, he would "pay him in ten days, on the faith of Abraham." The cashier returned word that by the rules of the bank, the endorser of the note must reside in the State!

More Cunning than Rothschild.

NOTWITHSTANDING his great forethought, sagacity, and penetration, Rothschild was occasionally surpassed in cunning. On one occasion a great banker lent Rothschild a million and a half on the security of consols, the price of which was then eighty-four. The terms on which the money was lent were simple and usual. If the price reached seventy-four, the banker might claim the stock at seventy; but Rothschild felt satisfied that, with so large a sum out of the market, the bargain was tolerably safe. The banker, however, as much a Jew as Rothschild, had a plan of his own. He immediately began selling the consols received from the latter, together with a similar amount in his own possession. The funds dropped; the stock exchange grew alarmed; other circumstances tended to depress it—the fatal price of seventy-four was reached, and the Christian banker had the satisfaction of outwitting the Hebrew loanmonger.

Voltaire's Dealings in Government Stocks.

THOUGH a literary man, Voltaire had an eye to the main chance, the angle of his vision finding its focus in government stocks. "Here I am," he says, "living in a way suited to my habits, and caring but little for to-morrow; for I have a friend, a director in the Bank of France, who writes to me whenever money is to be made in the public funds. Sometimes he writes to me desiring me to sell, because the bank is going to withdraw its notes. At other times he bids me buy—for 'we are going to issue a quantity of notes;' and so, through the kindness of my friend, I always make money, though living two hundred miles from Paris."

Jewish Money Lenders.

A PREJUDICE against Jews, on account of their sharpness in money transactions is almost universal. The simple fact is, however, just this: that when a man—not a Jew—is in a tight place, or broken down in his fortune, so that he can neither raise funds by the credit of his name nor by mortgage on his estate, he flies to the money lender. Now, Jews are essentially a financial people, and money-broking, in all its details, is their special avocation. The class of Israelite money lenders is, therefore, numerous; and it is ten to one that the broken-down individual who requires a loan addresses himself to a Jew, even if he take the money lender nearest to him, or to whom he is at first recommended. Well, he transacts his business with this Jew; and as his habits of life and shaky business condition are well known, he cannot of course obtain the loan he seeks, save on terms proportionate to the risk incurred by the lender. Yet he goes away, and denounces the Jew as a usurer; when, had he applied to a "Christian" money broker, the terms would have been equally high,—if any terms could have been effected at all, seeing that he had no real security to offer, and that his name was already tarnished. Perhaps, then, after all, Jewish "hardness" will compare favorably with the proverbially rapacious practices of Christian attorneys and the greedy exactions of Christian bill discounters!

Discounting a Hibernian's Note.

A TRANSPARENT Hibernian wanted a friend to discount a note. "If I advance this," said the lender, "will you pay your note punctually?" "I will, on my honor," replied the other—"*the expense of the protest and all!*"

Addison's Opinion of the Royal Exchange and its Frequenters.

ADDISON once pleasantly wrote: There is no place in the town which I so much love to frequent as the Royal Exchange. It gives me a secret satisfaction, and in some measure gratifies my vanity, as I am an Englishman, to see so rich an assembly of countrymen and foreigners, consulting together upon the private business of mankind, and making this metropolis a kind of emporium for the whole earth.

The Royal Exchange of London still exhibits one of the most remarkable assemblages in the world, if the stranger visiting it is fortunate enough to have the advantage of a city merchant as his cicerone; otherwise there is little in its general aspect differing from what may be seen daily at 'Change hour in any of the large cities. But it certainly interests the stranger, on walking into the quadrangle between two and three o'clock, "when merchants most do congregate," to see the representatives of the different nations of the earth, grouped in their respective places under the piazzas, and engaging in negotiations, which, more than the councils of cabinets, influence the policy of states; and to be told, for example, that the thoughtful-looking man, with strongly marked Jewish features, leaning carelessly against a pillar, is able by a dash of his pen to control the most powerful governments in Europe. In this quadrangle, too, resides the mysterious susceptibility to the variations in the political and commercial atmosphere, indicated upon the scale of that most sensitive of all barometers, the money market, with its constantly fluctuating prices.

Money Street of New York.

WALL STREET is not a long street, though it is felt a long ways. A man, without corns, can walk the length of it in five minutes—and then, if he should keep on, would find himself in the East River. It is not a wide street. Bids have been made from curb to curb. Wheels get locked there daily, especially near the head of it; and a vast deal of highly ornamental profanity is done by sweet-tempered carmen, who, having wedged themselves in, seem to think that, like the poor debtor, they can *swear* themselves out.

It is not a handsome street, still there is nothing wooden in it, except, perhaps, the heads of some stock buyers. White marble, brown freestone, terra cotta, and substantial granite bespeak its wealth. There is that wonderfully intricate building, the Merchants' Exchange—now the Custom House, where there is so much hard swearing over fraudulent invoices and political assessments.

On either side of the street is an illustrious row of banks and insurance offices, with foreign insurance agents, land agents, coal agents, railroad agents, steamship agents, and many other sorts of agents (Satan's too, perhaps), including some lawyers on the second and higher floors. The basements swarm with brokers. Every nook and cranny in all these buildings commands high rents. Add to this picture innumerable groups of earnest-talking, scolding, chaffing, gesticulating men, dividing the rapid currents of merchants, brokers, clerks, foreign consuls, financiers, and commercial editors, who are continually passing, and one who has never seen the notorious thoroughfare will have a tolerably graphic idea of Wall street.

It is admitted, even by Europeans, that, as a money-dealing street, this has no superior in the world. The nature and amount of transactions of this kind, for a single week, in this locality, would make a formidable portion of Doomsday Book.

Governor of the Bank of England taken by Surprise.

AT the half-yearly meetings of the proprietors of the Bank of England, it sometimes happens that one or more of the stockholders endeavor to elicit some information relative to the conduct of the governor, and also as to the cause of any particular loss sustained by the bank, and from what data the directors have fixed the dividend. These and similar questions are generally put in the most cautious manner; and, if answered at all—which is a rare occurrence—are met with an equal degree of caution on the part of the governor.

That functionary, however, is on some occasions taken by surprise, and betrayed into admissions which are contrary to practice. A singular instance of this occurred during the term of Governor Reid, at a meeting for the declaration of the dividends, when he stated that during the past year the amount of commercial paper discounted by the bank was forty millions of pounds. As this amount was unusually large, and as the rate of interest charged by the bank was five and one-half to six per cent., with only a loss of six hundred pounds, it naturally occurred to the stockholders to inquire why the dividend was not larger than the corresponding period of the last year; and, on one of them putting a question to the chair, as to whether the repayment of the money borrowed from the Bank of France had been attended with any considerable loss to the corporation, the governor was on the point of answering this question, when some kind friend, like a second Mentor, whispered something in the ear of the governor, which had the effect of immediately sealing his lips, and he refused to answer the question. At these meetings, as little as possible of the affairs of the bank is disclosed by the directors, from the fear that, should they be more explicit,

it might endanger their property by depreciating the value of bank stock; and, to such an extent is this system of secrecy carried, that it is a proverbial saying, "that if you met a bank director going across the Royal Exchange, and you asked him what o'clock it was, he would say, 'You must excuse me answering *that* question.'"

Picayunes and Coppers.

YOU "can't buy nothing" in New Orleans, or most Southern and Western cities, for less than a "picayune"—six and a quarter cents. And in connection with this fact in currency, a little incident took place on board one of the Western boats, the rehearsal of which can do no harm on a hot or rainy day. A man from the North, who happened to have quite a lot of coppers weighing down his pocket, but who, Yankee-like, had no idea of not getting their full value in a trade, essayed to pass ten of the filthy coin upon a " Sucker," for a dime.

" What *be* they ?" inquired the Sucker, in unfeigned ignorance.

" I calculate they are cents," replied the Northerner; " can't you read ?"

" I reckon not," said the other; " and what's more, old hoss, I allow I don't want to. What *is* cents, mister ?"

" I vow to the judges," said the Northerner, " you are worse than the heathen! Cents is money—'sartin! Ten of them are worth one dime. Can't you see ? It says ' E Pluribus Unum '—that's the Latin for ' Hail Columbia '—and here it's inscribed ' One Cent.' "

" Look here," responded the Sucker, putting the thumb of his hand into his ear, and inclining his fingers forward, " you may run a sew on a Hoosier or a Wolverine, but I'm blamed if you Yankee me with that contusive stuff!"

8

Bewitching a Bank Teller.

DURING the sojourn of Professor Anderson in the Quaker City, he used one of the banks for his deposits. One day he went to the bank for this purpose, with a large amount. It was principally in twenty and ten dollar gold pieces, and was handed in in packages of five hundred each. The teller, who did not know the wizard, and who is usually a very smart man, commenced counting the gold, but could not, for his life, satisfy himself of the numerous amounts. Opening one package, he found all right; then he took a second, and found it ten dollars short—recounted it, and found ten dollars over; and then again, and it was short. He then laid it aside, took another parcel, and found it contained twenty dollars over—recounted it, and it was only ten over; again he carefully and deliberately counted it, and discovered it was thirty short! The young man felt his head, to see if he was laboring under sickness, dreaming, or deranged. Finding his senses all right, he set to work again, commencing at the first package and got through five very well; the next he found twenty short, and, recounting it, discovered forty over! He finally called to his aid another teller, who was equally puzzled; but, turning round, his eye fell upon Professor Anderson standing near by, and he felt convinced it was the trick of the wizard. The professor blandly smiled, and desired him to proceed; and when he got through satisfactorily, he took the receipt for the amount. The teller then went to the table where he had left the piles of gold, in order to put them into the drawer, when lo! he could not lift any of them; the coins clung together and were immovable! The young man here looked fairly terrified, and sought a chair; but the professor, seeing his perplexity, told him not to be alarmed. He found his imagination had affected him, and told him to put the cash away; the professor then left the bank, passing the crowd of anxious customers who had been observing, in blank astonishment, the capers that were being cut up on the other side of the counter.

The Proud Broker Barnard.

JOHN BARNARD, usually styled "the proud broker," flourished extensively in the English money circles of the last century. The reduction of interest on money loans, in 1750, from four to three per cent., originated with this famous man, and he it was who defiantly made war upon time bargains. His pride was indomitable to such a degree that it passed into a proverb; the members of the exchange, who were always spoken of by Sir John with haughty contempt, thoroughly detested him, and greatly helped to fan the unpopularity which fell upon him when he opposed public feeling—as, with a most unflinching determination, he invariably did, if his conscience prompted.

On commercial subjects his opinion was greatly regarded; when any remarkable feature in financial politics occurred, the town echoed with, "What does Sir John say to this?— what is Sir John's opinion?" He once had the honor of refusing the post of chancellor of the exchequer.

It is somewhat at variance with the proud character of the man, that from the time the distinguished honor was paid him of erecting his statue in the Royal Exchange, he never so much as entered that building, but transacted his business in the front.

The blood of Sir John Barnard still flows in the veins of some of the best houses in the commercial world, his son having married the daughter of the great banker, Sir Thomas Hankey. Sir John's great enemy—and a powerful one, it may well be believed—was Sampson Gideon, the Jew broker,

" worth more than all the land of Canaan."

Four Money-making Rules of Rothschild.

ROTHSCHILD commonly ascribed his *early* success, in a great degree, to the following rules :

" First : I combined three profits; I made the manufacturer my customer, and the one I bought of my customer —that is, I supplied the manufacturer with raw materials and dyes, on each of which I made a profit, and took his manufactured goods, which I sold at a profit, and thus combined three profits.

" Second : Make a bargain at once. Be an off-hand man.

" Third : *Never have anything to do with an unlucky man or place.* - I have seen many clever men who had not shoes to their feet. I never act with them ; their advice sounds very well, but fate is against them—they cannot get on themselves—how can they do good to me ?

" Fourth : *Be cautious and bold.* It requires a great deal of boldness and a great deal of caution to make a great fortune ; and when you have got it, it requires ten times as much wit to keep it."

The last idea was one which Rothschild frequently expressed ; it forms a passage in his memorable conversation with Sir Thomas Buxton, and there is no doubt he was thoroughly impressed with its truth.

Albert Gallatin declining Baring's Offer of a Fortune.

THE financial talent and success of Albert Gallatin were equalled only by his inflexible business integrity—his name, through scores of years, standing forth as the very embodiment of rare good judgment and unspotted honor. One of the most interesting illustrations of his high-toned character, in business dealings, occurred while he was in Europe, on a mission in behalf of his Government, in 1818. While absent on his duty, he rendered some essential service to Mr. Alexander Baring in the negotiation of a loan from the French Government. Mr. Baring in return pressed him to take a part of the loan, offering him such advantages in it that, without advancing any funds, he could have realized a fortune. " I thank you," was Gallatin's reply ; " I will not accept your obliging offer, because a man who has had the direction of the finances of his country as long as I have, should not die rich."

Gresham's Scheme of Exchanges.

THOMAS GRESHAM was for many years the commercial pride of England ; and that his character has not been overrated is proved by the notable scheme he devised at Antwerp, for operating on the exchanges, so as to render them favorable to England. He promised Edward the Sixth, during the reign of whom this occurred, that if he might pursue his own views, he would remove all his sovereign's difficulties in two years. The following is his plan, in his own words :

My request shall be to his majesty and you, to appoint me out, weekly, twelve or thirteen hundred pounds, to be secretly received at one man's hands, so that it may be kept secret, and that I may thereunto trust, and that I may make my reckoning thereof assuredly. I shall so use the matter here in the town of Antwerp, that every day I will be sure to take up two or three hundred pounds sterling by exchange. And thus doing, it shall not be perceived, nor yet shall be the occasion to make the exchange fall. For that it shall be taken up in my name. And so by these means, in working by deliberation and time, the merchant's turn also shall be served. As also this should bring all merchants out of suspicion, who do nothing toward payment of the king's debts, and will not stick to say, that ere the payment of the king's debts be made, it will bring down the exchange to 13s. 4d., which I trust never to see that day. So that by this you may perceive if that I do but take up every day, but £200 sterling, it will amount in one year to £72,000, and the king's majesty oweth here at this present £108,000, with the interest money that was prolonged before this time. So that, by these means, in two years, things will be compassed accordingly, and my purpose set forth.

By this plan, he found means in a short space to raise the exchange from sixteen shillings Flemish for the pound sterling to twenty-two shillings, at which rate he discharged all the king's debts, and in this way money was rendered plentiful and trade prosperous.

First Run upon Bankers.

THE extravagant luxury of the court of King Charles, together with its utter want of principle, and incapacity to carry on the contest with Holland, produced the *first run upon bankers ever made*. The Government had suffered a succession of humiliating disasters. The extravagance of the court had dissipated all the means which Parliament had supplied for the purpose of carrying on offensive hostilities. It was determined only to wage defensive war; but even for defensive war the vast resources of England were found insufficient. The Dutch insulted the British coast, sailed up the Thames, took Sheerness, and carried their ravages to Chatham. The blaze of the ships burning in the river was seen at London; it was rumored that a foreign army had landed at Gravesend; and military men seriously proposed to abandon the tower.

The people, accustomed to the secure reign of Cromwell, were in utter consternation. The moneyed portion of the community were seized with a panic. The country was in danger. London itself might be invaded. What security was there, then, for the money advanced to the crown? The people flocked to their debtors; they demanded their deposits; and London now witnessed the first run upon the bankers!

The fears of the people, however, proved fallacious, for the goldsmiths—as the bankers were then called—met all demands made upon them. Confidence was restored by a proclamation from the king, stating that the demands on the exchequer should be met as usual; and the run ceased.

Queen Anne saving the Government Bank from Pillage.

HISTORY shows, in more than one instance, that the great wealth accumulated in the treasury of the Bank of England, has rendered it peculiarly liable to attack in times of public excitement and tumult. There are always idle and profligate men to whom the very name " bank " possesses a charm. In 1709 the piety of the people of London created a religious riot. One Dr. Henry Sacheverell, an apostate Whig, being appointed to preach the annual sermon at St. Paul's, before the Lord Mayor and court of aldermen, used the occasion as an engine of attack upon some of the Government officials. The measureless impudence of the preacher was rebuked—among others by Sir Gilbert Heathcote, a director of the Bank of England. The usual courtesy of having the discourse printed by the city was not extended; in the absence of which, Sacheverell himself had it printed, with an inflammatory epistle, dedicating it to Garrard, the Lord Mayor, at whose instance, he alleged, the publication was made. He was arrested and impeached, in revenge for the liberties he had taken with the Government. The populace chose to support the divine ; and a body guard of London butchers accompanied him to his trial at Westminster Hall, which the queen honored with her presence. "God bless the Church and Dr. Sacheverell" was echoed from mouth to mouth among the "pious" populace. Money was thrown among them, by some of the better classes, who followed in hackney coaches. The dissenting chapels were sacked. The queen and court were in the utmost consternation. Multitudes followed the Doctor, pressing about him, and striving to kiss his hand. Alarm seized every bosom.

The anxiety of the bank directors during this period of tumult was great, as every day rendered them liable to attack. At last, intelligence reached them that the rioters were moving toward their locality. As a pious mob was no more to be trusted, pecuniarily, than a political one, the court, assembled to "concert measures proper to be taken," and sent to the principal Secretary of State for a guard to prevent any attempt they might make on the bank. When the message was received the Earl of Sunderland made its tenor known to the queen, who immediately ordered both horse and foot out to quell the tumult, leaving her own person without protection. "God will be my guard," was her ready reply, when reminded of her danger. A detachment under Captain Horsey was immediately ordered into the city to prevent the meditated attack on the alarmed directors. "Am I to preach or fight?" was the question of the blunt soldier, on receiving his instructions. There proved, however, to be no occasion for either. The rioters retreated in alarm; *the bank was saved from pillage, by the self-sacrifice and devotion of the queen.*

Rendering Bank Notes Serviceable.

THE uses of bank notes are manifold; but the following is a novel mode of rendering them serviceable. One of these for £5 came in the course of busi-

ness to a mercantile house in Liverpool. On the back of it was written : "If this note gets into the hands of John Dean, of Longhill, near Carlisle, his brother Andrew is a prisoner in Algiers." The circumstance was interesting and appeared in a newspaper, in which the paragraph was perused by a person in Carlisle, who had known in past years one Andrew Dean, and was still acquainted with his brother John Dean, of the place named in the note. The son of the latter happened to be in Carlisle, and hearing the intelligence, gave such a report of his uncle that there was every reason to believe he was the Andrew Dean whose captivity became thus singularly known to his friends in England. Of these things are formed the romance of life; and the impossibility of assisting the Algerine slave must often have been a painful remembrance to the prisoner's brother.

Supposititious Will of the Bank-of-England Directors.

THE success which attended the operations of the Bank of England, in its early history, naturally provoked competition. A bank was proposed by Dr. Hugh Chamberlain, to advance money on the security of landed property, and though the Bank of England had no occasion to fear rivalry, they petitioned against it, and were heard by their counsel. All that the projectors required was money; and as that was not ready at the appointed period, "the romantic Land Bank" failed. A war of most sarcastic pamphlets ensued between the friends of the new scheme and those of the old institution, one of these pamphlets being entitled : "The Trial and Condemnation of the Land Bank, at Exeter 'Change, for murdering the Bank of England at Grocers' Hall." A will, by no means complimentary to the directors of the latter, is supposed to be produced at the trial. It runs as follows :

"Know all our creditors by these presents, that we, the Governor and Company of the Bank of England, being weak in body through the wounds received from the Land Bank at Exeter Change, to whom we lay our death, but of as good sense as ever we were, finding ourselves impaired in our credit and reputation, and despairing of recovery, do make our last will and testament.

"1st. We bequeath *our soul to the devil*, in order to serve the public out of our creditors' money; and as to the qualities of our mind, we dispose them as follows, namely, all our skill in foreign exchanges, and our probity and candor in making up the accounts of the loss thereof, we give to all and every of our directors, except four or five, jointly and severally, to hold to them, and to their successors, as heirlooms, and imperishable monuments of their skill and probity forever. All our obstinacy and blunders we give unto our present governor, upon trust, that he shall employ one equal third part thereof as one of the lords of the Admiralty, and the other part thereof as Governor of the Bank of England. All our oaths, impudence, &c., we give unto our present deputy governor and our dear Sir Henry Furnese, to hold in joint partnership during their lives, and the survivor to have the whole. All our shuffling tricks we give to our dear Sir William Gore. All our cynicalness and self-conceit we give to our directors, Sir John Ward and Sir Gilbert Heathcote, equally to be divided betwixt them, share and share alike, as tenants in common. All our blindness and fear we give unto our dear Obadiah Sedgwick, and we also give him £5 in money to buy him a new cloth coat, a new half-beaver hat, a second-hand periwig, and an old black sword to solicit with in the lobby, and also to buy him a pair of spectacles to write letters to lords with.

"As to the residue of our temporal estate (besides the said £5) we dispose thereof as followeth : *Imprimis*, we devise to our own members (when they shall have paid in our £100 per cent.) our fund of £100,000 per annum, charged and chargeable, nevertheless, with the sum of £1,200,000, for which it stands mortgaged, by bank bills, in full satisfaction of all their great expectations from the probity and skill of our directors, advising them to accept a redemption thereof by Parliament, whenever they can have it.

"*Item*—all our ready moneys, before any of our debts are paid, we give to our executors, hereinafter named, in trust, that they shall, from time to time, until 1st August, 1696, lend the same into the exchequer, upon condition to defeat the establishment of the Land Bank ; and from and after the 1st said August, then to lend out the same into the said exchequer, upon security of premises to establish our executors the next session, instead of the Land Bank, and for such other premiums as our said executors can give to themselves, for doing thereof. And we do direct our said executors to continue the stock and pensions already allowed to our past friends—they know where. And after all our ready moneys so disposed, we leave the residue of our effects for payment of bills and notes, at such days and hours, and in such manner and proportion, and with such preferences, as our said executors shall see fit. And we do hereby constitute our directors executors of this our will, giving each of them power, out of our cash, to discount their own tallies, bills and notes, at par ; and the bills and notes of other of our creditors at the highest discount they can get for the same.

"And *our body we commit to be burned*, with all privacy, lest our creditors arrest our corpse. In witness wherof, we have hereunto set our common seal, 4th May, 1696."

The epitaph was as follows :

"Here lies the body of the Bank of

England, who was born in the year 1694, died May 5th, 1696, in the third year of its age. They had issue legitimate by their common seal, 1,200,000, called bank bills, and by their cashier two million sons of —— called Speed's notes."

Immense Consignment of Gold to a New York House.

THE great business crash in 1837 was attended by a universal suspension of specie payments by the banks throughout the country. Under these circumstances, and in view of the extensive business relations between the United States and England, application was made to the bankers and capitalists of the latter country, for such aid as would encourage Americans then struggling to extricate themselves from embarrassments, and enable them to return to specie payments. To effect this, Mr. James G. King, of the house of Prime, Ward & King, New York, proceeded to England, and was warmly received and eagerly consulted by bankers and merchants in London. His calm and assured tone and judgment did much to allay the apprehension which panic and ignorance of the extent of resources possessed by the American commercial community and banks, had produced. He startled the bank-parlor in Threadneedle-street by a suggestion, that instead of embarrassing American merchants by discrediting, as they had been doing, paper connected with the American trade, it nearly concerned the solvency of many of their own customers, and thus their own interests, that liberal aid should rather be extended to that trade. He finally brought them over to these views, and proposed that the Bank of England at once send over several million dollars in coin, to strengthen the American banks and enable them to resume. In conformity with Mr. King's opinions and plan, the bank consigned to his firm the immense sum of *one million*

pounds sterling in gold, upon the sole responsibility of that house and the guaranty of Baring Brothers & Co. The receipt of this coin in America produced at once a realization of the result anticipated by Mr. King, and the transaction constitutes one of the most important events in the financial history of the United States, nor is it necessary to state that Mr. King added much to his already high renown as a merchant and banker, by the part he so grandly enacted. The affair was wound up without loss and with great promptness.

"Accommodation" offered at the Bank.

A CAPITAL example of what is often termed "taking the starch out," happened in a country bank in New England. A pompous, well-dressed individual entered the bank, and, addressing the teller, who is something of a wag, inquired:

"Is the cashier in?"

"No, Sir," was the reply.

"Well, I am dealing in pens, supplying the New England banks pretty largely, and I suppose it will be proper for me to deal with the cashier."

"I suppose it will," said the teller.

"Very well; I will wait."

The pen peddler took a chair and sat composedly for a full hour, waiting for the cashier. By that time he began to grow uneasy, but sat twisting in his chair for about twenty minutes, and, seeing no prospect of a change in his circumstances, asked the teller how soon the cashier would be in.

"Well, I don't know exactly," said the waggish teller, "but I expect him in about eight weeks. He has just gone to Lake Superior, and told me he thought he should come back in that time."

Peddler thought he would not wait.

"Oh, you may stay if you wish," said the teller, very blandly. "We have no objection to your sitting here in the daytime, and you can probably find some place in town where they will be glad to keep you nights."

The pompous peddler disappeared without another word.

Pennsylvania Bonds.

AT the time when Sidney Smith, the reverend canon of St. Paul's, was denouncing the "drab-coated men of Pennsylvania"·for neglecting to pay the interest on their State stock, of which he held a considerable amount, he was visited by a young author, exceedingly lavish in his compliments and flattery, and who declared that if he could only hope to attain to even a small degree of the fame and honor which he (Sidney) enjoyed, he would be the most happy man on earth. "My dear young friend," said the canon, "I would that you were not only almost, but altogether such as I am, *except these bonds*," laying his hand at the same time on the certificates of his Pennsylvania stock lying on the desk before him.

PART THIRD.

———•———

ANECDOTES AND ILLUSTRATIONS OF THE SUCCESSFUL
BUSINESS QUALITIES.

PART THIRD.

Anecdotes and Illustrations of the Successful Business Qualities.

INTEGRITY, ENTERPRISE, ENERGY, PERSEVERANCE, COURAGE, SHREWDNESS, PUNCTILIOUSNESS, PRUDENCE, AMBITION, GRATITUDE, BENEVOLENCE, GENEROSITY, ECONOMY; WITH PEN-CILLINGS OF STRIKING BUSINESS ADVENTURES, VICISSITUDES, EXPLOITS, AND ACHIEVE-MENTS, BOTH SERIOUS AND COMICAL.

> 'Tis not in mortals to *command* success ;
> But we'll do more, Sempronius, we'll *deserve* it.—ADDISON'S "CATO."

In all negotiations of difficulty, a man may not look to sow and reap at once ; but must prepare business, and so ripen it by degrees.—LORD BACON.

It is in vain to put wealth within the reach of him who will not stretch out his hand to take it.—JOHNSON.

A merchant who always tells the truth, and a genius who never lies, are synonymous to a saint.—LAVATER.

> Of plain sound sense life's current coin is made ;
> With *that* we drive the most substantial trade.—YOUNG.

Making Conditions—King James and the Corn Merchants.

DURING the reign of James the First, a great dearth of corn happened, which obliged his majesty to send for the celebrated Eastland Company of merchants. He told them, that to obviate the present scarcity, they must load their homeward-bound ships with corn ; which they promised to do, and so retired. One of the lords of the council, however, said to the king, that such a promise signified little, unless they agreed at *what price* it should be sold ; on which they were all called back, and acquainted that the king desired a more explicit answer. The deputy replied : " Sir, we will freight and buy our corn as cheap as we can, and sell it here as we can afford it ; but to be confined to any certain price, we cannot." Being still pressed for a more distinct answer, the deputy, who was not only a princely merchant but a great foxhunter, said to the king :

" Sir, your majesty is a lover of the noble sport of hunting—so am I, and I keep a few dogs ; but if my dogs do not love the sport as well as we, I might as well hunt with hogs as with dogs." The king replied : " Say no more, man, thou art in the right ; go and do as well as you can, but *be sure you bring the corn.*"

Shaking One's Business Credit.

A good story is told of old Mr. Fuller, once the famous banker of Cornhill, London—founder of the firm now located in one of the splendid bank palaces in Moorgate street, shining with plate glass, polished mahogany, brass railings, and bronze candelabra, a glance at which would have half driven its head and originator into Bedlam.

Mr. Fuller not only lived at his bank, but even had his washing done on the spot. On such days, for many a revolving year, every one who passed his door at or about noon might have seen a single pint of porter placed at the foot of the staircase; that was the washerwoman's allowance. In process of time this constant pint, so long a pint, became a pot, and forthwith there was a sensation at the bank, in Cornhill, and all along Lombard street! The twelve o'clock pint of beer that had stood so long, at Fuller's bank, had been increased to a *pot!* Every one talked of the event; and at last one customer—whether a dull, hardhearted, unhappy miser, or some solemn mocker, pleased to trifle with the infirmities of poor human nature, cannot be told—drew the senior partner's attention to the circumstance, in this formal manner: Entering the bank, one morning, and finding the old gentleman fixed, as usual, woodwork-like to his desk, as if he was a component part of that article, he drew near and thus began:

"I have banked with you now, Mr. Fuller, for a good many years."

Mr. Fuller hereupon bowed, not his head, but head, shoulders, and half his body, smirked, and replied: "Yes, many thanks for your favors; you have, sir."

"I have, Mr. Fuller," continued the other, "and have always felt great satisfaction in keeping my account with you until lately."

"Indeed, sir," interrupted the old gentleman, with quick anxiety, laying down his pen, and pushing his spectacles from his eyes up to his forehead; "pray, what has happened?—we are the same as ever."

"Pardon me, Mr. Fuller; I have noticed for many a year, that on a certain day in the week a pint of porter has regularly stood at the foot of your stairs. I always could tell, when I saw that pint, that it was washing-day with you, and greatly pleased I used to be at that proof of your economy; for, Mr. Fuller, the man who is intrusted with the keeping of other men's money, should know how to take care of his

own; and he cannot give any better or stronger proof of what he is capable of in that respect, than by being moderate and abstemious in his *housekeeping*. Therefore I was always, as I have just said, well pleased to see you were not wasteful with your washerwoman. I felt sure, while that continued, that my deposits in this house were safe—perfectly safe, sir. (This was said with an emphasis that weighed all of thirteen pounds, and with a look that set the tips of Mr. Fuller's fingers a-twirling, as if a small electric battery had been brought to play upon his nervous system.) But I see you are changing—you are breaking loose, Mr. Fuller; you now allow your washerwoman not a pint, but a whole pot of beer, every washing-day; and I must say, sir, that if you go on *doubling your expenditures* at that rate, it may be time for your customers to be looking after their balances."

Mr. Fuller, it is said, took this rebuke quite seriously, and with humble thanks, assuring his customers that business had increased — that more resident clerks were now employed than formerly—and that, as there was more washing to be done, helpers had been hired, and an extra allowance of beer permitted. But this he promised to retrench at once, and he kept his word. The pot of beer was countermanded, the "standard" pint replaced, and this was never afterward exceeded during the old banker's lifetime.

Yankee Shrewdness Handsomely Illustrated.

WHEN the prospect of founding a large manufacturing town on the Merrimac River was in contemplation, some of the persons interested in that great commercial enterprise sent up Mr. B., a young gentleman skilled as an engineer, and who was also fond of sporting, to view the water privilege carefully, and to make inquiry as to the prices of land in the vicinity. He went with his dog, gun, and fishing tackle, and obtained board in a farmer's house, a Mr. F. He spent his time in viewing the falls, the canal, the river and grounds, with occasional fowling and fishing.

After spending some time there, in talking with the farmer, one evening he told him "that he liked the place very well, and thought he should be pleased to come and live there." The man said "he should be pleased to have him." "Well, Mr. F., what will you take for your farm?" "Why, I don't want to sell it, Mr. B.; nor would I, unless I can get twice what it is worth, as I am satisfied here, and don't want to move." "Well, what do you say it is worth, Mr. F.?" "Why, it is worth fifteen hundred dollars, and I can't sell it for less than three thousand dollars." "That is too much," said Mr. B., "I can't give that." "Very well, you need not." Here the conversation ended.

Mr. B. continued his sporting, and, having received his instructions in the course of a few days, renewed his talk with Mr. F., and said to him, "Well, Mr. F., I have made up my mind that I should like to live here very well, and though you ask so much, I will take up with your offer, and give you three thousand dollars." "Why, as to that, Mr. B., you did not take my farm when I offered it to you, and I am not willing to sell it now, for anything less than six thousand dollars." "You are joking, Mr. F.!" "Not so, Mr. B., I am in earnest, and I shan't continue my offer more than twenty-four hours."

B., finding he was determined, went off for instructions, and the next day told Mr. F. he would give him six thousand dollars. The purchase was made, deed passed, and money paid.

Some time afterward, Mr. B. asked the farmer what reason he had in the course of a few days to double the price for his farm, and to insist upon it. "Why, Mr. B., I will tell you; a day or two after I offered you the farm for three thousand dollars, I saw two men on the opposite side of the Merrimac River, sitting on a rock, and talking for some time; then they got up, and one went up the river, and the other down, and after some time they returned, seemed in earnest conversation for half an hour or more, when they arose and went away. I did not know what it meant, but I thought *something* was in the wind, and I determined, if you asked me again to sell my farm, I would demand double the price." Thus began the purchase, by Boston merchants, of the land upon which the city of Lowell has been erected.

Queen Jane's Opinion of Merchants.

JANE, of France, wife of Philip the Fair, while residing a few days at Bruges, was mortified at the splendor of the appearance of the merchants' wives, judging by that of her own. "I thought," said the elegant and royal visitor, "I had been the only queen here; but I find there are above six hundred queens in this city!"

Boyhood Struggles of a Merchant.

"I REMEMBER," said Gideon Lee, in after life, "when I was a lad living with my uncle, it was my business to feed and milk the cows. And many a time, long before light in the morning, I was started off, in the cold and snow, without shoes, to my work, and used to think it a *luxury* to warm my frozen feet on the spot just before occupied by the animal I had roused. It taught me to reflect, and to consider possibilities; and I remember asking myself, "Is it not *possible* for me to better my condition?"

Lee and His Travelling Companion.

BEFORE establishing himself permanently as a leather merchant in New York, Gideon Lee made a voyage to St. Mary's, Georgia, taking with him some small ventures of leather. On returning to New York, the vessel in which he took passage was wrecked off Cape Fear, and he barely saved himself, with the few clothes he had on. Accompanied by a faithful friend, named Smith, who had nursed him while sick at St. Mary's, he had no other means of getting to the North than to trudge it on foot. The journey was a most tedious and dismal one; several days of it were through the pine barrens of North Carolina, not meeting with a house in a day's travel. Smith was a brother Yankee, and bore the hardships with great courage and good humor. Mr. Lee used to relate an anecdote of him, illustrating this latter trait, as well as the dismal character of the country through which they were travelling. "One day," said he, "we had been trudging along, nothing to be seen but the pitch-pine forests, before and behind, and on both sides of us; shoes worn out, and our feet bleeding, myself before, and Smith following after; neither of us had exchanged a word for some time, when Smith suddenly spoke out in his nasal twang—"Mr. Lee!" "Well, Smith, well, what about it?" "I wish I could hear it thunder!" "Hear it thunder! why do you wish so?" "Because they say thunder is God's voice, and if I could only hear it thunder I should know I was on God's earth; as it is now, I don't know where I am."

First Penny Gained by a Millionaire.

An eminent English millionaire, who rose—as most of that class have—from obscurity, says that the first money he ever recollects possessing, was gained in the following manner: I went, he says, to school, a distance of three miles. One day, on my way, I picked up a horse-shoe, carried it about three miles, and sold it to a blacksmith for a penny. *That was the first penny I ever recollect possessing;* and I kept it for

some time. A few weeks after, the same man called my attention to a boy who was carrying off some dirt opposite his door; and offered, if I would beat the boy, who was somewhat bigger than myself, to give me a penny. I did so; he made a mark upon the penny, and promised that if I would bring it to him that day fortnight, he would give me another. I took it to him at the appointed time, when he at once fulfilled his promise, and I thus became possessed of three pence; since which I have never been without money, except when I gave it all away. It is hard to tell which point involves the most difficulty—the art of first obtaining a little "nest egg," or the use and management of it when once possessed.

Benevolence of Goldschmid, the Old Jew Banker.

GOLDSCHMID's wealth seemed, on some occasions, hardly greater than his pure-minded benevolence. It is related that at one time a clergyman of the Church of England, who with a family had met with some unforeseen misfortunes, was in debt the sum of four hundred and sixty pounds. From the good character and conduct of the poor debtor, a number of friends and parishioners were induced to open a subscription for making up the amount; but being unable amongst themselves to raise more than one hundred and fifty pounds, the collectors were advised to try their success by applying to the benevolent Jew banker; this was accordingly done. On application, the collectors were ordered to call in the course of a day or two, when Mr. Goldschmid promised to inquire into the state of the facts. He did so without delay, and finding it a truly worthy case, on their second application, he presented them with a check for the whole amount of the debt, desiring them, at the same time, to return the amount of subscriptions raised elsewhere to the poor debtor, to begin the world with afresh.

Reynolds, the Charitable Quaker Merchant.

THE late venerated Richard Reynolds, a Quaker merchant in Bristol, Eng., who amassed a princely fortune, was accustomed to speak of himself, in connection with his wealth and the use of it, as merely a steward of the Almighty. Thus, his entire income, after deducting the moderate expenses of his family, was devoted to charitable purposes; and he thought his round of duty still incomplete, unless he devoted his time likewise. He often deprived himself of the slumber which his years craved, to watch beside the bed of sickness and pain, and to administer consolation to those in trouble. On one occasion, he wrote to a friend in London, requesting to know what object of charity presented itself, stating that he had not spent the whole of his income. His friend informed him of a number of persons confined in prison for small debts. . *He paid the whole, and swept that miserable abode of its distressed tenants.* Most of his donations were inclosed in blank covers, bearing the modest signature of " A Friend." A lady once applied to him in behalf of an orphan, saying, " When he is old enough, I will teach him to name and thank his benefactor." " Nay," replied the Quaker, " thou art wrong. We do not thank the clouds for rain. Teach him to look higher, and thank Him who giveth both the clouds and the rain. My talent is the meanest of all talents—a little sordid dust; but as the man in the parable was accountable for his talent, so am I accountable to the great Lord of all."

Liberality of Yakooleff, the Russian Merchant.

THE rich sheet iron merchant, Ivan Alexevitch Yakooleff, at one time most generously presented to the Czar, through Count Orloff, an order on the bank for one million of silver rubles, equal to *nearly eight hundred thousand dollars*, to make good the defalcation of Politkoffsky in the Invalid Fund, thus saving present and former members of the commission, with their families, from ruin, as their estates and other property were all to be taken to indemnify the government.

Politkoffsky was president of the commission for the management of the Invalid Fund, and possessed the unbounded confidence of his associates in the commission. His death revealed the defalcation, which probably had been increasing for years until raised to above a million of silver rubles; for all which the emperor held the commission individually responsible. This would have involved most of them in ruin, but from which the noble deed of Yakooleff rescued them.

French Mercantile Independence.

SOON after Colbert came into the management of the finances of France, he sent for the principal merchants of that kingdom; and in order to ingratiate himself with them, and to acquire their confidence, he asked what he could do for them ? They unanimously answered, " Pray, sir, do nothing ! *Laissez nous faire.*" " Let us do for ourselves."

Patriotic Merchants of the Revolution.

IN that immortal Congress that adopted the Declaration of American Independence, sat many merchants. It was the merchant John Hancock, that presided over its deliberations and that first put a bold and unshrinking mercantile signature to that perilous Declaration. With him, in glory and in danger, were the merchants, Robert Morris and George Clymer, of Pennsylvania ; Elbridge Gerry and Samuel Adams, of Massachusetts ; Wil-

liam Whipple, of New Hampshire;
Philip Livingston and Francis Lewis,
of New York; Joseph Hewes, of North
Carolina; and Barton Gwinnett, of
Georgia.

Old-fashioned Shopkeepers.

FORMERLY, the English shopkeeper
took short turns before his door, crying, "What d'ye lack, sir? What d'ye
lack, madam?" and then he rehearsed
a list of the commodities he dealt in.
When he became weary, this task was
assumed by his apprentice; and thus a
London street was a Babel of strange
sounds, by which the wayfarer was
dinned at every step. The articles of
shopkeeper were often of a very hetero-
geneous description in those days of
"auld lang syne." They were huddled
in bales within the proprietor's little
shop, and in the midst of them the
wife and daughter of the master were
ensconced, plying the needle or knit-
ting wires, and eyeing the passing crowd.
In one of the plays of the time, the
merchant thus explains to his idle apprentice the way in which he grew rich:
"Did I gain my wealth by ordinaries?
No. By exchanging gold? No. By
keeping of goldsmiths' company? No.
I hired me a little shop, bought low,
took small gains, kept no debt-book,
garnished my shop—for want of plate
—with good, thrifty, wholesome sentences, as: 'Keep thy shop, and thy
shop will keep thee;' 'Light gains
make heavy purses;' ''Tis good to be
merry and wise.'" But, although the
shops and warehouses of the London
traffickers were so humble, their houses
were of a very different description; so
that, even as early as the reign of
James, the dwelling of a chief merchant rivalled the palace of a nobleman in the splendor of its furniture,
among which cushions and window
pillows of velvet and damask had
become common.

At the hour of nine, the *Bow bell*
rang, which was a signal for the employed to leave off work, and repair to
supper and to bed—a bell which the
master thought too soon, and the apprentice too late. Only a great mag-
nifico, or royal merchant, was thought
worthy the honor and privilege of pre-
fixing "Master" or "Mr." to his name,
in those times—the addition of *gentleman,* or *esquire,* would have thrown
everybody in such a man's circle into
an uproar indeed.

Looking up Foreign Merchants in England.

LONDON is mentioned by Tacitus as
the chief residence of merchants, and
the great mart of trade and commerce.
Yet, before the charter of Runnymede,
foreign merchants were permitted to
visit England only during the period
of public fairs, and were restricted to
a residence of forty days. Afterward
a German company monopolized the
trade of the country for several centuries, and its members were regularly
locked up at night—getting comfort,
however, from this species of indignity,
by keeping the whole foreign commerce
of the realm to themselves. Singularly
enough, long after the importance of
commerce had been recognized in other
countries, the people of England, now
the most mercantile on the face of the
globe, neglected the occupation which
has mainly contributed to their greatness.

Merchants of the Golden Fleece.

THERE was formerly, and for many
years resident in London, a company
of Dutch traders, located at a place
called the Stilyard; it was granted
many privileges by Henry the Eighth,
in return for its occasional loans
which enabled him to carry on his
wars. Its profits and wealth became so immense that a rival company
of traders and merchants was finally
created, under the patronage of Queen

MUTATIONS OF A MERCHANT'S LIFE.

Elizabeth, and its title was that of "The Company of English Merchant Adventurers." This company had for many years the principal trade to Germany, the Netherlands, and the adjacent countries — establishing its marts in all the principal cities of western Europe, and doing an immense business, especially in the exportation of English woollens. It became abroad what the Stilyard merchants had been in England; its credit was in repute, and its wealth famous throughout Europe. The general estimation in which it was held abroad may be judged of from the fact that Philip of Burgundy, because of the great revenue ensuing to his treasury from the duties on English woollen, adopted as the name and emblem of his favorite order of knighthood, that of "The Golden Fleece."

Who were the First Whalemen?

THE interesting question has often been discussed—"Who were the first whalemen?" In answer to this it is stated, not the sea-ruling Briton, not the hardy Dane, not the steadily enduring, amphibious Dutchman, not the bold Norwegian, child of the sea kings. No: the Spaniards — Biscayans and Bosques—first dared attack the Leviathan on the high seas, so early as 1575. True, some have tried to prove the Norwegians were the first in the field, but they have not made out a clear case. It was probably the narwhal, grampus, and other small versions of the great whale, they hunted. The old ninth century navigator, Olithore the Norwegian, whose wonderful adventures were taken down from his own lips by no less a man than King Alfred, often speaks of having slain sixty whales in two days—flatly impossible, if right whales had been in question. Thus much is certain: the first whalebone which ever found its way into England, was picked up from the wreck of a Bis-

cayan ship, in 1594; and when, at the close of the sixteenth century, the English first began to fit out whaleships, they were obliged to call on Biscayans to direct them in their preparations, and to fill the more important offices in the ship.

Mutations of a Merchant's Life : the New Orleans Sockseller.

A STRANGE old man is he, who may be seen any day, be it cold or hot, in the neighborhood of the Poydras Market, New Orleans, with a bundle of socks in his hand or on the banquette beside him. Selling socks is now his only business; yet time was when it was not so. Of the multiform mutations of human life, that old man has experienced more than mortal's share. See how he. mutters to himself, and smiles, half insanely, as he praises his wares to his real or pretended customers! One eye is closed, and the lid is swollen, and the face of the sockseller is covered with scars. These are the traces left in the old man's face by assassin burglars, who once robbed him of his goods, and left him as one dead, in his house on Circus street. It was long before this old man recovered, and when he did, his intellect was a wreck, and nothing save his business habits was left to keep him from total insanity. Since then he has followed the business of selling socks.

But it were unjust to the old man to give so imperfect an abstract of his history. Let us roll back the tide of time some quarter of a century, and a tall, fine-looking gentleman may be observed walking down Broadway, in New York. Fair ladies ogle him as he passes, and feel flattered when he smiles on them. And is it strange? for the smiler of *that* day is a wholesale merchant, of princely fortune. After that changes come. The merchant, broken in fortune, removed to New Orleans, and his remains may now be found in the muttering sockseller of

9

the Poydras Market. There is a strange tale of love connected with the old man; but here let the veil drop.

Recovering a Wasted Fortune.

It is related of a young man, that, having fallen heir to a large estate, he engaged in a career of profligacy and wasteful expenditures, until he found himself utterly impoverished and destitute, cast off by his former associates, and having no resource to which to look for relief. His misery was so great that he resolved upon self-destruction, and wandering forth to find some suitable place for the execution of his desperate purpose, found himself on an eminence which overlooked the estates that once belonged to him. He sat down and thought of his folly. A long time he mused in silence. When he arose, a new purpose had taken possession of him. He said to himself, "Those estates shall again be mine," and at once he set about carrying out the plan he had thus cogitated in silence.

As he passed along, he saw some coal lying before a door, and he asked to be employed to carry it into the house. His wish was gratified, and after finishing his task, he was master of a shilling. He soon earned another by a similar process, and when hungry he satisfied his cravings in the most frugal manner. Month after month, year after year, he pursued his plan, and in process of time achieved his end. The estates once forfeited by his prodigality were regained by decision, energy, concentration of purpose upon a single end.

Fortunes at a Single Blow.

"I find," said a shrewd merchant, "I make most money when I am least anxious about it." There is practical philosophy in this remark. Caution,

prudence, sagacity, and deliberation are all necessary to business success. Some men, it is true, get rich suddenly, but the great majority do not, and cannot. Bonaparte once said, "I have no idea of a merchant's acquiring a fortune as a general wins a battle—at a single blow." Such fortunes too often vanish suddenly.

Merchant Patrons of Literature.

There are honored names, and not a few—such as Peabody, Bates, Girard, Lawrence, Perkins, Cooper, Astor, &c. —that might be dwelt upon in proof of the connection that may and does exist between trade and letters. Prominent among those of a former day, were Cosmo and Lorenzo de Medici, the wealthiest men of Europe in their day. And yet they were merchants and bankers, and were preëminent still for their generosity and devotion to letters. To this merchant family belongs the lasting honor of having restored the empire of science and true taste to Europe, after a dreary night of darkness. By their efforts, many valuable manuscripts were saved from total destruction. The Medici thought the discovery of a manuscript equivalent to the conquest of a kingdom. It is doubtful, indeed, if we are not indebted to them for most of the perfect copies now known of the Greek and Roman classics. It is remarkable, too, that they lived at a time when they were enabled to find and preserve so many valuable manuscripts just before the invention of printing, and previously to the wonderful extension of trade and commerce. The Medici were by education and pursuit merchants, yet they devoted their energies for a long lifetime, not only to extend their vast commercial relations, but also to collect and found great libraries, establish galleries, and encourage the fine arts. The names of Cooper, Astor, Perkins, Lawrence, Corcoran, Peabody, &c., of the present day, rank in the same noble category.

Napoleon and Byron on Trading.

NAPOLEON openly expressed his aversion to commerce and those engaged in it. When a deputation of commercial men came out from Antwerp to welcome him on his approach to that city, he met them with the words, " I don't like merchants ! A merchant is a man who would sell his country for a shilling !"—" Je n'aime pas les négociants ? Un négociant est un homme qui vendrait sa patrie pour un petit écu !" He despised the walks of trade, and in one of his consultations with the banker Ouvrard, uttered the reproach that he had degraded loyalty to the level of trade.

The curious opinion that there is something derogatory in trade, was exemplified, too, even in a distinguished British statesman, at the Congress of Vienna, who asserted, in the presence of the representatives of Europe, that England was not dependent on commerce. This was intended as an offset to the sneer of Napoleon against the "nation of traders," and arose from a desire to " sink the shop " before the plumed and epauletted array which dazzled and bewildered the civilian into an ungrateful forgetfulness of the very class, without whose aid emperors and kings, if suffered to retain power at all, would have dwindled to provincial governors.

Byron said, " If Commerce fills the purse, she clogs the brain ; " and yet he himself bravely encountered that peril by trafficking his own verses with a thrift that would have done credit to Baillie Nicol Jarvie, and a shrewd attention to detail which might have won the heart of Tim Linkinwater. His practice refuted his theory, and his driving a sharp bargain, at the highest market rates, for the proceeds of his genius, resulted in no apparent diminution of his acuteness.

Mercantile Character Comparatively Estimated.

A SHOPKEEPER at Doncaster had for his trading virtues obtained the name of the *little rascal*. A stranger once frankly asked him why this appellation had been given to him. " To distinguish me from the rest of my trade," quoth he, " who are all *great* rascals !"

Money Enough to Break On.

ONE of the richest men in the wealthy town of Zanesville, O., is Mr. S., who acquired some hundreds of thousands of dollars by his industry and business tact. He is a pleasant sort of a man, very nervous, and somewhat eccentric. Being one of the first settlers, he has not brought around his family those ruinous influences that so frequently destroy rich families. When his son William came of maturity, he asked the " old man " for capital to start on. The father gave the son $10,000, saying that it was enough for him *to break on.* " Bill " took the $10,000, and instead of breaking, acquired a fortune in ten years, equal to that of his father. He is an extensive private banker, engaged in milling, &c. Occasionally the youth ventures into deep water, and the father undertakes to restrain him ; but Bill's reply is, " Perhaps you want the ten thousand dollars ; if so, the chinks are ready for you, principal and interest."

Mohammedan's Reason for not Storing Goods.

SOME years ago, a Philadelphia merchant sent a cargo of goods to Constantinople. After the supercargo saw the bales and boxes safely landed, he inquired where they could be stored.

" Leave them here—it won't rain tonight," was the reply.

" But I dare not leave them thus exposed ; some of the goods might be stolen," said the supercargo.

The Mohammedan merchant burst into a loud laugh, as he replied— "Don't be alarmed, there ain't a Christian within fifty miles of here."

Value of a Good Credit.

A CELEBRATED gambler, of great address, but notorious bad character, meeting with a mercantile gentleman of the highest reputation for honor and veracity—one of that exalted class, whose "word is as good as their bond," observed to him, "Sir, I would give fifty thousand dollars for your good name." "Why so?" demanded the wondering merchant. "Because," replied the gambler, "I could make one hundred thousand dollars out of it."

Merchants and Legislators.

THAT the East India Company, at an early age of its existence, entertained a due consideration of the dignity of commerce, is evident from the bearing of Sir Josiah Child, the able manager of the affairs of the company at home, during part of the reigns of Charles II. and James II. Mr. Vaux, the manager in India, on being exhorted to "act with vigor, and to carry whatever instructions he might receive from home into immediate effect," answered—"that he should endeavor to acquit himself with integrity and justice, and would make the laws of his country the rule of his conduct." Sir Josiah replied, telling Mr. Vaux roundly that he expected his orders were to be his rules, and not the laws of England, which were a heap of nonsense, compiled by a few ignorant country gentlemen, who hardly knew how to make laws for the good government of their own private families, much less for the regulating of companies and foreign commerce!

Quaker Merchant's Idea of Privateering.

DURING the war between France and England, in 1780, Mr. Fox, a merchant of Falmouth, Eng., had a share in a ship, which the other owners determined to fit out as a letter of marque, very much against the wishes of Mr. F., who was a consistent Quaker. The ship's fortune resulted in the capture of two French merchantmen, and the share of the prize-money which fell to Mr. F., was about eight thousand dollars. At the close of the war, Mr. Fox sent his son to Paris, with the eight thousand dollars, which he faithfully refunded to the owners of the vessels captured. The young merchant, to discover the owners, was obliged to advertise for them in the Paris papers. In consequence of this advertisement, he received a letter from a small village near Nismes, in the province of Languedoc, acquainting him that a society of Quakers was established in that remote part of France, consisting of about one hundred families; that they were so much struck with this rare instance of generosity in one of their sect, that they were desirous to open a correspondence with him in England; which immediately commenced—the first correspondence of the kind which the Society had initiated for upward of a century.

Indian's Mode of Judging a Trader.

AN old trader among the Northern Indians, who had some years ago established himself on the Wisseoa, tells a good story, with a mercantile moral worth remembering, about his first trials of trading with his red customers. The Indians, who evidently wanted goods, and had both money (which they called *shune ah*) and furs, flocked about his store, and examined his goods, but for some time bought nothing. Finally, their chief, with a large body of his followers, visited him, and accosting him with, " How do, Thomas? Show me goods; I take four yard calico, three coonskins for yard, pay you by'm by—to-morrow," received his goods and left. Next day he returned with his whole band, his blankets stuffed with coonskins. "American man, I pay now; with this he began counting out the skins until he had handed him over twelve. Then after a moment's pause he offered the trader one more, remarking, as he did so, "That's it." I handed it back, said the trader, telling him he owed me but twelve, and I would not cheat him. We continued to pass it back and forth, each one asserting that it belonged to the other. At last, he appeared to be satisfied, gave me a scrutinizing look, placed the skin in the folds of his blanket, stepped to the door, and gave a yell, and cried at the top of his voice, "Come, come, and trade with the pale face, he no cheat Indian; his heart big." He then turned to me and said: "You take that skin; I tell Indian no trade with you—drive you off like a dog; but now you Indian's friend, and me yours." Before sundown I was waist deep in furs, and loaded down with cash.

Merchants getting to be Gentlemen.

By a statute of King Athelstane, grandson of Alfred, it was provided that any merchant who made three voyages, on his own account, beyond the British Channel, should be entitled to the privilege of a thane—that is, be regarded as a gentleman.

Not ashamed of Work—Astor's Diligence.

Some one has said, that the secret of success in business is to be beforehand with your affairs. No one was better able to fulfil this condition than Astor. Always an early riser, he generally left business at two o'clock in the afternoon. He was never at rest, but seldom in haste. His forces, his resources, were always marshalled and in order. An enthusiastic critic of this great business genius, declared that Mr. Astor could command an army of half a million men.

His unresting industry was not hampered by false pride. He would work with his own hands, and he was not ashamed of workmen's garb. He knew that the master's example must guide, that the master's eye must be on the work if it is to be well done. If his furs required sorting and beating, he would do it himself with the best of his men, and was as ready to work when worth millions as when struggling for success. No humble disciple of poor Richard was ever more plodding diligent in the practice of frugality and thrift, which the spirit of mere speculation is prone to overlook, than he.

Opulent New York Merchants.

Preserved Fish commenced life as an apprentice to a blacksmith, and his next situation was that of a seaman on board a whaling ship. From being a hand before the mast, he rose to be a mate, and finally commander, and in this hazardous pursuit amassed the foundation of his great fortune.

Saul Alley was bound, when a small boy, apprentice to a coachmaker, and during his apprenticeship his father died, leaving him totally dependent on his own exertions, so that the very clothes he wore he was obliged to earn by toiling extra hours, after the regular time of leaving off work had passed; the foundation of his fortune he acquired by the exercise of frugality and prudence, while a journeyman mechanic.

Cornelius W. Lawrence was a farmer's boy, and worked many a long day in rain and sunshine on Long Island; there were few lads, within twenty miles of him, that could mow a wider swath, or turn a better furrow.

Great Deeds of European Merchants.

THE tact and generosity of an English merchant, Thomas Sutton, are said to have materially aided in the defeat of the Spanish Armada, and thereby saved British liberty from torture and thumbscrews.

A fear of the power of merchants stopped Charles the Fifth from establishing the inquisition in Antwerp; while a merchant of that city lent this king a million of money, and, at an entertainment which he gave them, burnt the bond in a fire of cinnamon—at that time a most costly spice.

A merchant of France raised an army at his own expense, and lent millions to his country.

A Georgian of low birth was able, by the quiet arts of commerce, to obtain an immense revenue, and to keep six thousand troops in his pay.

Russia, with all her extent of land, was as nothing, until that half Goth, Peter, surnamed by his countrymen, "the Great," promoted the advancement of commerce. He gave his personal attention to the building of ships, training of seamen, opening of harbors, the establishment of ports, and the furtherance of commercial enterprise.

Peremptory Refusal of Hope & Co. to do Business with Girard.

GIRARD learned one of the most trenchant lessons in his eventful mercantile life, from his favorite correspondents in Europe, Messrs. Hope & Co., of Amsterdam.

Notwithstanding the reliance he placed in them, he had sent a Quaker, by the name of Hutchinson, to Amsterdam, with explicit instructions to watch those gentlemen closely, and see that they accounted for the real prices received by them for his consignments, etc., etc.

It was a rule in the house of Messrs. Hope, to compute one eighth per cent. more than the daily noted rate of exchange, when sending the regular receipts to bank, and this was done to cover a variety of minute office expenses, which could not be brought into a stated account. Thus, for instance, Mr. Hutchinson was informed that they had sold a thousand bags of coffee, at so-and-so much per cent. Hereupon, that gentleman came, next day, to the counting room, interrupted Mr. Labouchère in his meditations, and, running his finger along the printed price current he held in his hand, pointed out to him that the rate must be put at one eighth per cent. less. The oft-repeated hints Mr. Labouchère had given the young Quaker, who invariably came in with his hat on his head, and, without permission, marched directly up to the door, and pushed on into the private counting room—that sanctum sanctorum of Dutch merchants—had all proved of no avail; at last they got to let him stand there, without paying any attention to what he had to say.

Under these circumstances, Hutchinson wrote to Girard, who, in response, at once dictated, for his benefit, the most offensive letter to Messrs. Hope, which finally decided the latter to let him know, unmistakably, that there existed so wide a difference between their ways of doing business and his, and all attempts to teach him better had so signally failed, that, for the sake of their own comfort and tranquillity, they should be compelled to decline any further transactions with him. Then there came from Girard a sort of apology, a promise to manage differently in future, etc., etc. But the house in Amsterdam remained firm in the resolution they had taken, offering, however, to do him the favor of recommending to him, as his future correspondents, Messrs. Daniel Crammelin & Sons, their neighbors.

The astonishment of the latter gentlemen themselves, when the first important consignments began to reach them from Girard, and the surprise of the whole Amsterdam Bourse, that any one should reject such business as his, requiring no advances, may be readily conceived.

Mohammedan Mercantile Morality.

IN some of its phases, Mohammedan mercantile morality exceeds in its scrupulousness that of any other people, whatever their religious character or creed. A mercantile firm in Salonica had bills to a large amount on the principal inhabitants and merchants of the place, which, with their books and papers, were destroyed by fire. On the day following, a prominent Turk, who was largely in their debt, went in person and told them that, having heard that their papers had been destroyed, he had brought a copy of his account with them and fresh bills for the amount which was their due. This example was followed by *all* the Turkish debtors to them. It does not appear to be intimated that this course was one that they had ever learned from the *Christian* traders in their country.

Commencing in the Subcellar.

ONE of the wealthiest merchants of New York relates how he commenced business in that city. He says: I entered a store, and asked if a clerk was not wanted. "*No!*" in a rough tone, was the answer, all being too busy to bother with me—when I reflected, that if they did not want a clerk, they might want a laborer; but I was dressed too fine for that. I went to my lodgings, put on a rough garb, and the next day went into the same store and demanded if they did not want a porter, and again, "No, sir," was the response— when I exclaimed, in despair, almost, "a laborer? Sir, I will work at any wages. Wages is not my object—I must have employ, and I want to be useful in business."

These last remarks attracted their attention; and in the end I was hired as a laborer in the basement and subcellar at a very low pay, scarcely enough to keep body and soul together.

In the basement and subcellar, I soon attracted the attention of the counting house and chief clerk. I saved enough for my employers in little things usually wasted, to pay my wages ten times over, and they soon found it out. I did not let anybody about commit petty larcenies, without remonstrance and threats of exposure, and real exposure if remonstrance would not do. I did not ask for any ten-hour law. If I was wanted at three in the morning, I never growled, but told everybody to go home, "and I will see everything right." I loaded off at daybreak packages for the morning boats, or carried them myself. In short, I soon became—as I meant to be—indispensable to my employers, and I rose, and rose, until I became head of the house, with money enough for any luxury or any position a mercantile man may desire for himself and family in a great city.

Romance of Trade—"Blackguard Snuff."

LUNDY FOOT, the celebrated snuff-manufacturer of Dublin, originally kept a small tobacconist's shop at Limerick, Ireland. One night his house, which was uninsured, was burnt to the ground. As he contemplated the smoking ruins on the following morning, in a state bordering on despair, some of the poor neighbors, groping among the embers for what they could find, stumbled upon several canisters of unconsumed but half-baked snuff, which they tried, and found so grateful to their noses, that they loaded their waistcoat pockets with the spoil.

Lundy Foot, roused from his stupor, at length imitated their example, and took a pinch of his own property, when he was instantly struck by the superior pungency and flavor it had acquired from the great heat to which it had been exposed. Treasuring up this valuable hint, he took another house, in a place called "Black Yard," and preparing a large oven for the purpose, set diligently about the manufacture of that high-dried commodity, which soon became known as "Black Yard Snuff" —a term subsequently corrupted into the more familiar word "Blackguard." Making his customers pay liberally through the nose for one of the most "distinguished" kinds of snuff in the world, he soon raised the price of his production, took a larger house in the city of Dublin, and was often heard to say—"I made a very handsome fortune by being, as I supposed, utterly ruined!" When he was rich enough to own and use a carriage, he applied to Lord Norbury for an appropriate motto for his panels. The witty judge suggested the phrase—Latin or English as you please—"*Quid rides?*"

"Everything by Turns"—Girard's Example.

NOTWITHSTANDING the common adage, that a business man who puts too many irons in the fire, is not likely to get any one of them red hot, it seems to have been otherwise in the career of Stephen Girard. Thus, if one operation miscarried, with that versatility so peculiar to his countrymen he tried another, and another, until he tried the right one. This change of business gave rise to the story that he was at one time engaged in the manufacture of hair powder, as a partner of Boldasky & Co., who, about the year 1786, carried on that business, near Germantown, Pa. But whether or not Mr. G. had a concern in that establishment, the books of the latter show large accounts with Stephen and John Girard for that article, which they purchased for exportation to St. Domingo and the Southern markets.

It is certain that Girard left nothing untried, by which to make his fortune. Even the occupation of a merchant at length began to lose some of its charms for Girard, and failed to satisfy that boundless craving of his mind, which is so peculiar a faculty of genius. Thus it was that he turned banker; and then, this failing to yield him full satisfaction, he becomes a great builder, filling up streets, and skirting whole squares with his mansions, palaces and stores, careful to learn something as he went along, of the arts of those several professions, from the construction of a ship and the building of a palace, down to the erection of a wharf, the paving of a street, or the setting of a curb stone; adding to all this, that of being one of the first farmers, graziers, and butchers, in the State. A gentleman once went to him on business, but was refused an interview, because he was cutting up his hogs for his winter provisions—this job, however, being but small game for Girard; for, when he assisted to butcher on his farm, *fifty oxen* at a time sometimes smoked beneath his knife; or he slew a whole hecatomb, glorying, like a hero, in the gore around him. When to these varied occupations are added his knowledge of horticulture, his skill in planting and gardening, his extensive aviaries, together with the fact that he was an excellent nurse, and prided himself on his success as a doctor,—perhaps few men have ever lived, who could be quoted as his equal, or superior, for the variety as well as excellence and success of his pursuits, nor would it be safe for men in general thus to diversify their occupations. Girard was a man of such remarkable executive capacity, that it seemed almost impossible for him to touch anything without its turning into gold.

"Stick to Your Last."

THIS phrase, though seemingly referring to the disciples of St. Crispin, is of general application, and is accepted as such. Zadock Pratt was originally a tanner by trade,—a man of quaint manners and speech, and of very strong common sense. A speculator was once showing him a new method of tanning, by the use of which, he argued, great quantities of money might be made. Pratt told him he had no reason to doubt his assertion, but he was making money enough; and that he—the speculator—would better find some one who was not doing so well. He made it an invariable rule to resist all attempts to allure him from his legitimate business, and by this undeviating application rolled up a splendid fortune. The well known story of Plautus, the Roman comic writer, is an apt though ancient illustration of this principle of "sticking to your business." He acquired a very handsome fortune by his comedies. He was afterward tempted to embark in trade, and met with such severe losses that he was in consequence reduced to the necessity of working in a mill, as a day laborer, in order to obtain a support.

Controversy among Wine Dealers.

THE question, whether the wines of Champagne or Burgundy were entitled to the preference, was, during the reign of Louis the Fourteenth, a matter of sharp controversy among the wine dealers and their friends of that day. The celebrated Charles Coffin, head of the University of Beauvais, published, during this controversy, a pungent classical ode, in which Champagne is extolled, and its superiority vindicated, with a spirit, vivacity, and delicacy worthy of the most important theme. For this, the citizens of Rheims were not ungrateful to the poet, but liberally rewarded him with an appropriate and munificent donation of the wine he had so happily panegyrized. Gréneau wrote an ode in praise of Burgundy; but, unlike the subject which it treated, it was flat and insipid, and failed to procure any recompense to its author. The different pieces in this amusing controversy were collected and published in octavo, at Paris, in 1712. Erasmus attributes the restoration of his health to his having drunk liberally of Burgundy, and has eulogized it in the most extravagant terms. An epistle of his, quoted by Le Grand d'Aussy, shows that Falstaff and he would have spent an evening together more agreeably than might have been supposed.

Little Too Candid.

DURING a political campaign in Virginia, a democratic speaker was addressing a large audience, and descanting with great vehemence upon the proscriptive tenets of know-nothingism with regard to foreigners, when his eye fell upon a little German Jew, a peddler of ready-made clothing, who seemed to be very much impressed with the argument of the orator, and greedily swallowing everything he uttered. This was too good an opportunity not to be made the most of. Looking the peddler in the eye, he exclaimed:

"Furriner, didn't *you* come to this country to escape from tyrannical, downtrodden, and oppressed Europe? Didn't *you* flee to these happy shores to live in a land of freedom, where the great right of suffrage is guaranteed to all? *Didn't* you, furriner?"

He paused for a reply; when the little peddler squeaked out—

"No, sur; I comes to dis countrie to sell sheap ready-made clothes."

The astonishment of the orator, the shouts and roars of the multitude, cannot be described. The speech was finished, and the orator quit the rostrum, heartily cursing all "furriners" generally, and clothes peddlers in particular.

Hinges upon which Trade Swings.

A GRAVE discussion was once overheard, concerning shop-door steps, in which a young beginner was solemnly recommended not to adopt more than one step into his shop. People, it was said,—that is, commercial human nature,—wouldn't take the trouble to mount up two or three steps, when, by going a little farther on, a more easily accessible establishment might invite them in.

The same idea is involved in the widely-opened, easily-revolving door of our modern shops. Be the winter's frost ever so sharp, or the cold wind ever so keen, it is a standing rule with certain dealers, that the shop-entrance be never hindered by a closed door, or only upon the condition that a porter stand in continued readiness to bow in or bow out the purchasers.

There can be no doubt that, upon a hinge as slight even as this, many a man's fortune or ill-fortune has swung.

Expectations against Results.

A GOOD anecdote is told by an "old hand," illustrating the probability of business sales:

A young friend of ours called on us the other day in high glee; he was about concluding arrangements with two others to embark in the jobbing trade, and was quite sanguine in his expectation of brilliant results. As we did not express full faith in his anticipations, he rather chided us for our doubts, whereupon we questioned him a little as to his prospects. At our suggestion, he took pen and paper, and put down first of all his proposed expenses. We could see that he had not done this before, as he seemed quite startled to find that, even at the moderate estimates he had made, the total expenses for rent, clerk hire, and living of the several partners, amounted to the snug sum of $8,200.

"Now for the amount of business!" said we.

"Oh, as to that," he replied, "we hope to sell $300,000 worth of goods per annum."

"But what amount of trade do all of you at present influence?" we asked. "Make now a careful estimate of the business you can rely upon with some degree of certainty." He did so, and, to his surprise, it did not quite reach $125,000.

"Now, what profit can you average upon this?" After some debate, this was set down at seven and one-half per cent. This gave the sum of $9,375.

"Now, what shall we call the losses?" The latter was settled at two and one half per cent. on sales, amounting to $3,125, leaving the net income at $6,250, or $1,950 *less* than enough to pay his estimated expenses. He left us, proposing to show the estimate to his colleagues. He did so, and after figuring awhile without arriving at any more satisfactory result, they finally abandoned the undertaking. There is no doubt that, if all, when about to embark in trade, would thus boldly look at the figures, instead of closing their eyes and *hoping* for the best, there would be fewer failures among business men, and there would be less complaint that "trade is overdone."

Getting the Hang of Mercantile Transactions.

AN amusing account of the manner in which Vincent Nolte got "posted" in certain mercantile transactions, while holding a certain relation to the great banker Labouchère, is thus given by himself: This canvassing for consignments from the United States, and the kind of uneasiness which Mr. Labouchère betrayed, whenever his neighbors, Messrs. Hottinguers & Co., a branch of the Paris banking house, received important consignments from the United States—frequently whole fleets at a time—were to me inexplicable; so I asked my chief, what the real cause of this anxiety could be. His reply invariably was, " Large advances, probably ! " My next question was : " And who makes these advances ? how are they made ? " His answer : " I am ignorant of that ! " or, " I do not know." At length, however, I learned from one of the Hottinguer clerks, with whom I had struck up a friendship, that the house of Messrs. Baring accepted bills drawn as an advance, in the United States, took out the insurance, and after sale took charge of the remittances for the merchandise. From this information, I for the first time got a key to this whole system, so universally understood at the present day.

Sabbath Experiences of a Shipmaster.

I was in command of a vessel, says Capt. G., of W—, Mass., engaged in the hide trade, between N— — and a port in Brazil.

The custom of the Brazilian port, was to load vessels on the Sabbath. This labor was performed by gangs of negroes, under the direction of stevedores. These stevedores were few in number, and, in times of great hurry of business, in order to an equitable division of their services, the vessels were accustomed to take their turns in the order in which they were reported as ready to receive cargo. If, when the time came round for a particular vessel to load, she was not ready, her name was transferred to the bottom of the list. It was my lot to experience some of the effects of this custom.

My turn came to load. The work commenced and continued till Saturday night, when I ordered the hatches closed, and forbid any work being done on board till Monday morning. The stevedore and his gang, muttering curses, left the vessel, threatening to do no more work on board.

Monday came. I made application to the commission merchant, and was informed that I had lost my turn in loading, and must wait until it came round again, and that the stevedore and his gang had gone on board another vessel.

To aggravate my disappointment, I found that a hostile feeling had sprung up against me, and was participated in by all around. The merchant was studiously polite and respectful as before, but no longer familiar. Masters of vessels avoided my society. Evil disposed persons busied themselves in secretly doing me injuries, such as cutting my rigging in the night time, and the like. And thus things went on, until our turn came round again, when, there being no other vessel ready to load, we were left to do our own work in our own way. The loss of time, occasioned by the refusal to load on the Sabbath, amounted to several weeks. Whether it was actually a loss, or not, the result will show.

It was now Saturday night again, the loading of the ship was completed, and we were ready for sea. With the Sabbath came a fresh and fair wind ; but instead of sailing, the Bethel flag was hoisted, as an invitation for all the shipmates to come on board and observe the day in the good old way.

Monday morning, early, we were under sail for the lower harbor, several miles distant. On our way, we passed two brigs aground, with lighters alongside discharging their hides, in order to lighten them and get them off. They left the harbor on the Sabbath, and here they were. On reaching the lower harbor we found, to our surprise, lying at anchor, upward of forty sail of shipping waiting for a wind. · Among them were all the vessels that had cleared for the last month or more, including every vessel that had obtained an advantage over us in respect to loading.

We had now to obtain a pilot and get to sea, when the wind came fair and before it had spent itself. These were by no means matters easy to be accomplished. Pilots were few, and vessels many, and here, too, the principle of rotation was rigidly enforced. The winds, meanwhile, when fair, were shortlived and feeble, and the bar at the entrance of the harbor was too dangerous to pass without a pilot. A pilot who had been on a long visit to the interior, returned to the seaboard and resumed his duties on the very day when we reached the outer harbor, and presenting himself on board, offered to pilot us to sea.

Tuesday morning found us, with a fair wind, a pilot on board, and under way at daylight. We were the second vessel over the bar, and among the first to arrive in the United States. The getting out of cargo, its exposure and sale, were matters of no little interest. Our own cargo, owing to the delay in getting it on board, received unusual attention at our hands and was in perfect shipping order when stowed away, and came out in the same good condition. The cargoes of the other vessels came out very differently, with a loss in some cases of twenty, thirty, and even fifty per cent. This loss was occasioned in part by hurrying the hides on board in the first instance without their being thoroughly dried, in order to greater despatch, and in part to the unusual detention of the vessels at the port of loading. From these two causes combined, and the activity of the vermin that took possession of the hides, and riddled them through and through, several of those voyages turned out disastrous failures.

Celebrated Question of Conscience in Commerce put by Cicero.

ONE of the most celebrated points as affecting the obligations of one person or party toward another, in trade, is that put by Cicero, as follows : A corn merchant of Alexandria, he says, arrived at Rhodes in a time of great scarcity, with a cargo of grain, and with knowledge that a number of other vessels laden with corn, had already sailed from Alexandria for Rhodes, and which he had passed on the passage—was he bound in conscience to inform the buyers of that fact ? Cicero decides that he was. Other writers on the morals of trade decide in the negative.

Arab Honesty in Business Transactions.

WHEN Mr. Layard, the traveller, was at some brackish springs called Belaisse, he was awakened by the alarm that two of his horses were stolen. Sabuman, under whose escort he was travelling, felt his honor so much concerned, that he wandered till daybreak in search of the thieves. Finally, having tracked them, and pronounced with unerring sagacity of what tribe they were, he made an oath that the missing property should be returned. After six weeks' search and extensive journeyings, he fulfilled his vow and brought back the animals, without asking—apparently without permitting, any reward.

Suthun, another companion of Mr. Layard, was often sent across the desert, with perhaps three thousand dollars in money, and always with perfect confidence—his only reward being an occasional silk dress, or a few camelloads of corn for his family.

In commercial or business transactions the same holds true. Of late years, the wool of the Bedouin sheep has been in demand in the European market, and a large trade is even now going on in the region of the explorations. Money is generally advanced by the English representative, mostly before sheep-shearing, without any written or other guaranty, to tribes of whom nothing is heard after the payment until the receipt of the produce, amounting sometimes to thousands of dollars in value. And on the part of the Arabs such scrupulous honesty is observed, that one Bedouin made the whole journey from Bagdad to Mosul, solely to pay the balance of an old wool account not amounting to so much as one dollar.

Business versus Disease.

A TRADESMAN who had acquired a large fortune in London, retired from business, and went to reside in Worcester. His mind, without its usual occupation, and having nothing else to supply its place, preyed upon itself, so that existence became a torment to him. At last he was seized with the stone; and a friend, who found him in one of its severest attacks, having expressed his condolence—"No, no, sir," said he, "do not pity me; for I assure you what I now suffer is ease compared with the torment of mind from which it relieves me."

Retiring from Business—Engaging to Blow the Bellows.

THE misery of having "nothing to do" is oftentimes greater than that which comes from having "nothing to wear"—poetry to the contrary notwithstanding. A London tradesman, who had risen to wealth from the humble ranks of life, resolved to retire to the country to enjoy, undisturbed, the remaining years of his life. For this purpose, he purchased an estate and mansion in a sequestered corner in the country, and took possession of it. While the alterations and improvements which he directed to be made were going on, the noise of hammers, saws, chisels, etc., around him, kept him in good spirits. But when his improvements were finished, and his workmen discharged, the stillness everywhere disconcerted him, and he felt quite miserable. He was obliged to have recourse to a smith upon his estate, for relief to his mind, and he actually engaged to blow the bellows for a certain number of hours in the day. In a short

time, however, even this ceased to afford him the relief he desired; he returned to London, and acted as a gratuitous assistant to his own clerk, to whom he had given up his business.

Too Close Application to Business.

MR. RIPPON, late chief cashier of the Bank of England, furnishes an extraordinary instance of the manner in which the mind becomes warped by continual and close application to business. He always declared he felt himself nowhere so happy as in his business, and, though for upward of fifty years in the bank, he never solicited but one holiday, and that was on the recommendation of his medical adviser, on account of ill health. The permission for leave was instantly granted, and he left London with the intention of being absent a fortnight; but the *ennui* of an idle life and the want of his usual occupation so preyed upon his spirits, that he actually returned to his post at the expiration of three days, stating as a reason, that green fields and country scenery had no charms for him. Mr. R. was always remarkable for his sound judgment, preciseness, and extreme punctuality; and his long services and habits of economy enabled him to leave behind him a very large fortune.

Lending a Helping Hand: Abbott Lawrence.

THE genial nature and courteous manners of Abbott Lawrence were carried with him in the marts of trade. His unselfishness exhibited itself in his readiness to share with his contemporaries in trade the benefits of honorable enterprise. An anecdote in point will illustrate this, though only one of scores of the same kind that might be told of that noble and elegant merchant. A trader called at his counting room one day, and remarked to him that flannels were selling low, very low. "Buy, then," said Mr. Lawrence.

"I am afraid to; besides, I have not the money," said the other. "*Go buy them!* I will back you and share with you in the speculation"—was the ready and accommodating reply.

Agreement for a Loan.

A MAN in the town of D., years ago, went to a merchant in Portsmouth, N. H., who was also president of a bank, and stated that he lived on a farm, the home of his father, which had descended to him by right of inheritance; that this, his only property, was mortgaged for one thousand dollars to a merciless creditor, and that the time of redemption would be out in a week. He closed by asking for a loan to the amount of his debt, for which he offered to re-mortgage his farm.

Merchant: I have no money to spare; and if I could relieve you now, a similar difficulty would probably arise in a year or two.

Applicant: No; I would make every exertion—I think I could clear it.

Merchant: Well, if you will obey my directions, I can put you in a way to get the money; but it will require the greatest prudence and resolution. If you can get a good endorser on a note, you shall have money from the bank, and you can mortgage your farm to the endorser, for his security. You must pay in one hundred dollars every sixty days. Can you do it?

Applicant: I can get Mr. —— for endorser, and I can raise the one hundred dollars for every payment but the first.

Merchant: Then borrow one hundred dollars more than you want, and let it lie in the bank; you will lose only one dollar interest. But mind, in order to get along, you must spend nothing, buy nothing; make a box to hold all the money you get, as a sacred deposit.

The applicant departed. The note was discounted, and the payment punctually made. In something more than

two years, he came again into the store of the merchant, and exclaimed, "I am a free man—I don't owe any man ten dollars—but look at me!" He was indeed embrowned with labor; and his clothes, from head to foot, were a tissue of darns and patches. "My wife looks worse than I do." "So you have cleared your farm," said the merchant. "Yes," answered the other, "and *now I know how to get another one.*"

Late at a Dinner Party—George Hudson.

ON a certain occasion, George Hudson was engaged to preside at a dinner of fellow railway magnates; the guests were assembled, but Mr. Hudson was wanting—and, as he was always the most important person wherever he went, great was the concern felt lest he should not come at all. The explanation was simple, and much to the credit of his business qualities. It appears that as the railway chief drove to his appointment, his route lay by a new line, at the various posts of which the employés were ordered to be present. Unhappily, one of these was away; and, incensed at this neglect, Mr. Hudson ordered his instant dismissal. As he proceeded, it occurred to him that the punishment was harsh, that the man was a poor man, that he had a large family, and he determined to annul the sentence at some future period. He proceeded along yet further; and when he thought of the distress which the man would bear to his house, he drove back many miles to revoke his order—and he did revoke it, though he kept his courtiers waiting at the magnificent feast given in honor of himself.

Girard Trying to Raise Five Dollars.

AT the age of about thirty years, Girard's occupation is supposed to have alternated between that of captain and merchant, occasionally making a voyage to New Orleans or St. Domingo, and then remaining at home to dispose of his cargo and adjust his accounts for a second voyage. It was while prosecuting one of these adventures, that he was met at the capes of Delaware, by Capt. James King, of Philadelphia, and who has given the following curious and remarkable account of Girard's condition at that time:

On the first day of May, 1776 (says Capt. King), I was chased by a British man-of-war. I ran my vessel ashore, all sails standing, about eight miles southwest of Cape Henlopen. Whilst waiting at Lewistown for an opportunity to come up, the men-of-war were coming in and out every day, so as to prevent us from sailing. One morning I saw a sloop at anchor, within the cape, with a white flag flying. I applied to Major Fisher, who was then commandant, to send a pilot aboard of her. "No, no, King," said he, "that is only a British decoy to get a pilot; I shall not trust them." I then went over the cape, opposite to where the sloop lay at anchor. I hailed her, waved my hat, and did everything that I could, in order to attract their attention; they answered me in the same manner, but the surf made such a noise as to prevent us from understanding each other, from which I concluded to turn back, but, as I was returning, discovered a boat rowing toward me with a flag on a staff. I waited till they came up, when they told me that they had orders from Major Fisher, that if I would risk myself with them, to go alongside of the sloop, they would convey me; and if not, to return. I immediately stepped into their boat, and we proceeded to the sloop. On inquiring where she was from, informed me (in French) that they were from New Orleans and bound to St. Pierres, but that they had lost themselves. I explained to the captain, whose name was Girard, the dangerous situation they were in, and that if he

attempted to go out he certainly would be captured, as the men-of-war were in and out every day.

"My God, what shall I do?" said Girard.

"You have no chance but to push right up to Philadelphia," I replied.

"How shall I do to get there? I have no pilot and don't know the way."

"These men are all pilots," I answered.

"Oh, my good friend," said he, "can't you get one of them to take charge of me?"

I said that I would try, and accordingly spoke to them. They were willing, but insisted *they must have five dollars* to give to the men for rowing them off.

"Oh, my good friend," exclaimed Girard, "what shall I do? *I have not got five dollars aboard.*"

"Darn the Frenchman," was the reply, "we don't believe him, he hasn't come to sea without being able to muster five dollars."

I informed him what the men had said, and he replied—

"*It is really the case—it is out of my power to muster it—and what shall I do?*"

"Well," said I, "I cannot stay with you any longer, for I am going up to Philadelphia myself, and I see one of my shallops coming out of the Lewistown creek at this moment."

"Oh, you are going up to Philadelphia yourself, are you?" observed Girard; "can you not stand security to these men for the five dollars, and I will pay you as soon as I get up to the city?"

I told him that I would, and one of the pilots then took charge of his sl.p, and commenced heaving the anchor immediately. I jumped into the boat and parted with them. The boat put me on board of the shallop that was coming out of Lewistown with my goods, and both sloop and shallop proceeded up.

Before we had got out of sight of the spot where the sloop had cast anchor, we saw a British man-of-war coming in, and had we not started at the time, in less than an hour Stephen Girard would have been a prisoner to the British. We both arrived safe in Philadelphia.

The foregoing account certainly shows Girard's knowledge of navigation to have been very limited, and his circumstances far from being prosperous. For, although even a rich merchant might have been without five dollars in *cash*, under certain circumstances, yet the general description of the little sloop and her commander bespeak a considerable depreciation from his former condition. But the story of his actually having lost himself may very reasonably be supposed to have been some trick, or manœuvre, in Girard, to obtain a pilot, knowing, as he must have done, the extreme peril of his situation, owing to the constant visits of the British sloops of war; and this supposition is strengthened, when taking into account the close observation and uncommon sagacity of this singular man—who thus readily invented a specious fiction, in order to accomplish his purpose.

Confidence in Mercantile Success.

BUDGETT, the successful English merchant, not long before his death, heard some one saying he wished for more money: "Do you?" said he, "then I do not; I have got quite enough. But if I did wish for more, I should *get* it." He would often say that, place him in what position you might, he would work his way on—ay, leave him without a shilling, still he could rise. His faith in the power of *perseverance* was unbounded. In speaking to some of the poorest young men in his neighborhood, and urging them to self-improvement, he declared that there was no reason why they *might* not—though the reason was manifest why they *would*

not—every one of them be worth ten thousand pounds. He placed his confidence simply in "enduring powers and extraordinary application."

Astor's Early Prediction.

WHILE yet almost a stranger in New York, and in very narrow circumstances, Mr. Astor was one day passing by a row of houses which had just been erected in Broadway, and which, from the superior style of their architecture, were the talk and the boast of the city. "I'll build, one day or other, a greater house than any of these, in this very street," said he to himself;—a prediction which all will acknowledge has been most amply fulfilled in the stately and magnificent "Astor House"—one of the most impressive structures on this continent, and exceeded by only a few in Europe, of its class.

Erastus B. Bigelow's Boyhood Bargain.

THE name of Erastus B. Bigelow is a notable one among the many sons of New England who have risen from the smallest beginnings to the highest pinnacle of business success and renown.

In Erastus's youth, good John Temple was his neighbor—a substantial farmer. The latter had noticed the lad's capacity, and sometimes jokingly asked him to come and live with him, and learn *his* occupation. Erastus regarded this proposition as a business matter. With him, an offer was an offer. Accordingly, one Monday morning, in early spring, this boy of ten years presented himself at Mr. T.'s door, and demanded employment. It was given him, with no expectation that he would continue through the day. He worked on, however, and at the end of the week suggested to Mr. T. that it would be proper to come to some understanding in regard to wages. On being asked his terms, he offered to work six months, on condition of receiving at the close, a cosset lamb called "Dolly," to which he had taken a strong liking. The moderate demand was of course acceded to. But scarcely had a month elapsed ere a difficulty arose. Dolly could not live without eating, and how was he to provide for her? His fellow laborers discovered the cause of his anxiety, and teasingly aggravated it. At length he proposed and effected an alteration in the contract. He relinquished his claim to Dolly, and Mr. T. agreed to furnish, instead, a pair of cowhide boots, and sheep's gray cloth sufficient for a suit of clothes. The agreement was fully carried out on both sides. At the close of the period, an offer of four dollars a month for the ensuing summer was offered and accepted. The kind-hearted man, at parting, gave the young farmer and future capitalist, a silver dollar.

General Jackson's Interview with Samuel Slater.

WHEN making his Northern tour, President Jackson visited the town of Pawtucket. After he and his suite had been duly conducted through the town, and were expressing themselves as delighted with its appearance—its numerous and well regulated establishments of business, its ample and commodious churches, and especially its intelligent and well-ordered citizens—they repaired to the house of Mr. Slater, then confined by a rheumatic disorder, to pay their respects to a man whose business enterprise had thus produced such great results.

With the affability and complaisance so peculiar to General Jackson, he addressed Mr. Slater as the father of American manufactures, as the man who had erected the first valuable machinery, and who spun yarn to make the first *cotton cloth* in America; and who had, by his superintendence and direction, as well as by intense labor, erected the first cotton mill in Rhode

10

Island, which was the first in the land of the Pilgrims.

General Jackson, who had been informed of the particulars referred to, entered into familiar conversation on the subject. "I understand," said the President, "you taught us how to spin, so as to rival Great Britain in her manufactures; you set all these thousands of spindles at work, which I have been delighted in viewing, and which have made so many happy by a lucrative employment." "Yes, sir," said Mr. Slater, "I suppose that I gave out the Psalm, and they have been singing to the tune ever since." "We are glad to hear also that you have realized something for yourself and family," said the Vice-President. "So am I glad to know it," said Mr. Slater, "for I should not like to be a pauper in this country, where they are put up at auction to the lowest bidder."

A. T. Stewart's Success.

"IRELAND," says that genial writer, Walter Barrett, "has been the birthplace of many remarkable men, but never has she sent from her shore a more sagacious one than A. T. Stewart. Our land has fostered the Frenchman Girard, of Philadelphia, and the German Astor, and they died worth millions; but they never, even at a great age, reached the wealth of the merchant Stewart. He is yet in the gristle of his success, and not hardened into the bone of mammoth, overgrown wealth. Stewart is this day worth fourteen to twenty millions of dollars. He owns more real estate than Astor, and if he lives ten years longer, Mr. Stewart will probably be worth from twenty to thirty millions of dollars. In 1848, he moved to his present marble palace. He had bought Washington Hall of young John Coster for sixty thousand dollars, and for a few thousand dollars more two additional buildings and lots on Broadway, corner of

Chambers street. Upon this magnificent site he erected the present store. The whole cost of the ground and the palace erected did not reach three hundred thousand dollars. To-day it would sell at auction for from eight hundred thousand to one million dollars. He paid patroon Van Rensselaer five hundred and thirty thousand dollars for the Metropolitan Hotel and outbuildings. It is now worth and pays an interest of ten per cent. on one million dollars, and would bring at auction eight hundred thousand dollars. He owns more real estate than any other man in New York."

What John McDonogh said to a Lawyer.

THE following reminiscence of a familiar personal interview between the great millionnaire of New Orleans and a lawyer of that city—as narrated by the latter, is one of the rarest things of the kind to be found in mercantile annals :

I said to Mr. McDonogh, " You are a very rich man, and I know that you intend to leave all your property to be expended in charitable purposes. I have been thinking over your singular life, and I want you to give me some advice in regard to the success which has attended you, for I, too, would like to become very rich, having a family, so as to leave my heirs wealthy." " Well," said he, " get up, sir ; " and as I rose from my arm-chair, he took my seat, and, turning to me, as if he was the proprietor and I his clerk, said,—pointing to a common chair in which he had been sitting,—" sit down, sir, and I will tell you how I became a rich man, and how, *by following three rules,* you can become as rich as myself :

" I first came to Louisiana," continued Mr. McDonogh, " when it was a Spanish colony, as the agent for a house in Baltimore and a house in Boston, to dispose of certain cargoes of goods. After I had settled up their accounts and finished their agency, I set up to do business for myself. I had become acquainted with the Spanish. governor, who had taken a fancy to me, although I had never so much as flattered him, and through his influence I obtained a contract for the army, by which I made ten thousand dollars. After this, I gave a splendid dinner to the principal officers of the army and the governor, and by it obtained another contract, by which I made thirty thousand dollars.

" This is what the French and the Creoles do not understand. I mean the spending of money judiciously. They are afraid of spending money. A man who wishes to make a fortune must first make a show of liberality, and spend money in order to obtain it. By that dinner which I gave to the Spanish authorities, I obtained their good will and esteem, and by this I was enabled to make a large sum of money. To succeed in life, then, you must obtain the favor and influence of the opulent, and the authorities of the country in which you live. This is the *first* rule.

" The natural span of a man's life," observed Mr. McDonogh, " is too short, if he is abandoned to his own resources, to acquire great wealth, and, therefore, in order to realize a fortune, you must exercise your influence and power over those who, in point of wealth, are inferior to you, and, by availing yourself of their talents, knowledge and information, turn them to your own advantage." This is the *second* rule."

Here Mr. McDonogh made a long pause, as if lost in thought ; and seeing him remain silent, I asked, "Is that all?" " No," said he, " there is a *third* and *last* rule, which it is all essential for you to observe, in order that success may attend your efforts." " And what is that ?" I inquired. " Why, sir," said he, "it is *prayer.* You must pray to the Almighty with fervor and zeal, and you will be sustained in all your doings, for I never prayed sincerely to God, in all my life, without having my prayers answered satisfactorily." He stopped; and I said, "Is this all?" He answered, "Yes, sir; follow my advice, and you will become a rich man." And he arose and left.

Day and Martin, the Millionnaires of "High Holborn."

THE lucky incident which made millionnaires of Day and Martin, of "High Holborn," by the sale of their famous blacking, is as follows: Day was a hairdresser in a humble way, and was beneficent and charitable in the extreme. One day, a soldier entered his shop, and stated that he had a long march before him to reach his regiment; that his money was gone, and nothing but sickness, fatigue, and punishment awaited him, unless he could get a lift on a coach. The worthy barber presented him with a guinea, at which exhibition of kindness the grateful soldier exclaimed, "God bless you, sir,—how can I ever repay you this? I have nothing in the world except"—pulling a dirty piece of paper from his pocket —"a receipt for blacking; it is the best ever was seen; many a half guinea have I had for it from the officers, and many bottles have I sold—may you be able to get something for it, to repay this you have given to a poor soldier; your kindness I never can repay or forget."

Mr. Day, who was a shrewd man, inquired into the truth of the story, tried the blacking, and finding it good, commenced the manufacture and sale of it—with what results, the magnificent fortunes of the partners amply attest.

Jacob Barker's Success when a Youth.

DURING Mr. Barker's minority the whaling business of Nantucket became very much depressed, insomuch that many merchants wished to sell their vessels. This being made known by him to Robert Mott, a gentleman of great merit, he proposed to his friends, Messrs. Robinson and Hartshorn, to join him in the purchase of a ship at Nantucket, and to employ young Barker for the purpose. They offered to be concerned in such a speculation, but refused to intrust a boy with the mission, saying that their Mr. Robinson would go. Mr. Mott declined unless young Barker was employed. They finally compromised by agreeing that both should go. Application was made to Hicks (young Barker's employer) for permission, to which he consented on condition that he be paid a full commission of two and one half per cent., if a purchase was made.

They both went, Barker not appearing to have anything to do with the purchase. Robinson offered nine thousand dollars for the ship Portland; ten thousand was demanded. After several days' unsuccessful negotiation, he determined to offer five hundred dollars more; had a meeting with the owners, of whom an inquiry was made if they were disposed to divide the difference. They replied that "not a dollar less than ten thousand would be accepted." They separated, Robinson deliberating how far it would be best to yield to the demand of ten thousand dollars, when young Barker prevailed on him to repair to New Bedford for a few days, leaving him to make the purchase. He did so, and Barker succeeded—purchased the ship for nine thousand dollars, and this, too, in season to notify Robinson by the first mail, when he returned to Nantucket to attend to her dispatch. On arrival at New York, she was sold to George M. Woolsey, for thirteen thousand five hundred dollars, and young Barker employed to return immediately to Nantucket to purchase a ship for James Lyon, of New York, and John James, of Philadelphia, and another for Jacob Valentine, Samuel Hicks, and Samuel Robinson. He did so; the ship Rose for the former gentlemen, and the ship Beaver for the latter, for which service Mr. Hicks also received a full commission of two and one half per cent. on the amount of purchase.

In relation to the Rose: when that vessel was ready for sea the vendors refused to let her go without an indorser on the bills of exchange to be given in payment, amounting to ten thousand dollars, although it had not been before mentioned; this was very inconvenient. Barker, not having the means on the island to give a satisfactory indorser, had to proceed to New Bedford therefor. As there were not any steamboats running, and the mail-packet had been detained some days by a northwest wind, a change seemed probable, and in the afternoon it came round to west south-west—too scant, however, for the captain of the mail-packet to be induced to leave. Barker, impatient at the delay, took passage on a lumber-loaded vessel that had put in for a harbor, bound to the neighborhood of New Bedford, which he discovered making sail to leave, late in the afternoon. She proceeded twenty-five miles, when the wind turned back to northwest, which obliged the vessel to come to anchor at eight o'clock in the evening. At daylight the next morning a signal was set for a pilot; a boat soon appeared from the Vineyard, and was chartered to proceed to New Bedford.

On reaching Wood's Hole, the current was found running east too swift for the boat to encounter that passage with an unfavorable wind; she therefore beat up the Vineyard sound and passed through Quicksi's Hole, and arrived at New Bedford as the bells, according to the custom of the place, were ringing for twelve o'clock. The indorsement of William Rotch, jr., was procured.

"Walter Barrett's" Cotton Mission.

THE following well-told story belongs, of course, to a period when electric telegraphs did not, like a cobweb, cover our land: Goodhue & Co. (the great New York firm then and now) had many rivals to their line of packets, but none were successful. Robert Kermit once started a line of "Saint" ships. He owned the ship St. George, and he persuaded Stephen Whitney and old Nat Prime to become owners in a new ship called the St. Andrew. The line never succeeded, although the latter once made a very short passage in the year 1834, and brought the intelligence of an advance in the price of cotton in Liverpool. She came in late, one Christmas eve. Old Mr. Prime lived at that time at the corner of Broadway and Marketfield street (now Battery Place). Mr. Whitney lived only a few steps' distance on the corner of State street and Bowling Green Row, where he lived until he died very recently. These old heads and two or three younger ones had the exclusive news, and they intended to make the most of it. It was certain not to be made public until the day after Christmas. Letters of credit were prepared in the front parlor of No. 1 Broadway for one million of dollars. Walter Barrett was selected to leave next morning for New Orleans, by way of Wheeling, hoping that he would outstrip the great Southern mail, leaving two days ahead, carrying these credits in favor of Thomas Barrett and John Hagan, of New Orleans, both eminent merchants in those days. The letters ordered cotton to be bought so long as there was a bale in *first hands* in New Orleans. Mr. Barrett, the bearer of credits and orders, was told to spare no expense in order to beat the mail. It was now eleven o'clock, Christmas eve. No one had thought about money for the expense of the messenger to New Orleans. Banks were all shut—brokers too. Mr.

Prime seized a blank check, and went up with it to the City Hotel.

" Willard, for what amount can you cash my check to-night ? "

" How much do you wish, Mr. Prime ? "

" One thousand dollars."

Mr. Willard had the money, and gave it to Mr. Prime. It was in the pocket of Mr. Walter Barrett, the next morning, when he embarked at six o'clock in the boat for Amboy, commanded then by the since famous Capt. Alexander Schultz.

The messenger, by bribing stage drivers, paying Mississippi boat captains $50 or $75—*not* to stop and receive freight, reached New Orleans in eleven days. It was daylight when he got into the old City Hotel, in New Orleans, kept then by Mr. Bishop. Two hours after, John Hagan and Thomas Barrett had the letters of credit and orders to purchase cotton. The Southern mail did not arrive for three days. Before night, over fifty thousand bales of cotton had been purchased at eleven to twelve cents, or about sixty dollars per bale. That cotton was sold at seventeen and eighteen cents when cotton went up a few days after. Some was sent to Liverpool. The profit was on some lots over thirty dollars a bale, and was divided up among the New Orleans houses of Barrett & Co., John Hagan & Co., and the New York operators. The messenger had the profits of two hundred bales awarded him, and his expenses paid. This operation was a lucky one for some of the owners of the St. Andrew, but it did not aid Captain Robert Kermit particularly, and the " Saint " line went down.

We venture to say that that same Walter Barrett can " do " a good job now !

Privateering Exploit of a Salem Merchant.

JOSEPH PEABODY, the merchant-sovereign of Salem, left that place in 1781–'2, in the letter-of-marque Ranger, he being second officer. Proceeding to Richmond, they disposed of their cargo of salt, and then went to Alexandria, where they loaded with flour for Havana, and arrived safe. The Ranger returned to Alexandria, and after receiving on board another cargo of flour, on the 5th of July, 1782, dropped down the Potomac to near its mouth, where encountering head winds, she was obliged to anchor, and, after making the ordinary arrangements for the night, the officers and crew retired to their berths.

About eleven o'clock the watch ran aft for a speaking-trumpet, and announced to the officers the unwelcome news that boats were making for the ship. The captain, Simmons, directed Mr. Peabody not to let them come alongside; but they both rushed up the companion-way, and as they reached the deck, received a discharge of musketry, by which Capt. Simmons fell, badly wounded, and entirely disabled from further action. Mr. Peabody, having no time to dress himself, ran forward in his night-clothes, calling on the crew to seize the boarding-pikes, and grasping one himself, accompanied by a man named Kent, armed in the like manner, sprang to the bows, where they had a fierce encounter with several of the enemy already on the gunwale. The crew having armed themselves, a desperate conflict ensued, in the midst of which another boat came alongside and began a heavy fire on the other quarter.

The first officer being employed at the magazine in procuring ammunition for those who were armed with muskets, the command of the deck devolved on Mr. Peabody, who, wearing a shirt, was a conspicuous mark, even in a dark night. He now ordered cold shot to be thrown into the boats, and it was done with such effect that one of them gave way; both had been grappled to the Ranger before receiving any damage.

Perceiving the advantage thus obtained, he applied his entire force to the other boat, and cheering his men with the cry of "we have sunk one, my boys, now let us sink the other," the responding cheers of the crew so alarmed the assailants, that they dropped astern, and both were soon lost in the darkness of the night.

When the confusion was over, one of the crew only was found to be dead, and three wounded. Mr. Peabody was not aware, during the action, that he had received any wounds, but afterward found his arms stiff, and a ball lodged in his left wrist, that the bone of his right elbow was laid bare, and a ball had grazed his left shoulder. The Ranger was armed with seven guns, and had a crew of twenty, while the barges of the enemy contained sixty men. The assailants, a band of tories headed by two desperate characters, lost fifteen killed, and had thirty-eight wounded.

Patriotism and Prowess of French Merchants.

ONE of the chief merchants of Marseilles, M. de Corse, carried his patriotic zeal to such an extent, that in 1760 he published a manifesto, declaring war in his own private name against the king of England, and put to sea no less than twenty frigates, to cruise against British commerce !

This merchant, however, had a rival in M. Gredis, a famous Jewish merchant at Bordeaux. He fitted out, in 1761, the Prothée, of sixty-four guns, which captured the merchant ship Ajax, an Indiaman, worth about a million and a half dollars. He had also several frigates of thirty-six guns cruising at the same time, on his own account.

In both these cases, it may perhaps be doubted if, with a strong patriotic feeling, there was not *some* motive of commercial gain ; for it *has* occurred in England, as well as in France, and our own country, that vessels thus fitted out by merchants have done much in-jury to the enemy, and no small service to their owners.

Thomas H. Perkins's Deliberate Habits.

THOMAS H. PERKINS's self-possession and tranquillity seldom forsook him in any of his multifarious business or private cares. At one time, when he had decided to leave Boston in order to take a long journey of several thousand miles to the South and West, application had been made to him to give his guaranty for a considerable sum, to enable one whose welfare he wished to promote to engage in a commercial connection that seemed to offer great advantages.

As the magnitude of the affair required caution, it was expected, of course, that when he had considered the subject, explanations on various points would be necessary before he could decide to give it ; and it was intended to take some favorable opportunity, when he might be entirely at leisure, to explain everything fully. Suddenly, however, he found it best to commence the journey a week or two sooner than had been mentioned, and engagements of various kinds, previously made, so occupied him in the short interval left, that there seemed to be no time for offering such explanation without danger of intruding, and the hope of obtaining his aid at that time, in an affair that required prompt action, was given up. The applicant called at his house half an hour before he was to go, merely to take leave, knowing that the haste of departure in such cases usually precludes attention to any matter requiring deliberation. On entering the room, however, he found there was no appearance of haste. All preparations for the journey had been entirely completed in such good season that the last half-hour seemed to be one entirely of leisure for anything that might occur.

After a little chat, Col. Perkins introduced the subject himself, and made pertinent inquiries; which, being answered satisfactorily, he gave the guaranty and very kindly added a further facility by allowing, until his return, the use of a considerable sum of money which he was leaving in the bank. The arrangements were, in consequence, completed the next day; they proved in the result to be eminently successful, all pledges were redeemed, his guaranty was cancelled in due course, without the slightest cost or inconvenience to him; and the person whom he wished to oblige received very large profits, which happily influenced the remainder of his life, but which, perhaps, he might never have enjoyed, if that last half-hour before the journey had been hurried.

Rothschild and Astor Compared.

THE elder Rothschild was perhaps a richer man than Mr. Astor, but in other respects his inferior. Rothschild was a good arithmetician and a good banker. He wrought out, skilfully and successfully, the materials offered to his hand by the social condition of his time; but his was not an original, an inventive, a creative mind. That of Mr. Astor, on the contrary, was strongly marked by such characteristics. All his bold and grand operations were in scenes before untried; carrying out combinations before unthought of; opening up mines of hitherto undiscovered wealth; and all tending not more to his own advantage than to the prosperity of the country, in its material and commercial interests. Surely, the stock operations of Rothschild never partook of these characteristics.

Labouchere and Vincent Nolte.

VINCENT NOLTE became the American agent of the renowned Amsterdam house of Hope & Co., under the following curious circumstances, as narrated by himself: One day, after the close of the Bourse, Mr. L. placed his arm confiden-

tially in mine and said, "Let us take a walk; we will be able to converse undisturbed, and to better purpose, than in the counting room. I have very often been pressed, by my brother, to give him permission to send an agent to the United States, but would never listen to his request, until he made mention of you and your wishes. I think that I have a perfect knowledge of you, and understand you, from your correspondence, and that you may be useful to him, to yourself, and to us all."

The "us all" sounded very pleasantly in my ears, for under the word us I was given to understand a mission for the important house of Messrs. Hope itself. I instantly said, "How is that? Us all?"

"I will tell you," he continued: "To make your first appearance as agent for the house of my brother is a very good preliminary introduction to the United States, and you can, according to the directions and hints I will give you, carefully look about you a couple of months, until we shall have some further additional need of your services. Even were you not to make one single bargain, I should still be well enough satisfied; but I have something better in store for you. You will be intrusted with a mission that will make you catch your breath to hear of it. You will feel the ground heaving under your feet."

And here he began to sketch for me the outline of a really colossal undertaking he was then planning in his own mind. He then pointed out the position he had in view, and the heavy responsibility that would rest upon my shoulders. He was right. I did catch my breath at the magnificence of his project. Ere I had put a hand to it, I at once declared to Mr. L. that I was too young and inexperienced to assume such a responsibility, and that I should only in a moderate degree equal his expectations. His answer was:

"That is my business, and not yours.

I have but one thing to recommend to you: never commit any action which may one day cause you to blush before me, or in the presence of your own conscience!"

I was now placed upon the right ground. He had correctly judged me, and I had understood him perfectly. At length we touched upon the question, how much salary I was to receive for all this: He replied:

"Nothing! Your expenses will be liberally paid! That is all. If you cannot foresee what a position such a mission may secure for you in the commercial world, and the facilities which it cannot fail to open for you in the future, you had better stay at home."

My reply was, that his extreme confidence honored me, and that I would unconditionally agree to all that he saw fit to point out to me.

"In order to progress," he added, "you must renounce all impatience to succeed."

The business, of which Mr. Labouchere thus communicated only a rough outline, and which Mr. Nolte got to understand and form an opinion of, in its whole extent, only several months later, in the autumn of 1805, originated in one of the many conceptions and combinations of Ouvrard, the once celebrated French banker.

Scene in a Merchant's Counting Room, after the Peace in 1815.

THE promptness and energy of American merchants is established as characteristic of them wherever American commerce is known. Here is an illustration—the like of which it would be no difficult labor to find in every city and town in the country.

At the time of peace, in the winter of 1815, Mr. A., a New York merchant, proceeded to his office. The clerks, four in number, were already at their posts, and met their employer with a smile each. "Well, boys," said he, "this is good news—now we must be up and doing." He seldom used the first person, I, but spoke to his clerks, and of them, as being part and parcel with himself. "We shall have our hands full now," he continued, "but we can do as much as anybody."

Mr. A. was the owner and part owner of several ships, which during the war had been hauled ashore three miles up the river, and dismantled, and they were now inclosed by a bay of solid ice, for the whole distance, from one to two feet thick, while the weather was so cold that, when broken up, the pieces would unite and congeal again in an hour or two; but this proved no discouragement in the present case. It would be a month before the ice would yield to the season, and that would give time for merchants in other places, where the harbors were open, to be in the markets abroad, before him. The decision was therefore made on the instant.

"Reuben," said Mr. A. to one of the clerks, as soon as the "peace" greeting was past, and he had told them his intentions, "go out, and collect as many laborers as possible to go up the river, Charles, do you go and find Mr. ——, the rigger, and Mr. ——, the sail maker, and tell them I want to see them immediately; John, go and engage half a dozen truckmen for to-day and to-morrow; Stephen, hunt up as many caulkers and gravers as you can find, and engage them to work;" and Mr. A. then sallied out himself to provide the implements for ice breaking, and before twelve o'clock, more than one hundred men were three miles up the river, clearing away the ships and cutting ice, which they sawed out in large squares, and then shoved them under the main body, to open the channel. The roofing over the ships was torn off, and the clatter of caulkers' mallets was like the rattling of a hail storm—loads of rigging were passing up on the ice—riggers had buckled on their belt and knife—sail makers were plying their needles, and the whole was such a busy scene as had not been witnessed there for years. *Before night the ships were afloat*, and moved some distance in the channel, and by the time they had reached the wharf, which was eight or ten days, their rigging and spars were aloft, their upper works caulked, and everything in a great state of forwardness for sea.

It would not be safe to doubt that energy like this met with its reward.

Strong Point in Mercantile Success— Girard's Silence.

A POINT in the character of Girard, the Napoleon of commerce, gives a strong insight into the cause of his business success.' No man ever heard him boast of *what he could do*. He remained quiet and silent until the time came for action, and then he struck the blow with an unerring aim which insured him success. He was studious to learn all he could from others, and as careful to impart nothing in return.

Tudor, the Original Ice Merchant.

To Mr. Frederick Tudor, of Boston, is due the very creditable honor of originating the ice trade of our country, now so extensive and important. This gentleman, having previously sent agents to the West Indies to procure information, determined to make his first experiment in that region. Finding no one willing to receive so strange an article on shipboard, he was compelled to purchase a vessel, the brig *Favorite*, of about one hundred and thirty tons, which he loaded with ice from a pond in Saugus, Massachusetts, belonging to his father, and sent to St. Pierre, Martinique. This first enterprise resulted in a loss of about $4,500, but was, nevertheless, followed up until the embargo and war put an end to the foreign trade, up to which period it had yielded no profit to its projector. Its operations had been confined to Martinique and Jamaica.

After the close of the war with England, in 1815, Mr. Tudor recommenced his operations by shipments to Havana, under a contract with the Government of Cuba, which enabled him to pursue his undertaking without loss, and extend it in a short time to Charleston, S. C., Savannah, Ga., and New Orleans. In the mean time it had been tried again, by other parties, at Martinique and St. Thomas, and failed, and by Mr. Tudor at St. Jago de Cuba, where it also failed, after a trial of some three years. In 1833, the first shipment of ice was made to the East Indies by Mr. Tudor, in the ship *Tuscany*, for Calcutta, and shipments were subsequently made to Madras and Bombay. Up to this time the ice business was of a very complicated nature, and shipowners objected to receive it on freight, fearing its effect on the durability of their vessels and the safety of their voyages. It is now, however, one of the most conveniently conducted, extensive, and profitable kinds of mercantile business, and many parties are engaged in it.

First Greek Adventure to America.

THE first Greek ship that ever touched at an American port, arrived there in 1811. She was called the *Jerusalem*, and had a cargo of wines; but in entering the port of Boston, she ran aground, and sustained so much damage, that it took some months to repair her. The captain, having in vain endeavored to sell his cargo, proceeded to Havana, where he was not more successful. He then returned to Boston, and having become involved in lawsuits, his ship was seized, his cargo sold at great sacrifice, and himself reduced to such distress, that he was obliged to beg for subsistence, until a subscription was opened to defray the expenses of his return to his own country. All his crew died in prison.

Roman Idea of Merchants.

Among the Romans, the deity who presided over commerce and banking was Mercury, who, by a strange association, was also the god of thieves and of orators. The Romans, who looked upon merchants with contempt, fancied there was a resemblance between theft and merchandise, and they easily found a figurative connection between theft and eloquence; hence, thieves, merchants, and orators, were placed under the superintendence of the same deity. On the seventeenth of May, in each year, the merchants held a public festival, and walked in procession to the temple of Mercury, for the purpose, as the satirists said, of begging pardon of that deity for all the lying and cheating they had found it convenient to practise, in the way of business, during the preceding year.

"Monsieur Smith," Girard's Man.

It is known that Girard admired industry as much as he despised sloth, and there was never, it is related, an instance where he did not furnish employment or money to an industrious and worthy man in distress.

Early one morning, while Mr. Girard was walking around the square where the millionnaire's well-known houses now stand, John Smith, who had worked on his buildings in the humble capacity of a laborer, and whom Mr. G. had noted for his unusual activity, applied to him for assistance, when something like the following dialogue took place:

"Assistance—work—ha? You want to work?"

"Yes, sir; it's a long time since I've had anything to do."

"Very well, I shall give you some. You see dem stone yondare?"

"Yes, sir."

"Very well, you shall fetch and put them in this place. You see?"

"Yes, sir."

"And when you done, come to me at my bank."

Smith diligently performed his task, which he accomplished about one o'clock, when he repaired to Mr. Girard, and informed him that it was finished, at the same time asking if he would not give him some more work.

"Ah, ha! oui. You want more work? Very well; you shall go place dem stone where you got him. Understandez? You take him back."

"Yes, sir."

Away went Smith to his work, which having got through with about sunset, he waited on Mr. Girard for his pay.

"Ah, ha! you all finish?"

"Yes, sir."

"Very well, how much money shall I give you?"

"One dollar, sir."

"Dat is honest. You take no advantage. Dare is your dollar."

"Can I do anything else for you?"

"Oui. Come here when you get up to-morrow. You shall have some work."

Next morning, on calling, Smith was not a little astonished when told that he must "take dem stone back again," nor was his astonishment diminished when the order was repeated for the fourth and last time. However, he was one of that happy kind of persons who mind their own business, and he went on with his job, with all the indifference imaginable. When he called on Mr. Girard, in the evening, and informed him that the stones "were as they were," he was saluted thus in the most cordial manner:

"Ah, *Monsieur Smith*, you shall be *my man;* you mind your own business; you do what is told you; you ask no questions; you no interfere. You got one vife?"

"Yes, sir."

"Ah, dat is bad. Von wife is bad. Any de little chicks?"

"Yes, sir; five living."

"Five? dat is good; I like five; I like you, Monsieur Smith; you like to work; you mind your business. Now I do something for your five little chicks. There, take these five pieces of paper for your five little chicks; you shall work for them; you shall mind your business, and your little chicks shall never want five more. Good bye."

The feelings of the grateful man being too much overcome to allow him to reply, hé departed in silence; and by minding his own business, he became one of the wealthiest of his name in Philadelphia.

Thomas P. Cope's Integrity.

A PERSON highly recommended approached Mr. Cope, the Philadelphia merchant, one day, and invited him to embark in a certain joint-stock enterprise. In a careful exposition of the matter, he made it appear that the scheme was likely to succeed, and that the stock would instantly run up to a liberal premium, on being put into the market. "Well," said Mr. Cope, "I am satisfied on that point; I believe it would be as thou sayest. But what will be the *real* value of the stock?" "Why, as to that," answered the speculator, "I cannot say (implying by his manner what he *thought*); but that is of no account, for all *we* have to do is to sell out, and make our thirty or forty per cent. profit." "I'll have nothing to do with it—I'll have nothing to do with it," was the prompt and indignant reply. "And from that day," he used to say, in relating the occurrence, "I *marked* that man, and shunned all transactions with him."

Second Thought on a Trade.

A MAN had bought a pair of shoes from a dealer in that article, for which he promised to pay him on a future day. He went with his money on the day appointed, but found that the dealer had in the interval departed this life. Without saying anything of his errand, he withdrew from the place, secretly rejoicing at the opportunity thus unexpectedly afforded him of gaining a pair of shoes for nothing. His conscience, however, would not suffer him to remain at ease under such an act of injustice; so, taking the money, he returned to the shop, and casting in the money, said, "Go thy ways, for though he is dead to all the world besides, yet he is alive to me."

Three Merchant Voyages, and their Results.

A NEW YORK paper makes the following statement: Several years ago, there lived in one of our seaports, three merchants, whom we will designate as A, B, and C, and all of whom were owners of freight ships. Each of these men loaded a ship at the same time, which were to go first to Egypt, and to the Baltic, to one of the Russian ports. All being loaded, they waited for a favorable wind. The harbor was so situated, that there was no egress for ships unless the wind blew in a particular direction. One Sabbath morning, the wind was fair. The masters of the vessels went to their respective owners for sailing orders. A and B immediately had their ships put to sea; but C told the master that he must remain in port until the next day. Before Monday morning, however, the wind had changed, and remained contrary until the next Sunday, when it again came round fair. The master of the vessel again repaired to the house of C, to procure the ship's papers and orders. But, to his astonishment, C remarked that his ship must not leave the port on the Sabbath. The captain attempted to reason the point with him, but all in vain. He said if his ship *never* sailed, it should not put to sea on that day of the week; and he was willing to run all the risks of maintaining his principle.

Some time during the following week, the ship sailed with a fair breeze, and arrived in Egypt just as the ships of A and B were about to sail for the Baltic. In the mean time, information had circulated through the country, that American vessels were in port, wishing to sell their cargoes, and purchase a certain kind of their produce, namely, rice. The desired article was brought in such abundance that the market was glutted by the time C's ship arrived. In consequence of this, his cargo was sold at an advanced price, and his ship loaded at a much better rate than the others. C's vessel proceeded then on her voyage up the Baltic. The ships were to dispose of their rice in the Russian ports, and load for home with iron. C's ship arrived in the Baltic after those of A and B had purchased their freight and nearly loaded; and good success continued to attend the former, as it did in the Mediterranean. Abundance of iron was brought to the market, and there were enough purchasers for the rice. All these ships reached America about the same time, that of C having actually earned as much by the voyage as both the others.

Sharing in a Good Operation.

With the foibles generally attendant upon an aspiring, money-seeking man, Mr. Fordyce, the celebrated English banker, had many generous qualities. A young, intelligent merchant, who kept cash at his banking house, one morning making a small deposit, he happened to say in the office, that if he could command some thousands at present, there was a certain speculation to be pursued, which in all probablity would turn out fortunate. This was said carelessly, without Fordyce appearing to notice it.

A few months afterward, when the same merchant was settling his book with the house, he was very much surprised to see the sum of £500 placed to his credit, more than he knew he possessed. Thinking it a mistake, he pointed it out to the clerk, who seeing the entry in Mr. Fordyce's handwriting, said he must have paid it to him. The merchant knew he had not, and begged to see Mr. Fordyce—who, on appearing, said, "It is all right enough, for as I made £5,000 by the hint you carelessly threw out, I think you fairly entitled to £500." Mr. Fordyce did not stop here; for when, some years afterward, the merchant became embarrassed, he found a liberal friend in his previous benefactor.

Secrecy in Business Transactions Practised by Rothschild.

One cause of Rothschild's great advantage in his business transactions was the secrecy with which he shrouded them, and the tortuous policy with which he misled those the most who watched him the keenest. If he possessed news calculated to make the funds rise, he would commission the broker who acted on his behalf to sell half a million. The shoal of men who usually follow the movements of others sold with him. The news soon passed through the monetary circle that Rothschild was "bearing" the market, and the funds fell. Men looked doubtingly at one another; a general panic spread; bad news was looked for; and these united agencies sunk the price two or three per cent. This was the result expected; and other brokers, not usually employed by him, bought all that they could at the reduced rates. By the time this was accomplished, the good news had arrived; the pressure ceased; the funds rose instantly; and Mr. Rothschild reaped his reward. There were, however, periods when his gigantic capital seemed likely to be scattered to the four quarters of the globe. He lost half a million in one English operation; when the French entered Spain in 1823, he was also in the utmost jeopardy; but perhaps the most perilous position in which he was placed was with the famous Polignac loan, although his vast intelligence saved him, and placed the burden on the shoulders of others. With this, nevertheless, he suffered greatly, as the price fell thirty per cent.

Ladder of Commercial Success.

JAMES HALFORD rose step by step up the ladder of fortune until he stood securely at the summit, with fame, wealth, and honors surrounding him. Some twenty years back, this same James Halford was at the very foot of the ladder, pondering how he should rise. The ladder was very curious to contemplate, and still more curious was it to hear what the world said about it.

"It is all luck, sir," cried one, "nothing but luck; why, sir, I have managed at times to get up a step or two, but have always fallen down ere long, and now I have given up striving, for luck is against me."

"No, sir," cried another, "it is not so much luck as scheming; the selfish schemer gets up, while more honest folks remain at the foot."

"Patronage does it all," said a third; "you must have somebody to take you by the hand and help you up, or you have no chance."

James Halford heard all these varied opinions of the world, but still persisted in looking upward, for he had faith in *himself*.

"The cry of 'luck's all,'—what does it amount to in reality," thought he, "but that some people are surrounded by better circumstances than others? They must still, however, take advantage of these circumstances permanently to succeed; and I, having very indifferent circumstances around me, have the more need to use great exertion in order to better them; and when reverses come, I will not despair, as some

do, but persevere on to fortune. I want no friend to take me by the hand and do that for me which every healthy man can do better for himself. No, I will rise by myself alone."

The resolution was earnestly made, and faithfully carried out. From the humblest capacity in a store, to the post of highest trust, James Halford rose in a few years. He became a trader for himself, and amassed a heavy fortune.

Six days for Business and One for Rest.

A DISTINGUISHED capitalist and financier, charged with an immense amount of property during the great pecuniary pressure of 1836 and 1837, said: I should have been a dead man, had it not been for the Sabbath. Obliged to work from morning to night, to a degree that no hired day-laborer would submit to, through the whole week, I felt on Saturday, especially on Saturday afternoon, as if I *must* have *rest*. It was like going into a dense fog. Everything looked dark and gloomy, as if nothing could be saved. I dismissed all from my mind, and kept the Sabbath in the "good old way." On Monday it was all bright sunshine. I could see through—and I got through. But had it not been for the Sabbath, I have no doubt I should have been in the grave.

Boston Merchant's Opinion of Business Men's Honesty.

IT is said of Mr. Samuel Appleton, a "merchant prince" of Boston, that he was himself so thoroughly upright, that it was hard for him to doubt the honesty of other men—and, as is often the case, men were really to him what he expected them to be. On a certain occasion he was asked—and the answer threw light alike on his own character and on the character of merchants generally—"You have been long engaged in business, under a great variety of circumstances, and in different countries: what is your opinion in regard to the honesty of mankind?" "Very favorable," he replied; "very generally, I think, they mean to be honest. I have never in my life met with more than three or four cases in which I thought a man intended to be dishonest in dealing with me."

Philadelphia Young Merchant who was not Afraid of Girard.

A MAN who had just set up in the hardware business, and who had been a clerk where Girard had traded, applied to him for a share of his patronage. Girard bought of him, and when he brought in the bill, found fault and marked *down* the prices. "Cask of nails," said he, "which I was offered for so and so, you have charged so and so, and you must take it off." "I cannot do it," said the young merchant. "You *must* do it," said Girard. "I cannot and will not," said the merchant. Girard bolted out of the door, apparently in a rage, but soon after sent a check for the whole bill. The young man began to relent and say to himself: "Perhaps he *was* offered them at that price. But it is all over now; I am sorry I did not reduce the bill, and get it out of him on something else. His trade would have been worth a good deal to me." By-and-by, Girard came again and gave him another job. The young man was very courteous, and said, "I was almost sorry I did not reduce your former bill." "*Reduce a bill!*" said Girard, "had you done it, I would never trade with you again. I meant to see if you had cheated me."

Hiding the Dollar with a Dime.

BUCKLEY, in one of his lectures, made use of an illustration that will bear repeating: Holding a dime close to his eyes with one hand, and a half dollar at some distance with the other, said he: "Now, I cannot see the half dollar with

this eye, for the dime is so near it, it obscures my vision. So it is with men of business; in their eagerness to save a dollar, they often lose sight of the fifty within their reach."

Mercantile Defalcation made good after Sixty Years.

IN the month of January, 1821, a man of respectable appearance entered the Corn Exchange, in Mark Lane, London, and advancing to one of the principal factors, asked him if he was the legal descendant of the head of a very ancient firm in that line, long since extinct? Being answered in the affirmative, he made some further inquiries, confirmatory of the first question, and departed. On the same day in the following week, he again made his appearance with a bag, which he presented to the factor, and containing three hundred and seventy sovereigns. The factor, of course, surprised at the transaction, began to make some inquiries; but the person refused to answer any questions, observing, that the property was now returned to its rightful owner —that he wanted no receipt, and that it was a matter of no consequence who he was. On referring to some very old business accounts, it appeared that in the year 1762, the firm alluded to had a very extensive business contract, in the course of which a defalcation to nearly that amount occurred.

Mysterious Benefactor—Incident of the South Sea Bubble.

ONE day, late in the evening, in 1720 —a year celebrated for the bursting of the South Sea Bubble—a gentleman called at the banking house of Messrs. Hankey & Co., one of the heaviest in the British kingdom. He was in a coach, but refused to get out, and desired that one of the partners of the house would come to him; into the hands of this banker, when he appeared, he put a parcel, very carefully sealed up, and desired that it might be taken care of till he should return again, which would be in the course of a few days. A few days passed away, a few weeks, a few months; but the stranger never returned. At the end of the second or third year, the partners agreed to open this mysterious parcel, when they found it to contain the large sum of one hundred and fifteen thousand dollars, with a letter, stating that it had been obtained by the South Sea speculation; and directing that it should be put in the hands of three trustees, whose names were mentioned, and the interest to be appropriated to the relief of the poor.

Touro's Great Gift to a Beggar.

A POOR widow once called upon Mr. Touro, the benevolent Hebrew merchant of New Orleans, and opened to him a very moving budget of griefs—she had several children, her rent was due, and her landlord threatened to eject her, nor had she a cent with which to buy food or clothes. Long before she had concluded her affecting jeremiad, Mr. Touro had filled up a check and begged her to go and draw it at once. The poor woman proceeded accordingly to the bank, and eagerly presented the check at the counter. The teller carefully examined the check, and then surveying the poor, scantily dressed, woebegone looking woman, shook his head, and informed her that the check could not be paid. With a heavy heart, and a sense of mingled shame and indignation, that she should have been thus "cruelly trifled with, " she returned to Mr. Touro's store, and handing him the check, remarked that it ill became a rich man to subject a poor widow to insult and mockery. "My dear madam," exclaimed the astonished and philanthropic merchant, "it is all I can give you to-day; it is, I know, a small sum, but it is all I can spare now." "But the bank officer refuses to give me anything for it," replied the distressed widow. "Oh, yes! I see it all

—he requires proof of your identity. Here," turning to his clerk, "go down to the bank with this lady, and tell them to pay that check." No wonder that the teller refused to pay a *check for fifteen hundred dollars* to so poor and forlorn looking a holder!

Generosity of Chickering, the Pianoforte Maker.

MANY years since, a boy, who thought and dreamed of nothing but music, wandered into a certain large establishment in Boston, where his favorite instruments were manufactured. Passing into the extensive saloons where these instruments were displayed, he sought out a quiet corner, and seating himself at one of those magnificent pianos, he first looked around, to be sure that no one was listening, and then began to play some of those beautiful waltzes of Beethoven, which, at that time, so suited his capacity, and suited his heart. Borne away in a delicious musical reverie, he did not for some time observe that a figure had stolen up to him and was listening as he played. A benevolent face was over him, and a kind voice addressed words of commendation and praise, which, being the first the boy had received, sent the blood tingling to his cheeks. The proprietor of the establishment, for it was he, then asked the boy if he would like to come and live among those pianos, discoursing just such music to purchasers— thus forming, in a word, a connection with his establishment. · But books and college were before the boy; and wondering at the proposition, he timidly thanked the proprietor and declined.

Years passed away. School and college were done with, and the books thrown aside. The boy had reached manhood; but still the spirit of music haunted him, and again he found himself in those spacious saloons. He had just ceased playing upon one of those magnificent instruments again, and stood looking dreamily out of the window, and down upon the crowded "Washington street" below. Again a quiet figure stole up to him, and a most musical and pleasant voice began to speak. The person before him was of small stature, had the manners and garb of a gentleman, was dressed in black, with a single magnificent diamond pin in his bosom; the only contrast in his appearance was the clean white apron of a workman, which he wore. It was the proprietor of the establishment again; who, wealthy as he was, had his own little working cabinet, with an exquisite set of tools, and there put the finishing touch to each of his beautiful instruments—a touch he intrusted to no one else. The proprietor inquired kindly of the young man as to his plans for life. These, alas! were undetermined. The voice of music was more fascinating than ever; but a learned profession of some kind seemed to be the wish and expectation of his friends. Music, however, was his first and strongest love, and he had sometimes thought, if he could but go abroad to study, he would decide for that. His father had given him his college education and his blessing, as capital for life. A harsh struggle with the world was before him; music, therefore, was hardly to be thought of.

In the quietest tone of that low, pleasant voice, the proprietor, as though making an ordinary remark, rejoined, "Well, but then, if the sum of five hundred dollars a year for a period of four years would suit your purpose, I could easily supply you with that."

The world grew dim before him, and the young man almost staggered with surprise; but when he recovered himself, there was the same quiet gentleman standing beside him, and looking pleasantly out of the window. Two months afterward the young man sailed for Europe, where he passed the allotted time and longer, from means with which his own compositions in the mean time furnished him. And whatever of knowledge, and whatever of artistic culture, and whatever of success in life, as connected with art, have since been his,—and he has long been one of the most distinguished among American musical composers,—he ascribes entirely to that most generous and noble-hearted Mæcenas of art, Jonas Chickering.

Whale Fishery Enterprise by Americans.

THE first attempts at the whale fishery, in Massachusetts, were made from the south shore and the island of Nantucket, by persons who went out in small boats, killed their whale, and returned the same day. But the whales were in this way soon driven from the coast, the population increased, and the demand for the product of the fisheries proportionably augmented. It became necessary to apply larger capitals to the business. Whaleships were now fitted out at considerable expense, which pursued the adventurous occupation from Greenland to Brazil. The enterprise thus manifested, awoke the admiration of Europe, and is immortalized in the well-known description by Burke. But the business has grown, until the ancient fishing grounds have become the first stations on a modern whaling voyage; and capitals are now required sufficient to fit out a vessel for an absence of forty months, and a voyage of circumnavigation. Fifty thousand dollars are invested in a single vessel; she doubles Cape Horn, ranges from New South Shetland to the coasts of Japan, cruises in unexplored latitudes, stops for refreshments at islands before undiscovered, and on the basis, perhaps, of an individual house, in New Bedford or Nantucket, performs an exploit which, eighty or ninety years ago, was thought a great object to be effected by the resources of the British government. The "overgrown capitalist" employed in this business may be said to be an "overgrown lamplighter."

Enterprise of Yankees and Russians 'Cutely Illustrated.

A GOOD anecdote is told, illustrating the *rather* superior enterprise of the Yankees over the Russians. The squadrons sent out by the Russians to explore the South Seas, had attained a degree of latitude which it was supposed had never before been reached, when land was descried. The commander was congratulating himself upon a discovery which was thus to immortalize his name, when, standing out from the land, a simple schooner was observed, which proved to be a sealing vessel of thirty tons. Hoisting the stars and stripes, the captain of the Yankee craft, for such she proved, ran alongside of the commodore, and politely offered to pilot him in! The Russian was astonished "some," to find such a rig and such a crew at a spot which, in Europe, was not known to exist—though, indeed, it would be really more astonishing to find a place where Yankee trading enterprise had *not* penetrated. Working a gold mine on the top of Himmaleh, or speculating in dead horse flesh among the Usbecs—heading a caravan across the Siberia, or trapping bears at the North Pole—bartering yellow buttons for goats' hair in the capital of the Grand Lama, or exchanging fez-caps and coral for Soudan ingots, in the stalls of Timbuctoo—in any and all of these places and employments, the Yankee might be expected to be found.

Tempting Business Paragraph.

" WE are well acquainted," says the editor of a city journal, " with a young and very handsome girl, who has the principal management of a large mercantile establishment in a flourishing country town, who visits different cities alone, stops at hotels, purchases supplies of dry goods, dimity, hardware,

china, groceries, shoes, nick-nacks, and all the multifarious saleables which make up ' a stock' in a miscellaneous store. She gives notes, makes contracts, and attends to all such business as belongs to her; and we have never yet learned that she has sacrificed one iota of the dignity, admiration and respect, which are her just due as a young, amiable, and very pretty woman. *There!*"

Bone and Offal Millionnaire.

SOME years ago, a poor French woman, residing at Buenos Ayres, being exceedingly perplexed with regard to the " ways and means," set her inventive genius to work, and hit upon the following expedient:

Observing a vast quantity of bones and animal offal thrown away from the slaughter houses with which Buenos Ayres abounds, a thought struck her that she might turn this waste to a profitable account. Having procured a large iron pot, and collected a quantity of bones, etc., she commenced operations by boiling them, and skimming off the fat, which she then sold at the stores. Finding the proceeds of her industry amply rewarded her labor, she persevered, advancing from a pot to a boiler, and from a boiler to a steaming vat, until she possessed a magnificent apparatus, capable of reducing a hundred head of cattle to tallow, at one steaming. In course of time she sold her manufactory, and retired from business with a large fortune, rolling through the streets in one of the most sumptuous carriages in Buenos Ayres. There is now scarcely a respectable merchant in that place, or in Montevideo, who is not in some way connected with cattle-steaming.

"Five Years of Privation and a Fortune."

UNDER the arcades near the markets, in Havana, may be seen a number of shops, not ten feet square, with a show-

11

case in front, before which a restless being is constantly walking; reminding one of a caged wild animal that chafes for a wider range. At night, the showcase is carried into his little cabin, which serves him for a shop, dormitory, and kitchen,—and where he may be often seen preparing his frugal meal over a chafing dish of live charcoal. "*Five years of privation and a fortune,*" is his motto; and not a few of the wealthiest Spanish residents in Cuba are said to date the commencement of their prosperity from so humble a source. These are the Catalans—an industrious, shrewd, economical class, who have received the *sobriquet* of Spanish Jews. A large portion of the commerce of the island is in their hands, as well as a very great part of its wealth. In the interior of the island they appear to monopolize every branch of trading, from the pack of the humblest peddler to the country *tienda* with its varied contents; and, in the maritime towns, many a commercial house, whose ships cover the sea, is theirs.

McDonogh's Greatest Victory.

ONE of John McDonogh's favorite plans of operation, to increase his fortune, was to purchase the back lands of plantations on the river, the value of which would be increased enormously by the improvements in front of them. So he eagerly pounced upon all the lands in the neighborhood of the towns and villages in the State. One of the most brilliant of his feats in this sphere was the completion of his lines of circumvallation around the city of New Orleans. For many years he pursued this object with the greatest ardor and intensity. Commencing at the upper end of the city, he stole gradually around through the swamps, purchasing large belts of land, until at last, a few years before his death, meeting one of his old friends in the street, he

slapped him on the shoulder, and with his face full of enthusiasm and joy, exclaimed, "Congratulate me, my friend; I have achieved *the greatest victory of my life.* I have drawn my lines around the city, and now entirely embrace it in my arms—all for the glory of God and the good of my race."

James G. King's Treatment of Resentments.

AN incident in the life of James Gore King affords a pleasing illustration of the tenderness of heart which not unfrequently accompanies high mercantile character. A misunderstanding had for some years existed, and comparative estrangement between him and one who had been early connected with him by family ties. This state of things grieved him, for having no resentment or unkindness in his own heart, he was uneasy even under the appearance of cherishing any. A casual and most improbable meeting in a city omnibus, only four days before his death, with the person thus estranged, the inhabitant of another State, afforded him the opportunity of reconciliation. After exchanging friendly salutations in the omnibus, when the person alighted he too got out, and when alone together said, extending his hand, "If, without asking or giving any explanation, you are willing that we should be friends, let it be so;" adding, with that thoughtful prescience which sometimes goes before the event, "I want, before I die, to be at peace with all." The extended hand was taken; and the particulars of this interview comprised one of the last subjects upon which Mr. King conversed, and with much happiness, just before his death.

Noble Mercantile Trait of Jonathan Goodhue.

THE late Mr. Jonathan Goodhue was noted for the ready-flowing sympathy and fellow feeling which marked his character. It was especially manifested toward those in dependent situations and in the more humble walks of life. No laboring man, however low his condition, could be engaged in his service without perceiving that he had a considerate regard for his feelings and for his rights. No domestic ever lived in his family without being impressed by his condescension and kindness. This feeling made him reluctant to part with those who had faithfully served him, and few men have ever made so few changes in those who have held subordinate situations under them. The cartman who, on his first arrival in New York, took his baggage to his lodgings, was employed by him until old age obliged him to retire from active life. A principal book-keeper, well worthy of his confidence and esteem, remained with him for fifteen years, and then withdrew because of a change in his mode of life. A confidential counting-room porter, after being in his service for twenty-five years, still holds his place in the house of Goodhue & Co. These incidents show a trait of character indicating true nobility.

Redeeming Lost Time.

THE diligence and application displayed by Gideon Lee were remarkable; he usually worked sixteen hours out of the twenty-four. An anecdote which he used to relate of himself in this connection, is worthy of being told, as illustrating two traits in his character, which adhered to him through life —his great industry and his resolution. He had "made a bargain with himself," as he expressed it, to "labor each day a certain number of hours, and nothing but sickness or inability should make him break the contract. It was known to my young friends in the neighborhood, and on some convivial occasion, a quilting frolic, I believe, they came to my shop and compelled me to leave my work and go with them; there

being girls also in the deputation, my gallantry could not resist. I lost my night's rest in consequence, for the morning sun found me at work, *redeeming the lost time.*" After gratifying his *friends* by spending the evening in their society, he returned to the shop to gratify *himself*, by not violating his faith.

Restitution by a Shopkeeper.

A GENTLEMAN, passing through the streets of Newcastle, was called in by a well known and extensive shopkeeper, who acknowledged himself indebted to him to the amount of a guinea. The gentleman, much astonished, inquired how this was, as he had no recollection of the circumstance. The shopkeeper replied, that about twenty years before, as the gentleman's wife was crossing the river Tyne in a boat which he was in, she accidentally dropped half a guinea, as she took out her money to pay the fare. The now well-off shopkeeper, who had then a family at home literally starving, snatched up the half guinea. He had since been prosperous in his business, and now seized the first opportunity since his good fortune, of paying the money, with interest.

Spanish Mercantile Dealing.

THE Spanish galleons destined to supply Terra Firma, and the kingdoms of Peru and Chili, with almost every article of necessary consumption, used to touch first at Carthagena, and then at Porto Bello. In the latter place a fair was opened; the wealth of America was exchanged for the manufactures of Europe; and during its prescribed term of forty days the richest traffic on the face of the earth was begun and finished with unbounded confidence and the utmost simplicity of transaction. No bale of goods was ever opened, no chest of treasure examined; both were received on the credit of the persons to whom they belonged—only one in-stance of fraud being recorded, during the long period in which trade was carried on with this liberal and unsus-pecting confidence. It seems that all the coined silver which was brought from Peru to Porto Bello, in the year 1654, was found to be adulterated, and to be mingled with a fifth part of base metal. The Spanish merchants, with their usual integrity, sustained the whole loss, and indemnified the for-eigners by whom they were employed. The fraud was detected, and the treas-urer of the revenue in Peru, the author of it, was publicly burnt.

Not Disposed to Lie.

WHEN that model merchant, Abbott Lawrence, was at the height of his mer-cantile prosperity, he was offered the post of ambassador to the English Court—an elegant compliment to him-self personally, and to the honorable and influential class of whom he might almost be said to be the head. Before accepting, he asked Mr. Everett, who had already occupied the post, "wheth-er there was really any foundation in truth for the ancient epigrammatic jest, that an ambassador is a person sent to a foreign government to tell lies for his own," adding that, "if such was the case, his mind was made up; he had never yet told a lie, and was not going to begin at the age of fifty-six." Mr. Everett told him he could answer for himself as a foreign minister, that he had never said a word or written a line which, as far as his own character or that of his government was concerned, he should have been unwilling to see in the newspaper the next day. This ex-planation, the upright merchant re-plied, removed one of his scruples.

Polly Kenton's Lard Speculation.

WHEN Miss Kenton first came into Girard's employ, as his housekeeper or attendant, which was nearly four score years ago, he was making large ship-ments to the West Indies, and he or-dered her to procure some fifty kegs of lard from her father, who was a farmer, and ship them upon her own account. She did so ; and the product, from some unusual state of the market at that time was immense. This product remained on her hands until her death, and was afterward recovered from his executors.

Handful of Wool and a Bank of Money.

A MARSEILLES merchant had a daughter named Eugenie, who early married a Catalan officer, in the service of Don Carlos. He fell in battle, and after burying him in a grave dug with her own hands, this widow with her two children, wretched, and utterly pen-niless, fled to the solitude of the Span-ish mountains, taking refuge in a ruined convent. There, by various little ser-vices to the shepherds and peasants, she obtained a scanty crust and milk for her infants. Becoming thus more and more acquainted with the women who visited the mountains to carry food to their husbands, she invited them to bring with them their wheels and spin together in her place of abode, as more convenient and less lonely than for each to labor by herself. This they did in great numbers, and at the end of every week the grateful peasants presented her a handful of spun wool each. Out of this handful of wool she in due time made a bank of money and a vast estate.

Descending occasionally to the near-est town, she sold these little wool gatherings, and had in a few months accumulated, through this means, suf-ficient money to purchase the shep-herds' raw wool, and to beg for an hour's labor, instead of the handful of material from her guests. Before the summer season was over, and its occu-pations, she collected, by management and industry, enough funds to pay them for their work; and, at the next sheep-shearing, she became the purchaser of more than half the wool.

Encouraged by the rewards of her business skill thus far, she proceeded, the second spring following, under the escort of some of her shepherd friends, to the frontier, where she contracted with one of the greatest wool-buyers in the country, for the produce of the next winter's spinning. In the space of three years the old convent was converted into a spinning factory; became renowned throughout the north of Spain for the fineness of its produce; and proved both a source of social comfort and pecuniary prosperity to the poor peasants who had once, out of their humble means, exercised charity toward its then desolate and necessitous inmate.

Madame L——'s web of good fortune waxed after this agreeable fashion every year, until she became an exceedingly wealthy capitalist, with literally a bank of money, and credit unlimited. She has four factories in Spain, and seven in France, besides cotton and flax mills in Belgium. And all this great fortune has been extracted or irradiated from that handful of wool!

Johnson's Prejudice against Merchants.

DR. JOHNSON was bitterly prejudiced against the mercantile classes, whether of humble or high degree. At breakfast, says his entertaining jackal, Boswell, I asked:

"What is the reason that we are angry at a trader's having opulence?"

"Why, sir," said Johnson, "the reason is, though I do not undertake to prove there is a reason, we see no qualities in trade that should entitle such a man to superiority. We are not angry at a soldier's getting riches, because we see that he possesses qualities which we have not. If a man returns from battle, having lost one hand, with the other

full of gold, we feel that he deserves the gold; but we cannot think that a fellow sitting all day at a desk is entitled to get above us."

"But," responded Boswell, "may we not suppose a merchant to be a man of an enlarged mind, such as Addison in the Spectator describes Sir Andrew Freeport to have been?"

"Why, sir," quoth Johnson, "we may *suppose* any fictitious character. We may suppose a philosophical day laborer, who is happy in reflecting that, by his labor, he contributes to the fertility of the earth, and the support of his fellow creatures; but we *find* no such philosophical day laborer. A merchant may, perhaps, be a man of an enlarged mind, but there is nothing in trade connected with an enlarged mind."

Johnson's opinion—he who could say that Americans ought to be thankful for anything "short of hanging,"—will not have much weight at the present day.

Business Habits of A. T. Stewart.

IT is said of A. T. Stewart, that so accurate is his comprehension of all the departments of his great establishment, that his clerks have sometimes imagined that he has an invisible telegraph girdling the whole building. They also have a saying, that if any one of them is absent he is the one to be first called for.

But few of the thousands who trade at Stewart's ever get sight of the proprietor. He is only to be found at his office, which is situated on the second story, on the side of the house looking into Chambers street. Here he sits at his desk, absorbed by his responsibilities, directing the various energies of the great body of which he is the head. None, except a man of the highest executive ability, could endure the constant care, the earnest effort. He is the hardest worker in the concern. It is not generally known that during these hours of application, and while engrossed in the management of his immense operations, no one is allowed to address him personally until his errand or business shall have been first laid before a subordinate. If it is of such a character that that gentleman can attend to it, it goes no farther, and hence it rests with him to communicate it to his principal. In illustration of this system, the following incident is related: One day a person entered the wholesale department, with an air of great importance, and demanded to see the proprietor. That proprietor could be very easily seen, as he was sitting in his office, but the stranger was courteously met by the assistant, with the usual inquiry as to the nature of his business. The stranger, who was a Government man, bristled up and exclaimed, indignantly, " Sir, I come from Mr. L——, and shall tell my business to no one but Mr. Stewart." " Sir," replied the inevitable Mr. Brown, " if Mr. L—— himself, were to come here, he would not see Mr. Stewart until he should have first told me his business."

Thorburn's Flowery Path to Fortune.

One of the pleasantest stories of the casual manner in which a business was commenced which led on to fortune, is that given by Grant Thorburn, formerly the keeper of a small grocery, afterward the leading and most wealthy American seedsman and florist, his business relations extending to almost all parts. Here it is, in the easy and simple style of that remarkable man :

On the east corner of Nassau and Liberty streets, New York, there lived the venerable old gentleman, Mr. Isaac Van Hook, so well known as the sexton of the New Dutch church opposite his house, for nearly fifty years. In course of time, J. L. and W. S., both cabinet makers, and carrying on a respectable business, having in their employment ten or twelve journeymen and apprentices, took a mad resolution, gave up their business, sold their stock, hired the corner house over the head of poor old Van Hook, turning him and his tobacco pipes out of doors, and commenced the grocery business. · Theirs being a corner, took away the most of my customers; insomuch that · I was obliged to look round for some other mode to support my family. This, you may be sure, I considered a great misfortune; but, in the sequel, prepared the way to put me into a more agreeable and profitable business.

About this time the ladies in New York were beginning to show their taste for flowers, and it was customary to sell the empty flower pots in the grocery stores; these articles also composed part of my stock.

In the fall of the year, when the plants wanted shifting, preparatory to their being placed in the parlor, I was often asked for pots of a handsomer quality, or better made. As stated above, I was looking round for some other means to support my family. All at once it came into my mind to take and paint some of my common flower pots with green varnish paint, thinking it would better suit the taste of the ladies than the common brickbat-colored ones. I painted two pair, and exposed them in front of my window; they soon drew attention, and were sold. I painted six pair; they soon went the same way. Being thus encouraged, I continued painting and selling to good advantage. This was in the fall of 1802. One day, in the month of April following, I observed a man, for the first time, selling flower plants in the Fly market, which then stood at the foot of Maiden lane. As I carelessly passed along, I took a leaf, and rubbing it between my finger and thumb, asked him what was the name of it. He answered, a geranium. This, as far as I can recollect, was the first time I ever heard that the flower in question was a geranium; as, before this, I had no taste for, nor paid any attention to plants. I looked a few minutes at the plant, thought it had a pleasant smell, and that it would look well if removed into one of my green flower pots, to stand on my counter and thus draw attention.

Observe, I did not purchase this plant with the intention of selling it again, but merely to draw attention to my green pots, and let the people see how well the pots looked when the plant was in them. Next day, some one fancied and purchased both plant and pot. The day following, I went when the market was nearly over, judging the man would sell cheaper, rather than have the trouble of carrying them over the river, as he lived at Brooklyn —and in those days there were neither steam nor horse boats. Accordingly, I purchased two plants, and having sold them, I began to think that something might be done in this way; and so I continued to go, at the close of the market, and always bargained for the unsold plants. The man, finding me a useful customer, would assist me to carry them home, and show me how to shift the plants out of his pots and put them into the green pots, if any customers wished it. I soon found, by his tongue, that he was a Scotchman, and being countrymen, we wrought into one another's hands, and thus, from having one plant, in a short time I had fifty. The thing being a novelty, began to draw attention; people carrying their country friends to see the curiosities of the city, would step in to see my plants. In some of these visits the strangers would express a wish to have some of these plants, but, having so far to go, could not carry them. Then they would ask if I had no seed of such plants; then, again, others would ask for cabbage, turnip, or radish seed, etc. These frequent inquiries at length set me to thinking that, if I could get seeds, I would be able to sell them;

but here lay the difficulty. As no one sold seed in New York, none of the farmers or gardeners saved more than what they wanted for their own use, there being no market for an overplus. In this dilemma, I told my situation to G. I., the man from whom I had always bought the plants in the Fly market. He said he was now raising seeds, with the intention of selling them next spring along with his plants in the market; but added, that if I would take his seeds, he would quit the market, and stay at home and raise plants and seeds for me to sell. A bargain was immediately struck; I purchased his stock of seeds, amounting to fifteen dollars, and thus commenced a business, on the 17th of September, 1805, that became the most extensive establishment of the kind in the western world.

Bruised, but not Crushed—the Messrs. Brown, of Liverpool.

THE transactions of the eminent firm of the Browns, in Liverpool, are said to have amounted, in the year 1830, to fifty millions of dollars. In 1837, the American banks all over the country went down one after the other, and many together, almost with a universal crash. They fell, and their fall involved the Messrs. Brown. The latter, though bruised, were not crushed. American commerce was at that time a towering pile ·in course of erection— bank credit was the scaffolding. It fell; and the Browns were not far from being smothered in the rubbish. Had they possessed less than the strength of giants, they could not have extricated themselves—and, giants though they were, they would have struggled in vain, had not a powerful hand assisted them. The British government saw, and looked with apprehension as it saw, the struggles of this colossal mercantile house. From Inverness to Penzance, there was not a single town but would have felt its fall. In Sheffield and Birmingham, and the towns surrounding them, and in Manchester, Leeds, and all the great factory communities, a large number of the merchants and employers—and, as a matter of course, every man and woman employed—were more or less involved in the fate of this establishment. The government of that day saw the imminent peril, and so did the directors of the Bank of England. The latter met, and passed a resolution to give assistance to the extent of some two million pounds to Mr. Brown; the exact sum which he was authorized to draw—a loan of money, to a single individual, unparalleled in the history of the world, unless it be the case of George Peabody—was one million and nine hundred and fifty-nine thousand pounds, or nearly ten million dollars. Of this loan, Mr. Brown took advantage to the extent of between eight and nine hundred thousand pounds, which he afterward repaid, besides clearing up all other embarrassments, and ultimately possessing one of the greatest personal fortunes ever accumulated in the world. The solid romance of this page in the history of so world-renowned a firm is rarely surpassed in interest.

Wealthy Men of Cincinnati.

THERE is a man doing business on Main street, Cincinnati, who was refused credit in 1850 for a stove worth twelve dollars. He is now a director in one of the banks, and is worth $150,000, every cent of which has been made in Cincinnati during that period. There is another business man on the same street, who was refused credit in 1850, by a firm in the drug line for the amount of five dollars; eight years after, the same firm lent that very man five thousand dollars upon his endorsed note. An extensive dealer in Cincinnati, now worth $100,000, and who, it is said, can command more money on short notice for sixty, ninety, or one hundred and twenty days, than almost

any man in Cincinnati, went to a grocery store in 1850 to purchase a hogshead of sugar; it was sold to him with many misgivings as to getting the pay when it became due. A man whose credit in 1850 was such that when trusted by a clerk for a keg of saltpetre, the employer remarked that it might as well have been rolled into the Ohio, was worth, in 1857, $100,000, again a bankrupt in 1860, and now worth $20,000. A man, now good for $300,000, was ten years ago exhibiting a monkey in the streets of the city, for a living. Another heavy business man, a bank director, sold apples in a basket when a boy, through the streets. One of the first merchants in the place, in 1845, and who could at that time have bought entire blocks of houses on credit, and who was a bank director, subsequently died intemperate and insolvent. Another, who in 1837 was rated at half a million of dollars, has since died, leaving his estate insolvent.

Reverses of Mercantile Fortune.

THE array of agents, brokers, bookkeepers, and decayed gentlemen, who were but lately numbered among the merchants, bankers, and ship owners of New York, is quite a moving spectacle. Thus A. B——, for thirty years connected with trade, during most of which period he was a leading member of the great cloth house of ——, has been worth $200,000, but is now a bookkeeper for a concern in John street. J. S. has been forty years in trade, and was considered successful beyond all liability to future risk, being for many years ranked among the rich men of the street, failed, and is now poor. B—— and M., princes in the dry goods line, built two palatial stores in Broadway, and have been immensely rich, but after battling honorably with adverse fortune, failed. J. R——, a retired merchant, estimated at $500,000, holding at one time $50,000 in Delaware and Hudson Canal stock, subsequently got involved and lost all. Instances like these might be multiplied to any extent.

William Roscoe, the Poet Banker.

AFTER Mr. Roscoe had retired to private life, he was earnestly solicited to enter a banking house, the officers of which desired the attention of a person possessed of a great business capacity and talent. He had already acted as the confidential adviser of the house when in difficulty, and had rendered it valuable assistance. Yielding to the earnest request of his friends, he became a partner in said house, and for a time devoted himself exclusively to its concerns. Some seven years after, owing to the demands of the time and the scarcity of specie, the house was forced to suspend. At his solicitation, the creditors of the firm allowed them six years in which to discharge their debts. During all this period Mr. Roscoe's labors were unremitted. To meet their obligations, however, the private property of the members of the firm had to be sold, and under the most unfavorable circumstances. It was during this season of trial, that Mr. Roscoe wrote the celebrated and immortal sonnet, so well known to all who read the English language, and so evincive of his resignation during trials so severe.

Chinese Merchant's Gratitude.

A MERCHANT resided many years, highly respected, at Canton and Macao, when a sudden reserve of fortune reduced him from a state of affluence to the greatest necessity.

A Chinese merchant, to whom he had formerly rendered service, gratefully offered him an immediate loan of ten thousand dollars, which the gentleman accepted, and gave his bond for the amount; this the Chinese immediately threw into the fire, saying, "When you,

my friend, first came to China, I was a poor man. You took me by the hand, and, assisting my honest endeavors, made me rich. Our circumstances are now reversed—I see you poor, while I have affluence."

The bystanders had snatched the bond from the flames; and the merchant, sensibly affected by such generosity, pressed his Chinese friend to take the security, which he did, and then effectually destroyed it.

But the disciple of Confucius, observing the renewed distress this act occasioned the merchant, said he would accept the latter's watch, or any little valuable as a memorial of their friendship. The merchant immediately presented his watch, and the Chinese, in return, gave him an old iron seal, saying: "Take this seal—it is one I have long used, and possesses no intrinsic value; but as you are going to India, to look after your outstanding concerns, should misfortune further attend you, draw upon me for any sum of money you may stand in need of, seal it with this signet, sign it with your own hand, and I will pay the money."

Father Taylor and the Banker's Exhortation.

AN eminent banker from the West End, Boston, once visited Father Taylor's church during a warm revival, and somewhat varied the usual character of the prayer meeting, by an address setting forth the beneficence of the merchant princes, the goodness of the Port Society, and above all the duty of seamen to show their *gratitude to the merchants*. He was somewhat taken aback when Father Taylor arose, at the close of this rather presumptuous exhortation, and simply inquired, "Is there any other old sinner from up-town that would like to say a word?"

"An Error in Shipping the Goods."

TOWARD the close of the Revolutionary war, the owners of the North Church in New Haven, Ct., sent to a Boston merchant for some nails, to make repairs with, when one of the kegs sent in return for the order was found to contain Spanish silver dollars. The deacons wrote to the merchant in Boston, that there was " an error in shipping the goods ;" but he answered that the goods were sold as he bought them of a privateersman, and " he couldn't rectify mistakes." So the silver was melted up into a service of plate for the church, which is in use at the present day. Had the deacons been less shrewd, and stated the nature of the "error" to the merchant, that service of plate would never have turned up. As it was, they realized the full benefit of what is so much esteemed in business correspondence—brevity.

Persevering Traders.

AN old bachelor who resided in Brixton, in order to prevent itinerant traders annoying him by knocking at his door to dispose of their wares, affixed to his knocker a label to this effect: ' The inhabitant of this house never buys anything at the door—Hawkers, beware ! " He was dreadfully annoyed shortly after by a loud knock at the parlor window, from which he saw two fellows with clothes-lines, mats, and pegs to sell. Throwing up the sash in a pretty considerable rage, he accosted them thus : " Can you read ? " " Yes, master," answered the hawker. " Then don't you see a notice affixed to my knocker, that I never buy anything at the door ? " " To be sure we do ; so we thought we would make bold and try to do a little something at the parlor window." The fellow's wit pacified the old bachelor, who straightway (he had a good vein in him, after all) made a purchase. Immediately afterward,

however, he sent for a painter, and had the following addition made to his announcement : " Nor at the window either."

Aptness and Nicety in Business Illustrated

ON a certain Saturday night, the clerks of the Bank of England could not make the balance come out right by just one hundred pounds. This is a serious matter in that little establishment—not the cash, but the mistake in arithmetic ; for it necessitates a world of scrutiny. An error in the balancing has been known to keep a delegation of clerks from each department at work, sometimes, through the whole night. A hue and cry, therefore, was made after this one hundred pounds, as if the old lady in Threadneedle street would be in the *Gazette*, as an insolvent, for want of it. Luckily on the Sunday morning following, the clerk—in the middle of the sermon, perhaps, if the truth were known,—felt a suspicion of the truth dart through his mind quicker than any flash of the telegraph itself. He told the chief cashier, on Monday morning, that perhaps the mistake might have occurred in packing some boxes of specie for the West Indies which had been sent to Southampton for shipment. The suggestion was immediately acted upon. Here was a race — lightning against steam, and steam with eight and forty hours the start given. Instantly the wires asked, " whether such a vessel had left the harbor ? " " Just weighing anchor," was the reply. " Stop her ! " frantically shouted the telegraph. It was done. " Have up on deck certain boxes marked so and so ; weigh them carefully." They were weighed ; and one, the delinquent, was found heavier by just one packet of a hundred sovereigns than it ought to be." " Let her go," says the mysterious telegraph. The West India folks were debited with just one hundred pounds more, and the error was corrected without even looking into the boxes, or delaying the voyage an hour.

European and American Modes of Doing Business.

THE loose and careless manner in which business is done in this country —at least in these latter days of hurry and venture—as compared with the practice among European merchants— was a subject frequently commented upon by the late John Bromfield, well known as one of the "prince mer- chants" of Boston. In his familiar style, Mr. Bromfield used to say, "Here, if a purchaser is about to buy a cargo of box sugars, he will bore into one box, look at a second, kick a third —and take the lot; but in Europe, they thrust an iron searcher through and through every box, and carefully exam- ine every layer."

Minding One's Own Business.

"DURING my long commercial expe- rience," says Girard, "I have noticed that no advantage results from telling one's business to others, except to create jealousy or competitors when we are fortunate, and to gratify our enemies when otherwise." He was never known to disregard this theory in all his pro- tracted career as one of the greatest and most successful of merchants.

Hon. Peter C. Brooks, of Boston, who left one of the largest fortunes ever amassed in this country, on being asked what rule he would recommend to a young man as most likely to ensure suc- cess, answered: "Let him mind his own business;" and to a similar in- quiry, it has been said that Robert Lenox, of New York, well remembered as one of the most distinguished mer- chants ever known in that great city, and for his wide hospitality, once an- swered: "Let him be beforehand with his business." One answer seems to in- clude the other, as no man can be be- *forehand* with his business, unless he *minds* it unremittingly, instead of spend- ing his time and wits in looking after others.

John Jacob Astor's "Highway to For- tune."

"IT's what thee'll spend, my son," said a sage old Quaker, "not what thee'll make, which will decide whether thee's to be rich or not,"—Franklin's advice, only in another shape, "Take care of the pennies, and the pounds will take care of themselves."

John Jacob Astor used to say, that a man who wishes to be rich and has saved ten thousand dollars, has won half the battle—is on the highway to fortune. Not that Astor thought ten thousand much. But he knew that in making and saving such a' sum, a man acquired habits of prudent economy, which would constantly keep him ad- vancing in wealth. The habitual small expenses, which are designated as "only a trifle," amount, in the aggre- gate, like the sands of the shore, to something pretty serious. Ten cents a day, even, is thirty-six dollars and a half a year, and that is the interest on a capital of six hundred dollars; so that the man who saves ten cents a day only, is so much richer than him who does not, as if he owned a life estate in a property worth six hundred dollars.

Gideon Lee carrying the Lapstone.

IN the year 1834, the memorable panic year, a report was put in circula- tion among the New York business men, that the house of Gideon Lee, long so eminent and stable, had failed. In allusion to the report, Mr. Lee re- marked: "I commenced business, when poor, on credit; I thrived by credit; and I hold it to be my duty to sacrifice my property down to twenty shillings in the pound, before that credit shall be dishonored. *I have carried the lap- stone, and I can do it again; but I will* never suffer a promise of mine to be broken, while I have a shilling left that I can call my own."

Usurious Interest on Money—Peter C. Brooks's Rule.

ONE of the undeviating principles upon which Peter C. Brooks conducted his great business was that of never, either directly or indirectly, taking more than legal interest. Had he been willing to violate this rule, and that in modes not condemned by the letter of the law, nor by public opinion, he might easily have doubled his fortune. But many considerations led him to adopt and adhere to his rule on this subject. It was contrary to law to take more than legal interest, and he held it to be eminently dangerous to tamper with the duty of a good citizen, and break the law, because he might think the thing forbidden not morally wrong. This consideration was entirely irrespective of the fact, that at one period, by the law of Massachusetts, the contract was wholly violated by the demand of usurious interest, and the creditor placed in the debtor's power. But after the mitigation of the law in this respect, Mr. Brooks's practice remained unaltered. He believed and often said, that, *in the long run*, six per cent. is as much as the bare use of money is worth in this country; that to demand more was for the capitalist to claim the benefit of the borrower's skill in some particular business, or of his courage and energy; or else it was to take advantage of his neighbor's need. He frequently said that he would never put it in the power of any one, in a reverse of fortune, to ascribe his ruin to the payment of usurious interest to him. On more than one occasion, when some beneficial public object was to be promoted, he lent large sums at an interest below the legal and current rate.

Benevolence of Shai-king-qua, a Chinese Merchant.

AN interesting instance of generosity is given of a Chinese merchant, of the name of Shai-king-qua, who had long known a Mr. Anderson, an English trader, and had large business transactions with him. It appears that Mr. Anderson met with heavy losses, became insolvent, and at the time of his failure owed his Chinese friend upward of eighty thousand dollars. Mr. A. wished to go to England, in the hope of being able to retrieve his affairs; he called on the Hong merchant, and in the utmost distress, explained his situation, his wishes, and his plans. The Chinese listened with anxious attention, and having heard his story, thus addressed him :

"My friend Anderson, you have been very unfortunate; you lose all—I very sorry; you go to England; if you more fortunate there, you come back and pay; but that you no forget Chinaman friend, you take this, and when you look on this, you will remember Shai-king-qua." In saying these words, he pulled out a valuable gold watch, and gave it to Anderson.

Mr. Anderson took leave of his friend, but he did not live to retrieve his affairs, or to return to China. When the account of his death, and of the distress in which he had left his family, reached Canton, the Hong merchant called on one of the merchants of the factory who was about to return to Europe, and addressed him in the following manner : "Poor Mr. Anderson dead ! I very sorry; he good man; he friend, and he leave two childs; they poor—they have nothing —they childs of my friend; you take this for them; tell them Chinaman friend send it !" And he put into the returning merchant's hands several thousand dollars for Mr. A.'s children.

Money-getting Tact of Jews.

THAT the Jews are more successful in money-getting than any other people is a generally admitted fact. "As rich as a Jew," is a proverb. How to account for it—to what cause to ascribe it—has long been a puzzle. If the following be matter-of-fact, instead of romancing, it may be considered a partial solution of the puzzle: "The politest people in the world are not the French, the English, the American, the Italian, nor the German, but the Jewish. For the Jews are maltreated, and reviled, and despoiled of their civil privileges, and their social rights; yet are they everywhere polite, affable, insinuating, and condescending. They are remarkable for their industry and perseverance; indulge in few or no recriminations; are faithful to old associations; more respectful of the prejudices of others than those are of theirs; not more worldly-minded and money-loving than people generally are; and, everything considered, they surpass all nations in courtesy, affability, and forbearance. Few persons excel in address a bright and polished Jew. There is no rusticity among that people." Whether this representation be correct or not, we scarcely know, as the majority of the reputed Jews in this country, especially those in the clothing trade, are a mongrel race. But it is certain that much of business success depends on courtesy.

Sole Qualification of a Bill Broker.

AN ancient writer on money affairs compressed a good deal of shrewd truth in his brief description of what a bill broker should be: A bill broker ought to be a man of honor, and know his business; he should avoid babbling, and be prudent in his office, which consists in one sole point—*to hear all and say nothing;* so that he ought never to speak of the negotiations transacted by means of his intervention.

Peculiar Feature in Rothschild's Business Character.

ROTHSCHILD'S management of the business of exchanges was one of the most remarkable features in his character. He *never hesitated for a moment* in fixing a rate either as a drawer or purchaser of a foreign bill of exchange on any part of the world; and his memory was so retentive, that, notwithstanding the multifarious and immense transactions into which he entered on every foreign post-day on the Exchange, he never took a memorandum of them, but, on his return to his office, could dictate to his clerks the whole of the bargains he had made, with the various rates of exchange, and the names of the several parties with whom he had dealt, with the most perfect exactness.

Commercial Fortune of a Peer.

ONE of the most popular members of the British House of Lords is said to have purchased his peerage with a million of dollars in gold. One of the methods by which that mercantile house, of which he was the leading member, amassed the large fortune which they now enjoy, was this: they saw that the stock of a certain article, necessary for culinary purposes, was becoming scarce, and that the supply would be limited; they forthwith sent orders and agents to buy up that particular article, and thus swept the market. The demand for the article increased—as is usual—in proportion to its scarcity, the rice went up, and the house cleared within one week, at the expense of tens of thousands of consumers in very humble circumstances, hundreds of thousands of dollars.

Half-a-Million Profit by One of Girard's Operations.

IN the year 1813, an interesting circumstance occurred in the business operations of Girard, through his bank, by which he accomplished an enterprise of great importance to the city of Philadelphia, by the increase of its trade, as well as to his own funds in its profits, besides the advantages which were furnished to the Government by the duties which accrued to the national treasury. It happened that his ship, the Montesquieu, was captured at the mouth of the Delaware river, as was alleged, by a British frigate, and as this vessel had an invoice cargo of two hundred thousand dollars—consisting of teas, nankeens and silks—from Canton, it was determined by the captors, in preference to the hazard of being recaptured by an American ship in any attempt to carry their prize to a British port, to send a flag of truce to Mr. Girard, in order to give him the offer of a ransom. Applying to his well-stored vaults, the banker drew from them the sum of ninety-three thousand dollars in doubloons, which was transmitted to the British commander, and his vessel was soon seen coming into port with her rich cargo,—and which, notwithstanding the price of the ransom, is supposed, by the advanced value of every article on board, to have added a half a million of dollars to his fortune.

American Merchants of the Olden Time —Joseph Peabody.

JOSEPH PEABODY, of Salem, Mass., a name known wherever American commercial enterprise has been heard of, built and owned *eighty-three* ships, which, in every instance, he freighted himself; and for the navigation of which he shipped, at different times, *upward of seven thousand seamen.* From the year 1811, he had advanced thirty-five to the rank of shipmaster, who entered his employ as boys. He had performed by these vessels the following voyages, viz.: to Calcutta, thirty-eight; Canton, seventeen; Sumatra, thirty-two; St. Petersburg, forty-seven; other ports in the north of Europe, ten; the Mediterranean, twenty, before

the war of 1812. The voyages performed by his vessels to the West Indies, Spanish Main, and along our wide extended coast, are unnumbered. The aggregate of his annual state, county, and city taxes paid into the treasury, amounted to about two hundred thousand dollars. A business of such vast magnitude and enterprise has rarely, for so long a period, been conducted by the energy and industry of an individual.

Gresham's Fortunate Letter.

THOMAS GRESHAM, as is recorded in history, was one of the first English merchants that traded to the East Indies; and, having fitted out several ships, he miscalculated the time at which they would return—a circumstance that caused him much embarrassment. He, however, soon recovered from this temporary disquietude. One day, while despondingly walking about the Bourse, or Exchange, which then had its location in Lombard street, a sailor came up and presented him with a letter from the captain of one of his ships, which contained the gratifying information that two of his ships had arrived safe from the East Indies; and that the box, which the bearer would deliver, contained some diamonds and pearls of great value, as a sample of the immense riches the ships had brought home. This peculiar and somewhat romantic incident is said to be an explanation of the statue of Gresham, in the old Royal Exchange of London, which represents him as holding an open letter in his hand.

Private Mercantile Finances and Royal Fleets.

A SINGLE merchant secured Queen Elizabeth against all the danger with which she was threatened by the *soidisant* invincible armada of Spain. When the queen was apprised of the designs of Spain, she had no ships ca-

SIR THOMAS GRESHAM'S FORTUNATE LETTER.

pable of being opposed to the Spanish fleet; as a part of those which were lying in the ports and docks could only be used after twelve months. Mr. Thomas Sutton, however, the distinguished merchant who founded the Charter House, being well acquainted with the state of the French finances, knew that the Spanish fleet could not set sail, but through the medium of bills which were to be drawn upon the Genoese Bank. He therefore conceived the idea of buying up all the paper or bills that could be met with in every commercial town in Europe, and to deposit them in the Bank of Genoa, that by his large remittances he might have that bank so in his power, as to incapacitate it, whenever he chose, from giving any aid to the Spaniards. Being well aware that it only required to let those remittances remain at Genoa, until the season should obstruct the sailing of the fleet, he calculated that these exchange operations would cost about forty thousand pounds sterling, and he proposed to the queen to extricate her at this price from the dilemma. The proposal was accepted, and carried into effect with so much secresy, that Philip's hands were tied, and he could not send out the fleet until the following year.

Portuguese Pilgrim in the Streets of Venice.

On a morning of summer, in the year 1498, a poor Portuguese pilgrim, clothed in rags, and who had wandered on foot from his native hills, appeared in the streets of Venice, and announced to its citizens that one of those daring navigators sent out by his king, had doubled the Cape of Storms, and discovered a new route to India. He was surrounded and eagerly questioned by a throng of princes, merchants, and artizans. His answers struck terror in every heart. They saw at once that the partition wall of their commercial monopoly was broken down; they saw the lucrative trade of the east transferred from the Lagoon to Lisbon and the Tagus; they saw that the rich merchandise which they gathered and dispersed throughout Europe, was destined to pass through other hands; they saw their ships rotting in their docks, and their sailors wandering idly about the streets; they heard the last motion of those looms which had produced the choice silken and woollen fabrics in which the nobles of Europe clothed themselves; in a word, they rightly fancied they saw the destruction of that commerce whence came all their wealth, their luxury, and their pride; that commerce which had sent forth with the third army of the Crusaders, two hundred ships, and with the fourth, five hundred; that commerce whose mighty pulsations had been felt at the furthest extremities of the earth. Here was the remote, but the chief cause of the *Commercial Fall of Venice!*

Shopkeepers and Warriors.

When Napoleon applied to England the contemptuous epithet of a "nation of shopkeepers," he paid her a higher compliment than he intended; it was an unintentional tribute to the power she had acquired by trade, an extorted homage to that commercial policy by which her merchants had become the arbiters of Europe—of those elements of strength which the shopkeepers of the Royal Exchange and Threadneedle street had furnished to her rulers, by which she alone was enabled to prescribe boundaries to the ambition of the great Captain, and say to the mighty wave of Gallic usurpation, "Thus far shalt thou go, and no farther." Military prowess was held in check by mercantile combinations, and the shopkeepers proved an overmatch for the warrior.

Murdered Merchant Watched by his Dog.

An account, well attested, is related of two French merchants, who were travelling to a fair, and, while passing through a wood, one of them murdered the other, and robbed him of his money. After burying him, so as to prevent discovery, he proceeded on his journey. The dog of the person remained, however, by the grave of his master; and, by his long and continued howling, attracted the notice of several persons in the neighborhood, who, by this means, discovered the murder. The fair being ended, they watched the return of the merchant. The murderer no sooner appeared in view, than the dog sprung furiously upon him. He was apprehended, confessed the crime, and was executed. The kindness of the merchant had secured even the attachment of his dog to such a degree, that not even death could sunder the noble animal from the loved form of his master.

Aged Merchant Saved from Robbery by the Weather.

An aged merchant was one day returning from market. He was on horseback, and behind him was a valise filled with money. The rain began to fall with violence, and the good old man was soon wet to his skin. At this he was vexed, and indulged in some pretty audible murmurings that the weather should prove so bad while he was journeying.

He soon reached the borders of a thick forest. What was his terror on beholding, on one side of the road, a robber, with leveled gun, aiming at him and attempting to fire! But the powder being wet by the rain, the gun did not go off, and the merchant, giving spurs to his horse, fortunately had time to escape.

As soon as he found himself safe, he said to himself, "How wrong was I, not to endure the rain patiently, as sent by Providence. If the weather had been dry and fair, I should not, probably, have been alive at this hour, and my children would have expected my return in vain. The rain which caused me to murmur, came at a fortunate moment to save my life and preserve my property." It is almost needless to add, that thereafter the good merchant made the best of the weather, whichever way it turned up, indorsing with a good will the old adage, that it is an ill wind indeed that blows no good to *some* one.

English Merchant and Spanish Beggar.

It is related that an English merchant in the neighborhood of Madrid, having no money in his pocket, generously gave a handful of choice cigars to a beggar who approached him: the poorest Spaniard will be more gratified with a cigar than with money, so far as his personal feelings are concerned, as it is a compliment. Three years afterward, this merchant was seized near his country house by a band of robbers. While they were settling his ransom they were joined by an absent comrade, who instantly dismounted, and, approaching the Englishman, whom he had at once recognized, saluted him, and asked if he did not remember having given, at such a place and time, a handful of cigars to a beggar; then, turning to his comrades, he said, "This is my benefactor—whoever lays a hand on him lays it on me."

Good Word for Girard.

One of the most ingenious and plausible estimates of Mr. Girard's character as a business man—and the most favorable—which has ever appeared, is that uttered by Mr. Everett: He told me himself (says Mr. E.), that at the age of forty, his circumstances were so narrow, that he was employed as the commander of his own sloop, engaged in the coasting trade between New York or Philadelphia and New Orleans; adding that on a certain occasion he was forty-five days in working his way up from the Balize to the city. Few persons enjoyed less personal popularity in the community in which he lived, and to which he bequeathed his princely fortune. If this proceeded from defects of personal character, it is a topic to be discussed only in its proper place. Of the effect upon the public welfare of the community of such a fortune in one's hands, freedom of speech may of course be indulged in. While I am far from saying that it might not have been abused by being made the instrument of a corrupt and dangerous influence in the community, I have never heard that it was so abused by Mr. Girard; and, on general principles, it may perhaps be safely said, that the class of men qualified to amass large fortunes by perseverance and exclusive dedication to business, by frugality and thrift, are not at all likely to apply this wealth to ambitious or corrupt designs. As to the effect in all other points of view, I confess I see nothing but public benefit in such capital, managed with unrelaxing economy; one-half judiciously employed by the proprietor himself in commerce—the other half loaned to the business community. What better use could have been made of it? Will it be said, divide it equally among the community; give each individual in the United States a share? It would have amounted to half a dollar each for man, woman, and child; and, of course, might as well have been sunk in the middle of the sea. Such a distribution would have been another name for annihilation. How many ships would have furled their sails, how many warehouses would have closed their shutters, how many wheels, heavily laden with the products of industry, would have stood still, how many families would have been reduced to want, and without any advantage resulting from distribution?

In a country like this, where the laws forbid hereditary transmission, and encourage equality of fortune, accumulations of capital, made by industry, enterprise, and prudence, and employed in active investments, without ministering to extravagance and luxury, are beneficial to the public. Their possessor becomes, whether he wills it or not, the steward of others; not merely, as in Mr. Girard's case, because he may destine a colossal fortune after his decease for public objects, but because, while he lives, every dollar of it must be employed in giving life to industry and employment to labor.

Had Mr. Girard lived in a fashionable part of the city, in a magnificent house; had he dazzled the passer-by with his splendid equipages, and spread a sumptuous table for his "dear five hundred friends," he would no doubt have been a more popular man. But in my apprehension he appears to far greater advantage, as a citizen and a patriot, in his modest dwelling and plain garb; appropriating to his personal wants the smallest pittance from his princely income; living to the last in the dark and narrow street in which he made his fortune, and, when he died, bequeathing it for the education of orphan children. For the public, I do not know that he could have done better: of all men in the world, he probably derived the least enjoyment from his property himself.

The Banker's Seven-Shilling Piece.

IT was during one of the great national panics, that a gentleman—who may be called Mr. Thompson—was seated, with something of a melancholy look, in his dreary back room, watching his clerks pay away thousands of pounds hourly. Thompson was a banker of excellent credit—there existed, perhaps, in the city of London, no safer concern than that of Messrs. Thompson & Co.; but at a moment like the one referred to, no rational reflection was admitted, no former stability was looked to. A general distrust was felt, and every one rushed to his banker's to withdraw his hoard, fearing that the next instant would be too late—forgetting entirely that this step was that of all others most likely to insure the ruin that was sought to be avoided. The wealthy citizen named sat gloomily watching the outpouring of his gold, and with a grim smile listening to the clamorous demands on his cashier; for although he felt perfectly easy and secure as to the ultimate strength of his resources, yet he could not altogether suppress a feeling of bitterness as he saw constituent after constituent rush in, and those whom he fondly imagined to be his dearest friends eagerly assisting in the run upon his strong box.

Presently the door opened, and a stranger was ushered in, who, after gazing for a moment at the bewildered banker, coolly drew a chair, and abruptly addressed him:

"You will pardon me, sir, for asking a strange question, but I am a plain man, and like to come straight to the point."

"Well, sir," impatiently interrupted the other.

"I have heard that you have a run on your bank, sir."

"Well?"

"Is it—true?"

"Really, sir, I must decline to reply to your most extraordinary query. If, however, you have any money in the bank, you had better at once draw it out, and so satisfy yourself; our cashier will instantly pay you,"—and the banker rose, as a hint to the stranger to withdraw.

"Far from it, sir; I have not one sixpence in your hands."

"Then may I ask what is your business here?"

"I wish to know if a small sum would aid you at this moment?"

"Why do you ask the question?"

"Because if it would, I would gladly pay in a small deposit."

The money dealer started.

"You seem surprised; you don't know my person or my motive. I'll at once explain. Do you recollect some twenty years ago when you resided in Essex?"

"Perfectly."

"Well, then, sir, perhaps you have not forgotten the turnpike gate through which you passed daily? My father kept that gate, and was often honored by a few minutes' talk with you. One Christmas morning, my father was sick, and I attended the toll bar. On that day you passed through, and I opened the gate for you. Do you recollect it, sir?"

"Not I, my friend."

"No, sir; few such men remember their kind deeds, but those who are benefited by them ought not to forget them. I am perhaps prolix; listen, however, only a few moments, and I have done."

The great banker had become interested, and at once assented.

"Well, sir, as I said before, I threw open the gate for you, as I considered myself in duty bound—I wished you 'a happy Christmas.' 'Thank you, my lad,' replied you—'thank you; and the same to you; here is a trifle to make it so," and you threw me a *seven-shilling piece*. It was the first money I ever possessed, and never shall I forget my joy at receiving it, nor your kind smile in bestowing it. I long treasured it, and as I grew up, added a little to it, till I was able to rent a toll myself. You left that part of the country, and I lost sight of you. Yearly, however, I have been getting on; your present brought good fortune with it; I am now comparatively rich, and to you I consider that I owe all. So this morning, hearing accidentally that there was a run on your bank, I gathered all my capital, and brought it to lodge with you, in case it can be of any use; here it is—" and he handed a bundle of bank notes to the agitated Thompson; "in a few days I will call again." Snatching up his hat, and throwing down his card, he walked out of the room.

Thompson undid the roll—it contained thirty thousand pounds! The stern-hearted banker—for all bankers must be stern—burst into tears. The firm did not require this prop; but the motive was so noble, that even a millionnaire sobbed; he could not help it. This house is still one of the first in London.

The thirty thousand pounds of the turnpike boy has now grown into some two hundred thousand pounds. Fortune has well disposed of her gifts.

Commencing with Three Tobacco Boxes—Jacob Barker.

JACOB BARKER's disposition for commercial pursuits manifested itself at a very early period—his first essay in this line being with three tobacco boxes. The history of the tobacco boxes was this: Mr. Barker was, as a relaxation from the fatigues of attending store and other matters for his brother James, permitted to go as cabin boy in his packet to New York and Boston two or three times a year. On one occasion, the passengers presented him with thirty-one cents. This he invested in Boston in three iron tobacco boxes, and took them to Nantucket, where he sold two of them for a penny apiece profit; the other got a little rusty, and was sold at first cost. When at Nantucket, forty years after this, he met a poor old man hobbling along with the aid of a staff, who abruptly observed, "Jacob, will you take a piece of tobacco?" at the same time presenting the box. Jacob replied, "No, I thank you, I do not use tobacco in that way,"—when the old man said, "Do you know that box?" This brought its sale to the recollection of Jacob, who seizing his hand, said, "Is this you, Mr. Ellis?

How do you do? I am glad to see you looking so well after so long a period."

Washington as a Business Man.

AT the age of thirteen, Washington studied the intricate forms of business with great ardor. He copied out bills of exchange, notes of hand, bills of sale, receipts, and all the varieties of that class—all being remarkable for the precision and elegance with which they were executed. His manuscripts, even then, were of the utmost neatness and uniformity, the diagrams always beautiful, the columns and tables of figures exact; and all in unstained and unblotted order. His business papers, ledgers, and daybooks, in which no one wrote but himself, were models of exactness. Every fact had its place, and was recorded in a plain, clear handwriting, and there was neither interlineation, blot, or blemish. One of his rules, at this immature age, was, "Let your discourse with men of business be short and comprehensive."

From 1759 to 1764, Washington was, in some measure, an active merchant; for, in that calmest period of his eventful life, he regularly exported to London the product of his large estate on the Potomac. The shipments were made in his own name, and to his correspondents in Bristol and Liverpool, to which places his tobacco was consigned. In return for the articles exported, it was his custom, twice in each year, to import from London the goods which he desired to use; and as an instance of the accurateness with which he conducted his commercial transactions as an importer, it is stated that he required his agent to send him, in addition to a general bill of the whole, the original vouchers of the shopkeepers and mechanics, from whom purchases had been made. So particular was he in these concerns, that he recorded, with his own hand, in books prepared for the purpose, all the long lists of orders, and copies of the multifarious receipts from the different merchants and tradesmen who had supplied the goods. In this way he kept a perfect oversight of the business; ascertained the prices; could detect any imposition, mismanagement, or carelessness, and tell when any advantage was taken of him—of which, if he discovered any, he did not fail to remind his correspondents.

Present Prosperity of the Rothschilds.

HE who does not delay for casualties, and has knowledge enough to perceive that in all great affairs the success not only depends on the choice and use of the most favorable moment, but *especially on the pursuit of an acknowledged fundamental maxim*, has the two principles which are never neglected by this banking house, and to which—besides to a prudent performance of its business and to advantageous conjunctures—it owes the greatest part of its present wealth and renown.

The first of these principles was that which caused the five brothers to carry on their business in a perpetual and uninterrupted communion. This was the golden rule bequeathed to them by their dying father. Since his death, every proposition, let it come from whom it may, is the object of their common deliberations. Every important undertaking was carried on by a combined effort, after a plan agreed upon, and all had an equal share in the result. Though for several years their customary residences, being in the great capitals of Europe, were very remote, this circumstance could never interrupt their harmony; it rather gave them this advantage, that they were always perfectly well instructed as to the condition of things in every metropolis, and thus each of them, on his part, could the better prepare and initiate the affairs to be undertaken by

the firm. The second principle in perpetual view of this house is, not to seek an excessive profit in any undertaking; to assign certain limits—though, of course, proportioned to their vast means —to every enterprise; and, as much as human caution and prudence will permit, to make themselves independent of the play of accidents.

Mr. Everett and the Hindoo Merchant.

THE far-reaching influence which American commercial enterprise has abroad, is illustrated by the following anecdote told by Mr. Everett: "When I had the honor to represent the country at London," says Mr. E., "I was a little struck one day, at the royal drawingroom, to see the President of the Board of Control (the board charged with the supervision of the Government of India) approaching me with a stranger, at that time much talked of in London—the Babu Dwarkananth Tagore. This person, who is now living, was a Hindoo of great wealth, liberality, and intelligence. He was dressed with oriental magnificence—he had on his head, by way of turban, a rich Cashmere shawl, held together by a large diamond brooch; another Cashmere around his body; his countenance and manners were those of a highly intelligent and remarkable person, as he was. After the ceremony of introduction was over, he said he wished to make his acknowledgments to me, as the American minister, for the benefits which my countrymen had conferred upon his countrymen. I did not at first know what he referred to; I thought he might have in view the mission schools, knowing, as I did, that he himself had done a great deal for education. He immediately said that he referred to the *cargoes of ice* sent from America to India, conducing not only to comfort but health. He asked me if I knew from what part of America it came. It gave me great pleasure to tell him that I lived, when at home, within a short distance of the spot from which it was brought."

Earliest American Whaleship in England.

THE following interesting scrap is from Barnerd's History of England: "1783. On the third of February, the ship Bedford, Capt. Moores, belonging to Massachusetts, arrived in the Downs, passed Gravesend on the 4th, and was reported at the custom house on the 6th. She was not allowed regular entry until some consultation had taken place between the commissioners of the custom house and the lords of the council, on account of the many acts of parliament yet in force against the rebels of America. She was loaded with five hundred and eighty-seven butts of whale oil, manned wholly with American seamen, and belonged to the island of Nantucket, Mass. The vessel lay at the Horsley Down, a little below the river, and was the first which displayed the stars and stripes in any British port."

Explaining his Business.

THERE is an ancient volume of "Saxon Dialogues," preserved in the British Museum, in which the merchant, as one of the characters introduced, gives the why and wherefore of his occupation:

"I say that I am useful to the king, and to aldermen, and to the rich, and to all people. I ascend my ship with my merchandise, and sail over the sea-like places, and sell my things, and buy dear things which are not produced in this land, and I bring them to you here, with great danger over the sea; and sometimes I suffer shipwreck, with the loss of all my things, scarcely escaping myself." He is then asked, "What do you bring to us?" to which he answers, "Skins, silks, costly gems, and gold; various garments, pigment, wine,

oil, ivory; brass, copper and tin, silver, glass, and such like."

The principle of all commercial dealings is distinctly enough stated in the answer to the next question: "Will you sell your things here as you bought them there?" "I will not; because what would my labor benefit me? I will sell them here dearer than I bought them there, that I may get some profit to feed me, my wife, and children."

Aztec Merchants.

THE Aztec merchant was a sort of itinerant trader, who made his journeys to the remotest borders of Anahuac, and to the countries beyond, carrying with him merchandise of rich stuffs, jewelry, slaves, and other valuable ' commodities.'

With this rich freight the merchant visited the different provinces, always bearing some present of value from his own sovereign to their chiefs, and usually receiving others in return, with a permission to trade. Should this be denied him, or should he meet with indignity or violence, he had the means of resistance in his power. He performed his journeys with a number of companions of his own rank, and a large body of inferior attendants, who were employed to transport the goods. The whole caravan went armed, and so well provided against sudden hostilities, that they could make good their defence, if necessary, till reinforced from home.

It was not unusual for government to allow the merchants to raise levies themselves, for warlike purposes, and which were placed under their command. It was, moreover, very common for the prince to employ the merchants as a sort of spies, to furnish him information of the state of the country through which they passed, and the disposition of the inhabitants toward himself.

Thus their sphere of action was much

enlarged beyond that of a humble tra- der, and they acquired a high consider- ation in the body politic. They were allowed to assume insignia and devices of their own. Some of their number composed what is called by the Span- ish writers a council of finance. They were much consulted by the monarch, who had some of them constantly near his person, addressing them by the title of " uncle."

Sources of Wealth of the Medici Mer- chants.

THE two brothers, Lorenzo and Cos- mo de Medici, were in conjunction in their great mercantile affairs, until the death of the former, when his propor- tion of the riches they obtained, amount- ing to hundreds of thousands of florins, was inherited by his son Pier Francesco de Medici, for whose use it was retained by Cosmo until the year 1451, when a distribution took place among the two families. From that time it was agreed that the traffic of the family should be carried on for the joint benefit of Pier Francesco, and of Piero and Giovanni, the sons of Cosmo, who were to divide the profits in equal shares of one third to each—and immense riches were by them thus acquired.

Of the particular branch of traffic by which the Medici family acquired their enormous wealth, there is little doubt but that a considerable portion of it arose from the trade which the Floren- tines, in the early part of the fifteenth century, began to carry on to Alexan- dria for the productions of the East, in which they attempted to rival the states of Genoa and Venice. To this they were induced by the representations of Taddeo di Cenni, who having resided at Venice, and being apprised of the advantages which that city derived from the traffic in spices and other Eastern merchandise, prevailed upon his countrymen to aim at a participa- tion in the new trade. The initiative was consequently made, and, in 1422,

the Florentines entered on their new commerce with the most imposing pub- lic pageant.

But perhaps the principal sources of the riches of this family arose from the commercial banks which they had established in almost all the trading cities of Europe, and which were con- ducted by agents in whom they placed great confidence. At a time when the rate of interest principally depended on the necessities of the borrower, and was in most cases very exorbitant, an incon- ceivable profit must have been derived from those establishments, especially as they were at times resorted to for pe- cuniary assistance by the most power- ful sovereigns of Europe.

Remarkable Case of Conscience in a Business Man.

AN old Dutchman, named S——, who lived in one of the wretched hovels that stand in the rear of Sheriff street, and whose apparent poverty and sufferings from a *dreadful case of hernia* had long excited the sympathy of his humane neighbors, died of asthma and a com- bination of other diseases. He was well known to be of a very obstinate and eccentric disposition; and, al- though he had been confined to his bed for some weeks, he not only reject- ed all medical aid, but persisted to the last in sleeping in the whole of his wardrobe, which consisted chiefly in a pair of breeches that at some remote era had been constructed of blue velvet, and a sailor's jacket, and a frieze over- coat, all of which exhibited accumu- lated proofs of the old man's attach- ment. He sent for Mr. Van D., a re- spectable countryman of his, residing in the neighborhood, who had given him charitable relief, and privately re- quested him to make his will! To this gentleman's great surprise, he be- queathed various sums of money, amounting altogether to several thou- sand dollars, to children and grand- children residing at Newark and Albany, and confidentially informed him where his property was deposited. He then narrated to Mr. V. D. the following remarkable facts in his history:

He stated that about twenty-five years ago, he was a porter to a mercantile house in Hamburg, and having been long in its employ, was frequently intrusted with considerable sums of money for conveyance to other establishments. In an hour of evil influence he was induced to violate his trust, and abscond to this country. Having arrived, he invested the greater part of it in the purchase of two houses, which adjoined each other, and which, before he had effected an insurance upon them, were burned to the ground. Considering this a judgment of heaven upon his dishonesty, he determined to devote the remainder of his life to a severe course of industry and parsimony, with the single object in view of making full restitution to the persons whom he had injured, or to their descendants.

He adopted another name, and, with the means he had left, commenced business as a tobacconist, and, although his trade was a retail one, and he had again suffered a heavy loss from fire, he had succeeded, five years since, in acquiring sufficient property to accomplish his just and elevated purpose. He then, accordingly, sold his stock in trade, and was preparing to transmit the necessary amount to Hamburg, where the mercantile firm he had defrauded still continues, when he ascertained that it had a branch establishment or agency counting house in Philadelphia. Thither he went, and paid the sum of *fourteen thousand dollars*, being equivalent to the original sum he had embezzled, with a certain rate of interest. The latter, however, was generously returned to him by a son of one of the partners, and this, together with some surplus money, he bequeathed as above stated. This money was found by his executor, principally in doubloons, and curiously concealed in a certain private department of the tenacious breeches before specified; and it was thus ascertained, at last, that the old man's *dreadful case of hernia*, on account of which he had received so much sympathy, was a 'case' of something far less objectionable, and hardly coming within' the category of those dreaded "ills to which human *flesh* is heir."

Mr. Grinnell's Liberality.

THE name of Henry Grinnell will have an enduring place in American mercantile history, as that of the author, advocate, and patron of the United States' expedition in search of Sir John Franklin and his gallant party. With that enterprise and liberality so characteristic of his profession—and of Mr. Grinnell in particular—he promptly came forward at a time when that much talked of undertaking was in special need of influential countenance as well as of pecuniary aid. The various expeditions which Great Britain had sent out in search of the illustrious pioneer party, though well devised, seemed to suffer from various and peculiar drawbacks, so that, before the beginning of 1850, all further attempts were abandoned—almost without attaining the first threshold of inquiry. Their failure aroused everywhere the generous sympathies of men. Science felt for its votaries, humanity mourned its fellows, and an impulse, holier and more energetic than either, invoked a crusade of rescue. That admirable woman, the wife of Sir John Franklin, not content with stimulating the renewed efforts of her own countrymen, claimed the coöperation of the world. In letters to the President of the United States, full of the eloquence of feeling, she called on us, as a "kindred people, to join heart and hand in the enterprise of snatching the lost navigators from a dreary grave." The delays incident to much of our national legislation menaced the defeat of her appeal.

The bill making appropriations for the outfit of an expedition lingered on its passage, and the season for commencing operations had nearly gone by. At this juncture, that noble-spirited merchant of New York, Henry Grinnell, fitted out two of his own vessels, and proffered them gratuitously to the Government. Prompted by such munificent private liberality, Congress hastened to take the expedition under its charge, and authorized the necessary proceedings to that end.—Moses H. Grinnell, a brother of Henry, is also distinguished for his merchant-like love of "doing a good thing."

A Good Beginning—Old Moses Rothschild.

AN account is given, on another page of this work, of the circumstances under which the Prince of Hesse Cassel, in his flight from the French republican army, passed through the city of Frankfort-on-the-Main, and paid a hasty visit to one Moses Rothschild, a Jewish banker of limited means, but of good repute, both for integrity and ability in the management of his business. As is well known, the Prince's purpose in visiting Moses was to request him to take charge of a large sum in money and jewels, amounting in value to several millions of dollars. The Jew at first point blank refused so dangerous a charge; but, upon being earnestly pressed to take it, at the prince's own sole risk—nay, that even a receipt should not be required—he at length consented. The money and jewels were speedily but privately conveyed from the prince's treasury to the Jew's residence; and, just as the advanced corps of the French army had entered through the gates of Frankfort, Moses had succeeded in burying it in a corner of his garden. He, of course, received a visit from the republicans; but, true to his trust, he hit upon the following means of saving the treasure of the fugitive prince, who had placed such implicit

confidence in his honor. He therefore did not attempt to conceal any of his own property (the value of his cash and stock consisting of only forty thousand thalers, or about $30,000), but, after the necessary remonstrances and grumbling with his unwelcome visitors, and a threat or two that he should report them to the general-in-chief—from whom he had no doubt of obtaining redress—he suffered them to carry it all off.

As soon as the republicans had evacuated the city, Moses Rothschild resumed his business as banker and money changer; at first, indeed, in an humble way, but daily increasing and extending it by the aid of the Prince of Hesse Cassel's money. In the course of a comparatively short space of time, he was considered the most stable and opulent banker in all Germany.

In the year 1802, the prince returning to his dominions, visited Frankfort in his route. He was almost afraid to call on his Jewish banker; apprehending that if the French had left anything, the honesty of Moses had not been proof against so strong a temptation as he had been compelled from dire necessity to put in his way. On being introduced into Rothschild's sanctum, he, in a tone of despairing carelessness, said:

"I have called on you, Moses, as a matter of course; but I fear the result. Did the rascals take all?"

"Not a thaler," replied the Jew, gravely.

"What say you?" returned his highness. "Not a thaler! Why, I was informed that the sans-culottes had emptied all your coffers, and made you a beggar. I even read so in the gazettes."

"Why, so they did, may it please your serene highness," replied Moses; "but I was too cunning for them. By letting them take my own little stock, I saved your great one. I knew that as I was reputed wealthy, although by no means so, if I should remove any of my own gold and silver from their appropriate bags or coffers, the robbers would be sure to search for it, and, in doing so, would not forget to dig in the garden. It is wonderful what a keen sense these fellows have got! they actually poured buckets of water over some of my neighbors' kitchen and cellar floors, in order to discover, by the rapid sinking of the fluid, whether the tiles and earth had been recently dug up! Well, as I was saying, I buried your treasure in the garden; and it remained untouched until the robbers left Frankfort, to go in search of plunder elsewhere. Now, then, to the point: as the *sans-culottes* left me not a kreutzer to carry on my business; as several good opportunities offered of making a very handsome profit; and as I thought it a pity that so much good money should lie idle, while the merchants were both ready and willing to give large interest; the temptation of converting your highness's florins to present use haunted my thoughts by day and my dreams by night. Not to detain your highness with a long story, I dug up the treasure, and deposited your jewels in a strong box, from which they have never since been moved; I employed your gold and silver in my business; my speculations were profitable; and I am now able to restore your deposit, with five per cent. interest since the day on which you left it under my care."

"I thank you heartily, my good friend," said his highness, "for the great care you have taken and the sacrifice you have made. As to the interest of five per cent., let that replace the sum which the French took from you; I beg you will add to it whatever other profits you may have made. As a reward for your singular honesty, I shall still leave my cash in your hands for twenty years longer, at a low rate of two per cent. interest per annum, the same being more as an acknowledg-

ment of the deposit in case of the death of either of us, than with a view of making a profit by you. I trust that this will enable you to use my florins with advantage in any way which may appear most beneficial to your own interests."

Perseverance Badly Rewarded.

MANY years ago, when Texas was first admitted into the Union, George Ford, a well-known hardware merchant in Boston, visited that State on business. He had occasion to travel in distant and thinly-settled parts of the State on horseback, where sometimes he would not see a habitation for thirty or forty miles. He was told that on reaching the Brazos River, a quarter of a mile wide at a certain point in Washington County, he would find a bridge; but, on reaching the river, there were no signs of a bridge. The persevering merchant dismounted, undressed, and tying his clothes in his handkerchief, he fastened the bundle to the headstall of the horse, and drove him into the river, Ford swimming after him. Both arrived safely on the other side; and after dressing, he was very much perplexed to find three forks to the road or trail, and the question was now which one to take to reach his destination—a town some fifty miles distant. While pondering on the probabilities, he cast his eyes back over the river, and saw a signboard nailed to a tree. He resolved to swim back and read it. Undressing again, in he went, and reached the other side, and read these words: "Five dollars fine for crossing this bridge faster than a walk." It appeared the bridge had been carried away during a great freshet, some months previous, the only vestige remaining being the sign above on the tree. George said it was the only time he ever was "sold" in Texas.

Correct Appreciation of Mercantile Character by Mr. Astor.

WHILE in Liverpool, England, Mr. James G. King was brought into relations of business and much personal intimacy with Mr. John Jacob Astor, who was on a brief sojourn in Europe; and such was the impression made upon that sagacious observer and almost unerring judge of character, by the business tact and promptness of Mr. King, and his general character, that, upon his return to the United States, Mr. Astor invited him to come to New York and take the chief direction of the American Fur Company, with a very liberal salary. The offer was a tempting one, and made at a time when, owing to the mercantile disasters which had been battled with, the prospects of Mr. King's house in Liverpool were not very promising. But the business to which he was invited was wholly new to him; and, moreover, it was in his character to prefer an independent position—though it might be less lucrative—to any, however advantageous, of which the tenure was at the pleasure of others. Mr. King, therefore, declined, but with such expression of his sense of the liberal kindness of Mr. Astor as was both natural and fitting; and Mr. Astor continued his fast friend always, and had another occasion of proving his friendship about the close of 1823. Consulted by Mr. Prime, then at the head of the house of Prime, Ward, Sands & Co., as to his knowledge of some fitting person upon whom Mr. Prime might safely devolve a portion of the business of his prosperous house, Mr. Astor at once suggested the name of James G. King, and accompanied it with such eulogies as to determine Mr. Prime, who, it seems, from some business intercourse between their houses, had himself thought of Mr. King, to invite him to become a partner in his house; and this arrangement was in due time consummated. The brilliant commercial results of this copartnership, and the whole subsequent career of Mr. King, showed that Mr. Astor was not mistaken in his appreciation of the man.

Search for a New Route to China.

SIR HUGH WILLOUGHBY'S famous commercial exploring expedition in the fifteenth century—to discover a near route to China—met with a sad fate. By the sudden approach of winter he was compelled to seek refuge within an obscure harbor in Russian Lapland, where, with the crew of two of his vessels, he was frozen to death; and when the Laplanders, in pursuance of their annual custom, sought the seacoast in summer, for the sake of its fishery, they found the remains of the unhappy adventurer, who, meditating a great discovery, had met with an obscure death. It is a touching picture to contemplate him as he was found, sitting with his diary and papers before him as in life, and to think how little his aspiring but noble ambition meditated so melancholy a fate. The expedition, however, was not without its benefit, as one vessel escaped. Richard Chancellor, its commander, landed near Archangel, and inclined the Czar, Ivan Bazilowitz, then engaged in the Livonian war, to grant considerable commercial privileges to the English.

Extension and Profits of Mr. Astor's Fur Business.

IF there was anything left undone by Mr. Astor to extend and give success to his early and favorite trade in furs, then it was something which mortal shrewdness could not compass. He made himself thoroughly acquainted with the nature of that trade, coming in contact with the agents, and obtaining a complete knowledge of the methods and profits of the traffic. His great enterprise induced him to reach for ward to what others would have shrunk from.

When the revolutionary war closed, Oswego, Detroit, Niagara, and other posts, were in the hands of the British; and as these were the entrepots of the western and northern countries, the fur trade had languished after their capture and during their detention The traders had been either driven away or drafted into the armies; the trappers had ranged themselves on either side of the political contention; and the Indians obtained more fire-water and calico for the use of their mercenary rifles and tomahawks from Great Britain, in this her domestic quarrel with the colonies, than if they had employed them on beavers and squirrels. After much negotiation and surveying, and the advancement and consideration of claims, these posts were conceded to the United States, and Canada was opened to the fur trade. Shortly afterward the British retired from the west side of St. Clair, opening up to the enterprising merchants of America the great fur trade of the West.

Mr. Astor saw that the posts thus made free would soon be thronged by Indians eager to dispose of the accumulated produce of several years' hunting, and that the time had now come when he was certain to amass a large fortune by the traffic. He immediately established agencies, over which he exercised a sort of personal superintendence, visiting the stations sometimes, but chiefly devoting himself to the New York business. The results verified the sagacious predictions of Mr. Astor, for in a few years his gains from this source were very large.

The British fur companies had, however, built their block forts at almost every eligible site on the rivers of the northern and southwestern parts of the American continent, and were soon likely to acquire a monopoly of the whole of the fur trade, unless some bold measures were adopted to rescue it from them. This Astor attempted in 1803, by establishing the American Fur Company. The hardy adventurers who entered into this project, boldly pushed their outposts far into the hitherto unknown prairie, and raised their forts upon the banks of yet unexplored rivers. Tribes unused to see the white man, and who only knew him through vague tradition, or by a passing tale from some visitor of another tribe, now saw and knew him, and brought their abundance of beaver, otter, and buffalo skins, and laid them at his feet for muskets, powder, and fire-water.

No sooner was the American Fur Company established and in operation than Mr. Astor cast his shrewd eyes toward the region stretching from the Rocky Mountains to the ocean. He proposed to the United States' Government the establishment of a line of forts along the shores of the Pacific Ocean and on the Columbia River, in order to take from the hands of the British all facilities for establishing a trade west of the Rocky Mountains. The project was agreed to; and in 1810 sixty men, under the command of a hardy and adventurous leader, established the first post at the mouth of the Columbia, which took its designation of Astoria from the projector of the scheme. This became the germ of the budding State of Oregon. Then commenced a series of operations on a scale altogether beyond anything hitherto attempted by individual enterprise. The history is full of wildest romance. The whole scheme was the offspring of a capacious mind; and had the plans of Mr. Astor been faithfully carried out by his associates, it would, no doubt, have been eminently successful. But the enterprise soon failed. During the war a British armed sloop captured Astoria, and the British fur traders entered upon the rich field which Mr. Astor had planted, and reaped the golden harvest.

Honorable Distinction attained by Mr. Perit.

PELATIAH PERIT had at an early age marked out for himself a professional life, intending to devote himself to the ministry, and possessing a fine collegiate education and an unspotted religious character as the basis of such a career. But a partial failure of his health, and especially of his voice, required a reconsideration of his purpose. Compelled thus to relinquish the profession to which he was led by religious sympathies and aspirations, he chose the mercantile profession as better for him than any other secular employment.

He was in his nineteenth year when he began as a clerk in one of the large importing houses at Philadelphia, which had not then ceased to be the foremost of our American cities. Nor was he long in demonstrating that all his talents and attainments might be made serviceable to him in his chosen employment. After remaining about five years in connection with the house which he had entered as a clerk, and for which he had made several voyages to the West Indies and to South America, he returned to New York in 1809, just when all the commercial interests of our country were imperilled, and were coming to the brink of annihilation, by that series of measures which terminated in the war of 1812. When, however, peace was restored, and the business of the country had revived, and its foreign commerce once more began to traverse freely every ocean, he became a partner in the house of Goodhue & Co., and, through all the changes which time and death made in the partnership, he remained a member of that firm more than forty years. All commercial men know the character and standing of that house, and how much of it was the character and standing of Pelatiah Perit.

His place among his fellow merchants of the great metropolis was recognized by his election, eleven years ago, to the Presidency of the New York Chamber of Commerce. The rules of that body provide that no president shall be reëlected for more than three years in succession without a unanimous vote. Yet for ten successive years he held that place of honor, being nine times reëlected by the unanimous vote of his distinguished associates—a rare and honorable distinction.

PART FOURTH.

ANECDOTES OF TRADE AND BUSINESS IMMORALITIES.

PART FOURTH.

Anecdotes of Trade and Business Immoralities.

THE RAREST INSTANCES OF INGENIOUS FRAUD, FORGERY, COUNTERFEITING, AND SMUGGLING; USURY, ARTIFICE, TRICKS, AND MALPRACTICE; WITH EXAMPLES, EXTRAORDINARY AND AMUSING, OF AVARICE, COVETOUSNESS, PARSIMONY, EXTORTION, PRIDE, RUDENESS, VIOLENCE, AND EXTRAVAGANCE OF BUSINESS MEN.

A man of sense can artifice disdain,
As men of wealth may venture to go plain.—YOUNG.

A knave is like a tooth drawer, that maintains his own teeth in constant eating by pulling out those of other men.—BUTLER.

Lands mortgaged may return, and more esteemed;
But honesty once pawned, is ne'er redeemed.—MIDDLETON.

—— For a good old gentlemanly vice,
I think I must take up with avarice.—BYRON'S "DON JUAN."

He is rich whose income is more than his expenses; and he is poor whose expenses exceed his income.—BRUYÈRE.

Selling Salt by a Chalk Line.

AT one period in the changeful commercial life of Girard, he sold salt by the bushel; and, conceiving one day that his measure, or half bushel, was too large, he determined to regulate or readjust it himself. For this purpose he took a half-gallon liquid measure, and repairing to the wharf, which was at that time constructed with steps, for the convenience of supplying citizens with water from the river, he deposited the requisite number of half gallons into his half bushel, and then drawing a *chalk line* round the water mark, he found it was too large by an inch or more; on discovering this to be the case, he forthwith went to a neighboring cooper's shop, and borrowing a saw for the purpose, reduced the measure of his half bushel accordingly, thus making it what he conceived it ought to be. This gave rise to the saying, " that Mr. Girard was a just man, but it was according to his own *measure* of justice."

Rothschild and Lucas—Stratagem to learn the Former's Secrets.

When the great Hebrew financier lived on Stamford Hill, there resided opposite to him another very wealthy dealer in stock exchange, Lucas by name. The latter returned one night very late from a convivial party; he observed a carriage and four standing before Rothschild's gate, upon which he ordered his own carriage to go out of the way, and commanded his coachman to await his return.

Lucas now went stealthily and watched the movements at Rothschild's gate. He did not lie long in ambush, before he heard a party leaving the Hebrew millionaire's mansion, and going toward the carriage. He saw Rothschild, accompanied by two muffled figures, step into the carriage, and heard the word of command, " To the city!" He followed Rothschild's carriage very closely. But when he reached the top of the street in which Rothschild's office was situated, Lucas ordered his carriage to stop, from which he stepped out, and proceeded, reeling to and fro through the street, feigning to be mortally drunk. He made his way in this same mood as far as Rothschild's office, and *sans cérémonie* opened the door, to the great consternation and terror of the housekeeper, uttering sundry ejaculations in the broken accents of Bacchus's votaries. Heedless of the affrighted housekeeper's remonstrances, he opened Rothschild's private office, in the same staggering attitude, and fell down flat on the floor. Rothschild and his friends became greatly alarmed. Efforts were at once made to restore and remove the would-be drunkard; but Lucas was too good an actor, and was, therefore, in such a state as to be unfit to be moved hither or thither. "Should a physician be sent for?" asked Rothschild. But the housekeeper threw some cold water into Lucas's face, and the patient began to breathe a little more naturally, and fell into a sound, snoring sleep. He was covered, and Rothschild and the strangers proceeded unsuspectingly to their business.

The strangers brought the good intelligence that the affairs in Spain were all right, respecting which the members of the exchange were, for a few days previous, very apprehensive, and the funds were consequently in a rapidly sinking condition: The good news, however, could not, in the common course of dispatch, be publicly known for another day. Rothschild, therefore, planned to order his brokers to buy up, cautiously, all the stock that should be in market, by twelve o'clock that following day. He sent for his principal broker thus early, in order to intrust him with the important instructions. The broker was rather tardier, however, than Rothschild's patience could brook; he therefore determined to go himself. As soon as he was gone, Lucas began to recover, and by degrees was able to get up, being distracted, as he said, "with a violent headache," and insisted, in spite of the housekeeper's kind expostulations, upon going home. But Lucas also went to *his* broker, and instructed him to buy all the stock he could get by ten o'clock the following morning. About eleven o'clock, Lucas met Rothschild, and inquired, in a satirical manner, how he, Rothschild, was off for stock! Lucas won the day; and Rothschild is said never to have forgiven what he termed "that base, dishonest, and nefarious stratagem."

Financiering in Alabama.

IN the times of 1836, there dwelt in a pleasant town of Alabama, a smooth, oily-mannered gentleman, who diversified a common-place pursuit by some exciting episodes of finance—dealing occasionally in exchange brokerage, buying and selling uncurrent money, &c. His name may be supposed to be Thompson.

It happened that a Mr. Ripley, of North Carolina, was in T., having some $1,200 in North Carolina money; and, desiring to return to the old North State with his funds, but not wishing to encounter the risk of robbery through the Creek country, in which there were rumors of hostilities between the whites and the Indians, he bethought him of buying exchange on Raleigh, as the safest mode of transmitting his money. On inquiry he was referred to Mr. Thompson, as the only person dealing in exchange in that place. He called on Mr. T., and made known his wishes. With his characteristic politeness, Mr. Thompson agreed to accommodate him with a sight bill on his correspondent in Raleigh, charging him the moderate premium of five per cent. for it. Mr. Thompson retired into his counting room, and in a few minutes returned with the bill and a letter, which he delivered to Mr. Ripley, at the same time receiving the money from that gentleman, plus the "exchange." As the interlocutors were exchanging valedictory compliments, it "occurred" to Mr. Thompson that it would be a favor to him if Mr. Ripley would be so kind as to convey to Mr. T.'s correspondent a package of "documents" he was desirous of sending, which request Mr. Ripley assured Mr. T. it would afford him great pleasure to comply with. Mr. Thompson then handed Mr. Ripley a package, strongly enveloped and sealed, addressed to the Raleigh banker, after which the gentlemen parted with many polite expressions of regard and civility.

Arriving without any accident or hindrance at Raleigh, Mr. Ripley's first care was to call on the banker and present his documents. He found him at his office, presented the bill and the letter to him, and requested payment of the former. "That," said the banker, "will depend a good deal upon the contents of the package;" opening which, Mr. Ripley had the pleasure of seeing the identical banknotes, minus the premium he had paid Mr. T. for his bill, and which the banker now paid over to Mr. R. The latter was not a little surprised to find that the expert Mr. Thompson had thus charged him five per cent. for carrying his own money to Raleigh, to avoid the risk and trouble of which he had bought the exchange.

T. used to remark that *that* was the safest operation, all around, *he* ever knew. He had got his exchange—the buyer had got his bill and the money, too,—and the drawee was fully protected! There was profit without any outlay or risk.

Italian Picture Dealer Trapping an Experienced Connoisseur.

SIGNOR A—— has long been known as one of the most facetious London dealers in pictures and other objects of art,—not stopping at any clever ruse by which to make a good "sell." It is related, too, that one of his boldest tricks was successfully played off at the expense of an experienced purchaser and acknowledged connoisseur, the late Mr. C——. He persuaded the latter to look at a picture of high pretensions and of some merit in his house. While they were discussing it, the jingle of posting bells was heard in the street, and the prolonged crack of a courier's whip soon echoed in the doorway. A—— started, rushed out, and beheld an express, booted, spurred, and splashed, who handed him a letter. Tearing it open, he appeared struck with confusion, and exclaimed:

"Well, here is a fine scrape I have got into!"

"What is the matter?"

"Why, I am talking about selling you this picture, and here is the courier sent back from Ancona to buy it, by a Russian gentleman, to whom I offered it last week, for such a sum."

The price was a large one, and Mr. C. would not have thought of giving it for the picture, which did not interest him much; but so ingeniously did Signor A. contrive to transfer to it the importance of this dramatic scene, that, in the excitement of the moment, a bargain was struck, and the Englishman went off chuckling at the idea of having so nicely "done" the Russian,—the latter being an imaginary personage, and his courier a Roman postboy, hired to gallop up in the nick of time!

James Bolland's Financial Career.

ABOUT the middle of the last century, one of the most constant stock dealers in London, although in a small way, was James Bolland; a man of low extraction, but of great mind, of immense impudence, and unrivalled crime. There was nothing at which he would hesitate to obtain money with which to carry on his stock dealings; and, having once commenced, he soon found that the legitimate wants of his trade—that of a butcher—were not sufficient to support him. He formed, therefore, a wooden weight, which, resembling one of fifty pounds, weighed only seven, and thus, in his capacity of tradesman to one of the public institutions, practised his roguery with great success.

From butcher he turned sheriff's officer, revived every past iniquity, invented new frauds, and employed his money in buying lottery tickets, to which pursuit he was occasionally attached. He robbed the broker with whom he dealt, alike of his mistress and his money; and with the latter bought the place of city marshal. The citizens, however, discovered that his integrity was scarcely equal to his impudence, and refused to maintain their bargain.

Every moment he could spare was passed at the stock market, where his schemes were marked by a singularly bad fortune. Every speculation went against him; he never drew a prize in the lottery; and, finding there was a chance of his becoming penniless, he added forgery to his long list of crimes. The fraud was discovered, and he paid the penalty of his life.

Business Haggling in Scotland.

In England, when an article is offered for sale, it is immediately purchased, or at once rejected as being too dear. But in Scotland, there is a long haggling and cheapening of every article successively offered. The purchaser objects to the price. He will not buy. The seller urges him, but does not offer to make any reduction. Says he, "You are over dear, sir; I can buy the same gudes ten per cent. lower; if ye like to tak' off ten per cent., I'll tak' some of these." The seller tells him that a reduction in price is quite out of the question, and puts the sample of the article aside; but the Scotchman wants it.

"Weel, sir, it's a terrible price; but as I am out o' it at present, I'll just tak' a little till I can be supplied cheaper, but ye maun tak' off five per cent."

"But, sir," says the seller, "would you not think me an unconscionable knave, to ask ten per cent., or even five per cent., more than I intended to take?"

He laughs. "Hoot, hoot, man, do ye expect to get what ye ask? Gude Lord! an' I was able to get half what I ask, I would soon be rich. Come, come, I'll gie ye within two an' a half per cent. of your ain price, and gude faith, mon, ye'll be well paid."

He is told by the seller that he never makes any reduction from the price he first demanded, and that adherence to such a rule "saves much trouble to both parties."

"Weel, weel," says he, "since ye maun hae it a' your ain way, I maun e'en tak' the article; but really I think ye are over-keen."

So much for buying and selling—the settlement is another affair still, at a future time, as will now be seen:

"How muckle discount do ye tak' aff, sir?"

"Discount! You cannot expect it. The account has been standing a twelve-month."

"Indeed, but I do expect discount—pay siller without discount! Na, na, sir, that's not the way here; ye maun deduct five per cent."

He is told that no discount at all is made. "Weel, sir, I'll gie ye nae money at a'."

Rather than go without a settlement, the seller at last agrees to take two and one half per cent. from the amount, which is accordingly deducted.

"I hae ten shillings doon against ye for short measure, and fifteen shillings for damages."

"Indeed, these are heavy deductions; but if you say that you shall lose to that amount, I suppose that it must be allowed."

"Oh, aye, it's a' right; then, sir, eight shillings and four pence for pack-sheet, and thirteen, shillings for carriage and postage."

"These last items are astonishing. What, sir," said the seller, "are we to pay all the charges in your business?"

But if these are not allowed, he will not pay his account; so the seller acquiesces, resolving within himself that, since these unfair deductions are made at settlement, it would be quite fair to charge an additional price to cover the extortion. He now congratulates himself on having concluded his business with such a customer; but is disappointed.

"Hae ye a stawmpe?" asks he.

"A stamp,—for what?"

"Just to draw ye a bill," he replies.

"A bill, my good sir! I took off two and one-half per cent., on the faith of being paid in cash." But he says it is the custom of his place to pay in bills, and sits down and draws a bill at three months after date, payable at his own shop.

"And what can I do with this?"

"Oh, ye may tak' it to Sir William's, and he'll discount it for you, on paying him three months' interest."

"And what can I do with his notes?"

"He'll gie ye a bill in London, at forty-five days."

"So, sir, after allowing you twelve months' credit, and two and a half per cent. discount, and exorbitant charges which you have no claim on us to pay, I must be content with a bill which we are not to cash for four months and a half!"

"Weel, weel—and now, sir," says he, "if ye are going to your inn, I'll gang wi' ye, and tak' a glass of wine."

Dutchman Illustrating a Mercantile Principle.

An anecdote is told of a German, who, after it was known that a certain bank in Buffalo had closed its doors, went to one of the largest furniture establishments, and purchased articles amounting to $2.75, for which he off-handedly proffered a five dollar bill of said bank in payment. The clerk refused to take it, and the Dutchman insisted that it was all right, saying:

"It ish goot; te pank will open; deres lots of beeples dere; de pank ish opening already."

Still the clerk persisted in his refusal to take the bill. The proprietor, hearing the discussion, put in his oar, and the Teuton went through with his former lingo. Knowing that the bills are well secured against loss to the holders, he finally accepted the bill, and offered as change a quarter of a dollar in specie, and a two dollar bill on the same bank. The German was taken aback for a moment, but finally said:

"Ich no take dat."

"But you must take this, or the one you gave me is also bad," said the dealer.

"*I don't know as de pank ish so goot as it vas*," said Diedrich.

"Well, you must take this bill, or trade it out in those small chairs," said the furniture dealer, pointing to some juvenile affairs with round holes in their seats, and at which the Dutchman was intently gazing (he had a brood of children).

"Vell, I dink I'll dake de shairs," and he took them.

This anecdote illustrates the fact of the dislike of no small portion of mankind to swallow their own arguments, and illustrates a mercantile principle that much is good to dispose of, which it were quite undesirable to obtain.

Deadhead Customer—a Clincher.

YEARS ago, there dwelt in a certain town a divine, notorious for his parsimoniousness, which would sometimes run to almost fabulous extremes.

One day, this doctor of divinity stepped into a hat store in New York, and, after rummaging over the stock, selected an ordinary looking hat, put it on his reverend head, ogled himself in the glass, then asked the very lowest price of it, telling the vendor, that if he could get it cheap enough he thought he might buy it.

"But," said the hatter, "that hat is not good enough for *you* to wear—here is what you want," showing one of his best beavers.

"'Tis the best I can afford though," returned the theologian.

"Well, there, doctor, I'll make you a present of that best beaver, if you'll wear it, and tell whose store it came from; I'll warrant you'll send me customers enough to get my money back with interest; you are pretty extensively acquainted."

"Thank you—thank you!" said the doctor, his eyes gleaming with pleasure at raising a castor so cheaply; "how much, however, may this be worth?"

"We sell that kind of hat for eight dollars," replied the man of the *nap*.

"And the other?" continued the customer.

"Three."

The man of sermons put on the beaver, looked in the glass, then at the three dollar hat.

"I think, sir," said he, taking off the beaver, and holding it in one hand, as he donned the cheap 'tile,' "I think, sir, that this hat will answer my purpose full as well as the best."

"But you'd better take the best one, sir, it costs you no more."

"B-u-t—bu-t," replied the parson, hesitatingly, "I didn't know—but—perhaps—you would as lief I would take the cheap one, and leave the other —and, perhaps, you would not mind giving me the difference in a *five dollar bill!*"

Determining the Character of an Article by its Age.

QUITE a good story is told—and will bear telling again—of old Bunce, who prided himself upon never being mistaken in his judgment of a person's character from the phiz. He was in Washington market, New York, one day, to get a goose for dinner. In looking about, he saw a lot before a young woman who had a peculiarly fine, open countenance. "She's honest," said Bunce to himself; and at once asked her if she had a nice *young* goose. "Yes," said she; "here's as fine a one as you will get in the market,"—and she looked up in his face with that perfect sincerity that would at once have won his confidence, had he not already and at first sight made up his mind as to her character. "You're sure it's young?" "To be sure it is;" and Bunce took it home. All efforts to eat it were fruitless, it was so tough; and the next day he was at the market betimes, angry with himself, and more so with the honest-faced girl who had cheated him. "Didn't you tell me that goose was young, yesterday?" he exclaimed, stalking up to the girl wrathfully. "To be sure I did." "You cheated me," said Bunce as quickly; "it was a tough old gander." "You don't call *me* old, do you?" she asked. "No—I should think not," he replied. "No—*I* should think not, too. I am only twenty, and mother told me that goose was hatched just six months after I was born." Bunce had forgotten that a goose lives a hundred years.

"Genuine" Wines.

THE substitution of other wines for port was, it seems, practised in "great-grandfather's day" quite as extensively as at present. In an official investigation into the manufacture of wines by the English authorities a while ago, one witness, who had been engaged for many years in importing "Masdeu," a red wine from Roussillon, told the following curious story:

When I got to the port of shipment,

Port Veadres, I found very extensive warehouses constructed; and as it was in a very outlandish place, with not more than two hundred and fifty inhabitants in the port of shipment, such warehouses struck me as very remarkable. I inquired why these warehouses were built, and I was told that they had been put up by the proprietor's father—the age of the present proprietor was eighty-five. I inquired for what purpose the father had built them, and I was informed that he had built them in connection with a countryman of my own, a Mr. Ireland. "Had I ever heard of Mr. Ireland?" My answer was, no. But upon further inquiry, I was told that Mr. Ireland and his—Mr. Durand's—father had had large transactions in wine, and that Mr. I. stated that he wanted a wine for the supply of the troops and the navy, and I was told fine old wine. Upon my return to this country I went to the late Mr. George Hathorn, than whom a more respectable man never existed in any trade: being a very old man, I questioned him if he had ever heard of Mr. Ireland. He said, "Yes; he recollected Mr. Ireland had commenced life at Bristol in a very obscure position, and died one of the richest men in it."

"What course of trade did he follow?"

"He was an importer of red wines."

"Port wines?"

"*Port* wines."

"What reputation had his wines in the market?"

"*They were of the highest class.*"

Yet the old gentleman could not seem to tell why—it certainly was not from any want of funds—but, all at once, the house *suspended* its prosperous operations.

I supplied the wanting link; he could get no more Roussillon wines, as the first French revolution hindered him!

What it Means to be "Selling Off."

ONE of those generous, disinterested, sacrificing men, who had flaringly stuck upon every other pane of glass in his shop, "Selling off—no reasonable offer refused—must close on Saturday," once offered himself as bail, or security, in some case which was brought before a magistrate. The magistrate asked him if he was worth a thousand dollars: he said, yes. "But you are about to remove, are you not?" "No." "Why, you announce that you are 'Selling Off.'" "Yes—every shopkeeper's selling off." "You say, 'No reasonable offer will be refused.'" "Yes; I should be very unreasonable if I did refuse such 'offers.'" "But you say, 'must close on Saturday.'" "To be sure; you would not have me open on Sunday, would you?"

Espionage Practised by Girard.

GIRARD'S oversight of his hired hands was most arbitrary and exacting. He owned a farm a few miles from his residence in Philadelphia, which he kept under his own cultivation. It was superintended by a farmer who resided on the place, to which the owner often drove out to see how affairs were going on. He not unfrequently went in the morning—before breakfast. On one of those occasions, coming out perhaps somewhat earlier than usual, on arriving at a piece of stone fence which he was building along the roadside, he found his farmer absent. He immediately drove to the house, fastened his horse, and went in, searching the house for him, not overlooking those parts where he suspected the man might be found. Disappointed in his search, he mounted his chaise and returned to the fence—and, lo! the man was found very diligently at his work.

"Ah! how is this?" said the keen-eyed overseer; "you were too late at your work, this morning. I have driven out of town already, and you were not here." "Oh, yes, Mr. Girard," says the man. "I had been here, but I had only stepped aside for a few moments, to get something that I wanted, when you passed by." "You do lie!" said the keen-eyed master. "*I did go and put my hand in your bed, and it was warm.*" The man had been informed by his wife, of Girard's coming, when he jumped up in a hurry, and ran to his work. But Girard was too cute for him.

Quaker Ship Owner Economizing the Time of his Men.

THERE was once a wealthy ship owner in New Bedford, a member of the Society of Friends, and now deceased, who was very remarkable for economizing the time of his hired men. He had one of his ships hove down to the wharf to repair and copper. It was a cold winter's day, and there was a plank extending from the wharf to the floating stages around the ship, on which the carpenters and caulkers were at work. Among the men was one by the name of John, a man-of-all-work, a man of color, and on free and easy terms with his master. John was carrying matters and things up and down a slippery plank to the workmen, when he slid of a sudden and shot, heels over head, into the water. The old Quaker saw him, and as John came up to blow, called out to him, "Don't make a noise, John, you'll stop the men in their work —keep quiet, and I'll help thee out."

As good or bad luck would have it, the same day, the kind Quaker was coming down the plank, and away he went, souse into the briny deep. But John was close by, and as his master rose to the surface, and looked the image of ghastliness and despair, the tantalizing negro put on a long face, and cried, "Master, don't make a noise, to call off the men. I'll help thee out." And so he did, while the "men" *would* look on, laughing at the fun.

"A Little More."

A NEW ENGLAND merchant, who had accumulated a vast property by care and industry, yet still was as busy as ever, in adding vessel to vessel and store to store, though considerably advanced in life being asked by a neighbor, how much property would satisfy a human being?—after a short pause replied, "*A little more.*"

Royal Prize for Raising Money—Raid upon the Bankers.

AT one period of his reign, being very much distressed for money, and despairing of obtaining any from the House of Commons, King Charles the Second declared, in a private meeting with his ministers, that if any of them would invent a method by which to raise about one million and a half pounds, without a parliament, he should have the "White Staff," or, in other words, the lord treasurer's place. On the day following, Lord Ashley told Sir Thomas Clifford, *in confidence*, that there was a way to supply the king immediately with such a sum; but that it was hazardous to put it in practice, and might draw a train of ill consequences along with it, by inflaming both the parliament and the people.

Sir Thomas was impatient to know the secret, being bold and courageous, entirely in the French interest, and pleased with anything that might render the king unpopular with the parliament. Therefore, to discover the project, he plied his lordship with wine to excess, and then led the conversation to the subject of the king's wants. Lord Ashley unguardedly dropped the important secret.

The hint was immediately taken by Sir Thomas, who left his lordship, went directly to the king, and, falling on his knees, he demanded the white staff, according to promise. His majesty cried out:

"Odds fish! I'll be as good as my word, if you can find the money."

Sir Thomas then informed his royal master that *the bankers had a million and a half pounds in his majesty's exchequer*, which money he had an opportunity of seizing, by closing the exchequer, and refusing to pay the bankers. To this project the king readily assented; and at a privy council, his majesty being present, Sir Thomas proposed, " That, as the king must have money to carry on the war against Holland, in which his honor was staked, he knew of no other means at present than shutting up the exchequer. He desired none would speak against it without proposing some method more certain and expeditious." The king, after many apologies for this bold step, declared that " it should only be for the space of one whole year, and that then no new orders shall interfere to break the course of such property."

This conduct filled every one—especially the business classes—with consternation and dismay, and it was declared that the crown had published its own bankruptcy. The money thus forcibly seized did, in point of fact, belong to the trading community; and the failure of the bankers, which was the natural result, caused, for a time, a general suspension of all monetary transactions. Sir Thomas Clifford, for his services in the affair, was, according to the promise of the king, made lord high treasurer and a peer.

Ingenious Swindling of Pawnbrokers.

THE plundering of pawnbrokers has been reduced to quite a system in London by the " profession." The parties, it seems, are in the habit of sending to auction rooms, for sale, cases of very handsome medals and coins, finely finished, to represent gold. On the day of the sale, some of the party attend, bid a high price for the article, and, of course, become the purchasers. They then request the auctioneer to give a guaranty that they are gold, and he, not having any suspicions, at once gives the necessary certificate. The next step of the swindler is to go to a pawnbroker's and pledge the articles for the price they could fetch if they were gold, at the same time producing the auctioneer's certificate, which completely throws the pawnbroker off his guard.

Jack's Bargain for Rope.

IN one of our stores there is a mischievous young fellow by the name of George, who now and then acts as salesman. If his numerous friends ever make game of his short legs, they at least never deny him the possession of a long head. There came into the store one day a roving son of the sea, inquiring for rope. George immediately offered his services, and led him back to where the rope, in snaky folds, lay coiled. The sailor soon found the right size, and asked the price. The selling price was *twelve* cents the pound; but George, with an eye to the principles of merchandising in general, and the custom of Israelites in particular, was willing to put it to him at *fifteen* cents. To this the tar made no objection, and said he would take sixty fathoms; but as it was pretty well buried beneath a lot of old and somewhat heavy " truck," he very naturally inquired, " How'll you get it out? " Just then a bright idea shot through the aforesaid long head of George, and sparkled for a moment in his eyes, while he drawled out most innocently, " Well, if you'll pull it all out yo-ur-self, you may have it at twelve cents." Whereat the sailor, economically inclined, commenced a half-hour's tugging and hauling at the buried rope; while George, more humorously inclined, enjoyed a good half-hour's quiet fun.

Determined not to be overreached.

THERE lives, not a thousand miles from "Gotham," a dealer in small wares, whose greatest fear is that of being overreached. He goes without milk in his coffee, in dread of buying a spoonful of Croton, and never pays a newspaper subscription, lest it should not be published to the end of the year. His little shop is without gas, for he has no faith in the meter; and he even dips his own candles, to insure that they are all tallow. In one thing he is liberal; he makes large purchases of counterfeit detectors, and buys an "extra" if there are any whisperings of a broken bank. A neighbor of his was imposed upon the other day with a bank note which had been ingeniously altered from one to five; and the dealer had been sharply on the watch ever since, for fear of a similar imposition. The other day, a young girl from the country stepped into his store and purchased a pair of stockings, offering a one dollar note in payment. The old man eyed the girl so penetratingly that her face became suffused with blushes, and this was, to him, acknowledgment of guilt.

"How *dare* you offer me this?" he asked, in an angry tone.

"I thought it was good," she answered timidly and with quivering lip.

"What is the matter with it?" asked a bystander, who had been attracted by the dispute; "it looks like a genuine note."

"Genuine enough," said the shopkeeper, his face crimson with passion; "but, don't you see—it's a *one altered from a twenty!*"

Jemmy Taylor, the Miser Banker, and the Earl of Northumberland.

ONE of the longest, though not best, remembered of the old English stockbrokers was Jemmy Taylor. So acute and cunning did he become in all the trickery pertaining to that kind of business, that his profits were immense, and his wealth prodigious. He was as penurious as he was rich, and as wretched in his personal appearance and his mode of living as a pauper. A short time after the American war, it is said that the Earl of Northumberland, having occasion for about half a million dollars, applied to a broker, who accordingly appointed a certain day for the transfer. At the time and place for meeting, there was posted in waiting, old Jemmy Taylor, who, in appearance, resembled some itinerant vendor of matches. Upon the Duke's arrival, the broker brought Jemmy the banker forward to his grace, who, not knowing him, thought he was a beggar, and was about to bestow a trifle upon him, when he was informed that he was "a warm man." His grace immediately shook hands with the dirty usurer, and Jemmy accommodated him with £74,000 out of one stock, in the four per cents., and from whence, as it appeared by the books, he could have sold out as much more, and yet have had an abundance left. He used to say, that "if his successors had as much pleasure in spending his property, as he had in hoarding it up, they need not complain of their hard lot in the world." It does not appear that they were ever known to utter such a complaint *after* Jemmy's death.

Accomplished Canine Shoplifter.

A GENTLEMAN in Edinburgh owned a handsome spaniel, which he had bought from a dealer in dogs. The animal had been educated to steal for the benefit of its protector; but it was some time ere his new master became aware of this irregularity of morals, and he was not a little astonished and teased by its constantly bringing home articles of which it had feloniously obtained possession. Perceiving, at length, that the animal proceeded systematically in this sort of behavior, he used to amuse his friends, by causing the spaniel to give proof of its sagacity in the Spartan art of privately stealing, putting, of course, the shopkeepers, where he meant the dog should exercise this faculty, on their guard as to the issue.

The process was curious. As soon as the dog's master entered the shop, the animal seemed to avoid all appearance of recognizing or acknowledging any connection with him, but lounged about in an indolent, disengaged, and indifferent sort of manner, as if having come of its own accord, into the shop. In the course of looking over some wares, the master indicated by a touch on the parcel and a look toward the spaniel, that which he desired the dog should appropriate, and then left the shop. The dog, whose watchful eye caught the hint in an instant, instead of following his master out of the shop, continued to sit at the door or lie by the fire, watching the counter, until observing the attention of the people of the shop was withdrawn from the prize to be secured. Whenever he saw an opportunity of doing so, as he imagined, unobserved, he never failed to jump upon the counter with his fore feet, possess himself of the gloves, or whatever else had been pointed out to him, and escape from the shop to join his master.

"No Great Judge of de Hemp."

IT was one of Girard's ideas of success in business, that there was no stage in the process of the exchange of equivalents in trading, that might not be made to him an opportunity of present profit.

On one of these occasions, a merchant who had purchased of Girard a large quantity of hemp, sent a black man to superintend the weighing and loading of it. Girard was busy himself in putting it upon the scales, but a great part of it being damaged, the negro man watched him closely, and whenever Girard threw on a bad bundle, the negro would carefully throw it off. But this, Girard, of course, would not submit to, and would proceed to replace it, whilst the negro, in his turn, would as quickly fling it off—until, losing his patience, he commenced cursing the negro, and declared he should not touch the hemp, at the risk of chastisement. But Sambo, nothing intimidated by the threats of the rich merchant, continued to look after his master's interest, telling Girard that if he ventured to touch him, he would knock his other eye out. Girard became pacified, and seeing the determined purpose of the man not to suffer his employer to be wronged, he became reconciled to the negro, saying:

"Well, I believe you be one very honest fellow, but you no be one great judge of de hemp."

On another occasion of the same kind, the purchaser of his hemp *appeared* to be somewhat less inflexible than Sambo. Owing to some peculiar circumstances existing between the parties, the damaged hemp was taken by a ship chandler, Girard insisting that he would give no other; and very little, or none of the article being in the market, the buyer was obliged to submit to his eccentric humor, and take it as he gave it, or get none. It happened, however, that this ship chandler manufactured all Mr. Girard's cordage, and in order to mete out to him *measure for measure*, he ordered the *damaged hemp* to be selected and made up for Mr. Girard. This was done; and the retribution no doubt proved a more serious loss, than the profit on the unmerchantable hemp amounted to.

Raising the Price of Bread.

SOME years ago, the bread dealers in Lyons thought that they could prevail on M. Dugas, the provost of the merchants in that city, to befriend them at the expense of the public. They waited upon him in a body, and begged leave to raise the price of bread, which could not be done without the sanction of that magistrate. M. Dugas told them that he would examine their petition, and give them an early answer. The bakers then retired, having first left upon the table a good fat purse of two hundred louis d'or, intended as private pocket money for the provost.

In a few days the bakers called upon the magistrate for an answer, not in the least doubting but that the money had very effectually pleaded their cause. "Gentlemen," said M. Dugas, "I have weighed your reasons in the balance of justice, and I find them light. I do not think the people ought to suffer under a pretence of the dearness of corn, which I know to be unfounded; and as to the purse of money left with me, I am sure that I have made such a generous and noble use of it, as you yourself intended : I have distributed it among the poor objects of charity in our two hospitals. As you are opulent enough to make such large donations, I cannot possibly think you are incurring any losses in your business; and I shall, therefore, continue the price of bread as it was before I received your petition."

Trickery in the Clothing Trade.

A GENTLEMAN from the country, who makes a visit to Gotham once a year, dropped into a fine looking clothing establishment in that city, to buy a coat. Seeing one which pleased him, he inquired the price, which the tailor stated to be thirty dollars. Not exactly approving of that price for the coat, the seller fell to twenty-five dollars, and finally to twenty, at which price the coat was knocked down to him, as a bargain. It was immediately "bundled up," and the money paid for it, the buyer stating it to be his intention to leave the city in a few hours. On ar-

riving at his hotel, he thought he would examine the bundle he received; when, lo ! on unfolding the same, what a sight met his gaze ! *two old tweed coats*, worth three or four dollars, looked up pitifully in unconscious guilt, into his astonished face. How he felt, one might imagine; and mentioning the circumstances to the clerk in attendance at the hotel in which he supped and lodged, he was informed that such a thing was of daily occurrence. In a moment more, the buyer was on his way, with his "bargain," to the self-styled fashionable clothing establishment, and, on entering, accosted the man who sold him a *fine black broadcloth coat*, with a "Well, how do you do, sir ?" This pleasing *salut*, instead of receiving a salutation in return, equally as pleasant and agreeable, together with a desire to be happy to see a customer return again, was met with an indifference which showed to the customer that there was *no disposition or willingness manifested to know him !* Calmly, however, he proceeded to play *his* game upon the Peter Funk, or "clo' man," by informing that distinguished dealer in fine black broadcloth coats, that he had come back to his establishment to inform him of a mistake that he had committed a few hours before, in selling him two coats, when he had only bargained for and purchased one (here the clo' man became twitchy and somewhat uneasy)— that being a man who desired only what was right, his moral scruples would not permit him to go away without returning and satisfying (here the Peter Funk began to *smell* a Tartar !) the error that had been committed. "It cannot be a mistake; it is not possible; no, sir; it cannot be," were the expressions of the Funk at the close of the sentence above. "Now," said the customer, energetically, "you—*you*—had, no doubt, thought that YOU had in your power a verdant one (here Funk thought he was about to *catch* a Tartar), and that an opportunity was given you to indulge in your swindling operations, expecting, of course, that I would leave the city, and not call again, after discovering your fraud upon my purse."

The Peter Funk, now finding that he *had* caught a Tartar, began making explanations — declaring that the two coats were made for another gentleman, and that he would not for ten dollars that they had been kept out of his hands. This attempt to "get off," by telling a downright falsehood, especially in face of the fact that at least a dozen of bundles were on the counter, all of which, doubtless, were intended to be "changed" for *real* purchases, as was the case with the gentleman in question, did not "take." Apologies not suiting that individual, he departed with nothing less than the fine coat he had purchased, and the money for which was even then warm in the seller's pocket.

—◆—

Filibustering among Parisian Jewellers.

THE Parisian jewellers are now and then the victims of people in elevated stations—aristocratic, titled, possessed of everything to avert suspicion; and even of ladies in the highest social circles. These swindlers in high-born position find it convenient to take from jewellers what money bankers and usurers refuse to give them. They boldly enter the jewellers' shops, purchase and have delivered to them many bracelets and many diamonds, which they will return in a few days (so they say) if they find nothing to suit them. The objects thus intrusted to them go from the shop, after delivery, to the pawnbrokers. Time passes away; at first, the jeweller hesitates to produce scandal, and he accepts notes for the goods which have been taken as good as by force from the shop. At last the notes fall due; they are protested. The next step of such "patrons" is to offer to return the goods! And this is at the end of ten or twelve months, without interest or damages. So that the jewellers become the bankers of fashionable ladies and gentlemen pressed for money.

As an example of this kind of aristocratic filibustering, it is mentioned by a dealer, that M. de —— took sixty thousand dollars' worth of jewelry from seven or eight jewelry shops in Paris. A twelvemonth passed away, and nothing was paid; all had been sent to the pawnbrokers. Finally, M. de —— offered to return the jewels, but hooted at the idea of paying a single sou for merely "taking time to examine them and make up his mind." The dealers threatened to bring him before the police court; he laughed at them, and they abandoned it, fearing the loss of time and money. Another case was that of M'me de ——, who took from a certain dealer an immense quantity of jewels to "show to her mother," as she said; but really to carry to her "aunt" (the slang phrase for the pawnbroker), and they could not be got back but by the aid of the police.

—◆—

Window "Gazers" Employed by London Shopkeepers.

ONE of the most "exquisite" tactics of London shopkeepers is the hiring of regular *window gazers*. This leisurely employé, whose very existence is hardly known to one in a thousand (and of course is not intended to be), is a genteelly dressed, complacent-looking individual, having much the appearance and manners of an aristocratic "gentleman about town." It is but rarely that his services are monopolized by a single firm, unless they are the proprietors of several shops in different quarters of the city. It more frequently happens that he is the joint property of several individuals whose occupations and interests do not at all clash with each other.

These various traders manage to rig him out in fashionable trim by general contribution; a hatter takes charge of his head; a tailor of his back; the proprietor of the "pantaloononicon" contributes the trousers; the bootmaker indues him in a pair of the genteelest of boots; he supports a gold-headed cane or a handsome umbrella, supplied by the manufacturer of those articles; necktie and handkerchief of irreproachable style and pattern are bestowed by the haberdasher; while a jeweller finds him a gold watch, a showy ring, and a handsome double eyeglass.

Thus equipped, he "goeth forth to his labor," whenever the state of the weather is such as to support the probability of his genuineness. All he has to do is to walk leisurely from the shop of one of his patrons to that of another, stopping in front of the window, and scrutinizing with much apparent interest and complacency the various objects there displayed to public view. In so doing, he handles his gold eye-glass with aristocratic grace—taps his model boot with his splendid cane—drops a monosyllabic ejaculation of surprise or commendation, and when half a score of simpletons have gathered around to admire the astonishing cheapness and perfection of the goods, he pops into the shop, already commencing to give an order in a loud and pompous tone for a dozen of the article which the tradesman wants to push off—desires that they may be sent to May Fair before dark, and, naïvely leaving his card with the shopman, who bows him deferentially out, walks leisurely off to the next shop on his beat, there to repeat the same automatic ceremony. He contrives to arrive at the tailor's at the fashionable hour, when that functionary is engaged with customers, and there he spreads himself in giving his concise and liberal orders: "You have my measure—no immediate hurry—this day week will do—suppose you are driven as usual;" and he is off again on his way to the jeweller's.

He accomplishes his easy round in the course of the day, and betakes himself to his scurvy lodging, doffing his "show-toys" before dark. His pay varies from half a crown to three shillings and sixpence a day, according to his figure and effrontery; and he considers it easily and pleasantly earned, inasmuch as he is (according to his own notions), to all intents and purposes a *gentleman*—during the hours of duty.

One Price, but not the Same Article.

A LADY went into a drygoods store to buy a silk dress, and after being shown several pieces, at length fixed on one, for which, however, she would only give a certain price, and that considerably lower than the one demanded. But in accordance with the "One price —no deduction" rule of the house, no abatement could be allowed to be made, so the offer could not be taken.

The customer was just going away, when the salesman dexterously put aside the piece of silk in question, and replaced it by another of an inferior quality and lower price, though similar in appearance to that for which she had been offering. "Come this way, ma'am, you may have it!" he cried, as she was going out at the door. The dress was cut off, the full price paid, and the customer departed, highly pleased at having got it all her own way.

Drygoods Drummer "Sold."

THE following description, by the hero of a native romance bearing his name, of the manner and tactics of New York drygoods drummers, is a picture which the presiding genius of Harper's "Drawer" justly pronounces to be one that Dickens himself has rarely excelled. The scene succeeds the history of the hero's first acquaintance with a "drummer"—who, mistaking him for a country "dealer," had given him his card on board of a steamboat, taken him to his hotel, sent him his wine, given him tickets to the theatre, and requested him to call at his store in Hanover Square, where (though he didn't say so) it was his intention to turn these courtesies to profitable account. On a bright, pleasant morning, accordingly, our hero visits the store, where Mr. Lummocks, the drummer, receives him with open arms, and introduces him to his employer.

He shook me heartily by the hand, and said he was really delighted to see me. He asked me how the times were, and offered me a cigar, which I took, for fear of giving offence, but which I threw away the very first opportunity I got.

"Buy for cash, or on time?" he asked.

I was a little startled at the question, it was so abrupt; but I replied:

"For cash."

"Would you like to look at some prints, major?" he inquired.

"I am much obliged to you," I answered; "I am very fond of seeing prints."

With that he commenced turning over one piece after another, with amazing rapidity.

"There, major—very desirable article—splendid style—only two-and-six; cheapest goods in the street."

Before I could make any reply, or even guess at his meaning, he was called away, and Mr. Lummocks stepped up and supplied his place.

"You had better buy 'em, colonel," said Mr. Lummocks; "they will sell like hot cakes. Did you say you bought for cash?"

"Of course," I replied, "if I buy at all."

He took a memorandum out of his pocket, and looked in it for a moment. "Let—me—see," said he, "Franco, Franco—what did you say your firm was? Something and Franco, or Franco and Somebody? The name has escaped me."

"I have no firm," I replied.

"Oh, you haven't, hain't ye? all alone, eh? But I don't see that I've got your first name down in my 'tickler.'"

"My first name is Harry," said I.

"Right—yes—I remember," said Mr. Lummocks, making a memorandum, "and your references, colonel, who did you say were your references?"

"I have no reference," I replied; "indeed, I know of no one to whom I could refer, except my father."

"What—the old boy in the country, eh?"

"My father is in the country," I answered, seriously, not very well pleased to hear my parent called the "Old Boy."

"Then you have no city references, eh?"

"None at all; I have no friends here, except yourself."

"Me!" exclaimed Mr. Lummocks, apparently in great amazement. "Oh, ho! how much of a bill do you mean to make with us, captain?"

"Perhaps I may buy a vest pattern," I replied, "if you have got some genteel patterns."

"A vest pattern!" exclaimed Mr. Lummocks; "what! haven't you come down for the purpose of buying goods?"

"No, sir," I replied; "I came to New York to seek for employment, and, as you have shown me so many kind attentions, I thought you would be glad to assist me in finding a situation."

Mr. Lummocks's countenance underwent a very singular change when I announced my reasons for calling on him.

"Do you see any thing that looks green in there?" he asked, pulling down his eyelid with his forefinger.

"No, sir, I do not," I replied, looking very earnestly into his eye.

"Nor in there, either?" said he, pulling open his other eye.

"Nothing at all, sir," I replied, after a minute examination.

"I guess *not!*" said Mr. Lummocks; and without making any other answer, he turned smartly on his heel, and left me.

"Regularly sucked, eh, Jack?" asked a young man who had been listening to our conversation.

"Don't mention it," said Mr. Lummocks; "the man is a fool."

Harry was about to demand an explanation of this strange conduct, when the proprietor came forward and told him that he was not a retailer, but a *jobber*, and advised him, "if he wanted a vest pattern, to go into Chatham street!" The drummer was "sold," instead of his goods.

Deaconing both Ends of the Barrel.

IN preparing and packing fruit for the market, the practice of "deaconing," as it is called, is very extensively followed—that is, topping off a barrel of apples with the best specimens; the rather irreverent term "deaconing" having its origin, probably, from some one holding that office having been unfortunately distinguished for his frequent adoption of the plan, so as to put an inviting show on his fruit. A dealer down East, who happened to be "posted," sold a barrel of apples to a customer, at the same time recommending them as the choicest apples that had been raised in the town. In due time the barrel was opened, and found to contain a very inferior quality; whereupon the customer, feeling that he had been imposed upon, made complaint to the seller, who in turn very coolly made answer, that he guessed he must have opened the barrel at the wrong end! The only change this little episode was known to produce in the seller's practice was to make him careful afterward to "deacon" *both* ends.

Grocers' Raisin-Boxes and Nibbling Customers.

ALMOST every grocer, it may be safe to assume, is or has been infested with a customer who is perpetually infringing on the eighth commandment. This class of pilferers are constantly tasting the cheese, or munching convenient lumps of sugar, dried apples, etc. They occasionally stick their dirty fingers into the molasses hogshead, and suck them with infinite gusto.

A grocer, "not a thousand miles" from South Danvers, was the victim of such a bore. Whenever Mr. A—— came to the store, he would steer for the raisin-box, and deliberately abstract a handful; to the cheese, and take a generous slice; and, with a cracker and a glass of water, serve himself an excellent lunch. The grocer one day undid a box of nice Malaga raisins and placed it on his counter. Mr. A——, coming in, made direct tracks to them, and expressed his approbation of their quality by taking an unusually large handful. Our friend, the grocer, observing this, gave orders to his clerks not to sell or allow any one to touch the raisins in that box, except Mr. A—. He called frequently. At the end of six months, the box of Malagas was gone; Mr. A— had eaten them all. His bill for that time amounted to about forty dollars, the profits on which were three dollars. The raisins (to say nothing of other nibblings) amounted, at cost price, to $3.25. Thus the grocer, from that "customer," in that space of time, made twenty-five cents *out of pocket.* After that, he insisted upon having Mr. A— administer firm control over his fingers, or else withdraw his patronage.

Item—to whom it may concern: Don't imagine that when you purchase an ounce of pepper, the grocer can afford you the gratuitous privilege of his raisin box.

Artful Dodge.

AN ingenious rogue in Berlin, Prussia, lately practised one of the most artful dodges to be found in the records of any business. A member of the company of players at Kallenbach's theatre was to have a benefit night; and the question was, how to get together a good audience, as the usual attendance at that place of amusement, even if doubled, would produce far too slender a sum to satisfy the expectations of a benefit night. Accordingly, some days before the memorable evening, there appeared in all the Berlin papers an advertisement to the following effect:

" A gentleman, who has a niece and ward possessing a disposable property of fifteen thousand thalers, together with a mercantile establishment, desires to find a young man who would be able to manage the business and become the husband of the young lady. The possession of property or other qualification is no object. Apply to ———."

Hundreds and hundreds of letters poured in, in reply to this advertisement. On the morning of the benefit day each person who had sent a reply received the following note: " The most important point is, of course, that you should like one another. I and my niece are going to Kallenbach's theatre this evening, and you can just drop in upon us in Box No. 1."

Of course, the theatre was crammed. All the boxes, all the best paying places in the house were filled early in the evening with a mostly male public, got up in a style seldom seen at the royal opera itself. Glasses were levelled on all sides in the direction of " box No. 1," and eyes were strained to catch the first glimpse of the niece, when she should appear in company with the uncle. But uncles are proverbially " wicked old men;" and in the pre ent case neither uncle nor niece was to be found, and the disconsolate lovers—of a fortune—were left to clear up the mystery as best they could. The theatre had not had such an audience for years, and, of course, the chief person concerned reaped a rich harvest by the trick.

Half-hour's Experience with London Brokers.

I TURNED to the right (says an honest visitor to the rendezvous of English brokers, to see how the money-springs were touched), and found myself in a spacious apartment, which was nearly filled with persons more respectable in appearance than the crew I had left at the door. Curious to see all that was to be seen, I began to scrutinize the place and the society into which I had intruded. But I was prevented from indulging the reflections which began to suggest themselves, by the conduct of those about me. A curly-haired Jew, with a face as yellow as a guinea, stepped plump before me, fixed his black, round, leering eyes full on me, and exclaimed without the slightest anxiety about my hearing him:

" So help me Got, Mo', who is he ? "

Instead of replying in a straightforward way, " Mo " raised his voice as loud as he could, and shouted with might and main :

" Fourteen hundred new fives ! "

A hundred voices repeated the mysterious exclamation, " Fourteen hundred new fives ! "

" Where, where—fourteen hundred new fives—now for a look; where is he—Go it, go it ! " were the cries raised on all sides by the crowd, which now rallied about my person like a swarm of bees. And then " Mo," by way of proceeding to business, repeating the war-cry, staggered sideways against me, so as almost to knock me down. My fall, however, was happily prevented by the kindness of a brawny Scotchman, who humorously calling out, " Let the man alone," was so good as to stay me in my course with his shoulder, and even to send me back toward " Mo," with such violence, that, had he not been supported by a string of his friends, he must have infallibly fallen before me. But being thus backed, he was enabled to withstand the shock, and to give me a new impulse in the direction of the Scotch-man, who, awaiting my return, treated me with another hoist as before, and I found those two worthies were likely to amuse themselves with me as with a shuttlecock, for the next quarter of an hour. I struggled violently to extricate myself from this unpleasant situation, and, by aiming a blow at the Jew, inspired Moses to pause and give up his next hit, and to allow me for a moment to regain my feet.

The rash step which I had taken was likely to produce very formidable consequences. All present were highly exasperated and panting for a clinch. The war became more hot and desperate than ever. Each individual seemed anxious to contribute to my destruction; and some of their number considerately called out, "Spare his life, but break his limbs." My alarm was extreme; and I looked nervously round for means of escape.

"You ought to be ashamed of yourself to use the gentleman in that sort of way," squeaked a small imp-like person, affecting sympathy, and then trying to renew the sport.

"How would you like it yourself," cried another, "if you were a stranger?" shaking his sandy locks with a knowing look, and knocking off my hat as he spoke.

I made a desperate blow at this offender. It did not take effect, from the expedition with which he retreated, and I had prudence enough to reflect that it would be better to recover my hat than to pursue the enemy. Turning round, I saw my unfortunate beaver, or "canister," as it was called by the gentry who had it in their custody, bandying it backward and forward, between the Caledonian and his clan, and the Jew and his tribe. Covered with perspiration, foaming with rage, and almost expiring from heat and exhaustion, I at last succeeded in recovering my once glossy and respectable hat. I did not dare to rein-state it, but was forced to grasp it with both hands, in order to save what remained of it. I baffled several desperate snatches, one of which carried away the lining in shreds, and was now trying to keep the enemy at bay, afraid again to attack the host opposed to me; but not knowing how to retreat, when a person, who had not previously made himself conspicuous, approached and interfered, by saying, "Perhaps you had better go out;" at the same time pointing to a door which I had been too much in a hurry to have seen before.

One of the Operations in 'Change Alley.

WHILE the war in which the British nation was involved, in 1761, was going on, Mr. Dunbar, the eminent West India merchant in London, finding his affairs much less prosperous than usual, sought "the Alley," as the money street of London was then termed, to retrieve his failing fortunes—with what success, the sequel will show. From some private information of which he had come into possession, he believed that he had good grounds for supposing that a peace would soon be effected, and a rise in the funds at once ensue. He therefore ordered his broker to buy one hundred thousand pounds in stock for his account, telling him privately the opinion he had formed, with the intelligence on which it was based,—and the broker, in violation of his oath, jobbed extensively on his own account as well as for his client. February passed away without the expected peace, and Mr. Dunbar paid the difference. Confident, however, in his views, he continued the operation; but each account day proved that the price had been against him, and with great difficulty did he find money to pay the amounts due. In July, unable to pay cash, he gave notes of hand to the broker, who agreed to receive them. No objection being made, the account was continued on for

August. In that month the prospect of peace revived, the funds rose handsomely, and Mr. Dunbar, seeing a chance of paying a greater part of his losses, went with all speed to his broker. His distress may be imagined, when he was coolly told, that, since he had *given notes of hand*, no account had been opened, and no advantage could be reaped from the rise in price. Any appeal to law was useless; but, as Mr. Dunbar became a bankrupt, the members of the stock exchange subscribed to pay the amount claimed, in order that so flagrant a case might not become public.

His Ruling Passion.

A MR. L., a master in chancery, was on his deathbed—a very wealthy man. Some occasion of great urgency occurred, in which it became necessary to make an affidavit; and the attorney, failing of one or two other masters whom he inquired after, ventured to ask if Mr. L. *himself* would possibly be able to receive the deposition. The proposal actually seemed to give him momentary strength; his clerk was sent for, and the oath taken in due form. The master was lifted up in his bed, and with difficulty subscribed the paper; as he sank down again, he made a signal to his clerk, "Wallace?" "Sir?" "Your ear — lower — lower. *Have you got the half crown?*" He was dead before the morning.

Trick for "the Spashy."

WHEN the banks "shut down" on their specie, some people hold on to what coin they get a feel at, to the annoyance of the retail traders, who are importuned every hour to change a bill for some small purpose. An illustration of this fact is that of a Celtic woman who entered a grocery and called for "a cint's 'orth o' sand." The article was measured out, and put into

14

the customer's pail, who tendered a one dollar bill to have the pay taken out of it. "I can't change that for so small an amount," exclaimed the grocer; "you may take the sand, and be welcome to it." "Indade, sir, and shure it isn't the sand that I'm wanting at all at all; but it's the sulver—the *spashy* that ye'll be giving me back."

Game of the Money Packages.

NORTH, the noted insurance agent, banker, stock gambler, and speculator, who flourished upon such an extensive scale until the hour of his collapse—when he was found to be hundreds of thousands of dollars worse than nothing—was a most inveterate and persistent borrower of other people's money. He went to New York frequently, and took with him large packages of bank bills. Usually arriving in New York after business hours, it was his custom, on such occasions, to deposit the money packages, nicely sealed, with the clerk of the hotel he might decide to stop at. L. E. W., who had occasion also to go frequently to New York, and who often chanced to fall into North's company, had noticed that these deposits of money packages generally secured to North nice rooms and much attention at the hotels. He accordingly prepared two handsome packages, sealed them up with heavy seals, marked upon each, in bold characters, "$3,000," placed them in his carpet sack, and in two or three days after, on his way to Gotham, got into the company of North. They went together to the Astor. North booked his name, pulled a key from his pocket, unlocked his carpet sack, took out a sealed package marked "$2,000," and handed it to the clerk with a pompous request that it be taken care of till called for. L. E. W. then booked his name, and opening his carpet bag, drew out the two packages marked "$3,000," and handed them to the clerk with the same request. North looked on with evident satisfaction and surprise, but made no remark. The next day, after breakfast, he called L. E. W. aside mysteriously, spoke to him about having a bank note to pay, said he was " short," and ending by requesting a loan of one of the packages of three thousand dollars, which he had seen him deposit the evening before. The temptation was too great; and besides it was " All-Fool's Day." " You can have it for three days, if that can be of any accommodation to you," said W., looking wisely. Of course it would be an accommodation; so North wrote a note for three thousand dollars, payable one day after date, and the package was graciously passed to him. An hour later, and North went into a well-known bank in Wall street, with his usual bluster, bustle, and hurry. " I have a note here due to-day, I believe," said he to a teller. The note was produced. It was for five thousand dollars. A $2,000 and a $3,000 package were handed over in payment. The first was broken, and found to be correct; the second was then opened, and found to contain nought but blank tissue paper! The clerk looked inquiringly; poor North looked deeply mortified. He made a hurried apology, gathered up his two thousand dollars, and took his departure. North never afterward asked L. E. W. for a loan of a " money package."

King Charles in the Pawners' Clutches.

IN a curious pamphlet, published in 1676, an account is given of the outrageous advantage taken of the necessities of King Charles by the pawnbrokers; showing that the monarch who lives beyond his revenue, must pay the same penalty as the subject who outruns his income. He found himself at the mercy of the rich pawnbroker, who made the royal debtor pay ten, twenty, and thirty per cent. for ac-

commodation, while he allowed only six per cent. for the money which went to alleviate the difficulties of the "merry monarch." A business so profitable induced the pawnbrokers more and more to become lenders to the king, to anticipate all the revenue, to take every grant of Parliament into pawn as soon as it was given; also to outvie each other in buying and taking to pawn bills, orders, and tallies, so that, in effect, all the revenue passed through their hands.

Duplicity Practised by Furnese, the King's Banker.

THE name of Sir Henry Furnese figures largely among the bygone bankers who gave renown to the financiers of that period. Throughout Holland, Flanders, France, and Germany, he maintained a complete and perfect train of business intelligence. The news of the many battles fought was thus received first by him, and the fall of Namur added to his profits, owing to his early receipt of the news. On another occasion he was presented by King William with a diamond ring of immense value, as a reward for some important information, and as a testimony of that monarch's esteem. He was the king's friend and banker.

But the temptation to deceive was too great, even for this eminent and honored banker. He fabricated news; he insinuated false intelligence; he was the originator of some of those plans which at a later period were managed with so much effect by Rothschild. Thus, if Sir Henry wished to buy, his brokers were ordered to look gloomy and mysterious, hint at important news, and after a time sell. His movements were closely watched—the contagion would spread; the speculators become alarmed; prices be lowered four or five per cent.,—for in those days the loss of a battle might be the loss of a crown,—and Sir Henry would reap the benefit by employing different brokers to purchase as much as possible at the reduced price. Large profits were thus made, but a demoralizing spirit was spread abroad; and bankrupts and beggars sought the same pleasure in which the millionnaire indulged, and often with similar success.

Talleyrand and the Stock Jobber.

An extensive dealer in stocks, anxious about the rise and fall of the public funds, and eager to overreach those similarly situated, came once to Talleyrand for information respecting the truth of a rumor that George the Third had suddenly died, when the statesman replied in a confidential tone, "I shall be delighted if the information I have to give you, be of any use to you." The banker was enchanted with the prospect of obtaining authentic information from so high a source; and Talleyrand, with a mysterious air, continued: "Some say that the king of England is dead, others that he is not dead, but for my own part, I believe neither the one nor the other; I tell you this in confidence, but do not commit me."

Buying Cheap.

Some persons have a *penchant* for buying things cheap—a weakness, indeed, with which many are troubled, and it is oftentimes a most offensive one. Clapp tells a "good un" of a wandering Jew peddler, who stepped into the counting room of a Boston merchant, on a certain winter's morning, and after warming his hands, turned to the gentleman occupying the seat of authority, and politely inquired:

"Would you like to examine a vest pattern?"

"No, no, don't bother me. Very busy just now."

"It is the best article and the neatest pattern that you ever saw."

"Don't *want* any vest patterns!"

"But just look, sir,"—and the peddler had a piece of vesting unfolded, which was really quite neat, and the cogitator, unable to unravel the political web—he was conning the election returns as given by the rival journals—determined to unravel the web of the fabric.

"All silk, sir; warranted, and sufficient for two double-breasted vests, or three with rolling collars."

"What do you ask for it?"

"Twelve dollars. I bought it in Liverpool, and brought it over with me, and if you want it, you shall have it for just what it cost me—twelve dollars."

"It is too much, shan't give any such price—but will give you six dollars."

"Oh, my gracious!" exclaimed the peddler, as if astonished at such an offer, "I can't think of it." Off he walked. In ten minutes the door was opened, and the peddler thrust in his head: "You may have it for ten dollars."

"No," was all the reply he got.

"I will say eight, as the very lowest."

"No, *sir*," and away went the peddler the second time.

The gentleman was about relapsing into his revery upon the contradictory election returns, as given by the different political papers, when the peddler reëntered boldly, and laid the vesting upon the desk, exclaiming:

"Well, give us six dollars, and it is yours."

The money was paid, and the peddler was about leaving the door, when he turned round and took from his pocket another roll, and, undoing it, exposed to view a piece of vesting as far preferable to the other as possible.

The gentleman at once made a proposal to exchange. The peddler couldn't think of such a thing—he didn't mean to sell it on any account; he intended to keep it until he was able to have it made up for himself; but, after considerable trading and talking, he gave it up, received his first piece and two dollars, and walked off—making eight dollars for his piece of vesting. The gentleman, quite satisfied with the exchange, walked up to his tailor's, at noon, threw down the piece, ordering him to cut off sufficient for one vest.

"How many vests do you expect it will make?" inquired the tailor.

"Three, of course," was the reply.

The yardstick went down, and looking up, he informed the purchaser that it would make two, by piecing out the collar with black silk. The idea of measuring the article had not occurred to him before, but at this piece of news he felt a kind of film spread over his eyes, a lightness of pocket troubling his ribs, while the letters s-o-l-d, by a delusion of his optical nerves, appeared to be written on the outer walls of all the adjacent buildings. He then inquired the probable worth, and was informed that such vesting could be purchased at about two dollars and a quarter per yard! This was sufficient.

Business Suckers.

BUSINESS suckers, as they are appropriately termed, are no small class in modern times. They are most numerous out West, and ply their tactics after a style that leaves nothing wanting. An individual of this ilk, possessed of a moderate amount of money, commences business in some thriving town. He goes to one of the wholesale markets, and with one or two commendatory letters, but particularly with his money, he soon becomes acquainted—at first but limited—but he has only to manage his trumps (money) with a little professional tact, and his acquaintance will very soon extend. At first he purchases cautiously, and meets his obligations promptly, always managing to have his goods carefully packed and marked scientifically, and placed exposed on the street several days before he removes them ·

"Like books and money
Laid in show
As nest eggs
To make clients lay."

And he succeeds. He soon becomes known as a man of promptness and capital, and doing a dashing business; and such a business he *does* do, for the motto at home is to sell low for cash—never mind profits. His acquaintance is courted; he is be-drammed, be-dinnered and be-suppered. Everything goes on swimmingly, and finally he buys largely, goes in deeply, makes one grand manœuvre—a most prodigious swell, and then judiciously and *profitably* (to himself) explodes.

Fortune Making in Havana.

IT is a well-known fact, that nearly all the merchants and shopkeepers of Havana are native Spaniards. A large proportion of this class come to Cuba as adventurers—seekers of luck and fortune, and not particular as to the ways and means, though generally beginning their mercantile career as clerks, on small salaries. After accumulating, or getting, five hundred dollars, they will purchase a share in a joint-stock slave-trading company, and, in the course of a year or two, receive a profit in the shape of a dividend, amounting to ten thousand dollars, which sum, reinvested in the same business, soon makes them millionnaires. These nabobs then generally return to Spain to spend their ill-gotten fortunes, leaving a plentiful crop of clerks to follow in the footsteps of their predecessors.

Cheating the Oculist.

SIR WILLIAM SMYTH, of Bedfordshire, was an immensely rich money dealer, but most parsimonious and grinding in his dealings. At seventy years of age he was entirely deprived of his sight—unable to glont over his hoarded heaps of gold. In this condition he was persuaded by Taylor, the celebrated oculist, to be couched—who was, by agreement, to have sixty guineas if he restored the banker to any degree of sight. Taylor succeeded in his operation, and Sir William was enabled to read and write without the aid of spectacles during the rest of his life. But no sooner was his sight restored, than the banker began to regret that his agreement had been for so large a sum. His thoughts were now how to cheat the oculist. He pretended that he had only a glimmering, and could see nothing distinctly; for which reason the bandage on his eyes was continued a month longer than the usual time. Taylor was deceived by these representations, and agreed to compound the bargain, accepting twenty guineas instead of sixty. At the time Taylor attended him he had a large estate, an immense sum of money in the stocks, and tens of thousands in gold at his house.

Mr. Jones's Experience with Peter Funk.

A GREENHORN, named Mr. Jones, from Hartford, is stopped while careering down Broadway, by the sound of a stentorian voice from within, crying "Going." He hears the whack of the auctioneer's hammer, and sees six *gentlemen* standing round a table. "Things are selling mighty cheap in there," he says to himself, and goes in. Peter Funk holds a piece of linen in his hands, and is just on the point of knocking it down at six cents a yard—"fifty-five and one half yards, going, at six cents! an awful sacrifice." "*Seven,*" hastily shouts Jones. "Eight," says Stool Pigeon. "Nine," says Jones. Whack goes the mallet. "Sold," says Peter. "Mr. Jones, fifty-five and one half yards of linen, at fifty-*nine* cents," —touching lightly on the 'fifty.' The attentive clerk beckons to Jones, who steps back behind a mysterious desk with a screen in front. Clerk begins to make out the bill, while Jones lays

down a five-dollar bank note to pay for the linen; the money goes to the drawer. Clerk hands Jones the bill, which may read thus :—

Mr. Jones, bought of Peter Funk, 55½ yards Irish linen, at 59 c. per yd.,—$32.74.

Jones opens his eyes; clerk points to the sum, and holds out his right hand, with the remark, "Balance, $27.74." Jones opens his mouth, and essays to speak, but is dumbfounded; he has *hearn* of those pesky mock auctions, but never dreamed he should ever blunder into one in so *respectable* a place as Broadway. Mr. Jones ruminates and pinches himself to see if he is dreaming; he is awake—he is in New York, Broadway.

But Mr. Jones, though green, has Yankee presence of mind; he forks over the balance demanded, takes his linen under his arm and gapes at the auctioneer, until that functionary gets nervous, and announces that the sale is adjourned for the day. Mr. Jones, accordingly, to prevent being housed with the precious scamps, steps out and travels toward the Tombs, where he finds a policeman, and tells his tale of woe. In a few moments the swindling shop and the inmates, which meantime have got under full headway again, is taken all aback with an apparition—it is Mr. Jones with that linen under his arm, and a person with a brass shield on the lappel of his coat. The man with the shield takes the clerk by the nape of his neck, and starts him toward the Tombs; clerk remonstrates—explains—exclaims, and so on, but keeps custodially moving up Broadway and through Chambers street, when all of a sudden he concludes to disgorge the $32.74; which Jones takes, thanks the officer, and vanishes.

Connection between Small Bank Notes and Crime.

THE fact appears to be abundantly attested that the circulation of one-pound bank notes in England proved, at first, conducive to a melancholy waste of human life. Considering the advances made in the mechanical arts, at the time of their issue, they were rough and even rude in their execution. Easily imitated, they were also easily circulated; and from 1797, the executions for forgery augmented to an extent which bore no proportion to any other class of crime. During six years prior to their issue, there was but one capital conviction; during the four following years, eighty-five occurred. To prevent their imitation, most stringent penalties were ordained, and, in 1801, it was enacted that, to prevent forgeries, all the one and two pound notes should "be printed on a peculiar and purposely constructed paper, having waved or curved lines." But all these endeavors to repress crime fell sadly short of the necessity, and the connection between the issue of small notes and the effusion of blood because of their easy imitation was apparent enough. Thus, before 1797, the Bank of England could issue no notes under five pounds. In 1802, the average number of notes under that value was about three millions and a half. In the former period there were no capital executions; in the latter, one hundred and sixteen occurred

in four years. In 1817, there were thirty thousand forged notes of the one and two pounds class stopped at the bank, nine hundred of five pounds, fifty of ten pounds, and two of twenty. The crime is, therefore, imputed to the small notes; and the forgery of larger ones to the habits of criminality originating in the temptation of small notes.

Jacob Barker on "Thewdness" in Stock Dealing.

AMONG the new generation of Wall street, Jacob Barker, notwithstanding his present extensive business character, is comparatively unknown; but there was a time when Jacob made his mark upon the stock brokers and money changers of that monetary locality. He has long lived and thrived in the Crescent City. Jacob is as active and buoyant as most men at thirty-five; he cannot be said, however, to enjoy a green old age, unless it may be discovered in the suppleness he displays, so peculiar to youth. One of the many amusing stories told of him is where a gentleman called at his office and denounced, in the most unmeasured manner, certain persons who had swindled him—the gentleman (not Jacob, by any means)—in some stock transactions. Barker listened to the whole matter with professional zest, and finding that everything had been done "right," urged the indignant victim not to go on so, but to forget the thing entirely; "for," said Jacob, consolingly, "if you thwade in stock, you must call thealing *thewdness*, or you will constantly be out of themper!"

Stock Exchange Conspiracy.

A STOCK-JOBBING operation, which was undertaken in England, in 1814, and which has been celebrated in monetary annals because of its gigantic extent, will perhaps afford refreshing reading to that not small class who ply so dexterously similar expedients at the present day. The tale is most unique.

JACOB BARKER

P. C. BROOKS   J. & J.

PETER COOPER

J. C. HARNDEN   H. B.

Engraved for D. Appleton & Co.

On the 21st of February, 1815, about one o'clock in the morning, a violent knocking was heard at the door of the Ship Inn, at Dover. On being opened, the intruder announced himself as Lieutenant-colonel Du Bourg, aide-de-camp of Lord Cathcart. His dress supported the assertion. The richly embroidered scarlet uniform, the star on the breast, the silver medal suspended from his neck, the dark fur cap, with its broad band of gold lace, gave the wearer a military appearance. His clothes appeared wet with the sea spray, and he stated that he had been brought over by a French vessel, the seamen of which were afraid of landing at Dover, and had placed him in a boat about two miles from the shore. His news was important. Bonaparte had been slain in battle. The allied armies were in Paris. A great victory had been gained, and peace was certain.

He immediately ordered a post chaise and four horses to be prepared, and, after writing a letter in great haste to Admiral Foley, which was despatched by special messenger to Deal, he at once departed for London. Wherever he changed horses the news was spread, and the postboys rewarded with napoleons. In due time information reached the stock exchange; and it was not long before that resort was filled with rumors of general officers, despatches for Government, victories, and post chaises and four. Expresses from the various places where Du Bourg had changed horses poured into the principal speculators. The funds rose on the news. Application was made to the lord mayor, but, as his lordship had received no intelligence, they declined.

On the morning of the same day, about an hour before daylight, two men, in the habiliments of foreigners, landed in a six-oared galley, called on a Mr. Sandon, at Northfleet, and handed him a letter, purporting to be written by one whom he formerly knew, begging him to take the bearers to London, as they had great public news to communicate. The request was energetically complied with. Between twelve and one o'clock of that day, three persons, two of whom were dressed as French officers, proceeded in a post chaise and four, the horses of which were bedecked with laurel, over the then narrow and crowded thoroughfare of London bridge. While the carriage proceeded with an almost ostentatious slowness, small billets were scattered among the anxious gazers, announcing that Bonaparte was dead, and the allies in Paris. Through busy Cheapside and crowded Fleet street, the occupants of the carriage paraded their intelligence. They passed over the fine bridge of Blackfriars, drove rapidly to the Marsh Gate, got out, took off their military, put on round hats, and speedily disappeared. The news again spread far and wide. The neighborhood of the stock exchange was once more full of exaggerated reports. The funds rose. What could resist such accumulated evidence? The aide-de-camp of Lord Cathcart, at Dover; the foreigners at Northfleet with despatches; private expresses from various places, all tended to convince the members that there must be some foundation for the reports. Application was made to the ministry, but they knew nothing. Large bargains were made.

Altogether, the scene at the stock exchange at this time is spoken of by those who witnessed it as baffling all description. Yet still there was some doubt, so long as Government remained ignorant of the important intelligence. And as hour after hour of anxious doubt passed by, it would be difficult to imagine the feelings of many who began painfully to suspect that they were victims of a delusion. To the scene of unbounded joy and of greedy expectation of gain, there succeeded, in a few hours, that of disappointment, shame at having been gulled, the clenching of fists, the grinding of teeth, the tearing of hair—all the outward and visible signs of those inward commotions—disappointed avarice in some, consciousness of ruin in others, and, in all, boiling revenge. A committee was appointed by the stock exchange, and various circumstances tending to prove a huge conspiracy were discovered. On the Saturday preceding the Monday on which the deception was undertaken, consols and omnium, to the extent of eight hundred and twenty-six thousand pounds, were purchased for various individuals, many of whom were seriously implicated, and some of them suffered the penalties of fine and imprisonment.

Blinders for Stockholders.

EVEN railways have their reckonings, and the time of year comes when they are perforce made to show and disgorge their gains. Meetings are reluctantly summoned by the directors, and crowds of hungry shareholders are squeezed together for hours at a time. If this thing is not professionally understood in America, it certainly is in England.

The chairman pronounces a report, which is second only to a "speech from the throne," in vagueness, generality, and mystification. Anon comes the "clerk of the corporation," redolent of new shares, and he thickens the mist by a jumble of accounts, an incomprehensible hotchpotch of loans, debentures, calls, and balances, and generally winds up his abstruse financial puzzles by a prophetic announcement that the traffic next year is sure to be unprecedented and immense—at which every countenance is wreathed with the genial smiles inspired by hope.

All the details, however, are Greek to the poor shareholders, who really understand but one word in the whole railroad vocabulary — the welcome sound of "dividend;" but the fear of being thought a business nincompoop compels each one to be perfectly up to snuff, and wondrously sage. It is amusing, moreover, to observe how the directors manage (notwithstanding the "impertinent" interruptions of some inconveniently acute shareholder, whose sayings are recorded as those of "A voice"), somehow or other so to mix up this word dividend with other complicated details, as to leave the unhappy shareholders unable at the end to say whether they have to receive money or to pay it—the difference being the sum.

How refreshing, then, to find that the reports of one's own pet line are untainted by the faults alluded to! The public have a right to know this; and, as a pattern and incentive to other companies, the following extracts are made from the last report of the "Hum and Diddlesex Railway," England:

The chairman would now refer to their finance statement (*Hear!*). He felt bound to say it would be found most satisfactory. £7,000 had been mortgaged on annuities at par, and their debentures were now wholly independent of their stock of engines (*Cheers*, and cries of *Bravo!*). The permanent way was now in trust for the increased debits on the gradients (*Hear! hear!*). From this it was clear that there was £4,000 balance per contrà on the new half shares. (A voice, "What's the receipts?") The chairman could not be expected to go into such details. They had lately opened six miles of the "Navvey and Stoker Extension branch," which he had no doubt would pay well when a town had arisen at each end, and traffic was induced between them. (A voice, "What's the expenditure?") The chairman begged not to be interrupted in the midst of his statement. The meeting would observe one little item of £56,000 for law expenses. It was enough to say, they had triumphed over their opponents. True, they had incurred some trifling expense; but were they, he would ask, to be insulted by the " Grand Gumption ? " (*No!*)—or by any other line ? (*No, no!* and *cheers*). Then as to the dividend—(" *Hear, hear, hear !* " from all parts)—the clerk had recommended a net dividend of 10 per cent. (*Loud cheers*)—on the deficit, and this, after paying the surplus and the directors' salaries (which, in justice to those faithful servants, he was glad to say had been raised £500 each per annum), left the 4 per cent. incidental expenses as money in hand, which would simply render it necessary for the shareholders at once to pay up the late £20 calls. (Sensation. A voice, " What *is* the dividend to be ? ") The chairman put it to the meeting, whether the gentleman's question had not already been distinctly answered, and after some little confusion he vacated the chair, and the meeting—like the dividend—was dissolved.

Virginia Usurer Foiled.

PREVIOUSLY to the Revolutionary War, it was provided by an act of the Assembly of Virginia, that if any bill of exchange be drawn for the payment of any sum of money, and such bill is protested for non-acceptance or non-payment, it shall bear interest from the date, at the rate of ten per cent. per annum, until it shall be paid. The following curious circumstance, in connection with said law, took place at Williamsburg, Va., about the year 1760.

A usurious broker, not satisfied with five per cent. legal interest, refused to advance a sum of money to a gentleman, unless, by way of security, he would give a bill of exchange that should be returned protested, by which he would be entitled to ten per cent. The gentleman, who had immediate occasion for the money, sat down, drew a bill upon a merchant banker in London, with whom he had never

had any transactions, or carried on the least correspondence. The merchant, on receipt of the bill, observing the name of the drawer, very readily honored it, knowing the gentleman to be a person of large property, and concluding that he meant to enter into a correspondence with his house.

The broker, by this turn in the affair, became entitled to only five per cent. He was, therefore, exceedingly enraged at being, as he supposed, thus tricked, and complained very earnestly to his customer for having giving him a *good* bill instead of a *bad* one.

Kentucky Hams and Yankee Nutmegs.

SOME time since, the Kentucky nation commenced a rivalship with the Yankee land, in the manufacture of wooden eatables. A merchant in Port Gibson, Miss., desirous of procuring a lot of choice bacon hams, requested his agent at the Gulf to make the purchase for him, from the boats passing down the Mississippi. After many fruitless inquiries of the passing craft, he met with a Kentucky Jonathan, whose loading was composed of the nicest and choicest hams, all canvased, and that which was shown as a sample looked so well, and tasted so delightfully, that the confiding agent made the purchase on the spot.

The new Jonathan had such an innocent, unsuspected and unsuspecting countenance, too—giving forth no scintillations of vivacity, nor evincing the owner to possess brains more acute than a lobster, on any other subject than that of curing bacon—the art of which appeared to have become impressed on his cranium, as drippings wear the rock, or as the knowledge of law and physic reveals itself in the physiognomy of some members of those professions. Who would suspect *him* of perpetrating a Yankee or original art ? Straws show which way the wind blows; but, alas! the human countenance may present an unsolvable enigma, even to the most penetrating. Was it so in this case?

Jonathan's hams, when opened, proved to be wood, neatly turned in the shape of a hog's hind leg, and excellent for oven fuel—a recommendation, by the way, which, with characteristic modesty, he had not even alluded to. The Kentuckian showed that he was 'up to a trick or two,' and no one will deny that he threw down the glove, once and forever, to all Yankeedom.

Latest "Sell" of the Day.

THE latest 'sell' of the day originated in the fertile brain of a Baltimore clothes dealer. He placed in the pocket of a ready-made coat an old portemonnaie, and quietly awaited the advent of a fitting customer. Presently enters an individual desiring to be summer coated. After essaying several coats, the dealer says:

"Here is a coat made for a gentleman; he wore it one day and sent it back—it was too small for him—try it on. Ah! it fits first rate, like as if it was made for you. It is well made; buttons sewed on strong; with strong pockets."

The customer puts his hands into the pockets to try them, when his fingers come in contact with the pocket book. His imagination is kindled with the idea of appropriating the supposed treasure.

"How much did you say the coat was?" he eagerly asks.

The dealer names a good round sum.

The money is paid, and the self-duped customer walks off hurriedly with his supposed prize—not stopping to hear the suppressed chuckle of the dealer as he looks after him out of the corner of his eye.

Tompkins's Horse Trade.

TOMPKINS bought a fine horse—paid three hundred dollars for him. The horse, after a few months, proved to be lame in the right shoulder. Tompkins was distressed about it. Tried all sorts of remedies—embrocations, liniments, Mustang included, under the advice of the very best veterinarians, till the lameness was obstinate and grew rather worse. He became desperate, and hit upon this device to sell the horse. He drove an ugly tenpenny nail plump into the right fore-foot, and left it there for ten days; when he led the tortured animal limping to a neighboring blacksmith, to be shod. The blacksmith was a dealer in horses, and quite a jockey in his way. After a while, Tompkins called at the shop for his horse. "That's a splendid gelding of yours, Mr. Tompkins—pity he's so lame," says the smith. "He is, indeed," replied Tompkins; "but he is very lame, and I'm afraid he can't be cured." "Perhaps not, and may be he can," says Vulcan; "how much would you be willing to take for him, just as he stands, Mr. Tompkins, money down?" "Ah, well, I don't know what to say about that. If he is cured, he is worth all I paid for him, and even much more, as prices go now; but if his lameness should continue, you see he is worth nothing—not a dollar." The blacksmith began to chaffer. First he offered fifty dollars, then one hundred, and at last two hundred, for the animal. Tompkins was persuaded, and accepted the last offer. The money was paid, and the horse delivered on the spot. "Now," says the blacksmith, "as the bargain is finished, I will be frank with you, Mr. Tompkins. I suppose I can tell you just exactly what ailed that horse." "Can you?" says Tompkins, "well, I shall be glad to hear it. I *thought* you must know all about it, or you would not have paid me so much money for him."

The blacksmith produced the nail, and assured Tompkins, with great apparent satisfaction, that while paring down the horse's hoofs he had found that long piece of iron, and drawn it out of the frog of the near forefoot." "Is that *all* you know about it?" Tompkins asked, very quietly. "All!" replied the blacksmith—"all isn't that enough, for conscience' sake?" "Well," replied Tompkins, "I don't know as it is. I will be equally frank with you, since the bargain is finished. *I* drove the nail into the *foot*, but the lameness is in the *shoulder*."

"Old Vinter's" Bank Bills.

AWAY down East—that convenient but much abused locality for pointing a story—a wealthy old merchant, who was especially fond of a glass of good brandy, had established a bank, and, liking his own face better than any one's else, showed his frankness by placing it on both ends of his bank bills. One evening, a bill of this description was offered at the village hotel, and was thought to be a counterfeit. "Put a glass of brandy to the picter," proposed a wag, "and if his mouth opens, you may be sure it is one of old Vinter's."

Transactions in Worsteds.

A MAN some six feet three inches in height, and of herculean build, went into a Worcester shopkeeper's establishment, and asked if they had got any "whirlers"—by which he meant, stockings without feet, supposing, of course, that they were to be obtained of any "worsted" merchant.

"No," said the shopkeeper, "but we have got some famous big and strong stockings, as will just suit such a man as you."

"Let's ha'e a look at 'em," said the man.

The counter was immediately covered with a quantity. The working Hercules selected the largest pair—of mammoth size—and said:

"What's the price of them?"

"Four shillings and ninepence," was the reply.

"Can you cut the feet off of them?" was the next query.

"Oh, certainly," rejoined the shopkeeper.

"Then just cut them off," was the laconic direction.

No sooner said than done. The long shop shears were applied, and instantly the stockings were footless.

"And what's the price of 'em *now*?" asked the customer, with all the composure imaginable.

"Price of them *now!*" exclaimed the 'worsted' merchant, surprised beyond measure at the absurdity of the question; "why, four shillings and ninepence, to be sure!"

"Four shillings and ninepence!" exclaimed the customer; "I never gave but one shilling and sixpence for a pair of 'whirlers' in my life"—and he laid down that amount upon the counter.

"Well,' replied the tradesman, chopfallen and fairly outwitted, throwing the mutilations at him, "take them and be off with you! You've 'whirled' me *this* time, but I'll take good care that neither you nor any of your roguish gang shall do it again, as long as *I* live."

This case is similar to that of the cute Yankee auctioneer, who, after disposing of a violin, after a hard bidding, to a close-fisted buyer, went on—"Now, gentlemen, how much m' offered for the *bow?*—how much?—how much?—how much m' offered for the bow?" Expostulation was useless. The fiddle and the bow, he said, were in separate 'classes;' so that the former proved not so *very* cheap after all.

Bargains in "Cochin-Chinas."

IN the humorous account given by Burnham, of his experience in the fowl trade, which a few years ago went to such preposterous lengths, he thus sketches one of the " bargains " of that day:

A splendid open carriage halted before my door, one day, and there alighted from it a fine, portly-looking man, whom I had never seen before, and whose name I did not then learn; who, leaving an elegant dressed lady behind in the vehicle, called for me. I saw and recognized the carriage, however, as one of Niles's, and I was satisfied that it came from the Tremont House, Boston. As soon as the gentleman spoke, I was also satisfied from his manner of speech, that he was a Southerner. He was polite and frank, apparently; I invited him in, and he went to look at my fowls, that being the object, he said, of his visit. He examined them all, and said quietly:

"I'd like to get a half dozen of these, if they didn't come too high; but I understand you fanciers have got the price up. I used to buy these chickens for a dollar apiece. *Now*, they say, you're asking five dollars each for them."

I showed him my stock—the "*pure-bred*" ones,—and informed him at once that I had not sold any of *my* chickens, latterly, at less than forty dollars a pair. He was astounded. He didn't want any—much; that is, he wasn't particular. Shouldn't pay that, nohow; he could buy them for five dollars, wanted them for his boy; would come again and see about it, &c., &c. A five-year-old stag mounted the low fence at this moment, and sent forth an electrifying crow, such as would (at that period) have taken a novice " right out of his boots;" and a beautiful eight-pound pullet showed herself beside him at the same time. The stranger turned round, and said:

"There! What is your price for such a pair as that, for instance?"

"Not for sale, sir."

"But you *will* sell them, I s'pose?"

"No, sir, I have younger ones to dispose of; but *that* pair are my models. I can't sell *them*." The gentleman's eye was exactly filled with this pair of chickens.

"What will you *take* for those two fowls?"

"One hundred dollars, sir," I replied.

"I guess you will—when you can get it," he added. "Name your lowest price, now, for those? I want good ones, if any."

"I prefer to keep them, rather than to part with them at *any* price," I insisted. "If, however, a gentleman like yourself, who evidently knows what good fowls are, desires to procure the choicest specimens in the country, why, I confess to you that those are the persons into whose hands I prefer that my best stock should fall. But I will show you some at a lower figure," I continued, driving this pair from the fence.

"Don't you! Don't drive 'em away!" said the gentleman;—"let's see. That's the cock?"

"Yes, sir."

"And this is the hen?"

"Yes."

"One hundred dollars! You don't *mean* this, of course," he persisted.

"No, I mean that I would rather keep them, sir."

"Well—I'll—*take them*," said the stranger: "It's cruel. But, I'll take them;" and he paid me five twenty-dollar gold pieces down on the spot, for two ten-months-old chickens, from my "splendid" Royal Cochin-China fowls.

Messrs. Moan & Groan of Cypress Row.

THE "mourning" shopkeepers have a peculiarly benevolent eye to the griefs and necessities of those families into which death enters. This is condolingly manifested by their sending to such a family a remarkably neat envelope, with a handsomely embossed border, bearing the words, ' On especial service,' under the address, and winged with an appropriate stamp. The enclosure is a specimen of fine printing on smooth, thin vellum, in the form of a quarto catalogue, with a deep, black-bordered title page, emanating from the dreary establishment of Messrs. Moan & Groan, of Cypress Row.

Here commerce condescends to sympathy, and measures forth to bereaved and afflicted humanity the *outward* and *visible* symbols of their hidden griefs. Here, when you enter his gloomy penetralia, and invoke his services, the sable-clad and cadaverous-featured shopman asks you, in a sepulchral voice and with quivering lip, whether you are to be suited for inextinguishable sorrow, or for mere passing grief; and if you are at all in doubt on the subject, he can solve the problem for you, if you lend him your confidence for the occasion. He knows, from long and melancholy observation, the agonizing intensity of woe expressed by bombazine, crape, and Paramatta; can tell to a sigh the precise amount of regret that resides in a black bonnet ; and can match any degree of internal anguish with its corresponding shade of color, from the utter desolation and inconsolable wretchedness of dead and dismal black, to the transient sentiment of sorrowful remembrance so appropriately symbolized by the faintest shade of lavender or French gray.

Messrs. Moan & Groan also know well enough, that when the heart is burdened with sorrow, considerations of *economy* are likely to be banished from the mind as quite out of place, and disrespectful to the memory of the departed; and, therefore, they do not insult the lacerated sensibilities of their sorrowing patrons with the sublunary details of dollars and cents. They speed on the wings of the post to the house of mourning, with the benevolent purpose of comforting the afflicted household. They are the first, after the stroke of calamity has fallen, to mingle the business of life with its *regrets*, and to seek to cover the woes of the past with the allowable vanities of the present.

It is their painful calling to lead their melancholy patrons, step by step, along the cypress margin of their flowing pages—from the very borders of the tomb, through all the intermediate changes by which sorrow publishes to the world its gradual subsidence, and land them at last on the sixteenth page, restored to themselves and to society, in the front box of the Opera, glittering in 'splendid head dresses in pearl,' in 'fashionably elegant turbans,' and in 'dresses trimmed with blonde and Brussels lace.'

Strong in their modest sense of merit, Messrs. Moan & Groan make no sordid array of *prices*—oh, no ! They offer you all that in mourning you can possibly want; they scorn to do you the disgrace of imagining that you would drive a *bargain* on the very brink of the grave; and you are of course obliged to them for the delicacy of their reserve on so mercenary and plebeian a point—paying their bill in decorous disregard of the amount. It is true that certain envious rivals have compared them to birds of prey, scenting mortality from afar, and hovering like vultures on the trail of death in order to profit by his dart; but such 'caparisons,' as Mrs. Malaprop says, ' are odorous,' and we will have nothing to do with them.

Crœsus and his Avaricious Guest.

IT is related of this well-to-do *bullionaire*, that his messengers, having on one occasion been kindly treated by a family at Athens, he in return invited one of that family to visit him, and on his arrival made to him the offer of as much gold as he could personally carry. The visitor, with avaricious eagerness to enhance the value of the gift, provided himself with a large cloak, in which were many folds, and, with the most capacious boots that he could procure, followed Crœsus into the treasury, where, rolling among the gold, he first stuffed his boots or buskins as full as he could, and then filled all the folds of his robes, his hair, and even his mouth with gold dust. This done, with great difficulty he staggered from the place—from his swelling mouth and projections all around him, resembling anything rather than a man. Crœsus, who, probably from politeness, had left him alone to help himself, when he saw him come out, burst into laughter, and not only suffered him to carry away all he had got, but added other presents equally valuable.

Saving the Pieces. Girard and his Brother.

It is known that Girard entertained a perfect horror of parting with even the most trivial object in his possession, without receiving, in every case, a proper equivalent therefor. It seems that on one occasion, his brother, Captain John Girard, when fitting out a schooner for Cape Francois, had use for some pieces of glass for his cabin window, and observing the fragments of several boxes of that article in his brother Stephen's store, and knowing that the pieces were of little or no use to the owner, he so far presumed on the privileges of consanguinity, as to go and appropriate a few of the fragments for the purpose in question—when, while he was in the very act, Stephen suddenly pounced upon him, loudly deprecating the intended abstraction of his broken property, as if ruin would ensue from the loss of a few fractured panes of glass for which he had no earthly use. He continued to vent a torrent of ribaldry and invective upon his brother John— the very atmosphere was blue with his indignation. The temperament of John was of a milder and more conciliating

character than that of Stephen, so that he always retreated from the arbitrary and boisterous ebullitions of his brother.

"Merchant of Venice"—Shylock's Commercial Character Vindicated.

A NEW version of Shakspeare's "Merchant of Venice" has recently been given by a Jewish writer, which exhibits the commercial transactions of that renowned personage in quite a different aspect than heretofore. According to this authority, the play is *founded on fact*, with this important distinction, that it was the Jew who was to forfeit the pound of flesh if he had lost the wager. The circumstance transpired, not at Venice, but in Rome, during the pontificate of Sixtus the Fifth. The Jew lost; the other party demanded the pound of flesh; the Jew demurred and offered money, which was refused. Sixtus, to whom the matter was at last submitted, decided against the Jew, and that exactly one pound of flesh should be cut from him—not one grain more or less, on pain of the cutter being hanged; the latter very naturally declined the risk, and the pope fined both parties in heavy sums for engaging in such a transaction. Thus old Shylock's commercial character is vindicated at last —though the old version of the story will probably continue to be the popular one.

"P. D."

ENGLISH grocers have never enjoyed an immaculate reputation in the matter of adulterating goods. Not a few of their most costly wares are temptingly capable of easy and generally harmless mixture. Conscience is generally trained to the posture or practice habitual to the trade. Of course, the grocer has exceedingly good reasons for his apprentices, why they should adulterate. Yet if he went to the drygoods dealer, and found that for linen he had bought a mixture of cotton and flax, he would call that dealer a cheat. Or if he found that the silversmith had sold him plated spoons for silver spoons—zounds! It happens that only in his own line of business, such strong reasons exist for " doctoring" and " deaconing."

It happened that in the early business days of Mr. A., a grocer, pepper was under a heavy tax; and in the trade, universal tradition said that out of the trade everybody *expected* pepper to be mixed. Well, in the shop of said grocer stood a cask labelled " P. D.," containing something very like pepper dust, wherewith it was used to mix the pepper before sending it forth to serve the public. The trade tradition had obtained for the apocryphal P. D. a place among the standard articles of the shop, and on the strength of that tradition it was vended for pepper by men who thought they were doing the right thing—by themselves.

Now this P. D. began to give the clerk no little discomfort. Considering all that might be said, pro and con, he came to the downright conclusion that it was wrong. He instantly decreed that P. D. should perish. It was night; but back he went to the shop, took the hypocritical cask, carried it to a neighboring quarry, then staved it, and scattered P. D. among the clods and slag and stones.

But this P. D. is not wholly confined to grocers' traffic. The shipowner has a ship which has become too old to carry *sugar* from the West Indies, without damaging it by leakage; so he fits her out as a *passenger* ship, and advertizes her for Sidney, as " the well-known, favorite, fast-sailing ship"—and that is P. D. The corn merchant has a cargo damaged in a gale at sea; but as the underwriters will not pay unless the captain can swear that the vessel struck, the merchant, who was snug in his bed when the gale blew, tries to show the captain very conclu-

sively that, just off Flambeau Head, the keel did actually touch the ground, and that therefore he may safely take the requisite oath—and that is P. D. The director of some joint-stock company, who sees that the concern is hollow and all *dis-jointed*, sells out his own shares, but retains his place until the period during which he is liable is past, that no one else may take fright; —P. D. The jobber is standing by a parcel of goods which have been on his hands for a considerable time; a customer enters, and is received with smiles: " Are these new ? " " The latest things we have—just out, in fact. I almost thought you would look in to-day, and have this moment had the parcel opened for you; "—P. D. Well, there is more or less P. D. under every trader's roof. But it is bad. Stave the cask in pieces.

Bad Business.

KOHL, in his Travels in Russia, observes, that while at Moscow, he happened to take a stroll through one of the markets of that city. He saw there a man who was employed to sell frozen fish by the pound. " Friend," said he to him, " how do you come on in your business ? " " Thank God," replied the man, " very badly."

Commercial Milk.

A SUGGESTION has recently been made for the supply of London with pure country milk, in lieu of that wishy-washy triumph of art over nature, which flows, morning and afternoon, into jugs and mugs, from a thousand *milk* cans —so called.

Such an announcement has shaken, as if with a panic, all the metropolitan pans; and those purveyors who have dealt in new milk from the pump and chalk pit, without ever having been in possession of a single pair of horns, have been cowed all of a sudden by the very thought of the introduction of the bovine article. And yet, so unaccustomed are the Londoners to anything else but the well-known chalk mixture, that the probability is that the pure article will—like the genuine squeak of the pig in the fable—be pronounced far inferior to the imitation with which use or abuse has rendered us so familiar.

London, in fact, knows nothing of real milk, which differs as thoroughly as chalk is unlike cheese, from the spurious stuff which now finds its way into the coffee and tea cup. Commercial milk is a compound which any conscientious cow would indignantly repudiate. As has already been hinted, the Londoner literally knows nothing of milk; for of the stuff he has been taught to accept as "milk," he knows it would be idle to attempt even to skim the surface. It is understood that the chalk market immediately began to show symptoms of weakness at the bare rumor of real milk being introduced into the metropolis, especially when coupled with the current apprehension of a short supply of water in the city and suburbs.

Dangers of Legitimate Business Transactions.

THE dangers attending unlawful business transactions are sometimes fully matched by those which accompany dealings that are entirely legitimate. On one occasion, a merchant in London, having requested his broker to purchase a certain amount of stock, and having concluded his business, was surprised in the evening to hear his broker announced as a visitor. Some remark being made, the latter stated that a dispute had arisen with the jobber about the price which was in the receipt, and he should be glad to take it with him as an evidence of his correctness. Knowing that a stock receipt is in itself of no value, the buyer readily complied. His visitor thanked him, and

from that moment was never heard of. The receipt was false, the names were forged; and, secure in the possession of all evidence against him, the broker sought a foreign land in which to enjoy his ill-gotten gains.

Hardening Tendency of Business.

REMARKING on the state of trade in one of the large cities, a commercial editor states that "the hardening tendency of prices still continues." It is a pity that something cannot be done to counteract the hardening effect of business generally on the population of some of our mercantile and manufacturing cities.

Tragical Result of Losing Bank Notes.

ONE of the most tragical events in the business world took place a while ago in St. Petersburg. The agent of a banker, who had been to the bank to receive the value of fifteen thousand silver roubles, lost the package of bank notes on his return. The money was picked up by a clerk, who, instead of giving the funds at once to the owner, followed the agent to his destination, and in this way ascertained his name. The clerk then returned home, hesitating in his own mind how he should act. When he arrived there, a violent quarrel took place between him and his wife, the latter wishing to keep the money. The clerk, however, on the following day, went to the house of the owner to deliver the money, but the banker would not receive it, saying his agent had committed suicide in the night, on account of the loss. Overcome with remorse, the clerk returned home, where he found that during his absence his wife had hanged herself, from vexation at not having kept the money. He immediately cut down the body, and hung himself with the same rope.

Morocco Pocket Book Men.

THE " Morocco men," so called from the red morocco pocket books which they carried, were a remarkable feature in the London money dealings of half a century ago. They began their lives as pigeons; they closed them as rooks. They had lost their own fortunes in their youth; they lost those of others in their age. Generally educated, and of bland manners, a mixture of the gentleman and the debauchee, they easily penetrated into the society they sought to destroy. They were seen in the deepest alleys of Saint Giles's, and were met in the fairest circles as well. In the old hall of the country gentleman, in the mansion of the city merchant, in the butlery of the rural squire, in the homestead of the farmer, among the reapers as they worked on the hillside, with the peasant as he rested from his daily toil—addressing all with specious promises, and telling lies like truth— was the morocco man found, treading alike the finest and the foulest scenes of society. They whispered beguiling temptation to the innocent; they hinted at easy fraud to the novice. They lured the. youthful; they excited the aged; and no place was so pure, and no spot so degraded, but, for love of seven and one-half per cent., did the morocco man mark it with his pestilential presence. No valley was so lonely, but what it found some victim; no hill so remote, but what it offered some chance; and so enticing were their manners, that their presence was sought, and their appearance welcomed, with all the eagerness of avarice.

East India Company and the Missing Witness.

A century ago was the hanging century; and a great fraud was committed toward its close upon the East India Company—one of the most peculiar in the annals of crime, as related to busi-

15

ness. The leading witness—the only man who could prove the guilt of the accused—was accustomed to visit· a house in the neighborhood of the Bank, to be dressed and powdered, according to the fashion of the day. Shortly before the trial came on, a note was placed in his hands, informing him that the attorney for the prosecution was desirous of seeing him, at a certain hour, at his private residence, in or near Portland Place.

At the time appointed, the witness proceeded to the house; the door was opened, and the footman, without asking his name, ushered the visitor into a large room, where, discussing some wine upon the table, sat a group of gentlemen in earnest conversation. " There is a mistake," exclaimed the new comer, thinking he had been shown into the wrong room. " No mistake, sir," interrupted one, in a determined tone, while the remainder sat quietly but sternly by. Unable to comprehend the scene, and in some alarm, the visitor prepared to leave the room. " There is no mistake," repeated the same person, unostentatiously stepping before the door; "I am," he continued, " brother to that gentleman who is to be tried for forgery, and against whom you are the chief witness; the honor of a noble house is at stake; and your first attempt to escape·will lead to a violent death. There is nothing to fear, if you remain quiet; but all whom you see are sworn to detain you until the trial be over, or," he added, after a pause, " to slay you." The witness was a sensible man; he saw the determined looks of those around; and thought it best quietly to acquiesce.

In the mean time, great surprise was excited in the city. That the missing man had been inveigled away was universally believed; and every endeavor was made to track him. Whether the calmness with which he bore his confinement deceived his jailers, is not known; but it is certain that he effected his escape from the house, although not so securely but that his captors were after him before he could get out of sight. A mob collected; his pursuers declared that he was an insane nobleman, and that they were his keepers. The mob shouted with delight at the idea of a mad lord; and the unfortunate man was on the point of being again confined, when a carriage drove up. The inmate, a lady, desired the coachman to stop, and she listened to the counter statements of the pursued and his pursuers. Remembering the current story of a missing witness, she opened the carriage, he sprang in, the door was closed, and the lady, to whom he told his story, ordered the coachman to drive with all speed to the Old Bailey. It was the last day; the case, which had been postponed, was being tried; and the missing witness was just in time to place the rope around the neck of the unhappy forger.

Smugglers' Honor.

On the line between Prussia and Russia, smuggling is carried on by desperate bands of men, in a most desperately professional manner. These bands are also addicted to robbery. One of them, headed by a man named Krotinus, is very notorious; it has plundered the house of several of the richer Russian landowners on the frontier, returning across the line into Prussia to spend the proceeds. A party of this band once passed the day at a village winehouse, and were called out toward evening by a man who proved to be the captain himself, "for duty:" he was most particular in inquiring whether his men had behaved respectfully and paid for everything !

Characteristic Smuggling Ingenuity of Parisians.

Some of the curious expedients resorted to by Parisian smugglers are given in the following account by a

personal witness:—I saw, through one of the windows in the mayor's office, in the twelfth arrondissement, the body of a negro hanging by the neck. At the first glance, and even at the second, I took it for a human being, whom disappointed love, or perhaps an improvised people's tribunal, had disposed of thus suddenly; but I soon ascertained that the ebony gentleman in question was only a large doll as large as life. What to think of this, I did not know, so I asked the doorkeeper the meaning of it.

"This is the 'Contraband Museum,'" was the answer; and on my showing a curiosity to see it, he was kind enough to act as my cicerone.

In a large dirty room are scattered over the floor, along the walls and on the ceiling, all the inventions of roguery which had been confiscated from time to time by these guardians of the law, the revenue officers; a complete arsenal of the devices of smuggling, all in complete confusion.

As examples, there is a hogshead dressed up for a nurse, with a child that holds two and one half quarts. On the other side are logs, hollow as the Trojan horse, and filled with armies of cigars. On the floor lies a huge boa constrictor, gorged with China silks; and just beyond it a pile of coal curiously perforated with spools of cotton.

The colored gentleman who excited my sympathy at first, met with his fate under the following circumstances: He was built of tin, painted black, and stood like a heyduck, or Ethiopian chasseur, on the footboard of a carriage, fastened by his feet and hands. He had frequently passed through the gates, and was well known by sight to the soldiers, who noticed he was always showing his teeth, which they supposed to be the custom of his country.

One day the carriage he belonged to was stopped by a crowd at the gate. There was, as usual, a grand chorus of yells and oaths, the vocal part being performed by the cartmen and drivers, and the instrumental by the well-applied whips. The negro, however, never spoke a single word. His good behavior, through all this wild and unheard-of misusage, delighted the soldiers, who held him up as an example to the crowd. "Look at that black fellow," they cried, "see how well he behaves! Bravo, nigger, bravo!" He showed a perfect indifference to their friendly applause. "My friend," said a clerk at the barrier, jumping up on the footboard, and slapping our sable friend on the shoulder, "we are very much obliged to you." What surprise! *the shoulder rattled.* The officer was bewildered; he sounded the footman all over, and found he was made of metal, and as full as his skin could hold of the very best contraband liquor, drawn out of his foot. The juicy mortal was seized at once, and carried off in triumph. The first night the revenue people drank up one of his shoulders, and he was soon bled to death. It is now six years since he lost all the moisture of his system, and was reduced to a dry skeleton.

Terrible Career of Sadleir, the Speculator.

THE name of John Sadleir is still fresh in the annals of criminal speculation and its ofttimes tragical end. He was a provincial attorney in Ireland, in very moderate business; but being a man of talent and firmness of character, he was instrumental in establishing a bank in the county, and became a person of some consequence. He at length felt his field to be too small, and in an evil hour went to London, where his connection with the bank introduced him at once to the speculators and capitalists of that city; and this led to a large business as a parliamentary agent, and to his becoming chairman of a great joint-stock bank in London. The road of ambition was now fairly

opened. He got into Parliament, made himself the leader in the Irish Brigade, then deserted his party, and became a lord of the treasury. In the mean time, he was very busy with the Encumbered Estates Bill; and having procured from the commissioners under it almost unlimited authority, he organized an association in England for purchasing, and afterward selling at enormous advantage, properties sold in the Encumbered Estates Court. He now became chairman of the Swedish railway, arranged a new insurance company, established a newspaper of his own in Dublin, and plunged deep into English, Italian, Spanish, and American railways.

Such is a very brief outline of Sadleir's great business career; but when and where the pressure first began—when this originally obscure and moneyless man found that he could not pursue such schemes without funds—and what were the precise circumstances that originated his crimes, and led him on, step by step, to infamy, is not precisely known. It is known, however, that he obtained money on the security of forged titles, as, from the Encumbered Estate Court. He fabricated shares of the Swedish railway to the amount of over a million dollars; and besides the assignments of numerous deeds he held in trust, he forged on private individuals to the amount of at least half a million dollars.

It appears that for some time he must have contemplated his violent release from the fever of mind in which he had lived so long. But at length the occasion came; the forgery of one of the Encumbered Estates deeds was on the eve of discovery; and the wretched man went forth from his own house in the dead of night, with the instruments of death in his pocket—a midnight suicide!

Duplicity of French Speculators.

ONE of the most singular illustrations of the methods sometimes resorted to by speculators to accomplish their ends, is found in the history of the present ruler of the French. While Louis Philippe was king, a number of speculators in French stocks in London, desired, for a particular purpose, to depress said stocks for a few days. To this end they hired several ships, manned them, and gave them ammunition, bulletins, &c., and placed Louis Napoleon in secret command, in order to make a feint of invading France—using him as the unconcious tool for executing their own schemes.

Strange as it may seem, that reckless youth was under the delusion that the prestige of his name was sufficient, under the unpopularity of the then reigning monarch, to cause a general rising of the nation in his own favor. It was, however, *a plan gotten up by some cunning brokers*, who used him merely as an instrument, knowing his susceptibility to self-delusion; but they accomplished their end, and cleared large sums by their adroitly conceived mode of operating.

Two Playing at the Same Game.

DECIO was an extensive London merchant, who had large commissions for sugar from several foreign dealers. On a certain occasion, he treated about a considerable quantity of that article with Alcander, an eminent merchant in the West India trade; both understood the market very well, but could not agree. Decio was a man of substance, and thought nobody ought to be better able to buy than himself on favorable terms. Alcander was the same, and, not wanting money, stood for his price.

While thus engaged in attempts to bargain, at a tavern near the Exchange, Alcander's man brought his master a letter from the West Indies, which informed him of a much greater quantity of sugar coming for England than was expected. Alcander now wished for

nothing more than to sell at Decio's price, before the news was public; but, being a cunning fox, and that he might not seem too eager, nor yet lose his customer, he drops the discourse they were upon, and, putting on a jovial humor, commends the agreeableness of the weather—from whence, descanting upon the delight he took in his gardens, he invites Decio to go along with him to his country seat, about twelve miles out.

It was in the month of May, and as it happened to be Saturday afternoon, Decio, who was a single man, and would have no pressing business in town before Tuesday, accepted of the other's civility, and away they go in Alcander's coach. Decio was splendidly entertained that night and the day following. On Monday morning, to get himself an appetite, he goes to take the air upon an easy-paced horse of Alcander's, and coming back, meets with a gentleman of his acquaintance, who tells him news had come, the night before, that the Barbadoes fleet was destroyed by a storm, and adds, that before he came out, the news had been confirmed at Lloyd's coffee house, where it was thought sugars would rise twenty-five per cent. by 'Change time.

Decio returns to his friend, and immediately resumes the conversation about a sugar trade. Alcander, who, thinking himself sure of his chap, did not design to broach the matter until after dinner, was very glad to find his intention thus anticipated; but however desirous he was to sell, the other was yet more anxious to buy. Yet both of them, afraid of one another, for a considerable time affected all the indifference imaginable, till at last Decio, fired with what he had heard, thought delays might prove dangerous, and throwing a guinea upon the table, struck the bargain at Alcander's price. The next day they went to London; the news proved true, and Decio made his " pile " by the sugars. Alcander, while he had striven to overreach the other, was foiled in his mercantile tactics, and paid in his own coin.

Mysteries of Tea Smuggling.

On account of the high tax imposed upon tea by the Russian Government, the smuggling of that article is carried on as briskly as the wits of man can devise ways and means. The Government pays in cash the extraordinary premium of fifty cents per pound for all that is seized, a reward which is especially attractive to the officers on the frontier, for the reason that it is there paid down without any discount. Formerly, the confiscated tea was sold at public auction, on condition that the buyer should carry it over the frontier. Russian officers were appointed to take charge of it, and deliver it in some Prussian frontier town, in order to be sure of its being carried out of the country. The consequence was, that the tea was regularly carried back into Poland the following night, most frequently by the Russian officers themselves.

In order to apply a radical cure to this evil, destruction by fire was decreed as the fate of all tea that should be seized thereafter. Thus it is that from twenty thousand to forty thousand pounds are yearly destroyed in the chief city of the province. About this, the official story is, that it is tea smuggled from Prussia, while the truth is, that it is usually nothing but brown paper or damaged tea that is consumed by the fire. In the first place, the Russian officials are too rational to burn up good tea, when by chance a real confiscation of that article has taken place; —in such a case, the gentlemen take the tea, and put upon the burning pile an equal weight of *brown paper*, or *rags*, done up to resemble genuine packages of the "celestial leaf." In the second place, it is mostly damaged or useless tea that is seized.

The premium for seizures being so high, the custom-house officers themselves cause Polish Jews—regular commercial rats—to buy up quantities of worthless stuff and bring it over the lines for the express purpose of being seized! The time and place for smuggling it are agreed upon. The officer lies in wait with a third person whom he takes with him. The Jew comes with the goods, is hailed by the officer, and takes to flight. The officer pursues the fugitive, but cannot reach him! and fires his musket after him. Hereupon the Jew drops his package, which the officer takes and carries to the office, where he gets his reward. The witness whom he has with him—by accident, of course—testifies to the zeal of his exertions, fruitless though they were, for the seizure of the "unknown" smuggler. The latter afterward receives from the officer the stipulated portion of the reward. This arch trick is constantly practised along the frontier, and, to meet the demand, the Prussian dealers patriotically keep stocks of good-for-nothing tea, which they sell generally at the rate of twelve and a half cents per pound.

Spanish Contraband Trade.

Although the Spaniards have a dislike—so the idea prevails—to foreigners and foreign productions, yet the latter necessarily find their way into Spain, because she has no productions of her own, and must have them. But they hate custom houses and custom-house officers as much as they do foreigners, and they also prefer a smuggled article, even if it is a foreign production; hence it is that there is no scene in Spanish life without a smuggler—at least, so say the English. The peasant smuggles through necessity, the rich man through avarice, or the pleasure of cheating the revenue. Even the queen, it is told, robs her own exchequer, by wearing contraband finery.

The whole southern coast, from Barcelona to Cadiz, is said to be perpetually transformed, at night, into a strand for the loading of contraband goods. It is estimated that there are not less than four hundred thousand smugglers hovering continually about the mountains near the seacoast, who descend at night to hold communion with proscribed foreign smugglers, and receive from them the materials for rendering millions of the Spanish population comfortable, free of duty.

Prayers Requested for a New Business Undertaking.

THE ministers of the English Government made great use of lotteries in the eighteenth century, as an engine to draw money from the pockets of the people, and at a price alike disgraceful to the Government and demoralizing to all. The extent to which this evil had reached may be inferred from the fact that money was lent on these as on any other marketable securities; that in 1751, upward of thirty thousand tickets were pawned to the metropolitan bankers; and this when, to have an even chance for any prize, a purchaser must have held seven tickets—and it was ninety-nine to one that even if a prize were drawn, it did not exceed £50. Suicide, through lotteries, became common. All arts were resorted to. Lucky numbers were foretold by cunning women, who, when their art failed, shrouded themselves in their mysticism, or, if fortune chanced to favor them, paraded their prophecies to the public. Insurance of prizes—an art upon which hundreds grew rich, and thousands grew poor—was commenced with terrible success. Those who were unable to buy tickets, paid a certain sum to receive a certain amount, if a particular number came up a prize. The many iniquities, the household desolation, the public fraud, and the private mischief which resulted from this system, are beyond the power of recital.

Wives committed domestic treachery; sons and daughters ran through their portions; merchants risked the gains of honorable trade. " My whole house," wrote one, " was infected with the mania, from the head of it down to my kitchen maid and postboy, who have both pawned some of their rags, that they might put themselves in fortune's way." The passions and prejudices of the sex were appealed to. Lovers were to strew their paths with roses; husbands were plentifully promised, and beautiful children were to adorn their homes, through this kind of dealing. The melancholy history was occasionally enlivened by episodes, which sometimes arose from the humor, and sometimes from the sufferings of the populace. Religion itself was ingeniously used as a scapegoat in these transactions. Thus, it is recorded as a fact, that to promote the aid of the blind deity, a woman to whom a ticket had been presented, caused a petition to be put up in a church, in the following words:

" *The prayers of the congregation are desired for the success of a person engaged in a new business undertaking.*"

"He's a Country Merchant—Stick Him."

IN a certain city, Mr. A. established himself in business. Among the frequent visitors at his store was Mr. B., whose officiousness was never agreeable to the proprietor, and on one occasion at least his advice was both insulting and disastrous. It happened in this wise: A gentleman came into the store and inquired for sundry articles as to prices, &c. In the midst of the interview, Mr. B. asked Mr. A. to the door, and, taking him by the button, whispered confidentially, regarding the inquirer, "He's a country merchant—stick him!" Mr. A. turned away in disgust, and resumed his conversation with the new comer. But the whispered counsel had reached the ear of the latter, and he left the premises without purchasing a single article.

Spaniard and Chinaman at a Trade.

HERE is an old " trick at trade," and it still puzzles some people to get the right of it.

A Spaniard called at the store of a Chinese merchant shoemaker and bought a pair of boots at the price of ten dollars, and handed Jinnqua, the seller of the boots, an *ounce*, valued at seventeen dollars. As Jinnqua had no change, he stepped over the way to the Palo Gordo and got it changed; returned, and gave the boots and seven dollars to the Spaniard, who took them and his departure. Shortly after this, the proprietor of Palo Gordo called on the shoemaker with the ounce, which proved to be a bad one, and the shoemaker was obliged to pay him seventeen good dollars for the good-for-nothing metal. Now the question is, how much and what did the shoemaker lose by the operation? Some say he lost twenty-four dollars, and others twenty-seven dollars; but it is very plain that he lost just seven dollars and a pair of new boots. Whether they were worth ten dollars or not, is another question—one for China-tail and his customer to decide.

Buying Wine by Sample.

THE penetration and management of one of our old commodores in a Spanish port, some years ago, proved too much for the skill of a certain wine merchant, as the following will show.

He bought a cask of wine—he liked the flavor of it—in one of those enormous cellars, where the Spanish merchants store their immense stock, and where they, if the truth must be revealed, also mix, brew, and manufacture them.

"To what place shall I send the pipe?" inquired the merchant.

"Nowhere," said the blunt sailor, "I will take it with me;" and then appeared a competent number of sailors with a vehicle all ready for the purpose.

The merchant hesitated, demurred, and objected to delivering it for one reason or other, and finally offered a handsome sum if he would take another cask next to it, just as good, in its room, as this particular one had been disposed of. This made the commodore still more earnest and resolved; so he insisted on paying the Spanish trader his bill, and took away his prize without asking " by your leave."

It was worth double the sum he gave for it, as it was a sample cask of the pure article, which he and all who went to that cellar to purchase were to taste, as a criterion of the whole. When the article was sold and delivered, after the bargain, another was always put in its place. This time, however, the unlucky merchant was deprived of his decoy till he could prepare a new one, at considerable cost. It was a poor bargain that he made with the American commodore, who used to tell his friends at Washington, when he treated them to it, that it was the best battle he ever fought, and he had seen sharp service in 1813.

Smuggling on the Lace-Merchant's Dog.

WHO would have imagined that a dog had been made serviceable as a clerk, and thus rolled up for his master upward of a hundred thousand crowns? And yet a " big thing " like this happened some years ago.

One of those industrious beings who know how to make a chaldron of coals out of a billet of wood, determined, in extreme poverty, to engage in trade. He preferred that of merchandize which occupied the least space, and was calculated to yield the greatest profit. He borrowed a small sum of money from a friend, and repairing to

Flanders, he there bought a piece of lace, which, without any danger, he smuggled into France in the following manner:

He trained an active spaniel to his purpose. He caused him first to be shaved, and procured for him the skin of another dog, of the same hair and the same shape. He then rolled the lace around the body of the dog, and put over this the garment of the other animal so adroitly that it was impossible to discover the trick. The lace being thus arranged in his canine band-box, he would say to his obedient messenger, "Forward, my friend!" At these words, the dog would start, and pass boldly through the gates of Malines or Valenciennes, in the very face of the vigilant officers placed there to prevent smuggling. Having passed the bounds, he would wait for his master at a little distance in the open country. Then they mutually caressed and feasted, and the merchant deposited his parcels in places of security, renewing his ventures as necessity required.

Such was the success of the smuggler, that in five or six years he amassed a handsome fortune, and kept his coach. But—envy pursues the prosperous; a mischievous neighbor betrayed the lace merchant, and, notwithstanding the efforts of the latter to disguise his dog, he was tracked, watched, and detected. The game was up.

How far does the cunning of such an animal extend! Did the spies of the custom house expect him at one gate, he saw them at a distance, and instantly went toward the other. Were the gates shut against him, he overcame every obstacle—sometimes he leaped over the wall, at others passed secretly behind a carriage, or, running slyly between the legs of travellers, he would thus accomplish his aim. One day, however, while swimming a stream near Malines, he was shot, and died in the water. There was then about him

five thousand crowns' worth of lace—the loss of which did not afflict the master, but he was inconsolable for the loss of his faithful "clerk."

High-heeled Boots with Watches in them.

In the days when high-heeled French boots were the pride of fashion, there was a shoemaker in London, who made a fortune by the sale of the best Paris boots at a price which all his fellow tradesmen declared ruinous. He understood the trade, and obtained troops of customers. "These boots must be stolen," said his rivals, but there was no evidence that they were; certainly they were not smuggled boots—for any one could satisfy himself that the full duty was paid upon them at the custom house. The shoemaker retired from business with a fortune. Afterward his secret was accidentally discovered —although he had paid for the boots, he had not paid for everything that was in them. There was a heavy duty payable on foreign watches; and every boot consigned to him from Paris had contained in its high heel a cavity exactly large enough to hold a watch. The great profit obtained by the trade in smuggled watches made it possible for this tradesman, when he had filled up their heels, to sell his boots under prime cost. This was worth while again, because, of course, by the extension of his boot trade, he increased his power of importing watches duty free.

Philanthropy and Forty Per Cent.

Under the name of the Equitable Loan Company, there was many years ago started, in England, a mining scheme for taking money out of the pockets of the many, and putting it in the pockets of the few. In paragraphs, calculated to excite the sympathy of the public, the directors piously denounced the profits of the pawnbroker, arraigned his evil practices, and delicately concluded by hinting that a company formed upon the most philanthropic principles, and paying forty per cent., would soon be formed, and thus the public be saved from any further imposition. The philanthropy element in the scheme might have been proclaimed unavailingly for centuries, but *forty per cent.* was irresistible. The Duke of York good-naturedly lent his name; members of Parliament were bribed with shares; and when it was honestly said by one that "the bill would never pass the House," the ready reply of the philanthropic schemers was, "Oh! we have so many on the ministerial, and so many on the opposition side, and we are of course *sure of the saints!*" The shares, however, tumbled down to a discount; both opposition and ministerial members gave the nefarious scheme the go-by, and the philanthropy of the saints faded with the fading vision of "forty per cent."

Fate of a Clerical Dealer in "Fancies."

SOME time since an account appeared in the London journals of a practical joke—which, however, for one of the parties concerned, was no joke at all—having been played off upon a parson on the Stock Exchange. It appears that the said reverend gentleman in holy orders had been giving a series of most unholy orders to a variety of stockbrokers, who had thus been "let in" to a serious amount by said speculating clergyman. Having been persuaded to visit the "sanctum" of the stock exchange, the parson was forthwith surrounded, and an unceremonious punishment was improvised, without the slightest "benefit of clergy" being allowed to him. His coat was covered with flour thrown from bags, without the remotest respect for his cloth, and he was showered with eggs, of which there was an ample supply in readiness to make—as was remarked by an unhappy punster on the spot—a terrible eggsample of the defaulting dominie. The reverend financier's white choker was so besmeared with the batter thus hurriedly compounded, that he was obliged to rush from the stock exchange to exchange his stock at the nearest hosier's. The affair, happening as it did on or about "Shrove Tuesday," caused some who saw the parson covered with eggs and flour to suppose—naturally enough—that, while on some parochial call, he had unfortunately fallen into a mass of batter prepared for the manufacture of pancakes.

French Nicety in Trade Frauds.

ALL is false in wines; the color, the strength, the flavor, the age, even the name under which they are sold. There are wines which do not contain a drop of grape juice. Even science is impotent, in many cases, to distinguish the true from the false, so complete is the imitation, but it nevertheless greatly aids in the detection. This was developed in a memorable case which came before the French courts. The chemist, after reporting all the ingredients of which the wine was composed, observed that if *one* of them were in less quantity, he would have been unable to distinguish it from the natural wine. The prosecuted wine merchant, who was present, listened attentively to the chemist's report, and at last asked him *which* ingredient it was. The chemist very unguardedly told him, and the accused immediately answered, "I am very much obliged, sir, and I don't regret now my forty hogsheads of wine which will be destroyed, because now I am certain of my business."

Disposing of an Old Stock.

ONE Mr. P. G., a gentleman well known to many citizens of New Hampshire as a successful merchant of C., owed much of his good fortune to his knowledge of human nature, of which he always endeavored to take advantage. At one time, he opened, with another person, a " branch store " in a town in the north part of the State, and which they mostly filled with the unsalable goods from their principal store in C. These goods were " as good as new" among the rustics, and sold quite as well, with the exception of a large lot of that unique article of gentlemen's wear denominated hogskin caps.

G. generally kept himself at his house in C., though often visiting his country store, staying sometimes a week or more, and attending the country church—as a matter of course being looked at with astonishment by the go-to-meeting young men of the town. Indeed, he was honored by their imitation in almost all their acts, dress, &c. What Mr. G. wore to church of a Sunday, gentleman as he was, was the prevailing fashion there until he introduced a new style at some subsequent visit.

On one of these occasions, G. asked his partner about the business prospects and other matters in which he was interested, and received the reply that things went pretty quick at good prices.

" Keep those old caps yet. I didn't make a great bargain in buying them," said G., espying a large box filled with said caps. " Can't you get rid of them at any price ? "

" Haven't sold one yet; people don't like them, and I have had a great notion of throwing them out of the back window, and getting rid of the trouble of them. They won't go here, I think."

G. looked at them a moment, and exclaimed, " I have it ! You have kept them out of sight, I see ! Next Monday, you get them out and brush them up, and I'll send you a score of customers before the week is out."

The following Sunday, G. appeared in church with one of these identical caps tipped gracefully on one side of his head, and a splendid gold watch-chain dangling from his vest pocket. He was, as usual, the observed of all observers; and it is needless to say that, a fortnight after, when in his own store in C., he received an order for two dozen more of his " imperial " caps.

Bargaining for a Jar.

PASSING by the shop of a dealer in curiosities at Paris, a Neapolitan prince observed a superb Japan jar, five and one half feet high, and very large. He commenced bargaining for it, but the tradesman insisted on having four thousand francs for the article, while the prince was only willing to give three thousand francs; " but," said he, " if you had the fellow to it, its value would be infinitely greater to me." " No doubt, Excellenza ; the value of the pair would be fifteen thousand francs."

A few days elapsed, and the Neapolitan received a summons to return to his own country, and he went once more to try to obtain the jar. " I again offer three thousand francs," said he. " I will not take less than four thousand," said the tradesman. " I leave to-morrow." " No matter; I will keep my jar."

The next day, as the prince was superintending the packing up of his effects, a waiter of the hotel said, " Your excellency would no doubt be glad to find the fellow of the Japan jar ? Well, there is one in the faubourg St. Germain." " Is it possible ? " " It is quite certain." " Beppo, my carriage ! " Arrived in the faubourg, the prince saw that the jar was precisely the same as the one he had bargained for. " Where did you get it ? " he asked the tradesman who showed it. " At the sale of the Duchess de Montebello. There was a pair of them, but I was outbid for the other." " Ah, yes, I understand. And what do you ask ? " " Four thousand francs." " He does not know," thought the Neapolitan, "that the other jar is offered for sale in another part of Paris! If I give him four thousand for this, I can buy the other at the same price, and so have for eight thousand francs what is worth fifteen thousand."

He bought the jar at once, paid for it, and had it conveyed to his hotel. He then went to the other tradesman and asked for the jar. He was told that the tradesman was out, and that the jar had been taken away. He returned the next day, but could not see the dealer; but he learned subsequently that the jar which he had purchased for four thousand francs was the very one he had offered three thousand for, and that the waiter at the hotel had received ten francs to inform the prince of the existence of the jar in the faubourg St. Germain—a cool thousand being, by this trick, put into the pocket of the tradesman.

Three Millionnaires Quarrelling about One Farthing.

ELWES, the millionnaire banker and miser, notwithstanding his dislike of society, was a member of a club which occasionally met at his own village, and to which also belonged two other wealthy and miserly baronets, besides himself, viz., Sir Cordwell Firebras and Sir John Barnardiston. With these three, though all so rich, the reckoning was always a subject of minute investigation before they separated. One day, when they were at loggerheads in settling some trifling item, a wag, who was likewise a member of the club, called out to a friend that was passing, "For heaven's sake, step up stairs, and assist the poor! Here are three millionnaire baronets chafing and quarrelling about one farthing!"

Price of Extortion and Revenge.

IN one of our cities there occurred, some years ago, the following illustration of what sometimes comes from extortion. Mr. A., a wealthy merchant, built a very expensive warehouse on his lot, and after it was completed, B., his next neighbor, discovered that it was a couple or three inches on his lot. A surveyor was sent for, and A. discovered his mistake, and freely offered B. a large sum if he would permit it to remain. B. knew that he had his wealthy neighbor in his power, therefore he seemed unwilling to sell the narrow gore for twenty times the value of the land. He only *waited for a larger sum* to be offered, believing that before A. would pull down his warehouse, he would pay half its value. But A., finding that B. was determined to be satisfied with nothing but extortion, began to pull down his noble building. *Then* A. might have settled on his own terms, but he had no offer to make. The last foundation stone was removed.

But in order to revenge himself, A. ordered his builder to run up the new edifice a couple of inches *within* his own line, and it was done: and the noble building was again completed. A short time afterward, B. commenced the erection of *his* splendid warehouse, directly against his neighbor's, and, of course, two inches over on the lot of A. The trap laid had succeeded as was expected; and after B.'s building was completed, and his friends were congratulating him on his splendid warehouse, A. steps up and informs B. that his structure encroaches on his land! B. laughs at the thought, for amid the rubbish and deep foundations, a couple of inches cannot be detected by the naked eye. A surveyor was sent for, and conceive the blank astonishment that filled the mind of B., when he found himself at the mercy of one whom he had so deeply wronged. This was the moment for A. to show to the sordid B. what a magnanimous heart could do. But, no! A. was determined upon revenge, and that neighbor can name no sum at which he would even look. He offered him half the cost of his magnificent warehouse, if he would suffer him to let it stand. No, he must pull it down; and down it came to the very foundations. Such cases are rare indeed among merchants.

Knowing his Customer.

WHEN George the Second was returning from his German dominions, in his way between the Brill and Helvoetsluis, he was obliged to stay at an obscure public house on the road, while some of his servants went forward to obtain another carriage, that in which he had travelled having broken down. The king ordered refreshment, but all he could get was a pot of coffee for himself and Lord Delawar, and four bottles of gin made into punch, for his footmen; however, when the bill was called for, the conscientious Dutchman, knowing his customer, presented it as follows:

"To refreshments for his Sacred Majesty, King George the Second, and his household, £9."

Lord Delawar was so provoked at this imposition, that the king overheard his altercation with the landlord, and demanded the cause of it. His lordship immediately told him; when his majesty good-humoredly replied: "My lord, the fellow is a great knave, but pay him. Kings seldom pass this way."

A similar anecdote is related of another monarch, who, passing through a town in Holland, was charged at the rate of thirty dollars for two eggs. On this, he said, "that eggs were surely scarce in that town." "No, your majesty," replied the landlord, "but kings are."

"Old Guy" Putting Out the Light; or, Millionnaire Misers Rating each other's Frugality.

GUY, the broker and miser, was one evening seated in his little back room, meditating over a handful of half-lighted embers, confined within the narrow precincts of a brick stove; a farthing candle was on the table at his side, but it was not lit, and the fire afforded no light to dissipate the gloom. He sat there alone, planning some new speculation—congratulating himself on saving a pennyworth of fuel, or else perchance cogitating as to how he could bestow some thousand guineas in charity.

His thoughts, whether on subjects small or great, were interrupted by the announcement of a visitor—a shabby, meagre, miserable-looking man; but compliments were exchanged and the guest was invited to take a seat. Guy immediately lighted his farthing candle and desired to know the object of the gentleman's call. The visitor was no other than the celebrated Hopkins, whose fortune was about a million and a half, and who, on account of his avarice and rapacity, was known as Vulture Hopkins.

"I have been told," said Hopkins, as he entered the presence of Guy, "that you are better versed in the prudent and necessary art of saving, than any man now living. I now wait upon you simply for a lesson in frugality, an art in which I used to think I excelled, but I am told by all who know you that you are greatly my superior."

"If that is all you are come about," said Guy, "why then we can talk the matter over in the dark;" so saying, he with great deliberation put the extinguisher on his newly lighted farthing candle. Struck with this most ready instance of practical economy, Hopkins—having no need of any mere *verbal* lessons—at once acknowledged the superior ability of his host, and thoughtfully took his leave, imbued with profound respect for such an adept in the art of saving.

Discounting a Legacy.

TAYLOR, at one time one of the most eminent stock jobbers in London, and who died worth half a million dollars in cash, was so penurious that he scarcely allowed himself the common necessaries of this life; and this spirit he carried out as well in his financial and business dealings. A few days before his decease, the officers of the parish in which he resided, waited upon him at his request; they found the old man on a wretched bed in a garret, making his dinner on a thin slice of bacon and a potato, of which he asked them to partake. One of them accepted the offer; upon this, the miser desired his cook to broil him another—but, finding the larder was totally empty, Taylor harshly rebuked her for not having it well ·supplied with *a quarter of a pound*, to cut out in slices whenever it was wanted for company. He then informed the overseers of the poor, that he had left by his will, one thousand pounds sterling for their relief, and eagerly inquired if they would not allow him *discount* for *prompt payment:* this being assented to, apparently much delighted, he immediately gave them a check for nine hundred and fifty pounds, and soon after breathed his last.

M. Beautte and the Official Smuggler.

IT is difficult to imagine a collection more rich in those thousand wonders which tempt the female heart, than is seen at Beautte's, who stands at the head of the fashionable jewellers in Geneva; it is almost enough to drive a Parisian mad, or to make Cleopatra palpitate with longing in her grave.

This jewelry is liable to a duty on entering France; but, for a premium of five per cent., M. Beautte undertakes to smuggle it. The bargain between the buyer and seller is publicly made on this condition, as if there ·were no custom-house officers in the world—M. Beautte possessing wonderful address in setting them at fault, and thus securing a vast amount of profitable trade.

When the Count de Saint Crieg was director-general of the customs,. he heard of this skill, by which the vigilance of his officers was thwarted, and, so frequently was it mentioned, that he resolved to assure himself whether all was true that was said of it. He subsequently went to Geneva, presented himself in person at M. Beautte's shop, and purchased thirty thousand francs' worth of jewelry, on condition that it should be delivered, without paying the import duty, at his residence in Paris. M. Beautte agreed to the condition like a man accustomed to bargains of the kind, and merely presented to the purchaser a sort of promissory note, by which he undertook to pay the usual five per cent., besides the thirty thousand francs purchase money. The latter smiled; took up a pen, signed "De Saint Crieg, director-general of the French customs," and handed back the paper to Beautte, who looked at the signature, and contented himself with quietly answering, with a bend of the head, "*M. le directeur*, the article which you have done me the honor of buying, will arrive at Paris as soon as yourself."

M. de Saint Crieg, whose interest was now excited to the highest pitch, scarcely gave himself time to dine, sent to the post for horses, and set out an hour after the bargain had been concluded. M. de Saint Crieg made himself known to the officers who came to examine his carriage, told the principal one what had happened him, enjoined the most active surveillance on the whole line, and promised a reward of fifty louis to the officer who should succeed in seizing the prohibited jewelry.

Not a custom-house officer slept during three days. In the mean while, M. de Saint Crieg arrived at Paris, alighted at his residence, kissed his wife and children, and went to his room to take off his travelling costume. The first thing he perceived on the chimney piece was an elegant box, with the shape of which he was acquainted. He approached it, and read on the silver plate which ornamented the top, "The Count de Saint Crieg, Director-General of the Customs." He opened it, and found the jewelry he had purchased at Geneva!

Beautte had made an arrangement with one of the waiters at the inn, who, while assisting M. de Saint Crieg's servants to pack their master's luggage, had slipped the prohibited box among it. On his arriving at Paris, his valet, noticing the elegance of the case, and the inscription engraved upon it, had hastened to place it upon his master's chimney piece. Thus the director-general of the customs was the first smuggler in the kingdom.

Mode of Protecting the Money Drawer.

A YOUNG apprentice lad was very ingeniously detected in stealing money from the drawer of Mr. Throop's store. He had for some months made it a practice to call at the store when there was no one in excepting the owner or one of his clerks. He would generally then call for wine, or some trifling article kept in the store cellar, and, in their absence to procure it, it was suspected that he made somewhat too free with the money drawer. One day, Mr. Throop fastened a strong cord to the back of the drawer, and let one end pass through a small hole into the cellar. It was but a short time before the boy came in, and observing no one but the proprietor about the store, called for some wine. On entering the cellar, the owner perceived the cord to move, caught hold of it, and, with a sudden and violent jerk, made it fast. He then ran up stairs, and found the young rogue with his hand fast in the drawer, and he was taken, as Prince Hal says, "in the manner."

"Done for" Twice.

A FAT, burly English landlord was sitting one afternoon at the door of his inn, when a person entered the house, and after complimenting its cleanliness and snug appearance, ordered a good dinner and a bottle of wine. The dinner, when cooked, was laid in an upper apartment, looking out upon a pleasant garden; and after it had been thoroughly 'discussed,' and the wine sipped toothsomely to the bottom of the bottle, the satisfied guest sent for his host, and, when he had entered the room, thus addressed him: "You have a fine inn here, landlord—a very fine inn; everything is particularly nice—in fact, what I call comfortable." The landlord expressed his gratification.

"I shall have great pleasure," continued the guest, without noticing the interruption, "in recommending your house to my friends in town. Ahem! There remains only one thing more to mention, landlord; and as the subject is one which I have reason to think will be as unpleasant to you as to myself, I will express it in a few words: I have not, at this moment, any money; but I will be here again in—" "No money!" exclaimed the landlord, in a voice husky with anger—"NO MONEY!! Then why did you come to the 'Hen and Chickens,' and run up a bill that you can't pay? Get out of my house this instant! Go!"

"I expected this," replied the guest, rising; "I anticipated this treatment; nor can I much blame you, landlord, to tell the truth, for you don't know me. Because you sometimes meet with deception, you think I am deceiving you; but I pledge you my honor that a fortnight from to-day I will be with you again, and you will confess yourself ashamed of your suspicions." "Bah! you're a swindler!"

ejaculated Boniface; "this will be the last of you—take *that?*" and with a vigorous *coup de pied*, was "sped the parting guest." "You will live to regret this, landlord, I am sure; but I do not blame you, for you are ignorant of my character," was the meek reply to this gross indignity.

Just two weeks from that day, this same ill-used gentleman (with a travelling friend) was, with many apologies and protestations, shown into the best room of the celebrated "Hen and Chickens" inn. The landlord's profuse apologies were accepted; he was forgiven; and even invited to dine with the two friends upon the best dinner, flanked by the very choicest wines which his house afforded. When all was finished, and while the landlord, who had become exceedingly mellow, was protesting that he should never be so suspicious of a "real gentleman" again (referring, of course, to the little scene at the previous visit), he was interrupted by his first guest with—"But, landlord, there is *one* thing which we ought, in simple justice to you, to mention. *I* do not happen to have, at this moment, a single penny; and, I grieve to say, that my companion, who is a *good* man, but, in a mere worldly point of view, very poor, is not a whit better off. Under these unpleasant circumstances, it becomes, as it were, a necessity, to bid you a very good evening." It would be difficult to say whether the phiz of the amazed landlord was black or blue at this point. But, ejaculating, "Done twice! the Hen and Chickens done twice!—and both times exactly alike," he went down to set the swindle to the account of "Profit and Loss."

Looking Glass for Wall Street.

THE aptness of Mr. Kimball's description of a certain class of nervous, anxious people, who have to raise money from day to day, and whose business locality is Wall street, will be

appreciated by all who have seen a certain proverbial animal or his tusks. He says: It seems miraculous how this class can endure such a never-ending state of bondage. Some of these are fashionable, their connections are of the first distinction, their associations most desirable. They keep up handsome establishments; they earn by their pursuits $4,000 a year, and spend $5,000. They always anticipate what is due them, and are always harassed for ready money. They are honorable fellows, and would not plead usury under circumstances the most aggravating. They make notes, and get a broker to sell them. This broker, understanding their antecedents, and whom they are most intimate with, goes probably to some rich friend of the particular "party" wanting a loan, who is thoroughly acquainted with the "case," and who knows that the notes will be paid when due, although at the sacrifice of putting a new one on the market, and getting it shaved somewhere. So he cashes it at a fearful rate, puts the broker under an oath of secrecy not to reveal where he got the money, which oath it is for the broker's interest to keep, and our fashionable acquaintance is relieved. He hurries home in time for the opera or a dinner out, and, meeting several duns in the hall, he pays them off, and sets about his evening's enjoyment.

There are others who, having an excellent Government contract, either "General," "State," or "Corporation," need funds to help them through with it. They can afford to pay well, and they do pay well for cash accommodations. In fact, the street is full of persons *about* to realize, who want money in advance of the period, and who are ready to pay a large bonus for it. The result is, they do all the work, and the money lender gets nearly all the profits. Sometimes this latter personage mistakes his investment and makes a loss. But he can well afford it. And he never quarrels with the man who has been so unfortunate as to "let him in."

Hanging a Broker, One Hundred Years Ago.

JUST one hundred years ago, namely, in 1762, a London broker, named John Rice, was hung for malpractice in business. A female customer of Rice, and for whom Rice was in the habit of receiving stock dividends, was, under false representations, induced to grant a power to sell, as well as to receive the interest. The broker sold all his patron's stock, employed the proceeds to meet his losses, and kept up the deception by sending her the proceeds as usual. The lady, moved by doubt, or by some other impulse, in course of time intimated to Rice her intention of visiting the city. Unable to restore the principal, Rice took the alarm, and fled, leaving with his wife five thousand pounds of the misappropriated property. Ignorant of his deeds, and anxious to join her husband, she also embarked for Holland. The weather was rough; the vessel was driven back; and the person sent in search of the husband apprehended the wife, who yielded the money in her possession, leaving herself entirely destitute. The search continued for Rice, and being at last found, he was made to suffer the stringent penalty of the law.

Quaker Broker and the Stolen Doubloons.

THE Quakers were once, more than at present, a power in the commercial world in New York. They were an honest, industrious, and extremely shrewd race of merchants, not devoid of humor and sarcasm, and, though religious non-combatants, not in the least disposed to allow themselves to be the victims of roguery.

One of this fraternity—a dealer in specie and exchange, and a large purchaser of gold coin—one day left his counting house in haste, and crossed the street to accost a friend. He had just purchased a quantity of doubloons, which he had omitted to lock up in his safe. The office was empty. When the old Quaker returned, the room was in the same condition—no one was in it—but one of the bags of doubloons was missing. The Quaker now locked up the others, and opened not his mouth on the subject of the loss. Days passed, and weeks, but no reward was offered, no policemen were set on the track of the thief—the old Quaker stood his loss like a statue. Two or three months afterward, his neighbor, a small mercantile man, happened to be in his counting room, conversing on the topics of the day. Suddenly turning to the Quaker, he inquired:

"By the way, Mr. ——, did you ever hear anything of the bag of doubloons you lost?"

Up started the old Quaker in an instant.

"*Thee's* the thief, John! thee're the thief—*I never told any one I lost the bag!*"

Needless to say, the doubloons were restored, and the clumsy rogue pardoned, with a caution to go and sin no more.

Louis the Fifteenth's Opinion of his Own Paper.

THE fact of Louis the Fifteenth's being a stock jobber was a somewhat unfortunate one for those who fell into his financial clutches. He operated principally, in his exchange and loan transactions, through M. Bertin, his banker. The latter did his master's stock jobbing very profitably, too, by buying, on the spot, good paper at six and seven per cent., according to the scarcity of money. One day the banker proposed to Louis the Fifteenth an operation of several millions.

"Sire," said M. Bertin to the royal stock jobber, "the royal bills lose a great deal in the place; their discount is now considerable; it is the very moment to buy several millions. I am certain they will rise, and that there must follow a considerable profit to *some one* in a short time."

"That paper," replied the "prudent" monarch, "is not to be depended upon; the *risk* is *too great!*"

It was *his own paper* of which he was talking!

Consequence of a Simple Mercantile Speculation.

ACCORDING to a French authority, the war between England and France in 1777 was *the consequence of a simple mercantile speculation.* Several of our ministers (says a writer in high position at that period) have made among themselves an act of copartnership, in the commerce of America. The first expeditions proved very profitable; but as they have *a considerable outstanding fund*, they will not dissolve their partnership before they are reimbursed for their advances and receive the profits which are to arise, according to the calculations they have made. *Peace* would overturn all their speculations, and ruin the lenders of the various funds. The expenses, etc., of the "establishment" amount to an enormous sum. First of all must be paid their directors; their bookkeepers; their under clerks;—then follow the mistresses of the ministers, their sons or daughters, brothers, cousins, and even their grandchildren;—then those who lend their name to this speculation; courtiers and protectors. When this world of dependants is paid, ministers are to personally gain, notwithstanding all, cent. per cent. Then calculate the inferior profits which must be made before the net balance. Several of the ministers' *protegés*, who were known to have had at first only a salary of six thousand livres, afterward enjoyed, by these commercial operations priced with blood, an income of one hundred thousand, and became lords of

two or three manors. One of the chief clerks of a French mercantile house was heard to remark, in November, 1777: If peace took place at this moment, my principal would be ruined, and I too. We have all our fortune in America, and we wait for it with impatience. This is the reason for which the king has not yet declared for the Americans; he will only do this *when the ships we expect are safely arrived.*

City Merchant Securing a Customer.

AN eager merchant in New York, having heard of the arrival of a country trader who was known to be a large purchaser and of unquestionable credit, was resolved to get him to visit his establishment—and, once there, he felt sure that he could secure him as a customer. He accordingly sent out one of his drummers, of whom he had a large number, adapted to every taste and disposition. The one sent, however, returned without success. Number two was despatched, and with no better result; and again, number three, and so on, until all had gone and come back without their man. The merchant now determined to go himself; and, finding that brandy and water and free tickets to the theatre were of no avail, for the country trader did not take the one nor go to the other, and would not be persuaded by any such inducements, he was reduced to the necessity of a *ruse.* It was simple enough, but it proved effectual. On the merchant taking his leave, after a pleasant interview, he took care to commit the "mistake" of taking the trader's hat instead of his own. Next morning, as was expected, the merchant received a prompt visit at his store, from the country trader, who came to look up the hat which had thus, as he supposed, been hurriedly exchanged. This was, of course, all that was wanted. The visit was secured, and a good bill was the result.

Tradesmen's Ticketing System.

THE tendency of tradesmen to speak "by the card" is made manifest by the enormous extent to which goods are now-a-days ticketed. At one establishment articles are being "given away," while at the next door the proprietors are undergoing the daily torment of an "alarming sacrifice." One would imagine that self-immolation was a popular pastime with the tradesmen in our cities. Innumerable windows announce the determination of the proprietor "to sell considerably under cost;" from which it would seem that keeping a shop is a piece of disinterestedness, by which one man determines to victimize himself—and occasionally a few creditors—for the benefit of the public in general. These sacrifices, however, do not seem to be wholly without their reward, for, strange to say, the tradesmen who resort to them very frequently prosper, in spite of their recklessness of their own private interests. Thus, while the tickets in the windows bespeak a "ruinous reduction," the premises themselves display, from day to day, "a splendid enlargement," and when "sacrifices" are to be performed, the temples are often decorated in a style of gorgeous magnificence. That sacrifices *are* made, there can be no doubt, but it is another question who are the victims. In some houses it is in contemplation to keep a bankrupt permanently on the premises, to professionally preside at a counter set apart for giving things away and going to ruin.

Economical Hardware Merchant.

A FEW years since, a snug hardware merchant, who had made his fortune in the city of New York, determined to sell off his stock and retire. His goods were soon disposed of, and the shop empty. In sweeping out the store one day, however, he found in the crevices and corners a few stray shot—about twenty—of all sizes. These he gathered up in the hollow of his hand, and stood for some seconds gazing at them; at length, seizing his hat, he went into an adjoining liquor store, where they also sold shot, and thus addressed the proprietor : "In cleaning my store, I found a few shot—they are of no use to me, but to you they are worth something; I don't value them very highly, but perhaps (here he niggardly lowered his voice) you would give me *half a glass of beer* for them."

Unparalleled Parsimony and Benevolence of a Millionnaire.

WHEN, on a certain occasion, a public hospital was to be built in London, many benevolent individuals volunteered to solicit contributions by calling upon the inhabitants. Two or three gentlemen went to a small house in an impoverished neighborhood—for the pence of the poor were solicited as well as the pounds of the rich. The door was partially open, and as they drew nigh, they overheard an old man giving a female servant a thorough scolding for having thrown away a match, only one end of which had been used. Although so trivial a matter, the master appeared to be greatly enraged, and the collectors remained some time outside the door, before the old man had finished his angry .lecture, and could hear a knock from the outside. When the tones of his voice were somewhat subdued, they entered, and, presenting themselves to this strict observer of frugality and saving, explained the object of their application; but they did not anticipate much success. The millionnaire miser, however, for such he was reputed in the neighborhood, no sooner understood their object, than he opened a closet, and bringing forth a well-filled bag, counted therefrom four hundred guineas, which he presented to the astonished applicants. They expressed their surprise and thankfulness, and could not refrain from telling the old gentleman that they had overheard his difficulty with his domestic, and how little they expected, in consequence, to have met with such munificence from him.

"Gentlemen," replied the old man, "your surprise is occasioned by my care of a thing of such little consequence; but I keep my house and save my money in my own way; my parsimony enables me to bestow more liberally on charity. With regard to benevolent donations, you may always expect most from prudent people who keep their own accounts, and who pay attention to trifles."

Colloquy between a Storekeeper and his Customer.

STOREKEEPER: "That's a bad fifty-cent piece. I can't take it. It is only lead silvered over."

"Well," replies the customer, "admitting such to be the fact, I should say that the ingenuity displayed in the deception might well induce you to accept it. Admire, sir, the devotion of the artist to the divine idea of LIBERTY, the idol of us all! He, having wrought her effigy in humble lead, in order to make it worthier of that glorious impression, resorts to the harmless expedient of silvering it over! And shall we harshly repudiate his patriotic instincts—deny his work the paltry value of fifty cents? Oh, no, sir! you'll take it; I know you will!"

"Enough said:" he did take it, like a man!

Jew Losing a Bargain.

IT is not often that a Jew, bent on a nice little trade, is outwitted, or comes off second best. That such a contingency, however, is among the rare possibilities in business affairs, the following will show:

Some children were once playing in the Kent road, near Blackheath, England, amusing themselves with making grottos of oyster shells; and, in order to give effect, one of the children went home and begged of his mother to let him have two old pictures that were lying about the house and considered but as useless lumber, to adorn their grotto. This was readily granted, and the old pictures were placed one on each side of the grotto.

In a short time a Jew dealer came by, and after looking at the pictures for some time, he offered to give the children sixpence for them; the children refused, and said that they belonged to their parents. The Jew, at last, offered five shillings, but was still refused, and, at last, went to the parents, and offered ten shillings; but the extreme eagerness of the Jew excited some suspicion that the old pictures were of more value than had been supposed, and this was confirmed when the Jew offered five pounds and five shillings for them, which was also refused. The next day, the father of the children took the pictures to a connoisseur, to inquire if they were of any value, and that gentleman gave him a letter of recommendation to a person in London, who purchased them for fourteen hundred pounds, and they were afterward sold for much more.

Attention to Trivial Things by Girard.

EVEN after his head was white with the frosts of nearly fourscore years, Girard gave the minutest attention to the most trivial thing that could affect his fortune. "Take that lot of fowls away; the roosters are too many, they will keep the hens poor," said the old merchant to a farmer who had brought them for one of Girard's ships—"take them away—I will not buy them."

Jewish Opinion of Rothschild.

IT is very well known that, whatever may have been the redeeming traits in Baron Rothschild's character, the synagogue generally did not entertain the same respect for him as the German Jews do for the Rothschilds of Frankfort. Some thought he might have done more for his brethren than he did; and that if he had only used the influence which he possessed with Government and the many friends which he had at court, all the civil disabilities with which the British Jews were stigmatized would have been abolished, when the proposition was first mooted. "But Rothschild," as was said of him by an eminent English Jew, "was too great a slave to his money, and all other slavery was counted liberty in his sight."

Avarice of Osterwald, the French Banker.

OSTERWALD, the wealthy French banker, was a man remarkable for his penuriousness. So strong was this habit in its hold upon him, that, even within a few days of his death, no importunities could induce him to buy a few pounds of meat, for the purpose of making a little soup, in order to nourish him. "'Tis true," he remarked, "I should not dislike the soup, but I have no appetite for the meat itself; what, then, will become of that, if I cannot eat it?" At the time that he refused this nourishment, for fear of being obliged to give away two or three pounds of meat, there was tied around his neck a silken bag which contained eight hundred assignats of one thousand livres each. At his outset in life he drank a pint of beer, which served him for supper, every night, at a house much frequented, and from which he carried home all the bottle corks he could come at; of these latter, in the course of eight years, he had collected as many as sold for twelve louis d'ors —a sum that laid the foundation of his fortune, the superstructure of which was rapidly raised by his uncommon success in stock jobbing. He died possessed of the snug sum of one hundred and twenty-five thousand pounds sterling.

Estimate of his Own Life by a Miser.

AN old bachelor, whose trading skill, combined with the most grinding closefistedness, had enabled him to amass a clever fortune of some fifty thousand dollars, meeting a friend one day, began to harangue him very learnedly upon the detestable sin of avarice, and gave the following instance of it. "About three years ago," said he, "by a very odd accident, I fell into a well, and was absolutely within a very few minutes of perishing, before I could prevail upon an unconscious dog of a laborer, who happened to be within hearing of my cries, to help me out for a shilling. The fellow was so rapacious as to insist upon having twenty-five cents, for above a quarter of an hour, and I verily believe he would not have abated me a single farthing, if he had not seen me at the last gasp; and I determined to die rather than submit to his extortion."

Stephen Whitney's Charities.

NOTWITHSTANDING he stood in the front rank of New York merchants in point of immense wealth, Mr. Whitney's charities were extremely stinted. When the congregation of which he was a member were building a mission house, he was applied to to head the subscription, which he did with a trifling sum. The gift was refused, and a larger one was demanded, as in better keeping with his position. "Sir," was his reply, "if you go on in this way, there will not be a rich man left in the city of New York." It is also said that on a certain occasion he was called on to aid a political movement with his subscription. "Sir," was his reply, "I have no money to spare; but I'll come and sit up all night to fold ballots for you."

Skinflint Philosophy.

WHEN that respectable skinflint, Elwes, who left such an enormous fortune in gold to be divided between his two sons, was advised to give them some education, his characteristic answer was: "Putting things into people's heads is taking money out of their pocket."

Raising his Customer.

THE perseverance of trade hunters in some of our large cities will not lose anything in comparison with the tenacity of that griping little animal called the leech. One of this hunting or drumming class in Boston, seeing the name of a Western trader registered at one of the hotels, who he knew would be a desirable customer, and anxious to secure him first, put himself upon the said trader's trail in this wise: He sat down in the office of the hotel to watch the *key* of the Western man's bedroom till he should come in to claim it; but something kept the stranger out very late, and the drummer fell asleep. When he awoke, he found that his customer had escaped him by coming in and going to bed. He was obliged to give it up, therefore, for that night, but early on the next morning, he repaired to the door of the gentleman's bedroom, and seeing, as he expected to, his *boots* outside, he, with a lead pencil, marked them across again and again, until they could not be mistaken, and once more took up his position in the office, where he could examine at a glance, the boots of all who came down. Finally he discovered the ones with the well-known marks upon them, when, with much suavity, he cordially addressed the wearer by name, as if he had known him for years, and, with some other appropriate *finesse*, which it would be quite impossible to describe, "raised his customer."

Purloining Speculator in the French Funds.

X—— was a speculator upon the Bourse of Paris—sometimes successful and sometimes the contrary. He had wasted some years in this uncertain way of livelihood, when a sudden shifting of the funds made him utterly penniless. He wandered in a melancholy way about the Exchange for a week after, wishing very vainly for a few thousands, to make a new venture on; when one day he chanced to see a wealthy banker of the town put into his pocket a well-filled portemonnaie, containing some fifty thousand francs. He knew the old banker well—knew his habits—knew his absent habit of thought, and he seemed to him a good subject for an amateur bit of roguery. He therefore pushed after him in the throng which belongs to the closing hour of the Bourse, and, brushing with feigned carelessness against him, managed to transfer his bank bills to his own pocket.

The banker did not miss his purse until he was by his own office fire. It was too late to attempt to find it again in the hall of the Exchange. Indeed, all his inquiries proved vain. On the fourth day after his loss, he received a pleasant letter, informing him that his money was in good hands, and if affairs at the Bourse turned well—as the writer hoped might be the case—he would in time refund the money.

After a time, the banker, who had nearly forgotten the money and the note, received an enclosure of thirty thousand francs, on account of the fifty thousand missing four years before; and the writer condescended at the same time to inform him that his speculations were looking favorably, and, if there was no heavy fall within a month, he hoped to refund him the balance with interest.

The banker was grateful for the enclosure; but, on attentive examination of the handwriting, fancied he perceived some resemblance to letters addressed him by a certain broker of his acquaintance.

An "expert" was called, who pronounced unhesitatingly the different letters to be written by one and the same person. Upon this, the eager banker, just now in need of the additional twenty thousand, entered a prosecution against the broker, insisting upon immediate payment of the balance.

X—— very naturally defended himself. against a charge of robbery, which rested on so unsubstantial proof, and defied evidence of his misdeeds; with what result is best known to the parties.

In view of the uncertainty of the decision, it is a question if the banker would not have pursued the safer policy in receiving quietly the disgorgement of a rogue who had proved so prompt in his instalments.

Knavery of British and Chinese Traders Compared.

ACCORDING to a well-known mercantile writer, "A grocer is a man who buys and sells sugar, and plums, and spices, for gain."

Happy, says a London writer, is the English grocer, who can lay his hand upon his commercial heart, and, making answer to the text, can say—"I am the man." For of the men who take over unto their shop doors the name of grocer, how many are there who buy and sell sugar, and sugar only; who turn the penny upon spices in their purity; vend nought but the true mace —the undoctored clove?

Great is the villany of the Chinese; but it is written in certain books of the prying chemist, that the roguery of the Englishman—bent, it may be, upon the means of social respectability—doth outblush the pale face of the Tartar tricksters.

The Chinaman glazes his tea with Prussian blue; he paints his Congou,

and adds a perfume to his Twankay; but he—the pig-tailed heathen—does not recognize in a Britisher a man and a brother, and, in his limited sympathies, fails to acknowledge, in any British maiden, of any fabulous age soever, a woman and a sister. The China teaman is a benighted barbarian; the British grocer is an effulgent Christian. The Chinaman's religion is the gust of revenge; the Briton's creed is the creed of common love. (Oh!)

It is possible, if the effort be made, to drop a tear over the ignorance of the Chinaman who dusts his faded tea leaves over with chromate of lead; but shall not one's eyes flash fire at the enlightened British tea dealer, who to the withered leaf imparts the mortal glow of plumbago? Nevertheless, there are grocers, in the commercial form of men, who treat the stomachs of their customers as customers treat their stoves —namely, they bestow upon their internals the questionable polish of black lead, innocently swallowed in cups of liquid, worse and blacker than the Lacedemonian black broth. How many an innocent tea-loving spinster, proud of the jetty loveliness of her fireplace, would vent a spasm of horror did she know that the polish of her own stove and the bloom of her own black tea, fragrant and smoking at her lips, were of one and the same black lead—of lead that, in due sufficiency, is akin to coffin lead! And the English grocer, intent upon deceit, outvies—say the chemists—the teaman of the flowery kingdom. There is not a toss-up between the two; and if there be, though China beats by a tail, England fails not to win by a head.

Of coffee (a word still found in some of the dictionaries) it is hardly necessary to speak—the acres of chiccory, wherein the pious grocer as well as his customers may "walk forth to muse at eventide," have a language and a lesson of their own. It may be added, however, that perhaps there is not a more touching, a more instructive, and withal a more pathetic picture than either man or woman complacently employed in drinking what the drinker, in more than primitive innocence, believes to be coffee—grocer's coffee, at one shilling per pound!

"Cornering" among Brokers.

THE operation of "cornering," as the term is, is played by brokers in the following manner: Four, five, six, or ten (as the case may be) brokers enter into an arrangement with each other to buy and get control of the entire stock of some company. They commence by depressing the stock as much as possible. To do this, they must all appear to be sellers, and cry down the price, representing it to be worthless, and themselves heartily sick of everything pertaining to it. While they are publicly selling lots of one hundred or two hundred shares, their agents or tools are buying all that they can get hold of. As soon as they can buy all the cash stock they find in this way, they turn suddenly around and begin to buy on time. Parties not in the secret, of course, are willing to sell on thirty, sixty, or ninety days—even though they do not possess the stock—thinking that before the expiration of that time they will be able to buy it at a less price than they sold it at. In this way, thousands of shares are sold, to be delivered at a future day, to the very men who own every share of the stock that has ever been issued. When the time arrives for delivery, the sellers discover that there is no stock to be had but of the men to whom they have sold it. Of course they must pay whatever the owners choose to demand. If the game is well played, the cornerers will make as much in selling as they did in buying in. Should every one of the party prove true to his comrades, they will so manage as to get rid of the whole stock to outsiders at a high price. It will be

readily seen that this is a very dangerous game unless well played; for should any of the parties interested "let fly" without letting the others know it, the game is up, and although he may make a fortune, it will be at the sacrifice of all the others.

Stock "Washing."

WHAT is known as the game of "washing" among stock brokers, is when John makes a sale in public to Joe, with a previous understanding that Joe is not to take the stock. For instance, John holds a large amount of "Harlem," which he is anxious to get rid of. If he throws it into the market at once, he is pretty sure to knock the price down. His safety depends upon a stiff market; and he goes to Joe and makes an arrangement with him to take five hundred shares at full price or one eighth above. They both go into the board, and when Harlem is called, John offers one hundred shares at fifty-eight and one fourth, cash. No one takes them, but several bid fifty-seven, and fifty-seven and one fourth to one half. John comes down one eighth, and Joe "takes 'em;"—"a hundred more," "take 'em;" — "a hundred more," "take 'em;" — "a hundred more," "take 'em." John now "holds up," and Joe offers to take one hundred more. If some old stager sees through the game, he "sticks" Joe with a hundred, and the game is up; if not, why, John may be said to have succeeded, and the market for Harlem is firm. "Washing" will hardly go down at the board; the game is too old, and there is too much danger in playing it when there are none but old brokers present; but in the street it is very common, and many a "green" one is taken in by a "wash sale." The truth is, a man who does not understand the business had better go to California than speculate in stocks.

Commercial Croakers.

THE commercial croaker is a character with which every commercial city and neighborhood is infested. Does a friend embark in a mercantile speculation of any sort, he is the first to inform him that he has undertaken impossibilities, and that the chances of his failure are ten to one. Is a new movement proposed in the city, the croaker spreads his palms and rolls up his eyes with horror at the audacity, or turns up his nose with a sneer at your plans. If you speak of the growth of his native city, or its increased facility for business, he informs you oracularly that "all is not gold that glitters." He knows of at least one hundred houses which are for sale or rent, but which cannot find any tenants upon any terms. He informs you of some nameless friend who has sold real estate and stocks at an alarmingly low rate, in order to raise money to provide himself with a new location; and he lachrymosely expresses the belief that in less than five years the grass will be growing in the main streets of the city. If A fails for a couple of thousand dollars, the croaker goes snivelling round the streets, predicting that nine tenths of the merchants in the city will be in the same condition within the year. Does the severity of the winter suspend navigation, the croaker is sure that the spring business is ruined for that year, and that by midsummer half the names in town will be gazetted for bankruptcy. When political excitement runs high, the croaker is at the height of his enjoyment. Of course, he predicts the reduction of property, the want of money, and the prospect of an overwhelming commercial crisis.

Slavers Raising a Capital.

ONCE on a time, two young fellows, brothers, went to Jamaica, with the intention of commencing a mercantile business. They were by trade blacksmiths. Finding, soon after their arrival, that they could do nothing without a little money to begin with, but that with a few hundred dollars they might be able to realize a fortune, they hit upon the following novel and ingenious trick : One of them stripped the other naked, shaved him close, and blackened him from head to foot. This ceremony being performed, he took him to one of the negro dealers, who was so pleased with the appearance of the young fellow, that he advanced four hundred dollars currency upon the bill of sale to the "slavers;" and prided himself much on the purchase, supposing him the finest negro upon the island. The same evening, this manufactured negro made his escape to his brother, washed himself clean, and resumed his former appearance. Rewards were then in vain offered in handbills, pursuit was eluded, and discovery, by care and precaution, rendered impracticable. The brothers, with the money thus obtained, commenced commercial business, and finally left the island with a large fortune. Previous, however, to their departure from the island, they waited upon the trader from whom they had received the money, and, recalling the circumstance of the negro to his recollection, paid him the principal and interest with thanks.

Turtles and Gold Snuff-Boxes.

So strict is meant to be the searching at Russian custom houses, in order to prevent smuggling, that the ship captain, who is bound to give an inventory of every article on board, may fall into unheard-of trouble if he forget so much as his own private Canary bird.

There was an English captain once at Cronstadt who by accident forgot to enter a fine turtle upon his list. He told the leading custom-house official, plainly and honestly, of his unfortunate omission, and the functionary, who was a good-natured man, saw no plain way out of the difficulty.

He recommended that the matter should be glossed over by assuming that the turtle was intended for the emperor. The captain did, therefore, formally declare that, if he had not entered the turtle, it was because it had been brought expressly as an Englishman's gift to the czar, and to the czar the turtle was despatched accordingly. Soon after there arrived a Government messenger, inquiring for this most courteous of captains, who brought the gracious thanks of the czar Nicholas, together with the gift of a gold snuff-box, embellished with the autocratic cipher set in diamonds.

Instead of fine and persecution, there were royal gifts and honors for this lucky sailor. But when, afterward, some other trading captains, acting, as they imagined, cunningly upon the hint, brought turtle to exchange for gold snuff-boxes, his astute majesty quietly made the turtles into soup, but declined, by any act of exchange, to add snuff boxes to the articles of Russian trade shipped at the port of Cronstadt.

Tobacco in Loaves.

STREEN, a custom-house officer at Liverpool, apprehended a woman who had come as passenger on board an American vessel to that port, on suspicion of having some smuggled tobacco in her possession. Upon examining her dress, seventeen pounds of tobacco were found concealed under it; but the most remarkable of the expedients which had been resorted to for the purpose of deceiving the lynx-eyed deputies of the customs, was that of giving to the contraband leaf the resemblance of a loaf. A quantity of cut tobacco had been pressed into a tin, over which a thin layer of dough was spread, and this, being baked, had the appearance to the eye of a veritable and edible loaf. The quantity of tobacco which the woman had contrived to secrete in this and other modes, amounted to no less than seventy pounds.

Custom-House Swearing.

SOME time ago, says a lively writer, I had charge of a department in one of the Eastern custom houses. Holmes was an officer in the same room with me. On the monthly pay day it was necessary for him to make oath to two pay rolls—one, the account of the officer himself, and the other of the sum due to his assistant. One day, Holmes signed his pay roll, received his money after making oath to its correctness, and walked out, without signing that of his assistant. When the omission was discovered, I went for him, and he bustled in with a " What do you want of me?" " To sign the pay rolls." "But I have already." " You signed and swore to one, but not to the other." " Well," said Holmes, " I know I swore to something—I didn't know exactly what." Such swearing is said to be quite custom-ary in the custom house.

Cool Assurance of a Doomed Financier.

THE cool assurance of Sadleir, the greatest of modern swindlers, when the fearful guilt of his transactions had already become known in more than one quarter, is hardly paralleled in any similar case. This was particularly manifested in a conversation that passed in the office of one of the city newspaper writers at the time referred to. Even steeped as he was to his eyes in crime, he preserved admirable calmness, and betrayed not the least apprehension.

Scene: Lombard street, London, hour about 1 P. M.

John Sadleir (pale, cadaverous, but gentlemanly—introduced by a friend and brother director of a bank): " Oh, there has been some slight mistake respecting the announcement of the drafts of the Tipperary Bank having been refused over the way; it is all set straight; the remittances have been delayed passing through Hull, when they should have come direct to London. Just please mention it, so that the fact may be known."

Party addressed : " You are sure it is all right; because it will be awkward if there is any further difficulty."

Sadleir and his friend : " It is all made straight; you can ask over the way."

Party addressed : " You are sure there will be no *fresh hitch ?* "

Sadleir (plainly, but with great emphasis) : " I am sure there will be *no further hitch.*"

The inquiry was made " over the way ; " it was stated the drafts had been provided for, and the explanation as requested was afforded. But the party entertained his suspicions, and meeting the friend of Sadleir late in the day, he asked him if there was not something " doubtful " in the business. The reply was, " No, there cannot be ; the bank has just declared a dividend and bonus, and the report is most favorable." Two or three days afterward the explosion took place, with all its tale of Sadleir's infamy.

Terrible Sequel to Parsimony : M. Foscue's Case.

M. FOSCUE, who had amassed enormous wealth by the most sordid parsimony and disreputable extortion, applied his ingenuity to discover some effectual way of hiding his gold. With great care and secrecy he dug a cave in his cellar. To this receptacle for his treasure, he descended by a trap door, to which he attached a spring lock, so that, on shutting, it would fasten of itself. By and by the miser disappeared ; inquiries were made ; the house was searched ; woods were explored, and the ponds dragged ; but no Foscue

could they find. Some time passed on. The house where he lived was sold, and workmen were busily employed in its repair. In the progress of their work they met with the door of the secret cave, with the key in the lock outside. They threw back the door, and descended with a light. The first object upon which the lamp reflected was the ghastly body of Foscue, and scattered around him were heavy bags of gold, and ponderous chests of untold treasure ; a candlestick lay beside him on the floor. The worshipper of Mammon had gone into his cave, to pay his devoirs to his golden god, and became a sacrifice to his devotion.

Attempt to Overthrow Rothschild's Power in the Money Market.

REPEATED efforts, but always without success, and generally to the ruin of the party making the same, have been made to overthrow the power of Rothschild in the money market. It was clear that the only way in which this could be done, if it was to be done at all, would be by the party attempting it engaging in transactions of corresponding magnitude.

By far the boldest of these attempts was that once made by a young gentleman, a Mr. James H——. He made a number of most extensive purchases, and sold out again to a very large amount, all in a very short period of time ; and so far from imitating the character of the rival whose empire he sought to subvert, in the secrecy of his transactions, he deemed it essential to the success of his schemes that his operations should be performed as speedily as possible.

Mr. H. was the son of a wealthy banker in the country, and held, at the time of his introduction, money stock in his own name, though it actually was his father's, to the extent of £50,-000. The reputation of being so rich invested him at once with great importance as a banker. The £50,000, after

Mr. H. had been some time a member of the house, was privately retransferred to his father, the real owner of it. For some time, and until he became perfectly master of the rules and usages of the house, he acted with great prudence and caution, confining his transactions to small amounts; but he eventually began to astonish "the natives"—for so the members of the stock exchange are often called—by the boldness of his manœuvres. In a very short time he became the dread of all parties—the bulls and bears were anxious to follow him; but, like Rothschild, he evinced a disposition to act independently of every person and every party.

About this time consols were as high as 96 or 97. In a few months afterward symptoms of a coming panic began to manifest themselves; and a well-known writer on money matters, having at the time, for reasons best known to himself, begun to deal out his fulminations against the Bank of England, in an influential paper, the unhealthy state of the money market was greatly aggravated, though high prices were still maintained. Mr. H. watched the state of things with great penetration; and being satisfied in his own mind that a leader was only wanting to commence and carry on a successful war against Rothschild, he determined himself to become that leader—and it must be admitted that he acquitted himself as an able general. Going into the house one afternoon, he accosted one of the most respectable jobbers thus:

" What are consols ? "

" 96 and 98," was the answer.

" In £100,000 ? " continued he.

" Yes," said the jobber. " You have them; £100,000 more ? "

" I'll take £100,000 more."

" They are yours."

" Another £100,000 ? "

" No, I don't want any more."

On this transaction being finished, the adventurous young gentleman immediately turned round and announced aloud that "£200,000 had been done at 96, and more offered." Then walking backward and forward, "like a tiger in a den," he followed up the bold tactics he had commenced by offering any part of £1,000,000 at 94. For a great part of this amount he at once found purchasers. But he was not yet content with the extent of his transactions, great as they were; nor would he wait for buyers at 94. He offered them, viz., consols, at 93, at 92, and eventually as low as 90, at which price they left off that day. Next day he renewed his exertions to depress the market, and he succeeded to the utmost of his wishes; for consols did not stop in their descent till they reached 74. As was to be expected, contemporaneous with this sudden and extraordinary fall in the price of consols, there was a run on the Bank of England, which almost exhausted it of its specie. He then purchased to so large an extent that, when a reaction took place, he found that his gains exceeded £100,000.

The rivalry of Mr. H. was, however, of short duration, ending in this wise: In about two years after the above extensive "operations," he attempted another, on a scale of corresponding magnitude. But in this case, Rothschild, anticipating the tactics H. would adopt, laid a trap for him, into which he fell, and became a ruined man. He was declared a defaulter, and his name stuck upon the blackboard. It was only now that the discovery was made that the £50,000 money stock, supposed to be his own, was in reality his father's, and that it had been retransferred in his name. A deputation from the committee waited upon Mr. H. immediately after his failure, at his own house, in the neighborhood of Regent's Park, when one of the most rapacious of the number suggested a sale of his furniture and a mortgage of the annuity settled on his wife. He received the suggestion with the utmost indignation, and ringing the bell for his servant, desired him to show the deputation down stairs, adding that he would be —— (it need not be said what) before he would pay a sixpence after the treatment he had met with from them. "As for you, you vagabond, 'My son Jack', (one of the brokers who went by that name), who have had the audacity to make such a proposal to me—as for you, sir, if you don't make haste out of the room, I'll pitch you out of the window!" It is scarcely necessary to say, that "My son Jack" was the first who reached the bottom of the stairs.

Sharing in Rothschild's Fortune.

DURING the stormy days of 1848, two stalwart mobocrats entered the bank of the late Baron Anselm Rothschild, at Frankfort. "You have millions on millions," said they to him, "and we have nothing; you must divide with us." "Very well; what do you suppose the firm of Rothschild is worth?" "About forty millions of florins." "Forty millions, you think, eh? Now, then, there are forty millions of people in Germany; that will be a florin apiece. Here's yours."

Extravagant Business Rhetoric.

DEFOE, who wrote of the morals of mercantile trade in England, in former times, mentions among other manœuvres of retailers, the false light which they introduced into their shops for the purpose of giving a delusive appearance to their goods. He comments upon the "shop rhetoric," the "flux of falsehoods," which tradesmen habitually uttered to their customers; and quotes their defence as being that they could not live without lying. Add to which, he says, that there was scarce a shopkeeper who had not a bag of spurious or debased coins, from which he gave change whenever he could.

The giving and taking presents, as a·

means of obtaining custom, has become a great practice. An extensive dealer once remarked : " Every one of the buyers with whom I deal, expects an occasional bonus in some form or other. From time to time I have to make a handsome present—perhaps a dozen of choice port, or else to give a round sum as discount. Some require the bribe to be wrapped up, and some take it without disguise."

Getting wide glimpses through small holes, any one may easily get an idea of how trade is carried on, even by the sights and sounds of the street. Hearing the fruiterer cry all his fruit and vegetables as "fine," and the itinerant fish-vendor invariably describe his supplies as "fresh" and "alive," one might infer the generality of misrepresentation ; and he would find this inference strengthened when, on turning to the advertising columns of the daily newspapers, he found *all* the ships and packets characterized as "splendid," "first class," "very fast sailing," "beautiful," "celebrated," "magnificent ;"—when he read of the horses that they were all either "finest grown," or "first rate," or "invaluable," or "the handsomest in town," or "one of the grandest steppers," and in *every* case "sold for no fault ;"—or when he saw that all the properties for sale were "exceedingly valuable," "extremely well fitted up," "most eligible," "delightful site," "admirably adapted," etc. ; —or when he discovered that all the lodgings were "unsurpassed for comfort," all the medicines "infallible," all the references "unexceptionable."

Casting the eye over shop signs and door plates, and meeting with such titles as "mechanical operative dentist" —implying that other dentists are *not* mechanical and operative ; or "practical bootmaker," tacitly referring, as it seems, to some class of mere theoretical bootmakers—one gets further impressions that the screw which is loose is a very large one. Add to these the words " patent and registered," applied to commonplace objects, implying improvements where there are none; together with the glaring announcements of " great reduction," " selling off," " bankrupt stock," " tremendous sacrifices," " twenty per cent. below other houses "—and there can be no doubt that " bait " is used as plentifully on the land as in the sea.

Customs of the Store in Church.

IN a certain town, not more than fifty miles from Boston, as the clergyman was holding forth one Sabbath in his usual drowsy manner, one of the deacons, probably influenced by the narcotic qualities of the discourse, fell into a doze. In connection with the train of thought characterizing his sermon, the preacher happened to use the words, " What is the price of all earthly pleasures ? " The money-getting deacon (he kept a small store, and had a lively eye to the main chance), half consciously, thinking the inquiry was respecting some kind of merchandise, immediately answered, " Seven and sixpence a dozen."

Hoarding and Amassing—Noted Instances.

THERE died at Paris, in the year 1709, literally of want, the noted banker Osterwald. He deprived himself of almost every personal comfort and convenience, alike in sickness and in health, for fear of encroaching on his hoarded treasures. He died worth £125,000.

Another desperate case of this kind was that of the millionnaire Elwes, whose diet and dress were of the most revolting kind, and his penuriousness almost passing belief. His property was estimated at £800,000.

Daniel Dancers's miserly propensities were indulged to such a degree, that, among his eccentricities, was that of performing his ablutions at a neighbor-

ing pond, and drying himself in the sun, in order to save himself the extravagant indulgence of a towel; yet the yearly income of this poor mendicant was reckoned by thousands of dollars.

The well-known Nat Beatty, *alias* " Dirty Dick," of London, was the victim not only of a craving for gold, but even for old iron.

Another deplorable case was that of Tom Pitt, of Warwickshire. It is related that some weeks prior to the sickness which terminated his remarkable career, he went to several undertakers in quest of a cheap coffin. He left behind him a rich hoard in public funds.

Thomas Cook afforded a precious example of this kind. On his physician intimating to him the possibility of his not existing more than five or six days, he protested against the useless expense of sending him medicine, and charged the doctor never to show his face to him again. His property was rated at £130,000.

Jewish Money-Makers in the Holy City.

SOME of the Jews residing in the Holy City, though they are ready enough to accept alms from their European brethren, amass money, and are no more above a little sharp practice than are their kindred in Holywell street. " Dog ought not to eat dog," is a proverb, but here is a veritable anecdote, told by a close observer of the Israelites in Jerusalem, which shows some of their traits.

Sir Moses Montefiore brought with him in wooden barrels a large quantity of dollars in specie, and resolved, with his usual kindness of disposition, to give with his own hand a dollar to every poor person. It took many hours before his task was done and the miserable exhibition of poverty concluded. It so happened that the noble distributor, forgetful of himself, gave away the sum which he required to pay his travelling expenses home. He was obliged to borrow money. A man was soon found, who expressed his readiness to oblige him—*for a consideration*—and supplied him with the necessary sum, the amount of which was considerable, in specie. And yet this man, the previous day, seemed to be the neediest of the needy, and *had received a silver dollar from the hand of the benefactor of Palestine!* Sharp practice that.

Even among the leading Jews of Jerusalem, the ruling passion seems to be to pervert everything—even charity —to their pecuniary gain. Thus, an institution for advancing money as loans was founded by Mr. Cohen, and endowed by the Rothschild family with one hundred thousand piasters. M. Alterns, one of the Sepharedim, and an Austrian subject, being intrusted with the management of it, lent forty thousand piasters to the presidents of the Sepharedim. All of them regarded the money, not as a means of benefiting others by advancing loans without interest, but as a means of benefiting themselves by lending it out on usury. One half of the money thus advanced with the best intentions was lost, notwithstanding the efforts made to recover it.

Presents to Bank Officers—Curious Cases.

In his admirable exposition of banking in New York, Mr. Gibbons gives a few racy incidents in regard to the artifice of present making to bank officers, and what comes of such "favors:"

A cashier asked a director of the same bank if he could advise him where to purchase a certain description of tea. The latter engaged to find the article. On the same evening, a "quarter chest" was left at the cashier's house without a bill, and the matter was not again alluded to. The director was subsequently indebted to the officer for some "favors," which, however, did not keep him solvent. A dealer in fancy goods asked the same cashier for his address, without specifying any object. On going home, the latter found his parlor mantel furnished with some elegant ornaments.

A bank president inquired of a dealer in foreign porcelain, where he could best get an English dinner set at a cost of not over one hundred dollars. The latter answered that his acquaintance with the wholesale importers would enable him to purchase at a considerable discount, and he did so. The president never asked for a bill, but he discounted his friend's paper liberally "between the Boards."

Said a bank officer carelessly, to a jeweller, after serving him with a loan: "By the way—where is that gold-headed cane you promised me?" The jeweller smiled, but said nothing. In a week, the cane was sent; and when the donor called at the bank, subsequently, he was greeted with an expression of great surprise: "Why, Mr. D., you didn't suppose I was in earnest the other day, did you?"

Another officer called at the store of a drygoods merchant, after assisting the latter to a liberal discount of paper. While walking along the aisle, he was attracted by some ladies' kid gloves of superior quality. "Ah,' said he, "you keep these articles, do you? They are really very soft and beautiful!" "Yes, sir," answered the proprietor, at the same time wrapping up a dozen in some fine tissue paper—"put those in your pocket. Yes, yes, do!" overcoming the apparent reluctance of his visitor, by unaffected earnestness. The same scene was acted over again on the next occasion, when the merchant had paper discounted. A third rehearsal taught him to add a dozen of the finest kid gloves to the legal rate of seven per cent. whenever he obtained accommodation at that bank.

A dealer, who was impatient to rectify his accounts, urged a bookkeeper to balance his bank book; after wait-

ing several days, the request was repeated, and the clerk promised that it
should be done: "But," he added,
"you haven't sent me that umbrella
yet!" It was added to his wardrobe.

A clerk took lodgings at a hotel during the absence of his family in the
country, which led to the landlord opening an account with the bank. In the
"progress of human events," baskets
of brown stout were left at the residence of one of the officers, and dining
privileges were enjoyed without cost.
The result in this case was a loan of
twenty thousand dollars on inferior securities; and although it was finally
paid, the process involved transactions
of questionable propriety.

Mr. George Curtis, the first cashier of
the New York Bank of Commerce, and
late president of the Continental Bank,
was occasionally the unwilling recipient of "a present." His well-known
high sense of honor and propriety
would have protected him against all
suspicion of improper influence in the
administration of his trust; but so sensitive and scrupulous was he on the
subject, that he uniformly placed the
article, whatever it was, in the directors' room, and related its history at the
next meeting of the board of directors.

First Forged Note on a Bank--Execu-
tion for the Crime.

IT is a memorable fact that the Bank
of England had circulated its paper
with freedom for sixty-four years, before any attempt at imitation was made.
The name of the criminal was Vaughan,
a Stafford linen-draper, and he was executed for his crime.

It appears that the records of Vaughan's life do not show want, beggary,
or starvation urging him, but a simple
desire to seem greater than he was.
By one of the artists employed, and
there were several engaged on different
parts of the notes, the discovery was
made. The criminal had filled up to
the number of twenty, and deposited

them in the hands of a young lady to
whom he was attached, as a proof of his
wealth. There is no calculating how
much longer bank notes might have
been free from imitation, had this man
not shown with what ease they might
be counterfeited. But from this period
forged notes became common. And
the fact is, that the faculty of imitation
is so great, that when the expectation
of profit is added, there is little hope
of restraining the destitute or bad man
from a career which adds the charm of
novelty to the chance of gain.

The publicity given to this strange
and easy fraud, the notoriety of the
proceedings, and the execution of the
forger, tended to excite that morbid
sympathy which, up to the present
day, is apt to be evinced for any extraordinary criminal; and it is therefore possible, that if Vaughan had not
been induced by circumstances to star-
tle London with his novel crime, the
idea of forging notes might have been
long delayed.

Fauntleroy, the Executed Banker.

THE sensation produced by the
criminality of Fauntleroy, the great
banker and forger, has never been
exceeded by that attending any similar case, in Europe or America. In
September, 1824, Plank, the Bow-street
officer, might be seen proceeding in
the direction of the banking house of
Marsh, Stracey & Co. A person
who accompanied him entered first,
and, requesting an interview with
Mr. Fauntleroy, was ushered into his
private counting house. Within a
minute he was followed by Plank.
The interior of a bank is nearly sacred;
but the officer pushed boldly by the
clerk, who would have interrupted
him, merely saying he wished to speak
with Mr. Fauntleroy. On entering, he
closed the bar, announced his name,
and produced a warrant for the apprehension of Henry Fauntleroy on a

charge of forgery. A deadly pallor passed over the face of the latter; he was fearfully agitated, and hurriedly exclaimed, "Good God! cannot this business be settled?" Plank begged him to make no noise, but to walk out for a few minutes, and they could talk about it. Mr. Fauntleroy then signed a few blank checks for the business of the house with a hand so unsteady that it was difficult to recognize his signature; and said he should go out for a few minutes. He was then conducted to the private residence of Mr. Conant, the magistrate; and, after an interview of the prisoner with one of his clerks, Mr. Freshfield, accompanied by Plank, proceeded to the banking house to search the papers.

The search was successful. Documents unparalleled in the history of crime were discovered. In a private room, a box, bearing no name, was found. What must the surprise have been, on finding in it a list, in the prisoner's handwriting, of forgeries which he had committed on the Bank of England, amounting to one hundred and twelve thousand pounds, with the following extraordinary acknowledgment : "In order to keep up the credit of our house, I have forged powers of attorney, and have, thereupon, sold out all these sums, without the knowledge of any of my partners. I have given credit in the accounts for the interest when it became due. Henry Fauntleroy." These words followed : "The bank first began to refuse our acceptances, and thereby destroy the credit of our house. The bank shall smart for it." At the period of his apprehension he had a power of attorney by which he would have replaced the stock that produced the discovery.

In a conference the forger had with a partner, he expressed great anxiety to obtain possession of a "blue book." Mr. Graham searched, and brought one with a blue sheet for a cover. "No, no," he said, "this is not the one I want. It is a bound book." Mr. Graham informed him that it had reached the hands of Mr. Freshfield. "Then," said Fauntleroy, "I'm a dead man. I could have set the bank at defiance." This book was said to contain an account of all his forgeries.

The crime of Mr. Fauntleroy excited intense and universal interest. Hardly anything else was talked about. The newspapers teemed with anecdotes. His past life was inquired into. His portrait was in the windows. His behavior was analyzed. His person was described. The very way in which he held his hat was represented. The magistrate apologized for an intrusion; and, when the forger heaved a sigh, the scribe was ready to draw the attention of the public to so memorable a fact. The loss sustained by these forgeries was three hundred and sixty thousand pounds; and the interest alone, which was regularly paid, must have been nine or ten thousand pounds a year. The care required by these accounts, and the constant anxiety weighing on the mind of Fauntleroy, from the knowledge of his perilous position, were, in themselves, a punishment. His exertions at the banking house were extraordinary. So energetic was he, that his services were noticed as being equal to those of three clerks. The last time he received from the bank the warrants due to the firm was the day on which Thurtell and Hunt were tried. During the payment, he entered into conversation on the crime with the clerk who paid him; imagining but little—perhaps—that within a year the same judge who had tried them would try him; that the very list of warrants he was receiving would be brought in evidence, and that the clerk with whom he was so familiarly conversing would be a witness against him. Before the debtors' door at Newgate, and amidst a vast concourse of spectators, the unhappy man expiated his crime.

Restitution of Bank Notes.

On the 24th of November, 1844, Sunday, the "strong room" of the banking house of Messrs. Rogers, Towgood & Co., London, was opened, and property in bank notes, gold, and bills of exchange, taken therefrom, to the amount of nearly fifty thousand pounds. The notes, of various denominations—and of which there were thirty-six one-thousand-pound notes—amounted to about forty-four thousand pounds in all, and the gold to twelve hundred pounds; the rest consisted of bills of exchange.

On the day in question, one of the partners was in the house an invalid, and a clerk, whose duty it was to remain on the premises during the day, was also in attendance; yet the above property was abstracted, and never missed till the following morning, when the safe was opened.

A reward of three thousand pounds was immediately offered for the recovery of the property, and so ran the offer: "Her most gracious majesty's *pardon* will be granted to any one of the guilty parties who will give such evidence as will procure the conviction of the other offender or offenders;" and, although this offer, with a description of the notes stolen, which occupied three full pages in octavo, was published in almost every newspaper and periodical in the three kingdoms and on the continent, no clew could be obtained of the robbers, yet, after a considerable lapse of time, and when the circumstances had been almost forgotten by every one but the losers of the property, the bank notes were returned in a parcel, directed to the bankers in an unknown hand, and without any comment.

Tough Experience of a Business Drummer.

One cold January night, the hospitably huge fireplace of the best room of the best inn in —— was surrounded by a jovial company, composed of commercial travellers and their customers of the town. The air of solid comfort which pervaded the scene was heightened by its contrast with the cheerless aspect of the weather without; and the complacent manner with which each guest quaffed from his mug of flip, and gave a bland reflection to his neighbor's smile, told that the pleasantness of the situation was not unappreciated.

All were overflowing with jest and story, but the most amusing member of the party, was a gentlemanly looking person, rather smaller than the common size of men, and frank and open in his address. He gave his name as Morris, and (from remarks thrown out, as if casually, by himself, and from that fact alone, for of those present not one had ever seen him previous to that time) he was supposed to be the agent of a new Liverpool house. There was a rich, racy humor, and a power of imitation and description, about the man, allied to a knowledge of the light and dark spots in human nature, which lent to the stories that he told a fascination winning entire attention. Identifying himself for the moment with the character whose deeds and words he was narrating, he would seem at times the artless Scotch lassie, the Yorkshire lout, the rude sailor, the querulous beldame, the blundering Irishman, changing from one to another with a chameleon-like facility.

But his *chef-d'œuvre*, in this kind of narration, was a story of a finished freebooter, who accomplished much in his line of business, by first insinuating himself into the confidence of his intended victims in the guise of a gentleman. His personation of the easy impudence of the gentleman of the road was characteristic and excellent. When he had concluded, however, his "freebooter" was criticized by Mr. D. (an agent for a large house in London, connected with the coffee trade), whose

17

flip had made him flippant. He insisted that Morris had made but "a
tame bird" of his hero, instead of
a "roystering, rough-handed, ribald
rogue," as in nature, and swore with
a laugh that he could enact the highwayman better himself. Morris rejoined, in the same good-natured
way, that were it not so late, and the
calls of Somnus less inviting, he would
try a little competition of the kind
with him, and let the company then
present decide which was the better
of the two. However, he professed to
think that an opportunity might yet
occur, as they *would probably meet again
on the road at some time or another.* The
company laughed heartily at the joke,
and, drinking sundry parting toasts,
each of which was denominated, as
given, the *very* last and best, retired
for the night. Mr. D. was fain to
maintain his equilibrium by accepting
the arm of Morris to his bedroom.
Before he bade the latter a good night,
he had, in drunken bravado, defied all
the highwaymen in christendom, and
in confidence pointed out to his new
friend a secret pocket in his coat, containing a brace of small pistols loaded,
and a considerable amount of money
in gold.

In the morning, several of the "drummers" departed in their own vehicles.   Mr. D. was to take a seat in a
stage, but being invited by Morris to
take a seat in his chaise, concluded to
go with him, as their routes were alike.
During the ride of the first few miles,
D.'s good opinion of his companion
suffered no diminution, but it immediately fell below *par,* when, in a lone-
some part of the road, Morris presented
a pistol in juxtaposition with his head,
and begged leave to borrow the funds
then in his possession.   The altered
mien and determined look of the man,
as well as his own instinctive assurance
that he was in earnest, left no doubt in
the mind of the poor agent of the other's
character. He determined, however, not

to comply with the rascal's request,
without an effort to save his money for
loans more *profitable.* With the pretence of producing the desired funds,
he seized one of his pistols from his
pocket, and snapped it at the head of
the robber. It flashed, but it did not
explode. The quondam Morris laughed,
and mockingly remarked, as the other
grasped at the remaining weapon, that
he was obliged to him, but he was sufficiently helped, and that the contents
of his *pocket* would be equally acceptable, and much more effective, than
those of his pistols, inasmuch as the
last were *empty*—which was not the
case with the pocket, that being
charged with gold. He explained
the failure of the weapons to discharge, by saying that lest accident
should befall the esteemed friend
whom he had the pleasure of addressing, he had availed himself of the information given him on the evening
previous, and *drawn* the *charges* from
both of the pocket pistols. In effecting this friendly measure, he had
noticed with great satisfaction, that
his friend had the wherewithal to
make him the loan, which he now
desired receiving without delay. As
his fingers, he said, were rather tremulous, and the *persuader,* into the muz-
zle of which his esteemed friend did
him the honor to blink, had a hair
trigger, he begged leave to suggest
the expediency of a *speedy* delivery
of all his funds. Mr. D. cursed the
other's impudence, and with a pardon-
able ill grace gave up his money. He
also handed his watch to the robber,
but it was returned to him, with a
pathetic request that he would keep it
in remembrance of the "tame bird."
The poor, plucked agent remembered
his boasting of the previous evening,
and ground his teeth with vexation.

After Mr. D. had alighted from the
chaise, he was asked by his eccentric acquaintance whether or not he thought
it would be necessary to find referees

to decide which was the better highwayman of the two! Before he could answer, the robber was driving at a rapid rate toward the London road, and he was left to pursue his journey on foot. Poor D. never again sought to rival a freebooter.

Government Contractors in Russia.

IT would seem that American contractors for Government jobs are not alone in the *patriotic disinterestedness* of their mode of doing business; but that their equals in this respect may be found even among the rough and grizzly Russians. As for example:

A certain quantity of well-seasoned oak being required, Government issues tenders for the required amount. A number of contractors submit their terms to a board appointed for the purpose of receiving them, who are regulated in their choice of a contractor, not by the amount of his tender, but of his bribe. The fortunate individual selected immediately sub-contracts upon a somewhat similar principle. Arranging to be supplied with timber for half the amount of his tender, the sub-contractor carries on the game, and perhaps the eighth link in this contracting chain is the man who, for an absurdly low figure, undertakes to produce the seasoned wood. His agents in the central provinces, accordingly, float a quantity of *green* pines and firs down the Dnieper and Bay to Nicholaeff, which are duly handed up to the head contractor, each man pocketing the difference between his contract and that of his neighbor. When the wood is produced before the board appointed to inspect it, another bribe *seasons* it, and the Government, after paying the price of well-seasoned oak, is surprised that the one-hundred-and-twenty gunship, of which it has been built, is unfit for service in five years.

Muller, the Rich Merchant of Nuremberg—Fictitious Theft.

A PHILOSOPHER has said, "Take away interest and vanity from the heart of man, and humanity is perfect." A little story, apropos of this vanity of our age, concerning an eminent German merchant, will not be out of place in this volume.

Heinrich Heine, when very young, set out one fine morning, from Hamburg, and started for Germany. He arrived one evening at Manheim, enters the faubourg of the Golden Lion, and finds, in the dining hall, a man with white hair and a respectable appearance, digesting his dinner by reading a newspaper. From time to time he sighed heavily. Heinrich Heine moved—he was very young—and asked of the unknown the cause of his grief.

"Ah, monsieur!" he groaned, in reply, and ordered a bottle of Johannisberg. Our two Germans drank together; Heinrich Heine renewed his question, and the unknown, who was continually sighing, suddenly yielding to the desire of removing from his heart an enormous weight, said to him:

"Listen to me. My name is Muller; I am a very rich merchant of Nuremberg; I have two hundred thousand livres income, an adorable wife, and charming children; my health is excellent, and I am the—most unfortunate of men!"

"How is that?"

"Ah! (another sigh.) How to make you so terrible an avowal! I have committed a crime in my life. I have stolen!"

"Rich as you are, what hinders you from restoring the sum you have taken?"

"There does not pass a month that I do not give, in charities, in pious works, the double, the triple, the quadruple of what I have purloined; but the claw of the vulture does not leave me a moment of sweet repose."

"And how has a man like you been able to yield to the temptation of theft?"

"A vertigo. I had the honor of dining with the Duke of Nassau at his chateau at Biebrich; the prince, who has a very particular consideration for me, placed me on his right, and we talked during the dinner of one thing and another. "Monsieur Muller," said the Duke to me, "how is Madame Muller?" "Your highness is too good." "And the little Mullers?" "Very well. But your highness does me too much honor." The Duke de Nassau places me on the footing of a flattering familiarity. "Suddenly I saw shining before my eyes a little gilt spoon. What passed in my brain I know not, but the moment when the Duke turned his head I stretched my hand slyly along the cloth, took the spoon and put it in my pocket. This, sir, is what I did at the house of the Duke de Nassau."

And Mr. Muller, who had just finished his third bottle, tumbled off to sleep, and, in spite of so much remorse, snored like a bass viol.

Some days after this conversation Heinrich Heine made inquiries in regard to this man. He was truly Mr. Muller, a merchant of Nuremberg, possessed of two hundred thousand francs income, he was surrounded by a large family, but—he had never dined at the house of the Duke de Nassau. He had only invented the fable of the spoon to persuade the people that he was the friend of the Duke; willing to gratify his vanity by imputing to himself an act of theft.

Bank Teller Filing His Gold Coin.

A NEW business crime was discovered in 1767. The notice of the clerks at the bank of England had been attracted by the habit of William Guest, a teller, picking new from old guineas, without assigning any reason. An indefinite

suspicion, increased by the knowledge that an ingot of gold had been seen in Guest's possession, was awakened; and although he stated that it came from Holland, it was remarked to be very unlike the regular bars of gold, and that it had a considerable quantity of copper on the back. Attention being thus drawn to the movements of Guest, he was observed to hand to one Richard Still some guineas which he took from a private drawer, and placed with others on the table. Still was instantly followed, and on the examination of his money, three of the guineas in his possession were deficient in weight. An inquiry was immediately instituted, and forty of the guineas in the charge of Guest looked fresher than the others upon the edges, and weighed much less than the legitimate amount. On searching his home, four pounds eleven ounces of gold filings were found, with instruments calculated to produce artificial edges. Proofs soon multiplied, and the prisoner was found guilty. The instrument with which he had effected his fraud, and of which one of the witnesses asserted it was the greatest improvement he had ever seen, is said to be yet in the Mint, a memento of the prisoner's capacity and crime.

Ingenious Plot against a Banker.

A LONDON banker was severely grieved by the contents of a letter which, on a certain occasion, he received from a correspondent at Hamburg, the postmark of which place it bore. From the statement it contained, it appeared that a person most minutely described had defrauded the writer, under extraordinary circumstances, of three thousand pounds. The letter continued to say information had been obtained that the defrauder—the dress and person of whom it described—was occasionally to be seen on the Dutch Walk of the Royal Exchange. The object of the writer was to induce his correspondent to invite the party to dinner, and, by any moral force which could be used, compel him to return the money; adding that, if he should be found amenable to reason, and evince any signs of repentance, he might be dismissed with a friendly caution and five hundred pounds, as he was a near relation of the writer.

As the gentleman whose name this letter bore was a profitable correspondent, the London banker· kept a keen watch on the Dutch Walk, and was at last successful in meeting and being introduced to the cheat. The invitation to dine was accepted; and the host, having previously given notice to his family to quit the table soon after dinner, acquainted his visitor with his knowledge of the fraud. Alarm and horror were depicted in the countenance of the young man, who, with tones apparently tremulous from emotion, begged his disgrace might not be made public. To this the banker consented, provided the three thousand pounds were returned. The visitor sighed deeply, but said that to return all was impossible, as he had unfortunately spent part of the amount. The remainder, however, he proposed to yield instantly, and the notes were handed to the banker, who, after dilating upon the goodness of the man he had robbed, concluded his moral lesson by handing him a check for five hundred pounds, as a proof of his beneficence. The following morning, the banker, on depositing the money he had received, was told, to his great surprise, that the notes were counterfeit. His next inquiries were concerning the check, but that . had been cashed shortly after the opening of the bank. He immediately sent an express to his Hamburg correspondent, who replied that the letter was a forgery, and that no fraud had been committed on him. The whole affair had been plotted by a gang, some of whom were on the continent, and some in England.

Exchanging a Cheese for a Pinch of Snuff.

. JOHN TICE, a New Jersey grocer, came to Philadelphia a short time since, to replenish his stock. Completing his purchases, which in due time were deposited on the docks, to be shipped per river steamer, Mr. Tice thought proper to keep his eye upon his goods until they could be taken on board. Among them was a fine Bucks county cheese, weighing about sixty-five pounds, upon which, for want of better accommodations, the weary grocer seated himself as he watched the remainder of his property on the wharf. While thus seated, running over the events of the day, calculating the profits that he would realize on this purchase, and every now and then solacing his nasal organ from a "yaller" snuff-box, two nice young men approached, and entered into conversation.

"You take snuff, sir," asked young man No. 1. "Yes—couldn't do without it—took it for over eight years." "You use the maccoboy, I perceive" (No. 2). "Yes. That suits me the best for a steady snuff." "Let me recommend you mine," said the sharper, producing a silver-plated box, engraved with an American eagle and two harpoons; "I imported it from France. It is the identical snuff used by Marshal Pelissier and the officers of the French army." Mr. Tice said, "Certainly," and inserted his thumb and finger in the stranger's box. The moment he placed it to his nose, he was seized with sneezing. At every sneeze he lifted himself about a foot from the cheese upon which he sat. While he was doing this, sharper No. 2 was carrying out his share of the programme. As Mr. Tice gave the third sneeze, the rogue pushed the cheese from under him, and in its stead placed a peck measure; and as he was sneezing for the eighth and last time, the sharpers and cheese had disappeared.

The grocer continued rubbing his nose for about five minutes more, wondering as to the style of nose possessed by Marshal Pelissier and the officers of the French army, who took such remarkable snuff. By this time, the deck hands of the boat commenced to load up Mr. Tice's goods. Mr. Tice rose from his seat and said, "Take this cheese, too." Deck hand said, "What cheese?" The grocer looked around, and found that instead of the cheese, he had been sitting upon a peck measure. When he understood the manner in which the exchange had been effected, he was the most excited man of the season. He offered fifty dollars to any one who would give him an opportunity to fight the thieves with one hand tied behind his back.

Wanting to Pay the Cash.

In an interior town in old Connecticut lives a shaky character, named Ben Hayden. Ben has some good points, but he will run his face when and where he can, and never pay. In the same town lives Mr. Jacob Bond, who keeps the store at the corners. Ben had a " score " there, but to get his pay was more than Mr. Bond was equal to, as yet. One day Ben made his appearance with a bag and wheelbarrow, and said, " Mr. Bond, I want to buy two bushels of corn, and I *want to pay cash for it*." " Very well," replied Mr. Bond, " all right; " and so they both ascended the loft, and when the necessary operations were gone through with, they respectively returned. But by the time the trader had got down and looked around him, old Ben had got some distance from the door, and was rapidly making for home. " Halloo, halloo, Ben!" cried out the trader lustily; " you said you wanted to

pay cash for that corn." Old Ben deliberately sat down on one handle of his barrow, and cocking his head on one side, said, " That's all true, Mr. Bond. I *do* want to pay you the cash for the corn, but I can't!"

A Rustic Bargaining for a Hat.

A JOCKEY country merchant was trafficking one day with a rustic mountaineer, purchasing hay rakes in exchange for goods. Of course, the merchant's prices were what are called barter prices. Our rustic had need of a new hat, and inquired the price of one from a case just opened, from New York. " Only five dollars," said the merchant. " Isn't that rather dear ?" said the customer. " I never sold one for less," said the sharp merchant.

The clerk in the store inclined his head to the ear of a bystander, who was listening to the interesting confabulation, and whispered : " He never sold one at all." The case was bought at auction in New York for one dollar a piece.

Results of a Career of Overreaching.

One who knew well the late Gideon Lee, remarks of him that no man more thoroughly despised trickery in trade than did Mr. L. He used to say that " no trade can be sound that is not beneficial to both parties—to the buyer as well as to the seller. A man may obtain a temporary advantage by selling an article for more than it is worth; but the very effect of such operations must recoil on him, in the shape of bad debts and increased risks." A person with whom he had some transactions once boasted to him that he had, on one occasion, obtained an advantage over such a neighbor, and, upon another occasion, over another neighbor; " and to-day," said he, " I have obtained one over you."

" Well," said Mr. Lee, " that may be;

but if you will promise never to enter my office again, I will give you that bundle of goatskins." The man made the promise, and took them.

Fifteen years afterward, he walked into Mr. Lee's office. At the instant, on seeing him, Mr. L. exclaimed: "You have violated your promise; pay me for the goatskins!" "Oh!" said the man, "I am quite poor, and have been very unfortunate since I saw you." "Yes," responded Mr. Lee, "and you always will be poor; that miserable desire for overreaching others must ever keep you so."

Keen Ruse by a Yankee Peddler.

JUST before the Declaration of Independence, a Yankee peddler started down to New York, to sell a parcel of bowls and dishes he had made of maple. Jonathan travelled over the city, asking everybody to buy his wares, but no one seemed disposed to buy wooden dishes. It happened, however, that a British fleet was then lying in the harbor of New York, and Jonathan struck upon a plan of selling his dishes. So he got a naval uniform, by hook or by crook—for history doesn't tell where he got it—and, strutting up town one morning, in his assumed garb, asked a merchant if he had any nice wooden ware; that the commodore wanted a lot for the fleet. The merchant replied that he had none on hand; but there was some in town, and if he would send in the afternoon he could supply him. "Very good," said our naval officer—and out he went, *and cut for home.* He had scarcely doffed his borrowed plumage before down came the merchant, who, observing that Jonathan had sold none of his wares, now offered to take the whole, if he would deduct fifteen per cent.; but Jonathan said "he'd be hanged if he didn't take 'em home before he'd take a cent less than his first price." So the merchant paid him down in gold his price for the wooden

ware, which laid on his shelves for many a long day thereafter. If anything additional is necessary to be said in connection with this trade, it is not—that Jonathan trotted home in high glee at the success of his ruse, while the merchant cursed British uniforms and officers ever after.

Trading in Imaginary Candlesticks.

IN 1808, Vincent Alessi, a native of one of the Italian States, went to Birmingham, England, to choose some manufactures likely to return a sufficient profit in Spain. Among others he sought a brass founder, who showed him that which he required, and then drew his attention to "another article," which he said he could sell cheaper than any other person in the trade. Mr. Alessi declined purchasing this, as it proved to be a forged bank note; upon which he was shown some dollars, as fitter for the Spanish market. These were also declined. It would seem, however, from what followed, that Mr. Alessi was not quite unprepared, as, in the evening, he was called on by one John Nicholls, and, after some conversation, he agreed to take a certain quantity of notes, of different value, which were to be paid for at the rate of six shillings in the pound.

Alessi thought this a very profitable business while it lasted, as he could always procure as many as he liked, by writing for so many dozen candlesticks, calling them Nos. 5, 2, or 1, according to the amount of the note required. The vigilance of the English police, however, was too much even for the subtlety of an Italian; he was taken by them, and allowed to turn king's evidence, it being thought very desirable to discover the manufactory whence the notes emanated.

In December, John Nicholls received a letter from Alessi, stating that he was going to America; that he wanted to see Nicholls in London; that he required twenty dozen candlesticks, No. 5, twenty-four dozen No. 1, and four dozen No. 2. Mr. Nicholls, unsuspicious of his correspondent's captivity, and consequent frailty, came forthwith to town to fulfil so important an order. Here an interview was planned within hearing of the public officers. Nicholls came with the forged notes. Alessi counted up the whole sum he was to pay, at six shillings in the pound, saying: "Mr. Nicholls, you will take all my money from me." "Never mind, sir," was the reply, "it will be all returned in the way of business." Alessi then remarked that it was cold, and put on his hat. This was the signal for the officers. To the dealer's surprise and indignation he found himself entrapped, with the counterfeit notes in his possession, to the precise amount in number and value that had been ordered in the letter. Thus Mr. Nicholls found his business suddenly brought to a close, and the brisk trade in imaginary candlesticks finished.

The Bank Detectives Foiled.

THE desire of the London banks to discover the makers of forged notes produced, on a certain occasion, a considerable amount of anxiety to one whose name is indelibly associated with the fine arts. George Morland—a name rarely mentioned but with feelings of admiration and regret—had, in his eagerness to avoid incarceration for debt, retired to an obscure hiding-place, in the suburbs of London. At one period he hid himself in Hackney, where his anxious looks and secluded manner of life induced some of his charitable neighbors to believe him a maker of forged notes. The bank directors despatched two of their most dexterous emissaries to inquire, reconnoitre, search, and seize. The men arrived, and began to draw lines of circumvallation round the painter's retreat. He was not, however, to be sur-prised; mistaking those agents of evil mien for bailiffs, he escaped from behind as they approached in front, fled into Hoxton, and never halted till he had hid himself in London. Nothing was found to justify suspicion; and when Mrs. Morland, who was his companion in this retreat, told them who her husband was, and showed them some unfinished pictures, they made such a report to the bank that the directors presented him with a couple of bank notes of twenty pounds each, by way of compensation for the alarm they had given him.

Sharp at a Trade—Sharper in Getting out of it.

THERE once flourished in one of our commercial cities a little French merchant, who was very well known in said locality, and who himself "knew a thing or two." During the last war, our little Frenchman was doing a very thriving business in the drygoods line, and was supposed to be a little sharper at a bargain than most, at least, of his fellow tradesmen. There also flourished at the same time, and in the same city, an importing merchant, of Yankee origin, who was noted as a long-headed, close-fisted dealer.

It is well known that during the war English goods were sold at enormous prices. The Yankee merchant was in that line of trade; and a few days before the arrival in this country of the news of peace, he received private advices from the continent, which led him to anticipate it. As he had a large supply of English goods on hand at the time, the prices of which would of course instantly fall, he set about disposing of them as soon as possible to his less informed and unsuspecting customers. The little Frenchman was one of his victims. After much haggling, and the offer of a long credit, the importer effected a bill of sale of goods to him, to the amount of something like twenty thousand dollars, taking his notes on long time in payment. These he considered perfectly good, of course, as his customer's reputation in the money market was unsullied. The bargain being consummated, the two friends parted, each in a capital humor with himself; the Yankee to deposit the notes in his strong box, and the Frenchman to his store, where, receiving his newly purchased goods, he immediately commenced marking them one hundred per cent. above cost, thus making, before midnight, to use his own boast, a *profit* of twenty thousand dollars on his purchase!

Three days afterward the official news of peace came; English goods instantly fell one half, and our little Frenchman awoke in horror from his dream of cent. per cent. Nine persons out of every ten, under such circumstances, would have failed at once. But *nil desperandum* was the motto of our Frenchman. He saw that he had been *bit* by his commercial friend, and he immediately set his wits at work to turn the tables upon him. So, late in the evening of the next day, he repaired to the dwelling of the importer, and told a long and pitiful story of his embarrassments. He said his conscience already smote him for making so heavy a purchase while in failing circumstances, and that he had come to make the only reparation in his power—namely, to yield up the goods obtained of the importer, on the latter's cancelling the notes given therefor. The Yankee at first demurred; but on the Frenchman insisting that he was a bankrupt, and that he feared the moment he opened in the morning the sheriff would pounce upon him with a writ that would swallow up everything, he finally agreed to the proposition. "Half a loaf was better than no bread," he thought; so the notes and the bill of sale were accordingly cancelled.

By daylight in the morning, the Yankee was at the Frenchman's store, with his teams, as had been agreed

upon the night before, and every package of his goods was soon removed. The two merchants again parted, the Frenchman relieved of a heavy load, and the Yankee rather down in the mouth at the result of his trade.

Two or three days afterward, as the importer was passing the Frenchman's store, he observed his sign still up, and everything apparently as flourishing as ever. He stepped in to see what it all meant. "Hallo! Mr. S.," said he, "I thought you had *failed!*" "*Failed!*" repeated the little Frenchman, thrusting his thumbs in the arm holes of his vest, and sliding his legs apart from counter to counter, till he resembled a small Colossus of Rhodes: "*Failed?* No, be gar! Firmer than ever, Mr. H.; but I *should* have failed, *almosht*, if I hadn't got rid of dem tamn'd English goods at cost!"

Coal Dealer's Prediction Fulfilled—Perhaps.

AN English coal dealer, who was notorious for his continual and unprovoked swearing, had occasion to proceed with a boat to a neighboring port, with a cargo of coals, and ordered one of his men to take charge of it. As the boat was leaving the wharf, an acquaintance civilly accosted the man, asking where he was going. "I am going to hell," he characteristically replied, with an oath. Strange to relate, he died suddenly before reaching the port of his destination. Perhaps his profane prediction was fulfilled; he knows best.

Deserved Reward of Blasphemy.

IN the strait between Johor and Rhio there is a small white rock, called the "White Stone," only slightly elevated above the water, and so exactly in the centre of the passage that many vessels, unacquainted with it, have there been wrecked.

A Portuguese merchant passing this

strait, in a vessel of his own, richly laden with gold and other valuable commodities, asked the pilot when this rock would be passed: but each moment appearing to him long until he was secure from the danger it involved, he repeated his question so often that the pilot impatiently told him "the rock was passed." The merchant, transported with joy at this announcement, rashly exclaimed, that "God himself could not now make him poor." But in a little while, the vessel *did* reach and struck on the White Stone, and all his wealth was in a moment engulfed in the deep sea. His life alone was spared, which he spent in misery and remorse.

Friend Hopper and the Due Bill.

UPON a certain occasion a man called upon Isaac T. Hopper, the Quaker, with a due bill for twenty dollars against an estate he had been appointed to settle. Friend Hopper put it aside, saying he would attend to it as soon as he had leisure. The man called again a short time after, and stated that he had need of six dollars, and was willing even to give a receipt for the whole if that sum were advanced just then. This proposition excited suspicion, and the administrator decided in his own mind that he would pay nothing on that demand till he had examined the papers of the deceased. Searching carefully among these, he found a receipt for the money, mentioning the identical items, date, and circumstances of the transaction, and stating that a due bill had been given and lost, and was to be restored to the creditor when found. When, therefore, the man called again, Isaac said to him, in a quiet way :

"Friend Jones, I understand thou hast become pious lately."

He replied in a solemn tone : "Yes, thanks to the Lord Jesus, I have found out the way of salvation."

"And thou hast been dipped, I hear,"

continued the Quaker. "Dost thou know James Hunter ? ".

Mr. Jones answered in the affirmative.

"Well, he was also dipped some time ago," rejoined friend Hopper, "but the neighbors say they didn't get the crown of his head under water. The devil crept into the unbaptized part, and has been busy with him ever since. I'm afraid they didn't get *thee* quite under water. I think thou hadst better be dipped again."

As he thus spoke, he held up the receipt for twenty dollars. The countenance of the pretended pious man became scarlet, and he disappeared instantly.

Bit of Yankee Financiering in Wall Street.

A LITTLE colloquy, after the following fashion, is reported in the *Knickerbocker*, as having occurred in the counting house of a mercantile firm : "A man kind o' picks up a good many idees abeout. I larnt a few in Wall street." "In Wall street ? " "Yes ; 'see, I studied it eôut while I was stage drivin'. I got a little change together ; didn't know where to place it ; couldn't hire it eôut hum, 'cause I was pleadin' poverty all the time ; that, 'see, wouldn't deu : so I goes deôwn and claps it in the Dry Dock Bank ; got five per cent., tew. Had a brother thair who was teller. One day I 'gin a check for fifty dollars : all right. At last the bank got in trouble : I had some four or five thousand dollars ; I goes to my brother and draws eôut my money—he pays me in Bank of —— notes. Well, I took 'em hum, but they forgot to take côut my check for fifty dollars. So I goes, and sez I, 'I owe you fifty that you haint charged me ; will you take your own notes ? ' 'Sartin,' says they ; so I pays 'em in notes that I bought at twenty-five off. 'That's a good spec,' says I ; so I goes areôund, and buys up about tew hundred Dry Dock notes. When I got to the city, I couldn't pass 'em off. I tried a good many banks—no go. At last they creöwded me off the pavement in Wall street, the creöwd was so big, and I stood in the middle of the street, and calc'lated. 'I've got the idee,' sez I; 'I'll come country over 'em.' So I walked into the Bank of ——, took off my hat, and looked areöund as if didn't know what I was abeöut. I know'd the cashier; so he comes up : ' Sam ! ' sez he, ' what neöw ? —how's the family ?' ' All well,' sez I, ' but what's the matter with your banks ? I don't know who to depend on. Here's your neighbor, the Dry Dock's, gone, and maybe you'll go next; and I've got abeöut five thousand dollars of your money, and I guess I'll come deöwn to draw the specie.' I expect I must a-looked as if I was frightened to death ; for he said to once, ' Deön't do that, Sam ! ' sez he ; ' you'll frighten the hull country, and they'll come and run us.' ' Can't help it,' sez I; ' here's abeöut tew hundred dollars of the Dry Dock, and if I don't get the money somewhere before I go hum, I'll draw on you seöon.' ' Heöw much ?' sez he : ' Abeöut tew hundred.' ' We'll take it, Sam,' sez he, ' and you keep our paper.' ' Well,' sez I, ' on that condition I'll keep still.' I guess I made my twenty-five per cent. eöut of Wall street that time, ' if I am Dutch ' —as the saying is ! "

Taking him at his Word.

" WILL you give me a glass of ale, please ? " asked a rather seedy-ish looking person, with an old but well-brushed coat, and a'most too shiny a hat. It was produced by the bartender, creaming over the edge of the tumbler. " Thanky'e," said the recipient as he placed it to his lips. Having finished it at a swallow, he smacked his lips, and said : " That is very fine ale—very. Whose is it ?" " It is Harman's ale." " Ah ! Harman's, eh ? well, give us another glass of it." It was done, and

holding it up to the light and looking through it, the connoisseur said : " 'Pon my word, it is superb ale— superb ! clear as madeira. I must have some more of that. Give me a mug of it." The mug was furnished, but, before putting it to his lips, the imbiber said : " Whose ale did you say this was ?" " Harman's," emphatically repeated the bartender. The mug was exhausted, and also the vocabulary of praise ; and it only remained for the appreciative gentleman to say, as he wiped his mouth and went toward the door : " Harman's ale, is it ? I know Harman very well—I shall see him soon, and will settle with him for two glasses and a mug of his incomparable brew ! Good mawning ! "

Lodging a Banker in the Gutter.

THERE is a class of retail dealers in London who keep accounts with bankers, but who seldom, or perhaps never, have the privilege of the entrée to a banker's parlor or " sweating room." (A banker's parlor is called a " sweating room," a significant term, as all who have been under the necessity of asking for " accommodation " will readily allow.) This privilege is almost exclusively enjoyed by the merchants and wholesale dealers ; and on this account the retail tradesman scarcely knows the person of the banker with whom he lodges his money, or the banker that of his customer. This ignorance gave rise to a ludicrous scene between a wealthy London banker and a baker, one of his customers.

It happened on a certain day that the baker had paid in to his account a large sum of money, and on his retiring from the bank he paused on the step of the door, and began to reflect which way he should steer his course. While in this position of innocent uncertainty, as ill luck would have it, the banker came up ; and, as he could not pass the dusty baker without touching him, and thus soiling his own clothes —for the baker was in his working gear—he very haughtily said : "Move away, fellow.". This language, applied to a trader who had just paid five hundred pounds in to his account, which already had a large sum to his credit, was, to say the least of it, very irritating, and such as the baker thought, no doubt, he ought to resent, for he replied : " I shan't move for you nor any coxcomb like you ; and, what's more, if you give me your lip again in that manner, I'll put your nose in the kennel."

The banker, not being, in his turn, used to such a mode of address, still authoritatively ordered the baker to move and let him pass, or he would let him know who he was. Words ran very high. At last the pugnacious baker, unable any longer to restrain his passion, with one blow—for he was a powerful man—*knocked the banker into the gutter.* The banker's fall shook Lombard street ; but, unlike most bankers, who, when they fall, fall like Lucifer, never to rise again, he did rise, and, rushing into his banking shop, covered with mud, foaming with rage, and followed by the still bristling baker, eager for a clinch, he called loudly for the parties to fetch a constable to " take this fellow into custody."

The cashier, who but a few minutes before had attended upon the baker, to his utter amazement witnessed this extraordinary scene. He immediately ran to the banker, and whispered in his ear : " That is Mr. ——, our customer." These few words acted upon the excitable feelings of the banker in the same manner as oil upon troubled water ; for, without uttering another word, he retired to his room—which, on this occasion, might with peculiar propriety be called a " sweating room," and after a while requested the cashier to calm the belligerent baker, who, in a menacing attitude, was still chewing the

cud of his resentment outside the room. This the cashier soon effected ; and the customer was then, for the first time, formally introduced to him, when apologies were mutually interchanged, and the banker and baker were from that day well known to each other.

The Prince Regent's Wine and the Confidential Dealer.

AN anecdote is related in *Tait's Magazine* of the Prince Regent, which gives some insight into the mysteries of the wine trade. The incidents of the case relate to how the Prince Regent had, in a corner of his cellar, a small quantity of remarkably fine wine, of a peculiar quality and flavor ; how, this wine remaining untouched for some time, the household thought their master had forgotten it, and to make up for this inexcusable lapse of memory, took upon themselves to drink it nearly out ; how the prince, one day, expecting some illustrious connoisseurs to dinner, ordered this particular wine to be served, and thus threw " the household " into a state of consternation, and how one of them hastened thereupon to take *confidential counsel of a wine merchant* in the city, who quickly allayed his terrors. " Send me," said the ingenious dealer, " a bottle of what remains, and I will send you in return as much wine of that description as you want ; only you must take care that what I send is drunk immediately." This advice was followed, the success was complete. The Prince Regent and his distinguished guests (so the story goes) were delighted with this rare old wine, whose peculiar merits had been so long overlooked. Three or four times afterward, the prince, whose taste in wine was exquisite, ordered some from the same batch ; and on every occasion the confidential dealer had recourse to his private vineyard in his cellar, and " the mixture as before " was forthcoming. This process was continued until " the household," fearing a discovery, thought it prudent to inform their royal master that the stock of this favorite beverage was exhausted.

"Dummies," or Counterfeit Show Windows.

IT is stated that the demand for "dummies" has wonderfully increased in the large towns of England, as well as on the Continent, since the recent elevation and widening of shop windows. Though the shopkeeper may carry his magnificent crystal windows up to the first or second floor, as many of them do, it is out of his power to conveniently lift the heads of his customers to the same level; he consequently finds out, sooner or later, that it is a losing game to exhibit his perishable stock at a height of half a dozen feet or more above the heads of the public, and he has recourse to the maker of dummies, who can counterfeit any description of solid-looking goods, and save him from the deterioration which would befall genuine goods thus exposed to the glare and dust, damp, smoke, &c.

The dummies, therefore, go aloft, and economically fill in the ample background, and, for purposes of show, their attractive appearance enables them to be used about as advantageously as the real article. They are not, however, confined to the window solely; a young tradesman with a small capital may fill the major portion of his shelves with a "rich stock of goods," by means of dummies, displacing them gradually by real wares, as success enables him to do so.

Pieces of linen, rolls of broadcloth or Brussels carpeting, splendid brocades, whole fathoms of backs of elegantly bound books, chests of tea, huge tuns of "Old Tom," or real Jamaica rum, packets of patent medicines, and innumerable things besides, are counterfeited with such perfect effect as to reality and beauty, as to defy recognition by a stranger—nay, the tradesman himself will sometimes lay hands on the dummy, mistaking it for a genuine piece of goods.

Smuggled Needles and the American Eagle.

SOMEBODY tells the following anecdote, capital of its kind: In the time of the last war, there were two hotheaded politicians, whose contempt for John Bull was so hearty, that, taking their own word for it, they would not so much as eat with a knife and fork of English manufacture, if they could avoid it. During the war, the English had possession of Castine, at the head of Penobscot Bay, and smuggling English goods from that place into the country was extensively practised. The temptation was too great for the cupidity of our two republicans, and finally overcame all their scruples. I lived at that time (says the narrator) in an eastern town, and one bitter cold night in February, I was called, at two o'clock, from my bed, by two men whom I never knew before, to go and receive several loads of smuggled goods, which, by direction of my employer, I took into the cellar, through a back way in the store where I was a clerk, and secreted them carefully.

One of the sleighs was loaded with hardware, and in crossing the ferry over the Kennebeck, they met with a sad accident. The only ferry boat was a large, flat gondola. When they arrived on the opposite side, intending to stop for some refreshment, they drove the sleighs out of the gondola, except the hindmost one, which, being loaded with the hardware, was very heavy, and tipped the boat very much. This was permitted to remain, and while they were regaling themselves, the tide rose, overflowed the sides of the boat, and sank it. The goods were, of course, wet. Among them was a package of sewing needles, and being accustomed to handling such goods, our republicans employed me to open, dry, and repack them in emery, which I did very carefully, at the expense of several days' labor. Needles were many times as dear then as now, so that the case was valued at some hundreds of dollars, which, but for my care and industry, would have been spoiled entirely. And one day, when a custom-house officer came into the store to search for smuggled goods, I showed him every place in the store *except* where they were. The goods were delivered out again, and sent in small parcels to Boston and New York, for sale.

The pains I had taken, and the value of my services, led me to expect a generous reward, and I congratulated myself with the *anticipated profits of fidelity* to the trust reposed in me. When the last package of goods was removed, one of the smugglers came to me and said, " You are a capital little fellow; if I had you in my store you would be worth your weight in gold. Always be as faithful, and you will always be trusted."

Expectation was now on tiptoe; I would not have given a sixpence to insure a twenty-dollar bill in my hand the next moment, but, like most high worldly hopes, mine were doomed to disappointment. The republican smuggler put his hand in his pocket and *solemnly drew forth an American half dollar!* "That," said he, "is the real coin, the true *American eagle;* keep it, and be sure you always avoid an Englishman as you would an adder." He took his valise in his hand and walked toward the stage office; I looked after him till he was out of sight, and his gait, form, and figure, to the smallest outline, are as fresh in memory now as at that moment (I was then a boy), and the contempt I then felt for him has never been effaced. I have met him often in the streets of New York; he does not know me, but I never passed him without laughing, though I have kept his secret to this day.

Throwing Sawdust in the Eyes of Custom-House Officers.

AN ingenious *ruse* was played by a wag who, before the working of the saline springs of New York, made it a business to smuggle salt from Canada into the " States." One day, having got wind that he was suspected, he loaded his bags with sawdust, and drove past the tavern where the suspicious excisemen were waiting for him. He was ordered to stop, but he only increased his speed. At length he was overtaken, and his load inspected, with many imprecations from the eager officials, after which he was permitted to pass on. A day or two after he drove up again, with a full load of salt, and asked, banteringly, if they didn't want to search him again. " Go on! go on!" said the officials; " we've had enough of you!"

Snug Place for Bank Notes.

A GREAT number of false bank notes were at one time put into circulation within the dominions of the Czar. They could only have been imported; but although the strictest search was made habitually over every vessel entering a Russian port, no smuggling of false notes was discovered. Accident, however, at last brought the mystery to light. It happened that several cases of lead pencils arrived one day from England, and were being examined, when one of them fell out from a package, and the custom-house officer, picking it up, cut it to a point, and used it to sign the order which delivered up the cases to the consignee. He kept the one loose pencil for his own use; and a few days afterward, because it needed a fresh point, cut it again, and found that there was no more lead. Another chip into the cedar brought him to a roll of paper nested in a hollow place. This paper was one of the false notes engraved in London, and thus smuggled into the dominions of the Muscovite.

Parisian Female Smugglers.

THE smuggling of game and such taxable articles into Paris, under the petticoats of women, has become so frequent that a female has been attached to the bureau of the department, in order that she may search under the garments of suspected individuals of her sex. Recently a woman—known as the Hottentot Venus—presented herself at one of the gates. The agents, who are always jealous of stout people, requested the lady with the phenomenal contour to stop. She refused, and pushed by. One of the custom-house employés seized her, and commenced pressing his fingers on various parts of her fictitious body, as if he were feeling to see whether she was ripe. She screamed and fought, and in her struggles a partridge fell from under her skirts to the ground. Her contraband wares were probably strung like dried apples, and the escape of the partridge loosened the whole. Down came a quail, and then a snipe, and then another quail, and a woodcock, until the woman, whose *embonpoint* had now visibly diminished, was thrust into the office, where the female attendant of the establishment commenced a thorough investigation. When all was over, the victim was found to be a very spare person, not weighing over ninety-five pounds.

Smuggling by the Chinese.

ALTHOUGH the Chinese smugglers do not precisely fear the mandarin boats, they always endeavor to avoid them, unless they have come to some agreement. If, however, they cannot escape being overhauled, they endeavor to negotiate, and will offer the mandarin and his crew a *cumsha* (a present) in order to obtain permission to continue their voyage. They do not fight except at the last extremity, or unless the demands of the mandarin are too exorbitant—or, what is still more rare, unless that functionary shows himself inaccessible to corruption, and will not traffic his duties.

Doing Things on Shares.

HERE is a case illustrating the working of the "peculiar institution of" doing things on shares. A happened to have more pigs than he could keep, while his neighbor B had more milk than he could dispose of. One day, A brought two pigs over and deposited them in B's pen, saying that he wished B to keep them two months and have one of them as his share. B replied that, as he had plenty of feed, he would keep them four months and have them both, as, of course, that would amount to the same thing! A left, saying that he supposed it was all right, but guessed he wouldn't bring any more.

"Doing" and "Shaving" Customers.

"A FOOL and his money are soon parted"—a proverb not founded on fact, but a great favorite with merchant princes and cabmen on the occasion of their having, in their respective callings, succeeded in "doing" a liberal customer. With what gusto does the "gentleman" relate to his partner, over a bottle at his country seat, how easily the greenhorn took the bait! "An entire cargo—ten per cent. above the market price—said he supposed it was 'all right'—would take my word for it; ha! ha! ha!—a fool and his money are soon parted!" And listen to the humbler but not meaner chuckling of the hackdriver over his gin twist: "Charged him a dollar from Whitehall to the Astor—forked over the tin without a word! A fool and his money," etc. The fact is, an avaricious man sees no wit in liberality or open dealing. Shylock began it: "This

is the fool that lent out money gratis!"
It's all wrong. A Wall-street broker of
the best reputation once said that the
hardest man to "shave"—as he technically expressed himself—is a fool.
"Sir," said he, "you don't know where
to have 'em; you can't stick soft cheese
on a hook!"

Settling a Question of Taste and Trade.

*Mr. Jones was down to 'York once,
and being very fond o' sassengers, he
went into an eatin' shop to get some.
While he was a-hearin' of 'em fry, his-
sin' and sputterin' away, a man was
buyin' some of 'em raw at the counter,
and while he was a-tyin' of 'em up, a
chap came in with a fuz cap and a
dirty drab sustout, and laid down a little bundle at fur cend o' the counter.
He looked at the keeper, and see he
was a little busy; so he said, lookin'
sly at him as he went out, says he,
"'Tan't no matter about the money
now, but that makes eleven"— p'intin'
toward the bundle. Jones looked at
the bundle, and says he saw the *head
of a cat* stickin' out at the eend, with
long smellers onto it as long as his finger! He left *that* shop 'mazin' quick,
and has had no relish for the article
sence, tho' once so savory and tooth-
some to him.

"Newscloth."

A PUBLISHER in Greenock, Scotland,
having been fined for printing news on
unstamped sheets of paper—contrary to
the law in such cases—retaliated by
printing on *cloth*, which is not specified in the act—calling his journal the
"Greenock News*cloth*," in allusion to
the material.

Expedient of a Russian Miser.

A RUSSIAN merchant, who was so
immensely rich that on one occasion he
lent the Empress Catharine the Second

a million of roubles, used to live in a
small, obscure room in St. Petersburg,
with scarcely any fire, furniture, or attendants, though his house was larger
than many palaces. He buried his
money, in cash, in the cellar, and was
so great a miser that he barely allowed
himself the common necessaries of life.
He placed his principal security in a
large dog of singular fierceness, which
used to protect the premises by barking
nearly the whole of the night. At length
the dog died; when the master, either
impelled by his sordidness from buying
another dog, or fearing that he might
not meet with one that he could so well
depend on, adopted the singular method of performing the canine service
himself, by going his rounds every
evening, and barking as well and as
loud as he could, in imitation of his
more excusable beast.

Burns and the Drowning Merchant.

BURNS was standing one day upon
the quay at Greenock, when a most
wealthy merchant, belonging to the
town, had the misfortune to fall into
the harbor. He was no swimmer, and
his death would have been inevitable,
had not a sailor, who happened to
be passing at the time, immediately
plunged in, and, at the risk of his own
life, rescued him from his dangerous
situation.

The Greenock merchant, upon recovering a little from his fright, put his
hand into his pocket, and generously
presented the sailor with a—shilling!
The crowd, who were by this time collected, loudly protested against the
contemptible insignificance of the sum;
but Burns, with a smile of ineffable
scorn, entreated them to restrain their
clamor—"for," said he, "the gentleman is of course the best judge of the
value of his own life."

One Cent with Girard.

A GENTLEMAN from Europe purchased a bill of exchange on Girard, to defray the expenses of a tour to this country. It was duly honored on presentation; but in the course of their transactions, it so happened that *one cent* remained to be refunded on the part of the European; and, on the eve of his departure from this country, Girard dunned him for it. The gentleman apologized, and tendered him a six-and-a-quarter-cent piece, requesting the difference. Mr. Girard tendered him in change *five* cents, which the gentleman declined to accept, alleging that he was entitled to an additional quarter of a cent. In reply, Girard admitted the fact, but informed him that it was not in his power to comply, as the Government had neglected to provide the fractional coin in question, and returned the gentleman the six-cent piece, reminding him, however, in unmistakable language, that he must still consider him his debtor for the balance unpaid—the one cent.

Resolving to be Rich.

"I MEAN to be a rich man, cost what it may. A man is nothing in the world without wealth. With plenty of money he is everything. I mean to get rich, anyhow."

This was the soliloquy of a young merchant, who, with a small capital, had recently established himself in business. He made a stern resolve to be rich, and having great perseverance, he went busily to work in the execution of his project.

Everything was made subordinate to the realization of his golden vision. Ease and pleasure were out of the question. Domestic enjoyments were of no account. The merchant's brow ached with incessant care; his heart chilled and warmed with the rise and fall of the markets; the changes of commerce

shaped his dreams; money was his superlative idea. He had time for nothing but business. In vain did his wife languish under the weight of her domestic cares. He had no time to unbend himself at home, and contribute to the bliss of his little world there. Neither could he bestow attention to the wants of the world, nor the miseries of his fellow creatures around him. All calls were vain, for our merchant had neither eyes nor ears for aught but mammon.

After many years of toil and care—after enduring anxieties and labors sufficient to wear out his over-taxed energies—he had reached the goal. The merchant *had grown rich*—so rich that he could forsake the counting room, and live with princely splendor in a palace-like home!

This was the fulfilled vision of his youth. He had sought gold, and his massive coffers did, indeed, sweat beneath the weight of their glittering load; and when men passed him, they said, "That is old ——, the millionnaire."

Was the prize worth what it cost? Thirty years of sacrifice had been devoted to its pursuit! During that period, true enjoyment had been a stranger to his heart; how could it be otherwise? For thirty years he had not had *time* to be happy—he had surrendered all this for the expected advantage of future wealth! He had literally sold these for gold! He had his prize.

The merchant had not been many months out of the counting room before his mind, missing the stimulus of business, began to prey upon itself. For intellectual and philanthropic pursuits it had no sort of relish; they had been avoided so long for want of time, for the sake of the money god, that they would not now afford any satisfaction. Without occupation, the merchant's life became a blank. His mind sank into weakness, his memory failed, his energies dried up; first he sank into the imbecility of second childhood, and then into the stupidity of an idiot.

18

They carried him to the asylum of departed intellect, and there, ever talking of notes and ships, his soulless eyes gazing into vacancy, his fingers tracing figures in the air, the at last "successful" merchant ended his days with maniacs and fools, and the treasures which he had heaped up were gathered and enjoyed by others. This is no fancy sketch.

Hard Philosophy of an Annuity Monger.

AUDLEY, the old English banker, usurer, and what not, was equally ready to lend money to the gay gallants of the town on annuities, as he was to receive it from the thrifty poor who took, on "the security of the great Audley," the savings of their youth to secure an annuity for their age. But needy as the youngsters of that day might be, the usurer was as willing as they were needy. He lent them, however, with affected remonstrances on their extravagance, and took the cash they paid him with a well-feigned air of paternal regret. His money bred. He formed temporary partnerships with the stewards of country gentlemen, and having, by the aid of the former, gulled the latter, finished by smartly cheating the associates who had assisted him to his prey.

The annuity monger was also a philosopher. He never pressed for his debts when he knew they were safe. When one of his victims, mistakenly assuming Audley to possess a conscience, asked him where it was, he replied, "We moneyed people must balance accounts. If you don't pay me my annuity, you cheat me; if you do, I cheat you." He said his deeds were his children, which nourished best by sleeping.

His word was his bond, as many could testify to their sorrow; his hour was punctual, striking terror to the unprepared; his opinions were compressed and sound. In his time he was called "the great Audley," "old Audley," &c.;

and though the fathers of the church proclaimed the sin of usury to be the original sin, he smiled at their assertions, and went on his golden way rejoicing. As his wealth increased, he put himself in a position where his annuity jobbing increased—an office in the Court of Wards—the entire fortunes of the wards of Chancery being under his control.

When he quarrelled with one who disputed the payment of an annuity, and who, to prove his resisting power, showed and shook his money bags, Audley sarcastically asked "whether they had any bottom?" The exulting possessor answered in the affirmative. "In that case," replied Audley, "I care not, for in my office I have a constant spring." Here, indeed, he pounced upon encumbrances which lay upon estates; he prowled about to discover the cravings of their owners, and this he did to such purpose that, when asked what was the value of his office, he replied, "Some thousands of pounds to any one who wishes to get to heaven immediately; twice as much to him who does not mind being in purgatory; and nobody knows what to him who will adventure to go to hell." Charity forbids a guess as to which of these places Audley himself went.

Old-School Money Jobbers.

THE old English money brokers had arts peculiar to their day. They had a walk upon the Exchange devoted to the funds of the East India and other great corporations, and many of the terms now in vogue among the initiated arose from their dealings with that description of stock. Jobbing in the great chartered corporations was thoroughly understood—reports and rumors were as plentiful and well-managed as now. No sooner was it known that one of the fine vessels of the East India Company, laden with gold and jewels from the East, was on its way, than every method was had recourse to. Men were employed to whisper of hurricanes which had sunk the well-stored ship; of quicksands which had swallowed her up; of war, which had commenced when peace was unbroken; or of peace being concluded when things were actually in the utmost danger.

Nor were the brains of the speculators less capable than now. If at the present day an English banker condescends to raise a railway or other kind of bubble fifty per cent., the broker or money jobber of that day understood his craft sufficiently to cause a variation in the price of East India stock of two hundred and sixty-three per cent! Everything which could inflate the hopes of the schemer, was brought into operation by the brokers. If shares were dull, they jobbed in the funds, or tried exchequer bills; and if these failed, rather than remain idle, they dealt in bank notes at forty per cent. discount.

Sober citizens were entangled as well as the more adventurous. Their first impulse was to laugh at the stories currently circulated of fortunes lost and won; but when they saw men who were yesterday threadbare pass them to-day in their carriages—when they saw wealth which it took their plodding industry years of patient labor to acquire, won by others in a few weeks—unable to resist the temptation, the greatest merchants deserted their regular vocations for these more glittering avenues to fortune.

These jobbers came from all classes of society, and those who won were at once on a par with the nobility. As an illustration of these ups and downs, it is related that a worthy Quaker, a watchmaker by trade, having successfully speculated in the shares and funds, was of sufficient importance to invite to the marriage feast of his daughter such guests as the Duchess of Marlborough and the Princess of Wales, who, with three hundred others of "the quality," graced the wedding entertainment.

Making a Good Job of it.

A WORKMAN recently purchased, in a small provincial town of Germany, ten pounds of powdered sugar; but on examining it, he found that the grocer had generously mixed with it at least a pound of lime. On the succeeding day he advertised as follows in the public prints: "Should the grocer who sold me a pound of lime along with nine pounds of sugar, not bring to me the pound he cheated me of, I shall forthwith disclose his name in the papers." The next day the customer received nine pounds of sugar from several different grocers who had similar actions on their conscience, and feared publicity. The customer was so well satisfied, that at last accounts he was making a vigorous examination of his recent supplies of coffee, spices, etc., and the prospect was that he would soon be performing among the grocers what the bull enacted in the crockery shop.

French Usurers and Pigeons.

THE chronicles of the French money and credit system partake of that piquancy which might naturally be looked for among such a lively race. There are usurers, courtiers, pigeons, &c., &c., almost without number. But the usurer never sees the pigeon, or very rarely. He is banker, count, minister of state, director of theatres, lives in a grand hotel of his own, gives dinners to princes, dresses superbly à la mode, and is far above the acquaintance of a mere pigeon. This he leaves to the courtier, a genteel and knowing personage, who deals in everything. He tells the pigeon that if M. ——, not being inclined to part with his ready money, can only give wine or furniture in exchange for the bill, he, the courtier, will undertake the sale, and this he does, upon occasion. But in the majority of instances, wine, furniture, and all the rest of the old story, is a mere pretence. ,

The pigeon proposes a bill. The agent, or *faiseur*, goes to the banker and gets it done at fifty per cent. in ready money. He returns to the pigeon, says that the bill is discounted, but that the price is given in goods, which he will not undertake to sell. In two or three days he returns with the story that the goods are not to be sold. The pigeon is impatient. The faiseur then offers to take the goods at his own risk. at a discount. This the pigeon is only too glad to do, and gets one half of the money which was received by the faiseur—just one quarter of his bill. The faiseur gets the other half, without any risk whatever; and in half an hour is to be seen trotting down the Rue Vivienne, eager for the excitement of the new loan or the latest scheme.

Instances are known where the pigeon has taken a horse for a note of a thousand francs. The horse remains in the stable of the courtier, who in a few days sends in the bill for its keep—thirty francs. The pigeon orders the horse to be sold at auction. It fetches twenty-seven francs! All the pigeon gets by the transaction is the pleasure of paying three francs ready money, and the bill, when it becomes due. In another case, a young man is known to have signed a note of twenty-eight thousand francs; he was credited in return with sixty thousand blocks of marble, eleven thousand mouse traps, six thousand iron rods, and three thousand francs in money. The marble remained in the quarry; no one would buy it *in situ*, or advance the large sum necessary to remove it. The mouse traps and the rods sold for about one thousand francs, and the pigeon was finally credited four thousand francs, of which he received about half, the courtier pocketing the rest.

———

Imitating Signatures.

THE imitation of signatures with inconceivable accuracy was a quality possessed by John Mathison, an English mechanic, and probably never surpassed by any one in any country or age. Tempted by the hope of sudden wealth, he applied this faculty to the forging of bank notes, which, being discovered, a reward was offered, with a description of his person, and he escaped to Scotland. There, scorning to let his wonderful talent lie idle, he counterfeited the notes of the Royal Bank of Scotland, amused himself by negotiating them during a pleasure excursion through the country, and reached London, supported by his imitative talent. Here a fine sphere opened for his genius, which was so active, that in twelve days he had bought the copper, engraved it, fabricated notes, forged the watermark, printed, and negotiated several. When he had a sufficient number, he travelled from one end of the kingdom to the other, disposing of them. Having been in the habit of procuring notes from the bank—the more accurately to copy them—he chanced to be there when a clerk from the excise office paid in seven thousand guineas, one of which was scrupled. Mathison, from a distance, said it was a good one. "Then," said the bank clerk, on the trial, "I recollected him."

The frequent visits of Mathison, who was very incautious, together with other circumstances, created some suspicion that he might be connected with those notes, which, since his first appearance, had been presented at the bank. On another occasion, when Mathison was there, a forged note of his own was presented, and the teller, half in jest and half in earnest, charged Maxwell—the name by which he was known—with some knowledge of the forgeries. Further suspicion was excited, and directions were given to detain him at some future period. The following day, the teller was informed that "his friend Maxwell," as he was styled ironically, was in Cornhill. The clerk instantly went, and under the pretence of having paid Mathison a guinea too much on a previous occasion, and of losing his situation if the mistake were not rectified by the books, induced him to return with him to the hall; from which place he was taken before the directors. To all the inquiries he replied, "He had a reason for declining to answer. He was a citizen of the world, and knew not how he had come into it, or how he should go out of it." Being detained during a consultation with the bank solicitor, he suddenly jumped out of the window. On being taken and asked his motive, if innocent, he said "it was his humor."

In the progress of the inquiry, the Darlington paper, containing his description, was read to him, when he turned pale, burst into tears, and saying he was a dead man, added, "now I will confess all." He was, indeed, found guilty only on his own acknowledgment, which stated he could accomplish the whole of a note in one day. It was asserted at the time, that, had it not been for this confession, he could not have been convicted. He offered to explain the secret of his discovery of the water-mark, provided the corporation would spare his life; but his proposal was rejected, and he paid the penalty of his crime.

Bad Bank Bill.

A CITY journal, describing a new counterfeit bank bill, says the vignette is "cattle and hogs, with a church far in the distance." A good illustration of the world!

Selling a Bad Article.

AT a business meeting of one of the Methodist churches in Philadelphia, not long since, a rare incident occurred, as showing the relation which a man's business may sustain toward his standing as a church member. The question on the tapis, among the official members of said church, was to find a suitable man to fill a vacancy in the board of trustees. A gentleman in business as a wholesale grocer was named by a member present as a very suitable man for the place; but his nomination was vehemently opposed by another brother, who was very zealous in the temperance cause, on the ground that in the way of his business he sold liquor. And appealing to Brother A., one of the oldest members present, who, from his solid and clerical look, was called "the Bishop," he said, "What do you say, Brother A.?"

"Ah!" said Brother A., looking very grave, drawing up his cane with a view to emphasize and give point to what he had to say, "that is not the worst of it" (solemn shake of the head); "*that* is not the worst of it!"

"Why, Brother A.," said the others, crowding around and looking for some astounding developments, "what else is there?"

"Why," said Brother A., bringing down his cane with a rap, "he don't keep a good article—I've tried it!"

Prejudice against Yankee Clock Peddlers, and how it was Overcome.

NEAR one of the rural villages in Ohio there dwelt, a few years since, an elderly gentleman, who went by the familiar name of "Uncle Jonathan." He was a rigid member of the Lutheran church, sober, exemplary, and withal, possessed of considerable wealth. Like many of his neighbors in that region of the country, he entertained a bitter prejudice toward "Yankees;" and, notwithstanding his piety, he had avowed his intention of kicking out of his door the first Yankee clock-peddler that should enter.

One sultry day in summer a covered wagon was drawn up to his gate; a keen-eyed, gaunt-looking individual alighted, and rapping softly at the door, requested, in subdued tones, a drink of water. After drinking, the traveller asked permission of the old gentleman to sit and rest for a few minutes, saying he was overcome by the heat. The stranger said but little, and the old gentleman eyed him suspiciously. Presently the old man's eye began to brighten.

"What papers have you got there?" said he, pointing to the stranger's pocket, which bore the appearance of a travelling post office.

"Oh," said the stranger, "those are a few copies of our *Lutheran Observer* that I carry to read along the road."

"Indeed! Then you belong to the Lutheran Church?"

"Yes, sir. Would you not like to look at a copy of the paper?"

The old man was delighted; asked stranger to stay for dinner. Of course he accepted. As they were putting up the team, the old gentleman remarked, "You drive a queer-looking wagon."

"Yes," said the stranger; "I have been out West, and have suffered several months from chills and fever. Wishing to get home to my family, and having no means of defraying my expenses, I purchased a few clocks to sell along the way."

Stranger stayed, and fed himself and horses without money and without price. He did more. He sold Uncle Jonathan every clock on his wagon, and took his note, which he turned into money within two hours.

"Well," said the landlord, "didn't I tell you that he would abuse you?"

"Very much mistaken," said Yankee; "the old man is a gentleman. Here, take these papers [*Observers*]; I have no further use for them."

Uncle Jonathan is silent on the subject of Yankee clock peddlers.

Risks of the Currency.

A ROCHESTER darkey named Pete got a five-dollar counterfeit bill, and taking some friends to a lager beer saloon, treated them to the extent of forty cents, passed the bill, and got the change. The Dutchman soon found the bill was bad, and overhauling Pete, charged him with passing counterfeit money. Pete expressed great surprise, said he knew where he got the bill, and would take it and get a good one for it. This was agreed to, but day after day passed, and Pete did not bring back the money. The Dutchman overhauled him again, and Pete said the man who gave it to him was now trying to get it back from the man *he* took it from. The Dutchman was furious, and threatened to have him taken up for passing counterfeit money. "Guess you couldn't do that," said Pete; "can't took up a man for passing counterfeit money, when *you hain't got de bill!*" This was a new idea to Mr. Lagerbeer and Pete comforted him by paying him a dollar and a half of the change, as he said, "goin' halves" with him in the loss of the V.

Making Change at Railroad Refreshment Stands.

YEARS ago Lewis Holt kept a railroad refreshment stand at the station at Attica, on the road running west. He had a way which men of his persuasion have —not altogether abandoned—of taking the money of passengers, sweeping it into his drawer, and fumbling after the change till the cars were *off*, when the passenger would have to run and leave his money. Charlie Dean stepped out of the cars there one day, took a "ginger pop," price six cents, laid down a quarter, which Holt dropped into his till, and went hunting to get the change. Away went the cars, and Charlie jumped on without his change; but he had time to read the name of

LEWIS HOLT over the door, and, making a note of it, rode on.

Postage was high in those days, and was not required in advance. From Buffalo he wrote a letter to Holt— "Sell foam at 25 cents a glass, will you?" Holt paid ten cents on this letter, and ten more on one from Detroit, and twenty-five on another from St. Louis, and for two or three years he kept getting letters from his unknown customer, and would have got more to this day, but for the law requiring postage to be paid in advance. He had to pay two or three dollars in postage before the letters ceased to come, and as they were always directed in a new handwriting, he hoped each one was of more importance than the ones before.

Weighing Short.

A WESTERN man, too smart by half for his own interest or the good of his soul, drove into town with a load of wheat in bags, to be sold by weight, so many pounds to the bushel. Finding a merchant ready to purchase, the seller demurred to the proposal to drive upon the buyer's scales, as he was afraid he might not be fairly dealt with. "Very well," said the merchant, "if you prefer it, drive on and be weighed out there," pointing to the next platform. On he went, keeping his seat on the load; the merchant opened a little door in the floor, asked the seller how many bags there were, and being told twenty, pronounced the load to be forty-two bushels. "All right!" said the seller, and then returned and deposited his wheat at the buyer's store and went off, never finding out that he had been weighed on the platform of a fire cistern, and that he had sold fifty bushels of wheat for forty-two!

Italian Knavery in Picture Selling.

IF modern copies and paintings in Florence can be counted by myriads,

there seems to be equally a mine of old copies and originals as inexhaustible as the coal pits of England. For centuries Italy has been furnishing the rest of Europe with pictures, yet the supply still remains as plentiful as its beggars. Lumber rooms are stored with them; streets are lined with them; every tailor has his gallery; each Italian gentleman his heirlooms; in short, Florence is a vast picture shop. One would imagine that every man, woman, and child, for the last century, had been born with pencil in hand. There is no possibility of diminishing them. One dealer has sold *twelve thousand* in England alone—at least he says so—and yet his rooms are full to repletion, though he is diminishing his stock to give up business. Cargoes go annually to the United States—the matter being much after this wise:

A speculator arrives, and gives out that he is a purchaser of pictures by the wholesale. A flock of crows cannot light sooner upon an open cornbag, than do the sellers upon him. He is not after good pictures, but the trash that can be bought for the value of the wood in their frames. They are brought to him by wagon loads. He looks at the pile, and makes an offer according to its size. In this way he buys several thousand daubs at an average of a few dimes each, spends as much more in varnish, regilding, and a little retouching, sends them to America, where they are duly offered for sale as so many Titians, Vandykes, Murillos, or other lights of the European school. One lucky sale pays for the entire lot. No other art affords a wider scope for fraud. There are fair dealers, but Italian reputation in general, in this respect, is of a slippery character. A dealer will sometimes practise his trickery after this fashion: have a fine copy, in a frame, exposed as a sample, for which a buyer is found, at what appears a reasonable price, the bargain concluded, and the purchaser's name marked by himself on the back of the picture. Upon receiving it at home, however, he could not believe his own senses, so inferior did it appear to the one he selected; but on the back there was the veritable evidence of his own handwriting. Upon investigation, it was proved that the seller had two pictures in the same frame, the outer one being good and the inner bad, and that he had withdrawn the former and sent the latter.

"To what Base Uses have we Come at Last!"

WHEN poor Law's "Mississippi scheme" had run itself out, to the terrible damage of those who had invested in it, the excitement knew no bounds, and there were thousands of ruined and frenzied men seeking to lay revengeful hands upon the author of their misery. Law took good care not to expose himself unguarded in the streets. Shut up in the apartments of the Regent, he was secure from all attack, and, whenever he ventured abroad, it was either *incognito*, or in one of the royal carriages, with a powerful escort. An amusing anecdote is recorded of the detestation in which he was held by the people, and the ill-treatment he would have met, had he fallen into their hands.

A merchant by the name of Boursel was passing in his carriage down the Rue St. Antoine, when his further progress was stayed by a hackney coach that had blocked up the road. M. Boursel's servant called impatiently to the hackney coachman to get out of the way, and, on his refusal, struck him a spirited smack on the face. A crowd was soon drawn together by the disturbance, and M. Boursel got out of the carriage to restore order. The hackney coachman, imagining now that he had another assailant, bethought him of an ingenious feint to rid himself of both, and called out as loudly as he was able:

"Help! help! murder! murder! *Here are Law and his servant going to kill me!* Help! help!"

At this cry, the people came out of their shops, armed with sticks and other weapons, while the mob gathered stones to inflict summary vengeance upon the supposed financier. Happily for M. Boursel and his servant, the door of a church near by stood wide open, and, seeing the fearful odds against them, the two rushed toward it with all speed. They reached the altar, still pursued by the people, and would have been ill-treated even there, if, finding the door open leading to the sacristy, they had not sprang through, and closed it after them. The mob were then persuaded to leave the church by the alarmed and indignant priests; and, finding M. Boursel's carriage still in the streets, they vented their ill-will against it, and did it considerable damage.

Little did the once powerful and pampered Law imagine that he would thus ever be made the convenient scapegoat of a hackney coachman!

Plan to Ruin the Ancient Firm of Child & Co. by the Bank of England.

IT is well known that in the year 1745, on account of the domestic confusion which prevailed in some parts of England, bank notes were at a considerable discount. The notes, however, which were issued by Child's house, as well as those of Hoare & Co., still maintained their credit, and were circulated at par. The bank directors, alarmed at the depreciation of their paper, and attributing it to the high estimation in which the house of Messrs. Child still remained, attempted, by very unfair artifices, to ruin their reputation. This plan they endeavored to accomplish by collecting a very large quantity of their notes, and pouring them all in together for payment on the same day. Before the project was executed, her Grace, the Duchess of Marlborough, who had received some intimation of it, imparted the information to Mr. Child, and supplied him with a sum of money more than sufficient to answer the amplest demand that could be made upon them. In consequence of this scheme, the notes were sent by the bank, and were paid in their own paper—a circumstance which occasioned considerable loss to that corporation, their paper being circulated considerably below par. Perhaps this anecdote finds confirmation in the well-known circumstance of the hostility of her Grace to the administrators of that trust.

Bubble Prospectuses.

THE most laughable reading may be found by looking over the prospectuses of the joint-stock bubble companies which flourished in England in 1824. At that time mines were proposed in all parts of the world. One was issued at a premium avowedly for the benefit of the projector. Another was celebrated " for having a vein of tin ore in its bottom, as pure and solid as a tin flagon." A third was pronounced by the directors as " no speculative undertaking—no problematic or visionary scheme—it was founded on a sure and permanent basis, adopted after months of mature deliberation, after inquiries, surveys, investigations, and reports;" and this was dissolved almost immediately. Another declared that " lumps of pure gold, weighing from two to fifty pounds, were totally neglected," and that its mines alone would yield " considerably more than the quantity necessary for the supply of the whole world." The romantic aspect of the land was described in a fifth; while a sixth, proposing to supply England with granite, lamented, in plausible and poetic strain, the " soft and perishable materials " of the buildings of " the mighty head of a mighty empire." Innumerable laborers and artisans were to be employed, " and," continued the prospectus, " perhaps by the efforts of this company the dingy brick fronts, the disgrace of the metropolis, may give way to more durable and magnificent elevations, worthy of the throne of the queen of the isles."

PART FIFTH.

ANECDOTES OF FAMOUS COMMERCIAL RESORTS AND LOCALITIES.

NATHAN MEYER ROTHSCHILD.

Died at Frankfort. O.M., July 28, 1836.   Aged Sixty Years

PART FIFTH.

Anecdotes of Famous Commercial Resorts and Localities.

THE EXCHANGE, CUSTOM HOUSE, BOARDS OF TRADE, MARKETS, ETC.—THEIR ANNALS, USAGES, PECULIARITIES; WITH PERSONAL MISCELLANIES, APHORISMS, ODDITIES, WHIMS, AND CAPRICES OF THEIR HABITUÉS.

Business is the salt of life, which not only gives a grateful smack to it, but dries up those crudities that would offend.—ARION.

Long has this worthy been conversant in bartering, and knows, that when stocks are lowest, it is the time to buy.—TATLER.

I'll *give* thrice so much land
To any well-deserving friend;
But in the way of *bargain*—mark me!
I'll cavil on the ninth part of a hair.
SHAKSPEARE'S "HENRY IV."

And conscience, truth, and honesty are made
To rise and fall, like other wares of trade.—MOORE.

Custom-House Official Dealing with a Princess.

THE Princess of Prussia having ordered some rich silks from Lyons, which paid a high duty at Stettin, the place of her residence, the custom-house officer rudely seized them, until the duties were paid. The princess, highly indignant at such an affront, desired the officer to bring the silks to her apartments. He did so, when the princess seized them, and giving the officer a few cuffs in the face, turned him out of doors. The proud and mortified man of excise, in a violent fit of resentment, presented a memorial to Frederic the Great, in which he complained bitterly of the dishonor put upon him in the execution of his office. The king, having read the memorial, returned the following answer: "Sir, the loss of the duties belongs to my account; the silks are to remain in the possession of the princess —the cuffs with him who received them. As to the supposed dishonor, I cancel it at the request of the complainant; but it is itself null, for the lily hand of a fair lady cannot possibly dishonor the face of a custom-house officer. FREDERIC."

Rencontre between Rothschild and Rose the Broker, on 'Change.

There was no more constant attendant on 'Change, every Tuesday and Friday, than Rothschild, and, for years, he was in the habit of planting himself at a particular spot, with his back to the pillar known to every frequenter of that precinct as "Rothschild's pillar;" but, alas for human greatness! he was on one occasion doomed to the sad annoyance, that he had no especial right to that particular spot. A person of the name of Rose, possessed of great courage, one Tuesday afternoon purposely placed himself on the spot hitherto occupied by the world's financial dictator. On Mr. Rothschild's approach, he requested the party to move. This was just what the other expected, and what he was prepared to dispute. He argued that this was the royal exchange, free to all ; and he, as a British subject, had a right to stand there if he thought fit. This doctrine could not of course be disputed, but he was told that it was the spot that Mr. Rothschild invariably occupied, and, as such, ought to be yielded; but no ! Mr. Rose, being a powerful man, defied Mr. Rothschild and all his tribe to remove him. For nearly three-quarters of an hour—the most valuable portion of the exchange time—did he keep deliberate possession of the autocrat's pillar ; and not until the whole business of the exchange of the day was jeopardized did Mr. Rose, after having, as he said, established his right, retire, amidst the yells and howls of the friends of Rothschild there assembled.

Paying Government Fishing Bounties.

ON the accession of a new auditor in one of our custom houses, several years ago, he found considerable looseness in the machinery by which the fishing bounties were paid at that establishment. He determined to correct the proceeding, and then return with joy to the original and honest state of things.

Be it known, that the oath required of an applicant for this bounty is a long, rude complication of solemnities, and had usually been sputtered over with indelicate and unseemly haste.

One day a blustering and confident-looking skipper came to the desk with his bundle of papers, looking as if he had robbed the circumlocution office, and wanted some bounty. The new auditor rose to a tall majesty, took the great book of oath in his hand, fixed his keen eye on Mr. Skipper, requested him to uncover his head, hold up his right hand, and repeat after him the oath as he read it. They had not trav-

elled more than half way through the serious business, when the hand of the skipper fell as quick as if his arm had been struck by a chain shot.

" You may stop there," he exclaimed; "I can't swear to any more of that. Give me back the papers."

He nervously grasped the package, hurried out of the office, and to this day his fate and reflections are unknown.

Photograph of Wall Street.

THE view given of this great thoroughfare by Mr. Kimball, in his " Undercurrents of Wall Street," is admirable in its descriptive power. He says:—Its advantages for a universal mart are incredible. It is Lombard Street, Threadneedle Street, Old Broad Sreeet, Wapping, the Docks, Thames Street, and the Inns of Court, combined. In it is the Custom House as well as the Exchange. It is a good dog market, cow market, and bird market. If you want a pair of horses, and any description of new or second-hand carriage, wait a little, and they will be paraded before you. You will find there the best fruit, and the finest flowers in their season. If you would have a donkey, a Shetland pony, or a Newfoundland dog, a good milch cow and calf, a Berkshire pig, a terrier, white mice, a monkey or parroquets, they are to be had in Wall street. It is a strange spot. On Sunday or early in the morning during the week it is like the street of a deserted city. About ten o'clock it begins to show signs of extraordinary animation. Through the day the turmoil increases, people rush to and fro, and literally " stagger like drunken men." Toward three o'clock the street appears undergoing a series of desperate throes. Men rush madly past each other with bank books in their hands, uncurrent money, notes, drafts, checks, specie. Occasionally you may see an individual on the steps of a building, evidently waiting for something, with an air of forced calmness. From time to time he turns his eyes anxiously to the great dial-plate which is displayed from the church, and then up and down the street. The minute-hand has marked five into the last quarter. In ten more minutes it will be three o'clock. Occasionally an acquaintance passes; the man attempts as he bows to smile pleasantly; he can't do it, he only makes a grimace. What is he waiting for? That individual has a note to pay, or a check to make good before three. He has worked hard, but the fates are against him. One friend is out of town, a second is short, a third can't use his paper: he has sent to the last possible place. Look! the young man is coming. Yes? No? He runs eagerly up, thrusts the welcome little slip, a check for the desired amount, into the hands of the now agitated principal; it is rapidly indorsed, and on flies the youth to the bank.

Our hero relieved—he has probably borrowed the money for a day only, and has to renew the attack next morning—now proposes to leave his affairs, he lights a cigar, invites the first friend he meets to take a drink with him, and strolls leisurely up Broadway as unconcernedly as if he had not a care in the world. Perhaps he does not come off so luckily; perhaps his young man reports to him, while standing gloomily on the steps, that it is "no go;" then the fatal hand which points toward three, travels fast. He considers a moment; he sees it can't be done; he waits until he hears the chimes ring out the full hour, and then "his mind is easy." Your shrewd money-lender understands this perfectly. He knows how unsafe it is to let his victim pass the point unrelieved; for, once having gone to protest, he becomes demoralized, and in consequence indifferent. So, just before the hour, the money is generally "found."

Drinking the Health of Custom House Officers.

"WILL Watch," the bold smuggler, as a once popular song has it, sleeps, or rather slept for a considerable time, at peace with the dead. That is a pity certainly on one account,—for if Mr. Watch were, conformably to his surname, alive and wide awake, he would have a capital story told him of a somewhat novel importation.

It appears that among the cargo of the *Dane* steamer, unloaded at the Southampton docks, Eng., from the Cape of Good Hope, were seven cases addressed to Dr. Schwarz, Germany. The contents being unknown, they were taken to the "sight floor" for examination by the customs' officers, when they were found to contain, according to the judgment of the officials in question, various specimens of natural history, illustrating the science of anatomy. One case was filled with "human bones," and in another case were four tins, each containing the "head of a negro," *preserved in brandy* in a jar closely secured in the tin. The whole were pronounced to be in a most perfect condition.

The fact, which Mr. Watch would hardly have required to be pointed out to *him*, evidently is, that a very neat trick was in this instance played on the custom house officers, resulting in their being most cleverly "sold." The simple fact is that they, in their innocence, did not taste the brandy in which the heads of the blackamoors were preserved. If they had tried that formidable but, as it would have proved, safe experiment, they would have found the spirituous liquor none the worse for the preserves. By the art of the modeller and colorist, no doubt, heads, black or white, and of the right kind of material—as incapable of affecting as of being affected by brandy—may be manufactured in any required quantity; and it was not a very long time after the decision in question, that certain

gentlemen might have been seen, provided access could have been obtained
to the scene of their good cheer, convi-
vially and with a hearty gusto drinking
*the health of the Southampton custom house
officers* in the fluid supposed to have
served an antiseptic purpose in relation
to the heads of the black men.

It is wonderful that such expert officers were so easily done. The address,
" Dr. Schwarz," ought to have opened
their eyes. What would they have said
to "Mr. Smith," London ? The case
shows one more of the secrets of smuggling, which is an occupation much
more romantic than reputable, for the
smuggler inflicts a downright injury on
the really fair trader—assuming that
the latter character still exists. Such
a case also causes the imposition of a
very disagreeable duty on custom house
officers—those usually bland and accommodating persons. They will henceforth
have to assure themselves, beyond a
doubt, that the brandy in which alleged
anatomical preparations are imported,
really contain those objects of medical
science ; and it is only to be hoped
that they will find the means of determining this point by some other sense
than that of taste.

Manners at the English Stock Exchange.

THE manners—no less than the
morals—of the London Stock Exchange, are curious, to say the least.
Some time since, the papers reported
a limb broken " in sport ; " occasional
duels arise from the "fun" of the
members ; and the courtesies of life
are wanting on the part of many of its
habitués, if a stranger ventures among
them. When such an "intruder" appears, instead of the bearing of gentlemen, the first discoverer of the visitor
cries out, "Fourteen hundred fives ! "
and a hundred voices re-echo the cry.
Youth or age is equally disregarded ;
and the following description of what
occurred to an unconscious interloper,

and which is no rare instance, will
show that there are financial as well as
political " roughs."

Not long ago (according to an English journal), a rural gentleman, ignorant of the rule so rigidly enforced for
the expulsion of strangers, chanced to
" drop in," as he phrased it, to the
Stock Exchange. He walked about
for nearly a minute, without being discovered to be an intruder, indulging
in surprise at finding that the greatest uproar and frolic prevailed in a
place in which he expected there would
be nothing but order and decorum.
All at once, a person who had just
concluded a hasty but severe scrutiny
of his features, called out at the full
stretch of his voice the usual signal
in such cases—" Fourteen hundred."
Then a bevy of the " gentlemen " of
the resort clamorously surrounded him.
" Will you purchase any new navy five
per cent. ? " said one, eagerly and mena-
cingly looking him in the face. "I am
not—," the stranger was about to say
he was not going to purchase stock of
any kind, but was unceremoniously
prevented finishing his sentence by his
hat being, through a powerful application of some one's fist to its crown,
not only forced over his eyes, but over
his mouth also. Before he had time to
recover from the stupefaction into
which the suddenness and violence of
the eclipse threw him, he was seized
by the shoulders and whirled about
as if he had been a revolving machine,
accompanied by several smart cuffs
which told, with stinging effect, in the
region of his ears. He was then
dragged about, from one person to another, each having a fraternal " turn "
at him, as if he had only been the
effigy of some human being, instead of
a human being himself. After tossing
and hustling him about in the roughest
possible manner, abbreviating his coat
of one of its tails, and tearing into
fragments other parts of his wardrobe,
they carried him to the door, where,

INTERIOR VIEW OF THE LONDON STOCK EXCHANGE.

after depositing him on his feet, they left him to recover his lost senses at his leisure—but in some other place and company than theirs.

Origin of Boards of Trade.

CROMWELL seems, according to the best accounts we have, to have given the first notions of a board of trade. In 1655, he appointed his son Richard, with many lords of his council, judges and gentlemen, and about twenty merchants of London, York, Newcastle, Yarmouth, Dover, etc., to meet and consider by what means the trade and navigation of the republic might be best promoted. Charles the Second, on his restoration, established a council of trade for keeping a control over the whole commerce of the nation; he afterwards instituted a board of trade and plantations, which was afterwards re-modelled by William the Third. This board of commercial superintspection was abolished in 1772; and a new council for the affairs of trade, on its present plan, was appointed in 1786.

Attacks on the Stock Exchange.

THE character of the old stock exchange, of London, has been set forth in terms about as strong as language can express it. Even as far back as a century ago, a writer of that time says, "The centre of jobbing is the kingdom of 'Change Alley;'" and what was true then is by many regarded as the same at the present day. The enormous profits made by the association, the malpractices of the greater part of its members, and the insolence of the richer ones, excited long since the alarm of those unaccustomed to such manœuvres, and the public writers began to attack their increasing power.

"The villany of stock-jobbing is called a mystery or machine of trade," says one of these writers. "This destructive hydra! this new corporation

19

of hell!" exclaims another; while one of them gives directions, in order to besiege and bring to surrender "that infamous place, 'Change Alley," "to storm it," etc.

Another writer declares that "the general cry against stock-jobbing has been so long, and it has been so justly complained of as a public nuisance, that these people are hardened in crime; all their art is a mere system of cheat and delusion; their characters are as dirty as their employments; and the best thing that can be said of them, perhaps, is that there *happen* to be two honest men among them." "Exchange Alley is, in fact, as dangerous to the public safety as a magazine of gunpowder to a populous city."

But all these invectives did not obstruct the progress of the establishment; on the contrary, it continued to become more powerful, and increased in proportion as the government was more extravagant and careless of the public money. It became, in short, an indispensable engine of the government itself; but the latter was finally compelled, by public opinion against the detested operations of the exchange, and in order to keep up appearances, to pass several acts against the very operations and the very gambling it was so deeply, though secretly, fomenting. Avarice, idleness, and the hope of becoming rich in a short time without industry, eluded and evaded all laws. The members of this corporation have not only become the exclusive masters of the British money market, but have acquired the immense power of secretly controlling and regulating the funds and money market of almost the whole world.

Custom Houses and Star Chambers.

A MERCHANT in London, of the name of Richard Chambers, having sustained some loss by a confiscation of part of his property by the custom-house officers, in a moment of indignation said, in the hearing of some of the privy council, "that the merchants in England were more wrung and screwed than in foreign parts." For the offence of this language he was forthwith brought before "the honorable court of Star Chamber," as it was termed, and fined two thousand pounds, for refusing to pay which he was ordered to be imprisoned six years, and even this punishment was by some members of the court considered too small. It was also part of Chambers' sentence to sign a very mean submission, which was accordingly prepared. But when this was brought to him he absolutely refused, and, with all the terrors of a prison in view, wrote under it that " he abhorred and detested it as unjust and false, and never until death would he acknowledge any part of it." In consequence of his determined opposition to the tyranny of the government, on this and other occasions, Chambers was utterly ruined, and died of poverty and brokenheartedness at an advanced age.

———

Quotations of the New Exchange.

THE commercial phrases peculiar to the new Matrimonial Exchange, London, are from time to time delineated by the stock reporters for Punch—a journal which appears to be the exclusive organ of the dealers and habitués of that important mart. Quotations are given as follows—though the variations are so rapid and anomalous as almost to defy the reporter's skill :

The demand for hands has been flat. Rings have been heavy, and so were not fingered. Acceptances were at a discount—offers fluctuating. " Yes's " were in plenty, but no takers. Kisses were liberally showered on new visitors. Hearts that were to be had for love went off unsteadily, and, in some cases, at considerable risk ; those with high interest eagerly sought for, though, in many

cases, at a great risk, as permanent investments.

Banns might have been had with asking for ; but licenses kept their prices—there were very few transactions in this stock. Smiles and squeezes were unchangeable at par, and one gentleman who speculated boldly in foot touches, met with favorable returns. Sighs latterly were heavy, but small-talk continued brisk to the close. Bright eyes looked up occasionally, but soon fell again. Though some business, as usual, was done in blushes, silly looks were not in demand ; free-and-easies, however, rose to a high premium, and drove genuine modesty almost out of the market.

Maternal frowns were in considerable quantities, and prevented, it is thought, many imprudent bargains from being finally settled. Scandal kept its customary high ground ; and more transactions occurred in that line than in the three others put together. Serenades—particularly of wind instruments—were in great demand and in plentiful supply during the equinox. Slights were complained of by many dealers.

On the whole, at the close of the season and markets, the single per cents were not much reduced, as compared with the business of former years ; and there was a sluggishness in even improper flirtations, which had no doubt its share in casting a gloom and monotony over the general course of the Exchange.

P. S.—A later report gives the market an aspect of greater steadiness and encouragement. Liberal offers being more difficult to obtain, has caused acceptances to be had at a great discount compared with previous quotations. Not much doing in maternal frowns, on which account time bargains are settled without much difficulty. Heavy purses are much inquired for ; but stocks with small

SCENE IN AN ORIENTAL CUSTOM HOUSE.

capitals, have not once been sought after. Sly squeezes are very brisk. Blushes are remarked as quite scarce, none having been seen in the market for a length of time. Jealousy is rising considerably. Other stocks remain almost the same as before, with the exception of scandal, which may be said to be rather on the advance.

Scenes in a Turkish Custom House.

THERE is a slight difference between an American and a Syrian custom-house. On entering the latter, the Hadji dons a pair of spectacles, and taking a scrap of paper from the nearest applicant, carefully peruses the same before handing it over to some subordinate. The room is a long oblong one, with only one entrance door, and a few pigeon holes close to the ceiling, which do duty for windows. Round three sides are placed long, narrow divans, with equally low wooden desks before them. Only the Hadji, in compliment to the high office he fills, is accommodated with a lofty seat, which serves for manifold purposes; on it he sits, tailor fashion, himself; on it are his ink-horn, his pepper-box, full of steel gratings (to serve instead of blotting paper), his tobacco pouch, his private account book, his seal of office, a large pair of shears, to cut his paper with, a quire of paper, and a few envelopes. All the clerks have the same inventory of goods, with the exception of the signet, either on the desk before them, or on the divan beside them; and, as far as can be judged, very few of the clerks seem to pay any particular heed as to what is going on around them. Some are playing backgammon, shuffling the dice, and speaking or laughing as loudly as though the place were an hotel; others are playing at cat's cradle; some are narrating little episodes of private adventure; and one or two, with intense anxiety depicted in their faces,

may be seen endeavoring to unravel a sum in simple addition, adding up some six lines of figures, and arriving repeatedly at most unsatisfactory results.

At the farther end of the room, and nearest the door, are some half-dozen patient individuals, who, seeing the throng pressing around the Hadji's desk, despair of transacting any business for a good half-hour to come, and endeavor to while away the time with the stale old newspaper, or in desultory conversation. In the centre of the room, wrangling with each other in no measured accents, are a couple of Hebrews, the one the seller, the other the purchaser of a few barrels of sugar, which are warehoused in the custom house; the bone of contention between them is a couple of rusty old hoops, which have fallen off said casks, and which both lay claim to as their respective perquisites; their joint value might be somewhat under six cents— but six cents are six cents, and the dispute grows fierce and loud. At last they appeal to the Hadji; and the Hadji, who always has an eye to the main chance, claims them as his own. The customs charge nothing for warehousing, therefore he considers himself entitled to occasional windfalls. Vainly they expostulate against this, pale with anxiety and rage to think that they are both outwitted; the order is given to the warehouse scribe, who chances to be in the room at the time, to make an immediate memorandum of the matter; and this dignitary, who to all appearance is totally unfurnished with materials, squats down immediately upon the floor, and, producing ink-horn and paper, thrusts up one knee, which serves him as a desk, and the minute is forthwith entered. Then the two dealers go away, full of enmity toward each other, their tempers not being improved by a sly allusion, on the part of some witty individual, to the fable of the two cats and the

cheese—which fable itself was originally copied from the Arabs.

Every one is talking and clamorous,
when a hurried shipmaster, accompanied by a consular cawass and an interpreter, elbows his way up to the Hadji's
desk and demands, as the wind is fair,
to have his ship cleared out instanter,
"Shuay, shuay, ye ebney! Yauash!
yauash!" (Gently, gently, my son!
quietly, quietly!) "Does the man
think we work by steam in this
office?"

Thus demands the Hadji, to which
on due interpretation, the captain
allows that he would be mad or blind
to think so. Nevertheless, the Hadji
has a wholesome fear of the English
consul; wherefore, he takes the documents out of the captain's hands, and
gives them to his own private translator. This individual, who is clad in
hybrid costume, reads out the manifest, line by line, the Hadji making
note of the same, and comparing them
with his own entries of shipments,
which are found to tally exactly. Then
comes the most important question,
viz., Have all these shipments paid
the right export duty? The Greek
broker has made some omission, it appears, and matters cannot be proceeded
with till the mistake is corrected.
Upon this information, the shipmaster
is naturally annoyed, but there is no
remedy; he is obliged to go all the
way back to the broker's, thence to the
shipper, and in all probability is forced
to appeal to the consul. Meanwhile
the fair wind subsides, and the owners,
the underwriters, and all parties concerned, have lost a week, if not more—
a week of hardship, wear and tear, of
expenses in pay and sustenance, and
perhaps the cargo is about ruined by
so long confinement.

Manchester Cotton Merchants.

THERE is, perhaps, no part of the
commercial world in which so much is
done and so little said in the same
space of time, as among the merchants
of Manchester, Eng., at the time of
"high" change. A stranger sees nothing at first but a collection of gentlemen, with thoughtful, intelligent faces,
who converse with each other in
laconic whispers, supply the non-use
of words by nods and signs, move
noiselessly from one part of the room
to another, guided as if by some hidden
instinct to the precise person in the
crowd with whom they have business
to transact.

A phrenologist will nowhere meet
such a collection of decidedly clever
heads. The physiognomist who declared that he could find traces of
stupidity in the faces of the wisest
philosophers, would be at a loss to find
any indication of its presence in the
countenances assembled at the Manchester Exchange. Genius appears to
be not less rare than folly; the characteristic features of these habitués, collectively and individually, are those of
talent and sagacity in high working
order.

Whether trade be brisk or dull, high
'change is equally crowded; and the
difference of its aspect at the two
periods is sufficiently striking. In stir-
ring times, every man on 'change seems
as if he belonged to the community
of the dancing dervishes, being utterly
incapable of remaining for a single
second in one place. It is the principle of a Manchester man, that
"naught is done while aught remains
to do;" let him but have the opportunity, and he will undertake to supply
all the markets between China and Peru,
and will be exceedingly vexed if he has
lost the chance of selling some yarn at
Japan, on his way. When trade is
dull, the merchants and factors stand
motionless as statues, or move about
as slowly as if they followed a funeral—
the look of eagerness exchanged for
that of dogged obstinacy; it seems to
say—"My mind is made up to lose so

much, but I am resolved to lose no more." An increase of sternness and inflexibility accompanies the decline of the Manchester trade, and foreigners declare that the worst time to expect a bargain is a season of distress.

Free Trade.

THE well known Hussey Burgh, at the opening of the session of parliament in 1777, moved the usual address to the king, in which was the following sentence : " It is not by temporary expedients, but by an extension of trade, that Ireland can be ameliorated." On the reading of this paragraph, Flood, who was seated in the vice-treasurer's place, said, audibly. " Why not a *free* trade ?" The amendment electrified the house ; the words were adopted by his friend, and the motion was carried unanimously. It was a bold commercial stroke, accomplished with a master's skill and brevity.

Animated Scenes at the French Exchange.

THE spirit which animates the French Exchange wakes up at one o'clock precisely. The stroke of the clock gives the signal of business. At this sound everything is in motion ; a thousand cries are sent forth ; a universal shout fills the vast hall, and strikes the roof. The " basket "—corbeille—a kind of circular balcony occupying the east end of the hall, around which sixty brokers crowd, bristles with threatening arms, and furious memorandum books. In the wink of an eye, the floor is covered with a multitude of little torn bits of paper ; these are the orders of purchase and sale, sent by their principals, and the answers returned by the brokers. Iron railings keep off the profane vulgar, who besiege the basket on all sides, and whose continual buzz mixes with the shriekings of the brokers, and of the pages of the Exchange. A general stamping and

buzzing—a perpetual coming and going, as in an ant hill or a bee hive —seeming confusion yet perfect order ; —such is the aspect of the Exchange from one o'clock to three.

From the gallery above, which is also thronged with multitudes of the curious, a strange spectacle is presented by this furnace ·in full blast, where writhe, like twigs in the flame, the most violent passions of the human heart. The floor of fine and well-swept sand, which surrounds the centre of the parquet, or inclosure, is simply the spitting-box of the brokers. These threatening cries—this defiance—these exorcisms—are good natured words and pantomines, always the same, and meaning " I have fifty Northerns !" " I'll take ten thousand of the *Fives !* two thousand of the *Threes !* "   " Let me have some *Premiums*, early day—next day !" " Let me have some Piedmont !" " I'll sell some Gas !" " Who wants Zinc ?" Here is Bank !" " Here is City !" &c., &c.,

That personage who from time to time raises his voice in a corner of the Exchange, and whose purple face rises above all other heads, thanks to the stool which forms his pedestal, is the *muezzin* of this mosque—the auctioneer of the Exchange—the person whose duty it is to minute and announce the rates of public stock as they are ascertained. At right angles with the inclosure, on entering by the façade, a sort of human alley-way is opened through the crowd, in order to afford a passage for the brokers' clerks, who go and come. Two similar, but shorter alley-ways, run to the right and the left of the basket, like the two arms of a cross. These three openings of the inclosure are incessantly crowded with orders of sale and purchase, which are sent to the brokers by the busy messengers, who bear the official insignia embroidered conspicuously on the coat-collar.

The lower sides of the hall, furnished

with benches at wide intervals, serve as a promenade for the sages of the portico—the dreamers and the idle.

The Origin of the Clearing House.

NOT many years after the London bankers had ceased to issue notes, the inconvenience of making all payments in Bank of England notes and gold, had become so great, that some change was indispensably necessary; when the plan of adjusting each other's daily payments by an interchange of liabilities was adopted as the best mode of economizing the use of money. At first the system adopted was of the most primitive kind, and certainly not the safest. The clerks of the various banking houses used to perform the operation of exchanges at the corners of the streets, and on the top of a post. They then met, by appointment, at a public house; but, from the insecurity of these arrangements, it was at last thought best that the principal city bankers should rent a house near the old post office in Lombard street. This house was called the Clearing House.

Derivation of the Commercial Term Bourse.

THE original name of bourse, given to edifices for the accommodation of merchants, is thus stated: There was, in former times, a square commodiously situated in the middle of the city of Bruges, in which stood a large building that had been erected by the noble family of La Bourse, whose coat of arms, on its wall, was three purses. The merchants of Bruges made this old house the place of their daily assemblies; and when afterward they went to the fairs of Antwerp and Mons, they called the places they found there for the assembling of merchants, by the name of La Bourse, or the Bourse.

Reduction of Custom-House Duties:— "Death to the Beet-Root!"

THE news of the reduction of the customs duty on sugar was celebrated with great enthusiasm in the towns and cities of France—nowhere more joyously than in Havre. Not only were all the ships in the harbor gayly dressed, and the houses profusely adorned with tri-colored flags, but the laboring class, whose work had been so diminished by the smallness of the cargoes brought by ships from the colonies, paraded the streets in great numbers, preceded by a banner, with a sugarcane surmounted by a nosegay, below which was a beet-root covered with crape, and bearing the inscription "Death to the Beet-root!"

Ludicrous Custom-House Examinations.

NOTHING can exceed the lynx-eyed scrutiny and annoying detail of the British custom-house officers. Upon the arrival of a vessel from the Continent, for instance, the passengers are asked for their trunk keys, and they look as if they were about to offer to the British Government their entire stock of movables. Each has his single carpet bag, and waits his turn. The first bag opened may exhibit an old coat, a hair brush, a checked shirt, an empty flask, and a toothbrush; the next, a checked shirt, an empty flask, and a hair brush; the third contains an empty flask, a hair brush, and a checked shirt. Then comes a bag which actually contains a large portion of dirty striped linen, which one of the men engaged in the search begins to rummage with a minuteness and curiosity which, after the very general way of disposing of the other things, seems quite surprising. The truth is, the man has smelt brandy in the clothes, and is looking out for the bottle. His search for it is very much like that of Page for Falstaff in the buck-basket, and, as it turns out, is as little successful.

Business in London at Four o'Clock.

A GRAPHIC picture—though not very complimentary—of " Commercial London " at four o'clock in the afternoon, may be seen in the following, from the pen of North :—Attorneys are cheating their clients, or assisting them to cheat other people. Merchants are calculating the chances of the markets, like gamblers inventing martingales. Clerks are adding up figures as clocks add up minutes. Cashiers and secretaries are reflecting on the facilities of an impromptu voyage to California. Directors of companies are " cooking " the accounts of their shareholders. Waiters at Joe's, Sam's, Tom's, Betsy's, and other chop houses, whose proprietors are apparently more proud of their Christian names than usual, order countless chops, through patent gutta-percha telegraphs. Cooks baste themselves with half and half, while roasting before their fires, like Fox's martyrs, bound to the steaks of their tyrants. Crossing-sweepers are industriously cleaning streets as dry as carpets, and begging of passengers as charitable as cannibals. Usurers are meeting gentlemen who want to borrow money at any rate of—non-payment. Adventurers are keeping appointments with capitalists they hope to drag into speculations ; capitalists are contriving monopolies by which to crush non-capitalist adventurers. Stock brokers are playing money tricks on the Stock Exchange. Hebrew gold-kings are manufacturing intelligence to astonish the stock brokers. Couriers are dashing off with the commands of London financiers to foreign potentates. Messengers are arriving from the sham, entreating aid from the *real* sovereigns of Europe. And the plenipotentiaries of that greater monarch still—the daily press — are calmly overlooking the whole anthill, with sublime indifference to the struggles of its busy insects, and generalizing for millions the knowledge which, even to those in the midst of the bustle, is too often but semi-obscurity and chromatropic confusion.

Merchants and Business Resorts in Moscow.

THE mercantile portion of Moscow presents characteristics peculiarly its own. The quarter in which the retail business is carried on is called Kitai-gorod, or Chinese Town, a name which it obtained in the earliest times as the seat of the Chinese trade. At present it contains two Gostivie dvori, or bazaars, resembling that of St. Petersburg in arrangement, but far surpassing it in variety and amount of business. One can hardly think of a desirable object, for the sale of which a row of stalls is not to be found there. Each dealer both buys and sells in his own line of business. Specie is also ranked among the articles of commercial traffic. The current coins of all countries are to be purchased, as well as those which time or circumstances have converted into mere articles of curiosity.

The mercantile population of Moscow cling to the same antique habits which distinguish the commercial classes in St. Petersburg ; indeed, nationality is much more developed in the former place. St. Petersburg is a chameleon, the color of which changes from contrast. The foreigner thinks it Russian, while to the native of Moscow it appears a foreign city. The comfortable tradesmen in Moscow have a quarter to themselves ; and while their servants keep the shops, the bearded owners chat with one another in the street. They live in indolent resignation on whatever fortune sends them, and their language is proverbially that of careless indifference.

Railway Clearing House.

On account of the difficulty which the multitude of English railway companies found in keeping their mutual accounts, they adopted, some years ago, a system analogous to that of the "clearing house" established by bankers and merchants in large cities. The clearing house, carried on in the interest of mercantile classes, is, it is known, an establishment which keeps up a sort of imaginary debtor and creditor account with all the bankers and merchants. The latter send their bills and checks, not to each other, for payment, but to the clearing house, where they are sorted and classed under the name of the firm which is to pay them. As four o'clock approaches, each banker's debits for the day are arranged in one column in a printed form, and his credits in the other; and the payment of a small sum of money, either to him or by him, may balance a complicated list of large sums.

It is this convenient principle, as applied in their mutual dealings in respect to passengers, merchandise, mileage, and lost luggage, which the railway companies have adopted. In a street near the vast Euston station—the great root whence most of the railroad lines spring—is a plain doorway, with a plain plate bearing the plain inscription—RAILWAY CLEARING HOUSE. Few passers by ever think, or could think to any purpose, of what is done within that doorway; few would imagine that commercial accounts to a stupendous extent are there daily settled, by clerks more numerous and in rooms more extensive than those employed by the most world-renowned banker. The building was constructed at the joint expense of all the companies, who also bear the charge of salaries and office expenses. The companies all elect deputies or delegates, who form, collectively, a committee for managing affairs—or rather, there is a manager, to carry on all the operations of the establishment, while the delegates attend principally to seeing after the interests of their respective companies. There are several hundred clerks, who have the management and adjustment of accounts, and the amount involved annually is said to be from thirty to forty million dollars. There is an excellent library, news room, reading room, etc., combined with the vast business apartments of this great concern.

Lloyd's Establishment, London.

THE designation LLOYD'S, so well known in the mercantile world, originated with a person of the name of Lloyd, who kept a coffee house in Abchurch lane, Lombard street. From the vicinity of this house to the old royal exchange, it speedily became a rendezvous of merchants for news, and for the transaction of business. It was afterward removed to Pope's Head alley, and thence again, in 1774, to the Royal Exchange. After the destruction of the Exchange, in 1838, by fire, which originated in Lloyd's, the business was carried on in the South Sea House, in Old Broad street, where it remained until the opening of the present Royal Exchange in 1844, when it was removed to its now splendid apartments.

These rooms are frequented by underwriters, merchants, ship owners, ship and merchandise brokers, and others, chiefly for the purpose of obtaining shipping intelligence, and of transacting business connected with marine insurance. The principal room is that of the underwriters, in which two enormous ledgers lie constantly open; the one containing notices of *speakings*, or ships spoken with, and arrivals of vessels at their various destinations; the other recording distances at sea. The immense amount of insurance business done at Lloyd's may be appreciated when it is said, that the value of the interest annually insured at the present is estimated at about $200,000,000. The shipping intelligence received at Lloyd's is furnished by responsible agents, in the especial employ of the establishment, in almost every port.

One Thousand Million Pounds' Business Annually at the London Clearing House.

On his "Visit to the Bank of France," by Francis Lloyd, he says: I explained to the regents of the bank the operations of the London Clearing House; that system so economical of time and trouble, and without which concentration and rapid settlement the enormous balances between the banking houses in the great emporium of the commercial world could not be so promptly struck—the wheels of our complicated monetary system could not revolve so evenly and quickly. I have always thought that the system of making bills, drawn from whatever quarter of the world, or from whatever town or village in Great Britain, upon all parts of Great Britain, payable in one place—that is, as effected daily by one hour's adjustment of the clearing house—that such united regulation and acceleration of finance are to the complex machinery of banking what the flywheel and governor are to the steam engine.

Imagine the regent's surprise when I told him that in the London clearing room—a plain room, on part of the site of the old post office in Lombard street —a clerk from each private bank in London attended twice a day but for half an hour; and commercial obligations were collectively discharged to the amount of three millions sterling every day in the year, with not more than a fifteenth of this sum in bank notes. That, as to using coin (silver and copper), I could readily picture to myself the contemptuous and derisive expression of the face which the most juvenile of those clearing clerks would assume at the bare suggestion. A thousand millions of pounds sterling, I told him, were paid last year in this room by those clerks, not more than forty in number—a sum larger than the national debt; and that all the money used for the operation—this balancing of a year's commercial enterprise in all quarters of the globe—was effected without a single error or moment's delay, and with bits of paper only, viz., the promissory notes of the Bank of England.

'Change Alley as a Business Resort.

The centre of financial jobbing in London is in 'Change alley and its adjacencies. The limits are easily surrounded in a minute and a half. Stepping out of Jonathan's into the alley, you turn your face full south; moving on a few paces, and then turning due east, you advance to Garraway's; from thence, going out at the other door, you go on still east into Birchin lane, and then, halting a little at the swordblade bank, you immediately face to the north, enter Cornhill, visit two or three petty provinces there on your way to the west; and thus having boxed your compass, and sailed round the stock-jobbing globe, you turn into Jonathan's again. Such is the description given by a pamphleteer of this depot of the dealers and jobbers in the funds and stocks market—long so famous throughout the business world. Here assembled the sharper and the saint; here jostled one another the Jew and the Gentile; here met the courtier and the citizen; here the calmness of the gainer contrasted with the despair of the loser; and here might be seen the carriage of some minister, into which the head of his broker was anxiously stretched, to gain the intelligence which was to raise or depress the market. In one corner might be witnessed the anxious, eager countenance of the occasional gambler, in strange contrast with the calm, cool demeanor of the man whose regular trade it was to deceive. In another, the Hebrew measured his craft with that of the Quaker, and scarcely came off victorious in the contest.

Amusing Perplexities at the Custom House.

THE occasional importation of articles which are not enumerated in the tariff of custom-house duties is in some instances productive of amusing perplexity. A singular case of this nature occurred once at the London custom house, the *solution* of which was beyond the skill of all the officials, and was only reached at last by the native power of the article itself. This case was the importation of some ice from Norway. A doubt was started as to what duty it ought to pay, and this point was referred from the custom house to the treasury department, and from the treasury to the board of trade. Oddly enough, it was the opinion of the latter officials, that the ice might be introduced on the payment of the duty on *dry* goods—but, as the thing turned out, "the ice was dissolved before the question was solved." In another case, the officials came to an equally *dead* lock: A gentleman had imported a mummy from Egypt, and the officers of the customs were not a little puzzled as to what to do with this non-enumerated article. These remains of mortality—muscles and sinews, pickled and preserved three thousand years ago—could not be deemed a raw material, and, therefore, upon deliberation, it was determined to tax them as a manufactured article. The importer, anxious that his mummy should not be seized, concluded, before the decision was made, just to state its value at two thousand dollars—an unfortunate declaration, which cost him one thousand dollars, being at the rate of fifty per cent. on the "manufactured merchandise."

Duty on Pictures.

MR. N., an American, used to relate, with much good humor, the following adventure, which happened to him on his arrival at the custom house at Dover, England. Being an amateur of pictures, he had brought with him a view of the Falls of Niagara, which he had himself painted during his residence in Canada. The size of the picture was about six square feet, and as the duty on painted canvas was rated at one guinea the foot, the demand was consequently the very considerable one of six guineas. Mr. N. demurred to such a charge on a picture of no value to any one but himself, and appealed to the director of the customs, who, however, informed him that the regulation was positive, and could not be departed from. Mr. N. still complained of the exorbitant duty. "Very well," said the director, "I only know one way for you to avoid the payment of it; leave your picture here for six months; as you are the sole proprietor, no one will claim it, and at the end of that period I shall put it up for sale. Of course, no one will purchase such a *horrid daub*, which is certainly not worth six shillings, and you will then have it for nothing." With this timely advice Mr. N. complied, and in due season obtained his picture.

High 'Change Hours.

HIGH 'change hour is fixed at one o'clock by the merchants of Philadelphia. New York exchange assembles at two and three quarters o'clock, but is not fully attended until three and one quarter o'clock. In Liverpool, the hours are from two to five o'clock; and, if the visitor wishes to be sure of seeing the persons who frequent it, he may be obliged to wait or waste three hours before he can accomplish his purpose. In the London exchange, the crowd begins to pour in at four o'clock, and in a quarter of an hour it is "high 'change." At half past four it ceases, when beadles go round with large bells, with which they make such a deafening noise that the assembly is soon dispersed, the gates are locked, and no one is allowed to enter till the next day.

In European cities, all the principal houses or firms have regular places of resort on 'change. For example, Mr. Rothschild is always to be found, on foreign post days, on the "Italian Walk;" the Messrs. Baring, Brothers & Co. are to be found at the column which they have frequented for years; those merchants who are in the American trade frequent the "American Walk;" those who are in the Russian and Swedish trade frequent the "Baltic Walk;" and those in the German trade, frequent the "Hamburg Walk."

In Amsterdam, the exchange bell begins to ring at half past two o'clock, and if all persons who wish to enter the gates before the clock strikes three, do not succeed in getting in, they are compelled to pay a small fee, amounting to eight or ten cents, for admission. If any one wishes to enter at half past three, he is obliged to pay a fine of half a guilder. So much importance is attached to regular attendance on 'change, that if a house is not represented, either personally or by one of the confidential clerks, it is considered that a death has occurred in the family of some one of the partners, or that bankruptcy or some other misfortune has occurred. High 'change at Antwerp is at five o'clock in the afternoon, when the gates are closed, after which, to gain admittance, a fee of half a franc is paid.

First East India Company House.

THE tradition is, that the East India Company, incorporated December 31, 1600, first transacted their business in the great room of the Nag's Head inn, opposite St. Botolph's church, Bishops-

gate street. The maps of London, soon after the great fire of 1666, place the India House on a part of its present site in Leadenhall street. Here originally stood the mansion of Alderman Kerton, built in the reign of Edward the Sixth, rebuilt on the accession of Elizabeth, and enlarged by its next purchaser, Sir W. Craven, lord mayor in 1610. Here was born the great Lord Craven, who, in 1701, leased his house and a tenement in Lime street to the company, at one hundred pounds a year. A scarce Dutch etching, still preserved, shows this house to have been half timbered, its lofty gable surmounted with two dolphins and a figure of a mariner, or, as some say, the first governor; beneath are merchant ships at sea, the royal arms, and those of the company. This famous and grotesque structure was taken down in the year 1726, and upon its site was erected the old East India House, portions of which yet remain—although the present stone front, two hundred feet long, and a great part of the house, was built in 1798.

Romance and Trade.

THERE is nothing so sentimental in the columns of a daily newspaper as the article devoted to the state of the markets. We seldom peruse it—quoth Punch—without a tendency to tears, which are only checked by the recollection that it is only on bags of coffee, bales of cotton, parcels of pepper, and barrels of flour, that we are exhausting our useless sympathy.

We, however, defy any one to be otherwise than moved by the description of the markets, which is evidently the production of a writer who luxuriates in a strain of melancholy tenderness, that is excluded by universal consent from every other portion of the newspaper. The literary sentimentalist, finding no market among the booksellers for his goods, has gone to the very markets themselves, and has secured a corner in the journals, where he may indulge without restraint his tendency to pathos.

Let us take a specimen of that affecting style of writing, which has found its way, appropriately enough, to Mincing Lane: "An improved feeling has again begun to show itself in the coffee market, where dulness had until lately prevailed, and sugars began to assume a livelier aspect."

Surely this must be written by some fashionable novelist "out of luck," whose Rosa-Matilda-isms, that once used to cloy the circulating libraries with their sweetness, have rushed to the sugar cask as the only alternative to avoid the butter shop. Substitute Augustus Danvers for the "coffee market," insert Rosalie in the place of "sugars," and we get a sentence that would seem to form part of a melting novel of ten years back, when the writers of the same sort of stuff could command their three or five hundred pounds for an adequate lot of it. The paragraph, as amended, will stand thus: "An improved feeling had again begun to show itself in Augustus Danvers (the coffee market), where dulness had until lately prevailed, and Rosalie (sugars) began to assume a livelier aspect."

We know nothing of the mysteries of what is termed the "staff" of a daily paper; but we certainly picture to ourselves the writer of the markets as a pale gentleman, with a forehead bared to its highest, a Byron tie, a turned-down shirt collar, and a melancholy cast of countenance, with a feminine tinge of the romantic. We can imagine him walking moodily about the markets, looking out anxiously for a glimpse of gloom in sugars, and feeling an indescribable satisfaction in the dulness of peppers. Why is it necessary that wool should be "flat," Bengal figs "low," indigo "dull," rice "depressed," and everything that seems nice and eatable so wretchedly low-spirited? It is seldom we meet with a

bit of sensible "firmness" in something or other; but, even if we do, we are told of a "tendency to give way," before we get to the end of the article.

Hall of the St. Petersburg Exchange.

THE hall of the Exchange in St. Petersburg is one of the most rare places of business which our planet affords. It is built only for whispers. An audible conversation was never held there. Nothing is spoken aloud save mere bagatelles. "How is your good lady?" "Oh, we enjoyed exceedingly our water party yesterday; we were at this place and that, at such a one's and such a one's." "Yes, I admit that A gives excellent dinners, but I find myself more comfortable at B's." Nothing but this kind of conversation is spoken. But when two persons are seen to put their heads together, talk in the lowest whispers, and palisade themselves in a circle with their backs, so that not a wedge could get into it, then there is surely something in the wind, a *bargain* has been made—the whispering has led to some result. "Yes, sir." "No, sir." "Too much—three thousand—four—twenty—a hundred thousand." "October." "November." "London." "Hull." "Baltimore." "Well, I will take it." "Done! that is settled then, Mr. Curtins."

In the six side rooms, the sugar bakers, and the dealers in tallow, corn, and timber, have established themselves, though without any formal regulation to that effect; and each class has, from habit, taken possession of a particular spot. These are composed almost exclusively of Russians, with and without beard, some old men still in kaftans, others in modern French coats. Between them and the lords of the sea in the centre, are the German brokers, with silver marks at the button hole. Lastly, in the outermost circles, are the "artelschtschiki," a sort of messenger class, for carrying letters or money, and performing other errands, one of whom constantly attends every Petersburg merchant; and these are always Russians.

This assemblage of the mercantile classes of St. Petersburg is certainly the largest company of respectable and polished men that is to be seen in Russia, without order or cross of any kind. Besides these silver marks, which are worn by the brokers in their business, as a sign that they have been duly appointed and sworn, and medals of a pound weight hanging about the necks of a few of the Russian merchants, no distinctions are seen—nothing but black frocks and simple green surtouts. An observer has here an excellent opportunity of studying the Russian commercial character, and will be struck with the difference in manner and other respects between the merchants of St. Petersburg and those of any other city.

Men of Letters frequenting the Share Mart.

THE Hotel de Soissons, in Paris, was made famous for a time as the headquarters of John Law, while blowing his Mississippi bubbles. All classes were represented in the eager throng that besieged that mart of financial lunacy. This hotel was the property of the Prince de Carignan, together with the adjoining garden of several acres in the rear. Law became the purchaser of the hotel, at an enormous price, paying for it out of his prodigious stock-jobbing gains,—the prince reserving to himself the magnificent gardens for his personal profit. They contained fine statues, beautiful fountains, and various other embellishments and decorations.

As soon as Law was installed in his new abode, an edict was published (for there were high officials involved in Law's project), forbidding all persons to buy or sell stock anywhere but in the gardens of the Hotel de Soissons. In the midst, among the trees, about five hundred small tents and pavilions were erected, for the convenience of the stock-jobbers. Their various colors, the gay ribbons and banners which floated from them, the busy crowds which passed continually in and out— the incessant hum of voices, the noise, the music, the strange mixture of business and pleasure on the countenances of the throng, all combined to give the place an air of enchantment that quite enraptured the Parisians. The Prince de Carignan made enormous profits while the delusion lasted.

As is well known, all classes became enamored with Law's dazzling promises of cent. per cent. for their investments; at any rate, the exceptions were so rare as to attract attention. One day, two sober, quiet, and philosophic men of letters, M. de la Motte and the Abbé Terrason, were heard to congratulate each other that they, at least, were free from this strange infatuation. A few days afterward, as the worthy Abbé was coming out of the Hotel de Soissons, whither he had gone to buy shares in the Mississippi, whom should he see but his friend La Motte entering for the same purpose.

"Ha!" said the Abbé, smiling, "is that *you?*"

"Yes," said La Motte, pushing past him as fast as he was able; "and can that be *you?*"

The next time the two scholars met, they talked of philosophy, of science, and of religion, but neither had courage for a long time to breathe a syllable about the Mississippi. At last, when it was mentioned, they agreed that a man ought never to swear against his doing any one thing, and that there was no sort of extravagance of which even a wise man was not capable.

Something like this was the case of Gay, the poet. Receiving a present from his friend Mr. Scraggs of some

South Sea stock, he once supposed himself to be master of twenty thousand pounds. His friends persuaded him to sell his share, but he dreamed of dignity and splendor, and could not bear to obstruct his own fortune. He was then importuned to sell as much as would purchase a hundred a year for life, "which," says Fenton, "will make you sure of a clean shirt and a shoulder of mutton every day." This counsel was rejected ; *the profit and principal were lost,* and Gay sunk under the calamity so low that his life became in danger.

It will hardly be wondered at, however, that literary men should have been thus beguiled, in view of the fact that so multitudinous was the crowd around Law's quarters, and so eager were all classes of the population to buy the stock, that a hump-backed man who stood in the street gained considerable sums by lending his hump as a writing desk to the anxious speculators !

PART SIXTH.

Anecdotes of Commercial Art and Phraseology.

PART SIXTH.

Anecdotes of Commercial Art and Phraseology.

ADVERTISEMENTS, SIGN BOARDS, TRADE MARKS, TOKENS, ENVELOPES, LABELS, INSCRIPTIONS, MOTTOES, AND TERMS—QUAINT, CURIOUS, GROTESQUE, INGENIOUS, AND LAUGHABLE.

The great skill in an advertiser is chiefly seen in the style which he makes use of. He is to mention "the universal esteem or general reputation" of things that were never heard of.—TATLER.

Liberal trade is good scholarship popularized, and commerce is literature on a sign board.—ANON.

Adepts in Commercial Puffing.

PACKWOOD, some fifty years ago, led the way in England of liberal and systematic advertising, by impressing his razor strop indelibly on the mind of every bearded member of the kingdom. Like other great potentates, he boasted a laureate in his pay, and every one remembers the reply made to the individuals so curious to know who drew up his advertisements: "La, sir, we keeps a poet!"

But by universal consent, the world has accorded to the late George Robins the palm in this style of commercial puffing. His advertisements were really artistically written. Like Martin, he had the power of investing every landscape and building that he touched with an importance and majesty not attainable by meaner hands. He did perhaps go beyond the yielding line of even poetical license, when he described one portion of a paradise he' was about to subject to public competition, as adorned, among other charms, with a "hanging wood," which the astonished purchaser found out meant nothing more nor less than an old gallows. But then he redeemed

slight manœuvres of this kind by touches which displayed a native and overflowing genius for puffing. On one occasion, he had made the beauties of an estate so enchanting, that he found it necessary to blur it by a fault or two, lest it should prove too bright and good "for human nature's daily food." "But there are *two drawbacks* to this property," sighed out this Apostle of the Mart, "*the litter of the rose leaves and the noise of the nightingales.*" Certainly the rhetoric of exquisite puffing could no further go.

"Up to Snuff."

In the days when every London shopkeeper had a sign hanging out before his door, a dealer in snuff and tobacco on Fish-street hill carried on a large trade, especially in tobacco, for his shop was greatly frequented by sailors from the ships in the river. In the course of time, a person of the name of Farr opened a shop nearly opposite, and hung out his sign inscribed :

"The best Tobacco *by Farr*."

This—like the shoemaker's incription, "Adam Strong Shoemaker," so well known—attracted the attention of the

20

sailors, who left the old shop to buy "the best tobacco by far." The old shopkeeper, observing that his opponent obtained much custom by his sign, had a new one put up at his door, inscribed :

"*Far better* Tobacco than the best Tobacco by *Farr*."

This turned the tide of trade—his customers came back—and finally his opponent found himself so " far " in the background as to be obliged to give up business.

Irish Pun on a Sign.

AN Irishman once saw the popular sign of the Rising Sun near Seven Dials, beneath which the name of the jovial landlord, Aaron Moon, was written with only the initial letter of the Christian name, whereupon he exclaimed to a friend : "Och ! Phelim, dear, see here. They talk of Irish bulls ; why, here's a fellow now, who puts up the *Rising Sun*, and calls it *A Moon !* "

Dean Swift and the Barber's Sign.

DEAN SWIFT, while resident on his living in the county of Meath, was daily shaved by the village barber, who became a great favorite with him. Razor, while lathering him one morning, said he had a great favor to request of his reverence—that his neighbors had advised him to take the little public house at the corner of the churchyard, which he had done, in the hope that by uniting the profession of publican with his own, he might gain a better maintenance for his family.

"Indeed," said the dean, " and what can I do to promote this happy union?"

"And please you," said Razor, "some of our customers have heard much of your reverence's poetry ; so that, if you would but condescend to give me a smart little touch in that way, to clap under my sign, it might be the making of me and mine forever."

"But what do you intend for your sign ? " says the dean.

"The jolly barber, if it please your reverence, with a *razor* in one hand and a *full pot* in the other."

"Well," rejoined the dean, " in that case there can be no great difficulty in supplying you with a suitable inscription." So taking up his pen, he instantly scratched the following " smart little touch " of a couplet, which was affixed to the sign, and remained there for many years :

"Rove not from pole to pole, but step in here,
Where nought excels the *shaving* but—the *beer*."

Killbury and Maimsworth Railway's Advertisement.

THE Board of Directors of the Killbury and Maimsworth line of Railway, respectfully announce that they intend starting Excursion Trains during the present season, to run at greatly reduced fares, setting out from Killbury in the morning, getting to Maimsworth at twelve, and returning, with as many passengers as are capable of being brought back, every hour of the forenoon, up to twelve o'clock, or later, according to the state of the engines, and the breakdowns and collisions—depending on management of the engineers, brakesmen, and the rest of the Company's employés. Owing to the prevailing competition occasioned by the overcrowded state of the medical profession, the Company have been enabled to secure the services of a numerous staff of experienced surgeons, who will accompany each train, together with a large body of dressers from the principal hospitals, to act as their assistants—thus seeing practice, for which so large a field is afforded by the Killbury and Maimsworth line. Medical students will find splendid opportunities for amateur surgery in these excursions. Amputations (under chloroform, several carboys of which have been obtained expressly for these excursions) at the shortest notice. Tourniquets, with directions for use, in each car. Splints, bandages, and every other comfort and convenience for the mutilated, in abundance (supplied by the Company's own manufactory), gratuitously furnished.

Earliest Printed Advertisements.

The very first advertisement discoverable in any newspaper is one which refers to the theft of two horses. It is contained in an early number of an English newspaper called the *Impartial Intelligencer*, published in the year 1648, and consequently now considerably more than two centuries old. It was inserted by a gentleman of Candish, in Suffolk. After this, these notifications are very few and far between for several years, until the era of the *London Gazette*.

Next to the above, in point of precedence, so far as an active search among the earliest newspapers can be relied on, is an advertisement relating to a book, which is entitled:

"IRENODIA GRATULATORIA, an Heoick Poem; being a congratulatory panegyrick for my Lord General's late return, summing up his successes in an exquisite manner.

"To be sold by John Holden, in the New Exchange, London. Printed by Tho. Newcourt, 1652."

The above appeared in the January number of the Parliamentary paper, *Mercurius Politicus.* It is evidently a piece of flattery to Cromwell upon his victories in Ireland. Booksellers appear, therefore, to have been the first to take advantage of this then new medium of publicity, and they have continued to avail themselves very liberally of its benefits up to the present day.

Boston Merchants' Business Marks or Tokens.

There are some interesting specimens of New England merchants' marks, or tokens, of an ancient date, still in existence. Among these are those of Thomas Sandbrook, of Boston, and William Holmes—the former bearing the initials T. S., with the triangle and cross; the latter, W. H., with a rude figure of a tree between. Another is that of John Mills, of Boston, 1651; James Astwood, of Roxbury, 1653; and Nicholas Busby, of Watertown, 1657. That of Mills bears the initials I. M., the triangle and cross at top, a heart pierced with an arrow at the bottom, six stars, and some other figures; that of Astwood, the initials I. A., with a branch between them; and that of Busby, the initials N. B. united, the triangle, some scrolls, etc.

New York Business Tokens.

Occasional memorials of old New York business firms, of the last century, come to light, and are of peculiar interest. A piece in copper, issued by Messrs. Matts, New York jewellers, in 1789, appears to have been the first business token put in circulation in that city. It bears on one side a clock, on the other an American eagle; one of these was sold at auction, a short time ago, for $1.62½. Talbot, Allum & Lee, New York, merchants in the India trade, issued their "one cent" in 1794 —having an emblematic figure of liberty guarding a bale of goods on one side, and a ship under full sail on the other; one of these tokens, issued in 1794, was sold at auction for the sum of $1.25, and another, issued by this house in 1795, brought $2.25.

Inscriptions on Trade Coins.

The trade coins, once so common among British shopkeepers, usually bore on one side the issuer's name, and on the other his address and calling; sometimes a sign and date. Few trades were unrepresented in this way, as the coins still preserved show.

Some of these country trade coins bear a simple promise to pay, as "I will exchange my one penny;" or an announcement, "I pass for a half penny in Leeds;" "I am for a public good in Cockermouth." Another, combining a request and a prayer, "Send me to the mercer of Knox Hall — God grant peace." One says, "Paines bring gaines;" another that, "Plain dealing is best." W. Wakeling shows his loyalty with "Vive le Roy in Uttoxeter;" while another shopkeeper profanely exclaims, "Touch not mine anointed, and do my *profits* no harm." There is a mock humility in "Poore Ned, of Feversham;" unintelligible quaintness in "Pharaoh in Barley;" and a mingling of the practical and poetical in such inscriptions as

and

> "Welcome you be
> To trade with me,"—

> "Although but brass,
> Yet let me pass."

Scotch Tobacconist's Motto.

PERSONS who retire from trade are sometimes disposed, from a false shame, to conceal the mode by which they acquired their wealth. A notable exception to this occurred in the case of a Mr. Gillespie, a tobacconist, in the city of Edinburgh. Having acquired an ample fortune by the sale of snuff at the end of the American war, he set up a carriage; and, lest the public, or himself, might forget how he had acquired the means of keeping one, to arms of three snuff boxes rampant, he added the following doggerel couplet as a motto:

> "Who would have thought it,
> That noses could have bought it?"

Mottoes in Ancient Times.

WHEN printed books first became an article of sale, they found such eager purchasers, that spurious and imperfect editions of the more celebrated works began to be circulated. To remedy this evil, and to give security and protection to those printers whose publications combined great literary merit with rare typographical excellence, princes and potentates granted them permission to use on the title page some symbol and motto, to counterfeit which was legally as well as morally criminal.

Thus, Aldus Manutius, who established the famous Aldine press at Venice, and was the inventor of the type called Italic, adopted for his sign on his title pages a dolphin and anchor. Henry Stephens, the founder of the celebrated family of printers of that name, when established at Paris, took for his symbol an olive tree, and which long continued to be used by his son.

One of the earliest printers, of much celebrity in England, was Henry Day; upward of two hundred works issued from his press, all distinguished by his symbol—the rising sun, with a boy awaking his companion with the words, "Arise, for it is day!" in allusion to the dawning day of the Protestant Reformation. Christopher Plantin, of Antwerp, adopted for his emblem and motto a hand and pair of compasses, with *Labore et Constantia*—"By labor and perseverance:" he stuck to his own motto, and became very rich and eminent. Juan de la Cuesta, of Madrid, the printer and publisher of the first edition of "Don Quixote," took for his device a stork, surrounded by the words *Post tenebras, spero lucem*—"After the darkness, I expect light."

English Business Mottoes.

THE great trading and business companies in England, which were established before the Reformation, and enjoyed exclusive monopolies by royal grant, had each its patron saint, to whom altars were built in the churches of which they held the control—the saint being generally chosen from some relation, supposed or real, to the craft or mystery of the company. Thus, the fishmongers chose St. Peter, and met in St. Peter's Church; the drapers chose the Virgin Mary, "Mother of the Holy Lamb, or fleece," and assembled for their ecclesiastical services in St. Mary Bethlem Church; the merchant tailors selected as their patron saint, St. John the Baptist, as the messenger or prophet who announced the advent of the "Holy Lamb;" and the goldsmiths' patron was St. Dunstan, reputed to have been a fellow craftsman. Their liveries also bore their mottoes: that of the skinners was, "To God be all the glory;" that of the grocers, "God grant grace;" the clothworkers' was, "My trust is in God alone;" the ironmongers', "God is our strength;" and the drapers', "Unto God be honor and glory."

Fresh Gems from English Advertising Columns.

THE English journals continue to furnish, now and then, an emerald of the first water, in the way of ambiguous advertisements—as complete a triumph, indeed, over Lindley Murray, as was that of Wellington over Napoleon. The two specimens which follow, taken from a London paper, appeared under the head of "For sale:"

"PIANOFORTE—Cottage, 7 octaves—the property of a Lady leaving England, in remarkably elegant Walnut Case on beautifully carved supports. The tone is superb, and eminently adapted for any one requiring a first-class instrument. Price, 22 guineas, cost double three months since."

We have heard of Arion riding on a dolphin, and of the wise men of Gotham who went to sea in a bowl; we have heard of Helle on her ram, and of

Europa on her bull; but we never before heard of a lady designing to cross the English Channel in a remarkably elegant walnut case with beautifully carved supports. Indeed, we might go so far as to ask—as probably every reader of the advertisement would be led to—whether the "beautifully carved supports" are those of the walnut case or of the lady herself. In either case, they would seem equally ill adapted to struggle with the winds and billows.

The other advertisement referred to is as follows:

"BUSINESS CHANCE.—To be disposed of, a Genuine Fried Fish Business, at the West End."

The meaning of this advertisement is quite as obscure as that of the first. Does the genuineness apply to the business, to the fish as objects of ichthyology, or the manner in which they are fried? We can guess what is meant by Genuine Patent Medicines, Genuine Bear's Grease, etc., but "Genuine Fried Fish," and still more, a "Genuine Fried Fish Business," is something hopelessly beyond us. There was a time when we did not know what was meant by an "old fish for a mast," but, thanks to many kind friends, we know now very well. Perhaps a like confession of ignorance may lead to our enlightenment on the possibly kindred subject of this "Genuine Fried Fish Business, at the West End."

An Untried Method.

THERE seems to be no end to the new advertising projects which are daily springing up in all directions. There is, however, still one method of advertising left untried, and it is a wonder no one makes the experiment. *Umbrellas* are still left blank—their ample and conspicuous surface bearing no announcement of any new pill, new adhesive gum, bankrupt's sale, or "What is it?" It is pretty certain that the umbrella, with its little brood of para-solettes, sunshades, etc., is destined to become a tremendous vehicle for information. An umbrella maker might try the experiment by placing a puffing broadside on all the articles of his own manufacture. Or perhaps it would be a better plan—as some persons might foolishly object to carry an advertising or pictorial umbrella—that on wet days there should be stations, with placards ready printed, to be pasted on (for a consideration) to the umbrellas of any one who might be disposed to combine profit with convenience.

Classical Shop Language.

To use plain and pure English seems now quite foreign to the taste of many shopkeepers. French is pressed into their service quite as much as Greek and Latin, and by ill-educated tongues, which talk of " hany other harticle," it is not easy to imagine, without having the headache, how the French language must be mispronounced. One can hardly ever take up a newspaper, now-a-days, without seeing an advertisement of some " *recherché* stock of goods" which are to be disposed of forthwith, " *sans* reserve." A hair-dresser now styles himself in general an *artiste*, and advertises to the universe his famed *esprit de violette*, or *bouquet de Rhine*. One enterprising dealer has had the courage to combine his classics with his French, and to advertise for sale a lot of *broché madapolums*, which must be something rather curious if they at all be really like their name. *Corsets* and *chapeau* have quite supplanted such old English words as " stays " and " bonnet ; " and of course no upper-ten dressmaker would ever dream of naming petticoats by any other term than *jupes*. Why this is so, it would be difficult to say; nor is it very easy to guess why in a newspaper professedly intended for circulation among those who speak the English

language, *le sommier élastique portatif* should be advertised, when " portable spring mattress " is vastly more intelligible and far more easily pronounced.

Chinese Trade Puffing.

THE advertisement of Messrs. Chops & Co., the great Chinese firm in London—as it appears in the columns of *Punch*—is formed after the choicest models of English and American trade-puffers, as the following will show :

We, Chop-chin, Chop-lip, Circassian-cree, & Co-cree, having, in the plenitude of our hearts, set up a shop in the very bowels of this barbarian city, now graciously invite all to come and feast on the wonders of our celestial genius. If, after this glorious proclamation, ye will come and look, then most assuredly will we benignantly smile ; and if, further, ye should buy, we will as assuredly laugh very heartily. Delay not ! hasten, hasten ! ! be speedy ! !

Our luxuriant and nourishing Tartar Cream, so highly sought for by the Chinese to polish and finish off their tails, is much recommended for producing a beautiful head of hair.

The True Keying Cold Cream the Messrs. Chops can safely recommend, it having been used for many years on the nose of the Jolly Keying, when heated by a vast multitude of red bunkles, occasioned, it was believed, by a constant flow of good spirits.

Since the arrival of the Messrs. Chops into this country, they have witnessed the fashion of reducing all things to the smallest possible size and lightest conceivable weight. Under this impression, we have manufactured the smallest, lightest, and most shallow pots ever beheld ; two will go into a pillbox, and any six can be carried in a gentleman's waistcoat pocket. Each pot 4s. 6d., being only one shilling more than the usual large and clumsy pots sold at perfumers.

The Imperial Dentifrice, for procuring a beautiful set of teeth, is composed of pulverized bricks from the Porcelain Tower, Nankin. The wonders of this beautiful powder can be at once discovered by merely buying a pot.

Commercial Envelopes, Wrappers, Labels, etc.

To such a degree is the ornamental enveloping of the objects of commerce and the products of industry now carried on, in some departments of trade, that the outside aspects of certain goods, in the popular estimate, actually outvies the goods themselves—the decorated packing case surpasses its contents—the shell excels the kernel. Indeed, this is the *key* to the whole business: the plainest envelope would answer all the purposes of the most luxurious and ornamental one, with a single exception—it *would not sell* the article!

The most expensive of the articles which may be classed as commercial envelopes, is the envelope of the *jeweller*—the morocco case, lined with silk velvet. The gold watch, the costly ring, the bracelet, the gem, are presented to the buyer in a morocco case, which, however costly it may be in itself, forms a very trifling item in the bill. Much capital is invested and much skill employed in the manufacture of these articles.

It is the *paper maker* who is the great source of the commercial envelope. The dress boxes, cap boxes, flower boxes, pattern boxes, lace boxes, and all that legion of envelopes, of every shape and size, are made of paper, in some of its numberless forms, such as card board, mill board, etc. There is no limit to articles of this description, comprising the finest and whitest, or plain, or grained, or embossed, with the most elaborate designs, or spread with gorgeous arabesques and radiant with gold.

The *pictorial* element comes largely into play in the various kinds of paper boxes and envelopes; and it is said

that none of the pleasing discoveries in chromo-typography, chromo-lithography, and block printing in colors, would have proved profitable, but for the use to which they are applied by the makers of paper boxes and ornamental wrappers of various kinds. The perfumer, the fancy stationer, the lace man, the glove maker, are the wholesale patrons of those beautiful arts, and not the public, who admire their *chefs-d'œuvre* in the shop windows, but rarely purchase. It is by the sale of tens and hundreds of thousands of small colored designs and vignettes, which are in demand to envelope the scents, the soaps, the cutlery, the conserves, the toilet gear of the ladies, or the choice filigree stationery they use, that the chromo-photographer is paid. For every picture which the chromo-typographist sells *as* a picture, a hundred at least are nominally given away as part and parcel of the envelope to some kind of merchandise. This luxurious species of envelope originated in Paris, and is there manufactured most extensively, and sent in exquisite parcels to almost every part of the world.

A rival of the paper-box maker is the *worker in metal*. The thinnest sheet or film of lead, or tin, or brass, or bronze, may be pressed in the form of a box and its cover, with an endless variety of most attractive patterns. Millions of these metal envelopes are used, some of them being exceedingly handsome and perfect in design, and of course helping largely the sale of the articles to which they are applied.

The *glass blower* is another important agent in the fabrication of commercial envelopes. The dealers in scents and odors know full well that it is the *bottle*, more than anything else, which recommends and sells the perfume, and they spend infinitely more time and trouble, and—it may as well be told—capital, too, in elaborating a new toilet bottle, than they do in the composition of its contents. A delicious scent—the

" extract of a thousand flowers," for instance—may be concocted from essence of lavender, a modicum of eau de Cologne, and a trifle of attar of roses, homœopathically diffused in an ocean of *aqua pura*—and may be varied *ad infinitum* by the least change in the ingredients ; but the *bottle*, which is to glitter on the toilet table, demands all the genius of the artist and the skill of the craftsman. It is here the chief difficulty lies—to achieve a two-ounce bottle of classical design, toned down to the modern standard of dressing-room elegance ; he is a lucky man indeed who will accomplish it, and may reckon upon an influx of profit compared to which cent. per cent. is mere zero.

The *potter* is in still greater request than the glass blower, among a certain class of dealers. Not to detail the various jars and earthen bottles which he makes for trade purposes, there is a shallow pot and cover, varying in diameter from two inches, or less, to eight inches or more, and formed of every species of ceramic compound, from plainest delf to finest porcelain, the demand for which is almost incredible. They are used as the deposits of pomatums, hair paste, cold cream, " bear's grease," and so on. There are also larger ones, for other purposes, some of which are moulded with great care, and delicately painted by hand with groups of flowers or small landscapes.

Literature and Groceries.

POPE's saying, that " a little learning is a dangerous thing," is pretty well verified in the following inscription over the door of a trader in Holton East, England, and which very naturally arrests the attention of the passers by :

> WATKINSON'S
> Academy;
> *Whatever man has done man may do.*
> Also
> Dealer in Groceries,
> &c.

Signboard Punctuation.

PAINTERS of signboards are too often negligent or incompetent in the matter of punctuation. They either indulge themselves in a redundancy of stops, or totally omit them. In the latter case there will sometimes be met with such non-punctuated inscriptions as—" A Wood Smith," " Lamb Butcher," " Clay Baker," " Winch Turner," " Peacock Builder," " Gay Painter," " Church Saddler," " Moon Gilder," &c.

"For Her Majesty."

A TRAVELLER in England, in a pedestrian tour through the principal business streets, speaks of the amusement afforded him on reading the inscriptions on the ancient signboards ; one was coat maker, hat maker, boot or spur maker, and so on, " for *his* Majesty." Another—frock maker, cape maker, corset, or glove maker, " for *her* Majesty." Thousands are " licensed " to sell tea, sugar, and coffee, provisions, snuff and tobacco, porter and pies, hay and straw, etc., and this is duly specified on the board. On the front of a three-story building, in large letters, reaching from top to bottom, was the following : " Sight restored, and Headache cured, by Grindstone's celebrated Eye Snuff—sold here ; " something rather hard and gritty, it would seem, this process of curing eyes by a grindstone. Many have on their signboards, under their name, the number of years they have done business in that house ; as " John Thomas, Wine Dealer, since 1794,"—thus signifying that he is a man of steady habits to reside and do business in the same house for scores of years. Some of the signs state that father and son have done business on the same spot for one hundred years and upward.

Evasions of Trade Marks.

AN English journal gives an account of several remarkable evasions of trade marks, some of which, at least, can scarcely be heard of without a smile. A Burlington Arcade "Perruquier" introduced a Medicated Mexican Balm, to which he prefixed his name; whereupon a neighbor speedily advertised *his* Medicated Mexican Balm. A quarrel and a lawsuit ensued, ending in the award of protection to the trade mark.

Prof. H.'s pills and ointments may or may not be worthy of the puffery which surrounds them; but by all business men it must be regarded as an obviously mean trick when another person, taking advantage of the same name, opened a shop within the distance of a few houses, and advertised, in the same surname, pills and ointment, and which was another case brought before the law courts.

A third, and quite a curious case, exhibited the following facts: Mr. Crawshay, the eminent ironmaster of South Wales, marks his iron " W. Crawshay," or " W. C.," enclosed in a ring. One day he observed on a wharf some bars of iron bearing a mark which he supposed to be his own, but which, on closer inspection, he found to be " W. O.," enclosed in a ring. He ascertained, moreover, that this mark commonly passed in the Turkish market for his own (Crawshay's) mark. Although this trade mark was not exactly like Crawshay's, yet the O, which was substituted for the C, was, when combined with the W and the ring, a proof of imitation. That Thompson, the proprietor of this iron, was aware of the imitation, was made clear; but there was an absence of technical proof of an *intention* to imitate.

Mr. Linnell, the distinguished painter, painted a picture, and put his name to it; a copy of this picture, name and all, got into the market. That this was an infringement of a trade mark, and something worse, was clear enough, yet, through the inconsistencies of the law, the perpetrator of the fraud escaped both on the charge of forgery and on that of obtaining money on false pretences.

One George Borwick invented what he called baking powder, and egg powder, sold in packets, with his name printed on the wrapper. Another dealer, failing to sell his own baking powder, applied to a printer to print ten thousand labels as nearly as possible like Borwick's, except the signature. This signature had been rendered invisible by the peculiar wrapping of Borwick's packets, until the wrapper was torn off; and therefore the cunning cheat deemed himself in this particular safe. Many of these deceptive packets were sold as Borwick's, before the scheme was discovered.

Foreign manufacturers have in many cases had to vindicate themselves against the arts of nimble-witted and unprincipled English adventurers. The never-dying Jean Maria Farina had once to go into an English court of law, to demand justice for his trade mark. Relying on the confusion between the many eau-de-Cologne makers who, in almost every part of the world, assume that cognomen, an English printer imitated a label with the signature, " Jean Maria Farina, gegenüber dem Julich Platz," with a peculiar flourish, and also a stamp and seal. Although a Prussian subject, Farina was able, in this particular instance, to obtain justice in an English court of law.

Another instance is that of the Collins Company, manufacturers of edge tools, Hartford, Conn. They stamp on their manufactured articles the words, " Collins & Co., Hartford, cast steel, warranted," and also affix labels on which is printed, " Look out for the stamp *Hartford*, if you want the genuine Collins & Co." A Birmingham

(England) merchant was clearly proved to have imitated the trade mark and labels of this company, and to have been in the habit of selling and exporting tools so stamped as being the tools of the company. The latter got the merited justice in this case.

Shop and Business Signs: Ancient Examples.

THE bearing of devices over the doors of shops and other places of business, was a very common practice before the introduction of the plan of numbering the houses, which did not take place until about one hundred years ago. The sign of the house in Bread street, where Milton's father resided, was a spread eagle, which appears to have been the arms of that family. Remains of this custom are still to be observed in several parts of London, and, as is pretty well known, the Messrs. Hoares, the bankers, in Fleet street, retain to this day over the door the symbol of a leather bottle, gilt; and the same was also represented on their notes' which they formerly issued. The Messrs. Gostlings also retain their sign of the three squirrels, and Strahan, Paul & Co., the sign of the golden anchor. The three gilt balls so commonly hung out as signs at pawnbrokers' shops, and by the mass humorously said to indicate that it is two to one the things pledged are never redeemed, were in reality the arms of a set of merchants from Lombardy, who were the first that publicly lent money on pledges; these merchants borrowed this triple symbol from the great merchant, De Medicis. They dwelt together in a street, from them named Lombard street, in London, and also gave their name to another in Paris. The appellation of Lombard was formerly all over Europe considered as synonymous with that of usurers.

The barber's pole has been the subject of many conjectures, some conceiving it to have originated from the word poll or head, with several other conceits as far-fetched and unmeaning; but the true intention of that party-colored staff was to show that the master of the shop practised surgery, and could breathe a vein as well as mow a beard. The white band which encompasses the staff was meant to represent the fillet thus elegantly twined about it.

Fresh Sea-water.

OVER a door on the road from Brighton to Lewes, is a signboard with the very intelligible announcement—"*Fresh sea-water sold here.*"

Titles of Business Firms.

ONE of the most expressive titles of a mercantile firm that could be met with, is that of "Call & Switchem," which is painted in golden letters on a sign in one of the eastern cities; also another, that is equally unique, viz., "Bangs & Swett;" and that of "Lanceman & Payne." "Neal, Pray & Co.," is the title—sufficiently devotional, certainly —of another firm. But the following "beats all." Two attorneys, who were many years ago in partnership, had for the name of their firm, "Catchum & Chetum;" but as the singularity and ominous juxtaposition of the words led to many a disparaging joke from the passers by, the men of law attempted to destroy in part the effect of the odd association, by the insertion of the initials of their Christian names, which happened to be Isaac and Uriah; but, in reality, this made the matter ten times worse, for the inscription ran, "I. Catchum & U. Chetum," and people could not, for the life of 'em, dispossess their minds or imaginations of "high doings" in said law office.

Arms and Seal of the Bank of Ireland.

THE arms and seal of the Bank of Ireland are: Hibernia bearing a crown, as a symbol of her independence; an anchor in her hand, to denote the stability of her commerce, with the words "Bank, of Ireland;" and under the anchor, "*Bona fide republicæ stabilitas*" —intimating that the existence of a people depends upon the faithful discharge of their public debts.

Unexampled Enterprise: The Chinese Wall for Advertisements.

AN enterprising and opulent billsticker has, it is privately understood, made offers to the leader of the Chinese insurgent forces to rent of him, in the event of his being made emperor, the renowned wall of China. The sum offered has not transpired, but it is said to be something extremely munificent.

It is the bill sticker's intention, as soon as he obtains an imperial grant, to form a company of persons who spend large sums of money every year in advertisements, and to cover the entire length of the wall with their bills and posters, a larger price being, of course, charged for those which will be posted outside than for those inside the wall, where comparatively but few people will be able to see them. The bills will be in English, or specially translated into Chinese, at the option of the advertiser. In the event of China being thrown open to universal commerce—and there is, at present, every prospect of such a fact—it will be at once seen what "a desirable medium for advertisements" this national posting-station will be. So favorably is the scheme entertained, by some leading advertisers, that already twelve thousand miles of that part of the wall which runs through the most densely populated districts of the empire, has been bespoken at an enormous rental.

The company will be announced at a future day, and it is expected that the shares will be quoted on 'Change at a heavy premium the very first day. A good judge has been heard privately to say, that next to a celebrated millionnaire's property, it will be the largest hoarding in the world, and there is no doubt it will be. All the puffing tailors, pill merchants, quack-medicine sellers, etc., are actively on the look out—though, in the present case, instead of trying to "drive one another to the wall," as is too generally the case among competitors, each one is doing all he can to keep the rest from that position. Professor Liebig's testimonial in favor of bitter beer is already printed in all the Chinese dialects, only waiting to be posted up.

First Trade Advertisement.

WITH the exception of quack-medicine and book advertisements, the first record of a tradesman turning the newspaper to account in making known his goods to the public, is in 1658. Independently of its being in itself a curiosity, it possesses a very strong interest, from the fact that it marks the introduction of a new article of food and commercial traffic. The advertisement reads thus:

THAT Excellent and by all Physitians approved *China* drink called by the *Chineans Tcha*, by other Nations *Tay alias Tee*, is sold at the *Sultaness Head Cophee House* in *Sweetings* Rents, by the Royal Exchange, London.—*Mercurius Politicus*, September 30, 1658.

This is undoubtedly the earliest authentic announcement yet made known, of the public sale in England of this now universal beverage. The mention of "cophee house" proves that the sister stimulant had already got a start.

"Tight Times."

THAT financial visitor, of such bad renown, "Tight Times," is thus set off:

He may be seen on 'Change every day. He bores our merchants, and seats himself cozily in lawyers' offices. He is everywhere.

A great disturber of the public quiet, a pestilent fellow, is this same Tight Times. Everybody talks about him; everybody looks out for him; everybody hates him; and a great many hard words and not a few profane epithets are bestowed upon him. Everybody would avoid — "cut" him, if they could; everybody would hiss him from 'Change, hustle him out of the street, kick him from the banks, throw him out of the stores, out of the hotels —but they can't. Yes, Tight Times is a bore—he will stick like a brier.

An impudent fellow, too, is Tight Times. Ask for a discount, and he looks over your shoulder, winks at the cashier, and your note is thrown out. Ask a loan of the usurers at one per cent. per month, he looks over your securities, and marks "two and a half." Present a bill to your debtor, Tight Times shrugs his shoulders, rolls up his eyes, and you must "call again." A wife asks for a fashionable brocade and a daughter for a new bonnet; Tight Times puts in his caveat, and the brocade and bonnet are postponed.

A great depreciator in stocks is Tight Times. He steps in among the bankers, and down go the "favorites of the market." He goes along the railroads in process of construction, and the Irishmen throw down their shovels and walk away.

A famous exploder of bubbles is Mr. Tight Times. He looks into the affairs of gold companies, and they fly to pieces; into "kiting" banks, and they stop payment. He walks around "corner lots," draws a line across lithograph cities, and they disappear. He leaves his footprints among mines, and the rich metal becomes dross. He breathes upon the cunningest speculations, and—they burst like torpedoes.

A hard master for the poor is this Tight Times—a cruel enemy to the laboring classes. He takes the mechanic from his bench, the laborer from his work, the hod carrier from his ladder.

He runs up the prices of provisions, and he runs down the wages of toil. He runs up the prices of food, and he runs down the ability to purchase it at any price. His picture is hung up in everybody's memory.

Irish Advertisement.

THE Edinburgh Review, in an article on Plowden's History of Ireland, wherein the historian has much to say of the splendid efforts of the Irish literati—their essays, histories, and learned effusions, or rather the assumed absence of such, on account of the wicked irruption of the Danes in the ninth and tenth centuries—says that in such an apology there is something that strongly reminds one of the Irish advertisement:

"Lost, on Saturday last, but the loser does not know when or where, an empty sack, with a cheese in it. On the sack the letters 'P. G.' are marked, but so completely worn out, as not to be legible."

Carmeline the Dentist's Sign.

CARMELINE, the famous toothdrawer and maker of artificial teeth, had his portrait painted and placed in his chamber window, with a motto taken from Virgil's line of the Golden Bough, in the sixth book of the Æneid:

"Uno avulso, non deficit alter."

The application of this line [When one is drawn out, another is never wanting] was extremely happy.

Criticism of a Hatter's Sign.

A JOURNEYMAN hatter, a companion of Dr. Franklin, on commencing business for himself, was anxious to get a handsome signboard with a suitable inscription. This he composed himself, as follows: "John Thompson, hatter, makes and sells hats for ready money," with the figure of a hat subjoined. But he thought he would submit it to his friends for criticism—and amendments, if susceptible of any.

The first he showed it to thought the word *hatter* tautologous, because followed by the words "makes hats," which of themselves showed he was a hatter. It was struck out. The next observed that the word *makes* might as well be omitted, because his customers would not care who made the hats—if good, and to their mind, they would buy, by whomsoever made. He struck that out also. A third said, he thought the words *for ready money* were useless; as it was not the custom of the place to sell on credit, every one who purchased expected to pay. These too were parted with, and the incription then stood, "John Thompson sells hats." "*Sells* hats!" says his next friend; "why, who expects you to *give* them away? What, then, is the use of the word?" It was struck out, and "hats" was all that remained attached to the name of John Thompson. Even this inscription, brief as it was, was reduced ultimately to JOHN THOMPSON, with the figure of a hat subjoined.

Cabalistic Sign for an Alehouse.

THE keeper of a paltry Scotch alehouse having on his sign, after his name, the letters M. D. F. R. S., a physician, who was a member, or fellow, of the Royal Society, asked him how he presumed to affix those letters to his name. "Why, sir," said the publican, "I have as good a right to them as you have." "What do you mean, you impudent scoundrel?" replied the doctor. "I mean, sir," retorted the other, "that I was Drum Major of the Royal Scots Fusileers."

Pleasant History of a Familiar Word.

SOME signboards have much of history connected with them. A slight instance of this sort is as follows: Before the year 1730, the English publicans sold to the thirsty souls of their day three sorts of beer, which they drew from different casks.into the same glass, and gave to this mixture the name of half-and-half. The owner of one of these resorts (history has handed down the name), Horwood, wishing to spare himself the trouble of performing this task so constantly during the day, hit upon brewing the beer which would combine the qualities of all these beers. To this compound he gave the name of "Entire," which has adhered to it till this day, at least on the signboards. It was afterward christened "*porter*," because principally drunk by that class.

Streets and Shop Signs in Canton.

.THE streets of Canton present, to a stranger, an extraordinary sight; they are very narrow, and hung about in all directions with signs and advertisements. Every shop has a large upright board on each side of the door, usually painted white, and on it, in red or black letters, is inscribed a list of all the articles sold. Other signs are hung over the street, and some are fixed to poles reaching from one side of the street to the other. Many of these display puffing advertisements, such as— "*This Old Established Shop*," etc. ; "*The Refulgent Sign: Original Maker of the finest quality of Caps*," etc. ; "*Canton Security Banking Establishment ;*" and "*No two Prices at this Shop*" is a very common notification. The Chinese.writing looks very well in this way; and being generally red letters upon white, black upon red or yellow, and blue upon white, the array of signs presents a most gaudy and extraordinary appearance.

Ancient Pictorial Signboards.

IT became quite customary, in the seventeenth century, among English traders, to have emblazoned some animal or object spreading upon the signboards, in order more effectually to catch the eye. In course of time, when fancy became capricious, something more grotesque or piquant was adopted, such as blue boars, black swans, red lions, flying pigs, hogs in armor, swans with two necks, and all such queer skimble-skamble stuff. Then there were multitudes of compound signs, such as the fox and seven stars, ball and neat's tongue, dog and gridiron, sheep and dolphin, pig and whistle. These comical combinations seem to have originated in the apprentice quartering his master's symbol with his own, like the combined but very dissimilar arms of a matrimonial heraldic alliance. Some curious instances of this kind are given on another page of this department of Anecdotes.

In not a few instances—which can be traced to the ignorance of the people, or the customary contraction or abbreviation of speech—these absurd emblems became most ridiculously perverted. Thus, the Bologne mouth, the mouth of the harbor of Bologne, in France, became the "bull and mouth;" a noted traveller's inn in St. Martin's lane, the Satyr and Bacchanals, became the "devil and bag of nails;" and the praiseworthy legend or phrase, "God encompasseth us," became, after being many times mouthed over by various provincialists, profanely metamorphosed into the "goat and cow passes." These signs, which then projected into the street at all lengths and angles, where they swung from their elegant and elaborately curled iron supports, creaked to and fro, most hideously, with every blast.

———

Joke upon a Boston Sign.

A SOLEMN-LOOKING fellow, with a certain air of dry humor about the corners of his rather sanctimonious mouth, stepped quietly, one day, into the well-known establishment of "Call & Tuttle," Boston, and quietly remarked to the clerk in attendance, "I want to *tuttle*." "What do you mean, sir?" "Well, I want to *tuttle:* noticed the invitation over your door, so I '*called*,' and now I should like to *tuttle!*" He was ordered to leave the establishment, which he did, with an assumed look of angry wonder, and facetiously grumbling to himself, "If they don't *want* strangers to 'call and tuttle,' what do they put up a sign for, calling 'em in to do it?"

———

"Cotton is Quiet."

IN consequence of the snow, says Punch, Liverpool was last week in a state of isolation from the rest of the world, there being no traffic by rail or news by letter, and indeed nothing by which any idea could be formed of the doings or condition of the Liverpoolians. Of course, indefatigable efforts were made to open the communication with the metropolis; but all was in vain, for the ordinary electric telegraph had got into a state of entanglement through the ice and snow, thus baffling all hopes of hearing anything from Liverpool.

Bills were falling due in London, and were being dishonored for want of "advice;" commercial firms were falling into discredit, and all for want of communication with the north; when at last, after almost superhuman endeavors, it was announced that the magnetic telegraph had succeeded in bringing news from Liverpool. Everybody rushed to the second edition of the morning papers, to drink in the long looked-for news, when public curiosity was put in possession of the fact, that by tremendous energy, a communication had reached London, bringing the news that "Cotton is quiet." We cannot judge of the effect of this intelligence on the commercial world, but, to us, it seems as though the result of the telegraphic achievements had, after "much cry," ended in "little *wool*"—though there might be a fair supply of cotton.

We had no idea that the condition of this raw material was of such vital consequence as to make it paramount to every other subject of curiosity. We shall, however, henceforth, look out for the bulletins about cotton with unprecedented anxiety and interest. If we can only be assured by the paper on our breakfast table that " cotton has had a quiet night and is better," we shall have all our mental trepidations soothed, and shall even be contented with the knowledge that " cotton is not worse "—or worsted.

Stock Terms in the Sickroom.

M. DE CHIRAC, a celebrated physician, had bought some joint-stock shares at what proved an unlucky period, and was very anxious to sell out. The stock, however, continued to fall for two or three days, much to his alarm. His mind was filled with morbid concern in regard to the subject, when he was suddenly called upon to attend a lady who imagined herself unwell. He arrived, was shown up stairs, and at once felt the lady's pulse. "It falls! it falls! good God! it falls continually!" said he musingly though audibly, while the lady looked up in his face all anxiety for his opinion. "Oh, M. de Chirac," said she, starting to her feet and ringing the bell for assistance, " I am dying! I am dying! it falls—it falls—it falls!" "What falls?" inquired the doctor in amazement. "My pulse! my pulse!" said the lady; "I *must* be dying!" " Calm your apprehensions, my dear madam," said M. de Chirac, " I was speaking of the stocks. The truth, is, I have been a great loser, and my mind is so disturbed, I hardly know what I have been saying."

Phenomena Extraordinary.

THE following announcement of facts, taken from a city advertising column, may fairly be said to come under the head of " phenomena extraordinary." In one place it is announced that there may be had " An airy bedroom for a gentleman twenty-two feet long by fourteen feet wide ; "—the bed room ought, indeed, to be airy, to accommodate a gentleman of such tremendous dimensions. Again, one may read of " A house for a family in good repair," which is advertised to be let with immediate possession ;—a family in good repair meaning, no doubt, one in which none of the members are at all " cracked." Another oddity in this line, is an announcement of there being now vacant " A delightful gentleman's residence ; " the " delightful gentleman " must be rather proud of his delightful qualities, to allow himself to be thus strangely advertised A rare bit in this way, in addition to the above *morceaux*, is an advertisement offering a reward for " a large Spanish blue gentleman's cloak, lost in the neighborhood of the market." The fact can easily be realized, of a gentleman looking rather blue at the loss of his cloak; still there is something rather unaccountable in his advertising the fact of his blueness in connection with the loss of his garment.

Quack Advertisement Two Centuries Ago.

THAT great—though not quite the earliest—progenitor of the newspaper tribe, the *London Gazette*, of Nov. 16th, 1660, shows that the quack fraternity of that day were the first to avail themselves of its pages to make known their nostrums. It is really astonishing to see what an ancestry some of the quack medicines of the present day have had. " Nervous powders," specifics for gout, rheumatism, etc., seized upon the newspapers almost as early as they were published. Here is a specimen of the above date—rising two hundred years ago—which might still serve as a model for such announcements:

"*Gentlemen, you are desired to take notice, That Mr. Theophilus Buckworth doth at his house on Mile-end-Green, make and expose to sale, for the publick good, those so famous Lozenges or Pectorals approved for the cure of Consumption, Coughs, Catarrhs, Asthmas, Hoarseness, Strongness of Breath, Colds in General, Diseases incident to the Lungs, and a sovereign Antidote against the Plague, and all other contagious Diseases, and obstructing of the Stomach: and for more convenience of the people, constantly leaving them sealed up with his coat of arms on the papers, with Mr. Rich. Lowndes (as formerly), at the sign of the White Lion, near the little north door of Paul's Church; Mr. Henry Seile, over against S. Dunstan's Church in Fleet Street: Mr. William Milward at Westminster Hall Gate; Mr. John Place, at Furnival's Inn Gate in Holborn; and Mr. Robert Horn, at the Turk's head near the entrance of the Royal Exchange, Booksellers, and no others. "This is published to prevent the designs of divers Pretenders, who counterfeit the said Lozenges to the disparagement of the said Gentleman, and great abuse of the people.— Mercurius Politicus, Nov. 16, 1660.*"

Baking and Banking.

A SAD blunder is mentioned by a writer in "Harper's," showing that the best signs *do* fail sometimes. He says that old Mr. Spoon kept a cake and beer shop in the village, and made a fortune in the business, leaving his money and the stand to his only son, who has long been flourishing on his father's profits, and turning up his nose at the baking business as altogether beneath a sprig of his quality. As soon as the old man was fairly under the sod, the rising son fitted up the shop on the corner, put in a show window, through which a heap of

bills and shining gold was seen, and over the door he spread a sign in handsome gilt letters—"BANKING HOUSE." He was now in a new line, adapted to his taste and genius. One day, as he was lolling over the counter, a stranger drove his horses close to the door, and called out to the new broker: "I say, Mister, got any crackers?" *Spoon* (very red and indignant): "None at all; you've mistaken the place." "Any cakes, pies, and things?" "No, *sir!*" —accompanied by a look intended as an extinguisher. *Stranger* (in turn getting red): "Then what on airth makes you have 'BAKIN' HOUSE' writ in sich big letters over your door for? Tell me *that!*" The difference between "baking" and "banking" was not so great as young Spoon supposed.

Questionable Sign for a Clothier.

A SIGN painter being called upon to letter the front of a large general clothing establishment, finished one line across the whole front thus:

"DEALER IN ALL SORTS OF LADIES'"

—and finding his ladder too long to paint the next line, returned to his house to get one of suitable length; but stepping unguardedly upon a stone, it turned his foot up, spraining his ankle, so that he could not finish the lettering till the next day.

In the mean time, the people—reasonably enough—stared at the new sign, and many of them, knowing the character of the man to be strictly in keeping with that of a good husband, father, and citizen, it was certainly unaccountable; as "*all sorts of ladies,*" in a city like New York, comprised commodities at their antipodes, the best and worst on earth.

The citizens made themselves busy that day in surmises, scurrilous innuendoes, and injurious quizzings; which could be hardly overcome when the finishing lettering, "*and Gentlemen's ready-made Clothing*," was at last added.

Out of Style.

ONE of the most eminent painters of signs, in London, was Mr. Wale, one of the founders of the Royal Academy, and who was appointed the first professor of perspective in that institution. The most notable of his achievements in signboards, was a whole length of Shakspeare, about five feet high, which was executed for and displayed at the door of a public house, at the northwest corner of Little Russell street, Drury Lane. It was enclosed in a sumptuously carved gilt frame, and suspended by rich ironwork, the cost being several hundred pounds. But this splendid and costly object for attracting trade did not hang long, before it was taken down, in consequence of the act of parliament which was passed for removing signs and other obstructions from the streets of London. Such was the total change of style and fashion, and the universal disuse of such signs, that this costly representation of the great dramatist was sold for hardly more than its value as oven wood, to a broker, at whose door it stood for several years, until it was totally destroyed by the weather and various accidents.

Natural Advertising.

SEVERAL years ago, and soon after the " anti-license law " went into force in the Green Mountain State, a traveller stopped at a village hotel and asked for a glass of brandy. "Don't keep it," said the landlord; "forbidden by law to sell liquor of any kind." "The deuce you are!" retorted the stranger incredulously. "Such is the fact," replied the host; "the house don't keep it." "Then bring your own bottle," said the traveller, with decision; "you needn't pretend to me that

you keep that face of yours in repair on water." The landlord laughed heartily, and his " private " bottle, advertised so well in his phiz, was at once forthcoming.' No mere decanters or artificial signs were needed in his case.

Class Advertisements in City Papers.

BOTH in Europe and the United States there are newspapers which are distinguished by class advertisements. The London Times, in its multifarious announcements, may be said to have no speciality in this respect. But the Morning Post, of the same city, almost exclusively monopolizes the advertisements which relate to fashions and high life; the Morning Advertiser, the organ and property of the liquor vendors, obtains the lion's share of whatever pertains to that craft; the Morning Herald, even yet, though its circulation is greatly reduced, contains a goodly array of auction sales of property; the Era, and Sunday Times contain a majority of theatrical advertisements; the Shipping Gazette chronicles the times, rates, and ports of departure, for the commercial marine; Bell's Life is devoted to the sporting fraternity; the Athenæum has the principal portion of the book advertisements—and so on, through an extensive series.

In the city of New York, the Herald and the Sun may be said to engross the greater part of the "wants" and "boarding" advertisements; the Tribune and Evening Post have a considerable proportion of the literary and real estate announcements; the Courier and Enquirer, or the World, is a favorite organ of the auctioneers; the Journal of Commerce, Commercial Advertiser, and Express, have their full share of the shipping notices; the Daily Times engrosses a liberal share of the banking and financial advertisements; and the other dailies and weeklies combine, more or less, all these varie-

21

ties, without being considered the medium of any one kind in particular.

First Advertisement in America.

THE first newspaper in America (with the exception of a solitary copy issued in 1690), the "*News Letter*," published in Boston, Sept. 24th, 1704, contained a notice by the publisher, inviting advertisements; and in the succeeding number, May 1st, 1704, was one response—the *first newspaper advertisement in America*, as follows:

"Lost on the 10. of *April* last, off Mr. Shippens's Wharf in *Boston*, Two Iron Anvils, weighing between 120 and 140 pound each: Whoever has taken them up, and will bring or give true intelligence of them to *John Campbel*, Post-Master, shall have a sufficient reward."

The charges for advertising then, as given in the first number of the "*News Letter*," were to be "at a Reasonable Rate, from *Twelve Pence* to *Five Shillings*, and not to exceed: Who may agree with *John Campbel*, Post-master of *Boston*."

Compare the above with the seven solid columns which sometimes constitute a single advertisement in city newspapers at the present day!

"Punch" on Commercial Phraseology.

IN the intelligence from the Brazils, last week, we met, says Punch, in one of the papers, with the following curious paragraph: "Dry Germans opened at 59½ reals, but declined to 58 for half ox, half cow, and 60 for ox, this quotation being merely nominal."

The above is a complete mystification. Of course, in our travelling experiences, we have met with many "dry Germans," but we little suspected that they ever formed an article of commerce. Besides, who could wish to *purchase* a "dry German"? Then the question arises, how do you dry a German? After this, comes the further mystery of his being "opened." It is rather undignified to talk in this way of a "dry German," as if he were no better than a dried haddock, or a cured herring, or a Teutonic mummy, that had the accumulated dust and cobwebs of centuries upon him. However, we are so far pleased as to notice that "dry Germans" fetch so good a price—in the "dry goods" market, we suppose. It is more than *we* should feel inclined to give for such a specimen of dried metaphysics and transcendentalistic Kantism.

But another puzzle that bewilders us still more is the revelation that your "dry German" is "half ox, half cow." We have heard of the multifarious nature pertaining to an Irish *bull*, and of a *vache Espagnole*, and of other curiosities belonging to the animal kingdom; but we must confess that such an ethnological specimen as a "dry German," who was at the same time "half ox, half cow"—having the head of an ox and the tail of a cow, perhaps—never, fortunately for us, crossed our scientific path before. We are so mystified that we must write to Prof. O. on the subject, though it looks very suspiciously as if Barnum, under a strong attack of "animal" spirits, had had a hand in stitching this new hybrid together, for the enrichment of his Museum. However, our Foreign Office, that always evinces such a strong sympathy for German interests, should take the matter up. If slavery is abolished, why, we want to know, are "dry Germans" thus offered publicly for sale?

Dialects of Different Trades.

EVERY trade has its own peculiarities and its own dialect. Stage drivers and hostlers have a language of their own. Hod carriers and masons always speak understandingly to each other, if not to strangers. Thieves and gamblers have their own phrases, and housebreakers their signs; all of which is as unintelligible to the uninitiated as so much Greek.

Drygoods dealers and grocers have a language of their own. In speaking of the standing of a countryman, they often say he is *good*—they have sold him, or are going to sell him—which means, not that they have sold *him* for a price, but that they have trusted him with a certain amount of goods. They are never heard to say they have *bought* him. So at auction sales they have signs; if they want to bid two dollars a dozen for a box of gloves, or two dollars apiece for a box of ribbons, they hold up two fingers;—and if a business man is in an omnibus and wants the driver to take pay for one, when he hands up a quarter he will hold up one finger to him, while a lawyer or mechanic will bawl out, " *One*—take out one, *one*, ONE."

Grocers talk about things in their trade being heavy, hard, quick, slow, and easy. Thus feathers may be heavy, cotton down, pork slow, beef quick, oranges flat, &c.

Brokers have, like all others, a language of their own. Thus, "b 3" means that the buyer has the privilege of taking the stock any time within three days; "b 30," within thirty days. If, for instance, A buys one hundred shares of Canton, of B, b 30, he can call upon B to-morrow, or next day, or next week, or whenever he chooses, for the stock, and B must deliver it. "S 30" means the seller has the privilege of delivering it at any time he chooses within thirty days. The seller is always entitled to interest on stocks sold on time. "Thwk" means this week; "nwk," next week; "opg," opening of the transfer books, which are closed for the time to make dividends.

Trade Placards and Shop Bills.

NOTWITHSTANDING the frequent announcement to be met with, " *Stick no*

Bills," bills *are* stuck somewhere, everywhere, and the trade of the bill-sticker, though not down in the cyclopædias of commerce, is such as makes him a definite, genuine, distinct character— one who keeps alive other trades—and who may also be said to live in the eye of the public as literally as any other man of his day. If not a literary man, he may at least rank as a commercial publisher, largely patronized by almost all trades.

There is one singularity in the follower of this profession, which to many is a mystery—that he invariably pastes over his bills on both sides; having stuck them to the wall or boarding, he is not content with that, but immediately gives them a coat of paste on the outer and printed side as well. This, which appears to others a sheer work of supererogation, is perhaps mysteriously connected with some important element in the process; he knows.

But if in this point of his art he puzzles others, he himself is sometimes in as odd a predicament—for instance, when he has a batch of announcements in Hebrew, addressed to the " children of Israel." While conning the square letters, he will get perplexed indeed as to which end of the poster has the most right to stand uppermost on the wall; and, when the spectators cannot help him to a conclusion, he will solve the problem in a sort of hit-or-miss way, by placing a couple of copies side by side, one on its head, the other on its feet, in accordance, it may be supposed, with the prudent maxim, that it is better to lose a part than to risk the whole.

This bill sticking is, after all, more of an art than shopkeepers who make use of it are accustomed to consider. Said an adept in the business—the very apostle of it in one of the large cities —a little old man with a wooden leg, equipped with a long cross-stick and an equally long hook upon his shoulder, and a majestic pot of paste in front—" These *young* fellows, sir, are quite unfit for their business. They do not know what they ought to do, and sometimes they will not even do what they know they ought. When *I* undertake a bill, I go over the whole town with it. I paste it *from end to end!* I also take care never to cover over a bill too soon. In fact, sir, I do *justice* to my business as a business man, which they never think of doing. Then, sir, how can they pretend to paste a bill with me? Why, *they have not the machinery!* (glancing at his cross-stick and hook).

He added—'I'll give out a shop-bill, too, sir, with any man in the country. Some that pretend to do it, give their bills to anybody who will take them. Now, *I* give them only to people who are going in the direction of the shop. Some give them to people who they can see at a glance are too poor to buy goods—*I* give them only to people who can. It requires some study, sir, to give out a shop bill rightly!"

Odd Comminglings.

THE subject of commercial art finds abundance of material, and of the greatest variety, in the pictorial signs and embellishment of ware now so much in vogue. Painting stops to make progress along with the crafts of buying and selling; nor is the sister art of sculpture discountenanced by the disciples of trade, for now and then the bust of some great man is found presiding over the stock of some petty trade—Sir Isaac Newton among piles of potatoes, and Shakspeare and Milton imbedded among the thread, wax, heel ball, and sparables of the retail leather seller.

Sometimes a tradesman shows historical proclivites. Some remarkable event of ancient or modern days—some battle, siege, earthquake, or terrible volcanic eruption is delineated in his shop window, as a background to his goods. Thus, the earthquake of Lisbon, the overwhelming of Pompeii, or the forcing of the Northwest Passage, are events sought to be illustrated to the spectator's mind by the destruction of vermin by Dosem's Patent Cockroach Exterminator, or the newly invented heel tips by Simon Bend-leather.

With eating houses and coffee shops, the pictorial subject generally consists of a loaf, or two loaves, of bread, a wedge of cheese on a plate of the willow pattern, a lump of "streaky bacon," a cup appearing to be full of coffee, or a tankard of beer, a lump of butter on a plate, and a knife and fork—perhaps a bunch of radishes and a red herring, eloquent of relish.

The fishmongers are not so generally given to the public patronage of art, but the pedestrian will come now and then upon a really well-painted picture gracing the wall or panel of the fishmonger's stand. It may be a group of fish in the grand style—salmon, cod, frost or silver fish, among which crabs and lobsters seem temptingly dripping with the salt ooze; or, it may be, a coast scene, with the bluff fishermen up to their waists in the brine, dragging their nets upon the beach, which is covered with their spoils. But whatever it is, it is sure to be pretty well done, if executed under the artistic auspices of the fishmonger.

Very Express-ive.

THE symbol long adopted by the American Express Company was the picture of a dog guarding a safe. Their new building upon Hudson street, New York, is adorned with a fine bas-relief of that appropriate emblem of care and fidelity, sculptured in marble. A symbol, less felicitous, used by an express manager, was a greyhound running at full speed—in-

THE HIDE DEALER'S SIGN.

tended probably to indicate despatch. Unfortunately for his customers it obtained at length a more pregnant significance, for the manager himself ran away. It only wanted a sack of gold on the back of the " hound," to render the picture perfect. Another express emblem, used somewhere, has been that of a deer, going at the rate of 1.20, to signify speed. Harnden's emblem upon a circular advertising the first express between the New World and the Old, was a vignette representing the two hemispheres, with himself striding from one to the other—one foot being on the American shore, and the other on " the chalky cliffs of Albion ; " while upon his back he carried a bag of newspapers, letters, etc. If, in spanning the ocean in that figurative way, it ever occurred to the fruitful brain of Harnden that a suspension bridge might at some future day serve the same purpose, he wisely kept the crotchet to himself.

Pawnbrokers' Three Balls.

THOUGH the fact is generally admitted that the three golden balls of the pawnbrokers had their origin with the Italian bankers—the Lombards—it is an interesting point quite generally overlooked in connection with this fact, that the greatest of those traders in money were the celebrated and eventually princely house of the Medici of Florence. They bore pills on their shield—and those pills, as usual then, were gilded—in allusion to the professional origin from whence they had derived the name of Medici ; and their commercial agents in England and other countries put that armorial bearing over their doors as their sign, and the great reputation of that house induced others to put up the same sign.

Hide Dealer's Sign : Rare Bit of Philosophy.

THE proprietor of a tanyard adjacent to a certain town in Virginia, concluded to build a stand, or sort of store, on one of the main streets, for the purpose of vending his leather, buying raw hides, and the like. After completing his building, he began to consider what sort of a sign it would be best to put up for the purpose of attracting attention to his new establishment ; and for days and weeks he was sorely puzzled on this subject. Several devices were one after the other adopted, and, on further consideration, rejected.

At last a happy idea struck him. He bored an *auger hole through the door post*, and *stuck a calf's tail into it, with the bushy end flaunting out*. After a while, he noticed a grave-looking personage standing near the door, with his spectacles, gazing intently on the sign. And there he continued to stand, dumbly absorbed, gazing and gazing, until the curiosity of the hide dealer was greatly excited in turn. He stepped out and addressed the individual :

" Good morning," said he.

" Morning," said the other, without moving his eyes from the sign.

" You want to buy leather ? " said the storekeeper.

" No."

" Do you want to sell hides ? "

" No."

" Perhaps you are a farmer."

" No."

" A merchant, maybe."

" No."

" Are you a doctor ? "

" No."

" What *are* you, then ? "

" I'm a *philosopher*. I have been standing here for an hour, trying to see if I could ascertain *how that calf got through that auger hole !* "

Latin on Business Signs.

THERE went from the good city of Baltimore, some years ago, to Norfolk, Va., a painter of signs, who professed to know a thing or two beyond the general run of his craft. He took very readily, for in truth he was no mean workman. Upon every sign that he painted, he put his " imprint," SPRAGUE (that was his name), to which he complacently added the Latin word *fecit.* The unlearned, " the little boys and all," supposing the two words to constitute the name of the painter, accosted him everywhere as Mr. Fecit, Mr. Sprague Fecit, until the poor fellow, annoyed to death by the ridicule which his little learning had brought upon him, ran away. He was some years after succeeded by another knight of the brush, from the same goodly city, who was something of a humorist, and disposed to throw Latin, like physic, to the dogs. He, too, painted many signs there, but was content to boast of his work in plain English, as might be seen by the modest inscription, customary with him—" *Coppuck did it.*"

Shopkeepers' Nomenclature of Goods.

ONE can hardly get an idea of how extensively diffused is the knowledge of languages in a community, at the present day, without taking notice of the signboard and shop announcements which meet the eye at every turn. Indeed, a walk along any of the principal shopping thoroughfares of a city, will very naturally excite one's curiosity as to the *source* whence so many traders derive their Greek, etc.

Thus, a tailor draws attention to his " anaxyridian trousers"—presumed to convey the idea of braceless and stayless trousers, using Greek as the tailor would have it used. A shop is called an " emporium" or " bazaar." Sometimes the names given to *woven* goods is an elaborate combination of Greek or Latin syllables, to denote in some degree the quality of the cloth; sometimes it is an imported French or Italian or Spanish name.

Among *cotton* goods may be found saccharillas, nainsooks, tarlatans, surougs, grandvilles, Selampores, denims, panos da Costa, Polynesian swansdown (did the cotton come from the breast of a swan, or did it grow in Polynesia ?), doeskins and moleskins and lambskins, coutils (sometimes inelegantly corrupted into " cowtails "), and a host of other examples.

The *woollen* and *worsted* people are not less liberal in nomenclature, for they give us anti-rheumatic flannel, swanskin, valencias, reversible Witneys, double-surfaced beavers, Himalayas, satin-faced doeskins (a doe would *hardly* know himself with such a face), fur James beavers, Moscow beavers, Alpa Viennas, three-point Mackinaws, barége-de-laine, Saxe-Coburgs, Orleans, napped pilots, double Napiers, elephanta ribs, elephant beavers (unknown to naturalists, certainly), rhinoceros skins, paramattas, barracans, moskittos, stockinettes, wildboars, uravenas ponchos, princettas, plainbacks, fearnoughts, chameleons, figured Amozonians (*exclusively* for *female* wear ?), alpaca inkas and madelinas, velillos, and cristales, and cubicas, and Circassians, madonnas, balzarines, durants, and cotillons, Genappes, Henriettas, rumswizzles—all, be it observed, varieties of woollen and worsted goods.

Nor do the *silk* dealers forget to supply us with mayonettes, diaphanes, glacé gros d'Afrique, brocatelles, barratthcas, armayine royales, Balmorals, paraphantons, Radzimores, moiré antiques, Algerias, levantines, and other oddly named goods.

The *linen* folks, too, have their own favorite list; such as dowlases, ducks, drills, huckabucks, gray Baden-Badens, drabbets, crankies, commodores, Wellingtons, dustings, paddings, Osnaburgs, Ficklenburgs, Silesias, platillas, estapillas, bretanas, creas legitimas, etc.

The *boot* and *shoe* fraternity give us a verbal crash in the "red morocco leg patent goloshed vandyked button boot," and the "ladies' ottoman silk goloshed elastic button gaiter;" and the more classical "soccopedes elasticus." The "pannuscorium boots" ought, surely, to be worn by every Latin schoolboy; and the "resilient boots" must not be forgotten by fastidious pedestrians of a lexicological turn.

But the *tailors* beat the shoemakers all hollow in their Latin and Greek. The "subclavien sector" is tremendous—it sounds so surgical-like; it is, however, simply a tailor's measure, and another tailor's measure is the "registered symmetrometer." It would be somewhat hazardous to say how many learned names besides "siphonia" are given to waterproof garments. There is also the "unique habit," the "bisunique or reversible garment," and the "monomeroskiton" (long enough to form a very pretty Greek lesson), or "single-piece coat, cut from one piece of cloth." Then we have the "duplexa," the "registered auto-crematic gown," and the "patent euknemeda."

Nor have *hats* and *bonnets* and hosiery and shirts been left unadorned with Greek and Latin trimmings; witness the "ventilating chaco," or foreign hat. But the "korychlamyd"—a helmet cap—is a crusher. The "novum pileum" hat suggests the very dubious query, whether the Latins ever wore silk hats. The "areophane bonnet," a pretty name for a pretty garment, is too transparently beautiful to seem like hard Greek. As to "goffered crinoline," we can only hint that it is used for garments which men folk are supposed to know nothing about. The "brayama gloves" we cannot interpret, and flatly "give it up!"

Of *shirts*, the "el dorado" must surely be a *golden* fit; if not, then we can try the "eureka," the "corazza," the "giubba," the "élastique transpirante," the "tourist sottanello," the "registered sans-pli," and others so bedizened with names that one can hardly recognize them as plain, honest, well-meaning shirts.

As to the florid and prolific nomenclature of the *patent-medicine* people, we can give no accurate information, until we have time to walk leisurely among them, with a Greek or polyglot dictionary in hand.

Pottery used to be pottery, but now it is "ceramic" manufacture. *Burnt clay* would be a poor, dull name indeed, but "terra cotta" has a fine æsthetic sound about it. *Fine China* is not a good enough name for statuette material—it must be called "Parian." The good people of yore delighted to look at a *magic lantern*, but now it must be a camera obscura, or a phantasmagoria, or both; and if public, the exhibition must be called by the name of diorama, cosmorama, cyclorama, panorama, polytechnic, pantechnicon, etc.

A rush has likewise been made into Greek and Latin by *musical instrument makers*, who give us piccolos, harmoniums, microchordions, microphonic pianos, æolians, ophicleides, cornopeans, floetinas, flutinas, accordions, concertinas, melodeons, seraphines, autophons, serpentcleides, euharmonic guitars and organs, symphonions, æolophons, etc.

Paying at "Maturity."

A PROMINENT mule dealer, doing business in Kentucky, sold a lot of stock to a trader, who was to pay him in *four* months—lawful tender in Bourbon. At the expiration of two months the trader sent him an accepted bill on New York for half the money, and wrote him he would pay the balance at *maturity*. After overhauling all the maps and school geographies, he goes down to the store, and says, "See here!

where is this place they call *Maturity?*
I can't find it on the map, and I have
a note payable there; and I fear I
won't be able to get there, for I can't
find it on the map!"

"Ditto."

An honest old man, rather ignorant
of the improved method of abbreviation or phraseology in business accounts, on looking over his grocer's
bill, occasionally found charges like
the following: "To 1 lb. tea—to 1 lb.
ditto." "Wife," said he, "this 'ere's a
putty business; I should like to know
what you have done with so much of
this 'ere *ditto.*" "Ditto, ditto," replied
the old lady, "never had a pound of
ditto in the house in all my life!" So
back went the honest old customer, in
high dudgeon that he should have been
charged with things that he had never
received. "Mr. B.," said he, "shan't
stand this—wife says she hain't had a
pound of this tarnal *ditto* in the house
in her life." The grocer, thereupon,
explained the meaning of the term, and
the customer went home satisfied. His
wife inquired, if he had found out the
meaning of that "ditto." "Yes," said
he, "as near as I can get the hang on't,
it means that I'm an old fool, and
you're ditto."

Where "Tariff" came from.

Everybody knows the *meaning* of
the word "tariff"—viz., a fixed scale
of duties, levied upon imports. Let
any one turn to a map of Spain, and he
will notice at its southern point, and
running out into the Straits of Gibral-
tar, a promontory which, from its position, is admirably adapted for commanding the entrance of the Mediterranean sea, and watching the exit and
entrance of all ships. A fortress stands
upon this promontory, called now, as it
was also called in the times of the
Moorish domination in Spain, "Ta

rifa;" the name, indeed, is of Moorish
origin. It was the custom of the Moors
to watch, from this point, all merchant
ships going into or coming out of the
midland sea; and, issuing from this
stronghold, to levy duties according to
a fixed scale on all merchandise passing
in and out of the Straits, and this was
called, from the place where it was
levied, "tarifa," or "tariff," and, in
this way, the word has been acquired.

Meaning of "Fund" and "Stock."

The term *fund* was applied originally to the taxes or funds set apart as
security for repayment of the principal
sums advanced, and the interest upon
them; but when money was no longer
borrowed to be repaid at any given
time, the term began to mean the principal sum itself. These facts, of course,
apply to the English monetary operations. In the year 1751, the Government began to unite the various loans
into one fund, called the consolidated
fund—though not to be confused with
that of the same name into which part
of the revenue is collected; and sums
due in this are now shortly termed
"consols." These come under the general denomination of "stocks."

Merchants' Religious Formulæ or Phrases.

There are many little *religious* for-
mulæ, or terms, now fallen into disuse,
which once prevailed universally among
those engaged in the various departments of trade and commerce. "*Laus
Deo*" (Praise be to God) was once the
usual heading of every page of a merchant's journal. When goods were sent
to some foreign port, the bill of lading,
as it is technically termed, invariably
stated that they had been "shipped *by
the grace of God* in and upon the good
ship"—called by such a name. A policy of insurance against sea risks still
begins with the words, "*In the name of
God, Amen;*" and, up to a late date,

all commercial appointments were made "God willing."

Responding to an Advertisement.

AN important mercantile house in New York had occasion to advertise for sale a quantity of *brass hoppers*, such as are used in coffee mills. But instead of brass hoppers, the newspaper read *grass hoppers*. In a short time the merchant's counting room was thronged with inquirers for the new article of merchandise thus advertised.

"Good morning, Mr. Invoice; how do you sell grasshoppers ?" said a fat merchant; "what are they worth a hogshead ?"

The importer was astonished; but before he had time to reply, in came a druggist, who, being bent on speculation, determined to purchase the whole lot, provided he could get them low. Taking the importer aside, for fear of being overheard by the merchant, he asked him how he sold those grasshoppers—if they were prime quality, and whether they were to be used in medicine. The importer was about opening his mouth to answer in an angry manner to what he began to suspect was a conspiracy to torment him, when a doctor entered, smelling at his cane, and looking wondrous wise.

"Mr. Invoice," said he, "ahem ! will you be good enough to show me a specimen of your grasshoppers ?"

"*Grasshoppers ! grasshoppers !*" exclaimed the importer, as soon as he had a chance to speak, "what, gentlemen, do you mean by grasshoppers ?"

"Mean ?" said the merchant, "why, I perceive you have advertised the article for sale."

"Certainly," said the druggist, "and when a man advertises an article, it is natural for him to expect inquiries relating to the price and quality of the thing."

"Nothing in the world more natural," said the doctor. "As for myself, I

have at present a number of cases on hand, in the treatment of which I thought the article might be serviceable. But since you are so—ahem ! so uncivil—why, I must look out elsewhere, and my patients—"

"You and your *patience* be hanged !" interrupted the importer; "mine is fairly worn out, and if you don't explain yourselves, gentlemen, I'll lay this poker over your heads !"

To save their heads, the advertisement was now referred to, when the importer found out the cause of his vexations, by reading the following: "Just landed, and for sale by Invoice & Co., ten hogsheads prime grasshoppers."

Business Puffing Two Hundred Years Ago.

SOME two centuries ago, the number of shopkeepers in England had got to be so numerous, that they commenced the practice of genuine, downright puffing—the art assuming some shapes hardly ventured upon even by the boldest at the present day. Sometimes, for example, a shopkeeper, scorning a direct puff advertisement of his articles, commenced with apparent anger, thus: "Whereas it has been maliciously reported that A. B. is going to leave off business;" and then would follow an earnest assurance that such was not the case—"that he continued, as before, to sell the undermentioned articles, at lowest prices." A more ingenious plan was for H. Z. to advertise in the public prints that a purse of gold, of large amount, with other valuables, had been, in the great hurry of business, dropped in his shop, and would be restored to the proper owner on describing its contents. Of course, every one was disposed to deal with such an honest tradesman, and the latter soon found his supposititious purse becoming a golden reality to him.

Transactions in the Cab Market.

THOUGH the numerous fluctuations in the money market are made the subject of acute comments in the public journals, it does not appear that any notice is taken of the fluctuations in the cab market, which are upon a very wide and extensive scale. A reporter for one of the English papers—more enterprising than its contemporaries—quotes as follows:

During the gloom which prevailed for a portion of the past week, the patent safeties without the coupon—or blind for wet weather—were done at a shilling a mile; and the reduced fives—or old clarences, that will hold five at a cram—were buoyant at eighteen pence, with a prospect of improvement. Open cabs during the rain were steady at nothing, and the list shows no transactions.

There was a rush of bears from the Adelphic Theatre, which caused the cab market to assume a very active appearance for a short time; and fathers of families, with their children, were done at a very high figure, with a prospect of advance at the settlement.

White handkerchiefs and polished boots were freely taken at lower rates than those demanded in the earliest part of the day, when it was understood that they had made bargains for time, and they were accordingly made to pay for the accommodation somewhat heavily. In one concern there was a breaking down, and a consequent failure in making the deposits at the time and place appointed. This is the only smash in the cab market which we have to report, and in this the getting out was ultimately arranged to the satisfaction of all parties.

Striking a Bargain.

AUBERY, in his manuscript collections, relates that in several parts of England, when two persons are driving a bargain, one holds out his right hand, and says, "Strike me;" and if the other strike, the bargain holds; whence the phrase "striking a bargain." The practice is retained in the custom of saying "Done" to a wager offered, at the same time striking the hand of the wagerer.

"Five Per Cent."

A VERDANT-LOOKING person called upon a jeweller in Montreal, and stated that he had managed to accumulate, by hard labor, for the few past years, seventy-five dollars, which he wished to invest in something, whereby he might make money a little faster; and he had concluded to take some of the stock and peddle it out. The jeweller selected what he thought would sell readily, and the new peddler started on his first trip. He was gone but a few days when he returned, bought as much again as before, and started on his second trip. Again he returned, and greatly increased his stock. He succeeded so well, and accumulated so fast, that the jeweller ventured, one day, to ask him what profit he obtained on what he sold? "Well, I put on 'bout five per cent." The jeweller thought that a very small profit, and expressed as much. "Well," said the peddler, "I don't know as I exactly understand about your *per cent.;* but an article for which I pay you one dollar, I generally sell for *five.*"

Historical and Poetical Signs.

IT is related of a barber in Paris, that, to establish the utility of his bag wigs, he caused the history of Absalom to be painted over his door; and that one of the profession, in an English town, used this inscription: "Absalom, hadst thou worn a periwig, thou hadst not been hanged." It is somewhere told of another, that he ingeniously versified his brother peruke-maker's inscription : under a sign which represented the death of Absalom, and David weeping, he wrote thus :

"O Absalom ! O Absalom !
O Absalom ! my son,
If thou hadst worn a periwig,
Thou hadst not been undone !"

Jemmy Wright's Modesty.

OLD Jemmy Wright, an eccentric barber of wide and harmless fame in his day, opened a shop under the walls of the King's Bench prison. The windows being broken when he entered it, he mended them with paper, on which appeared "Shave for a penny," with the usual invitation to customers. Whether his proximity to the gray walls of a prison had a salutary influence in developing his honest traits, cannot with certainty be stated; but over his door were scrawled the following words, which exhibit the rare business quality of a man speaking a better word for others of his craft than for himself :

"Here lives Jemmy Wright,
Shaves as well as any man in England,
Almost—not quite."

"Take Down that Old Sign."

ONE summer morning, quoth the *Knickerbocker*, Mr. Leupp—well known as an honored merchant in New York —was standing in the vestibule of the great "Leather House," No. 20 Ferry street, in the "Swamp," when *some* one, passing by at that time, and looking up, said, "Leupp, why don't you take down that old sign, ' GIDEON LEE' ? It's all worn out; the wood has dropped away from the letters, and the paint has e'en a'most rolled off *o' them.* Why don't you take it down and split it up ?" Leupp *looked* at his interlocutor, with that watery, blue, full-pupiled, interior German eye of his, and with a motion of his hand waved the questioner on his way, without

saying a word in reply. The memory of that name was precious in the esteem of Mr. Leupp. And there it is still, in the old place.

Signs are very curious things. Down in Murray street, there may be seen some rusty, dingy, forbidding-looking iron chests—but, like Gideon Lee's sign, they are types of something worthy to be remembered ; they are safes that have been tried by fierce flames for hours upon hours together, and yet delivered their precious and otherwise irrecoverable contents unharmed. And in West street, toward the Battery, there is another " case in p'int,"—a ship chandler's sign, an anchor, that "held wonderful onto a schooner," in a celebrated September gale, and a block and tackle that seem coeval with Sol Gil's midshipman sign, so reverenced by himself and Captain Cuttle.

Charging for Advertisements.

THE practice of charging for advertisements commenced at a very early period. A few might at first have been inserted gratuitously, but the revenue flowing from this source was so obvious a consideration, that the system soon began of charging a fixed sum for each. In the *Mercurius Librarius*, a bookseller's paper, it is stated that, " to show that the publishers design the public advantage of trade, they will expect but sixpence for inserting any book, nor but twelve pence for any other advertisement relating to the trade, unless it be excessive long." The next intimation of price is in the *Jockey's Intelligencer*, which charged a shilling for each, and sixpence for renewing. The *Observator*, in 1704, charged a shilling for eight lines ; and the *Country Gentleman's Courant*, in 1706, inserted advertisements at two pence a line. The *Public Advertiser* charged for a length of time two shillings for each insertion.

The Napoleon of Advertising.

PERHAPS the crowning fact in modern advertising is that which is stated by Thackeray, in his " Journey from Cornhill to Cairo," namely, that " *Warren's Blacking* " is painted up over an obliterated inscription to Psammetichus on Pompey's Pillar !

The greatest man of the day, however, as an advertiser, is Holloway, of London, who expends the enormous sum of one hundred and fifty thousand dollars annually, in advertisements alone.

His name is not only to be seen in nearly every paper and periodical published in the British Isles, but, as if that country were too " pent up " for this individual's exploits, he stretches over the whole of India, having agents in all the different parts of the upper, central, and lower provinces of that immense country, publishing his medicaments in the Hindoo, Ooordoo, Goozratee, Persian, and other native languages, so that the Indian public can take the pills, and use his ointment, as a cockney would do within the sound of Bowbells.

We find him again at Hong Kong and Canton, making his medicines known to the Celestials by means of a Chinese tranlation. We trace him from thence to the Philippine Islands, where he is circulating his preparations in the native languages. At Singapore he has a large depot ; his agents there supply all the islands in the Indian seas. His advertisements are published in most of the papers at Sydney, Hobart Town, Launceston, Adelaide, Port Philip, and indeed in almost every town of that region of the world.

Returning homeward, his pills and ointment are found on sale at Valparaiso, Lima, Callao, and other ports in the Pacific. Doubling the Horn, we track him in the Atlantic : at Monte Video, Buenos Ayres, Santos, Rio Janeiro, Bahia, and Pernambuco, he is advertising in Spanish and Portuguese.

In all the British West Indian Islands, as also in the Upper and Lower Canadas, and the neighboring provinces of Nova Scotia and New Brunswick, his medicines are as familiarly known, and sold by every druggist, as they are at home.

In the Mediterranean, we find them selling at Malta, Corfu, Athens, and Alexandria, besides at Tunis, and other portions of the Barbary States.

Any one taking the trouble to look at the *Journal* and *Courier* of Constantinople, may find in these, as well as other papers, that Holloway's medicines are regularly advertised and selling throughout the Turkish empire.

And even in Russia, where an almost insurmountable barrier exists—the laws there prohibiting the *entrée* of patent medicines—Holloway's ingenuity has been at work, and obviates this difficulty by forwarding supplies to his agent at Odessa, a port situated on the Black Sea, where they filter themselves surreptitiously by various channels into the very heart of the empire.

Africa has not been forgotten by this determined " benefactor " of suffering humanity ; he has an agent on the river Gambia, also at Sierra Leone, the plague spot of the world, the inhabitants readily availing themselves of the ointment and pills.

Thus it is that Holloway has made the complete circuit of the globe, commencing with India, and ending with the Cape of Good Hope, where his medicines are published in the Dutch and English languages.

Business Signboards in Different Nations.

THE Roman traders and venders had their signs ; and at Pompeii a pig over the door represented a wine shop within.

The Middle Ages adopted a bush— " Good wine needs no bush," &c., answering to the gilded grapes at a modern vintner's. The bush is still a common sign. At Charles the First's death, a cavalier painted his bush black. Then came the modern square sign, formerly common to all trades.

Old signs are generally heraldric, and represent royal bearings, or the blazonings of great families. Some of these will be found briefly noticed in another part of this volume, under the title of "Ancient Pictorial Signboards." The White Hart was peculiar to Richard the Second; the White Swan, of Henry the Fourth and Edward the Third; the Blue Boar, of Richard the Third; the Red Dragon came in with the Tudors, and also the Rose and Fleur de Lys; the Bull, the Falcon, and Plume of Feathers commemorated Edward the Fourth; the Swan and Antelope, Henry the Fifth; the Greyhound and Green Dragon, Henry the Seventh; the Castle, the Spread Eagle, and the Globe were probably adopted from Spain, Germany, and Portugal, by inns which were the resort of merchants from those countries. Then there were the Bear and Ragged Staff, etc., and some the origin of which is lost in obscurity. Monograms are common to the same period—as Balt and Ton for Balton; Hare and Tun, for Harrington. The three Suns is the favorite bearing of Edward the Fourth; and all Roses, red or white, are indications of political predilections. Other signs—and these are naturally very numerous—commemorate historical events.

The Pilgrim, Cross Keys, Salutation, Catharine Wheel, Angel, Three Kings, St. Francis, etc., are mediæval signs. Many of these became curiously corrupted, as already mentioned in the anecdotes of ancient pictorial signboards above referred to. As additional examples of this amusing verbal change may be mentioned that of the Cœur Doré (Golden Heart) to the Queer Door; Pig and Whistle—Peg and Was-

sail Bow; the Swan and Two Necks—Two Nicks; the Goat in the Golden Boots—from the Dutch, Goed in der Gooden Boote—Mercury, or the God in the Golden Boots; the Cat and Fiddle—the Caton Fidele.

The Swan with Two Nicks represented the Thames Swans, so marked on their bills under the "Conservatory" of the Goldsmiths' Company. The Coach and Horses pertain to the times when the superior inns were the only posting houses, in distinction to such as bore the sign of the Packhorse. The Fox and Goose denoted the games played within; the country inn, the Hare and Hounds, the vicinity of a sporting squire.

The Puritans altered many of the monastic signs, during their sway; such as the Angel and Lady, to the Soldier and Citizen. The Crusaders brought in the signs of the Saracen's Head, the Turk's Head and the Golden Cross.

In the various business signs of different periods may be read every phase of ministerial popularity, and all the ebbs and flows of war—as, the Sir Home Popham, Rodney, Shovel, Duke of York, Wellington's Head, etc. One such sign, in Chelsea, called the Snow Shoes, still indicates the excitement of the American war.

The chemist's sign was that of a dragon—some astrological device; the haberdasher and wool draper, the golden fleece; the tobacconist, the snuff-taking Highlander; the vintners, the ivy bush and the bunch of grapes; and the church-and-state bookseller, the Bible and crown.

———

Harlow's Sign Painting Extraordinary.

THERE is a clever anecdote connected with the ancient and celebrated sign of the Queen's Head, Epsom. This sign—that is, the original, for the board has been repainted—was executed by Harlow, an eminent artist, and a pupil of the renowned Sir Thomas

Lawrence. He was a young man of consummate vanity, and having unwarrantably claimed the merit of painting the Newfoundland dog introduced in Lawrence's portrait of Mrs. Angerstein, the two artists quarrelled, and Harlow took his resentment as follows: He repaired to the Queen's Head, at Epsom, where his style of living having incurred a bill which he could not discharge, he proposed, like Morland, under similar circumstances, to paint a signboard in liquidation of his score. This was accepted. He painted both sides: the one presented a front view of her Majesty, in a sort of clever, dashing caricature of Sir Thomas's style; the other represented the back view of the queen's person, as if looking into the signboard—and underneath was painted, "T. L., Greek street, Soho." When Sir Thomas met him, he addressed him with, "I have seen your additional act of perfidy at Epsom; and if you were not a scoundrel, I would kick you from one end of the street to the other." "There is some privilege in being a scoundrel, for the street is very long," replied Harlow, unabashed, but moving out of reach of the threatened demonstration.

Free Shave and a Drink.

THERE was once a barber who had on his sign the words—

"What do you think
I will shave you for nothing
And give you something to drink."

A man went in on the supposed invitation, and, after he was shaved, asked for something to drink. "No," said the barber, "you do not read my sign right. I say, 'What! do you think I will shave you for nothing, and give you something to drink?'"

"Words have their Meaning."

A MEDICINE man many years ago had a shop in Beekman street, New York, where he sold various medicaments, which were duly *sign-ed* at the door, as well as sealed and delivered within. Conspicuous among these signs, was one which bore the following inscription, namely, "The Celebrated Cure for the Spanish Piles." It was an infallible specific for a painful malady, the vender said one day to a friend, "but, by gar! nobody come to buy him! Yet his sign is biggest one at de door!" The friend looked at the sign. "I see how it is," said he; "nobody *here* has the *Spanish* piles—your *sign* is wrong. Have it changed to 'The celebrated *Spanish cure* for the piles.'" This advice was taken, and a few days after, the foreign pot'ecary met his adviser in the street, when, holding out his hand, with a cordial smile and a fervent grasp, he said, 'Aha! it is ver' good; *now* I sell de Spanish *cure* ver' moch! Everybody say he ver' most good t'ing!"

French Ideas of Advertising.

A MARCHAND de papier—or paper merchant—took an advertisement of such wares to a provincial newspaper in France, whose *régisseur* was proprietor, printer, and all—besides carrying on a little of *another* kind of paper business. The gentleman refused to insert the advertisement.

"Why not?" asked the dealer, in astonishment. "Here's the money down, if you are afraid of that!"

"Heu! heu!" said the editor, "I neither want your money nor your advertisement. I, too, sell paper—foolscap, quarto, letter paper, fine, coarse, and demi-fine, besides envelopes, cards, and letters of *faire-part*, of deaths and marriages, all in the newest style—a very large assortment. I cannot publish the advertisement of any one who would undersell *my* paper. What would you have?"

Too proud to make vain remonstrance, the customer went away. But in a few days returned to the office, and humbly asked:

"Monsieur, have you an attic to let?"

"What do you mean? I don't understand your question. Pray, now, what project can you have in respect to my attic?"

"Before I can explain my intentions," the merchant replied, "you must answer my question, whether you have an attic to let?"

"No, I have not."

"Very well, monsieur; I can now proceed to business without fear of a rebuff. Please insert this in your next number. *I* have an attic to let, but I thought I would ask whether *you* had one to let also, before I ventured to present the advertisement."

Pathos and Puffing Extraordinary.

THE tone of sentiment adopted in advertising the death of a trader or man of business, in England, not unfrequently affords matter of peculiar entertainment. There is sometimes a facetious—not to say barefaced—union of puff and despondency. Here is one of these pseudo-lachrymose specimens of a death: "Died, on the 11th ultimo, at his shop in Fleet street, Mr. Edward Jones, much respected by all who knew and dealt with him. As a man he was amiable, as a hatter upright and moderate. His virtues were beyond all price, and his beaver hats were only £1 4s. each. He has left a widow to deplore his loss, and a large stock, to be sold cheap, for the benefit of his family. He was snatched to the other world in the prime of life, and just as he had concluded an extensive purchase of felt, which he got so cheap that the widow can supply hats at a more moderate charge than any house in London. His disconsolate family will carry on the business with punctuality."

Alliteration in Advertising.

ADVERTISING, now-a-days, has become reduced—or elevated!—to a science. Somebody *alliterizes* in this manner, in an advertisement of an asserted superior article of marking ink: to wit, that it is remarkable for "requiring no preparation, preëminently preëngages peculiar public predilection; produces palpable, plainly perceptible, perpetual perspicuities; penetrates powerfully, precluding previous prerequisite preparations; possesses particular prerogatives; protects private property; prevents presumptuous, pilfering persons practising promiscuous proprietorship; pleasantly performing plain practical penmanship; perfectly precludes puerile panegyrics, preferring proper public patronage."

"Universal Stores."

ROYAL TYLER, the famous New Hampshire wit, thus set off, in parody, the advertisements of the "Universal Stores," so common in former times:

VARIETY STORE.

To the LITERATI:

MESSRS. COLON & SPONDEE,
wholesale dealers in

Verse, Prose, and Poetry,

beg leave to inform the PUBLIC, and the LEARNED
in particular, that

—previous to the ensuing

COMMENCEMENT—

They propose to open a fresh Assortment of

LEXICOGRAPHIC, BURGURSDICIAN, AND
PARNASSIAN

GOODS,

suitable for the season,

At the Room on the Plain, lately occupied
by Mr. FREDERICK WISER, *Tonsor,*

· if it can be procured—

Where they will expose to Sale—

Salutatory and Valedictory Orations, Syllogistic and Forensic Disputations and Dialogues among the living and the dead—Theses and Masters, Questions, Latin, Greek,

Hebrew, Syriac, Arabic, and the ancient Coptic, neatly modified into Dialogues, Orations, etc., on the shortest notice—with Dissertations on the Targum and Talmud, and Collations after the manner of Kennicott—Hebrew roots and other Simples—Dead Languages for living Drones—Oriental Languages with or without points, prefixes, or suffixes—Attic, Doric, Ionic, and Æolic Dialects, with the Wabash, Onondaga, and Mohawk Gutturals—Synalæphas, Elisions, and Ellipses of the newest *cut—v's* added and dovetailed to their vowels, with a small assortment of the genuine Peloponnesian Nasal Twangs—Classic Compliments adapted to all dignities, with superlatives in *o*, and gerunds in *di*, *gratis*—Monologues, Dialogues, Trialogues, Tetralogues, and so on, from one to twenty logues.

Anagrams, Acrostics, Anacreontics, Chronograms, Epigrams, Hudibrastics, and Panegyrics, Rebuses, Charades, Puns, and Conundrums, by the *gross* or *single dozen*. Sonnets, Elegies, Epithalamiums; Bucolics, Gearics, Pastorals; Epic Poems, Dedications, and Adulatory Prefaces, in *verse* and *prose*.

Ether, Mist, Sleet, Rain, Snow, Lightning, and Thunder, prepared and personified after the manner of Della Crusca, with a quantity of *Brown Horror, Blue Fear*, and *Child-Begetting Love*, from the same Manufactory; with a pleasing variety of high-colored *Compound* epithets, well assorted—Farragoes, and other Brunonian Opiates—Anti-Institutes, or the new and concise patent mode of applying *forty letters* to the spelling of a monosyllable—Love Letters by the Ream—Summary Arguments, both *Merry* and *Serious*—Sermons, moral, occasional, or polemical—Sermons for Texts, and Texts for Sermons—Old Orations scoured, Forensics furbished, Blunt Epigrams newly pointed, and cold Conferences hashed; with *Extemporaneous* Prayers, *corrected and amended*—Alliterations artfully allied—and Periods polished to perfection.

Airs, Canons, Catches, and Cantatas—Fugues, Overtures, and Symphonies, for any number of instruments—Serenades for Nocturnal Lovers—with *Rose Trees* full blown, and *Black* jokes *of all colors*—Amens and Hallelujahs, trilled, quavered, and slurred—with Couplets, Syncopations, Minim and Crotchet Rests, for female voices—and *Solos*, with the *three* parts, for hand organs.

Classic College Bows, clear starched, lately imported from Cambridge, and now used by all the topping scientific connoisseurs in hair and wigs, in this country.

Adventures, Paragraphs, Letters from Correspondents, Country Seats for Rural Members of Congress, provided by Editors of Newspapers—with Accidental Deaths, Battles, Bloody Murders, Premature News, Tempests, Thunder and Lightning, and Hailstones, of all dimensions, adapted to the Season.

Circles squared, and Mathematical Points divided into quarters, and half shares; and jointed Assymptotes which will meet at any given distance.

Syllogisms in Bocardo, and Baralipton; Serious Caution against Drunkenness, etc., and other coarse Wrapping Paper, *gratis*, to those who buy the smallest article.

☞ *On hand, a few Tierces of Attic Salt—also, Cash, and the highest price, given for* RAW WIT, *for the use of the Manufactory, or taken in exchange for the above Articles.*

Buying a Claim.

FROM the oil diggings a correspondent of Harper's "Drawer" writes, under date of Oleana: The world is full of good things. You also are in a similar state of repletion, and yet the half is not told. There are many things yet unknown, and, let us hope, many more yet to happen. We live in the midst of a good thing—oil; good for everything under the sun but to smell; it is not good for that. Three friends were discussing "THE SUBJECT" (oil, of course). Says A: "Old Billy G—— has bought a good claim." "What does he give?" says B. "One thousand dollars, and a quarter of the oil for a quarter of the claim," replied A. "Then," says C, "as a matter of course, had he bought the whole claim he would have had to pay four thousand dollars and *all the oil*." This is an opinion as is an opinion.

Very Racy.

PREVIOUS to the destruction of the National Theatre in Boston, one of the stores in the basement was occupied by one Patrick L Grace. A wag meeting a friend in the street, and knowing his penchant for rare and exciting sights, inquired if he had seen the pig race ? "

"Pig race !" repeated Dupee, "no ; I never heard of one before. Where is it ? "

"Down to the National Theatre ; you had better go down ; it's worth seeing," was the answer.

Dupee, who had been " spoiling " for something new in the way of amusements, started for the National at once, but of course found the doors closed, and no signs of any race around there, except the human race. Feeling that he was the victim of a " sell," he turned dryly away, when his eye caught Mr. Grace's sign. The stupid painter had omitted to insert any punctuation, and it read thus : PIGRACE.

"Very good," remarked Dupee ; "that does look like a pig race, sure enough !" and off he hurried, to find a victim in his turn.

Getting rid of his Neighbor's Customers.

IN the pleasant city of Canton, Mississippi, lives a worthy landlord by the name of Colonel Pierce. Next door to the Pierce House was a gunsmith's shop, kept by Bob Leonard, whose chief failing was the love of fish, squirrels, etc. When Bob wanted a day in the woods he had no scruples about closing up his establishment. Of course Bob's customers would be more numerous on the days the shop was closed. Now no place was so handy as Colonel Pierce's for the disappointed to inquire, " Do you know where Bob Leonard is ? " The Colonel, getting heartily tired of the annoyance, bethought him of a plan for ridding himself of the trouble of answering. He had a sign painted, and hung up in the most conspicuous part of the office, with this inscription : " I want it distinctly understood that I don't know where Bob Leonard is."

Broadway Signs.

NOT long since there could be seen a very singular and purely accidental collection of occupations in one building on Broadway—the signs across the front standing out like some great Ogre's eyes, nose, and mouth, ready to gobble a person up. The first floor, occupied by the " *Broadway Restaurant*," where you could be taken in, fed, and prepared ; the second floor, occupied by the " *Office of the West Point Foundry*," where you could be killed by the latest inventions ; the third floor occupied by the " *Office of Greenwood Cemetery*," where you could be buried in the most approved style. *Feed, kill,* and *bury,* all in one building.

Pat's Definition of Railroad "Stock."

PAT DONAHUE was a " broth of a boy," right from the " Gem of the Say," and he had a small contract on the Conway Railroad, New Hampshire, in the year of grace 1855, in which he agreed to take his pay part in cash, part in bonds, and part in stock. The stock of this road, be it remembered—like many others—was not worth a " Continental," and has always kept up its value with remarkable uniformity. In due time Pat, having completed his job, presented himself at the treasurer's office for settlement. The money, the bonds, and the certificate of stock were soon in his possession.

" And what is this now ? " said Pat, flourishing his certificate of stock, bearing the " broad seal " of the corporation.

" That is your stock, sir," blandly replied the treasurer.

22

"And is this what I'm to git for me labor? Wasn't me contract for sthock?"

"Why, certainly; that is your stock. What did you expect?"

"What did I expect!" said Pat, excitedly; "what did I expect! Why pigs, and shape, and horses, shure!"

Silk-Dyer's Poetical Sign.

POOR Goldsmith's familiar and touching lines:

"When lovely woman stoops to folly,"

fare sadly in the hands of a silk-dyer, who puts on his sign and circular this wicked parody:

"When lovely woman tilts her saucer,
    And finds too late that tea will stain—
Whatever made a woman crosser—
    What art can wash all white again?

"The only art the stain to cover,
    To hide the spot from every eye,
And wear an unsoiled dress above her,
    Of proper color, is to dye!"

Full-size Headings to Advertisements.

As the editor of "old KNICK." vouches for the strict ter-ruth of the following little *legend*, it may be safely assumed to be strictly ter-rue, especially in view of the extrinsic probability which is so obvious in the narration:

A few years since, the writer of the following sketch was one of the editors and proprietors of a daily and weekly newspaper, published in one of the large towns of Western New York. Among the numerous patrons of the paper was a man whom I shall describe as Levi Lapp, a carpenter by trade, and a very clever man in his way, but as the sequel shows, entirely unacquainted with the art which claims as its shining lights the names of Guttemberg and Faust.

Having considerable Yankee adaptedness to one thing or the other, in the useful as well as ornamental line, Mr. Lapp had recently purchased the right to manufacture a patent pump, which he was very desirous of introducing to the public, through the columns of our paper. In other words, he wanted to advertise it, and in the course of conversation about the price and other details, mentioned to me that he would like a cut of his new pump inserted as a heading to the advertisement. I replied, "Very well," and immediately asked, "Have you the cut here?" He replied, "No, but I have got one at my house, and will fetch it in."

In a day or two Mr. Lapp came into the office with a hand-bill, which he unfolded, and which contained a *fac simile* of the pump he was manufacturing.

He said to me: "Now you can get in my cut, and do so at once, for I wish to see it in print in your paper."

"Where is your cut?" I asked.

"On the bill," he replied, with all the seriousness of a post captain.

I then told him that it would require a block of wood cut by an engraver in the shape and likeness of the pump; that this was called a cut or engraving, and that it would have to be used in the press, in connection with the types, to make up such an advertisement as he desired. I further told him who could do the job, and the probable expense—some fifteen or twenty dollars.

A bright idea appeared to influence Mr. Lapp, and he informed me that he thought he could do the job himself, and save just so much outlay. I told him if he could it would suit me equally as well; but I thought he would find it a trifle difficult.

We separated, and I saw no more of Levi Lapp for several weeks. In fact, I had forgotten all about the matter. One morning, bright and early, as I was busy at the desk, in came Mr. Lapp, in a great hurry and bluster. He quickly explained himself, and said he had his cut finished, and had brought it as a heading to his advertisement.

I said : " Very well. Where is it ? " He answered : " Down stairs."

Without giving the matter a moment's thought, I said to him, " Bring it up ; " and he instantly left the room for that purpose.

His back was hardly turned, however, before the thought struck me that he had rather a huge engraving for a paper of limited size like ours. And calling to the foreman to see if I was not correct in my opinion, I turned again to the desk.

The foreman was back in an instant, and I was soon aware that Levi Lapp's bright idea had grown into giant proportions, and that the engraving or cut he had brought for our press was no less than *a veritable wood pump of full size, even to the pump log, chain, crank and water spout.*

Lapp was proceeding to bring his " extended cut " into our establishment, but at that very moment was deterred from executing his plan by the shouts and laughter of the entire printing office force, including the devil himself, who stood at the windows making merry at his expense.

The true condition of affairs slowly dawned upon Mr. Lapp's vision ; and when informed that he had made a much larger " cut " than the present condition of the art preservative would justify, he hurriedly replaced his " engraving " on the wagon that brought it to our door and drove off, evidently making a greater " impression " in this way than the pump could, by any possibility, have made in our limited establishment.

Rush's Celebrated Figure-Heads.

EDWARD CUTBUSH was considered the best carver of his day. Among his apprentices, at the close of the last century, was William Rush, of Philadelphia. When Rush first saw, on a foreign vessel, a walking figure—most unusual, in that day—he instantly conceived the design of more tasteful and graceful figures than had been before executed. He at once surpassed his master ; and having thus opened his mind to the contemplation and study of such attitudes and figures as he saw in nature, he was very soon enabled to surpass all his former performances. Then his figures began to excite admiration in foreign ports. The figure of the " Indian Trader " to the ship " William Penn " (the Trader was dressed in Indian habiliments), excited great admiration in London. The carvers there would come in boats and station themselves near the ship, so as to sketch designs from it. They even came to take casts of plaster-of-Paris from the head. This was directly after the Revolution, when she was commanded by Captain Josiah. When he carved a river god as the figure for the ship " Ganges," the Hindoos came off in numerous boats to pay their admiration, and perhaps reverence, to the various emblems in the trail of the image. On one occasion, the house of Nicklin & Griffiths actually had orders from England to Rush (fifty years and more ago), to carve two figures for two ships building there. One was a female personation of Commerce. The duties charged in that instance amounted to more than the first cost of the images themselves.

PART SEVENTH.

---

*ANECDOTES AND THINGS MEMORABLE CONCERNING
BUSINESS TRANSIT AND COMMUNICATION.*

PART SEVENTH.

Anecdotes and Things Memorable concerning Business Transit and Communication.

SHIPPING, STEAMBOATS, RAILWAYS, EXPRESSES, TELEGRAPHS, COACHES, OMNIBUSES, ETC.,—
THEIR OWNERS, OFFICERS, PATRONS, AND ATTACHÉS.

—— The heaven-conducted prow
Of navigation bold, that fearless braves
The burning line, or dares the wintry pole.—THOMSON.

Soon shall thy power, unconquered Steam! afar
Drag the swift barge and drive the rapid car.
DARWIN (*more than ninety years ago*).

Now there is nothing gives a man such spirits
As going at full speed.—DON JUAN.

No longer gee-up and gee-ho,
But fiz—fiz-z! off we go!—ANON.

Purchase of Jacob Barker's Ship "United States" by the Emperor Nicholas.

AT one period of his business career, Jacob Barker was extensively engaged in the Russian trade, and gave the name of "Russia" to the last ship he had built. Among the vessels employed by Mr. Barker in his Russian business, was a very fine New-York built ship, named the "United States."

This ship was lying at anchor at Cronstadt, in 1829, when the young emperor, Nicholas, passing by in his barge, on his way to the inspection of his fleet, being attracted by her fine appearance, the boatswain's whistle was sounded, and the men peaked their oars, while the emperor took a full view of the vessel; it again sounded, the boat went round the ship, and then landed; the captain was invited on shore, when the emperor inquired of him if his ship was for sale—and if so, what was the price. The reply was, "She was for sale until yesterday, when a charter was obtained, to take a cargo of copper, &c., to Bordeaux—price, $50,000; she cannot now be sold without the consent of the charterers." The emperor responded: "I will send down commissioners to inspect the vessel; if they report favorably, I will obtain the consent of the charterers, and give you the required $50,000 for the ship."

On the czar's return to the city, he directed his minister of marine to confer with the charterers; he did so, and stipulated to pay a specified amount for their annulling the charter, provided she, on inspection, should prove satisfactory—allowing three days for the examination. She proved satisfactory. But the minister of marine omitting to give the notice within the three days, the cargo was sent down, and the ship commenced loading. The emperor passed again the next day, and perceived her to be a foot and a half deeper in the water than when he resolved to make the purchase. He returned immediately to the city, and sent for the minister of marine, from whom he obtained an explanation. In place of directing him to disregard the delay in giving the answer, as a frivolous objection, he directed him to inform the captain that he might proceed to Bordeaux with his cargo; and as it would be too late to return that season to Russia, he might go to the United States and procure another cargo, come back with it to Europe, and then return to St. Petersburg, when he, the emperor, would take the ship at the same price. She did return, was received, and promptly paid for, the royal purchaser personally superintending the consummation of his bargain.

Such high-minded conduct, such business-like attention to mercantile usage, on the part of a crowned head, is seldom met with, though in this instance quite consistent with the autocrat's well-known respect for American merchants.

"Considering" a Ship Builder.

JOHN MORGAN was a merchant and ship owner, formerly residing in Pennsylvania. He made a contract with a builder to build him a vessel. When the vessel was partly finished, and he had received payment for all he had done, he went to Mr. M., and told him that he had ascertained that he could not build the vessel for the price agreed, as he should lose all he was worth, and perhaps more, and had therefore concluded he must abandon the job where it was, and let him get some one else to finish it. This was a poser to Morgan, who, after thinking of it for a few moments, said to him, "Well, well, you go on with it, and when we settle, I'll consider you;"—which, to the builder, was satisfactory. He therefore went on until the job was finished, Morgan advancing money from time to time. When they came to settle, Morgan drew his check for the balance due

according to contract. The builder stood and hesitated for a while, and then said, "You know, Mr. Morgan, you said that if I would go on with the job, you would—consider me." "Well, well," gruffly replied the old man, "I *have* considered yer, and considered yer a great fool for *doin'* on't so cheap."

Imaginative Expressmen—an Artificial Corpse.

IT is quite usual, now-a-days, to send corpses by express. But the business is *very* unpopular with expressmen, especially if the body has far to travel.

One morning, a messenger, having among his freight, in the express company's car, one of those ominously oblong boxes, declared confidentially to the conductor of the train, that the body inside "must be very far gone indeed—the smell of it fairly upset him." In vain he tried to forget it, or salubrify the odor by smoking a magnificent cigar. The smell became more offensive to him every minute during the long night that he was whizzing away with it over the rail track; and before the train arrived in New York, it affected him so much that he could not stay in the car.

When the drivers, with the wagons of the New York office, went to the depot for the express freight, the illness of the unfortunate messenger was obvious, and in answer to inquiries, he explained the cause. All eyes at once fell on the oblong box, and every man held his nose. It was decided unanimously that it was too far gone to be taken to the office, and as the railroad men swore (through their suppressed olfactories) that they would not suffer it to remain in the depot, the strongest-nerved and most accommodating driver present took it to the "dead house," up town.

No one knew where the obnoxious box came from. It was usual to make a special bargain in such cases, but no allusion was made to it on the way bill. In the course of the day, however, the mystery was solved. A gentleman came into the express office in Broadway, and called for the box.

"It has been taken to the dead house," was the reply of the clerk.

"The dead house!" exclaimed the applicant.

"Yes, sir," rejoined the clerk, firmly; "we couldn't stand it, sir. Too far gone, sir."

"Too far gone!" was the quick retort; "I should think so, if you have sent it way up to —th street. Explain yourself! What do you mean?"

"I mean that the body *smelt too bad*, sir!" responded the clerk.

"Smelt bad!" cried the visitor; "I have handled it for ten years past, and I never yet smelt anything but the varnish, and that not at all unpleasantly. Hang it, sir, that box contains my mannikin, an *artificial* anatomy or model of the human body. I am Dr. W——, the lecturer on physiology."

Risks and Accidents Insured Against.

IT would appear that the notion, broached so long ago, of a railway insurance office, has been carried into execution. A company has been actually started at Paris, to insure persons against railway risks and accidents. The directors promise to give so much for the loss of an arm, a leg—and even the value of a burn is calculated to a nicety. They offer annuities, also, to surviving relations, and undertake, free of expense, to bury any one who has been killed. Similar companies, it is thought, would be desirable in other parts—say in our own Western States. The only apprehension is, that so many railways in that section would have to be rated "Doubly Hazardous;" and that a person travelling by them, would be charged at the same rate as a medical insurance office would charge a person

who is on the point of sailing for Sierra Leone.

Floating Railways.

SOME ingenious gentleman of a practical turn of mind, who seems to think that capital does not get sunk rapidly enough in railways of the usual construction, has, as the result of much speculation, proposed a floating line, which will, of course, if carried out, be exposed to more than the ordinary fluctuations to which those things are liable. The scheme may work well enough when matters go on smoothly, but when Neptune has a bill—or a billow—to take up, and Boreas may be raising the wind to help him out, it is to be feared the traffic on the floating line would be entirely swamped, to say nothing of the difficulty the engineers might experience in taking their loads. However, the committee who have the subject under consideration, may be able to show that it will be practicable to outride these difficulties—which merely suggest themselves at first thought.

Superseding Steam.

A LETTER in Galignani's *Messenger* having fully proved the facility with which tables can be moved by means of a "company" through mere volition, after the hands of the company have been placed for a short time on the table, it is proposed that a company shall be formed for the application of tabular locomotion to practical purposes—transportation of merchandise and the conveyance of passengers; to be called the Locomotive Table Company. The principal object of the association will be to supersede steam engines on railways; an improvement in travelling by which it is hoped many serious accidents will be prevented which would otherwise have occurred. The table will be placed where the engine is at present, in front of the train. It will go on grooved castors, and a certain number of the directors of the company will be seated at a board in connection with it, which will insure that additional guarantee of safety so much wanted on railroads. The expenses involved in carrying out the company's object will not, it is expected, be very considerable; but shareholders will be required to pay down the whole of their subscriptions, as the projectors anticipate some little difficulty in obtaining credit.

Universal Salvage Company.

AMONG the various enterprises to which the ingenuity of the day has turned itself, is that of a company which advertises to raise sunken or wrecked vessels, all over the world, and divide the profits. It is not impossible that this very promising association may in time be followed by the Incorporated Mudlarks, or Joint-Stock Dredging Company—which, indeed, the first-named concern seems in fact to be, only on a somewhat extended principle. Directors are already appointed, and "a manager afloat" is advertised. It is to be hoped that "shareholders aground" will not be the end of this very useful nautical enterprise.

Dismissing a Shipmaster.

ONE of the most faithful shipmasters in the employ of Stephen Girard was Captain Guligar. He had been seventeen years in his service, from an apprentice until he rose to the command of one of his favorite and finest ships. Having thus by diligence and industry been promoted to the berth of first officer, he sailed in that capacity to Batavia, in the Voltaire or Rousseau. At Batavia the captain died; and Guligar, as first officer, took the command of the ship, sailing for Holland with a very rich cargo, and arriving at an excellent

market. From Holland he brought the ship safe into the port of Philadelphia, making altogether an immensely profitable voyage for his owner.

Girard having concluded to repeat the voyage to Batavia, Captain Guligar, being either averse to the climate, or from some other cause, observed to Mr. Girard, "that if he had no objection, he would prefer taking the command of such a ship," naming her, which Girard was then loading for a port in Europe. Girard, without uttering a syllable in reply, called to his clerk, and directed him to make out the accounts of Captain Guligar immediately. He discharged him on the same day from his employ, saying: "I do not make the voyage for my captains, but for myself," a declaration which no one acquainted with him could possibly venture to dispute.

Commercial Importance of the Cat.

THE peculiar relations which grimalkin sustains to commerce is not generally known. It is stated in a London journal that marine insurance in some parts of Europe does not cover damage done to cargo by the depredations of rats; but if the owner of the cargo thus damaged can prove that the ship was not furnished with a cat, he can recover compensation from the owner of the ship. Again, a ship that is found under certain circumstances, *without a living creature on board*, is considered a *derelict*, and, according to certain conditions, a forfeiture to the sovereign, lords of the admiralty, and other interested parties. And it has not unfrequently occurred, after all the crew have been lost, or the ship otherwise abandoned, that a live canary bird, domestic fowl, but most frequently a *cat*, being found on board, has saved the vessel from being condemned as a derelict. Consequently, the ship owners, considering the cat's proverbial tenacity of life, as well as its presence being a bar to claims of damage by rats, always take care not to send a ship to sea without having a cat on board.

Reading the Annual Report.

A CERTAIN little railway, the route and character of which will presently appear, has been following the example of larger companies, by holding a general meeting, presenting a report, and performing, on its own snug little scale, all the operations of a line of first-rate magnitude. A few extracts from the report, as read to the meeting, are here given in advance of its publication:

"Your Directors had hoped to render this a favorite trunk line for the conveyance of baggage belonging to the boys and girls going home for the holidays from the various boarding schools in the neighborhood; but as there is not as yet any scholastic establishment at Wormwood Scrubs, nor any probability of a large juvenile population in the Canal Basin, which form the two termini and the only stations on the permanent way, there has been as yet no chance of pushing the resources of the line as a trunk, or even a carpet-bag line, into full development.

"It is with regret that your Directors have to state that the 'branch' concerns, commenced last year, have not yet borne any fruit, though the asparagus cuttings yielded a small revenue —applicable to the Holfast Fund intended as superannuation money for the one fireman—and some of the cuttings remaining uncut from last year, have in due course run to seed, with a view to forming the seeds of future prosperity.

"A negotiation was undertaken by your Directors with the Great Western, for the sale of the whole of their plant (fixture and tools); but as the most valuable portion was a lot of cabbage plants, the negotiation fell to the ground just as the cabbages were shooting out of it.

"The canal has been looked at with great caution by your Directors, and they have in fact gone very deeply into it. They have also, after due deliberation, abandoned that part of the line known as the Shepherd's Bush Clothes Line, though the laundresses have been hanging out for better terms; but your Directors prefer the chance of the dry-goods to the prospect of having a damp thrown on any of their lines by a class of people who refused to stir a peg—or even a clothes peg—to meet the views of the proprietors.

"Your Directors are still undecided what to do with the first-class car originally built for the passenger traffic on this line, and are now considering a proposition from the Messrs. Wee, the great nurserymen, who have made an offer for the car without its wheels, with a view to its conversion into a Chinese summer house, or an extensive melon frame."

Every separate sentence of the above report was received with shouts of applause; and, after voting, by acclamation, to the chairman of the Board, a teacup of peanuts, to be debited to the company's treasury when the receipts should warrant the expenditure, the meeting broke up with a vote of confidence in everybody and everything.

Ask any Committee Man.

DID you ever know a railway from a place no one knows where, to a place no one ever heard of before, with branches everywhere, of which the gradients were not easy, the cuttings few, the tunnelling next to nothing, and the traffic immense?

Unparalleled Railway Damages.

THE transaction of Lord Petrie with the directors of the Eastern Counties Railroad, England, stands unparalleled, of its class, in railway annals—the Shylock, perseveringly exacting his full bond.

Previous to the company's obtaining a bill, or charter it appears that a secret engagement was entered into with his lordship by the provisional committee, who engaged to pay him the enormous sum of six hundred thousand dollars, nominally for the land through which the rail was to pass, but really for the withdrawal of an opposition which might have been disastrous to the road. When, however, the bill was passed, there seems to have been some objection to fulfilling the contract, on the pretended ground of misrepresentation. Nor did the directors hesitate to assert that to fulfil it would be a fraud on the proprietors, the legislature, and the public.

But if the company were unwilling to pay the money, his lordship was equally unwilling to give it up. He obtained an injunction against them; he opposed and prevented them from passing through his grounds; he harassed and irritated them as they had irritated him, and with far more effect. But the stake was too great to yield quietly. In addition to the money involved, Lord P.'s pride was touched to the quick by the treatment he received.

The company, wishing to be safe, appointed seven eminent surveyors to report as to the damage likely to be caused to his lordship's estate; copies of their reports were forwarded to Lord P., and an offer was made to use them as the basis of an amicable arrangement. His lordship, however, positively and squarely declined any change in the terms of the bond. Finally, the directors thought it best to stay proceedings, and, seeing the hopelessness of their case, urged a decision by arbitration. Lord P., however, flatly refused all such interference, and the company was emphatically grounded; the amended bill, too, which they had caused to be brought in their favor before the legis-

lature, seemed little likely to result in any good. Still, if the bill were abandoned, the compulsory power of the company by its first act would soon cease to exist; and even if they gained a chancery suit and annulled the contract, their opponent might refuse to sell his land at all, and thus a gap of six unfinished miles grace the line.

It only remained, therefore, for the company to pay the money. Thus his lordship beat the board, and exacted the full amount of his bond—the prodigious sum of six hundred thousand dollars, with interest, being paid for land said by appraisers to be possibly worth twenty-five thousand. This is believed to be a case which stands alone by itself, in respect to the immense amount involved and the peculiar circumstances investing the whole affair.

Rather Ominous.

THE directors of a railway company, it is announced, made a few days since a preliminary "trip" upon the newly completed line. There have been so many *trips* and *slips* on the various railways, that a little preliminary practice of that work might prove beneficial to persons who prefer making a rapid transit by steam to another world, to the old-fashioned and tedious mode of travelling by post.

Up Trains and Down Trains.

"WHAT do you mean by an 'Up Train'?" inquired a rural passenger.

"A train whose engine explodes and blows up the whole concern, of course," replied the conductor.

"Then, what do you mean by a 'Down Train'?" asked verdant.

"What else could it be but a train whose engine gets off the track and plunges down the bank or into the river, with the cars after it?"

"To which of the two does this 'ere belong—eh?"

"We can answer no such question in advance!"

The Ladder of Gold.

In 1845, when the new railroad mania had so frantically seized upon the English populace, the iron track was familiarly, and yet seriously, termed the *ladder of gold*, and all classes struggled for a foothold that should enable them to ascend its beckoning heights of speedy affluence. The facts almost exceed belief. A colony of solicitors, engineers, and seedy accountants settled in the purlieus of Threadneedle street. Every town and parish in the kingdom blazed out in zinc plates over the doorways. From the cellar to the roof, every fragment of a room held its committee. The darkest cupboard on the stairs contained a secretary or a clerk. Men who were never east of Temple Bar, before or since, were now as familiar to the pavement of Moorgate street—the great rendezvous of the railway craft—as the stock brokers. Ladies of title, lords, members of Parliament, and fashionable loungers thronged the noisy passages, and were jostled by adventurers, by gamblers, rogues, and impostors. The choicest phraseology was employed in picturing the advantages and profits of the different roads. Everything was to pay a large dividend; everything was to yield a large profit. The shares of one company rose 2,400 per cent. From his garret in some nameless suburb the outcast scamp; from his West-end hotel, the spendthrift fop; from his dim studio, the poor artist; from his starved lodging, the broken-down gentleman; from his flying address, the professional swindler; from his fine mansion, the man of notoriety, whose life was a daily fight to keep up appearances—all these poured into Moorgate street, side by side, and with kindred purposes, every day. Fraud, fiction, and fun made up the staple of these flash projects. On one of the contracts the name of a half-pay pensioner for £54 a year was down for £41,500; a curate, known to be poor, was down for £35,000; a clerk, for £50,000; and two brothers, sons of a charwoman living in a garret, were down for £12,000 and £25,000 respectively. Duchesses' delicate fingers handled scrip; old maids inquired with trembling eagerness the price of stocks; young ladies' eyes ceased to scan the marriage list—deserting this for the table of shares, and startling their lovers with questions respecting the operations of bulls and bears. One person was a director in twenty-three companies, a second in twenty-two, a third in twenty-one, and a fourth in twenty. Thus "madness ruled the hour." On Thursday, October 16, 1845, the Bank of England raised the rate of interest; the effect was immediate. Men looked doubtfully and darkly at each other. The panic came, and the crash that followed brought a haggard shadow upon the path of peer and peasant, and a frightful page to almost every family history.

Oldest Vessel in America.

It is believed that the oldest vessel in this country, of American build, is the barque Maria, of which a New Bedford (Mass.) paper of Aug. 11, 1859, thus speaks: The bark Maria arrived at this port last evening, from a three-years' cruise in the Indian ocean. She was built at the town of Pembroke, now called Hanson, for a privateer, during the Revolutionary war. She was bought by William Rotch, a merchant of Nantucket, afterward of this city, in the year 1783, and in the same year she made a voyage to London with a cargo of oil. Her register is dated A.D. 1782, and she is consequently in her seventy-seventh year. She claims to be the first ship that displayed the United States flag in a British port after the Revolutionary war, which flag is now in existence, though in shreds. Her model is of the old French construction, tumbling home, or rounding very much in her top sides, and she is consequently very narrow on deck, in proportion to her size, two hundred and two tons. It is said that there stands to her credit over two hundred thousand dollars; and from the earliest history of this ship, she never has been any expense by loss to underwriters except once, and that to a very small amount.

Names of Vessels and Trade of New York in 1680.

A LIST of the clearances from the port of New York, for the year 1680 and a few years subsequent, shows the following quaint names of vessels: Restore Peace, Bachelor's Delight, the Golden Hind, Happy Returne, Prudent Mary; and in the way of "adventures" —The Brothers' Adventure, John's Adventure, Nathaniel's Adventure, the Friends' Adventure, the Best Adventure, the Drovers' Adventure, and the Owners' Adventure.

The foreign ports with which trade was carried on in those days were Barbadoes, Jamaica, the Caribee Islands, Madeira, Nevio, Surinam, Curaçoa, Bermuda, Providence Islands, Fayal, Madagascar, Antigua, the Leeward Islands, St. Christopher's, Monserrat, Newfoundland, St. Augustine, St. Jago, Honduras, London, Amsterdam, Isle of Man, Falmouth, Dover, Cowes, Carlisle.

Curious Division of Ships into Ounces.

IT was lately stated in evidence in a bankruptcy case in Wales, that the sixty-four shares into which a vessel, the ownership of which was connected with the case, was divided, were considered equal to one pound avoirdupois, the owner of four shares being called the owner of an ounce, of two shares of

half an ounce, and so on. This resembles the mode of division among the Romans.

First Vessel in the World.

THE first vessel of which we have any authentic account—the first not only in point of time, but in size, and the magnitude of purpose for which it was intended, is the Ark. The more the dimensions, proportions, and arrangement of this wonderful vessel (as given in the simple but comprehensive directions for its construction found recorded) are considered, the more does one's admiration of it increase, as a work of nautical art, and as the most perfect adaptation of a means to an end. Her tonnage, estimated from the data of size given, must have been forty-two thousand four hundred and thirteen tons, equal to about eighteen ships of the line.

English Hares by Express.

A TRICK practised considerably of late years, by rogues in the name of expressmen, is to call upon people at their houses with bundles, purporting to have come by express from a distance, upon which they have the hardihood to collect charges. Their demands are usually paid, and their victims too late discover that they have got in exchange for their money only a parcel of paper rags, or other trash. In one instance, a box of "game" was left at a house up town, New York, and "twenty shillings charges" collected— the rascal remarking that he believed it was *English hares*. The lady was delighted with the idea that it was a present from a very dear friend in England, and she was dying of impatience until her servant man had opened it, and discovered that it contained only a deceased cat!

Telegraph vs. Express.

"CAN you take a box to Albany to-day?" was the question of a good-looking young gentleman, who was trying to raise a crop of hair on his upper lip, but which seemed more like the down on the south side of a peach.

"We will start it to-day, and it will arrive in Albany some time during the night, provided the train has the good luck to arrive here."

"Oh, but it *must* reach there by nine o'clock to-night, at the farthest."

"Had you not better send it by telegraph?—then there will be no doubt of its arriving in time."

"The telegraph man laughed at me when I asked him to do it, and said I had better carry the box to Albany myself."

"As it is now near five o'clock, and it 'must' be there by nine, you had better follow his advice. Those gentlemen who work the telegraph understand velocity in a remarkable degree, and I have no doubt they judged correctly when they advised you to take it there yourself."

"I suppose they judged me to be a *fast* young man, from the observations they made, and I was not pleased with them."

"They seldom form an incorrect opinion of those persons who visit them, and I doubt much whether they were mistaken with you."

"What must I do, then?"

"Take the advice of the telegraph operator."

"What! and carry the box there myself?"

"Certainly. You know it *must* be there by nine o'clock, and I know of no other way of its getting there."

And such impossibilities are expected by persons every day, of those engaged in the express business.

Church and State vs. Railways.

A TRANSACTION peculiarly illustrating the character and policy of George Hudson is thus related: In negotiating for the Newcastle and Darlington line, he had outwitted the Dean and Chapter of Durham, showing the vanity of the idea that the "Church and State" could interpose to stay such great industrial undertakings. He now again visited that ancient archiepiscopal see, in company with George Stephenson, for the purpose of outwitting the shareholders of the Durham junction, by buying up the railway between them. Great was the astonishment of the public when they came to hear the particulars of the affair. A railway put into the pocket of an engineer and director! The proprietors did not so slowly recover from their surprise. Mr. Hudson, by this purchase, which he handed over to the company, had gained a further step on the new highway to the north, a further security for carrying out unchecked all his plans, and sustaining without impediment the whole fabric of his power.

Lloyd's Nautical Book.

AN examination of this curious British commercial catalogue, and in which ten thousand five hundred and forty-eight vessels are registered, affords some little amusement in connection with the *names* most popular, or contrariwise, among British merchants. The largest proportion are named after their owners, or some member of their immediate family. The royal family also, the nobility, and eminent characters, seem to be favorite names with shipmasters: for example, there are twenty-five Victorias, thirteen Alberts or Prince Alberts, seven Prince of Wales, and fourteen Princess Royals; while each junior prince or princess has their representatives as well.

There are sixteen Dukes, besides the

Iron Duke, and six Wellingtons, and one called, par excellence, THE Duke, and six Duchesses. Descending a step in the peerage, there are found six Marquises and seven Marchionesses, thirty-three Earls and twenty-one Countesses, forty-four Lords, and exactly double that number of Ladies.

The army is represented by eighteen Generals, and the navy by thirteen Admirals. The bench has one solitary representative in Baron Martin; and the only literary characters are Burns, Byron, and Boz. Some of those good men whose names are as household words are also remembered, such, for example, as John Wesley, John Bunyan, Heber, Hedley Vicars, General Havelock, and Livingstone.

Names expressive of speed are naturally favorites, there being eleven Actives, and several Velocity, Alacrity, Alert, Flying Foam, Driving Mist, Arrow, and Faugh a Ballagh, or Clear the Way.

Some names let us into a little bit of family history; thus, there is something of filial affection in calling a vessel the Faithful Mother, and her owner can easily be imagined to be one who respects the fifth commandment. On the other hand, the Only Son is doubtless a tribute of parental love. There are numbers of Brothers, Sisters, Friends, and Cousins—quite a large family—even excluding the Seven Brothers, Five Sisters, and the Twins. *The Girl I Love* tells her own tale.

Several names have an airish smack of defiance; thus, Cock-o'-the-Walk, Touch me Not, and Let me Alone, seem to imply that any competitor has but a poor chance, and had better not try a race with them. *Come On*, on the contrary, invites a trial of speed, which I'll Try apparently accepts. There's something cheering about All Right, Fear Not, and Better Luck Still; and something a little conceited in Wide Awake, Look Out, Matchless, and Mark That! It is presumable that Bloomer and Cri-

noline belong to the same owner, and, no doubt, if he builds a third vessel, he will call her—well, the Sky Reacher. The man who put his savings in a ship, and named her the *Ascendant*, can comfort himself with the pleasurable feeling that he *must* be growing wealthy, for are not all his fortunes in the ascendant? So, too, the owner of Profit and Loss, doubtless, hopes the results of his vessel's earnings may be represented by the first part of her name; and likewise the owner of Cornucopia, that she may indeed prove to him a horn of plenty.

National characteristics are often exhibited in the names given to vessels in different countries. The Spaniard evinces the somewhat superstitious tendency of his mind by such titles as Santissima Trinidada, St. Joseph, Mother Mary, the Twelve Apostles, &c.

The French, again, manifest their *gaieté* and gallantry, by such titles for their ships, as La Belle Julie, La Bayadere, La Prima Donna, Mademoiselle, &c.

The Dutch, being an industrious, frugal people, may naturally be expected to confirm their character in these respects, by naming their vessels the Beaver and the Gold Hunter.

John Bull's crustiness and pugnacity are abundantly exemplified by such names as the Badger, Lion, Gladiator, Spitfire, Boxer, Julius Cæsar, Vengeance, Retribution, Bull Dog, and the like.

Rival Steamboat Lines.

IN the month of September, 1809, says Prof. Renwick, I was a partaker in the exciting scene, then first enacted, of a steamboat race. A company from Albany had been formed for the purpose of competing with Fulton. The first vessel of this rival line was advertised to leave Albany at the same time with Fulton's. Parties ran high in the hotels of Albany. The partisans of Fulton were enrolled under Prof. Kemp, of Columbia College; those of the opposition under Jacob Stout. The victory was long in suspense; and it was not until after the thirtieth hour of a hard struggle that the result was proclaimed by Dr. Kemp, on the taffrail of Fulton's vessel, and holding out, in derision, a coil of rope to Captain Stout, for the purpose, as he informed him, of towing him into port. When the age, high standing, and sedate character of these two gentlemen are considered, it did not surprise me—remarks Prof. R., who witnessed the excitement—when I afterward heard of Western women having devoted their bacon to feed the fires of a steamboat furnace!

Arrival of the Steamer.

COLONEL SNOW, a most incorrigible wag, came in one morning to Grant's tonsorial establishment in Ann street, New York, and with a face beaming with honest excitement, remarked, "Well! the steamer's in at last. She has made quick time; but she brought away her pilot, and carried away her pipes. She had a fine lot of passengers; more than one hundred and fifty. The news she brings is not—" Here half a dozen listeners, "under treatment," arrest the barber's hand, and wiping the lather from their faces, inquire with eagerness: "What steamer is it—the Hibernia, or Caledonia?" "Oh, bless you, no!" replies the colonel; "oh, no; the Olive Branch ferry boat from Brooklyn; she came over very full this morning, and in about six minutes; she carried back the pilot she brought away, and at the same time she carried away her pipes!"

Railcar Privileges.

EVERYBODY who has travelled much on the Northern railroads, must have noticed that in many of the cars, the name of the makers, "Eaton, Gilbert & Co.," is conspicuously posted. Not long

since, in one of these cars, a passenger of the name of *Gilbert* was travelling with a company of his friends, and seeing another notice just over the above, to the effect that "passengers are requested not to crack nuts in the cars," his innate love of fun was awakened. At the first stopping place he filled his pockets with peanuts, and distributing them among his friends, they were all soon busily engaged in eating them, and strewing the floor with the shells. The conductor, in passing, gently intimated that it was against the rules, and pointed to the printed notice.

"Oh, yes," said Gilbert, "I see, I see that; but you see by your own rules that *we* are privileged."

The conductor, thinking that they would soon stop, without any further trouble, passed on. On his next rounds, he found the same party still at the nuts, and making a great display of shells on the floor. Out of patience, he now spoke up quite sharply, and said to Mr. Gilbert:

"You must comply with the rules of the company, if you travel in these cars."

"Certainly, certainly, we will, but you do not seem to be aware that I and my company are excepted from the rule you refer to."

"No, I do not know anything of the sort, nor you either, and there is no use having any words about it; you must stop or quit the cars."

"Be quiet a minute," replied Mr. Gilbert, "and I will convince you. To be sure it says, 'Passengers are forbidden to crack nuts in the cars,' but right underneath is written, '*Eato*n, Gilbert & Co.' Now, my name is *Gilbert*, and this is my *company*, and we are doing as we are told."

The conductor "gave it up."

First Railroad in Europe and America.

THE first instance of the use of rails appears to have been some time previous to the year 1676, at the collieries near Newcastle-upon-Tyne, England. At that time, the coals were conveyed from the mines to the banks of the river, " by laying rails of timber exactly straight and parallel; and bulky carts were made, with four rollers fitting those rails, whereby the carriage was made so easy that one horse would draw four or five chaldrons of coal."

An advance was made about the year 1767, in the use of iron bars as a substitute for the upper rail of the road; they were cast five feet long, four inches wide, and one and three fourths inches thick, with holes for the spikes by which they should be secured to the lower rail.

The first railroad company opened for conveying passengers was the Stockton and Darlington road in 1825, and this was worked with horse power. In 1826, the French engineer, M. Seguin, successfully introduced locomotives upon the railways from St. Etienne to Lyons, and to Andrezieux.

In the United States, a horse railroad was built of pine rails, in 1826, from the granite quarries of Quincy, Mass., to the Neponset river, a distance of three miles. This was the first in America, except a temporary railway with two tracks in Boston, for removing gravel from Beacon Hill; this was so arranged, that while one train descended the hill with its load, the empty train would thereby be hauled up for loading. The first use of a locomotive in this country was in 1829, and was used on the railroad built by the Delaware and Hudson canal company in 1828, from their coal mines to Honesdale, the terminus of the canal.

Mode of Getting Money Transmitted.

In the bankerless twelfth century, so great was the difficulty of conveyance for the transmitting of money from Spain to Rome—which was generally done by pilgrims returning from Santiago—that

for every ounce of gold brought safely to the treasury of St. Peter's, a year's indulgence was granted to the soul of the bearer, by the Roman pontiff.

Thomas Gray, the Originator of Railways.

It is now a little more than forty years since a thoughtful man, Thomas Gray, travelling in the north of England on commercial business, stood looking at a small train of coal wagons impelled by steam along a tramroad which connected the mouth of one of the collieries of that district with the wharf at which the coals were shipped.

" Why," asked Gray of the engineer, " are not these tramroads laid down all over England, so as to supersede our common roads, and steam engines employed to convey goods and passengers along them, so as to supersede horse power ? "

" Just propose you that "—said the engineer, looking at the questioner with the corner of his eye—" to the nation, sir, and see what you will get by it! Why, sir, you would be worried to death for your pains."

Nothing more was said; but the intelligent traveller did not take the engineer's warning. Tramroads, locomotive steam engines, horse power superseded ! —the idea he had conceived continued to infest his brain, and would not be driven out. Tramroads, locomotive steam engines, horse power superseded ! —he would talk of nothing else to his friends. Tramroads, locomotive steam engines, horse power superseded !—he at length broached the scheme openly; first to the public men by means of letters and circulars, and afterward to the public itself by means of a printed book. Hardly any one would listen to his words, or be bothered with his fancies; the engineer's words seemed likely to prove true.

Still he persevered, holding the public by the button, as it were, and dinning into its ears the same wearisome words. From public political men, including the cabinet ministers of the day, he received little encouragement; a few influential *commercial* men, however, began at length to be interested in his plan. Persons of eminence took it up, and advocated it almost as eulogistically as the original projector. It having thus been *proved*, according to Dogberry's immortal phrase, that the scheme was a good scheme, it soon went near to be *thought* so. Capital came to its aid. In 1826, Parliament passed an act authorizing the construction of the first British railway, properly so called.

Largest Ship-owner in England.

The number of ships belonging to Mr. Dunbar, of Limehouse, the eminent Protectionist ship-owner, has been set down at thirty-three, the aggregate burthen of which is twenty-two thousand tons, or about one thousand more than the Messrs. Green. Nearly the whole of these vessels were bought while the repeal of the navigation laws was under agitation, or since they were repealed—some of them very lately. And yet Mr. Dunbar has been the leader among those who declared that British shipping has been and is in a state of ruin, during the whole of the period which he has employed in accumulating this enormous mercantile fleet—the largest ever owned in that country by an individual ship-owner.

Literature of the Cabin.

Many a downeast man has made a crack sea-captain, while he was a poor hand at spelling. Capt. Ezekiel Jenkins was one of these men; he knew the ropes well, but writing letters was not his forte. He sailed the ship *Jehu*, from Boston to South America, while the republics were in a disturbed condition, and the port he designed to make was blockaded; he could not enter, and his cargo could find no market. He informed his owners of the state of things, in a letter so remarkably condensed as to incline toward the obscure. It was in these words: " Sir— Own to the blockhead the vig is spilt." The owners could not make it out, but a friend of the captain, more familiar with his laconic style, read it thus: " Sir—Owing to the blockade, the voyage is spoilt."

Paying off Jack.

A ship-owner, in despatching a vessel, had a good deal of trouble with one of his men, who had got very "top-heavy" on his advance wages. After the vessel had accomplished her voyage, on settling with the crew, it came to this man's turn to be paid. " What name ? " asked the merchant. " Cain, sir," was the reply. " What! are you the man who slew his brother ? " facetiously rejoined the merchant. " No, sir," was the ready and witty reply of Jack, with a knowing wink, and giving his trowsers a nautical hitch, " *I'm* the man that *was slewed !* "

"No Swearing among the Crew."

A merchant in one of our seaports, on fitting out a ship for India, told the captain at the time of making the contract for the voyage, that there must be no swearing among the crew; that he, the captain, must engage not to swear himself nor permit others to be profane; that he must do as he pleased, with respect to taking command of the ship on these terms, but, if he accepted the employment, it would be expected that he should rigidly adhere to the stipulation, and that it should be known as the law of the ship, that no profaneness could be permitted.

The captain seemed to have no objection to reforming, but inquired: " How can I suddenly break off an inveterate habit ? " " I will take care that you be reminded of your duty," said the owner; "wear the ring that I shall give you, and let the law of the vessel be explicitly known." Accordingly he procured a ring for the captain, with this motto engraved upon it: "Swear not at all."

The vessel soon sailed, and after performing the voyage, returned to the seaport from whence she sailed. On being inquired of respecting the subject, the supercargo declared that there had been no profanity on board, excepting a little within the first twenty days after sailing. At the close of this short period, the old habit was entirely mastered; and during the remainder of the voyage, both at sea and in port, the success of the experiment was complete.

Usefulness of Steamboats in Reducing the Population.

ACCORDING to one of the most observing of modern writers, it is to the over-population of a country that its social or commercial depression is due. Of the numerous remedies applicable to this evil, none have been found so effectual as steamboats; and, although their superiority over the small-pox and railroads has sometimes been sharply disputed, yet, from the increased favor in which every succeeding season they are held, as engines of destruction, it is clear that the highest opinion is entertained of their efficacy.

In proof of this, any one who doubts may safely be cited to the cheap excursion boats on their Sunday trips. The deck crammed, and no convenient standing-room on the paddle-wheels, he will be wedged in by the crowd so tightly as to save him from any use of his limbs when the accident, which is sure to occur, takes place. Exactly at the moment of the start, an opposition boat will also set off, so that the speed will be deliciously exhilarating, and everything will be done to realize, to the most ardent expectant, the usual catastrophe. In trying to give "Hell turn" as narrow a berth as possible, each captain will foul his adversary, and a few passengers will be missed from the paddle boxes, to make an additional hole or turn in the water. As they will very likely amount to a dozen or so—quite enough to help one another—it would be nonsense to stop either vessel, and so the burthen being thus lightened, the speed is doubled.

In furtherance, too, of the praiseworthy object for which these vessels were originally started (the reduction of the population), they are ordered to "go on" at the precise moment a passenger is stepping off.

American Shipnology.

PERHAPS nothing so strikingly indicates the change which has taken place in the mercantile marine of this country—at least so far as mere taste is concerned—as the ingenuity displayed in the invention of names for ships. Formerly, merchants were satisfied with a plain and modest nomenclature, calling their vessels after their wives, or their friends, or by the name of some ancient worthy or modern hero, or by some homespun adjective, expressive of strength and safety. Now all this is changed. We have the Courser, the Bucephalus, the Storm King, the Flying Cloud, the Flying Dutchman, and the Flying Childers; the Stag Hound, the Wild Pigeon, the Sea Gull, and the Bald Eagle; the Sea Foam, the Billow Crest, the Ocean Spray, and the Ocean Wave; the West Wind and the Whirlwind, the Simoom and the Sirocco; and lastly, the Thunder Cloud, the Phantom, the Tornado, the Tempest, the Wings of the Morning, Ocean Monarch, Leviathan, Fury of the Billow, Hurricane, Wildfire, Thunderer, &c.

Origin of the Express Business: Harnden's First Trip.

WITH the innovations of railways, the stage drivers and wagoners found, like Othello, their "occupation gone." The loss of their services seriously incommoded the public, but the railroad offered no remedy. Years passed, trade and intercommunication between town and country suffering, in the meanwhile, from this cause. At length, hardly realizing what an improvement he was about to effect, William F. Harnden, then a railroad conductor, started the express business. The idea was not original with him exclusively, as will presently be seen, but to him is due the honor of having been the first to put it into execution.

It was in 1839 that Major Pullen and Mr. Harnden were both in the employ of the Boston, Providence, Worcester and New York Railroad and Steamboat Companies. Mr. Harnden's health was so bad, at this time, that he was unfitted for his accustomed duties. His pecuniary circumstances were such that he could not remain idle. In this crisis of his affairs he knew not what to do to sustain himself and his family.

Speaking to his friend, Major Pullen, on the subject, who was agent of the Steamboat Company at Boston, he asked his advice as to what he had better do. They were, on this occasion, in the office on board the steamer John W. Richmond; near them, a number of small packages were lying about, which were intrusted to the care of the agent for delivery, as was the custom at that time. Major Pullen says to Mr. H. substantially as follows: " I think you can make a good living by taking care of these packages and delivering them. If you will try it, I will give you all the packages and errands that are left with me, and give you all the aid in my power to help you along in the business." Some friends standing by advised Mr. H. to do so. After some deliberation, Mr. Harnden commenced his new avocation.

From this small beginning, expressing has attained its present prominent position, as among the first class of business occupations in the country. The only through route from Boston to New York, at that time, was by railroad to Providence, and thence to New York by the steamer John W. Richmond. The old line of steamboats ran from Stonington to New York. Harnden had no paid agent in the latter city at the outset. The messengers (called, during the first year or two, conductors), attended to all the business. Harnden himself acted in that capacity, usually making the trip in the " J. W. R.," and carrying his entire express in an ordinary valise. Upon his arrival in New York or Boston, he would hasten to deliver the parcels intrusted to him by his customers, who were mostly booksellers and brokers.

Out of compliment to Mr. Harnden, as the originator of that line, and the first one in the business, the line still retains the name of " Harnden's Express," though none of his name or kin, now he is dead, are connected with it.

The express tries to do everything for everybody—any and all kinds of service. They carry the exchange for the banks; they collect notes, bills, drafts, accounts, rents, etc.; they carry all the small and large packages which are either too valuable, or otherwise unsafe to intrust to the mails; and they extend over all sections of our own continent, besides forming one of the most important links in the great commercial chain which connects us with the old world.

Selling a Brig—The Ruling Passion.

A VERY good story is told of old embargo times and the war of 1812. Under the impulse of the removal of embargo, there was a sudden rise in the value of property, and such a demand for it that merchandise was sometimes carried off from vessels before the owners arrived at their place of business; and the parties taking it came in afterward to say that they were at the owner's mercy, and must pay what they chose to ask.

A brig was lying at Boston harbor, which had come up from Plymouth just before the embargo was laid, fit for sea. The Plymouth owner thought it was a good time to sell the brig, and sent up his son for the purpose, telling him to demand $8,000 for her, and not take less than $6,000. John went to Boston, found how things stood, sold the brig in a moment, as it were, and hurried home, elated with his bargain. As he neared the house, he saw the old man marching up and down the piazza, and presently he hastened out to meet his son, and hear the result of the sale.

" Have you sold the brig, John ? "

" Yes, father."

" For how much, John ? "

" For *ten thousand dollars !* "

" Ten thousand dollars ! " cried the old man, with staring eyes, at hearing a price more than double what the vessel cost—" *Ten* thousand dollars ? I'll bet you've sold her to some swindler, who don't care what the price is, and never means to pay his notes."

" Notes, did you say, father ? Why, there are no notes in the case ; I got the money, and put it in the bank. Draw, and you will get it."

The old gentleman's excitement was suddenly cooled, and as the ruling passion rose in its place, he said :

" I say, John, couldn't you have got a *leetle* more ? "

Forwarding by Telegraph.

Of all the telegraphic absurdities to be met with, none can be much more amusing than that relating to a man in the south of France, who received a letter from his son in the army before Sebastopol, begging his father to send him a pair of new shoes, and a five-franc piece. The old man was very willing to comply with the request, but having no readier means of forwarding the articles than the telegraph, which

conveniently passed within half a mile of his house, he procured the shoes, and hung them on the wire, with the money inside. A laborer returning homeward, seeing the shoes dangling to the wires, took them down, and finding they fitted him, carried them off, leaving his old ones in their place. In the evening, the old man came out to see how the wires had performed their work, and was delighted at the result : " My poor boy," said he, " has not only received the shoes I sent him, but has already returned the old ones."

Jumel the Merchant, and the Carman.

STEPHEN JUMEL was among the early merchant princes of New York. One morning, about ten o'clock, in the year 1806, this gentleman, in company with William Bayard, Harmon Leroy, Archibald Gracie, and some dozen others, were reading and discussing the news just arrived from Liverpool, in the extra short passage of seven weeks. The matter mostly concerned Napoleon the First and the battle of Wagram. While thus engaged, a carman's horse backed his cart into the Whitehall slip, at the head of which these gentlemen were grouped together. The cart was got out, but the horse was drowned, and every one began pitying the poor carman's ill luck. Jumel instantly started, and placing a ten dollar bill between his thumb and fingers, and holding it aloft, while it fluttered in the breeze, and with his hat in the other hand he walked through the length and breadth of the crowd, exclaiming, " How much you pity the poor man ? *I* pity him ten dollars. How much *you* pity him ? " By this ingenious and noble coup-d'état, says Barrett, he collected, in a few moments, about seventy dollars, which he gave over at once to the unfortunate and fortunate carman.

Scene in an Express Office.

" How much will you charge to take this package to Illinois ?."

" One dollar."

" Outrageous ! It is only worth fifty cents, and you have the conscience to charge twice the worth of it."

It is not our fault that the cost was only fifty cents; you can make the package twice as large and a hundred times as valuable, and the cost of transportation will only be the same."

"But that I do not want to do, as it will be so much out of my pocket for nothing."

" Yet you do not think it will be ' outrageous ' for *us* to be out of pocket in carrying this to your friend ! "

" I cannot see that you will be at any loss by taking it for fifty cents. If you can explain it to me I will be satisfied."

" Sensible to the last, and I am truly glad that you ask for the information. Well, in the first place, we charge you two shillings to carry this to B., then *pay* two shillings to get it to C., two shillings from C. to M., and two shillings from M. to S., where your friend resides, thus making one dollar. If we take it for fifty cents, we will be obliged to carry it to B. for nothing, and *pay* from B. to C. two shillings out of our own pocket, thus losing cash two shillings, and the freight from here to B., which we pay to the railroad—thus actually losing about forty cents, besides assuming the responsibility of delivering your package to your friend in Illinois."

" I was not aware that such was the case, and pardon me for speaking so abruptly when I came in."

" Granted, my dear sir; and it always affords us pleasure to give any information in our power in regard to business. And I assure you, that if many persons who think we are extortioners and swindlers, and call us many other hard names, would only ask for a reason, they would be as satisfied as you are."

Luxuries in the Car.

THE smoking saloon, it now appears, is only the first of a series of luxuries which it is intended to bestow upon travellers by railway. Thus, it is in contemplation to run a refreshment-room with every train, so that people will have their time allowed them to eat the articles sold, instead of being restricted, as at present, simply to the privilege of payment.

Various plans have from time to time been suggested, to enable passengers to swallow a cup of boiling tea or coffee, or a basin of hot soup in a minute and a half at the stations; but it has been over and over again proved that the time specified is absolutely insufficient for such a purpose. It has even been suggested that there might be kept and sold at all the refreshment-rooms a preparation similar to that which enabled a certain Frenchman some years ago. to swallow melted lead without any inconvenience. Others have proposed that parties should be allowed to take soup or tea into the car with them, and send back the cup or basin by the up or down train, with a return ticket fastened to the piece of crockery as a proof of its contents having been paid for.

The most feasible scheme, however, is believed to be the one above hinted at, namely, a portable refreshment room, one of which should travel with every train; and it might be advisable to have the boiler of the engine supplied with soup instead of plain water. It has been calculated that the steam produced from the former liquid—being somewhat spicy—would have much greater strength or force than the vapor arising from the latter; and the power of *propulsion* natural to *pea* soup would have a wonderful influence on the speed of a powerful locomotive.

On one line there has for some time been a shaving saloon, the want of which had long been sadly felt. The length of time on the journey by this line was so considerable that a person quitting the car on arriving at his destination felt ashamed to go forth, in consequence of his beard and hair having grown to a most unsightly length since he left the terminus he started from.

On another line, something has been said about a course of lectures on anatomy, amputation, life insurance, and kindred subjects, likely to possess an immediate interest to persons travelling on railways, but the plan has not been matured,—an almost insuperable difficulty being the frequent interruption of the lecturer occasioned by the shrieks and thinning off of the passengers, on account of collisions and similar catastrophes along the line.

Probable Origin of Schooners.

THE first schooner ever launched in this country, is said to have been built at Cape Ann, in 1714,—that is, a vessel of the build and rig described by that word. In regard to the origin of the name or term " schooner," Cotton Tufts says: "Being in Gloucester, Mass., Sept. 8, 1790, I was informed, and committed the same to writing, that the kind of vessel called schooners, derived their name from this circumstance, viz.: Mr. Andrew Robinson, of that place, having constructed a vessel which he masted and rigged in the same manner as schooners are at this day, on her going off the stocks into the water, a bystander cried out, " Oh, how she schoons!" Robinson instantly replied, " A schooner let her be,"—from which time vessels thus masted and rigged have gone by the name of " schooners," but before which instance vessels of this classification were not known in Europe or America. This account was confirmed to me by a great number of persons in Gloucester. I made particular inquiry of an aged sea captain, who informed me that he had not, in any of his voyages to Europe or in America, seen any of those vessels prior to Robinson's construction."

Female Shipmaster from Cape Horn to San Francisco.

THE name of Mary Patten will long be remembered as that of one of the most heroic of her sex. She was the wife of a merchant shipmaster, who, far off on the lonely Pacific, with no eye to witness, and no voice to cheer her, when her husband was taken down by illness, now tended him in his cabin, now took his place at the quarter-deck of his forlorn vessel,—took her chief observation every day with the sextant, laid down the ship's course on the chart, cheered and encouraged the desponding crew, arrested the mutinous chief mate, who was for creeping into the nearest port—and, poor young wife as she was, hardly twenty years of age, yet with a strong will and a stout heart, steered her husband's vessel, through storm and through calm, from Cape Horn to San Francisco.

Prussian Ship navigated by a Lady.

IN Prussia, as well as in Holland, captains in the merchant service, of small property,—which generally consists of a small class vessel commanded by themselves—make the vessel their home, and live there constantly, with their families, who accompany their head in all his voyages.

One of these Prussian captains, M. Hesser, was navigating his galliot Minerva, from Konigsberg to Riga. On board his vessel was his young wife, with three small children, and his crew, composed of a mate and four sailors. In the Baltic, during a violent storm in the night, while Hesser and his men were on deck, the galliot was run into by an English merchant-ship; and the shock of the two vessels was so great that Captain Hesser and one of his sailors was thrown against the prow of the English vessel, to which they clung, and from whence they crawled on board that ship. The three other sailors fell into the sea and disappeared immediately, so that there remained on the galliot only Mrs. Hesser, her three children, and the mate—the latter having, during the accident, met with a severe fall, by which he was so seriously wounded as to be unable to work.

In this state of things, Mrs. Hesser had the courage to take upon herself the charge of navigating the ship. By turns captain, mate and sailor, using the little nautical knowledge she had been able to acquire in her former voyages,—this intrepid young woman succeeded, by incessant labor, in gaining, with her vessel, the port of Riga. The native and foreign sailors at Riga, having learned the courageous conduct of Mrs. Hesser, caused a medal to be struck in her honor, and the corporation of seamen at Riga presented her with one thousand dollars. Captain Hesser and his sailor, who were saved on board the English vessel, were carried in the latter to Rostock, where they arrived safe and sound at Riga.

Royal Schemers in Railways.

THE madness of railway speculation which some years since spread like a contagion abroad, involved royal blood and the peers of more than one realm. Prince de Joinville mounted a tender; Lord F. Egerton sought to make a railway all by himself; Earl Lonsdale bought one; Lord Belhaven condescended to speak at meetings; Lord Worsley even took the chair; the Marquis of Ormonde trundled a wheelbarrow in the presence of his admiring peasantry; and Lord Wharncliffe, "high in the councils of her Majesty," cut turf on correct geometrical principles. The schemes in which these illustrious names figured were got up, in many cases, somewhat on the following plan: A flattering prospectus is issued, promising ten per cent., and perfect prosperity. Some secret agent of the directors is on the stock exchange, puffing up the shares. A price is named; it is eagerly accepted by him, the bargain is made, and the price of the scrip established. The agents continue to buy; the jobbers, calculating on plenty of scrip being in the market, are willing to sell on the liberal term which the agent pays; and they enter into engagements to deliver a large quantity of scrip. When a sufficient number of shares are sold to satisfy the grasping avarice of the directors, they profess to consider the applications; and it is announced that no more letters will be received, and that letters of allotment have been forwarded to the fortunate applicants, taking care, however, not to issue a tenth part of the number previously sold in the market. The letters applying for shares are burnt by bushels, without even the trouble of opening them; and those who have sold at five pounds a share cannot even buy at three times that sum, if the consciences of the directors are sufficiently elastic to allow so enormous a robbery. Premiums, patronage, and pay, made the brains of the directors swim and swell. Men who were known to have been penniless a year before, suddenly kept their broughams or started barouches. Valuable diamonds gleamed from fingers which had hitherto been guiltless of the bright adornment. Railway papers and railway pantaloons, railway ties and railway tricks, abounded. It was railway-madness indeed. London was to be tunnelled that the train might run beneath her mighty heart; colonnades were to be formed in the air that the engine might pass over the path of the pedestrian, and it was finally suggested that there should be one great terminus for all the companies, and that that terminus should be a lunatic asylum!

The system was fruitful, and every one said there was no risk. When shares were demanded of a company, and they only came out at par, the letter of allotment was put into the fire; if they arrived at a premium they were sold. Men without a shilling wrote for hundreds of shares. Journeymen mechanics styled themselves esquires, and signed deeds for thousands. The names of men well known in the city as gamblers, whose notorious character had banished them from the society of all good men, suddenly reappeared on the lists of the proprietors and directors, their names graced by the cheap "esquire," and their residences given in some far distant county. Tricks of all sorts were played; and in one instance the whole of the type and stock in trade of a printer was purchased by one company, to prevent its rival from publishing an important document by a particular period—this *ruse* proving successful, and the document behind its time.

On the last day allotted for the reception of plans by the Board of Trade, a most astonishing scene was witnessed. As the time approached, an anxiety which passes belief was evinced. Higher wages were paid to those who could or would work in preparing the plans. Night after night witnessed the earnest workman still snatching a brief repose for an hour or two, that he might resume his labors with greater energy. Post-horses were in demand. Special trains brought plans from all sections. Railway companies refused trains which would assist opposition projects; and the exertion made to lodge those which were ready, is almost incredible. The clerks were overwhelmed with them; and though an additional number of those gentlemen were employed, it was impossible to keep pace with the incessant arrivals. The place became crowded. The last hour was approaching. An alarm seized on all that the necessary forms could not be gone through in time. The clock struck, and the doors were closing, when a gentleman, with the plans of a proposed railway for Surrey, rushed in, and succeeded in lodging his charge. The doors were then closed, and, in a short time, a postchaise, with foaming steeds, galloped up to the entrance. Down the passage, and toward the office, rushed the three occupants, with their cherished papers. The door was shut; but railway persons deemed themselves privileged, and the bell was loudly rung. The unsuspicious inspector of police answered the ring; and the huge documents were thrown in at a venture; but were again thrown into the street. Many were too late for the appointed hour. The labor of anxious days and weary nights, the results of plotting heads and crafty brains, were rejected.

Laughable Opposition to Steam Trains.

PERHAPS the most interesting and romantic pages that could be furnished readers at the present day, might be found in the literature of early railways —gleanings from the speeches, pamphlets, reports, etc., which the proposal of such schemes brought forth. A few scraps will meet the purpose of this volume.

It was contended by the opponents of these enterprises, that canal conveyance was quicker; that the smoke of the engines would injure gentlemen's seats and villas; and one writer, more imaginative than perceptive, described the locomotives as "terrible things," although, on further questioning, he admitted he had never seen one. It was boldly declared, too, that a gale of wind would stop the progress of the carriage; that there would be no more practical advantage in a railway than in a canal; that Mr. Stephenson was totally devoid of common sense. The plan was asserted to be based on fraud and folly; that balloons and rockets were as feasible; and that the whole line would be under water for two or three weeks in succession.

"It is quite idle and absurd," said one, "to say that the present schemes can ever be carried into execution, under any circumstances, or in any way." "Whenever," said another, with the authority of an oracle, "Providence in Lancashire is pleased to send rain or a little mizzling weather, expeditious it cannot be." A third gave it as *his* opinion, that "no engine could go in the night time, because," he added, more scripturally than pertinently, "the night time is a period when no man can work!"

The public benefits of a railroad were put in disparaging competition with the annoyance which an individual would receive from the smoke of the engines coming within two hundred and fifty yards of his house, and it was pathetically asked, "Can anything compensate for this?" Gentlemen objected because it would injure their prospects, and land-owners because it would injure their pockets! Of Mr. Stephenson it was declared, "he makes schemes without seeing the difficulties." "Upon this shuffling evidence, we are called to pass the bill." "It is impossible to hold this changing Proteus in any knot whatsoever." "It is the greatest draught upon human credulity ever heard of."

"There is nothing," said one, "but long sedgy grass to prevent the train from sinking into the shades of eternal night." Another appealed to the pocket: "If this bill succeeds, by the time railroads are set a-going, the poor, gulled subscribers will have lost all their money; and, instead of locomotive engines, they must have recourse to horses or asses, not meaning to say which." Numberless were the sneers at the idea of engines galloping as fast as five miles an hour. One sapient gentleman thought, however, that the trains might go at four and one-half miles in fine weather, but not more than two and one-half in wet.

"When we set out with the original prospectus," was the remark of the counsel, "we were to gallop—I know not at what rate. I believe it was twelve miles an hour, with the aid of a devil in the form of a locomotive, sitting as postilion on the fore house, and an honorable member sitting behind him to stir up the fire, and keep it up at full speed. *I* will show they cannot go *six*. I may be able to show we shall keep up with them by the canal." "Thus, sir, I prove that locomotive engines cannot move at more than four and a-quarter miles an hour; and I will show the scheme to be bottomed on deception and fallacy."

Lady Ship-master.

THAT Irish ladies are 'smart,' abundant evidence might be forthcoming, if necessary. But the following single instance will do much to establish the general assertion. Amongst the fleet lately wind-bound in Lamlash, not the least, but perhaps the greatest wonder, was the good old brig Cleotus, of Saltcoats, which for more than twenty years has been commanded by an heroic and exceedingly clever lady, Miss Betsey Miller, daughter of Mr. W. Miller, shipowner and wood dealer of that town. He was concerned with several vessels, both in the American and coasting trade. Miss Betsey, before she went to sea, acted as "ship's husband" to her father, and seeing how the captains in many cases behaved, her romantic and adventurous spirit impelled her to go to sea herself. Her father gratified her caprice, and gave her the command of the Cleotus, which she holds to the present day; and she has weathered the storms of the deep when many commanders of the other sex have been driven on the rocks. The Cleotus is well known in the ports of Belfast, Dublin, Cork, etc.

Lucky and Unlucky Names of Ships, and Sailing Days.

THAT there is ill omen as well as bad luck attending vessels having certain names has long been believed by many, and curious instances are cited to prove that it is not mere superstition. Among the memorable in this respect is the bark Raleigh, fitted out and called after his family name by the great Sir Walter, and intended to assist his half brother, Sir Humphrey Gilbert, in his North American researches. This vessel sailed with Sir Humphrey, and, we are told in the sad record of his fate, appeared to predict the fatal termination of the expedition by returning in less than a week, through a contagious distemper which seized on the ship's crew. She was lost on a similar expedition to the one which hastened Sir Walter's sad doom. So of the Amazon, and Birkenhead, which sailed on Friday, and were lost so disastrously.

An attempt was once made to prove, once for all, that *Friday* was not the unlucky day poor Jack always fancied it to be. A ship was built with such an intention some years ago; she was named Friday, was launched on Friday, commanded by a captain whose name was Friday, sailed on a Friday, which no ship does if it can conveniently be helped, and was never—heard of afterward! But against all this, and other similar instances, must be placed the fact that vessels with even the luckiest names, have, in innumerable cases, perished, and that for each and every day of the week alike there is the fruitful record of mischance and disaster.

Columbus sailed on his great voyage of discovery, on Friday, August 21st. On Friday, October 12th, 1492, he made his first discovery of land; on Friday, January 4th, 1493, he sailed on

his return to Spain, which if he had not reached in safety, the happy result would never have been known; on Friday, March 15th, 1493, he arrived at Palos in safety; on Friday, November 22d, 1493, he arrived at Hispaniola, on his second voyage to America, and on Friday, he, though unknown to himself, discovered the continent of America. The Mayflower, with the pilgrims, made the harbor of Provincetown on Friday, November 10th, 1620. Surely, in a maritime and commercial sense, such facts send Friday up to a premium, and ought to disarm seamen of their ill-starred theory of that day.

Locomotion and Amalgamation.

PASSENGER : " What's the matter, conductor ?

CONDUCTOR (with accustomed presence of mind) : " Oh, nothing particular, sir. We've only been run into by an excursion train ! "

PASSENGER : " But, good gracious ! there's a train just behind us, isn't there ? "

CONDUCTOR: " Well, yes, sir ! But a boy has gone down the line with a signal, and it's very likely they'll see it ! "

New Rules for Railways.

SOME new regulations, recently proposed for the benefit of all concerned, have found their way into print, and are now being seriously considered by the various railways. A few are given below.

No stoppage at a railway station is to exceed half an hour.

No railway dividend is to exceed one hundred per cent. and no bonus to be divided oftener than once a month, otherwise shareholders shall have a right to throw up their certificates.

Lectures and dramatic representations are to be given at the stations to entertain the passengers when they are detained beyond the limit above specified, and payment of one shilling an hour is to be made to every laboring man for every hour of such detention.

Every tunnel must be illuminated with one candle at least, except during the season of fireflies, when it may be dispensed with.

A magistrate is to be in attendance at every station to grant summonses, on complaint, against the directors; and all law expenses incurred are to be paid by the Company.

Never less than one minute is to be allowed for dinner or refreshment.

One director must always travel with every train, either in one of the cars or in front of the engine—he having the liberty to choose.

Hospitals are to be built at every terminus and a surgeon to be in attendance at every station.

All the fines and damages levied upon a railway are to be paid into a fund for building a series of almshouses, for the maintenance of indigent persons mutilated from day to day by accidents on the railways.

There must be some communication between every car and the conductor, either by a bell, or a speaking tube, or a portable electric telegraph, so that the passengers may have some means of giving information when their car is off the track, or falling over an embankment, or a maniac has broken loose, or a robbery by chloroform has taken place.

———

Yankee Calculation of Railroad Speed.

" WELL, it's curous how we du git over the ground! Why, the trees all look as if they was a-dancin' a jig to double-quick time. I kin recollect ten or twelve years ago, that if I started from Bosting on a Wednesday, I cud git in Filedelphy on the next Saturday, makin' just three days. Now I kin git from Bosting to Filedelphy in one day; and I've been cal'latin' that if the power of steam increases for the *next* ten years as it has been doin' for the *last*

ten years, I'd be in Filedelphy jist two days before I started from Bosting ! "

———

Railroad Damages : The Tables Turned.

A CERTAIN community somewhere in Texas had made it a pretty frequent practice to get all the money they could from the railroad corporation thereabout, by allowing their cattle to get upon the track and obtaining damages when they were killed by the locomotive. At last, however, a law with due penalties was enacted, against the roaming of cattle upon the track of said road.

A new president of this corporation, Mr. Blank, was chosen, whose management proved him to be considerably *ahead* of some with whom he was soon called to deal. When Mr. Blank assumed the presidential control, it was in a dark day indeed. Acres of woodland, fields of grain, houses and barns had been consumed by the locomotive sparks, and cattle without number had been killed on the track. Demands against the company and impending law suits were more numerous than agreeable.

One day a man made his appearance at Mr. Blank's office. He was the champion of his neighborhood in this kind of business, and had come down to enforce payment for a valuable pair of oxen, suddenly converted into jerked beef by the iron horse. Our claimant entered the office as bold as a lion.

"I want payment for my cattle you killed last Saturday," said he.

" Your cattle ! " inquired Mr. Blank; " were those your cattle that were killed ? "

" Mighty apt to be," was the answer, " and I want two hundred for them."

"And *I*," said Mr. Blank, " want proof. You must make an affidavit of the particulars, and then we will come to a settlement."

Right willingly did the claimant assent; but when the instrument was

properly drawn up, signed, and authenticated, Mr. Blank turned to him with—
"Now, sir, I want two hundred dollars from *you*."

"From me ?" exclaimed the amazed rustic.

"Yes, sir, from *you*," reiterated the president. "Here I have proof, under your own hand, that your cattle were, contrary to law, upon the track, and thereby our engine was damaged to the extent of two hundred 'dollars. Are you prepared to settle the affair amicably, or must I proceed legally ?"

The applicant spoke no word, but rushed open-mouthed from the office, sought his wagon, and upon reaching his house advised his friends generally to pocket their grievances, or worse would come of it. From that day the demands upon the road were few indeed.

Telegraphing against Time.

An incident occurred at Niagara Falls during the Prince of Wales' stay, which illustrates some of the fortuities of telegraphic operating, and which has been frequently, but—excepting by a writer in Harper's Magazine—never correctly reported ; so it is stated.

The special reporter of a New York journal had ordered the telegraph line to be kept open, one Sunday evening, when the offices were usually closed, and had engaged to pay the operators liberally for their extra work. Before he had finished telegraphing his usual reports, along came the reporter of another New York journal, who, having obtained some exclusive news, and finding the line in fine working order, asserted his right to have his despatches transmitted to New York also. Reporter the first resisted. Reporter the second insisted. Reporter the first appealed to the telegraph operators, and after a great deal of conversation between the Niagara and Rochester offices, the operator decided that both re-

ports must be telegraphed. Reporter the second was calmly triumphant, and coolly prepared his notes. Reporter the first attempted to bribe the operators, and finding them incorruptible, began a long and desultory argument over the wires, in order to kill time and crowd out his opponent. Reporter the second, therefore, obtained an interview with the Hon. John Rose, the Premier of Canada, who sent down a message to the operators that he was, or had been, President, Vice-President, or Director —he really could not tell which—of the Telegraph Company, and that by virtue of his authority, he ordered both despatches to be telegraphed immediately. This order added fuel to the fire of indignation which glowed in the bosom of Reporter the first. A Canadian official dictate to an American reporter ? Never ! Meanwhile the moments slipped hurriedly away, and the hour was approaching when it would be useless to attempt to send a despatch to New York in time for publication in the morning papers. Observing this, Reporter the first suddenly recovered his self-control, and referred all the parties concerned to the standard rule of the Telegraph Company, that "despatches must be sent in the order in which they were received, and that one despatch must be finished before another could be transmitted." This rule was acknowledged to be telegraphic law. Reporter the first then claimed priority for his report. This point was also conceded. The reporter then eloquently but briefly informed the bystanders that they might as well go to bed, as his report could never be concluded while a chance of a despatch reaching New York that night remained to his competitor. Immediately he set to work to telegraph against time. His original report having been despatched, he jotted down every item worth sending, and ransacked his brains for any little incident of the Prince's doings which might possibly have been forgotten. His pencil flew over the paper like lightning. Click—click—click—the operator hurried off page after page almost as rapidly as the reporter could indite them. Reporter the second stalked gloomily up and down the office, despairing, but unconquered. To him the minute-hand of the clock moved with terrible swiftness. To Reporter the first the moments seemed shod with lead. Every item being exhausted, a description of Niagara Falls, carefully reserved to be sent by mail, was handed to the operator and flashed over the line at a cost of six or eight cents a word. This done, there was a moment's pause. Reporter the first reflected. Reporter the second breathed more freely, and even ventured to smile hopefully, and nervously finger his detained despatches. Alas! Reporter the first again writes—this time a note to the Rochester operator: "Which would you prefer to telegraph, a chapter of the Bible or a chapter of Claude Duval, the Highwayman? These are the only two books I can find in the hotel." The lightning flashes off with the query, and returns with the answer: "It is quite immaterial which you send." The Reporter seizes the Bible, transcribes the first chapter of Matthew, with all its hard genealogical names, adds this to his previous despatches, tacks portions of the twenty-first chapter of Revelation—describing the various precious stones—to the incongruous report, hands it all to the operator, sends his blessing and an injunction to be careful of the spelling to the Rochester office, and gleefully awaits the result with his eyes on the clock. Before this scriptural news is fully transmitted, the hour arrived when no more telegrams could be sent. Reporter the first retired in glory; but although his telegrams reached New York safely, the Biblical portions were unfortunately never published. Reporter the second telegraphed his news the next morning, at the same time

good-naturedly acknowledging his defeat.

Telegraphic Capers.

ON a certain occasion, says a London journal, the French telegraph made the following announcement:
"Abd-el-Kader has been taken"—but it was mentioned that a fog enveloped the remainder of the sentence in obscurity. The excitement, however, in the money market was at fever height, at the supposed capture of that adroit enemy, and the funds rose tremendously.

The following day, the sentence being completed, the intelligence ran thus:
"Abd-el-Kader has been taken with a dreadful cold in his head."

The funds fell, but the *coup*—which was worthy of a Rothschild—had been sufficiently successful for those who made the telegraph play into the hands of their agents at the Bourse. A fog in Paris is frequently a great windfall in a monetary and commercial point of view.

Guarding the Track.

THE Hon. Erastus Corning, President of the New York Central Railway, notwithstanding his remarkable activity, has the misfortune to be lame. He was one day hobbling over the railroad track at Albany, when an Irishman who was placed to guard the track, sang out, with marked Celtic accent, "Will ye leave the track?" Mr. Corning smiled inwardly and stumbled on, when the Irishman again cried, "Begone, ye stumbling high-binder, or the 11.30 Express will be forninst ye, and Mister Corning will have to pay for ye the full price of a well man with two legs. Begone! sare!" This was too much for "Old Central;" he yielded the track for the 11.30 Express, and sent a reward and commendation to the faithful watchman, who had never once suspected the name or position of that "stumbling high-binder."

A Deep Design.

A PLAN is about to be carried out by some enterprising London capitalists for passing an electric telegraph under the streets of that city. That *walls have ears* has been heard by all; but this is a plain matter-of-fact sort of scheme for giving *tongues to the streets*, which will enable them to rival the celebrated stones that were nearly rising up to remonstrate, in a certain exigency, to say nothing of those stones of the poet, in which he assures us there are sermons. It is presumed that an undertone will be best adapted to this subterranean language.

It has been decided that this telegraph, when completed, shall be let out to the whole public at so much a message. This plan will do very well, unless the whole population wants, as usual, to talk at once, when the effect would be most extraordinary. Nor is any statement made, as yet, to prevent the wrong people from receiving the messages that are thus sent by the telegraph. It would be very awkward if a somewhat general observation should arrive at a station, for there would be a difficulty in finding an owner for remark of such a common-place character.

The project seems a good one, but it will require much modification to render it effectual. One regulation provides that ladies who avail themselves of the telegraph shall be charged by the length of the message, an immense revenue being calculated from this source alone; in order, however, that all may share the benefits of such an enterprise, no one female is to be allowed to monopolize the use of the subterranean tongue for a longer time at once than thirteen hours.

Unsociable Travelling Companion.

A RARE incident occurred in an English stage-coach, on a certain occasion, before railroads came into vogue. Two passengers, one a merchant, set out from a London inn early on a December morning. It was dark as pitch; and one of them, not being sleepy, and wishing for a little conversation, endeavored, in the usual travelling mode, to stimulate his companion to discourse. "A very dark morn, sir. Shocking cold weather for travelling! Slow going in the heavy roads, sir." None of these very civil observations producing a word in response, the sociable merchant made one more effort. He stretched out his hand and feeling the other's habit, exclaimed, "What a very comfortable coat, sir, you have got to travel in!" No answer was made, and the merchant, fatigued and disgusted, fell into a sound nap, nor awoke until the brightest rays of a winter's sun accounted to him for the taciturnity of his comrade, by presenting to his astonished view a huge bear (luckily for him muzzled and confined) in a sitting posture.

Decoration of Railroad Depots.

AT one of our railway stations, a passenger on looking round saw the bill announcing the arrival and departure of the train, and by its side was posted —with most innocent candor on the part of the directors—another bill, advising him, in the most alluring terms, to insure his life. Of course the two things thus placed in juxtaposition, put him in a reflecting mood.

Railway companies might improve on this system of starting trains of serious thought. They should illuminate the walls of their waiting-rooms with moral sentences, expressive of the uncertainty of human existence, such as Memento Mori, Mors Janua Vitæ, &c.; which, executed in appropriate characters, might be made to have a picturesque and pleasing, as well as profitable effect. The intermixture with these legends, of tombstone cherubs, skulls, and femoral bones, and views in cemeteries well painted, would be very suitable; and to these æsthetic decorations might be added the figure of old Time with his scythe and hourglass. It may be mentioned, as a matter not unrelated to these suggestions, that some of the newspapers have adopted the plan of inserting their "Railway Intelligence" next to the "Obituary."

Punch's Own Railway.

THIS snug little suburban line (says its proprietor) occasionally makes a mild demand on public attention, by a sort of popgun-like proceeding, known as the issuing of its annual report, which is usually accompanied with a very little smoke, and somewhat less fire. Everything is on the smallest possible scale; and the rolling stock includes a garden roller, which is kept for the purpose of rolling the gravel walks by the side of those cabbage beds which form the vegetable wealth of the company. The property of the railway is understood to have somewhat increased; but there has been a loss of one engine and two buffers, the former being the moral engine which the company once possessed in the support of a now apathetic press; and the latter consisting of two old buffers who have got better places, after having been for some years in the service of the line as gardeners.

The balance at the banker's had been augmented by a few pounds, and the goods traffic is nearly eight ounces more this year than it was last—an increase which, considering the level of former times, may be considered feverish. Of coal, there is a skuttle more in the company's cellars than there was last year; and the directors propose that this surplus shall not be disturbed, but that it shall be added to the "rest," and carried over to the credit—the very great credit, of the company.

The engineer of the line has inspected the boilers, and reports that "the concern is not yet out of hot water, nor likely to be for some time to come,"—nor have the law proceedings been brought to a termination. Thanks were voted to the chairman, who had lent a Bath chair for a visit of the resident director to the terminus.

Stage Coach Experience of two Merchants.

ONE of the very pleasantest episodes to be found in the range of mercantile travelling experience, is that of the interview between Vincent Nolte, the great merchant of two hemispheres, and John McNeil, a Liverpool merchant of celebrity. It is one of those "happenings" which do not need to be read of more than once, as one reading will serve the memory ever after. It is almost worth the full price of Nolte's Autobiography, an admirable translation of which, from the German, has been published in this country. Mr. Nolte says:

I took a place, at five o'clock in the morning, in the Birmingham coach, the best conveyance then between Liverpool and London. It was a troubled, misty, unpleasant morning. In the corner of the coach opposite me, wrapped in his cloak, sat a gloomy looking person, besides myself the only passenger. More than two hours elapsed before the spirit moved us to any conversation. At length my companion roused himself, and brought forward the subject which always opens a conversation in England—the weather.

"We have a very nasty, disagreeable day before us, I fear," he remarked.

Whereupon I asked him if he were going all the way to London.

"No, no," he answered, "I will get out at a pottery near Wolverhampton, where I have to buy some hundred

24

baskets of crockery for my ship, the 'Peter Ellis.'"

"In order to send it to New Orleans, I suppose," said I.

"Certainly," he said, "but I beg your pardon, how did you know that?"

"I did not know it," I replied, "I only guessed it. I have seen the ship several times in New Orleans. She was consigned to my friends, Denistoun, Hill & Co."

"Oh, ho," said he, "so you have been in New Orleans."

"Very often," said I.

"How is the credit of the firm?" was his next question.

"Admirable," said I; "Mr. Hill is a man much esteemed and beloved."

"So I have always thought," he replied.

"Those gentlemen," I continued, "very often have ships to their address —for instance, the Liverpool brig 'The Brothers,' the ship 'Mary Wood,' and others. The Liverpool ship 'Ottawa,' was in other hands (namely, in ours), as well as many others."

"You appear to know our vessels well," said he, "and also most of the English houses in New Orleans."

"Oh, yes," I said; "I know nearly all the houses of any position there, pretty well."

"I am glad to hear it," said my companion, and then our dialogue continued.

"Do you know Munro, Milne & Co.? How do they stand?"

"Very well. They are the established correspondents of James Finley & Co., of Glasgow."

"Do you know P. W. & Co.? How do they stand?"

"So, so, no general credit."

"Do you know G., F. & Co.?"

"G. is a clever business man, and F. is a windbag, who, however, has thrown into the firm a large capital inherited from his aunt."

"The devil!" quoth my interlocutor; "you appear to know them all.

You must have lived some years in New Orleans."

"Yes, several."

"Do you know *Vincent Nolte?*"

"As well as he knows himself."

"What sort of a man is he?"

"Well," said I, "he has many friends, and perhaps quite as many foes; take him all in all, however, I believe he is a good sort of a fellow, with whom folks like to deal."

"Yes," he said, "our captains like him very much. He was prompt and expeditious, and when he had freighted a vessel, the goods came down as fast as they could be received on board."

"I believe," said I, "that this praise is not undeserved. It was always his custom to do quickly whatever he undertook."

Thereupon our conversation ended; and in half an hour the coach stopped before a large pottery belonging to Baker, Bourne & Baker. As he got out, my companion gave me his card— "John McNeil, Liverpool," saying:

"I have found so much pleasure in your conversation, that you must promise to pay me a visit when you return to Liverpool. I will present you to my two daughters, and we will all receive you with pleasure."

I was of course obliged to give him my card in exchange. He glanced at it twice, and in a doubtful sort of way read it over.

"Vincent N-o-ble!"

"No, sir," I said; "Vincent *Nolte*, the very gentleman you were inquiring about."

"Ah! so, so," he said. "Well, sir, glad to have had a sight of you. Do not fail to call when you come to Liverpool again. Farewell, sir!"

And so the coach rolled on.

An Interesting Consignment.

ONE of the most interesting consignments—at least in an historical point of view—of which there is any record, is that which was received from London, by Mr. Jacob Barker, of New York, viz., the first steam engine ever in successful operation for propelling vessels. It was made by Messrs. Bolton and Watts, celebrated for constructing steam machinery in that day. After its arrival it remained in Mr. Barker's store in South street many months before Mr. Fulton could raise the funds to pay for it. This engine was placed on the first steamboat that navigated the Hudson, and Mr. Barker thinks that she attained the speed of four miles an hour. Little did he then think that this discovery of the immortal Fulton would in less than half a century regulate the commerce of the whole world, saving time and shortening space to such a degree that to be deprived of its use would be universally considered a calamity of the first magnitude.

Squelching a Director's Impertinence.

THE plenary indulgence conceded to Mr. Hudson, the English railway monarch, by which his will was made law —all complaints of those who naturally esteemed themselves not fairly dealt with in various operations being silenced by his mere beck—cannot be better comprehended than in an anecdote of Mr. H. in his palmy days; being a circumstance which occurred at the board meeting of a certain line. The honorable gentleman had allotted to himself six hundred shares, and to another member of the board, two hundred. These shares having risen to five pounds premium, the latter gentleman thought he ought to have a larger number, and accordingly intimated his opinion to Mr. Hudson. "I have been accustomed, Mr. ——," replied the dictator, "to have gentlemen with whom I am associated, satisfied with my arrangements; and if you are not, I'll retire and leave the affairs in your custody, which I dare say you'll manage better than I do, as I have so much other business on my hands." "Oh, certainly not; by no means, Mr. Hudson," bowingly responded the crest-fallen director; "I am sure all you do is right, and I am quite satisfied with your arrangement." It is pretty certain that no further complaint was made by any of George's colleagues at *that* board!

Rare Passenger in an Omnibus.

JOHN McDONOGH, of New Orleans, was one of those who rarely spent tenpence for an omnibus ride, his habit being to economize to the last extremity in these minor as well as in larger things. He was an untiring pedestrian, being ever on foot, on some errand pertaining to his vast money concern. Suddenly, one day, while pursuing so eagerly his imaginary goal, he was seized with faintness on the street. Other men would have taken a cab, and ridden home, or at least to a physician's; but when did John McDonogh turn aside from business to relieve any weakness or want? He had an important document to file in court. It must be done that day. He is too weak to walk. There is the omnibus; the fare is only a dime—but that dime is so much taken from the poor, for John McDonogh is only an agent for the poor, so appointed and called of God. Such were the reflections, probably, that passed through his mind before he could be induced to perpetrate this serious violation of the settled rules of a life—this single blot and stain on a career of unbroken self-abnegation. With a sigh he took his seat in the omnibus. It was his last ride.

First Ship at St. Petersburg.

THE first ship which entered the port of St. Petersburg, was a Dutch vessel, the same in which Peter the Great acquired in Holland a practical knowledge of seamanship. She was received with extraordinary rejoicings and festivities, and whatever she might at any future period bring into the country was sacredly exempted from duty. This privilege she enjoyed until the end of the last century, when she was obliged to discontinue her trips, because it was found impossible to patch her up any longer so as to be seaworthy. The first ship that arrives in May, like the swallow proclaiming the return of spring, is still greeted with unusual demonstrations of joy, and has various favors granted her.

Proposed Line from England to China.

In consequence of the extreme difficulty at present experienced in making the voyage to China and India, together with the delay and chances of shipwreck, it has been proposed by gentlemen connected with the London *Punch* —under the advice of an eminent engineer—to construct a railway direct from that city to the Celestial Empire.
The plan suggested is the very feasible one of penetrating the bowels of the earth, through the medium of a suitable tunnel from London to Canton, passing through the centre of the globe, —thus obviating altogether the enormous expense usually incurred in the purchase of land, and avoiding the opposition likely to be encountered from hostile nations.
From the Report made to the Committee by Sinko Shaft, Esq., the engineer, who has descended some of the deepest wells and sewers in and about the metropolis, and has sounded the earth in various places at the outskirts, there is every reason to believe that the centre of the globe consists of a mass of softest soil, except where intersected by solid rocks of gold and silver, and caverns of precious stones; and that, from his examination, there is no reason whatever to believe, as some have conjectured, that the earth is a mere crust,

filled in the interior with *nothing at all* —a state of things which would naturally have rendered the cutting of a tunnel through it an expedient of some difficulty. As it is, however, the cutting will be exceedingly easy, except where the masses of precious metals and jewels interpose an obstacle; but inasmuch as this material, when removed, will be immensely valuable, and, according to the most moderate calculations of the engineer, will be many hundred times more than sufficient to cover the entire expense of the undertaking, but little fear need be apprehended upon this point.
It is intended that the terminus in England shall be at what is now the building known as St. Paul's Cathedral, London, which for the purposes of this line is to undergo the necessary architectural alterations, after permission has been obtained from the metropolitan bishop.
The journey by this route will, it is calculated, be accomplished as soon as the passengers get from one terminus to another. And as the railway will pass immediately under Mount Vesuvius, a station will be erected there, at which trains will stop for the purpose of taking in coals and lava, or blacksmiths, should there be any residing in those parts. Another stoppage will be made immediately under the Mediterranean, with a view of getting a supply of water—conveniently drawn down through a pipe from the sea above.
As regards the *intermediate* traffic between the two termini, there is, from the recent investigations into the subject by the learned members of the University Nhowhere, strong reason for believing that the population swallowed up at various periods by earthquakes, as at Lisbon, Port Royal, etc., etc., have only disappeared from the surface of the globe to colonize and people the interior. Should this be proved to be the case the most interesting results are likely to follow upon

the establishment of this undertaking —which indeed may be the means at once of opening an immense market for manufactures and a passage for the inhabitants of the interior regions of the earth of the most profitable and advantageous description. In addition to this it is confidently expected that most of the Continental nations will establish branch tunnels running into that of the parent Company, which will be both a most lucrative source of revenue, and be the means of opening an immense field to commercial enterprise.

Assuming the Responsibility.

HUDSON, the railway king, knew well how to make steady, gradual, and permanent encroachments in the conduct of those vast undertakings of which he was the body and soul; so as to compel others to concede to him the absolute influence necessary for that free individual action on which he felt the very existence of the organizations he brought about, and the success of the negotiations into which he entered, depended. He further knew how to make capital out of the feelings of reverence and admiration he excited. Having entered into some arrangements for the famous Midland Company which he had not vouchsafed to disclose to the board of directors, these gentleman, after having vainly endeavored, to worm out the coveted secret, screwed up their courage one day to demand it. They accordingly met much earlier one day than usual, and when their superior arrived, they were all exceedingly quiet.

"How now, gentlemen," said Mr. Hudson, "has anything happened?"

"Only," replied one, "that we being equally responsible with yourself for what is done, are desirous of knowing the nature of your future plans."

"You are, are you?" rejoined the premier; "then you will not!" And the business of the board proceeded.

Rothchild's Omnibus Fare.

THERE is a good story told of Baron Rothschild, which shows that it is not only money which"makes the mare go," —or *horses* either, as in this case,—but *ready* money, "unlimited credit" to the contrary notwithstanding. On a very wet and disagreeable day, the Barron took a Parisian omnibus, on his way to the Bourse or Exchange, near which the nabob of finance alighted, and was going away without paying. The driver stopped him, and demanded his fare. Rothschild felt in his pocket, but he had not a "red cent" of change. The driver was very wroth:

"What did you get in for, if you could not pay? You must have *known* that you had no money!"

"I am Baron Rothschild," exclaimed the great capitalist, "and there is my card!"

The driver threw the card into the gutter.

"Never heard of you before," said Jehu, "and don't want to hear of you again. But I want my fare—and I must *have* it."

The great banker was in haste: "I have only an order for a million," he said; "give me change?" and he proffered a "coupon" for fifty thousand francs. The conductor stared, and the passengers set up a horse laugh. Just then an "agent de change" came by, and Baron Rothschild borrowed of him the six sous. The driver was now seized with a kind of remorseful respect; and turning to the money-king, he said—

"If you want ten francs, sir, I don't mind lending them to you on my own account."

Great North Pole Railway.

THERE is a railway enterprise on foot, which, according to the prospectus, is to literally rise above everything in the line of that class of transit undertakings. It is styled, with that modesty of terms which distinguishes all real enterprises from those which are merely chimerical, the "Great North Pole Railway, forming a junction with the Equinoctial Line, with a branch to the horizon. Capital, two hundred millions. Deposit, three pence." The directors named for the North Pole terminus are J. Frost, Esq., chairman of the northwest passage; and Baron Iceberg, keeper of the great seal on the Northern Ocean. Director for the horizon, Hugh de Rainbow—admiral of the red, blue, and orange, etc., etc. And in addition to these are Simon Scamp, Esq, chairman of the East Jericho Junction Railway; Thomas Trapper, Esq., manager of the General Aerial Navigation Company; and Sir Edward Alias, non-resident director of the Equitable Coal and Slate Association;—with power to add to their number, by "taking in" as many as possible.

The proposed line will take the horizon for its point of departure, and, passing near the equator, will terminate at the North Pole, which will be the principal station of the company.

It is calculated that sunbeams may be conveyed along the line by a new process, which Professor Twaddle has been employed by the provisional committee to discover; and the professor's report will be laid before the subscribers at the very earliest opportunity.

By bringing the Equator within a week of the North Pole, and coöperating with the proprietors of the Great Equinoctial Line (long so vigorous in its operations), the advantages to the shareholders will be so obvious, that it is hardly necessary to allude to them.

It is estimated that the mere luggage traffic, in bringing up ice from the North Pole to the readiest market, will return a profit of sixty-five per cent. on the capital.

Should any unforeseen circumstance occur to prevent the Railway being carried out, the deposit will be returned, on application to Messrs. Walker, Gammon & Co. (Solicitors to the Company), at their temporary offices in Leg Alley.

Protective Costume for Travellers.

IT is in contemplation to provide, at all the stations on a certain western railway, a dress adapted for travellers along that celebrated line, by which it is thought they will be secured from the chances of injury by the collisions that are continually happening.

Considering that *padding* is not unfrequently resorted to, for the purpose of improving the figure, it has been thought quite reasonable that the fashion should be extended to the purpose of *protecting* the limbs as well as merely adding to their symmetry. A good pair of false calves, got up at a reasonable price, would doubtless be in very great demand, among those who risk their legs whenever they set their foot in a car on the line alluded to. The public would have no objection to a slight addition to the fares, for the purpose of insuring something like protection against accident.

The tariff of the Company might easibe so varied as to allow of the "first class, with paddings," being available at a small extra cost; while the "second class, with calves or knee-caps," might be charged something lower.

Waghorn's Great Scheme.

THE great pioneer of the Overland Communication with India was poor Thomas Waghorn. It is now upward of thirty years since Waghorn arrived in Bombay, full of a scheme for navigating a steamer round the Cape of Good Hope, which steamer, that it might carry a sufficiency of fuel for the whole trip, was only to take the mails and one passenger. On the day of Waghorn's arrival a meeting was held by the merchants to receive proposals from a Mr. Taylor for the formation of a company which was to open a communication with India *via* the Red Sea. Waghorn's scheme was scouted. Taylor received great encouragement, as far as promises could be relied upon, and he started for Europe with a party of friends, travelling up the Persian Gulf and Euphrates *en route* to Constantinople; but the whole party was murdered by the Vezedees near Diarbekir.

On the receipt of the news in India, Waghorn changed his tactics, and declared for the Red Sea route, offering to return to Europe with mercantile letters. But the "Ducks"—as the Bombay people are familiarly called in India—thought him mad or eccentric. Certainly he was afflicted with monomania—he could think, speak, dream of nothing but "steam." It became necessary, when in his company, to avoid all allusion to anything which could supply him with an excuse for bursting out on his favorite topic. Kettles, smoking tureens, condensed vapor, one shunned; for he watched, as a cat watches for a mouse, for an opportunity of bringing in steam navigation. On one unfortunate occasion (says the narrator of this), I introduced him to a Major Hawkins, a military engineer, saying: "Waghorn, make the acquaintance of my esteemed friend, Major Hawkins." "*Steamed*, sir, did you say?" exclaimed Waghorn; "I am delighted!" He seized Hawkins by the buttons and victimized him. Mad as he was, however, Waghorn contrived to carry his point with the London merchants and the ministry. He besieged the office of the Foreign Secretary, he worried the Premier, tortured the Duke of Wellington, and bullied the public through the press. At length the merchants consented to test his repeated asseverations that letters could be carried to India, *via* Egypt and the Red Sea, in half the time that it required to send them around the Cape of Good Hope. They intrusted him with a large packet and the means of paying his expenses. He set out: travelled express to Marseilles, went on a French vessel to Alexandria, hasten-

ed across the desert on a canal, hired a small vessel at Kosseir, and sailed down to India, accomplishing the feat in less than two months. All scepticism now vanished. If this feat could be accomplished by sailing vessels, what might not a steamer achieve? A company was formed; Waghorn was rewarded with a lieutenancy in the Royal Navy, and soon drank himself to death; and thenceforward India was brought ten thousand miles nearer to England. Mighty have been the results!

———

Rather Dry.

A FRENCH merchant—as usual vivacious and polite in the extreme—while travelling in a coach, had for his fellow traveller, a demure and taciturn old English banker. With characteristic French courtesy, he endeavored to engage his British companion in a little social chat, by addressing him thus: "Sare, I hope you are well;" he however received no reply, and therefore repeated the remark more emphatically,—"Sare, I hope you are *ver* well." To this the old nabob sulkily rejoined, "I was very well, sir, when we came away; I am very well now; and when I get ill, I'll let you know."

———

New York to Boston in Four Days.

THE first stage coach from New York to Boston, started on the 24th of June, 1772, from the "Fresh Water." It was to leave each terminus once a fortnight. The fare was four pence, New York currency, per mile. It reached Hartford, Conn. in two days, and Boston in two more. The proprietors promised a *weekly* stage, "if encouraged in their great enterprise."

———

Good Land for Railroad.

AT an early stage in the proceedings of the Erie and New York City Railroad, while the directors were negotiating with the chiefs for the land around Jennison Hill, the colonel and others had made some strong speeches depicting the worthlessness of the land and enlarging considerably upon the fact that it was good for nothing for corn, and, consequently, should be leased very cheap.

When the colonel sat down, the old chief replied in the Seneca tongue to the interpreter, to the effect that "he knew it was poor land for corn; but *mighty good land for railroad!*" The shrewdness and force of this remark will be fully appreciated when it is known that the little strip of land around Jennison Hill was the only possible place for a railroad that did not involve the building of two expensive bridges across the Alleghany.

Disinterested Railroad Contractor!

It has become so common for persons to engage in railroad enterprises, and seek to become directors, presidents, or contractors, for the purpose of speculating—in the opprobrious use of that term,—that it is really refreshing to record the instance of one who sacrificed his own interest for that of the persons whom he represented. Mr. F. C. went to New York, with authority to purchase iron for twenty miles of the railroad of which he was president. When in market, he found he could purchase enough for seventy miles more at good rates, but his limit by the directors was to twenty miles. He determined to close the contract for the *seventy* miles on *private* account, which he did. Iron soon rose in value so much so that his contract was $300,000 above what he had agreed to pay. It was, of course, legally and fairly his, but with a disinterestedness almost without a parallel, he gave the company the entire benefit of his bargain without a cent of compensation. A disinterested railroad contractor!

No wonder that the speedy dawn of the millennium has been so confidently expected, of late years!

Rigid Obedience of Shipmasters Exacted by Girard.

It is stated as a fact peculiar to Girard's management of his business, that he was always his own insurer upon his ships, and he never forgave the slightest disobedience of his orders on the part of any captain or supercargo in his employ.

He would at once dismiss his captains, even if they saved the ship through disobedience of his orders; and this practice he carried out in the most arbitrary manner, no matter how long a period the offender may have been in his employ, nor how faithful and valuable the services rendered by them. Such conduct is without a parallel among American merchants.

Scale of Railway Politeness.

The classification adopted in the management of English railways appears not to be confined to the cars; but the distinctions of first, second, and third class are as scrupulously observed in the degree of politeness shown by the employés of the company to the passengers. The old maxim that civility costs nothing seems to be treated as a fable by the railway managers, who calculate perhaps that politeness at all events takes time, and, as time is money, the officers of the company are not justified in giving it without an equivalent. Any one who doubts the fact of this discrimination has only to present himself at different times as an applicant for information at a railway station, in the different characters of a first, a second, or a third class passenger.

If he is going in the first class, he will get speedy attention from the clerks in the office; bows, and even smiles, from the policemen on the plat-

PAYING THE FIRST STEAMBOAT MONEY,

form; and perhaps a touch of the hat from the conductor. The second class passengers will get bare civility—but rather more of the bear than the civility, from the officials who deliver the checks; these latter are very fond of trying to cheat themselves into the belief that they are quite on a par with the petted "gentlemen in government office," whom the railway clerks chiefly resemble in an assumed nonchalance, which, however, the plain speaking of a passenger who *will* be attended to, and who *may* be a shareholder, is pretty sure to dissipate. A second class passenger will get little else than a "Now, sir," from the policeman, and a "Come, jump up!" from the conductor; while, alas! the third class passenger will perhaps suddenly find himself catching a smart poke in his chest from the conductor's staff, by way of keeping him back till it is convenient to let him enter.

In fact, there are short answers as well as short trains, and each class has a set of rules of courtesy or "attention" applied to it, which the officers are bound to obey as scrupulously as they do the railway signals.

───◆───

"Pleasure Excursions."

ONE would imagine that railways were of that "grave" nature that would drive away joking. One would about as soon expect to fall upon a comic churchyard, as to meet with a jocund railway—for smash-ups and mutilations, somehow, are not very favorable to fun. One style of joking which has been adopted by a certain railway company that has always been the most fruitful in accidents, is that of advertising "Pleasure Excursions." The directors' notions of amusement must have been learned in the slaughter house. One day of such pleasure, it would rationally be supposed, must suffice a man his entire life—his day of pleasure and his life or limb will

probably prove in this case to be neck and neck. The words "Last Chance," which commonly wind up such advertisements, are also intensely suggestive. The names of the engines, too, are frequently conducive to anything but pleasant emotions—there seems to be a cruel delight in christening them after the gloomiest objects: One railway, for instance, has the following lively stud of engines—"Lethe," "Styx," "Minos," "Pluto,' and several others, introducing every member of the latter gentleman's interesting family, as if it was absolutely necessary that every traveller should be on companionable terms with them, preparatory to what is to follow. One cannot help thinking that the very bad names which directors are in the habit of giving their engines may have had some influence in making them, as they so often prove, such emphatically thorough-going engines—of destruction.

───◆───

The First Steamboat Passage-Money ever Paid.

ONE of the most interesting incidents of a business nature is that which concerns the first steamboat fare paid to Fulton. The narrator of this, who was also one of the actors in the scene, says: "I chanced to be at Albany on business when Fulton arrived there, in his unheard-of craft, which everybody felt so much interest in seeing. Being ready to leave, and hearing that this craft was going to return to New York, I repaired on board and inquired for Mr. Fulton; I was referred to the cabin, and there found a plain, gentlemanly man, wholly alone, and engaged in writing.

"Mr. Fulton, I presume."

"Yes, sir."

"Do you return to New York, with this boat?"

"We shall try to get back, sir."

"Can I have a passage down?"

"You can take your chance with us, sir."

"I inquired the amount to be paid, and, after a moment's hesitation, a sum, I think six dollars, was named. The amount, in coin, I laid in his open hand, and, with his eye fixed upon it, he remained so long motionless, that I supposed there might be a miscount, and said to him, 'Is that right, sir?'"

This question roused him as from a kind of reverie, and as he looked up to me the big tear was brimming in his eye, and his voice faltered as he said, "Excuse me, sir; but memory was busy as I contemplated this, the first pecuniary reward I have ever received for all my exertions in adapting steam to navigation. I should gladly commemorate the occasion over a bottle of wine with you but, really I am too poor, even for that, just now; yet I trust we may meet again when this will not be the case."

That voyage to New York was successful, as all know, and terminated without accident.

Some four years after this, when the Clermont had been greatly improved, and her name changed to the North River, and when two other boats, viz., the Car of Neptune and the Paragon, had been built, making Mr. Fulton's fleet three boats regularly plying between New York and Albany, I took passage upon one of these for the latter city. The cabin in that day was below; and, as I walked its length, to and fro, I saw I was very closely observed by one I supposed a stranger. Soon, however, I recalled the features of Mr. Fulton; but, without disclosing this, I continued my walk. At length, in passing his seat, our eyes met, when he sprang to his feet, and, eagerly seizing my hand, exclaimed, "I knew it must be you, for your features have never escaped me; and, although I am still far from rich, yet I may venture that *bottle*

now!" It was ordered; and during its discussion Mr. Fulton ran rapidly, but vividly, over his experiences of the world's coldness and sneers, and of the hopes, fears, disappointments, and difficulties, that were scattered through his whole career of discovery,—up to the very point of his final, crowning triumph, at which he so fully felt he had arrived at last.

And in reviewing all these, said he: "I have again and again recalled the occasion, and the incident, of our first interview at Albany; and never have I done so without renewing in my mind the vivid emotion it originally caused. That seemed, and does still seem, to me, the turning point in my destiny—the dividing line between light and darkness, in my career upon earth; for it was the first actual recognition of my usefulness to my fellow men."

George Hudson, the Railway King.

GEORGE HUDSON, who will always be known as the English railway king, may be said to have left his counter as a linen draper and sprang upon the steam engine. His first notable movement in this line was the subscription for several hundred shares in the York railway enterprise, and by a natural progress, under a strong and vigorous, bold and determined mind like his, he soon became known as the railway monarch. His influence extended seventy-six miles over the York and North Midland railroads; fifty-one over the Hull and Selby and Leeds and Selby; over the North Midland, Midland counties, and another, one hundred and seventy-eight miles; over the Newcastle and Darlington, and the Great North of England, one hundred and eleven miles; while over the Sheffield and Rotherham, the York and Scarborough, the North British, Whitby and Pickering, it affected near six hundred miles more, making a total of more than one thousand miles, all of which were successful in developing traffic, and equally successful in paying good dividends.

For a time, no other name was heard in the great world of railways. In the journals of the day men read of his wonderful doings. The press recorded his whereabouts; the draughtsman pencilled his features. His name was connected with preference, shares, and profits. He wielded an influence unparalleled and unprecedented. Peers flattered the dispenser of scrip, and peeresses fawned upon the allotter of premiums. It was told with pleasure and repeated with delight, that his empire extended over one thousand miles of railway. His fortune was computed with an almost personal pride. Almack's was deserted when Albert house was full. The ducal crest was seen on the carriage at his door. The daintiest aristocracy of England sought his presence. Foreign potentates sued for his society. The coronet of the peer was veiled before the crown of the railway king. The minister paid his court, and the bishop bent in homage. The ermine of the judge lost its dignity, and the uniform of the officer its pride. The Christian banker and the Hebrew capitalist alike acknowledged his greatness. Stories were plentiful of the fortunes he had won, and the dividends his enterprises had paid. The prince consort was proud to be introduced to him, "shook hands very heartily with the member (he was in the House of Commons), and remained in conversation with him for some time."

When his name graced an advertisement, men ran to buy the share. In regard to lines known to be worthless, and on which no business was doing, if a rumor was skilfully spread that Hudson was after them, the stock exchange was in a ferment, and prices rose enormously, to the cool loss of the holder, however, when the contradiction came. He was their railway potentate, their iron king—their golden

god. His appearance on the platform was a perfect ovation. Sober, steady-minded men shouted with joy—shrewd speculators ditto; and one intense, universal homage greeted the image they had set up. The thought of ten per cent. enraptured them, and the loud applause which hailed his tramway periods would only have been justified by the discourse of a Macaulay or the oration of a Peel. Over railways and railway managers he maintained an imperial sway.

His exertions in behalf of the projects he espoused were absolutely astonishing. Nothing seemed to wear his mind; nothing appeared to weary his frame. He battled in parliamentary committees, day by day; he argued, pleaded, and gesticulated with an earnestness which rarely failed in its object. One day in town cajoling a committee—the next persuading an archbishop. In the morning adjusting some rival claim in an obscure office; in the afternoon astonishing the stock exchange with some daring *coup de main.*

But his connection with the railways of the Eastern counties, the bad management of which brought things to such a desperate pass, turned the scale of his fortune at last. The unwise experiment was made of declaring dividends which had not been earned, and paying them out of the capital, in order to keep up the value of the stock, and the prestige of Mr. Hudson. The imprudence was bitterly paid for. In a short time the railway king, stripped of crown and sceptre, was sent into ignominious exile! The revulsion in popular feeling was fierce, and he was now as intensely hated as he had been before admired. The more sweet had been the accents of praise, the more bitter were now the objurgations uttered by the same tongues against that name. It was a malignant delight to repeat and repeat over again the thousand stories of his unheard-of villanies. The railway king had now become the railway demon, and his many roads were but iron ways for transporting the whole realm to the infernal latitudes.

Personally, he was a plain, solid-looking man with a large and heavy build; a keen, penetrating, gray eye; a broad, wrinkled, and severe face; gray and scanty hair; a nervous and rather peculiar gait, somewhat shuffling; in dress inclined to be careless. His speech was rapid, without grace of delivery, his utterance somewhat thick, and he affected no refinement of manner. He pitched at once into his subject, and said what he had to say in the fewest words he could put it in.

Among the causes of his success, one was an excellent arithmetical capacity, enabling him to form in his head the most elaborate combinations of figures in a very brief time. Another thing was his close personal attention to the minutiæ; nothing was too small to be overlooked or to be left to others, if he could see to it himself. He examined personally every department of the roads under his management, and knew the duties of every man.

Stephenson, the Pioneer in Railway Construction.

To Mr. Stephenson is commonly awarded the honor of first constructing a railway for general transportation. Three years elapsed from the commencement of the work, and those interested began to be impatient. They wished—as was natural—for some returns from the vast amount of capital they had expended.

"Now, George," said Friend Crupper to him one day, "thou must get on with the railway, and have it finished without further delay. Thou must really have it ready for opening by the first day of January next."

"It is impossible," said Stephenson.

"Impossible! I wish I could get Na- poleon at thee. He would tell thee that there is no such word."

"Tush! Don't speak to me about Napoleon. Give me men, money, and materials, and I will do what Napoleon couldn't do—drive a railroad from Liverpool to Manchester over Chat Moss."

Mr. Grigg's Mode of Overcoming Obstacles.

On the death of Mr. Warner, the eminent Philadelphia bookseller, with whom Mr. John Grigg was for a considerable time associated in business, the settlement of the affairs of the firm was devolved upon Mr. G. Nor was this a slight undertaking. The business of the house had been immense; connected with it were numerous branches and agencies; it had dealings with various houses at the South and West, and the settlement of affairs rendered frequent journeyings necessary. During one of those journeys, an incident occurred which is too characteristic of the days of stage-coach travelling, and of the determined energy of Mr. Grigg's character, not to be worthy of mention. He was at Charleston. It was the latter part of December, 1825, and by Christmas day he must be in Philadelphia. He pushed forward, travelling day and night; at Baltimore, the steamboat which usually connected was found to have left off running, and the travellers were forced to take to the mail coach. But every seat was full when Mr. Grigg arrived; there was no alternative for the determined traveller, weary and excited as he was by incessant journeying for seven long days and sleepless nights, but to ride outside with the driver. The day, or rather the night, was cold, the air was full of sleet, the road miry. But to the driver's seat he mounted and pushed on. At Havre de Grace another driver took the reins, who was unacquainted with the road; it was long after dark, and the "insides," who began to be fearful of their necks as the coach plunged and tossed in the mire, grew clamorous for putting back till the morning. But Mr. Grigg was determined that the stage should go ahead and be in Philadelphia by Christmas day, and, besides, they carried the mails, and a public conveyance must not be delayed! So he procured a lantern, and going before the coach piloted the travellers though the darkness and mire for about two miles. Finally, mounting the box again, he took the reins into his own hands, and daylight saw the delighted travellers arrived at Elkton, and well on their way. They at once entreated him to take a seat inside. And early on Christmas morning Mr. Grigg *was* in Philadelphia.

Southern Accommodation Trains.

OUR railroad is a slow coach (writes a Southern traveller); going along at the usual speed of six or eight miles an hour, we came to a dead halt; several passengers left the cars, and went to climbing the trees by the side of the track. I asked the conductor what they were after. "Grapes," he answered. "Why," said I, "is it possible you stop whenever the passengers wish to get some grapes?" "Oh, certainly, this is the *accommodation* train!"

"Your Ticket, Sir!"

ON one of the Georgia railroads there was a conductor named Snell, a very clever, sociable, gentlemanly man, a great favorite with the company he was connected with, and the travelling public in general—fond of a joke, quick at repartee, and *faithful in the discharge of his duties.* During one of his trips, as his train, well filled with passengers, was crossing a bridge over a wide stream, some seven or eight feet deep, the bridge broke down, precipitating the two passenger cars into the stream.

As the passengers emerged from the wreck they were borne away by the force of the current. Snell had succeeded in catching hold of some bushes that grew on the bank of the stream, to which he clung for dear life. A passenger less fortunate came rushing by; Snell extended one hand, saying, "Your ticket, sir; give me your ticket!" The effect of such a dry joke in the midst of the water may be imagined.

Thompson's Travels in California.

IT is not unlikely (though the capital contributor to "Harper's" does not say so) that Thompson, who figures in the following whirligig of fun, was a Yankee, having an eye to "sites," "water privileges," etc., and ready for an "operation" when the opportunity should present itself. Assuming this very reasonable probability, we are only too happy to give it a place in these pages.

In the northern part of California is a stream called Yuba River. Across it some enterprising individual built a bridge; and on the banks somebody else built three or four houses. The inhabitants called the place Yuba Dam. Three bars were instantly erected, and the "town" increased rapidly. About noon one cool day a traveller and a sojourner in the land passed this flourishing locality, and seeing a long-legged specimen of humanity in a red shirt smoking before one of the bars, thus addressed him:

"Hello!"

"Hello!" replied the shirt, with vigor, removing his pipe from his mouth.

"What place is this?" demanded the traveller, whose name was Thompson.

The answer of the shirt was unexpected:

"Yuba Dam!"

There was about fifty yards between them, and the wind was blowing. Mr.

Thompson thought he had been mistaken.

"What did you say ?" he asked.

"Yuba Dam ! " replied the stranger, cheerfully.

"What place is this?" roared Mr. Thompson.

"Yu-ba Dam," said the shirt, in a slightly elevated tone of voice.

"Lookee here ! " yelled the irate Thompson; "I asked you politely what place this was; why in thunder don't you answer ? "

The stranger became excited. He rose, and replied with the voice of an 80-pounder,

"YU-BA DAM ! You hear that?"

In a minute Thompson, burning with the wrath of the righteous, jumped off his horse, and advanced to the stranger with an expression not to be mistaken. The shirt arose, and assumed a posture of offence and defence. Arrived within a yard of him, Thompson said :

"I ask you for the last time. What place is this ? "

Putting his hand to his mouth, his opponent roared :

"YU-BA DAM ! "

The next minute they were at it. First, Thompson was down; then the shirt; and then it was a dog-fall—that is, both were down. They rolled about, kicking up a tremendous dust. They squirmed around so energetically that it appeared as though they had a dozen legs instead of four. It looked like a prize fight between two pugilistic centipedes. Finally, they both rolled off the bank and into the river. The water cooled them. They went down together, but came up separate, and put out for the shore. Both reached it about the same time, and Thompson scrambled up the bank, mounted his warlike steed, and made tracks, leaving his foe gouging the mud out of one of his eyes.

Having left the business portion of the town, that is to say, the corner

where the three bars were kept, he struck a house in the "suburbs," before which a little girl of about four years of age was playing.

"What place is this, sissy?" he asked.

The little girl, frightened at the drowned-rat figure which the stranger cut, streaked it for the house. Having reached the door, she stopped, turned, and squealed, "Oo-bee Dam ! "

"Good Heavens ! " said Thompson, digging his heels between his horse's ribs—"Good Heavens ! let me get out of this horrid place, where not only the men, but the very babes and sucklings, swear at inoffensive travellers ! "

From Honolulu to Kaui.

Two citizens of Honolulu, Judge B. and Dr. N., had occasion to go to the island of Kaui, the land of sugar and coffee. They returned in a schooner, and among the passengers was the governor of the island, who was coming to visit the metropolis—the great city of Honolulu. The governor is a native, and so is the captain of the schooner—a first-rate seaman as long as land was in sight. There came up a gale that blew them off; and having no compass, and a short supply of provisions, they were soon in a sad plight indeed. On and on, for nine days, they sailed, when they ought to have been in port in two. The judge and the doctor thought it about time to take matters into their own hands, or they would all be starved to death; for neither law nor physic would serve them without something to eat. They deemed it proper to ask the governor what he thought best to be done. His excellency took the subject into consideration, and with great sagacity remarked, " Well, now, as we are lost, I think we had better go back to where we started from." The poor captain would have been but too happy to comply with the governor's suggestion, had there been any such thing as knowing where that place was; but that day a whaler hove in sight, and supplying them with provisions, led them into port. They were actually on the way to America.

Not Posted in Geography.

THERE was once an old gentleman of the utmost integrity of character, but keen as a brier in all business matters, who, not having had early opportunities of acquiring knowledge, sometimes made sad mistakes in his use of language. Although largely engaged in shipping, he was profoundly ignorant of geography. He came one day, with a letter in his hand, which he had just received, into the insurance office, and asked to see a chart of the Mediterranean. It was promptly unrolled, and spending a long time in an apparently unsatisfactory examination, the curiosity of the president of the office was excited, and he offered his aid to assist him in his trouble. "Why," says the old gentleman, "I have just got a letter from one of my captains, who states that he has experienced a violent hurricane, and consequently put in great jeopardy. Now, I know Great Jeopardy is a port in the Mediterranean, but I can't find the plaguey place on the map."

Working a Hand Car.

THE thriving town of Scranton, Pennsylvania, where railroad iron and other products of the same substantial metal are extensively manufactured, is situated on the Delaware, Lackawanna, and Western Railroad. There is a very heavy ascending grade for several miles westward from this place, to overcome which requires not a little power of steam with an ordinary train of cars. Just before this part of the road was opened, an officer connected with it had occasion to go three or four

miles west to superintend some operations.

He took a light hand car and two powerful men to work it, one of whom was a German, not an accomplished engineer, nor very familiar with the working of railroads. They toiled hard at the crank, working their way up the steep grade, landing their passenger at his destined point, who sent the car back to Scranton by the German alone, knowing that no labor was required to descend, excepting when it was necessary to hold back by putting on the brake. Not having received any specific directions, however, as to the manner in which he was to work his way down, the German mounted the car, and thinking as it had been such a severe labor for *two* men to take the car out, it would require still more exertion for *one* to work it back, he applied all his strength to the crank, and was soon moving with tremendous velocity, down the hill toward the town and the terminus of the road. As he passed through the town over the last half mile, all unconscious of what was before him, his danger excited universal apprehension, and the cry was raised on every hand, "Put on the brake! Put on the brake!" Interpreting the cry to mean "Put on more strength," he laid out all his power upon one last grand effort. Reaching the end of the road, where there was some heavy obstruction, sufficient to stop a train of cars, the hand car was instantly converted into kindling wood, and the poor German was thrown head over heels some twenty-five or thirty feet beyond where it struck. As he was picked up, in a mangled condition, some one asked him,

"Why didn't you put on the brake?"

"Put on the prake," said he, "vy, it ish preak all to pieces!"

And this was the end of that ride.

Amending the Charter.

A LITTLE transaction between a New York merchant and a Frenchman is thus related by the former: He was a captain of a coasting craft, and I chartered his vessel for a round sum, to take a cargo of wheat up the river to a mill, and to return with a load of flour in barrels. There was a written agreement between us, which required him to load without *unnecessary delay.* Having a limited knowledge of English, and being a cautious skipper, he took the agreement, before signing it, to a compatriot—who was, or pretended to be, in the legal profession—whose knowledge of our language was much more contracted than his own, and gave him a small fee to read it over and see if it was correct. They came together to my office, and the lawyer addressed me with much politeness and gravity, while his countryman stood by with approbative visage: " Sare, I have read this little papier. It is entierement cor-r-rect, except von vord. I do not like zat expr-r-ression *unnecessa-rie !* " " Very well," said I, with great frankness, " I will scratch it out," and I did so. The skipper and lawyer both seemed relieved immensely now that the former was obliged to load his vessel " *without delay.*"

"Soaking" the old Coach.

IN olden times, before the introduction of railroads, there lived in the town of Chambersburg, Pennsylvania, a certain tavern keeper named Ramsay, proprietor of all the stage coaches in that region of country. His house was not one of those miserable, dirty holes usually selected as the stopping places of the stages, but a fine, spacious, old-fashioned inn, where one was sure to find cleanliness and comfort—the best of everything that rich country could afford, and plenty of it. Squire Ramsay had become rich, and was much respected by all his neighbors. Unfortunately, however, he became also a little too fond of his " pure old rye," and was likely to become a regular drunkard. His friends felt the necessity of cautioning him against this besetting sin; but the Squire, being a high-spirited old colt, required careful handling.

Finally, it was agreed that the doctor of the place, one of his oldest friends, should deal with him in the most delicate manner possible. The doctor thought best to approach his friend in the way of a parable, as Nathan did David, and felt certain of success. At their next interview he led the conversation intentionally to the subject of stage coaches—how long they would last, etc.

" Now, Mr. R.," said he, " suppose you had a fine, well-built, old coach, that had done good service and was yet sound, though perhaps a little shackling, and the seams a little open; would you put it to a team of fiery young horses on the roughest part of the road, or would you not put it to a team of steady old stagers, and on the smoothest part of the road you could find ? "

" Well, doctor," said the squire, in perfect ignorance of the doctor's drift, " if I had such a stage as you describe, *I would soak it !* "

The doctor was silenced, but, whether from the advice of his friends or the promptings of his own good sense, the squire ceased to run the " old coach " so hard, and died highly esteemed and respected.

Strange Terminus to a Railroad.

THERE is a small town on the North Missouri Railroad called Renick ; and Renick is a hard place—a *very* hard place. In one of the cars on this road, on a certain occasion, sat—with his feet upon the cushions and his hat down over his eyes—a flashy but dirty-looking individual, evidently some "three sheets" gone; indeed, he was "maudlin drunk."

The conductor, in coming around, gave him a shove, and aroused him with a short "Ticket, sir!"

"Aint got none," said loafer.

"Pay your fare, then."

"How much is it?" demanded the fellow.

"Where are you going to?" inquired the conductor.

"Guess I'm—[hic]—goin' [hic]—to the devil!" spoke loafer, with some air of truthfulness.

"Then," said the conductor, "pay your fare to Renick—$5.70!"

Drinking Success to the First Railway.

IN 1823 the second Stockton and Darlington Railway Act was obtained from Parliament. Mr. Stephenson was appointed the company's engineer, at a salary of £300 per annum. He laid out every foot of the ground himself, accompanied by his assistants. He surveyed indefatigably from daylight to dusk, dressed in top-boots and breeches, and took his chance of bread and milk, or a homely dinner, at some neighboring farmhouse; for the country people were fond of his cheerful talk. One day, when the works were approaching completion, he dined at Stockton, and after dinner the great engineer ordered in a bottle of wine, to drink success to the railway. He then said to the young men assembled: "Now, I will tell you that I think you will live to see the day, though I may not live so long, when railways will come to supersede almost all other methods of conveyance in this country; when mail coaches will go by railway, and railroads will become the great highway for the king and all his subjects. The time will come when it will be cheaper for a workingman to travel on a railway than to walk on foot. I know that there are great and almost insurmount-

able obstacles that will have to be encountered. But what I have said will come to pass, as sure as I am now alive. I only wish I may live to see the day, though that I can scarcely hope for, as I know how slow all human progress is, and with what difficulty I have been able to get the locomotive adopted, notwithstanding my more than ten years' successful experiment at Killingworth." The anticipations of the great engineer were more than realized. At the opening of the road in question—the first public railway—Mr. Stephenson himself drove the engine. The train consisted of thirty-eight vehicles, among which were twenty-one wagons fitted up with temporary seats for passengers, and a carriage filled with the directors and their friends. The speed attained in some parts was twelve miles an hour. It was a complete success; and the goods and passengers soon exceeded the expectations of the directors.

In surveying a line for the Liverpool and Manchester railway, great opposition was exhibited on the part of the proprietors of the lands through which the line was to pass. Lord Derby's farmers and servants, and Lord Sefton's keepers, turned out in full force to resist the aggressions of the surveying party. The Duke of Bridgewater's property-guard threatened to duck Mr. Stephenson in a pond if he proceeded; and he had to take the survey by stealth, when the people were at dinner.

Change of "Packet Day."

To show what was the nature of Pelatiah Perit's influence as a Christian, in mercantile circles, and how much of that influence was the effect of his rare judgment and skill in dealing with men, an illustration is afforded in the change which he accomplished, perhaps thirty years ago, in the regulations of the packet-ships sailing from the port of New York.

25

Formerly the packets for Liverpool and other trans-atlantic ports were advertised to sail regularly on certain days of the month, and whenever the appointed days for sailing fell on Sunday, the Christian Sabbath was disregarded. To the house of Goodhue & Co. this was an inconvenience. It interfered with the Sabbath of the partners, and with the Sabbath to which their clerks and other employés were entitled. It interfered also with the religious feelings of all the passengers who honored the Christian Sabbath, and were unwilling to violate their consciences by commencing a voyage on that day. At the same time it interfered with the Sunday rest—religious or irreligious—of every merchant, who had occasion to send by every packet, the latest advices to his correspondents beyond the sea. But the practice was a settled one, and how could it be changed? Those were the days when tide and time waited for no man; and was not the sailing of a packet ship on her appointed day, even though that day happened to fall on Sunday, a work of necessity and mercy?

How, then, should the ship-owners and merchants, many of whom had no religious regard for the sanctity of the Sabbath, be brought to agree upon a change? Some men undertaking such a reform, would have begun with a public agitation on purely moral and religious grounds, and with denunciation of all persons implicated in upholding the existing arrangement, and the result would have been a failure. The personal influence of Mr. Perit with men who, whatever may have been their own position in relation to Christianity, could not but honor his Christian character, was such that he found no difficulty in effecting a new arrangement. He succeeded in convincing all parties that the change of "packet day," from a certain day of the month to a certain day of the week,

was no infringement of any man's religious liberty, and was required not only in the interest of religion and Christian morals, but also in the interest of merchants and their clerks, and in the general interests of commerce.

Palmerston and the Station-Master.

AT one of the chief stations on the Great Western Railway, England, is a station-master, noted for self-conceit and flunkeyism. His reverence for a person with a handle to his name is equalled only by the esteem in which he holds himself. One day he descried a gentleman pacing the platform with a cigar in his mouth—contrary to the rule. Official at once accosted the audacious offender, and requested him forthwith to stop smoking. The gentleman, absorbed in the most abstract thought, took no notice whatsoever of his command, but continued his walk with the utmost *nonchalance*, emitting a silvery cloud. Irritated by this disobedience, Official repeated his behests more peremptorily than before; but still the owner of the Havana maintained a provoking disregard. A third time the order was repeated, accompanied with an emphatic threat that if the obstinate sinner did not obey, he would at once be collared by the porters. The stranger took no more heed than before, and so at last, enraged beyond all further patience, Official pulled the cigar out of the smoker's mouth and flung it away. This violent act produced no more effect than the previous commands and threats, and the peripatetic philosopher continued his walk with imperturbable serenity. Presently a carriage and four drove up, an equipage well known to Official as that of the Duke of Beaufort. To his now inconceivable horror, the refractory smoker entered the said chariot, and drove off in style to Badminton. Official asked, in tremulous tones, who the stranger was, and he felt ready to sink into the earth when told that it was Viscount Palmerston, K. G., First Lord of the Treasury. He did not hesitate long, however; he at once ordered a chaise and pair, and drove off to Badminton. Arrived there, he sent in his card, and urgently requested a private interview with Lord Palmerston. His lordship soon appeared, when Official began a most abject apology for having "so grossly insulted his lordship : "

"Had I known who your lordship was, I would not have so treated your lordship for the world!"

The Premier heard the station-master out, then looking down upon him sternly, and with his hands in his pockets, said :

"Sir, I respected you because I thought you were doing your duty like a Briton; but now I see you are nothing but a snob."

Captain Macalester and his Fast Ship "Fanny."

ABOUT the beginning of the present century, the shipwrights of Philadelphia had attained great celebrity for the beauty of the models of their vessels, which united, in a remarkable degree, celerity in sailing and fitness for the purposes of commerce. Among the most skilful of these was Mr. Grice. Captain Macalester—eminent as a shipmaster and subsequently as a merchant —engaged him to construct a ship, called the "Fanny," in building which Mr. Grice exhibited his ablest skill in the adaptation of the principles of naval architecture, and Captain Macalester added the suggestions derived from his own experience as a practical and observing navigator. The result was

that the "Fanny," when launched' proved to be the fastest sailing merchantman of the day. Captain Macalester accomplished his first voyage in her, from Philadelphia to Cowes in the Isle of Wight, in seventeen days, a rapidity of passage of which there was no previous record. He took with him, as passengers on that occasion, the wealthy and distinguished merchant of Philadelphia and Senator of the United States, Mr. William Bingham, with his beautiful and accomplished wife. It is probable that this incident was the foundation of a particularly friendly intercourse, which, from his correspondence, appears to have existed between him and Mr. Alexander Baring (afterward Lord Ashburton), who was the son-in-law of Mr. and Mrs. Bingham.

In London, Captain Macalester engaged to make a voyage in the "Fanny" to Batavia and back. What was the surprise of the consignees of his vessel in London, when he presented himself in their counting house, having accomplished the entire voyage in seven months and twenty days, a speed, at that time, without a parallel. It was in the course of this voyage that he was chased by a British frigate, which fell in with him at daylight in the morning, but could not overtake him until ten o'clock at night. When the British boarding officer stepped upon his deck, he said to Captain Macalester :

"Sir, you have a very fast ship."

"I thought so until to-day," was the reply.

"Our frigate," answered the officer, "is reputed to be the fastest in the navy, and we never before have had such a chase."

 END OF VOL. I.